D1476384

WORKS ISSUED BY
THE HAKLUYT SOCIETY

———

JOÃO RODRIGUES'S ACCOUNT OF
SIXTEENTH-CENTURY JAPAN

THIRD SERIES
NO. 7

ARTE DA LINGOA DE IA-
PAM COMPOSTA PELLO
Padre Ioão Rodriguez, Portugues da Cõpa-
nhia de IESV diuidida em tres
LIVROS.

COM LICENÇA DO ORDI-
NARIO, E SVPERIORES EM
Nangafaqui no Collegio de Iapão da
Companhia de IESV
Anno. 1604.

Plate 1: Title page of João Rodrigues, SJ, *Arte de lingoa de Iapam*, Nagasaki, 1604. *Bodleian Library, University of Oxford.*

JOÃO RODRIGUES'S ACCOUNT
OF
SIXTEENTH-CENTURY JAPAN

Edited by
MICHAEL COOPER

THE HAKLUYT SOCIETY
LONDON
2001

Published by The Hakluyt Society
c/o Map Library
British Library, 96 Euston Road,
London NW1 2DB

SERIES EDITORS
W. F. RYAN
ROBIN LAW

© The Hakluyt Society 2001

ISBN 0 904180 73 5
ISSN 0072 9396

British Library Cataloguing-in-Publication Data
A catalogue record for this book is
available from the British Library

Typeset by Waveney Typesetters, Wymondham, Norfolk
Printed in Great Britain at
The Bath Press, Bath

To Toyoko U. McGovern
and in memory of
Melvin P. McGovern
1912–1992

CONTENTS

This table of contents does not appear in the original Portuguese text, and has been compiled by the translator.

Book 2

LIST OF ILLUSTRATIONS

INTRODUCTION

Summary

The Jesuit mission in Japan was founded in 1549 and continued until the 1620s when government persecution finally eradicated the Christian church in the country. Among the priests working on the mission during its period of expansion was the Portuguese João Rodrigues (c. 1562–1633), who was appointed to collect material for the compilation of a history of the mission. All that is left of his efforts are two books, written 1620–21, dealing with Japan and its people, and a third book recounting the history of the mission, 1549–52.

Rodrigues's original Portuguese text, *Historia da Igreja do Japão*, is no longer extant, and the present translation of the two books on Japanese life is based on a copy made in Macao during the 1740s and now preserved in the library of the Ajuda Palace, Lisbon (MS Jesuítas na Asia, 49–IV–53, ff. 1–83, *Historia da Igreja do Japão*). In this account, the author describes the country, its people, their customs, etiquette, and culture, as well as Chinese astronomy and astrology.

The spelling of Japanese names and terms varies greatly in the Ajuda copy, and for the sake of uniformity, I have consistently rendered them according to the modern Hepburn system of transliteration. This avoids the strange appearance of words such as *xixxi*, *xuxxi*, and *xogiqiraxij*, decidedly odd-looking by modern standards yet spelled quite consistently in the Portuguese fashion of Rodrigues's time. In accordance with modern convention, macrons have been omitted in well-known names and terms, such as Kyoto, Osaka, shogun, and *daimyo*. The spelling of Chinese names and terms has been rendered according to the modern *pinyin* system, although admittedly the former Wade-Giles orthography more closely approximates the spelling found in the original text. The Portuguese who dictated the text in Macao, and the copyist who transcribed it more than a hundred years after the author's death, were ignorant of Japanese (and possibly Chinese as well), and to list all the irregular variations in the spelling of foreign words would have no philological value and would inflict an unnecessary burden on readers. On a minor point of usage, I have retained the now obsolete English forms Tartar and Tartary since the popular etymology deriving these words from Latin *tartarum* (Hell) would have been known to Rodrigues, and he uses Tartaria as a regional name. Tatar or Mongol, depending on context, would, of course, be more appropriate in a modern text.

In the notes I refer to the writings of contemporaneous European merchants and missionaries in Japan and China to corroborate, amplify, and occasionally disagree with Rodrigues's statements, thus offering a more universal presentation of European observations on these two countries rather than the testimony of only one man. When citing relevant books and articles, I have not hesitated to refer to seemingly outdated works published fifty or a hundred years ago, for such sources tend to be more descriptive than the theoretical content of recent books, and are therefore more useful in checking the accuracy of Rodrigues's account. In addition, the Japan and China described in these writings more closely resemble the Japan and China of his day.

VOCABVLARIO
DA LINGOA DE IAPAM

com adeclaração em Portugues, feito por
ALGVNS PADRES, E IR-
MAÓS DA COMPANHIA
DE IESV.

COM LICENÇA DO ORDINARIO,
& Superiores em Nangasaqui no Collegio de Ia-
PAM DA COMPANHIA DE IESVS.
ANNO M.D.CIII.

Plate 2: Title page of *Vocabulario da lingoa de Iapam*, Nagasaki, 1603. The Japanese-Portuguese dictionary contains more than 32,000 entries. *Bodleian Library, University of Oxford.*

Rodrigues spent more than three decades in Japan, was renowned for his fluency in the language, and met most of the leading personalities of his time, which made him well qualified to describe the country and its culture. The two introductory books translated here form, it is true, part of his major work, *Historia da Igreja do Japão*, but do not deal with missionary history as such. For this reason, the present translation has been titled *João Rodrigues's Account of Sixteenth-Century Japan*, which more accurately reflects its contents. Despite its lack of elegance, his text offers a perceptive study of Japanese life that is unrivalled among European reports on Japan in the sixteenth and seventeenth centuries.

Rodrigues's account has even greater significance when viewed in a larger context. Just as China considered itself the centre of culture and civilization, so Europeans took for granted that their own culture and religion were superior throughout the known world. Yet the fact that Japan and China in the furthest reaches of Asia, 'where the people are out of contact with, and have no knowledge of, other world sages' (p. 333), had independently developed a highly sophisticated society and refined culture came as a salutary surprise to Europeans, and in time produced far-reaching revisions in Western thought and outlook. That intelligent European observers such as Rodrigues, Alessandro Valignano, Luís Fróis, and Matteo Ricci were willing to spend so much time and labour describing Asian countries and analysing their cultures implies a latent awareness of these societies' equality, even superiority in some respects, and inadvertently sowed seeds of doubt regarding the self-proclaimed European monopoly of civilization and culture.

João Rodrigues was born about 1562 in or near the rural town of Sernancelhe in the province of Beira in northern Portugal.[1] Nothing is known of his family or early boyhood, and the first definite information available is his arrival in Japan in 1577 at about the age of fifteen. The annual Portuguese trading ship reaching Japan in that year was commanded by Domingos Monteiro and carried on board fourteen Jesuit missionaries, and so the young Rodrigues likely came under their religious influence while on board. The official commercial carrack, or *não*, bound for the Indies always departed from Lisbon, and usually made lengthy stopovers at Goa and Macao awaiting favourable winds before ending its outward two-year voyage at Nagasaki; it can therefore be presumed that young Rodrigues passed through these four cities during his long journey. In his extensive writings, he never explains why he left his native country for Asia at such a tender age, but there are recorded cases of Portuguese orphans sailing to India and beyond to serve Catholic missionaries as acolytes and interpreters. It is also possible that he set out as a merchant's servant in the hope of earning his fortune in the fabled Indies.

The Japan that Rodrigues reached in 1577 was in a state of political and social transition. As he notes in his somewhat idealized account of Japanese history, the country had once been ruled by a long line of emperors claiming descent from the sun-goddess, Amaterasu. In the course of time the power of the throne waned as royal authority was increasingly usurped by powerful *daimyo*, or regional barons, and central administration disintegrated. As a result, Japan was plunged into its lengthy Period of Civil War (*Sengoku Jidai*) in which rival *daimyo* constantly strove to increase their holdings by war and treachery. Rodrigues personally experienced the turmoil of this confused period and years later would

---

[1] The present account of Rodrigues's eventful life and career is based on his biography (Cooper, *Rodrigues the Interpreter*), to which readers are referred for further details.

Plate 3: Toyotomi Hideyoshi, virtual ruler of Japan from 1582 until his death in 1598, whom Rodrigues knew well.
Rodrigues, *This Island of Japon*.

graphically describe the unstable situation: 'Men chastised and killed one another as they saw fit. They banished people and confiscated their possessions in such fashion that treachery was rampant and nobody trusted his neighbour' (p. 131).[1] Eventually there emerged in succession three powerful rulers who finally brought about a united Japan. At the time of his death in 1582 the *daimyo* Oda Nobunaga controlled about half of the country. His work was continued by his lieutenant Toyotomi Hideyoshi, whom Rodrigues came to know extremely well, and then by Tokugawa Ieyasu, whose family continued to rule Japan for more than two centuries. Thus the Europeans, who first reached Japan in 1542 or 1543, witnessed this process of national unification, and some of the Jesuits have left valuable reports on political developments.

The Catholic church in Japan was founded with the arrival of St Francis Xavier and two Jesuit companions at Kagoshima on 15 August 1549. In time the number of missionaries steadily increased, and after a slow start the enterprise flourished; by 1580 there were reportedly more than 100,000 Japanese Christians,[2] and by the end of the century several influential *daimyo* had joined their ranks. But evangelization was not allowed to continue, for in the early seventeenth century government persecution brought an end to the Church in Japan, and the country retired into self-imposed isolation from which it would not emerge until the middle of the nineteenth century.

According to his own account, young Rodrigues visited Kyoto (then called Miyako), the capital, soon after his arrival, and inspected the dilapidated imperial palace. In December 1578 he was with a group of missionaries accompanying the troops of the Christian *daimyo*

---

[1] Writing in 1565, the Jesuit Gaspar Vilela described the situation with some exaggeration: 'There are sixty-six kingdoms [in Japan], and not even four of them enjoy peace': *Cartas*, 1, f. 193.

[2] Schütte, *Introductio*, p. 429.

of Bungo, and they were obliged to beat a hasty and dangerous retreat when their patron's army was vanquished in battle. Rodrigues entered the Society of Jesus, or the Jesuit order, at about the age of eighteen in December 1580 and, after his two-year novitiate, studied for the priesthood and taught Latin to Japanese students in the seminary at Arima in Kyushu, one of the three main islands comprising Japan at that time. As there was no bishop residing in the country, Rodrigues sailed to Macao for ordination to the priesthood in early 1596, returning to Nagasaki in the summer of that year.

The Interpreter

Possibly on account of his youth at the time of his arrival, Rodrigues learned to speak Japanese with remarkable fluency and contemporaneous reports often refer to him as 'the Interpreter'. It was this linguistic skill that brought him to public notice and made him one of the most prominent Europeans in Japan in the late sixteenth century. In 1591 the Jesuit Alessandro Valignano (1539–1606), in his capacity as ambassador of the Viceroy of India, was received in audience by Hideyoshi in Miyako, and Rodrigues acted as interpreter on the occasion. The young and fluent Jesuit obviously caught Hideyoshi's attention, for he was invited back to the palace that afternoon and spent some hours conversing with the ruler. On the following day he was summoned again to explain to a bemused Hideyoshi how to regulate the European clock he had received as a gift.

This was the beginning of Rodrigues's relations with the all-powerful Hideyoshi and the first of his many meetings with high-ranking officials when dealing with mission business and Portuguese trade matters. When near the end of his life an increasingly irrational Hideyoshi condemned a group of twenty-six Franciscan friars, Jesuit brothers, and Christian laymen to death, Rodrigues was allowed to stand by their crosses at Nagasaki on 5 February 1597, exhorting and encouraging the martyrs. The memory of this traumatic experience never left him, and thirty-six years later he alludes to the event in his last letter, written in Macao on the anniversary of their deaths.

Rodrigues's relationship with Hideyoshi ended in September 1598 when, on two successive days, the missionary visited the ailing ruler only a week before he died. Although not enjoying such close contact with his successor, Rodrigues also met with the shogun Tokugawa Ieyasu on many occasions. Whenever any issue arose between the civil authorities and the Europeans, the Interpreter was invariably called in to use his diplomatic and linguistic skills to negotiate and settle the problem. Possibly on account of his dealings with some of the most powerful figures in the land, Rodrigues was appointed the Jesuit mission's procurator, or treasurer, and took part in the annual deliberations in Nagasaki to determine the bulk price of the coveted raw silk brought from China by Portuguese merchants.

These negotiations were sometimes prolonged and acrimonious, and it was only too easy for Rodrigues to make enemies in the process. The fact that, on the admission of his Jesuit colleagues, he could at times be tactless and involve himself too deeply in commercial matters served to aggravate the situation. One Jesuit report mentions, 'He is clever, but somewhat thoughtless by nature both in judgement and prudence, although he is virtuous and has good will.' While admitting that 'he is expert and clever in such negotiations,' another colleague believed that Rodrigues involved himself in business affairs 'with less caution and religious prudence than is fitting.' At a later date he was said to have

erred in greatly involving himself towards the end in trade and the administration of

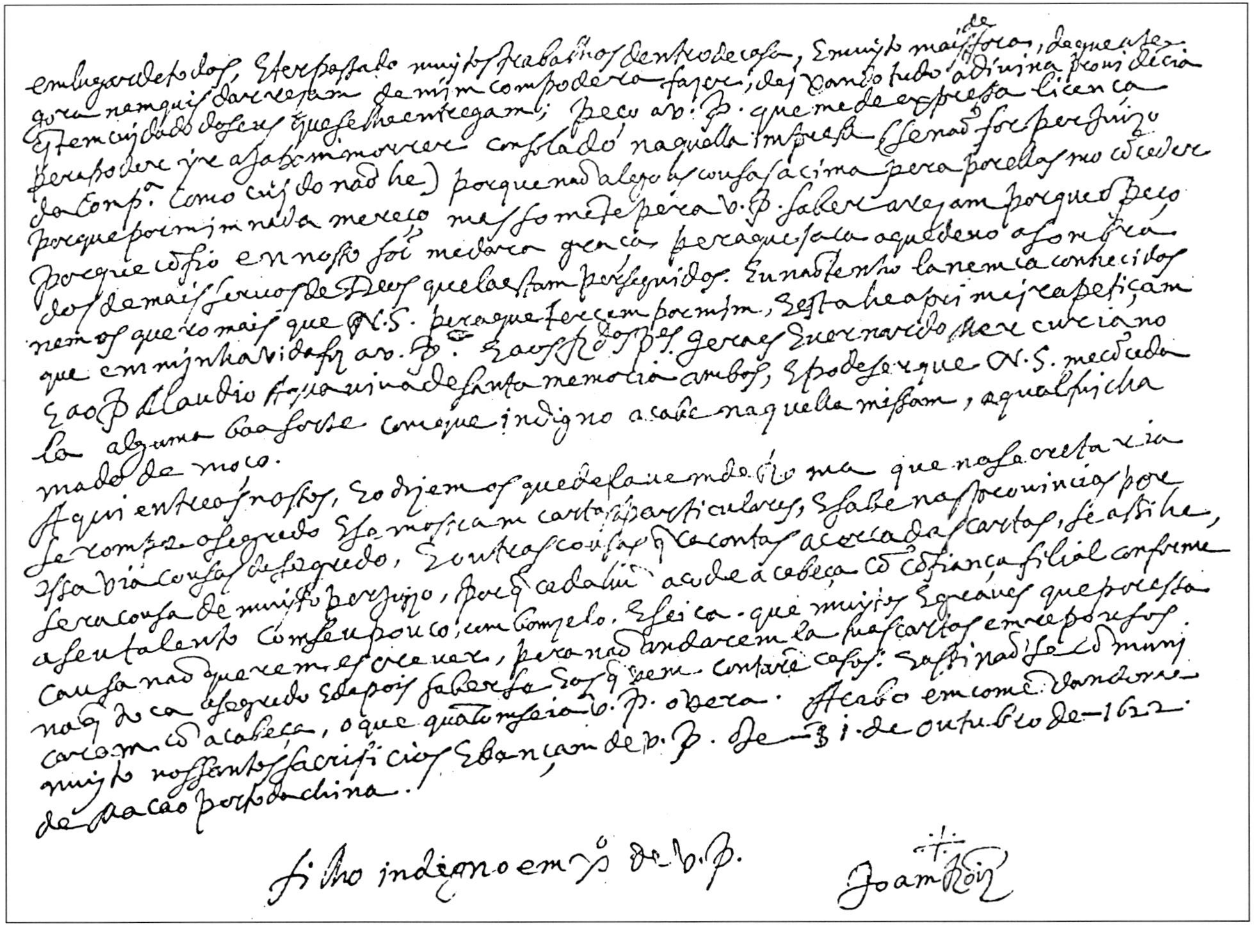

Plate 4: The last page of an autograph letter written by Rodrigues in Macao on 31 October 1622, in which he asks the Jesuit General in Rome for permission to return to Japan. Jesuit Archives, Rome: JapSin 18, f. 9v. *With permission of the Director of the Archivum Romanum Societatis Iesu.*

Nagasaki. ... He took rather a lot of liberties in this, and he made many enemies outside the house. ... They persecuted him (unjustly, I believe) and forced him to leave Japan.[1]

Despite growing tension, Rodrigues visited the retired Ieyasu in 1607, and then, at the ruler's suggestion, he travelled to Edo (present-day Tokyo) to pay his respects to his son, the shogun Hidetada. He made further visits to Ieyasu in the following two years. But the affair of the Portuguese ship *Madre de Deus* at the beginning of 1610 brought matters to a head, although Rodrigues was not directly involved. Claiming that the carrack's crew had mistreated Japanese sailors in Macao, local forces unsuccessfully attacked the ship in Nagasaki harbour. After a valiant three-day defence, Captain-Major Andre Pessoa realized that further resistance was useless and resolutely blew up the vessel, causing Japanese casualties and the loss of its rich cargo. This incident created much resentment on the Japanese side, and the Jesuit authorities reluctantly decided that, for the well-being of the mission, Rodrigues would have to be sacrificed and leave the country. And so, after residing in Japan for more than three decades, the Interpreter sailed from Nagasaki in the second half of March, bound for exile in Macao.[2] Although he requested permission to return (see Plate 4), his wish was not granted, and he spent the remaining twenty-three years of his life in Macao and the interior of China. Four years later, in 1614, the Tokugawa authorities issued a decree expelling missionaries from Japan and the era of anti-Christian persecution began.

China

During his Macao exile, Rodrigues made lengthy journeys inside China, and in his correspondence speaks about his experiences during extended stays in the interior, one of which lasted more than two years. During at least the first years of his travels, he was unable to speak Chinese and needed an interpreter, although he appears to have eventually learnt the language; his prior knowledge of Chinese characters used in written Japanese would have been helpful in this regard. In his letters he recounts some of his experiences within China. He attended a banquet given by the military governor of Canton (Guangzhou) at which he presented the official with a treatise on Christian teaching and promised to arrange the dispatch of terrestrial and celestial globes from Macao to the Beijing court. On a later occasion he travelled along the mighty Yangzi and was impressed by the system of great locks that made river transport possible for hundreds of boats. He reported the discovery of the Nestorian Stone near Xianfu about 1623, being the first European to present a detailed and accurate summary of the monument's lengthy inscription.

Never one to shirk an argument, Rodrigues took part in the heated Rites Controversy, and although revering Matteo Ricci as a saintly man, he was inexorably opposed to religious adaptation, both in liturgy and terminology, to Chinese traditions.[3] Within a few years of leaving Japan, he comments modestly about his contribution to the debate, 'The Fathers in China knew nothing about this, and as Our Lord has enlightened me in this

---

[1] These quotations are found in Cooper, *Rodrigues the Interpreter*, pp. 66, 254, 260.

[2] This is merely a summary of the complex developments leading to Rodrigues's departure; a full account is given in ibid., pp. 248–68.

[3] Perhaps because Xavier during his stay in Japan had for a while erroneously identified the Buddhist Dainichi with the Christian deity, the Jesuits in Japan were cautious about religious adaptation, and avoided using Japanese terms in their teaching, employing instead transliterated European words. Further details in ibid., pp. 284–6, and Üçerler, in Gómez, *Compendium*, III, pp. 52–5.

matter, they will receive much light from my going into China.' In his last letter, written only a few months before his death in 1633, he confidently claimed that colleagues in China who did not agree with him had 'shown some kind of passion where there should be none'.[1]

In late 1628, Rodrigues set out from Macao with a crew of Portuguese gunners and cannons to Beijing at the request of the faltering Ming dynasty under attack by Mongol troops. On his reaching the capital in February 1630, rumour spread that the Jesuit, then sixty-eight years of age, was no less than 250 years old, and crowds pressed around, trying to touch him so that his alleged longevity might be transmitted to them. By order of the Chinese court, he returned to Macao to recruit reinforcements, and on 31 October 1630 he started out with a regiment of some four hundred soldiers. At Nanchang the contingent was halted and not allowed to proceed further, but Rodrigues was able to press on with a small band of soldiers. By chance he met up with a Korean embassy in 1631 on its way to Beijing, and ever ready to establish new relations he presented it with Christian books, a telescope, and a pair of guns as a gift to the king of Korea.[2] Before reaching Beijing, Rodrigues and his companions were trapped for a month in the besieged city of Dengzhou. When traitors opened the city gates and allowed the enemy to enter, Rodrigues and nineteen others escaped by jumping from the city walls into a bed of snow. They then continued on to the capital, where the elderly Jesuit received official commendations and honours from the grateful court.

Rodrigues returned to Macao in January 1633 and died there in the summer of that year at the age of seventy-one; the cause of his death was a hernia, an injury possibly incurred during his extensive travels and exertions in the Chinese interior. He was buried on 1 August under the floor of St Paul's Church, whose grandiose and impressive façade exists to this day.

Writings

As far as his written work is concerned, Rodrigues's main claim to fame has so far been his two grammars of spoken Japanese. Newly arrived missionaries in Japan were required to study the language, and there was an obvious need for a standard textbook and dictionary. The latter was eventually provided by *Vocabulario da lingoa de Iapam*, Nagasaki, 1603–4, a monumental Japanese-Portuguese dictionary compiled by a committee of Jesuits, both Japanese and foreign, and printed on the European press imported in 1590. Containing some 32,000 entries, this remarkable work offers concise and objective definitions, distinguishing Buddhist, Shinto, literary, women's and children's words, and providing examples to show correct usage. Some of its listed colloquial terms are not found elsewhere in any written source and would have been lost but for their inclusion in the *Vocabulario*. Francisco

[1] Cooper, *Rodrigues the Interpreter*, pp. 352, 282. Rodrigues's self-confidence in this matter may be called into doubt. At least in his early visits to China he was unable to speak the language and required an interpreter. More generally, Superiors' confidential reports about him in Japan more than once refer to his *sciencia mediocre* (JapSin 25, ff. 44, 107v, 114), although in fairness this should be translated as 'average learning' in the context. But Rodrigues's rambling and disorganized style of writing in his letters, the two editions of his *Arte*, and the present work indicates a certain lack of intellectual discipline.

[2] As a result of this largesse, Rodrigues is mentioned (as 'Jo-han') in *Kukcho Pogam*, the Korean dynastic records, where he is described as '97 years old and with a noble spirit and graceful appearance'. Cooper, *Rodrigues the Interpreter*, pp. 348–9.

Rodrigues was the general editor of the project until his departure from Japan in 1603. The learned José Luis Alvarez-Taladriz detected a slight change in editorial policy from f. 270 in the work, and has suggested that João Rodrigues, the acknowledged expert in Japanese, might have taken over the task of editing the dictionary at that point.[1] This hypothesis cannot be definitely proved, but in view of Rodrigues's fluency, it is certainly plausible.

If there is uncertainty regarding his participation in the compilation of the dictionary, there can be no doubt about Rodrigues's authorship of a grammar of spoken Japanese, *Arte da lingoa de Iapam*, Nagasaki, 1604–8 (often referred to as *Arte grande*), for the title page clearly gives his name as author. Following the example of the Chinese, the Japanese have always shown greater interest in their literary language than in their colloquial, and the *Arte grande* can probably claim to be the first grammar of spoken Japanese to be published. Valuable though the work may be today for philologists studying the language spoken in the early seventeenth century, the grammar leaves a great deal to be desired as a textbook for beginners. Long lists of rules, followed by equally long lists of exceptions, would have daunted even the most zealous student.

Rodrigues based his work on Manuel Alvarez's celebrated Latin grammar, *De institutione grammatica*, Lisbon, 1572. Just as Alvarez begins his textbook with tables declining *dominus*, 'lord', so on the first page of his grammar, without offering any general introduction to the Japanese language, Rodrigues abruptly starts by declining *aruji*, 'lord'. It would, of course, have been far more useful to have produced a textbook based not on Latin principles but on Japanese as an entirely different language, requiring an entirely different approach to its study. But as the Jesuit representative, travelling constantly on mission business and paying frequent visits to court to lobby lords and senior officials, Rodrigues was a busy man and may well not have had the time and experience to compose an entirely original work.

In addition, Rodrigues's departure from Portugal at such a young age meant that he could have received little formal education in his home country. True, he studied Western philosophy and Catholic theology in Japan in preparation for the priesthood, but he himself candidly admits in one of his letters, 'I came from Europe as a child ... so I possess neither style in our Portuguese language nor method of writing briefly what is necessary.'[2]

For anyone interested in Japanese history and culture, the most fascinating part of *Arte grande* is the third and final section in which the author no longer depends on the Alvarez model. Here Rodrigues deals with Japanese poetry, history, money tables, ranks of Buddhist monks, letter writing, and a list of emperors (together with a table of Biblical figures such as Adam, Enoch, and Abraham), all of which demonstrates his wide knowledge of Japanese life and culture, even though the information provided has admittedly little or no relevance to the Japanese language as such.

In the preface of his grammar, the author candidly acknowledges that some readers (presumably his Jesuit brethren) had criticized his diffuse style and had suggested that a more concise work would be of greater use. Taking this advice to heart, he promises to bring out a shorter version for beginners, although insisting that the present edition is essential for

---

[1] In Valignano, *Sumario*, p. 421, n. 27. Doi does not agree, pointing out the differences in the spelling of Japanese words in *Vocabulario* and in Rodrigues's known works. Doi, *Kirishitan Gogaku*, pp. 55–106; summarized in Doi, 'Sprachstudium', pp. 456–7. But Rodrigues himself used slightly different spelling systems in the two editions of his Japanese grammar.

[2] Cooper, *Rodrigues the Interpreter*, p. 297.

anyone wishing to study Japanese in depth. His shorter *Arte breve da lingoa iapoa*, Macao (or *Arte breve*), was finally published in 1620, and was intended, as its full title states, 'for those who are beginning to learn the first principles [of the language]'. Although its title tells us that it is 'taken from *Arte grande*', the 1620 grammar is not merely an abridged edition of the earlier work, for it presents a new and improved approach to learning Japanese. Its first pages are taken up with an exposition of the author's views on language study, and instead of plunging immediately into nouns and verbs he discusses the need for correct pronunciation. But old habits die hard, and the second book still contains some forty pages listing interesting but extraneous information about the sixty-six provinces, the civil service, titles of emperors, and the organization of the various Buddhist sects.

In addition to these two grammars, Rodrigues reports in his letters that he wrote various polemical treatises in China expressing his views on the thorny problem of the Chinese Rites, but these tracts have yet to be discovered and presumably have not survived. The same fate was suffered by a three-volume atlas of Asia that he mentions in a letter written in 1627, and his knowledge of contemporaneous European understanding of Asian geography will become apparent below. As regards his correspondence to Europe, the texts, either in his own distinctive writing or in copy, of ten letters have come down to us. As he spent more than thirty years in Japan, it is disappointing that only one letter has been preserved from that period (Nagasaki, 28 February 1598), while the rest were written during his exile in Macao and the interior of China. Some of these letters are extremely long and amply demonstrate Rodrigues's meandering and repetitive style, a feature found in his description of Japanese culture.[1]

The *History* of the Japanese Mission

There was considerable interest in Europe about Japan in the sixteenth century, for Marco Polo's hearsay (and erroneous) account of its wealth of gold had aroused intense interest in his fabled island of Zipangu. One of the objectives of Columbus's voyages of discovery was in fact to locate the mysterious island, and he believed that he had succeeded in this quest when he landed at Cuba in 1492. Despite this interest, the missionaries faced formidable problems in Japan, for the country was remote from Europe, lack of manpower impeded evangelization, and the mission was chronically short of cash to cover expenses and finance new projects. Rodrigues was not the only writer to mention these problems, for the Jesuit Visitor (or inspector) Valignano, who visited Japan three times, discusses the matter in his numerous and lengthy letters.[2] To foster greater interest in Japan and gain further resources of manpower and finance, Valignano hit on the imaginative plan of sending to Europe a mission of four well-born boys representing three of the Christian *daimyo* in Kyushu. The delegation left in 1582 and achieved considerable success in Catholic Europe, where the youthful representatives were feted and feasted, meeting Philip II twice, two popes, and a future pope.[3]

---

[1] An English translation of his letters written in China is given in Rodrigues, 'Rodrigues in China'. His Nagasaki letter is discussed at length in Cooper, *Rodrigues the Interpreter*, pp. 163–81.

[2] For biographical information about Valignano, see p. 5, n. 2. Rodrigues alludes to the mission's financial problems in the preface to his *History*, on p. 6, below. For these problems, see Schütte, *Valignano's Mission Principles*, 2, pp. 35–7, 237–9; Boxer, *Christian Century*, pp. 104–21; Cooper, *Rodrigues the Interpreter*, pp. 239–47. The Jesuits owed more than 11,700 taels in Japan when they were expelled in 1614; ten years later the Japanese mission's debts had risen to 30,000 taels. Lisbon, Ajuda, 49–V–6, f. 154, and 49–V–7, f. 95.

[3] A useful summary account of this expedition is given in Lach, *Asia*, I, pp. 688–706.

Another way of keeping the Japanese mission before European eyes was through the printed word. A Jesuit instruction issued in 1565 suggested that missionaries should describe in their letters not only their apostolic work but also the region in which they laboured – 'the weather, the degrees of longitude, the dress, food, housing, numbers and customs of the inhabitants … ; just as other accounts are written to satisfy curiosity, so let our men write in the same way.'[1] The letters written by Jesuit missionaries working in Japan, the mysterious and long-sought island of Zipangu, met with popular response in Europe, and many of these reports were published in Latin, Spanish, or Portuguese editions.[2] But piecemeal letters (some written about local affairs) contained only piecemeal information, and Valignano clearly saw the need for an integrated history of the mission in Japan to provide European readers with a succinct and balanced account of the Jesuit enterprise.

It was not difficult to choose a well-qualified candidate to compile such a record, for the Jesuit Luís Fróis (1532–97) was the chronicler par excellence of the Japanese mission. Not only did he write many letters and treatises about Japan, but for years he had served as the Jesuit Provincial's secretary and Valignano's amanuensis, and thus was well informed about the mission's affairs.[3] In the course of his career in Japan, he had met and conversed with leading figures such as Nobunaga and Hideyoshi, virtual rulers of the country in their day. In addition Fróis possessed a singularly felicitous literary style, albeit (by today's standards, at least) a trifle verbose, and his zeal for recording in orderly fashion not only the affairs of the mission but also aspects of Japanese life was proverbial. Fróis had arrived in Japan in 1563, and although he had not worked in the mission during its first fourteen years of existence, he obtained first-hand information by interviewing some of its earliest members. He had, moreover, personally known Xavier in India.

So Fróis was commissioned to compile the history of the first fifty years of the Japanese mission. He began work in 1585, but it was no easy task, as he enjoyed indifferent health and for many hours a day was occupied as Valignano's secretary. Eight years later he reported to Rome that the text was finally completed. Thanks to his neat and orderly reports, we know a good deal about the structure of his history. To place the work in context, he composed an introductory book of thirty-seven chapters about Japanese life. The first thirteen dealt with general topics such as the climate, people, monarchy, government, housing, food, weapons, medicines, writing, and tea ceremony. As the entire work was to deal with the Christian mission, it was only appropriate that the remaining chapters in this introductory book should cover Japanese religion – Buddhist monks and sects, temples, preaching, and the indigenous Shinto religion.[4] The inclusion of this introductory book is not without relevance, for some thirty years later Rodrigues, perhaps following Fróis's

---

[1] Cooper, *Southern Barbarians*, p. 99. In February 1592 the senior Jesuits in Japan held a provincial meeting (or 'Congregation') at Nagasaki. They drew up 43 decrees, the 36th of which deals with the need to keep Europe well informed about Japan through official annual letters. Latin text in Valignano, *Sumario*, p. 729.

[2] The best collection of such letters is found in the bulky *Cartas*, 2 vols, Evora, 1598, a work often quoted in the following pages.

[3] A listing of Fróis's 130 extant letters and other writings is given in Fróis, *História*, 1, pp. 34*–42*. For biographical information about Fróis, see p. 3, n. 4.

[4] Fróis, *História*, I, pp. 11–13. It is unfortunate that Fróis's account of Japan and its Buddhist sects has not survived.

example, himself composed a similar account of Japan, a translation of which forms the basis of the present volume. As regards the history of the mission as such, Fróis compiled two more books with a total of eighty chapters, continuing his account down to 1593, methodically dealing in his elegant style with mission activity year by year.

Fróis was naturally anxious that his lengthy account, the fruit of so many years' labour, should be sent to Rome for publication. But alas for the overworked, infirm, and now elderly author, his work did not meet with the approval of Valignano, who considered the history to be too diffuse and unsuitable for publication without extensive editing and reduction in length. Here one can extend a certain sympathy toward Valignano, as Fróis often goes into excessive detail when only a succinct one-volume history was needed. His detailed hearsay account of Nobunaga's violent death in June 1582, for example, makes fascinating reading for the present-day historian, but there is hardly need for an entire chapter to be devoted to the subject in a history of the Christian mission.

While admitting that his text contained passages that could be amended, Fróis protested that a wholesale revision was neither necessary nor possible. But Valignano's decision prevailed, and as an unhappy result, the valuable record remained unpublished until the 1970s, when at last, after nearly four hundred years' delay, it finally appeared in its entirety.[1]

The over-committed Valignano then decided to compile his own version of the history, and devoted himself to this enterprise between March and July 1601 in Nagasaki during the last of his three visits to Japan. He already had material at hand, because in 1583, during his first visit, he had composed *Historia del principio y progresso de la Compañía de Jesús en las Indias Orientales*, covering the years 1542–64. The work contains no less than seven chapters dealing with Xavier in Japan and also a general description of the country and its people. His projected history of the Japanese mission was to consist of five books covering its foundation in 1549 to the end of the sixteenth century. In the event, Valignano was able to complete only down to 1570 and thus his history remains incomplete. Lacking Fróis's linguistic skills and years of experience in Japan, he was at an obvious disadvantage, and much of his text is in the form of a commentary on the account contained in Giovanni Pietro Maffei, *Historiarum indicarum libri XVI*, Florence, 1588, based on letters from Japan, and Orazio Torsellini, *De vita Francisci Xaverii*, Rome, 1594. Ironically, he made considerable use of Fróis's *História,* and incorporates or paraphrases passages from the earlier work without acknowledgment.[2] The fact that Valignano did not have the time or opportunity to complete a history of the mission is unfortunate, for he spent a total of nine years in Japan, travelled widely, and met both Nobunaga and Hideyoshi. With a doctorate in law from the University of Padua, he shows considerable administrative talent as well as intellectual acumen in his writings. His masterly treatise on Japanese land tenure, for example, reveals a high order of analysis and grasp of detail.[3] But Valignano's contribution suffered the same fate as Fróis's work and remained unstudied at any depth until recent years.[4]

[1] Fróis, *História,* Lisbon, 5 vols, 1976–84. A German translation of the first part of his *História* is given in *Die Geschichte Japans,* 1926, while most of the second part was published in *Segunda parte,* 1938.

[2] Üçerler, 'Sacred Historiography', 2, pp. LII–LIV.

[3] Alvarez-Taladriz includes this text in Valignano, *Sumario,* pp. 318–30.

[4] Valignano's text is in the British Library, Add.MSS 9857, and Ajuda, Jesuítas na Asia, 49–IV–53, ff. 244–420. It has been thoroughly studied in Üçerler, 'Sacred Historiography'.

Rodrigues's *History*

Despite the evident need for such an account, a full-scale history of the Japanese mission had yet to appear in print, and so the Jesuit superiors appointed yet another man for the work. This was to be João Rodrigues. A vague and indirect reference to this matter was made by the Jesuit Nicholas Trigault in 1615 when he published his *Rei christianae apud japonios commentarius,* based on the 1609–12 annual letters from Japan. He notes in the preface that having published an account of the Chinese mission, he has now turned to bringing out a record of events in Japan, 'but certainly not a complete history, for this is being written separately by one of the Jesuits residing among the Japanese.'[1] Trigault does not identify this author, but he was presumably not referring to Rodrigues, who had already left Japan for Macao in 1610. It is likely that the writer in question was Mateus de Couros, for in 1624 the Jesuit superior in Japan, Francisco Pacheco, wrote to Rome:

> Fr Couros has been very ill for eleven years and can do little or no work on the *History of Japan,* and so Fr Visitor [Jerónimo Rodrigues] has excused him from this task. I have asked Fr Visitor to give the work to Fr João Rodrigues, the Interpreter, so that he may gather the material and put it in order, and then write it up in the best style he can manage, so that afterwards someone else may arrange it better. For this reason I have sent to Macao (and am sending even this year) all the documents relevant to the *History* that we have here.[2]

The reasons for this choice of author were evident. Rodrigues had spent more than thirty years working in Japan, spoke the language fluently, had witnessed many of the events to be mentioned in the mission history, and had personally met most of the outstanding Japanese personalities of his time. Another reason might well have been to keep the elderly but still active Rodrigues busily occupied. After bringing out his second grammar book in 1620, it is possible that, between his travels in the interior of China, he had considerable time on his hands in the small enclave of Macao.

But Rodrigues had been entrusted with the project some years before Pacheco wrote the above letter in 1624. The catalogue of the Jesuits working in the Japanese mission, compiled in September 1620, reports about him: 'The Interpreter; ... is compiling the *History of Japan.*'[3] Further, as will be seen below, internal evidence shows that Rodrigues wrote at least part of the work in 1620–21. By 1622 he had completed a considerable portion of the *History,* and in a letter to Rome from Macao he shows that he fully understood his commission, as mentioned by Pacheco, to gather material for someone else to write up in elegant style.

> The *History of Japan* ... is now being concluded. Although I have not got an elegant style, I am doing the *History,* and later someone who has style will arrange it. So it will be a work full of mistakes and unfounded conjectures of those who compose it and not true facts. ... The Visitor, Fr Jerónimo Rodrigues, spoke to me and at the persuasion of the Japanese Fathers, I applied myself to the first part of this history, because I know more than anyone else about the things of Japan both before and after the persecution of Kampaku [Hideyoshi] up to the present time. I know the language and the history of the country well, and about the sects better than anyone else because I studied them. I have done a large part of it, including a true account both of the things and customs of

---

[1] In the Introduction to Trigault, *Rei christianae,* no page number.
[2] Schütte, *Archivo,* pp. 31–2.
[3] Cooper, *Rodrigues the Interpreter,* p. 297.

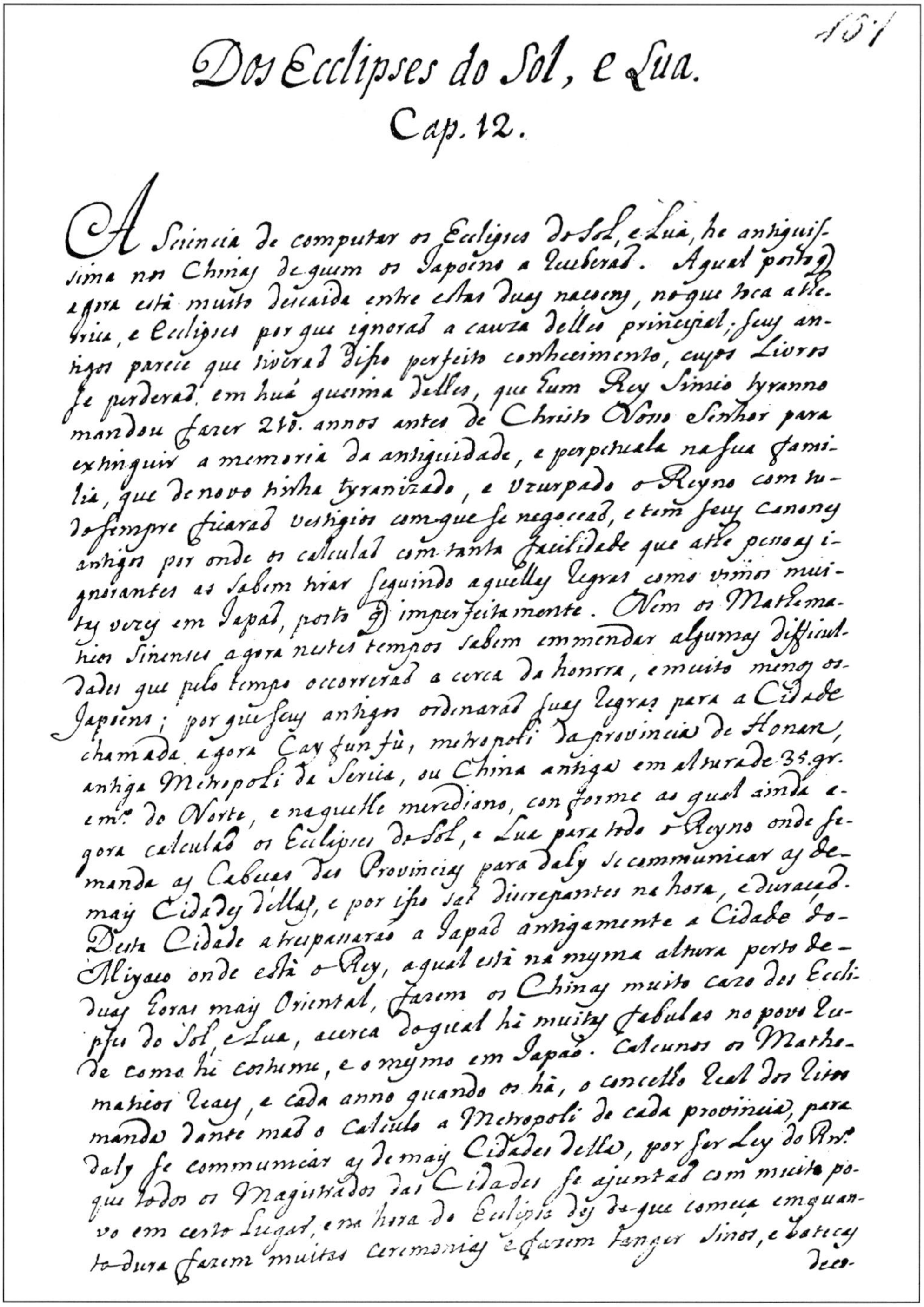

Dos Ecclipses do Sol, e Lua.
Cap. 12.

A Sciencia de computar os Ecclipses do Sol, e Lua, he antiquissima nos Chinas de quem os Japoins a receberad. A qual porem agora está muito descaida entre estas duas naçoeis, no que toca a theorica, e Ecclipses por que ignorad a causa delles principal; seus antigos parece que tiverad diso perfeito conhecimento, cujos Livros se perderad em hua queima delles, que hum Rey Sinico tyranno mandou fazer 2.0 annos antes de Christo Noso Senhor para extinguir a memoria da antiguidade, e perpetuala na sua familia, que de novo tinha tyranizado, e vrurpado o Reyno com tudo sempre ficarad vestigios com que se negoceia, e tem seu canon antigo por onde os calculad com tanta facilidade que atte pessoa ignorantes as sabem tirar seguindo aquelly Regras como vimos muity very em Japad, posto q imperfeitamente. Nem os Mathematicos Sinenses agora nestes tempos sabem emendar algumas difficuldades que pelo tempo occorrerad a cerca da honrra, e muito menos os Japoins; por que seu antigo ordinarad suas Regras para a Cidade chamada agora Cay fun fù, metropoli da provincia de Honan, antiga Metropoli de Sericia, ou China antiga em altura de 35.gr. em.o do Norte, e naquelle meridiano, conforme as qual ainda agora calculad os Ecclipses do Sol, e Lua para todo o Reyno onde se manda as Cabeças das Provincias para daly se communicar as may Cidady d'ellas, e por iso sat discrepantes na hora, e durações. Desta Cidade atrespasarad a Japad antigamente a Cidade do Miyaco onde está o Rey, a qual está na mysma altura perto de duas horas may Oriental, fazem os Chinas muito caro des Ecclipses do Sol, e Lua, acerca do qual hi muitas fabulas no povo Lusde como hi costume, e o mymo em Japad. Calculos os Mathemathicos Reay, e cada anno quando os ha, o conceito Real dos Ecclimando dante mad o Calculo a Metropoli de cada provincia, para daly se communicar as demay Cidades delles, por ser Ley do Rro. que todos os Magistrados das Cidades se ajuntad com muito povo em certo Lugat, e na hora do Eclipse dos de que começa emquanto dura fazem muitas ceremonias e fazem tanger Sinos, e baterej
deso-

Plate 5: The first page of Book 2, Chapter 12, 'The Eclipses of the Sun and Moon', in the copy of Rodrigues's *History* transcribed in Macao about 1746. *Library, Ajuda Palace, Lisbon.*

the kingdom, and of the arrival of our holy Fr Francis Xavier [in August 1549] up to the death of Father Cosme de Torres [in October 1570], the period of the first twenty years.[1]

Rodrigues goes on to observe sadly that neither the previous Visitor, Jerónimo Rodrigues, nor the present one, Gabriel de Matos, had afforded him any help or favour towards completing the project, an echo of the elderly Fróis's earlier complaint that he had received no assistance in bringing his major project to a conclusion. Five years later Rodrigues again wrote to Rome and had this to say about his progress:

> The insects and the fire will consume everything, and us with it too, if God so wishes, as also the *History of the Church of Japan*, at least the first forty years of its foundation, which I have now finished in two bulky parts. Those of us who have true knowledge of these events and have seen nearly everything at first hand are now dying off. Some days ago Fr Visitor [André Palmeiro] told me to carry on with this work, but I am old.[2]

This letter shows that by 1627 Rodrigues had written the first forty years of the *History*, that is, 1549–90. Whether he completed any more is not known; as it is, only the first two introductory books on Japanese life and the first book dealing with the foundation of the mission, 1549–52, have so far come to light.

Fortunately there still exists a general plan of the projected work and this gives some idea of the complete *History* as envisaged by its author. The full table of contents, written in Rodrigues's hand with many corrections, occupies four folios and goes into considerable detail. There was to be a Prologue, to be followed by Part 1, consisting of ten books, of which the first two are still extant and are translated in the present volume. These two books cover 'the position and antiquity of Japan… Japanese letters, liberal and mechanical arts.' There is no indication whether he completed the remaining eight introductory books, which were to deal with the Japanese king, nobility, Buddhist sects, Confucianism, Shinto, and Taoism.

Part 2 was to consist of the actual history, from the mission's foundation in 1549 down to 1634, with each of its ten books covering the period of office of a mission superior. This was a somewhat awkward division for there was no fixed length for Jesuit superiors to remain in office and their terms varied considerably. Thus Book 6 would cover thirteen years (Francisco Pasio, superior 1600–1613), while Book 8 would deal with only three (Mateus Couros, 1619–22). It is interesting to note that Book 10 was to continue down to 1634. Couros was appointed superior of the mission for a second time in 1626, and presumably Rodrigues believed that he would continue in office until 1634.[3] As it was, both Couros and Rodrigues died in 1633, another indication that Rodrigues never completed his ambitious project. Finally, Part 3 of the *History* would not deal directly with Japan at all, but would describe the missions in China, Siam, Cambodia, and Korea.[4]

The similarity between the structure of Fróis's and Rodrigues's histories is apparent,

---

[1] Ibid., p. 297.
[2] Ibid., pp. 297–8.
[3] Rodrigues's reference here to 1634 was not a slip of the pen, for the same date is mentioned again in the work's title and Preface.
[4] The table of contents is found in Madrid, Real Academia de la Historia, Jesuítas 7237, ff. 3–6.

for both were to deal with Japanese life in the first part and the actual history of the mission in the second.[1] Whether Rodrigues had read the earlier *History* is not known. He was, of course, certainly aware of its existence, for he refers to it in the Prologue of his own work.

There still exists an autograph seven-folio fragment titled *Bispos da Igreja do Japam*, in which Rodrigues describes the work of the first six bishops of Japan,[2] and in the course of this essay includes interesting information not found elsewhere. Internal evidence shows that this brief account was written in 1624. Presumably the author intended it to be incorporated into his *History*, but it is difficult to know exactly where and how it can be included as the fragment is not mentioned in the table of contents, nor does its subject matter fit easily into the work's general scheme.[3]

One further point may be raised regarding the dating of Rodrigues's *History*. There is still extant in Madrid a ten-folio autograph manuscript titled *Breve aparato para a história de Japam melhor se entender*, and its text corresponds more or less to Part I, Chapter I of the *History*, 'General Description of Asia.' In many passages the texts are completely identical, while in others additional information is provided, usually in *Breve aparato*; parts of the essay may also be found elsewhere in the *History*. From internal evidence it appears that the brief work was written in 1633, and indeed the author's death in the summer of that year must have cut short his composition of the account for the piece is obviously unfinished.[4] Rodrigues certainly intended *Breve aparato* to form part of his *History* for he inserted its title immediately after the Introduction in his autograph table of contents of the entire work, but his purpose in composing the *Breve aparato* is not at all clear. Obviously there is no room in the *History* for both this piece and the practically identical Chapter I. On his return from the interior of China in early 1633, the indefatigable author probably decided to rewrite the opening chapter in somewhat different form. As he did not complete this revision before his death, a later copyist transcribed the original version of Chapter I. Whatever the reason, it is surely remarkable that the 71-year-old Jesuit had enough energy after his exhausting journey through China to begin revising his work and to continue the task as far as the heading 'The ancient nobility of China'. These may well be the last words he wrote before his death.

Dispersion of the Texts

Whatever its value, Rodrigues's work was to suffer the same fate as Fróis's and Valignano's accounts, and remain buried away and unpublished until recent times. It would have stayed in Macao, unread and unappreciated, except that the Real Academia da Historia Portuguesa, founded in Lisbon in December 1720, began seeking in Asia historical material related to Portugal and its overseas possessions. Before setting out for his diocese in 1742, the newly appointed bishop of Macao, Hilário de Santa Rosa, OFM, and his companion

[1] When writing about the Church in China, Alvaro Semedo followed the same pattern: the 31 chapters of the first part of his *History* deal with China in general, while the 13 chapters of the second relate the history of the Christian mission.

[2] Of these six Portuguese bishops, the first two were given ecclesiastical jurisdiction over China as well as Japan, while the rest were assigned only to Japan. Only two of them ever reached Japan.

[3] Madrid, Real Academia de la Historia, Jesuítas, 7236, ff. 317–23. For more information about this short work, see Schütte, 'Historia inédita'. A Japanese translation of the text is given in Rodrigues, *Nihon*, II, pp. 605–67.

[4] Madrid, Real Academia de la Historia, Jesuítas 7237, ff. 6v–16.

José de Jesús Maria, OFM, had been in contact with the Real Academia, and on their arrival at Macao in November of the same year, the latter began the task of sorting and copying documents of historical value. Also travelling with them on the same ship was the Jesuit José Montanha (1708–64), and he too began work on copying materials in the Jesuit archives to send back to Portugal. Montanha personally examined hundreds of documents, and employed a staff of eight or ten scribes to make copies of the more important items. Two years after his arrival in Macao, Montanha sent to the Real Academia historical material dealing with the Macao diocese.[1]

When Montanha was posted to the mission of Siam in 1745, his work was taken over by his assistant, Brother João Álvares. For reasons unknown, from then onwards the copies were sent, not to the Real Academia, but to the Lisbon office of the Jesuit Procurator of the Japanese mission. Some of the manuscript volumes preserved in Lisbon still carry today a note written by Álvares:

> I am sending this book to the office of the Procurator of the Japanese Province in Lisbon in this month of January 1747, on the ship *S. Pedro e S. João*. It is to be kept in the said office and not removed therefrom. 1st day of January 1747. João Álvares.[2]

As regards Rodrigues's work, Álvares appears to have found only Volume 1, Books 1 and 2, that is, the description of Japan, and Volume 2, Book 1, 1549–52, of the actual history, for he noted at the beginning of the transcribed text: 'As it says in the frontispiece, this work ought to include the history of Japan from 1549 to 1634, but the volume contains only 1549–52.'[3] As noted above, Rodrigues definitely completed the first forty years of the mission's history, but as the careful Álvares could not find the part dealing with 1552–90, we may presume that the bulk of the work had already been lost by the middle of the eighteenth century. Thus comparatively little of Rodrigues's *History* is extant today.

Soon after the arrival of the copies in Europe, the government in Portugal suppressed the Society of Jesus in its domains and confiscated its property. The books and manuscripts found in Jesuit houses were assigned to the library of the Palacio Real in Lisbon in order to replace the material destroyed in the great earthquake of 1755. They were stored in the Ajuda district of the capital, and when a royal palace was built there early in the nineteenth century, the materials were deposited in its library. Cataloguing the manuscripts was delayed by the Napoleonic invasion and later by revolution, and only at the end of the nineteenth century was it discovered that the collection contained some sixty volumes of manuscripts relating to Jesuit missions in India, Japan, and China.[4]

The story of the dispersion of the Jesuit archives in Macao does not end here. In September 1759 the Portuguese authorities commandeered the Jesuit houses in Goa and confiscated their possessions. Brother Álvares realized that it was only a matter of time before the Jesuit property in Macao would suffer a similar fate, and to safeguard the archives on which

---

[1] For Montanha and his work in Macao, see Fróis, *História*, I, p. 16*; Schütte, *Archivo*, pp. 41–5; Üçerler, 'Sacred Historiography', 2, pp. LXIX–LXXII. Although the Franciscans were definitely in contact with the Real Academia, the relations between Montanha and that institution remain unclear.

[2] Lisbon, Ajuda, 49–IV–51, f. 1; similar notices appear in 17 other volumes. Cooper, 'João Rodrigues', p. 62; Üçerler, 'Sacred Historiography', II, p. LXXI.

[3] Lisbon, Ajuda, 49–IV–53, f. 1.

[4] Schütte, *Archivo*, pp. 38–44; Braga, *Jesuítas*, pp. 19–21.

he had expended so much time and labour, he made arrangements for the original documents and a second set of copies to be sent to the Philippines and safely preserved there, outside the Portuguese sphere of influence. The original manuscripts and new copies were accordingly packed into four large crates (the extant autograph part of Rodrigues's *History* travelled in the second crate) and in 1761 were shipped to Manila, where they were stored in the Jesuit college of S. Ildefonso. Álvares acted just in time, for in the following year the Macao Jesuits were deported to Goa and from there, with much hardship and suffering, to Europe.[1]

But the persecution of the Jesuits was not confined to Portugal and its possessions, as Álvares had supposed, and in May 1768 the Jesuits in Manila were arrested, the four crates of documents confiscated, and a catalogue made of their contents. The papers were then repacked, and in January 1773 were sent to Madrid, where the original documents remain in La Real Academia de la Historia to this day.[2] But Álvares's second set of copies somehow found their way into private hands and were bought by Sir Thomas Phillipps (1792–1872) for his own magnificent library. In 1946 two London book dealers, Lionel and Philip Robinson, bought part of the Phillipps collection, and in 1988 Sotheby's auctioned various items, including the Madrid copy of Rodrigues's *History*, which went to the well-known antiquarian bookstore Isseidō in Tokyo.[3] In May 1991, during his last visit to Japan, I accompanied the late Professor Charles Boxer to Isseidō, and was there shown the much-travelled manuscript. Unfortunately I was unable to compare it with my own photocopy of the Ajuda text or examine it in any detail.

To sum up this somewhat complicated account, the following scheme shows the present locations of the relevant manuscripts in public archives. Underlined items appear in translation or summary form in the present volume.

Lisbon: Biblioteca da Ajuda

Jesuítas na Asia, 49–IV–53, ff. 1–183. *Historia da Igreja do Japão, na qual se contem como se deu principio a pregação do Sagrado Evangelho neste Reyno ...* (Volume 1, Book 1, ff. 3–141; Book 2, ff. 141v–83. Copy.)

Madrid: La Real Academia de la Historia

Jesuítas 7236, ff. 317–23. *Bispos da Igreja do Japam, e ordem per que foram soccedendo ate este presente anno de 1614.* (Autograph.)

Jesuítas 7237, ff. 1–16. *História da Igreja de Japam, na qual se tra[ta] co[mo] S. Franicsco Xa[vier] da Companhia de Jesus, deu principio...*
(*Proemio ao leitor*, ff. 2–3; *Indice de los libros*, ff. 3–6; *Breve aparato*, ff. 6v–16. Autograph.)

Jesuítas 7238, ff. 1–88. *Segunda parte da historia eclesiastica de Iapam ...* (Volume 2, Book 1, dealing with the events of 1549–52. Autograph corrections.)[4]

This, in brief, is the history of the extant parts of Rodrigues's *History*, but two further

---

[1] Schütte, *Archivo*, pp. 46–74; Üçerler, 'Sacred Historiography', II, p. LXXIII.

[2] Schütte, *Archivo*, pp. 130–52; Üçerler, 'Sacred Historiography', II, pp. LXIII–LXXV.

[3] For the life and career of Phillipps, an avid bibliophile, see *Dictionary of National Biography*, XV, pp. 1078–81. I am indebted to Professor M. Antoni Üçerler, SJ, for the information about Phillipps's purchase and the subsequent fate of the manuscripts. Üçerler, 'Sacred Historiography', II, pp. LXXVI–LXXVII.

[4] Schütte, *Archivo*, pp. 176, 327–8, 329–30.

points may be raised. Neither the Macao copy of the *History* in Lisbon nor the second part in Madrid bear Rodrigues's name as the author. The latter manuscript has nothing at all to say about authorship, while in its lengthy title the former states that the work was 'composed by Religious of the same Society of Jesus who from the year 1575 to the present year 1634 have resided in these parts ...' Rodrigues is clearly named as author on the title pages of both *Arte grande* and *Arte breve*,[1] and it is not known why his name does not appear in his *History*. Perhaps as he was only preparing material for someone else to revise later in better style, he wished his contribution to remain anonymous. Also, as Fróis, Valignano, and possibly Couros had prepared the ground before him, Rodrigues may have modestly preferred to attribute the *History* to joint and anonymous authorship. Fortunately there is no lack of evidence, both direct and indirect, to prove that he was in fact the sole author.

The dating provided in the title ('who from the year 1575 to the present year 1634 have resided') presents a further problem. Why Rodrigues intended to continue his account down to 1634 has been tentatively explained above, but there appears to be no reason why the year 1575 should have been chosen as the year from which the compilers of the work began residing in Japan, for neither Rodrigues, Fróis, Valignano, nor Couros arrived in the country in that year. The significance of the year 1575 in this context defies explanation, and I can make only the unsatisfactory suggestion that the Macao copyist erred here and should have written 1549.[2]

The Contents of the *History*

Although it may be regretted that the bulk of Rodrigues's *History* has not survived, we can be consoled by the consideration that, judging from the extant 1549–1552 segment, the disappearance of most of his account is no great historical loss. It is possible that, when writing about events of which he had personal experience, Rodrigues could have contributed original material of considerable interest;[3] but when describing Xavier's foundation of the mission, he was recounting events that had taken place more than twenty years before his own arrival in Japan. Thus, writing some seventy years after these events, Rodrigues would have had to rely, just as any other author in Europe, on the limited number of sources compiled by the first missionaries in Japan.

Biographies of Xavier had been published by Orazio Torsellini at Rome in 1594, and by João de Lucena at Lisbon in 1600, and so there was no lack of material dealing with the work of the mission's founder in Japan. In addition, Sebastião Gonçalves completed his history of the Jesuits in Asia in 1614, and there was a manuscript copy of this work at

---

[1] The title page of *Arte grande* gives as author 'Fr Ioão Rodriguez of the Society of Jesus', while *Arte breve* has 'Fr Ioam Rodriguez of the Society of Jesus, Portuguese, of the diocese of Lamego'. The more specific reference in the second book was probably made to distinguish the author from his contemporary Portuguese colleague, Fr João Rodrigues Giram (or Girão), who arrived in Japan in 1586 and died in Macao in 1629, only four years before the death of the Interpreter in the same city. For centuries the two men have been mixed up, and even today it is not rare to find the first *Arte* attributed to Rodrigues Giram. Schurhammer deals with this confusion of authorship in 'Doppelgänger', pp. 124–6.

[2] This in fact is a continual problem in the translation that follows. When obvious errors occur, it is sometimes difficult to determine whether they first appeared in Rodrigues's original text or whether they are more likely due to the copyist.

[3] For example, in his brief essay *Bispos* (see pp. xxviii and xxx), Rodrigues recounts in considerable detail the events leading up to Bishop Pedro Martins's audience with Hideyoshi in 1596. Rodrigues was much involved in organizing this event and provides information not available elsewhere.

Macao.[1] When several authors deal with a short period of limited documentation, a certain amount of repetition and overlapping is inevitable, but it becomes only too apparent that similarities in Rodrigues's version go far beyond the limits of coincidence. Just as Gonçalves had freely borrowed from Lucena, so Rodrigues in his turn freely borrowed material from both authors. This dependence is somewhat ironic, for in his correspondence Rodrigues refers to the inaccuracy of works written by authors who had no firsthand experience of Japan. In fact, Rodrigues's dependence on Gonçalves and Lucena becomes positively embarrassing as he increasingly lifts the other writers' material without the courtesy of acknowledgement. While it is true that he mentions the two men by name in his Chapter 9, he offers no direct indication of his extensive dependence on them. As a result, all three works have one particular chapter with more or less an identical title and starting off with the same line.[2]

One may even hazard a guess that Rodrigues himself came to realize the futility of the exercise. The first few pages of the copy of his *History* preserved in Madrid are heavily scored with his marginal comments and corrections, but these become progressively fewer during the course of the work, as if the writer was losing interest in the project. Whereas the first of the twenty-eight chapters has about twenty-two corrections made in his distinctive writing, the last seventeen can muster a total of only seven emendations. Thus Rodrigues's account of Xavier's arrival and work in Japan makes disappointing reading and adds little to our existing knowledge. Experienced European historians, who had never set foot in Japan, but relied on the letters of the early missionaries, could and, in fact, did produce far more valuable accounts.

The two extant introductory books describing Japan and its culture tell a different story, for here Rodrigues falls back on his personal experience over a period of more than thirty years. Most of the work can be dated to 1620–21, shortly after the publication of his *Arte breve*. There are several references in the text to 'the present year of 1620', and this date may be inferred from other passages.[3] Halfway through Book 2 the author mentions 'the present year of 1621'. There are, it is true, several references, both direct and indirect, to later dates in Book 1, and these indicate subsequent additions to the text. At one point, Rodrigues refers even to 'the present year of 1633', the year of his death, and this is not an improbable date for, as noted above, his *Breve aparato* was composed in that year. After completing these two books, the author presumably made marginal additions to his manuscript from time to time to amplify and update his account, and the Macao copyist duly incorporated them into the text.

A summary perusal of the two books shows that Rodrigues obtained material from a wide range of authors and that he includes a number of quotations, especially in Book 2. Among the works or authors directly quoted are the Bible, St Basil, John Cassian, Cajetan, Clavius, Diogo de Couto, St Isidore, Josephus, Pomponius Mella, Sextus of Sienna, and the Coimbra textbooks of scholastic philosophy. References are also made to the works of

---

[1] Sebastião Gonçalves (1557–1619) wrote about the Jesuit missions in the Indies; the text is preserved in Ajuda, 49–IV–51. Two examples of Rodrigues's borrowing from Lucena are given in Cooper, 'João Rodrigues', p. 76.

[2] Cooper, *Rodrigues the Interpreter*, p. 304. Details of these borrowings are given in Cooper, 'João Rodrigues', pp. 74–6.

[3] The traditional date of Jimmu's accession is 660 BC (*Arte grande*, f. 236), and so if he began his reign '2,280 years ago', then the passage on p. 80 must have been written in 1620. Rodrigues also notes, p. 164, that 286 years had passed since 1334. As regards subsequent additions to the text, he refers to the martyrdoms of Jerónimo de Angelis (1623) and Diogo Carvalho (1624), p. 75. Other examples are given in Cooper, 'João Rodrigues', pp. 67–70, and Rodrigues, *Nihon*, I, pp. 51–2.

João de Barros, Confucius, Ise, Magini, Marinus of Tyre, Ogasawara, Ortelius, Pliny, Marco Polo, Ptolemy, and Strabo. Whether Rodrigues had read all the relevant works of these authors, or whether he had taken the quotations and references from other works, cannot be known for certain, but it may be doubted that such a busy, active man, whose formal education had been interrupted by his early departure from Europe, would have been familiar with such a wide range of scholarship. More than likely Rodrigues found many of the references in the standard scholastic textbooks used during his study of philosophy and theology for the priesthood.

It is difficult to determine what European books were available to Rodrigues in Macao while he was compiling the *History*. When the Jesuits were expelled from Japan in 1614, they took with them to Macao a small library of 145 books, most of them dealing with religious matters.[1] In addition, on the death of Diogo Valente, Bishop of Japan, in Macao in 1633, his library was found to contain more than 300 titles, dealing mostly with theology, liturgy, devotion, and patristics.[2] Neither of these collections would have afforded Rodrigues much source material, and it may be presumed that he used the Macao college library for references to European works. He could have obtained much useful information, especially dates in Japanese history, from the two editions of his own *Arte*. He presumably had kept copies of both of these works, and in any case there was a copy of *Arte grande* among the books brought from Japan in 1614.

In addition to directly quoting and citing other works, Rodrigues undoubtedly lifted material from Giovanni Magini's *Geographia* (Cologne, 1597) and incorporated it without acknowledgement. This is true only of the first chapter of Book I, in which he gives a general description of Asia and deals with matters not experienced at first hand. He borrowed material from Magini at least three times and I provide here just one example, leaving the quotations in their original languages to show their similarity.

Magini

Ptolemaeus eam [Asiam] in 47 regiones, ac provincias distribuit, cuius descriptionem tradit in quinto, sexto, ac septimo Geographiae libris, duodecim scilicet tabulis absolutam. ... Nostra tempestate Ioannes Barrius distinguit Asiam in novem partes; alii in quinque, inter quos Ortelius, qui secundum eius Imperia, quibus administratur, partitur, quem sequi volumus in harum partium distributione

Rodrigues

Ptolemeu divide toda a Azia em 47 Regions ou Provincias, cuja particular descripção poem elle no quinto, Sexto, e setimo Livro de sua Geographia por doce taboas geographicas, ... João de Barros a distinguio em nove partes, Abraham Ortelio ... com outros Authores a devide em sinco, João Antonio Magino na sua Geographia a destribuyo pelos Imperios em sete partes principaes.[3]

There are other passages in this first chapter that follow fairly closely the thought and plan of Magini, while Rodrigues's reference to Asia being the site of scriptural events bears a strong resemblance to a paragraph in Ortelius. Once, however, this introductory chapter

---

[1] For the contents of the Jesuit library in Japan at an earlier date, see López-Gay, 'Primera biblioteca'.

[2] For the bishop's library and other material, see Schütte, *Archivo*, pp. 30–37; Humbertclaude, *Recherches*, and 'Supplement'.

[3] Magini, *Geographia*, f. 211; Rodrigues, p. 14. Rodrigues obviously borrowed other material from Magini, *Geographia*, f. 211, and this appears on pp. 9–10 and 12. The relevant texts are quoted in Cooper, 'João Rodrigues', p. 75.

is completed, the author appears to have written from his own knowledge and experience, and I have detected only a few instances of unacknowledged borrowing of material from other works. For example, when talking about the three Portuguese who landed in Japan in 1543, Rodrigues quotes, without acknowledgement, from Gonçalves's history. In addition, writing about the introduction of Chinese ideographs into Japan, he seems to have borrowed some lines from his own *Arte breve*, 1620. He may also have taken sentences from Lucena's biography of Xavier.[1] I suspect that he must have borrowed material in his detailed treatise on Chinese astronomy, although he obviously knew a good deal about the subject. [2]While studying scholastic philosophy in Japan, he had as a teacher the talented Pedro Gómez, who lectured on cosmology and natural science. From an extant copy of a compendium of his lectures, we see that Gómez's course was largely based on the treatise *De sphaera*, compiled by the thirteenth-century astronomer John of Holywood (Joannes de Sacrobosco), and in his *History* Rodrigues quotes three times from Christoph Clavius's commentary on Sacrobosco.[3]

In 1627 Rodrigues wrote an informal letter to Nuno Mascarenhas, a Jesuit working in Rome, in which he noted:

> As you know, I came from Europe as a child and was brought up in these parts among the wilds and forests of these nations, so I possess neither style in our Portuguese language nor method of writing briefly what is necessary. So I do what I can, rather along the lines of a collection of stories without any order, in order to explain my ideas. Thus I feel ashamed to write unless I am obliged to do so, because I don't want to bore the recipients of these dull letters.[4]

Rodrigues wrote these lines with his personal letters in mind, but much of what he so frankly admits here can be equally well applied to his *History*, for it must be admitted that he seems quite incapable of 'writing briefly what is necessary'. His concept of the proposed *History* was far too ambitious, and when he drew up the plan of the projected work he set himself and others a task practically impossible to accomplish. A history of the Church in Japan should certainly contain some introductory material to describe the country and set the scene before actually dealing with the mission. But to plan no less than ten introductory books (and Book 1 runs to some 120,000 words) surely indicates a certain lack of judgement and proportion. Book 2 contains about 30,000 words, and with this disparity in length between the two extant books, it is impossible to estimate the total length of the projected ten books of Part 1, but it is reasonable to suppose that it would have been more than half a million words – a somewhat lengthy, if not unwieldy, introduction by any standards. In contrast, Fróis's introduction to his *História* follows a more logical and rational structure – thirteen chapters on Japanese life in general, followed by twenty-four chapters on Japanese religion.[5]

As regards the material of Rodrigues's two books, the selection leaves much to be

---

[1] Further details of Rodrigues's borrowing of material is provided in Cooper, 'João Rodrigues', p. 74–6.

[2] As regards European astronomy, Nicholas Trigault returned to Macao in 1619 from his six-year mission to Europe with a plentiful supply of European books on the subject as well as various calendars. Dunne, *Generation*, pp. 111, 179. Rodrigues may well have had access to these works in Macao before they were distributed to the Jesuit houses in China.

[3] Further details about Rodrigues's studies are given in Cooper, *Rodrigues the Interpreter*, pp. 59–60.

[4] Ibid., p. 297.

[5] Fróis's table of contents is given in Fróis, *História*, pp. 11–13; Rodrigues's table of contents, still unpublished, is in Madrid, Real Academia de la Historia, Jesuítas. 7237, ff. 3–6.

desired. As readers of the English translation, below, will appreciate, there is considerable repetition and superfluous material in Book 1. However helpful it may have been to include introductory material to set the history in context, it was hardly necessary to provide such detailed information about, for example, Japanese and Chinese etiquette, and technical information on Asian astronomy. In fact, when Rodrigues gets into full stride, he seems to forget that he is compiling an introduction to the history of the Christian enterprise in Japan, and he happily writes at great length about the minutiae of Japanese etiquette and social life. While this excessive detail does not make for a well-considered structure to the work, it does provide modern readers with much first-hand information, together with the views of a perceptive and experienced European.

The disparity in chapter lengths is striking: Chapter 1, Book 1, runs to about 12,000 words (or 10% of Book 1), while Chapter 14 consists of only forty-three words. Book 2 is, on the whole, better organized, but fails to live up to the promise of its title. Almost nothing is said about Japanese poetry (and Rodrigues knew a great deal about the subject),[1] yet no less than seven chapters, out of a total of sixteen, are extraneously devoted to astronomy and astrology.

As we have seen above, Rodrigues admits his poor literary style and this defect is evident in his *History*. His limited vocabulary and constant repetition of basic words often make the text monotonous, and although a translation should normally reflect the style and quality of the original text, I have believed it advisable to produce an English version that reads a little more smoothly than the original text. This improvement would not be permissible if the value of the *History* depended primarily on the elegance of its literary style and composition. But as the purpose of the present work is to show what Rodrigues has to say about Japan and not how he says it, any attempt to present his somewhat rough-and-ready draft in more readable form is surely justified. As it is, parts of the translation make tedious reading on account of rambling repetition, but the tedium would have been far more pronounced had not synonyms been used in translation. To give but two examples, here is a literal translation of two sentences:

> The common cup on its ordinary tray with wine, and the ordinary sakana which goes with it, is the common and ordinary Japanese courtesy

And,

> The natural humour and nature of the Japanese in general is melancholic; whence naturally led by this natural inclination... .[2]

Any doubt about the advisability of adapting his style was finally dispelled when I came to translate a sentence of exactly 286 words ungraced by any punctuation.[3]

Such criticism of the work could be extended almost indefinitely, and yet perhaps fails to do justice to Rodrigues, who on more than one occasion pointed out that because of his poor literary style he had been told only to collect relevant materials for someone else to work over and reproduce in a more elegant form.[4] Believing, therefore, that all he was

---

[1] He includes a short but comprehensive treatise on the subject in his *Arte grande*, ff. 180–84; English translation in Rodrigues, 'The Muse Described'.

[2] See pp. 239, 283.

[3] This is the first sentence in Book 1, Chapter 1.

[4] See p. xxv.

required to do was produce a rough draft, Rodrigues should not be censured unduly if the structure and style of his book leave much to be desired.

After this somewhat negative appraisal of Rodrigues's text, let me turn to a feature that I find appealing in his written work: he modestly seldom speaks about himself. Time and again in the *History* he names famous Japanese, but in only two or three cases does he tell us that he personally knew the men. He makes dozens of references to Hideyoshi, but never mentions his many meetings with the all-powerful ruler. He refers to Valignano's audience with Hideyoshi in March 1591, but is silent about his role as interpreter at the event and the beginning of his acquaintance with the dictator. Nor do we learn in his account that he sat by the prostrate and ailing Hideyoshi and conversed with him only a week or so before the ruler died. There are other people appearing in the *History*, Tokugawa Ieyasu, for example, whom Rodrigues knew well and visited often, but he says nothing about this in his account, except to mention that he was once present at the ruler's court. A lesser man would have revelled in the chance to drop names in the course of the lengthy text, and it is to Rodrigues's credit that he did not take advantage of these opportunities.

The copy

As regards the Ajuda copy from which the present translation has been made, the eighteenth-century scribe appears to have performed his task somewhat carelessly in places. Obvious mistakes can be found, and it is difficult to believe that these errors were contained in Rodrigues's original manuscript. For example, the peculiar term 'asssilabaxy' turns out to be 'a sílaba xi', while the phrase 'com hospedes calcados' should be 'com os pedes calçados'. The author was probably not responsible for the misquotation 'Erat probatione voluntas', for he correctly wrote 'Erat pro ratione voluntas' in a letter dated 1616.[1] Many of these mistakes indicate that the copyist transcribed the text from dictation. Had he been reading the original manuscript himself, he would not have written 'todos 2° o modo sinico' for 'todos sequem o modo sinico'. Some short gaps were left in the copy where it was presumably impossible to decipher the original script, but none of these omissions is of any significance. That the copyist was ignorant of Japanese is shown by his consistently writing the term *tenka* as *tença*; Rodrigues himself spelled the word as *tenca* in his *Arte*, but would never have dreamt of adding a cedilla and thus softening the second syllable.

There is, however, evidence that the copyist's work was on the whole accurate, for the same scribe also transcribed Book 1 of Part 2, dealing with the 1549–52 period of mission history, and an earlier copy of this part, corrected in Rodrigues's handwriting, is still extant.[2] A comparison of the two manuscripts, one in Lisbon and the other in Madrid, shows that the eighteenth-century Macao scribe was a fairly reliable copyist and that the accuracy of his work can by and large be trusted. Comparing these two versions also helps to settle a further point, for it shows that the copy, made in Macao in the eighteenth century, is practically identical with the text corrected and amended by Rodrigues a hundred years earlier. It will be recalled that his task was to gather material for someone else to write up more elegantly, but a study of the two documents shows that no subsequent editing in fact was made, nor do the Jesuit records refer to anyone being appointed for such a task. In

---

[1] Rodrigues, 'Rodrigues in China', p. 301.
[2] Ajuda, 49–IV–53, ff. 181v–236v, and Madrid, Jesuítas 7238, ff. 1–88.

any case, the author's repetitive and unimaginative style is apparent throughout the work and shows no trace of subsequent editing.

Rodrigues's insight into Japanese culture

Whatever the lack of organization and style in the *History*, its actual content is full of interest to anyone studying the early cultural contacts between Europe and Japan. Rodrigues spent more than three decades in the country, spoke the language fluently, travelled widely, mixed with political rulers, and was thus in an ideal position to send back to Europe an authoritative account of Japanese life. He was, of course, a man of his times, and gravely mentions a 700-year-old Japanese, a 300-year-old Indian, and fish that turn into birds. But these marvels, so popular among Europeans reading about the mysterious Orient, are few and unimportant.[1] In Book 2, he often mentions the Creation, Adam, and the Confusion of Tongues, but such references, quaint though they may appear to modern eyes, were not uncommon in his day. The fact that the author, when writing about Japanese social life, has mostly the gentry is mind is hardly surprising. His background in dealing with the nobility well qualified him to dwell on this topic, and in any case, the customs of impoverished peasants would not, rightly or wrongly, have been of great interest to European readers.

The author was unique among his contemporaries in that he lived in Japan and China for many years, probably being the only European to visit both Miyako and Beijing. This experience enabled him to take a comparative approach in his account of the two countries and their cultures, and, alone among Western authors, Rodrigues time and again points out the Chinese origins of Japanese customs and traditions.[2] In addition, he often refers to the simplification of social customs from the time of Nobunaga and Hideyoshi, and as he was living in Japan in that period, he was in a good position to make this observation. In Book 1, Chapter 30, he tells us that 'since the reign of Nobunaga and Taikō [Hideyoshi], ... practically everything was reformed'; later in the same chapter, he observes that since the times of those two rulers, 'many things have been reformed'.[3] Unfortunately he does not elaborate on this interesting observation, and explain what changes, apart from banquets, he has in mind.

As a zealous seventeenth-century missionary Rodrigues shows little sympathy for Japanese religions, yet he was ahead of his time in his assessment of Shinto legends. Some seventy years later the learned Dr Engelbert Kaempfer, who lived in Japan 1690–92, would express the customary European view by condemning Shinto as 'a heap of fabulous and romantick stories of their Gods, Demi-gods and Heroes, inconsistent with reason or common sense'.[4] Alone among the early Europeans, Rodrigues was sufficiently discerning

[1] As mentioned on p. xx, Rodrigues had personal experience of alleged longevity while in Beijing in 1630, when a rumour spread that he was 250 years old.
[2] See, for instance, the examples Rodrigues mentions at the beginning of Book 1, Chapter 15 (p. 174). In *Arte breve*, f. 83, he goes into considerable detail about the extent of Japanese borrowing from China. 'For about 600 years they took from China the costumes and ceremonies of the court, and the ranks, dignities, offices, and tribunals, adapting them to their kingdom and its administration.' He then lists the many offices that had been adopted 'in imitation of the ancient manner of China.' In his Preface to the present work (p. 5), Rodrigues stresses the need for knowledge of China in order to fully understand Japan.
[3] Rodrigues mentions these changes several times, especially on p. 264.
[4] Kaempfer, *History of Japan*, II, p. 13.

to recognize the historical basis of these legends and to point out that 'these fables are founded on some historical truth' (pp. 56–7).

Buddhism was considered the chief impediment to the spread of Christianity in Japan, yet he offers a remarkably lyrical description of the ideal of Zen monasticism. The monks 'give themselves up to contemplating the things of nature, despising and abandoning worldly things. They mortify their passions by certain enigmatic and figurative meditations … and attain by their own efforts to a knowledge of the First Cause.' (pp. 288–9) This ascetical training produces a 'resolute and determined character, without any slackness, indolence, mediocrity, or effeminacy' (p. 289). His perceptive observation about Buddhist beliefs in a plurality of worlds is also noteworthy (p. 359).

It is in his account of Japanese art and culture, however, that Rodrigues displays his talent to advantage, and his description of etiquette, the tea ceremony, flower arrangement, painting, and calligraphy is unrivalled in European reports. His understanding of the ethos of the Japanese artistic and cultural temperament is remarkable, as he sympathetically portrays the elusive feeling of *sabi*, the transcendental loneliness of *homo viator* in this transient world. This is apparent in his account of the Eight Views so often depicted in Chinese and Japanese monochrome painting,

> They are fond of melancholy subjects and colours rather than happy ones. … The first scene is a certain famous place with the clear autumn moon reflected in the water. They go out on autumn nights to gaze at the moon in a sad, nostalgic mood. The second view is of a valley or remote wilderness where a hermitage bell, rung at sunset or at night, is heard sounding softly from afar. (pp. 151, 317)

His explanation of terms such as *nurui, iyashii, kedakai, tsuyoi*, etc., used to assess cultural appreciation and accomplishment, shows an insight unique among the Europeans writing about Japan at that time. While Valignano comments that a certain tea bowl, bought for 14,000 ducats, was fit for nothing more than serve as a water-trough in a birdcage,[1] Rodrigues tries to explain the intrinsic beauty and value of such pieces. While Matteo Ricci remarks that the bells of Buddhist temples emit a note of poor quality because they are rung by a hanging log instead of a metal clapper,[2] Rodrigues maintains (and surely rightly) that such bells emit an evocative mellow sound precisely because of this arrangement (p. 317).

Living in his Macao exile the elderly Rodrigues perhaps tended to paint a somewhat idealized picture of various aspects of Japanese life. It is possible, for example, that relatively few Zen monks lived up to his described ideal of religious asceticism. Then he notes that Ashikaga Yoshimasa retreated to the shady woods of Higashiyama, 'adapting himself to a solitary and retired life' (p. 284), whereas the life of the retired shogun was not nearly so solitary and retired as the author would have us believe.[3] But such hyperbole is understandable. Rodrigues spent half his life in Japan and obviously admired its culture, and he may be forgiven if at times he allows a certain nostalgia to colour the description of his adopted country.

Rodrigues's deepest admiration is reserved for the tea ceremony and he devotes more than three chapters in his *History* to the pursuit. His lengthy account is of considerable interest, for *chanoyu*, as we know it today, was still in the formative stage of its development.

---

[1] Valignano, *Sumario*, p. 45.
[2] Ricci, *Fonti*, I, p. 32, and *China*, p. 22.
[3] See p. 284, n. 4, for further details.

Missionaries, especially Valignano, encouraged the practice as it involved no religious superstition, and in fact some of the outstanding tea masters of the time were Christian. There is no record of Rodrigues ever participating in the pastime, but his sympathetic and detailed report leaves no doubt that he was writing from personal experience when he explains not only the mechanics but also the ethos of the tea gathering.

Rodrigues observes:

> This gathering for *cha* and conversation is not intended for lengthy talk among themselves, but rather to contemplate within their souls with all peace and modesty the things they see there ... and thus through their own efforts to understand the mysteries locked therein. In keeping with this, everything used in this ceremony is as rustic, rough, completely unrefined, and simple as nature made it, after the style of a solitary and rustic hermitage. (p. 282)

He writes about tea masters:

> Hence they have come to detest in *suki* any kind of contrivance and elegance, any pretence, hypocrisy and outward embellishment, which they call *keihaku* in their language. ... Instead, their ideal is to promise little but accomplish much; ... always to use moderation in everything; ... finally, to desire to err by default rather than by excess. ... The more precious [the utensils] are in themselves and the less they show it, the more suitable they are. (p. 292)

It would be difficult to improve on this summary description of the Japanese canon of taste. Such sentiments expressed today by a Westerner would indicate a commendable understanding and appreciation of an essentially alien culture. To have been written nearly four hundred years ago reveals João Rodrigues as a unique interpreter not only of the language but also the artistic and cultural genius of the Japanese people.

Publication history

The first scholar to make extensive use of the material in the *History* seems to have been Léonard Cros, SJ, who worked in the Ajuda archives in December 1894 and January 1895, and incorporated some of the text in his biography of Xavier. But Cros was not aware of the author's identity and constantly referred to him as 'the Annalist of Macao'.[1] Neither did James Murdoch, historian of Japan, guess the identity of the anonymous Annalist of Macao, although he often mentions Rodrigues by name in the course of his history of Japan.[2] In 1906 Christovão Ayres published a study on Fernão Mendes Pinto and transcribed, not without errors, some twenty-two pages of Rodrigues's history.[3] When writing in 1946 about Fernão Mendes Pinto and the Europeans' arrival in Japan, the Jesuit scholar Georg Shurhammer included various passages.[4] José Luis Alvarez-Taladriz brought out Spanish translations of three sections of the text, and of the chapters dealing with the tea ceremony.[5]

The full Portuguese text of the first two books of Part I of the *History* was published by

---

[1] Cros, *Saint François de Xavier.*

[2] In his *History 1542–1651*, Murdoch often refers to Rodrigues (e.g., pp. 265–6, 271, 274, 475–5), but then cites Cros's reference to the 'Annalist of Macao' on p. 160, n. 6, without realizing that the two are one and the same author.

[3] Ayres, *Fernão Mendes Pinto e o Japão.*

[4] Schurhammer, 'Descobrimento'.

[5] Alvarez-Taladriz, tr., 'Perspectiva de la historia'; 'Miyako visto'; 'Pintura japonesa'; and *Arte del cha.*

João do Amaral Abranches Pinto in Macao in 1954–5, but this barely annotated edition is extremely faulty and unreliable.[1] Using this text, I translated into English lengthy excerpts and included them in an anthology of European eyewitness reports on Japan.[2] I subsequently made a complete translation of the first two books of the *History* using the Ajuda text, and this formed part of my doctoral thesis.[3] Four years later I published more than half the text in English translation, but for reasons of space was obliged to omit sixteen chapters, adequate annotation, and scholarly introduction.[4] Finally, Doi Tadao, the doyen of Rodrigues studies in Japan, teamed up with other scholars to publish in 1967–70 a generously annotated translation of Volume 1, Books 1 & 2, and Volume 2, Book 1, of the *History*.[5] As far as I know, this is the only published version of Volume 2, Book 1, dealing with Japanese mission history from 1549 to 1552.

Plate 6: Rodrigues's signature, 'João Rõiz', actual size, appearing at the end of a letter written in Macao on 22 January 1616. The cipher of a cross with a dot in each compartment usually accompanies his signature. Jesuit Archives, Rome: JapSin 16:1, f. 288v. *With permission of the Director of the Archivum Romanum Societatis Iesu.*

---

[1] Rodrigues, *Historia*. There are many omissions and errors of transcription; on p. 56, for example, two entire paragraphs have been omitted.

[2] Cooper, *They Came to Japan* [*TCJ*].

[3] Cooper, 'João Rodrigues'.

[4] Rodrigues, *This Island of Japon*.

[5] Rodrigues, *Nihon*, 2 vols.

ACKNOWLEDGEMENTS

I am grateful to the director of the library of the Ajuda Palace, Lisbon, for permission to publish this translation of João Rodrigues's work (manuscript 49–IV–53) and to Kodansha International Ltd, Tokyo, for allowing me to reproduce the material appearing in *This Island of Japon*, 1973. I owe much to the late Professor Charles Boxer, my thesis supervisor, who urged his inexperienced student to remain on the trail of Rodrigues and was unfailingly generous in helping to locate rare sources, some of which were contained in his own library. Professor Beatrice Bodart-Bailey, Ōtsuma University, Tokyo, has been a constant source of not only information about the Edo period but also encouragement, and I am happy to acknowledge my deep debt of gratitude to her. Professor M. Antoni Üçerler, SJ, Sophia University, Tokyo, most generously provided me with a copy of his recent thesis on Valignano, and supplied valuable information about the subsequent fate of the Jesuit papers sent from Macao to Manila in 1761. Professor Paul Varley, University of Hawaii, kindly allowed me to consult various works in his personal library. Professor Reinier H. Hesselink, University of Northern Iowa, and Tony Campbell, British Library, helped me track down the source of the map of Miyako appearing on p. 160, and Hunter Golay patiently converted my miscellany of Wade-Giles spellings of Chinese names and terms into standard *pinyin*. Tokiko Yamamoto Bazzell, University of Hawaii library, dealt with my many questions with unfailing efficiency and good cheer. Dr N. Golvers of the University of Leuven and the F. Verbiest Foundation, and Professor Charles Burnett of the Warburg Institute have given valuable help on obscure points in the text. To all these kind people I offer my grateful thanks. I also wish to thank Professor W. F. Ryan for his careful and helpful editing of this book.

Honolulu, 2001   MICHAEL COOPER

THE HISTORY OF THE CHURCH OF JAPAN

Wherein are recounted how the preaching of the Holy Gospel in this kingdom was begun by the Blessed Father Francis Xavier,[1] one of the first ten men who, with the glorious Patriarch Saint Ignatius,[2] founded the Society of Jesus, and the great work that Our Lord accomplished through him and his sons in the conversion of the pagan people to our holy Catholic Faith during a period of 85 years, from the year 1549 (when the Law of God was introduced into Japan) up to the present year of 1634.[3]

Composed by the religious of the same Society[4] who have resided in these parts from the year 1575[5] up to the present year of 1634, and have personally witnessed almost everything that has taken place during this entire period, and have known many of the first members of the same Society who from the beginning continued this work of conversion begun by the blessed Father.

---

[1] St Francis Xavier, or Francisco de Javier (1506–52), was born in Spanish Navarre, met Ignatius of Loyola at Paris University, and is considered one of the founders of the Society of Jesus. He sailed to the Indies as a missionary in 1541 and after laboring in India and elsewhere in Asia, he reached the port of Kagoshima in Japan on 15 August 1549 with two companions. He died while attempting to enter China. His standard biography is Schurhammer, *Francis Xavier*, 4 volumes; the text of his letters is given in Xavier, *Epistolae*.

[2] Ignatius of Loyola (1491–1556) was wounded during the siege of Pamplona in 1521 and experienced a religious conversion during his convalesence. While studying at Paris University, 1528–35, he formed a group of like-minded men (including Xavier) who are regarded as the founders of a new religious order, the Society of Jesus, formally approved by the pope in 1540. Ignatius was elected the first General Superior and remained in this office until his death.

[3] The reason for choosing 1634 is discussed in the Introduction, p. xxvii, above.

[4] That is, the Society of Jesus, or the Jesuit order.

[5] Concerning this date 1575, see the Introduction, p. xxxi, above.

A PREFACE TO THE READER[1]

It has been the wish of the Superiors of this Province that a book should be written concerning the origin and development of the Christian religion in this new Church of Japan. This was also desired by the early Fathers of our Society who came to Japan with St Francis Xavier and remained in that kingdom to continue the work of conversion to our Holy Faith, as well as by those who later succeeded them. For they wished to send to Europe a true and accurate account of the administration of this great nation, and of the number and size of these islands, situated between the two worlds – the world known to the ancients and the New World – and thus forming the boundary between the two. In this way it will be possible to appreciate more fully the great difficulties experienced in spreading the Holy Gospel therein and the power of divine grace that overcame all these obstacles.

With this in mind some of our first members of this mission committed various things to writing. For example, there were Fr Cosme de Torres[2] and Brother Juan Fernández.[3] Both of them accompanied St Francis Xavier to Japan and the latter was his interpreter. Then there was Fr Luís Fróis,[4] a truly single-minded man of integrity and zeal for souls, who came after Fr Cosme de Torres and Brother Juan Fernández, and was a great labourer in Japan. More than anyone else in Japan he diligently noted down in writing what happened in that Church both before and in his time. For many years he wrote the Annual Letters that were sent from Japan every year.[5] He knew Fr Cosme de Torres and Brother Juan Fernández for a long time, and he inquired from them everything that had happened and how Fr St Francis Xavier had begun the preaching of the Holy Gospel in Japan.

---

[1] An autograph copy, with many corrections and additions, of this Preface is found in Madrid, Jesuítas 7237, ff. 2–3 (a photograph of f. 2v forms the frontispiece of Rodrigues, *Nihon*, 1). The manuscript is in poor condition, with the first folio disfigured by a long tear and the bottom of the page torn away. As a result, some guesswork is occasionally required to make sense of the text.

[2] Cosme de Torres (1512–70) was born in Valencia and worked as a priest in Mexico. He met Xavier in Amboina in 1546, entered the Jesuit order in 1548, and accompanied him to Japan in the following year. After Xavier's departure, Torres was Superior of the Japanese mission until the year of his death. Schütte, *Textus*, pp. 1312–13

[3] Juan Fernández (c. 1526–67), a native of Córdoba, entered the Society of Jesus as a lay brother in Lisbon in 1547, sailed to India in 1548, and accompanied Xavier to Japan in the following year. He died in Hirado. Schütte, *Textus*, p. 1171

[4] Luís Fróis (d.1597), mentioned in the Introduction, pp. xxiii–xxiv, was born in Lisbon and there entered the Society of Jesus in 1548, setting out for India in the same year. He arrived in Japan in 1563, and as secretary of the Jesuit Superior and of Valignano, wrote, in addition to his *História*, more than a hundred letters, some of them lengthy, about Japan. Schütte, *Textus*, pp. 1176–7; Fróis, *História*, pp. 3*–10*. A symposium, held in Tokyo in 1997, on Fróis's work and contribution was published under the title *Luís Fróis* in 1998.

[5] On Valignano's instructions, the custom of sending an official annual report from Japan to Rome was begun in 1579 and many of these letters were written by Fróis. Valignano, *Sumario*, pp. 65*–7*.

Fr Luís Fróis lived in Japan in those early days for a period of thirty-seven years, that is, from the year 1560 to his death in 1597.[1] He wrote a history of the foundation and development of the mission of his day, and he also described the customs and political administration, the cult and religion of this nation.[2] But he was unable to finish and revise the work by the time Our Lord took him to Himself, because he had many commitments and the whole of Japan was involved in civil wars at that time. In addition, the things of Japan were not so well known by Ours as they are today, and thus there are some matters that should be corrected and further developed.

Moreover, some members of our Society in Europe (for example, Fr Orazio Torsellini) have written the life of St Francis Xavier,[3] while Frs Giovanni Antonio Maffei,[4] João de Lucena,[5] and others have written various descriptions of Japan based on the letters of the missionaries therein and on other accounts of these regions. But as these authors wrote, albeit elegantly, from secondhand accounts and not from personal experience, they erred in many things, while in others they strayed from the truth, which is the quality most esteemed in history.

Various letters written by Ours[6] in Japan have also been printed, and these deal with certain aspects of the kingdom. Now although they are accurate as regards the conversion and fruit that were accomplished (for they deal with affairs that the writers personally experienced), they were not composed as historical accounts of the things of Japan, nor with the clarity and distinction required for proper understanding. For they were merely letters written in different times and places about various topics in the style of informal letters between brothers.

Some of Ours wrote these letters as soon as they reached Japan, recounting things that they had heard from others. They did not know the language or have any knowledge or experience of the country. There were others who knew various things, but they did not write these letters with the idea of having them printed, and moreover they wrote only about the events that happened in their time. This was, so to speak, the foundation and infancy of this Japanese Church and afterwards there were many big changes.[7] The missionaries were very few in number and were kept extremely busy in the conversion of souls. The whole of Japan was divided among the lords, who disregarded the head, their proper and lawful king in former times,[8] and also the Kubō or Shogun,[9] the High Constable, and thus the entire country was embroiled in wars. Ours had neither time nor competence to

---

[1] This is an error, possibly the copyist's mistake, for Fróis arrived in Japan on the ship of Pedro da Guerra in July 1563. Schütte, *Textus*, p. 1176; Fróis, *História*, p. 9*.

[2] For Fróis's *História*, see the Introduction, p. xxiii–xxiv, above. Rodrigues here discreetly deals with the non-publication of this work.

[3] Orazio Torsellini (1544–92) was the author of *De vita Francisci Xaverii*, Rome, 1594. Sommervogel, *Bibliothèque*, VIII, cols. 140–42; Laures, *Kirishitan Bunko*, p. 189; Lach, *Asia*, I, p. 327.

[4] Giovanni Pietro [not Antonio] Maffei (1533–1603) was the author of *Historiarum Indicarum libri XVI*, Florence, 1588. Sommervogel, *Bibliothèque*, V, cols. 298–300; Laures, *Kirishitan Bunko*, p. 183; Lach, *Asia*, I, pp. 325–6.

[5] João de Lucena (1550–1600) was the author of *Historia da vida do Padre Francisco de Xavier*, Lisbon, 1600. Sommervogel, *Bibliothèque*, V, col. 159; Laures, *Kirishitan Bunko*, p. 195; Lach, *Asia*, I, pp. 327–8.

[6] That is, members of the Society of Jesus.

[7] Valiganano (*Del Principio*, f. Iv) also mentions this change and lack of stability as reasons for delaying writing his own *Historia*.

[8] That is, the emperor.

[9] The origin and office of the shogun are described in Book 1, Chapter 11, below.

investigate thoroughly the kingdom's proper administration and customs, for this greatly depends on knowing the ways of the kingdom of China.[1]

* * * * * * * * * * * * * *

Finally in this third stage of the history of Japan, the last writer was Fr Alessandro Valignano,[2] who wrote part of the history of the Church by order of our Fathers General Everardo Mercurian[3] and Claudio Aquaviva.[4] He was twice the Visitor to these parts of India and Japan and of these same provinces, and lastly Visitor of Japan.[5] He sent many men (of whom there was a great shortage) thither and founded colleges, a novitiate, three rectorial houses, many residences, and seminaries for the natives to study humanities.[6] He began to have some of the Japanese brothers ordained priests,[7] and in many other ways he rendered great service to Our Lord. He began the China mission.[8]

Although very busy in administration he decided to write a history of the Church of Japan, on account both of his great zeal and the orders of our reverend Fathers General. He began the part from the foundation of the mission up to the death of Fr Cosme de Torres.[9] But he did not know the Japanese language, and when describing the things of Japan he had to rely on the information of others, which was sometimes confused and uncertain, as he himself said. He expounded those things that caused doubt and perplexity in the printed works on Japan and in the things written about Japan by Frs Maffei and Torsellini. He took what they had written in their books as his base and text, commenting and simplifying in various places.[10]

Thus it can be seen that everything that has been written so far about the political administration of Japan, the names and qualities of the land, was done piecemeal and, moreover, expressed in a confused way. So far there has been no knowledge in Europe of

[1] There follows at this point a short account of Japanese history, which is repeated in Book 1, Chapter 11, below, and so is omitted here.

[2] Alessandro Valignano (1539–1606) was born in Chieti and obtained a doctorate in law at the University of Padua. He entered the Society of Jesus in 1566 and studied under the renowned scholar Christoph Clavius in Rome. Despite his youth, in 1573 he was appointed Visitor, or inspector, of the Jesuit missions in the Indies, in which capacity he made three extended visits to Japan. He was renowned for his urging Jesuits in Asia to adapt themselves to local culture and customs, a policy that bore much fruit in China, to which mission he sent talented young priests such as Matteo Ricci. Valignano died in Macao on 20 January 1606, leaving a testament in which he mentions Rodrigues. Schütte, *Textus*, pp. 1318–20; Schütte, *Valignano's Mission Principles*, I.

[3] Everardo Mercurian (1514–1581) was elected the fourth Superior General of the Jesuit Order in April 1573 and, as is the Jesuit custom, held that office until his death. Valignano, *Sumario*, p. 1, n. 4.

[4] Claudio Aquaviva (1543–1615) was elected the fifth Superior General in 1581. Valignano, *Sumario*, p. 1, n. 2.

[5] Valignano worked in Japan as Visitor 1579–82, 1590–92, and 1598–1603. As Rodrigues correctly states, on the first two occasions he was the Jesuit Visitor of all Asia (except the Philippines), but Visitor of only Japan and China during his last stay in the country.

[6] Valignano founded a Jesuit novitiate at Usuki in 1580, and two boys' schools in Azuchi and Arima in the same year.

[7] The first ordination of Japanese to the priesthood took place in 1601. By 1614 fifteen Japanese had been ordained, of whom eight were Jesuits and the rest were diocesan priests. Cieslik, 'Training', pp. 75–7.

[8] In 1582 Valignano sent instructions to Goa that young Matteo Ricci should leave for Macao, where he was to prepare himself for work in China.

[9] A reference to Valiganano's *Del principio, y progresso*, 1601, in BL, Add.MSS. 9857, and Lisbon, Ajuda, 49–V–53, ff. 244–420. He wrote the history down to 1570, the year that Cosme de Torres died. See p. xxiv, above.

[10] Valignano quotes or cites the works of Maffei, Torsellini, and Lucena in his *Del principio*, and, as Rodrigues notes, he modifies and corrects these texts whenever he believed necessary.

how the Fathers of the Japanese Province have preached the Holy Gospel with so much fruit to souls.[1] There has been even less knowledge of the great things that Providence has brought about, daily working marvels in this young Church through the religious of the Society of Jesus. As a result of this lack of information among all the provinces that are working for the conversion of souls to the faith of Jesus Christ, Our Lord, this most noble Province lacks the necessary aid to support itself and make further progress. Such help would certainly not be lacking if the Province were nearer to Europe, or if the Supreme Pontiff, the Vicar of Jesus Christ on earth, and other Christian kings and princes, both ecclesiastical and lay, had clearer and more complete knowledge of the mission.[2]

In order to remedy this defect (inasmuch as we are able, placing our trust in that true wisdom, who opened the mouths of the dumb and made the tongues of infants eloquent),[3] we will write about the origins and development of this young Japanese Church and about the singular providence with which it has been governed for a period of eighty-five years, that is, from the year 1549 to that of 1634. This account will show how it has been guided by Our Lord and will describe the copious fruit achieved for it by many outstanding martyrs and zealous confessors. Every part of the kingdom has been watered by the blood of the holy martyrs. This is the seed of Christians[4] by which the Church of God was founded and spread throughout the world, and we trust that it will swiftly spread in this kingdom and that the whole nation will be converted to our Holy Faith.

We have divided this history into two parts.[5] To avoid confusion and interrupting the text of the ecclesiastical history, there are several books in the first part describing the islands of Japan, their position, number, and size, the provinces into which they are divided, the smaller states into which each province is divided, the political administration of the kingdom, the cult and religion of the various pagan sects founded by ancient philosophers.[6] The second part deals with the ecclesiastical history in chronological order.[7]

---

[1] The translation of this sentence is conjectural as a complete line of the Portuguese text is missing at this point. As it stands, the statement is incorrect as the published letters written by the Jesuits in Japan contain plenty of information about their work.

[2] Here Rodrigues obliquely refers to the mission's financial problems, which obliged the Jesuits in Japan to request and receive papal dispensation to participate in the Portuguese silk trade. Details in Cooper, *Rodrigues the Interpreter*, pp. 239–47. See p. xxii, n. 2, above.

[3] Wisdom 10, 21. The quotation is given in Latin.

[4] A reference to Tertullian's saying, 'Semen est sanguis Christianorum', in his *Apologeticum*, 50, 12.

[5] Yet a few folios later, Rodrigues clearly shows in his Index that the work was to be divided into three parts. See p. xxvii, above.

[6] As noted in the Introduction, p. xxvii, Rodrigues planned to write ten books about Japan by way of an introduction to Part 2, the actual history of the mission. The first two books are translated here. It is not known whether he completed any of the remaining eight projected books.

[7] As noted in the Introduction, p. xxvii, Rodrigues intended to write the actual history of the mission in ten books, each one dealing with the period of office of a Jesuit superior. He completed at least the first four books down to 1590, but only Book 1, 1549–52, is extant.

PART ONE

Wherein are described the kingdom of Japan, its customs, its religion and worship, the state of Japan when the holy Gospel was introduced therein, and the beginning and progress of its preaching from the year 1549 to that of 1560,[1] throughout the period of 21 years when Father Cosme de Torres,[2] companion of the Blessed Fr Francis and first Superior of the Society in Japan, governed this Christian mission.

BOOK 1

Wherein are related the position, description, and nature of the islands of Japan, as well as some general customs of its people.

[1] An obvious slip for 1570. In the transcription of Part 2, Book 1 (Madrid, Jesuítas 7238), the copyist made a similar error on f. 15, where the text mentions a period of '72' years between 1549 and 1627. This figure was corrected to 78 by Rodrigues, who jotted down the dates in the margin to calculate the length of the intervening period:

1627
1549
0078

[2] For Torres, see p. 3, n. 2.

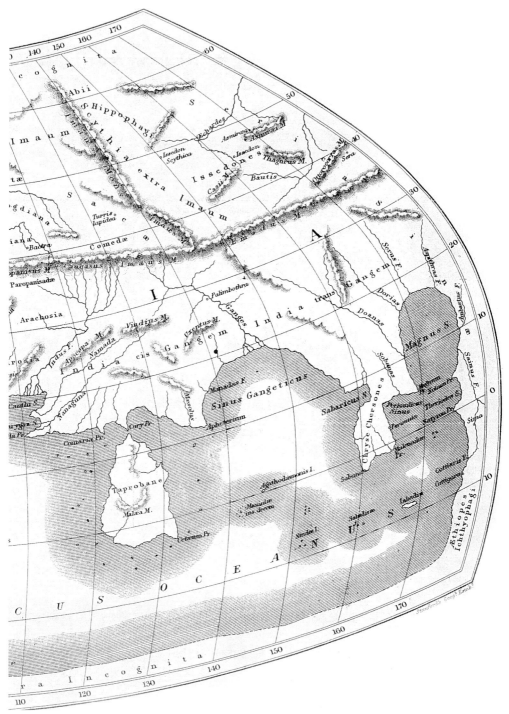

Plate 7: East Asia according to Ptolemy. Note the enormous size of Taprobana (Ceylon) and the Magnus S[inus], mentioned by Rodrigues on pp. 41, 26. Bunbury, *A History of Ancient Geography*, III.

8

CHAPTER 1

A GENERAL DESCRIPTION OF ASIA AND THE ISLANDS OF THIS ORIENTAL SEA[1]

In the course of this history reference is made to many of the principal parts of Asia with which the kingdom of Japan has been in contact on account of either trade or war. From some of these parts Japan obtained its writing and sciences, the religion and cult of the idols that it professes,[2] and many other customs and rites, while from other parts Japan was first populated. Above all, the very islands of Japan are situated in Asia itself. In order, therefore, to fulfil our purpose of providing a complete account of these islands and their situation, we believed it relevant to provide at the beginning a general description of the whole of Asia (especially the part lying east of the River Indus), with a geographical map showing its principal parts and its islands in this Oriental Sea.[3] This has been drawn up and executed here in these same parts with great accuracy and certitude. As regards the inland regions lying to the east of the River Indus as far as the New World, it differs a great deal from the information hitherto given in the charts and maps of European authors who have dealt with these areas, for no news about these parts has so far reached Europe. In this way the reader may gain a clearer and more exact understanding of what is said about these regions in the course of this history.

In addition, the real and true position of each of these regions will be seen, as well as the true shape of the land of the Orient, with the principal rivers that water it and the famous mountains, and also the similarities that these regions have with each other and with the islands of Japan.[4]

A new and true description of Asia

Asia, the third of the regions known to antiquity,[5] is a very illustrious part of the world

[1] By 'this Oriental Sea' (or 'the great Orientall Ocean sea', in Mendoza, *History*, I, p. 8), Rodrigues uses an already dated term to probably refer to the North Pacific Ocean. In maps according to Ptolemy, dated 1540 and 1548, the Oriental Ocean is shown south of China and India, extending over the equator. Nordenskiöld, *Facsimile-Atlas*, pp. XLIV, XLV. Ortelius's later map of India Orientalis (in *Theatrum orbis*, 1570) shows the Oriental Ocean lying between Japan and the Philippines.

[2] A reference to Buddhism, which reached Japan in 552 via Korea. See p. 48, n. 3, below.

[3] Unfortunately this map is not included in either the Lisbon or Madrid manuscripts. It probably formed part of Rodrigues's atlas of Asia, mentioned in the Introduction, p. xxii.

[4] The whole of this opening paragraph forms one long sentence in the Portuguese text, and, as regards structure, is strikingly similar to the introduction (also one long sentence) to the Constitutions of the Society of Jesus, with which Rodrigues, as a Jesuit, would have been familiar.

[5] For example, Pliny (*Natural History*, 3, Introduction) wrote: 'The whole globe is divided into three parts, Europe, Asia, and Africa.' The first two sentences of this paragraph appear almost word for word in Magini, *Geographia*, f. 211.

and is the largest as regards size. It is bigger than Europe and Africa combined, even without including its innumerable and mighty islands that have been discovered in our own day during recent voyages and are larger than the whole of Europe. Of all the regions of the world, Asia has always been renowned for its wealth because it produces everything that men consider precious and valuable, such as all kinds of precious stones, the best and most prized pearls, every sort of spice, and every existing variety of aromatic and perfumed products, such as balsam, incense, benzoin, musk, amber, civet, camphor, aloes wood, eaglewood, and sandal wood.[1] It also provides countless medicinal herbs and stones, such as rhubarb, bezoar, the highly esteemed and useful porcupine stone, and many other precious things that are produced here.[2]

Asia was very renowned on account of the monarchies of the Babylonians, Assyrians, Medes, Persians, Parthians, Greeks, Tartars, Turks, Mongols, and Chinese, which existed (and even now still exist) in this region. In addition it was celebrated for the famous nations therein and their flourishing kingdoms, such as those of the ancient Trojans, Mithridates, Croesus, Antioch, Galatians, Phrygians, the ancient King Porus of India, the Massagetes, Bactrians, the ancient Seres (who are the Chinese), and many others.[3] The principal events of the world took place in this region. It was here that God established the Garden of Eden, and created the first parents of the human race. It was here that man was redeemed and the mysteries of our Redemption were enacted. It was here that the Eternal Word assumed human nature, appeared in our flesh, and lived among men. The religion and worship of the true God with temples, priests, and sacrifices first thrived here before anywhere else. It was here that the patriarchs and prophets flourished, and the human race was saved from the Flood and then once more began to populate the entire world. Here it was that the history of the Old Testament and the greater part of the New Testament was worked out.[4] It was here that the sciences and the first use of writing began, and here were to be found the world's first sages, not only among the Hebrews and the people of God but also among the pagans and gentiles, long before they appeared among the Greeks or even the Egyptians.

Here began the other liberal and mechanical arts – the use of silk (a commodity so

---

[1] A similar list of perfumes is given in Magini, *Geographia*, f. 212v. For information concerning some of these exotic products, see Orta, *Colloquies*, pp. 4–18, 20–27, 58–65, 86–98, 393–9 (this work was first published in Goa in 1563 and may have been available to Rodrigues); Linschoten, *Discours*, pp. 117–22. Further references to aloes and eaglewood are given in Rodrigues, *Arte del cha*, p. 56, nn. 152, 153.

[2] Rhubarb formerly enjoyed great esteem as a medicine and especially as a safe laxative. Commissioner Lin Zexu (1785–1850) wrote to Queen Victoria in 1839, 'Rhubarb, tea, silk are all valuable products of ours, without which foreigners could not live' (Waley, *Opium War*, p. 29). The exhaustive history of rhubarb, Foust, *Rhubarb: The Wondrous Drug*, contains a great deal on the trade in China rhubarb. See also Orta, *Colloquies*, pp. 390–92. For bezoar, see ibid., pp. 470–72 and Yule, *Hobson-Jobson*, s.v. bezoar. *Breve aparato*, f. 6v, adds: 'In addition there is found in various parts [of Asia] an abundance of gold, silver, and all the other metals, as well as wild animals, tigers, lions, elephants, unicorns, and also tame animals.' As mentioned in the Introduction, p. xxviii, *Breve aparato* is a ten-folio autograph text written by Rodrigues in 1633, duplicating and sometimes expanding the material of this present chapter.

[3] This confused list is missing in *Breve aparato*, but similar catalogues can be found in Magini, *Geographia*, f. 212v. Porus was a king in northern India in the 4th century BC and was defeated by Alexander the Great in 326 BC.

[4] Similar passages may be found in Ortelius, *Theatrum orbis*, p. 3.

highly esteemed in the world),[1] the invention of writing and printing,[2] the use of gunpowder,[3] medicine,[4] and astrology, the material globe[5] with its circles (used in China 4,000 years ago) and with the movement of the planets, the map of the starry sky with its constellations and signs of the zodiac, the division of the sky into $365\frac{1}{4}°$ in a dozen parts or signs, the solar and lunar years with their intercalations, the equinoxes and solstices, and the method of recording the eclipses of the sun and moon.[6] All this happened in antiquity at the same time as the Confusion of Tongues,[7] or even earlier, so that those of us who have found the ancient use of these things here do not doubt that all of them have come down to us from the first Fathers before the Flood,[8] and that as a result of the Confusion of Tongues they were disseminated throughout the world and have been preserved here at the ends of the earth until now. Neither did these regions lack the use of the mariner's needle, for although it is something new among us the Chinese have possessed the compass, albeit an imperfect type, for more than 2,743 years.[9] In these parts were produced the first and most ancient writings in the world. These are the Sacred Text written by holy Moses and the writings of the Chinese concerning their first origin and roots,[10] written at the time of the patriarch Abraham.[11] These are the earliest of all the texts of which we have record.

---

[1] The invention of silk is traditionally attributed to Leizu (whose title was Xiling Shi), the consort of Emperor Huangdi, said to have flourished about 2640 BC. Giles, *Biography*, p. 270. Ricci (*Fonti*, I, p. 10, and *China*, p. 6) dates the invention at 2636 BC.

[2] Block printing appears to have been invented in China in the 8th century, and movable type was first used there three centuries later. Carter, *Invention*, pp. 40–41, 212. In 1609 Ricci (*Fonti*, I, p. 30, and *China*, p. 20) reported that the Chinese knew the art of printing 'at least five centuries ago'. Francisco de Escalona (in Wyngaert, *Sinica*, III, p. 233), who reached China in 1637, asserted that the Chinese had used printing for as long as 1,300 years. Further information is provided on p. 346, n. 1, below.

[3] Writing in the early 17th century, Bernadino de Avila Girón (*Relación*, p. 11) asserted that gunpowder had been invented in China more than 2,000 years earlier, but this is far too early. Chinese references to saltpetre date to the 9th century, while the use of gunpowder in simple bombs and grenades was reported in the year 1000. Needham, 'Science and China's Influence', pp. 245–52. Summarizing a lengthy chapter on firearms in China, Partington, *History of Greek Fire*, pp. 287–8, states that saltpetre was known in the Song period (960–1279), 'proto-gunpowder' was used in 1232, and true gunpowder was employed in the later Yuan period (1279–1368)

[4] The mythical founder of Chinese medicine was Emperor Huangdi, who is later mentioned on p. 350.

[5] Rodrigues repeatedly mentions the *hesphera material* and seems to be referring to both terrestrial and celestial globes, although 'material sphere' is an old term for a terrestrial globe. Terrestrial globes were a Western invention and one was taken to Beijing by Jamāl al-Dīn (in Chinese, Zhamaluding) in 1267. Chinese references are vague, but the celestial globe appears to have been used in China by the 5th century. *SCC*, III, pp. 382–90, and IV, p. 506, note g.

[6] Rodrigues deals in detail with Chinese astronomy in Book 2, chapters 9–13, where he discusses all the items listed in this sentence.

[7] In *Arte grande*, ff. 238–9, Rodrigues lists the ages of the world from the Creation until the time of Christ. Although the Tower of Babel is not actually mentioned, it would have been built, according to his calculations, about 2400 BC.

[8] According to Rodrigues's chronological list in *Arte grande*, ff. 238–9, the Flood took place in 2418 BC.

[9] *Breve aparato*, f. 6v, reads: '… the Chinese have possessed the compass, albeit an imperfect type, for more than 2,750 years, since 1120 BC' Rodrigues's dating is far too early. The earliest clear description of a Chinese magnetic compass is dated 1088, although there is a reference to the 'south-controlling spoon', involving magnetism, in 83. For a complete survey of the subject, see *SCC*, IV:1, pp. 229–334; Needham provides a convenient summary in his article, 'Science and China's Influence', pp. 252–7.

[10] Perhaps a reference to *Shujing*, the Book of History, the first of China's Five Classics. A collection of records (some of which are more fable than history), the work is traditionally attributed to Confucius, although his editorship was not asserted until four centuries after his death. For a translation of the text with copious notes, see Legge, *Chinese Classics*, III.

[11] According to *Arte grande*, f. 238v, Abraham was born in 2035 BC.

The whole of Asia is situated in the northern hemisphere, except for some of the islands that either overlap the equator or lie south of it. Geographers usually fix its western boundaries at the Red Sea, the isthmus separating it from Africa (although some ancient geographers place them as far as the River Nile and thus include Egypt),[1] the Mediterranean, the Euxine,[2] Lake Meotis with the River Tanais,[3] and the River Dvina, by which Asia is separated from Europe. In the north the region is bounded by the Scythian Sea of Ice;[4] in the south, by the Indian Sea and the Persian Gulf; in the east, partly by the Oriental or China Sea, partly by the island regions of 180° longitude where some people imagine that the Strait of Anian, separating Asia from America, is situated. But it seems more probable that there is no such strait, but that this region is contiguous with the New World, a part of which, before reaching the said meridian, is still Eastern or Lower Tartary, as may be seen on this map.[5]

Mt Taurus encircles all this region and stretches through the middle of the interior from west to east like a girdle as long as Asia[6] itself. According to Strabo,[7] it begins at the western shore of Rhodes and continues eastwards to the most distant parts of Eastern Tartary. Beginning between Caria and Lydia in Asia Minor, it is known by sundry names, and in various places sends out different branches or arms, some towards the north and others towards the south. That part of it that separates Lower Scythia or Upper India (embracing

---

[1] For example, Pliny, *Natural History*, 5, 9. But Ptolemy (*Geographia*, IV, 5, 3; in Magini, *Geographia*, p. 98) places Egypt in Africa. The first part of Magini's *Geographia* is paginated and reproduces Ptolemy's *Geographia*, while the second part, in folio, consists of Magini's description of the world. Magini's text of Ptolemy, first published in Venice in 1596, is not critical, but since it was almost certainly the version used by Rodrigues (see Introduction, p. xxxiii), I have checked all his references to Ptolemy in it.

[2] The Black Sea was formerly known as the Pontus Euxinus.

[3] Lake Meotis is the Sea of Azov, while Tanais was the former name of the River Don.

[4] The Scythian Sea of Ice (or simply the Scythian Sea) was the ill-defined ocean to the north of the Asian landmass. A map in Magini (*Geographia*, f. 229v) has its beginning at 60°N; in his map of Tartary, Mercator (*Atlas*, pp. 413–14) places its lower limits at more or less the same position and calls it Mare Tartaricum.

[5] Rodrigues is here returning to the old tradition of joining the American and Asian continents. The Anian Strait, roughly corresponding to the Bering Strait, was first introduced into European maps by Bolognino Zaltieri (Zalterius) in his 1556 map of America: Dahlgren, *Débuts*, p. 18–19; Bagrow, *History*, p. 136. For the supposed position of the strait, see Ortelius's map (Plate 9) and Mercator, *Atlas*, pp. 413–14. Jerónimo de Angelis, a Jesuit contemporary of Rodrigues and the first European to visit Ezo (Hokkaido), at first doubted the existence of the strait: Cieslik, *Hoku-hō*, p. (8). But in 1601 Valignano (*Principio*, f. 15) reported that the English were certain that there was a northern passage and that Asia and America were not joined in the northern regions. The English interest in this route is reflected in Richard Cocks's letters (Farrington, *English Factory*, I, pp. 99, 259, 592).

At this point in *Breve aparato*, f. 7, Rodrigues describes the size of Asia: 'The length of Asia begins in the west at the shore of Rhodes on the meridian that passes through Constantinople, 50° from the meridian that passes through the Canary Islands between Tenerife and the Grand Canary Island; in the east it begins at 180° of longitude, where Asia is divided from America. It thus has a length of 130°. Its breadth begins at the equator and ends in the north on the 70th parallel.'

Europeans at the time generally used the Canary Islands as the prime meridian after the example of Ptolemy, who regarded the islands as the westernmost part of the inhabitable world but miscalculated their position. About 18° must be subtracted from the longitude based on the Canary Islands to convert to the Greenwich meridian: Bunbury, *History*, II, pp. 566–7; Brown, *Story*, pp. 282–3.

[6] The copyist made an obvious slip by writing 'Africa' here, but *Breve aparato* correctly has 'Asia'.

[7] Both Strabo (*Geography*, XI, 1, 2–4) and Pliny (*Natural History*, 5, 27) describe this fabulous mountain chain, whose length Strabo puts at 45,000 *stadia*. For its position and size, see Ptolemy's map in Plate 7. Rodrigues's description of Mt Taurus is similar to the account in Magini, *Geographia*, f. 211v.

Bactria and Sogdiana) from India intra Gangem is called Caucasus by the Greeks,[1] Imaus by Ptolemy,[2] Conglingshan by the Chinese, and Sōreisan by the Japanese.[3] The Iron Gates, rather like a customs barrier, through which travellers pass from Bactria to India, are in a part of this mountain close to Bactria.[4]

There are, moreover, in the eastern part of Asia some famous deserts that the Chinese call Shamo, meaning 'sea of sand'. In shape they are like a long belt and separate Scythia extra Imaum in the south from Lower Scythia and China, and in the east from Inner or Eastern Tartary. The belt starts in the east at 144° longitude and 54°N, whence it descends roughly southwestward to 42° above the Great Wall of China and Beijing. Thence it continues westward until the province of Turkestan, where it finishes by dividing up into branches towards the south. One of these branches is the Lup or Lop desert, the boundary of ancient Serica. The width of this desert belt at its broadest is almost 2°, while its length is beyond all calculation.[5] The two deserts mentioned by the Venetian Marco Polo are situated in these sandy regions; the larger one is called Karakorum and the smaller one Lop.[6] Part of these desert lands is inhabited by the Tartars who dwell in wagons, covered with animal skins, which serve as houses and tents. Whence originated the fable among our authors who declare that the Chinese navigate on land in carts with sails, just like ships at sea. These are the Tartars dwelling in their wagons in these deserts above China, and they are continually on the move in search of pasture for their cattle.[7]

[1] For the possible origin of this name, see Arrian, *Life of Alexander the Great*, 5, 5.

[2] Ptolemy, *Geographia*, 6, 13, in Magini, *Geographia*, p. 155. In the map of Asia according to Ptolemy, Imaus is depicted as running north-south through Scythia. For origin of name, see McCrindle, *Ancient India*, p. 35.

[3] For what the Chinese understood by the Congling Mountains, see Bretschneider, *Mediaeval Researches*, I, p. 27, n. 47. Soreisan is the Japanese reading of the Chinese ideographs used in writing Conglingshan.

[4] Ruy Gonzales de Clavijo has left a famous description of the Iron Gates pass near Derbend, through which he travelled in 1403 on his way to the court of Tamberlaine. Clavijo, *Narrative*, p. 121–2; also Bretschneider, *Medieval Researches*, I, pp. 82–5, n. 211; Beal, *Buddhist Records*, I, p. 36. Identification of Rodrigues's reference is made easier by additional information in his *Breve aparato*, f. 7: 'This pass is called Diemanguan by the Chinese, and travellers pass through it on their way to India or from India to Bactria and Bogdiana. Alexander the Great passed here after defeating King Porus' in May 326 BC. According to a late legend, Alexander is said to have built a wall between two mountains in the Caucasus to keep out the barbarian subjects of the kings Gog and Magog, names appearing in Genesis, Ezechiel, and Revelations, and in time this fabled wall appears to have merged in popular imagination with the barrier near Derbend and came to be called Alexander's Iron Gate. This is presumably the pass, mentioned in Chinese records, to which Rodrigues is referring. For details, see Polo, *Book*, I, 4; Yule, *Book*, I, p. 50; Silverberg, *Great Wall*, pp. 151–6; Anderson, *Alexander's Gate*. There were legends even identifying Alexander's wall with the Great Wall of China.

[5] *Breve aparato*, f. 7, adds here: '… from east to west the belt is more than 7,000 leagues long between the parallels of 42° and 44°N,' so the 54° in the text must be a slip for 44°.

Shamo (in Japanese, Sabaku) is the Chinese name for the Gobi Desert and literally means Desert of Sand. Ricci, *Fonti*, I, p. 16, n. 2. If Rodrigues's longitude is converted to the Greenwich meridian, 144°E becomes 126°, but this is still too far east. The width of the desert belt is obviously more than 2°, but its length is far less than Rodrigues's estimate. Francesco Carletti (*My Voyage*, p. 160) reckons it to be 2,160 miles long. See Martini, *Atlas*, pp. 44–5, for contemporaneous European ideas of the desert's extent.

[6] Polo (*Book*, I, 39, 46; Yule, *Book*, I, pp. 196–7, 226–7) mentions Karakorum and Lop as cities on the edge of the great desert area. At Lop a month's rations were needed before entering the terrible desert where the singing sands lured many to their death.

[7] European reports about sailing vehicles in Asia enjoyed much popularity, and references and illustrations may be found in the maps of Ortelius and Mercator. These accounts inspired Milton to mention the vehicles in *Paradise Lost*, 3, 437–9. For an account of Chinese sailing wheel-barrows, see *SCC*, IV:2, pp. 274–81, and Needham, 'Science and China's Influence', pp. 275–7. Rodrigues's English contemporary, Richard Cocks (Hirado, 10 December 1614, in Farrington, *English Factory*, II, p. 254), mentions that the Koreans use 'great waggons or carts, which goe upon broad

Division of Asia into its parts or empires

The ancients divided this part of the world into Asia Major (or Universal) and Asia Minor, thus called after one of the provinces in Asia Minor that strictly is called Asia but is now commonly known as Anatolia or Great Turkey.[1] Ptolemy divides the whole of Asia into 47 regions or provinces, and he includes his specific description of them in the fifth, sixth, and seventh books of his *Geographia*.[2] His account is divided into twelve geographical sections, the tenth of which concerns India intra Gangem. The eleventh refers to India extra Gangem and China, to which the islands of Japan belonged; Ptolemy himself did not leave any information about these islands and designated everything as Terra Incognita.[3]

Many geographers divide Asia in various ways according to its state at the time of their writing, because from ancient times to the present day it has always been involved in continuous change. João de Barros recognized nine regions,[4] while Abraham Ortelius in his *Theatrum Orbis* [*Terrarum*] and other authors divide Asia into five parts.[5] Giovanni Antonio Magini divided it by empires into seven principal parts in his *Geographia*.[6] We ourselves make a division into nine parts as this best suits our purpose.

1. The Empire of the Muscovites
2. The Turkish Empire
3. The Persian or Sofian Empire
4. India intra Gangem
5. India extra Gangem
6. Asiatic Scythia or Tartary
7. The Chinese Empire

---

or flat wheeles under saile, as ships doe. So that observing monsoons they transport their goods to and fro in these sayling waggons.'

[1] The first person to use the term 'Asia Minor' was probably Paulus Orosius, born in Portugal between 380 and 390, who noted (*The Seven Books of History against the Pagans*, 1, 2), 'Asia Regio or, to speak more correctly, Asia Minor.' But it is possible that the Romans may have used this or a similar term to distinguish their province of Asia, east of the Aegean, from the rest of the continent.

[2] Magini (*Geographia*, f. 211v) gives exactly the same information about Ptolemy's division of Asia, adding that Strabo divided the region into five parts. See p. xxxiii.

[3] Quoting this passage from Rodrigues, Schurhammer ('*Descobrimento*', pp. 486–90) rightly rejects the theory that Ptolemy knew of the existence of Japan.

[4] João de Barros (1496–1570) was sent to Guinea in 1522 by John III, and after his return to Lisbon acted as Crown Agent for Portugal's Asian and African colonies. An indefatigable reader of reports from abroad, he used these first-hand materials to compile his celebrated *Décadas*. His work was continued under the same title by Diogo do Couto. Faris, *Vida de João de Barros*; Boxer, 'Three Historians', pp. 15–44. Barros's division of Asia into nine geographical, as opposed to political, regions is given in *Década primeira*, 9, 1 (ff. 172–172v).

[5] Abraham Ortelius (Ortels) was born in Antwerp in 1527 and died there in 1598. In 1570 he published his famous *Theatrum orbis terrarum*, which went through four printings in the same year. Often described as the first modern atlas, the work contains 70 maps drawn by 87 cartographers: Karrow, *Mapmakers*, pp. 1–31; Tooley, *Maps*, pp. 29–30. Rodrigues was obviously familiar with the work. Apart from this reference, he relates in a letter (Macao, 30 November 1627, in Rodrigues, 'Rodrigues in China', p. 257) that he has prepared an atlas of Asia 'of the size of a *Theatrum orbis*'. Ortelius divides Asia into five regions: Muscovy, Persia, Tartary, the Turkish Empire, and the Indies.

[6] A celebrated astronomer and cartographer. Born in Padua in 1555, he professed mathematics at Bologna from 1588, but later transferred to Mantua. He opposed the teachings of Copernicus and Galileo, and invented a complicated theory to explain celestial movement. He first published an Italian edition of Ptolemy's *Geographia* at Venice in 1596. He died in 1617. *Enciclopedia italiana*, XXI, pp. 897–8; Bagrow, *History*, p. 258. Magini (*Geographia*, f. 212) divides Asia into seven regions: Sarmatia, Persia, Tartary, the Turkish Empire, India, China, and the Islands in the East.

8. Various mighty islands in the Indian Ocean and the Oriental Sea, excluding the Islands of Japan.

9. The Islands of Japan, which we intend to describe in this history.

1. The first, second, and third parts of Asia

The first part of Asia bordering on Europe is Asiatic Sarmatia, now called Muscovy. It takes its name from a region in the middle of this part that is strictly called Muscovy and is the capital and metropolis of all the inner regions and cities under the sway of the Muscovite Empire. The region terminates in the west at the River Tanais, which separates Europe from Asia; in the north it is bordered by the Sea of Ice, while in the east it borders on to Tartary, or Scythia intra Imaum. In the south it is bounded partly by the Caspian Sea and partly by the isthmus lying between this sea and the Black Sea.

The second part is the region that the Turk possesses in Asia. It is bounded by the Black Sea, the Aegean Sea, the Mediterranean, Egypt, the Arabian Sea, the Persian Gulf, the River Tigris, the Caspian Sea, and the isthmus lying between this sea and the Black Sea. This part embraces the whole of Anatolia (which in ancient times was Asia Minor), the island of Cyprus, and all of Syria (which includes Palestine, Judea, Coelesyria, Phoenicia, Babylon, and other regions). It also includes the whole of Arabia Deserta, which the Hebrews call Kedar,[1] as well as Arabia Petraea or Nabataea (called thus after its capital Petra), which Scripture calls Petra Deserti[2] and also Arabia Felix.[3]

The third part of Asia is the Persian or Sofian Empire. Strictly speaking, Persia is the land now called Fars or Farsistan, situated below Parthia, or Arach, and Carmania, or Kirman, and between the provinces of Media and Hyrcania, with Arabia to the south. Shiraz, the capital and principal city, used to be called Persepolis in ancient times and was burned down by Alexander the Great.[4] Situated on the River Bendirmir, it is like a customs post and transit centre for the Chagatai merchants en route to India. The states of Lar, which border on to Ormuz, and the Sofian Kingdom, whose capital Shushter is on the River Saimarreh,[5] belong to Persia or Farsistan. But people usually mean by Persia everything included in the empire possessed by the kings of Persia reigning at the present time. Its latitude includes both the Caspian Sea and the Persian Gulf. Its longitude extends from ancient Chaldea, Syria, Mesopotamia (or Diarbekr) between the Euphrates and the Tigris, right up to the boundaries of Lesser Georgia and Northern Tartary. In the north it is

---

[1] For example, Psalm 120, 5, and Ezechiel 27, 21.

[2] Isaias, 16, 1: 'Emitte Agnum, Domine, de petra deserti ad montem filiae Sion.' This scriptural 'petra deserti' does not necessarily refer to the historical Petra, capital of Edom.

[3] Quaintly called Happie Arabia, or Arabia the Happie (Mercator, *Atlas*, p. 402), on some maps, Arabia Felix derives its name from Eudaimon, by which it was known to ancient geographers (e.g., Ptolemy, *Geography*, 6, 7, in Magini, *Geography*, p. 147). An explanation may be found in the native name Yemen, or Yamen, meaning right-hand side, with its traditional beneficial associations. Hansen, *Arabia Felix*, pp. 300–301.

[4] The identification of Shiraz with Persepolis is mistaken, as the ruins of the latter are some 40 miles northeast of modern Chirz: Curzon, *Persia*, II, p. 115. Alexander took Persepolis in the winter of 331–30 BC, but may have burnt down only Xerxes's palace.

In *Breve aparato*, f. 7v, at this point, Rodrigues adds a lengthy note that the Greeks called this region Perses, the Romans Parthia, the natives themselves Pars, and the Arabs Fars.

[5] Shushter is the ancient capital of Khuzistan, and I presume that 'Zeimana' in the Portuguese text may be identified with the River Saimarreh (now Simarsh), which flows in this region. Shushter stands on the River Karun. Curzon, *Persia*, II, pp. 363–82.

bounded by part of Muscovy up to the boundaries of the River Eden, or Volga, while in the south it borders on the two Arabias, Deserta and Petraea. Thus an imaginary circle is formed from the Caspian Sea, the Persian Sea, and Lake Giocho,[1] to the River Tigris and the River Oxus (or Abiano), right up to the River Indus. All the kingdoms under the sway of the Persian crown are included in this circuit and compass, extending 15°[2] of latitude and 21° of longitude from east to west. The kingdoms subject to the Persian crown are as follows:

1. Persia, or Fars or Farsistan, to which are subjected the states of Sofia and Lar; its capital is Shiraz, formerly called Persepolis.

2. Parthia, or Arach, whose capital is Isfahan, the present court of Persia. It is known as Nisf-i jahan, meaning 'half the world'.[3] This is the ancient Hekatompylos, which means City of a Hundred Gates, but in their stead there are now a hundred towers.[4]

2. The fourth and fifth parts of Asia: India intra and extra Gangem

Information in greater detail must be given about the position and division of the region of India because it is often mentioned in Japan and in the sects of the idols. Sacred Scriptures normally refer to it as Ophir, meaning the golden region, thus called on account of the gold and riches that it possesses such as *obryzum*, as St Jerome says, including both Indias in this term.[5] But Josephus holds that it is thus called on account of Ophir, son of Joktan, who some people believe populated that region which the ancients called India extra Gangem.[6] Others say that India extra Gangem is the region called Havilah in Scripture after another son of Joktan who, they suppose, populated the area.[7] But it is most unlikely that these two sons of Joktan populated these two parts and gave their names to the regions. Instead they peopled places nearer to Juda. Many reasons make it more certain that India in general is called Ophir in Scripture on account of the gold and riches that it produces and for which the ships of King Solomon and the kings of Juda came seeking.[8] Job mentions it when speaking of 'the dyed colours of India'. Here the Latin translator has rendered the name

---

[1] Lake Giocho is shown on a map in Magini, *Geographia*, f. 235, and appears to correspond to Lake Van in Asiatic Turkey, west of the Caspian.

[2] 18°, in *Breve aparato*, f. 7v.

[3] *Isfahan nisf i jahan*, 'Isfahan is half the world', was a phrase glorifying the splendour of the magnificent city. Curzon, *Persia*, II, p. 23.

[4] The ruins of Hekatompylos are found near the town of Damghan and the ancient city cannot be identified with Isfahan. Tarn (*The Greeks*, pp. 13–14) dismisses the pleasing image conjured up by the name of the city, stating that it merely means that 'the place had more gates than the stereotyped four of Hellenistic town-planning.'

[5] There are various references to Ophir in Scripture (e.g., 1 Kings 10, 11), but it is not certain that the name referred to India, and different writers have identified the place with Somaliland, Rhodesia, Malacca, Sumatra, Abyssinia, Spain, Peru, and even the Ryūkyū Islands. In fact, Ophir was probably situated on the southwest coast of Arabia, whence products of India were distributed. Acosta, *Natural and Moral*, I, 13, 14 (I, pp. 37–42); Dahlgren, *Débuts*, p. 13. Rodrigues explains the reference to St Jerome in *Breve aparato*, f. 8: '… as may be seen in Job, where it says, *India tinctis coloribus*, although the Hebrew version has *Ophir*. St Jerome says that it means *Aurea regio obryzum*'. The reference is to Job 28, 16.

[6] The scriptural reference to Ophir, son of Joktan, is Genesis 10, 29. Josephus merely records: 'Now Joktan had these sons …Ophir … [and 12 others]. These inhabited from Cophen, an Indian River, and in part of Aria adjoining to it.' Josephus, *Antiquities of the Jews*, 6, 4.

[7] Havilah, son of Joktan, is mentioned in Genesis 10, 29, and two different places bearing this name appear in Genesis 2, 11, and 1 Kings 15, 7. In *Breve aparato*, f. 8, Rodrigues makes it clear that he is referring to the latter. Mercator (*Atlas*, p. 419) believed that India was to be identified with the Scriptural Havilah: 'India beyond Ganges is called in the Holy Scriptures Hevila, or as some write Havilath, or Evilath.'

[8] 3 Kings 9, 26–8.

Ophir in the Hebrew text as India.[1] It is believed that the particular place to which Solomon's ships went is Sumatra, called the Golden Chersonese by Ptolemy, and Java the Less by Marco Polo.[2] As may be seen in Ptolemy, the ancient writers used to divide this region of India into India intra and extra Gangem.[3]

India intra Gangem, which we said is the fourth part of Asia, lies between the two rivers Indus and Ganges, and is called by its inhabitants Hindu or Hindustan, meaning the Province of India. Thus our name of India is derived from the name of the River Indus, which is now called the River Sind because it passes through the kingdom of Sind. It was called Sinthu by Ptolemy and Pliny,[4] and empties into the sea there. The Chinese, from whom the Japanese heard this name, call it Yinduguo, or Xifanguo, or Xitianguo, or Tianzhuguo, Xinduguo, and also Xiyu. This last name includes Upper India, or Lower Scythia. They also call it Tianzhu, which the Japanese know as Tenjiku.[5] It is bounded in the south by the Indian Sea, beginning at $7\frac{2}{3}$°N at Cape Comorin, which Ptolemy calls Cori Promontorium.[6] The northern limits are formed by Mt Caucasus, or Imaus, by which it is separated from Lower Scythia, which some people call Upper India in relation to the part that we are describing. In the west the region ends at the River Indus at 97° longitude and 32°N, where the river flows into the Indian Sea. The eastern boundary is formed by the River Ganges at 122° longitude in Bengal, where the region is separated from India extra Gangem, or Satigan and Arakan.[7]

In ancient times its inhabitants used to divide the country into five regions that they called the Five Indias (which the Chinese call Wuyindu, or Wutianzhu, and the Japanese Goindo, or Gotenjiku), that is, Northern, Southern, Western, Eastern, and Central India.[8] Northern India is that part that ends at the Caucasus and borders on the Bactrians and

[1] Job 28, 16. The Vulgate reads: 'Non conferetur tinctis Indiae coloribus.' The Douai version, based on this, runs, 'It shall not be compared with the dyed colours of India.' But a more accurate translation of the original text would be, as Rodrigues (and the King James version) suggests, 'It cannot be valued in the gold of Ophir.'

[2] For the references to the Golden Chersonese, see Ptolemy, *Geographia*, 7, 2 (in Magini, *Geographia*, p. 170), and McCrindle, *Ancient India*, pp. 197–8. Wheatley (*Golden Chersonese*, pp. 141–76) proves fairly conclusively that the Golden Chersonese was the Malay Peninsula, in which case Rodrigues's identification of it with Sumatra was not far wrong.

[3] Ptolemy, *Geographia*, 7, 1 and 2 (in Magini, *Geographia*, pp. 162–72). India extra Gangem was often called Further India by European writers.

[4] Ptolemy, *Geographia*, 7, 1 (in Magini, *Geographia*, p. 164), and Pliny, *Natural History*, 6, 23. On this point, see also Barros, *Década primeira*, 4, 7 (f. 73).

[5] Tianzhu ('Tiencio') is also mentioned by Ricci (*Fonti*, I, p. 122, and *China*, p. 98). See also Bretschneider, *Mediaeval Researches*, II, pp. 25–6. 'Tenjiku' often appears in early European reports, as the index of Fróis's *História*, I, shows.

[6] Ptolemy, *Geographia*, 7, 1 (in Magini, *Geographia*, p. 163). The exact position of Cape Comorin is 8°03′N.

[7] The text is corrupt here, as *Breve aparato*, f. 7v, shows: 'Its eastern boundary is formed at the easternmost mouth of the River Ganges in the kingdom of Bengal, where the port of Satigan is situated at 122° of longitude; this divides it from India extra Gangem and the kingdom of Arakan.' Rodrigues may have taken the names of Satigan and Arakan from Magini, *Geographia*, f. 259, or from Mercator, *Atlas*, f. 415v, who show the two places on opposite sides of the Ganges. For eyewitness descriptions of the 'fair citie' of Satigan by Ralph Fitch (c. 1583) and Caesar Frederick (1567), see Hakluyt, *Principal Navigations*, V, pp. 411, 483; see also Barros, *Década primeira*, 9, 1 (f. 175v). For modern accounts of Arakan, in West Burma on the bank of the Irawaddy, and of Satigan, north of Calcutta, see *Imperial Gazeteer*, V, pp. 397–8, and 22, p. 129.

[8] According to the ancient Hindu concept, India was likened to the lotus flower, the middle being Central India and the surrounding petals the eight principal divisions of the compass. In the Chinese plan, only the central part and the four primary divisions were retained: Cunningham, *Ancient Geography*, pp. 5–13.

Massagetes in the province of Turkestan. Bucephala Regio[1] is situated in this part, and is made up of the kingdoms of Kashmir and Lahore, the Mogul court, and other states that belonged to King Porus in ancient times. The Chinese call this India Beiyindu or Beitianzhu, while the Japanese know it as Hokuindo or Hokutenjiku, and this is the name used in the books of the Shaka sects.[2] Southern India begins at Cape Comorin and ends in the north at 20°N with the Ghats, which lie across the region from Bassein in the west to Bengal in the east. Ptolemy calls this mountain Batio Mons and it has only one approach from the north, the Gates of Varara.[3] A branch of this mountain running from north to south ends at Cape Comorin and divides this India into two parts. This is called Magoia, or more properly the Ghats.[4] This part includes the kingdom of Bisnaga, or Narsinga,[5] and Orissa (which Ptolemy calls Brachimarum Regio),[6] Malabar, Kanara, Deccan, Konkan, and the area belonging to the Portuguese as far as Bassein. It also includes the River Nagotana, which seems to be what Ptolemy calls Simylla Promontorium.[7] To the north of this part begins Gujarat, or Cambay. This is called in Chinese Nanyindu or Nantianzhu, and in Japanese Nan'indo or Nantenjiku, and this also is the name used in the sects of Shaka, whose disciples were the Brahmans belonging to this region.

Western India begins from this Cape of Damao and continues up to the most westerly mouth of the River Indus; it includes Sind and Gujarat, which modern writers call Cambay. This part is called Xiyindu or Xitianzhu in Chinese, and Sai-indo or Saitenjiku in Japanese, and this name can also designate the whole of India in respect to China. Eastern or Oriental India ends with the River Ganges at 122° longitude, where it is separated from India extra Gangem. Bengal, which Ptolemy calls Gangarida and the Chinese know as Bangala, is situated here.[8] This India is called Dongyindu or Dongtianzhu by the Chinese, and Tōindo or Tōtenjiku by the Japanese, and is very renowned on account of the River Ganges. Central India is bounded in the north by Northern India and ends in the south with the above-mentioned Mt Batio; this is the region that Ptolemy calls Gymnosophistarum Regio and

---

[1] Named after Alexander's favourite horse which died in 326 BC, the old Indian city is supposed to have marked his grave. Arrian, *Life*, 5, 19; Tarn, *The Greeks*, p. 16.

[2] That is, Buddhism.

[3] Ptolemy, *Geographia*, 7, 1 (in Magini, *Geographia*, p. 165); see also McCrindle, *Ancient India*, pp. 59, 78. For early European description of the Ghats, see Barros, *Década primeira*, 4, 7 (f. 74). 'The Gates of Varara' is undoubtedly a reference to the pass across the Western Ghats called Borghāt, situated 40 miles southeast of Bombay. *Imperial Gazetteer*, IX, p. 5.

[4] The Portuguese text is corrupt at this point, and some words or a whole line have been omitted. Rodrigues, *Nihon*, I, p. 101, n. 19, suggests that 'Magoia' may refer to the Venetian Maiolo (or Maggiolo) family, who produced sea charts in the sixteenth century, but it is impossible to verify this. An alternative explanation is offered in n. 6, below.

[5] Bisnaga is derived from Vijayanagara, the name of a dynasty replaced about 1487 by Narasinha, a prince who ruled until 1508 – hence the Portuguese Narsinga. See Pires, *Suma oriental*, I, pp. 63–5; Barbosa, *Book*, I, pp. 200–228; Yule, *Hobson-Jobson*, pp. 97, 618–19. Explanation of the names is supplied in Rubruck, *Journey*, p. 63, n. 1.

[6] Ptolemy, *Geographia*, 7, 1 (in Magini, *Geographia*, p. 168, and McCrindle, *Ancient India*, p. 170) actually calls this region Brachmanae Magoi. Perhaps this name has some connection with 'Magoia' in the previous sentence?

[7] According to Barros (*Década primeira*, 9, 1; f. 174), Nagotana was four leagues from Chaul, which itself is 23 miles south of Bombay. Ptolemy's reference to Symilla Promontorium may be found in his *Geographia*, 7, 1 (in Magini, *Geographia*, p. 162). The place is generally identified with Chaul: McCrindle, *Ancient India*, pp. 42–4. For detailed references to Chaul, see Barbosa, *Book*, I, pp. 158–63.

[8] Ptolemy (*Geographia*, 7, 1, in Magini, *Geographia*, p. 168, and in McCrindle *Ancient India*, pp. 173–5) refers to the region as Gange Regia and to its inhabitants as Gangaridai.

from ancient times has always been the principal and leading part of all.[1] It now includes the kingdoms of Delhi (where the ancient King Porus held his court), Agra, and other states. The sect of the Indian gymnosophists originated in this region and thence spread throughout the whole Orient. This is the sect of the bonzes that exists in Japan and China, and continues to this day among the Brahmans in this India and in all of India extra Gangem. Its author and founder was Shaka, or more properly Shakia as they call him in India and China. He is also known by another name, Buddha, meaning sage or philosopher. His father was the king of this region and he was the prince.[2] It will be necessary to speak about this sect at length in this history, and that is why we have given this information about the region. This part is called Zhongyindu or Zhongtianzhu by the Chinese, and Chūindo or Chūtenjiku by the Japanese.

At present the whole of India intra Gangem is divided into two parts. The first and principal part is the Mogul Empire, which included the four[3] Indias, Northern, Central, Eastern, and Western, with the kingdoms of Kabul and Kandahar, the province of Little Tibet,[4] and other states lying beyond the Indus in the direction of Persia. This Mogul state is bounded in the north by Mt Caucasus at 32°N, in the south by Mt Batio at 20°N, in the west by the River Indus (except for the part that it possesses towards Persia), and in the east by India extra Gangem and the province of Greater Tibet.[5] The second part is Southern India and contains the states that we have mentioned.

The fifth part of Asia is India extra Gangem. Its western boundary is the River Ganges in Bengal and the Liusha or Ryūsa Desert,[6] along the length of which flows that part of the Ganges that has its source in China; the Chinese call this river Liushahe and the Japanese Ryūsagawa. In the east the region partly borders on to China in the provinces of Shaanxi, Sichuan, and Yunnan, and partly on the Oriental Sea that washes the coasts of Champa and Cauchi, or Hainan.[7] In the south it reaches the Indian Sea, and in the north it is bounded

---

[1] Ptolemy (*Geographia*, 7, 1, in Magini, *Geographia*, p. 166, and McCrindle, *Ancient India*, pp. 130) merely states that 'further east are the Gymnosophistai ['Naked philosophers'].' Reports about these Hindu ascetics were brought back by Alexander's army and they are mentioned several times in classical literature, e.g., Strabo, *Geography*, XVI, 2, 39. Mercator (*Atlas*, p. 520) likens them to the Druids of Britain. Rodrigues errs in identifying them as Buddhists.

[2] S'ākya [Japanese, Shaka] Muni, the historical Buddha, was born in north India about 563 BC and died about 483; in *Arte grande*, f. 235v, Rodrigues gives 1027 BC, the traditional date of the Buddha's birth, and adds that he renounced his kingdom at the age of 19 years, became a buddha at 30, and died at the age of 79. For early European reports from Japan about Shaka, see *TCJ*, pp. 311–12, 316–18. It was sometimes said that the Buddha was born in Siam (Fróis, *História*, I, p. 139) and hence Tenjiku was occasionally identified with that country. Rodrigues puts the record right in *Breve aparato*, f. 9: '… hence the error of some of Ours is quite clear, because for lack of information they wrote that Shaka belonged to the kingdom of Siam and that this sect originated there. This is not true, although the sect flourishes even today in Siam and in all of India extra Gangem, whither it was carried from India.' Rodrigues neglects to mention that he himself, in his *Arte grande*, f. 235v, erroneously states that Shaka was 'the native king of Siam, which they called Tenjiku.'

[3] An obvious slip, probably on the part of the copyist, has 'the five Indias' here.

[4] Writing from the court of the Tibet king on 15 September 1626, Antonio de Andrade explains (*Nuevo descubrimiento*, II, p. 9) that Little Tibet is the region north of the kingdom of Kashmir, inhabited by Moslems.

[5] For a map showing the extent of the Mogul Empire about this time, see Davies, *Historical Atlas*, p. 47.

[6] For the Liusha desert, see Bretschneider, *Mediaeval Researches*, II, p. 27, n. 47.

[7] For a description of the ancient kingdom of Champa, see Polo, *Book*, III, 5 (Yule, *Book*, II, pp. 266–72); Pires, *Suma oriental*, I, pp. 112–15; Maspero, '*Royaume de Champa*'. The alternative name for Cauchi was Annam, not Hainan, and Rodrigues repeats this slip a few lines later; the same error is found in Martín de Rada (in Boxer, *South China*, p. 264). As the Portuguese called the island of Hainan 'Aynam' (e.g., Barros, *Década terceira*, 2, 7; f. 44v), it was easy to confuse the two names. Rodrigues gives the correct name Annam on p. 26.

by the Chinese province of Shanxi at the garrisons of Ganzhou and Xuzhou, which Marco Polo calls Campion and Succiur, while the Moors of Persia now know them as Cangiu and Sogiu. This is where the Wall of China ends and where people enter Cathay or China from the west through the gates of the Wall. A part borders on Tartary and here are to be found the gates for the west in the region of Shazhou, which Marco Polo calls Sachiu.[1]

This region includes a multitude of various nations, many of which are tributaries of China, such as Cauchi (or Hainan), Champa, Cambodia, Siam, Patani, Malacca, Pegu,[2] Burma, Tangu,[3] Mien,[4] the Mongols mentioned by Marco Polo bordering Bengal,[5] Tufan or Xifan, which Marco Polo calls Tibet,[6] and other regions that the inhabitants group under the name of Burma, such as Burma Ava, Burma Prome, Burma Bassein, Burma Lima,[7] and also the people of Laos, such as Chiengmai, Chiengrai, Chieng Khouang, and Lanchang,[8] on the western borders of Cauchi. All these regions border on to China and are subject to the province of Yunnan. A large part of what is now China was India extra Gangem in Ptolemy's time,[9] but was incorporated into China by Chinese force of arms. For example, the provinces of Nanjing (the part that lies south of the river),[10] Zhejiang, Fujian, Guangdong, Jiangxi, Guangxi, Guizhou, and Yunnan.

[1] For references to these Chinese garrisons, see Polo, *Book*, I, 40, 43, 44 (Yule, *Book*, I, pp. 205–7, 217–18, 219–21); for their position, see the reconstructed map at the end of Polo, *Book*, I. Ricci (*China*, pp. 514–18) mentions the fortified cities of Ganzhou and Xuzhou on the Chinese north-western frontier when describing the epic journey of Bento de Goes, who died at Xuzhou in 1607. Martini (*Description*, p. 65) names the nine principal forts along the Great Wall, and of these Xuzhou and Shazhou are the most westerly ones.

[2] For Pegu, a kingdom in south Burma, see Pires, *Suma oriental*, I, pp. 97–103; Barbosa, *Book*, II, pp. 152–7; Fitch, in Hakluyt, *Principal Navigations*, V, pp. 486–94; Lach, *Asia*, I, pp. 540–50.

[3] Tangu (or Toungoo) was a state in central Burma, often at war with Pegu. For a contemporaneous description of Burma, see Couto, *Década quinta*, 6, 1 (ff. 119v–121v). For modern accounts of ancient Burma, see Yule, *Narrative*, pp. 204–19, and Lach, *Asia*, I, pp. 539–60.

[4] Mien was a state in northern Burma, although the Chinese designated the whole of Burma by this name: Polo, *Book*, II, 51–4 (Yule, *Book*, II, pp. 98–114); Yule, *Narrative*, p. 207. The position of the state is shown in Ortelius's map in Hakluyt, *Principal Navigations*, I, p. 1.

[5] *Mien os Mogos de que falla Marco Paul, confinse a Bengala*. The clause, omitted from *Breve aparato*, is far from clear. I take *Mogos* as a corruption of *Mogores*, yet with some misgiving as Rodrigues later (p. 381) refers to the *Mogos* of Mien. It is possible that he had in mind the Mongol occupation of Mien in 1283, mentioned by Polo (*Book*, II, 54; Yule, *Book*, II, pp. 110–11), and inasmuch as they occupied Mien they could be said to border on Bengal. For Portuguese use of the name 'Mogor', see Dalgado, *Glossário*, II, pp. 63–4.

[6] Polo, *Book*, II, 45, 46 (Yule, *Book*, II, pp. 42–53). For the identification of Tibet with Tufan and with Xifan, see Bretschneider, *Mediaeval Researches*, II, pp. 22–4.

[7] These were minor states within Burma itself, and Rodrigues probably took the list from Barros, *Década terceira*, 2, 1 (f. 38v), who gives the same names but in different order. Yule (*Narrative*, p. 253) provides historical maps of Burma, and Rodrigues's account comes closest to the map of 1500. Yule (ibid., pp. 204–19), and Lach (*Asia*, I, pp. 542–60) describe early European visitors to the country.

[8] The Portuguese text gives these names as *Iagoma, Chancray, Chencran, Lanca ou Laoco*, and Rodrigues probably took the list from either Magini, *Geographia*, f. 260v, or Barros, *Década terceira*, 2, 5 (f. 38v). Lanchang was a Lao state that emerged in the 14th century, but split into three at the end of the 17th century. For its early history, see Barros, *Década terceira*, 2, 1 (ff. 37v–38); Le Bar, *Laos*, pp. 10–14. For early European references to Jangoma, or Chiengmai, see Couto, *Década quinta*, 6, 1 (f. 120); Pires, *Suma oriental*, I, p. 109; Fitch, in Hakluyt, *Principal Navigations*, V, pp. 495–6. See also Gastaldi's map in Nordenskiöld, *Periplus*, plate 56, and the map in Le Bar, *Laos*, p. 9.

[9] Ptolemy, *Geographia*, 7, 2 (in Magini, *Geographia*, p. 169). According to Ptolemy, the southern limit of Serica was about 35°N.

[10] Presumably a reference to the Yangzi, on the south bank of which stands Nanjing.

3. The sixth part of Asia: Asia Scythia or Tartary

The sixth part of Asia, Asiatic Scythia, is the largest of all and is generally called Tartary by modern geographers after the name of a nation in Scythia that is properly called Tartary. This nation dominated all this region and nearly all of Asia. This part includes many diverse nations and for the most part was not known by the ancients, who placed most of it under the title of Terra Incognita. They included Serica in it under the impression that it was different from China, and they divided the whole part into Scythia intra Montem Imaum and Scythia extra Montem Imaum.[1] In general its borders are formed in the west by the River Volga and Muscovy, while the Sea of Ice lies to the north. To the south it borders partly on the Caspian Sea, partly on the River Oxus and Regestan, partly on Mt Caucasus (or Imaus) by which it is separated from India, partly on the Wall of China, and, finally, partly on the Oriental Sea that lies north of the islands of Japan and flows between them and this Scythia from east to west[2] until it reaches America. In the east the region ends at 180° longitude where it is separated from America at a place where some people imagine the Strait of Anian exists.

Modern writers, whom we follow, divide the region into Upper and Lower Scythia. Lower Scythia (also called Upper India by some people) has its western border on the Caspian Sea, while to the north lie the River Jaxartes and the long deserts of Tartary. Its borders are formed in the south by Mt Caucasus (or Imaus), which separates it from India intra Gangem, and in the east by the desert called Liusha by the Chinese and Ryūsa by the Japanese, meaning 'shifting sands'. This is the Lop Desert, a branch of the great desert, and stretching from north to south it separates this region from India extra Gangem.[3] This part includes the provinces of Sogdiana, Bactria, Margiana, and the Saccae (both Pliny and Herodotus say that the Persians call Scythia by this last name).[4] These nations are now in the province of Turkestan, in which the city and kingdom of Samarkand and part of Chorassan are situated. The inhabitants call it Thoholma, or Thogorma, after a descendant of Noah of the same name who is said to have populated the place.[5] Thogorma was corrupted into Thure, whence comes the name Turkestan (that is, Province of Thure). In ancient times the genuine Turks originated in and came from this place, whence Mela declares, 'Thogorma frequens populis Turcarum gentis origo'.[6]

---

[1] See the map of Ptolemy's Asia on p. 8.

[2] 'West to east' would surely be more correct, unless Rodrigues means that the sea flows from the east of Asia to America, which is to the west of Europe.

[3] *Ryūsa* is, in fact, a common noun in Japanese, meaning quicksands. For the Lop Desert, see Polo, *Book*, I, 39 (Yule, *Book*, I, pp. 196–7).

[4] Pliny (*Natural History*, VI, 19; Herodotus (*Works*, I, 153; III, 93; VII, 64) does not mention the Persians.

[5] Genesis, 10, 3. Togarmah was the great-grandson of Noah.

[6] A reference to Pomponius Mela, who wrote a geographical treatise, *De situ orbis*, about the year 43. Details in Bunbury, *History*, II, pp. 352–68. The quotation, however, is not found in Mela's work, but this theory regarding the origin of the Turks was commonly held and is given by Rodrigues's Jesuit contemporary, Cornelius a Lapide, *Commentarii*, I, p. 140. In *Breve aparato*, f. 10, Rodrigues provides the full name of Pomponius Mela and continues: '... although in the histories of the Persians it is said that a king called Turc, son of a king of Persia, gave his name to this province. Perhaps Thogorma, the descendant of Noah, peopled it and then this king Turc later gave it its name. About the year 1230 the region was also called Chequetis or Chacatay after the name of a son, called Chacatay, of Temochin [Genghis Khan], the first Grand Cham, King of the Tartars. After he had overcome that kingdom, he left his son there as governor; he gave his name to the kingdom, calling it Chacatay after his own name. This name has been corrupted into Zagatay in the writings of our authors. At present, native lords called Usbeki rule there. Hence some call this province Usbequi.' This account of Genghis Khan (1162–1227), his son Chagatai, and the Uzbeks is substantially correct.

Upper Scythia is the Universal Scythia mentioned above, and the ancients divided it into Scythia intra Imaum and Scythia extra Imaum. Scythia intra Imaum is bordered in the west by Asiatic Sarmatia and the River Volga, and in the east by Mt Imaus, which the Chinese call Yinshan and place it in the same position as did Ptolemy. The southern borders are formed by the Caspian Sea and the River Jaxartes in Sogdiana, while the Sea of Ice forms the northern limit. In relation to their own kingdom, the Chinese divide Scythia extra Imaum into a northern part, which they call Beidi and the Japanese Hokuteki (meaning 'barbarians of the north'), and into an eastern part, which the Chinese call Dongyi and the Japanese know as Tōi (meaning 'barbarians of the east'). This is as if we were to call the two parts Northern Scythia and Eastern Scythia. We ourselves divide it into Western Scythia extra Imaum and Eastern (or Inner) Scythia extra Imaum.

Western Scythia lies to the north of China and includes those Scythias that Ptolemy places next to Serica and calls them Scythia extra Imaum; it in fact corresponds to the place that Ptolemy gives them.[1] This is that part of Tartary that now lies in Lower Scythia, which borders on to China in the west and northwest in a part where people enter China through the gates in the Wall near the city of Xuzhou. Shazhou (which Marco Polo calls Sachiu) and Kabul are situated in this region.[2] Ptolemy had no information about Scythia north of China, and Eastern (or Inner) Scythia, and left them under the heading of Terra Incognita.[3] Western Scythia terminates in the north at the Scythian Sea, while its southern limits are formed by the great desert above the Wall of China. This desert begins at 144° longitude, 14°N,[4] whence it descends southwest to 42°N, and from there turns towards the west until the province of Turkestan and then this part ends in the south.

In the west the region ends at Mt Imaus, the kingdoms of Thoholma, or Thogorma, or Turkestan, and Samarkand. This part is the real Tartary and is properly called Tartary. It was from here that the Tartars went forth to conquer the whole of Scythia and Asia, part of Europe, the kingdom of China and all its neighbouring realms. It was these Tartars who set out against Japan with a mighty army in the Year of the Lord 1278.[5] The kings of these Tartars are known among us as the Grand Cham, which comes from taijun, a Chinese name meaning 'great lord'. The Chinese call these people Dazi, or Dada, or Dadaer, and so we get the name Tartar[6] after one of their tribes thus called. This part includes the desert or region of Karakorum, the kingdom of Walach (or Walachia), the plains or regions of Bargu, and other parts mentioned by Marco Polo.[7] Among the tribes or nations that inhabited this region was one called Mongug, which the Chinese call Menggu in their records and the

---

[1] Ptolemy, *Geographia*, 6, 15, in Magini, *Geographia*, p. 151. See map on p. 8.

[2] See p. 20, n. 1.

[3] Ptolemy labelled as Terra Incognita the whole region north of the Imaus range, Scythia extra Imaum, and Serica. See the map in Lach, *Asia*, I, following p. 52.

[4] An obvious slip for 54°, as given on p. 13 and in *Breve aparato*, f. 7.

[5] Rodrigues recounts the attempted Mongol invasion of Japan at greater length on pp. 61–2, 96.

[6] For early explanations of this term's origin, see Barros, *Década terceira*, 2, 7 (f. 44v) and Couto, *Década quarta*, 10, 1 (ff. 188v–189v). Martini (*Bellum Tartaricum*, p. 255) uses the Great Wall as a convenient, if not accurate, marker for defining the Tartars. 'I call that Nation, *Tartars*, which inhabiteth the Northern parts, behind that famous Wall which stretching out above 300 *German* Leagues from East to West, hath ever served for a Rampart to hinder their irruptions into the said Empire.' For origin of 'Cham' or 'Khan', see Yule, *Cathay*, I, p. 149, n. 1.

[7] For Karakorum, see Polo, *Book*, I, 46 (Yule, *Book*, I, pp. 226–37); Rubruck, *Journey*, pp. 220–21. Polo (*Book*, IV, 22; Yule, *Book*, II, p. 487) mentions the kingdom of Lac, and Yule assumes this to be Walachia. I have taken 'Cegu' in the text to mean Bargu, northeast of Karakorum and mentioned by Polo (*Book*, I, 56; Yule, *Book*, I, pp. 269–73).

Japanese Mōko. This was the most illustrious nation of them all, for after conquering China their leaders were titled taijun, or Grand Cham, Mongug, or Mongal, whence is derived the name Mongol, or Mongali, or Mogor as they commonly say.[1] After these Tartars had been driven out of China, they helped in the conquests of the great Tamburlaine, or Temorlao, by allying themselves to him and afterwards to his younger son. They helped him to take India and he styled himself King of the Mongols.[2]

The western part of Inner (or Eastern) Scythia extra Imaum begins at 144° longitude next to the desert that stretches away to the southwest, and ends in the east at 180°, where it is separated from America at the place where the Strait of Anian is imagined to be. But it is more likely that there is no such strait, that this Inner Scythia is contiguous with New Spain, and that a part of what is now taken to be America at this meridian is really a part of Tartary, for the natives there live with their herds just like the other Tartars. Its southern limits are formed partly by the Wall of China and partly by the northern reaches of the Sea of Japan; its northern frontier is on the Scythian Sea. This part includes some nations of organized Tartars who are immediately […].[3] The Chinese call them Qitan and the Japanese Keitan, while the western Moors knew them as Kytai, or Katay, and thence came this name. The northern part of China was called Katayo or Kitai after this nation overcame and occupied the region for several centuries. The name continued to be used even in the time of the Grand Cham who succeeded them, and it continues to be used to this day by Westerners who come overland to China for trade and call China Cathay.[4]

Further to the east of these people and above the kingdom of Korea, there are other civilized Tartars whom the Koreans call Orancay.[5] They overcame part of China and the kingdom of Korea, spreading to the north above Japan. The island of Ezo[6] that borders on Japan at the Tsugaru district of Ōshū, belongs to them. Within this part of Tartary are included

[1] For suggestions regarding the origin of the term Mogul, see Yule, *Book*, I, p. 294, and Rubruck, *Journey*, p. 112, n. 1.

[2] Tamburlaine, 'the scourge of God and the terror of the world', had at least four sons, but Rodrigues is probably referring to his grandson, Pir-Muhammad Jahangir, who played a leading role in the Indian campaign. The supporters of the Yuan (or Mongol) dynasty were driven out of China in 1368, and some of the Mongol pretenders accompanied Tamburlaine to India: Hookham, *Tamburlaine*, pp. 185–202, 269. See also Couto, *Década quarta*, 10, 2 (ff. 193–4).

[3] There is an omission in the text at this point. Rodrigues, *Nihon*, I, p. 122, translates: '… who are immediately next to China.'

[4] D'Elia (in Ricci, *Fonti*, I, p, 7, n. 5) and Yule (*Hobson-Jobson*, p. 174) substantially agree with Rodrigues's explanation of the origin of the term Cathay. Cathay, reached overland, and China, reached by sea, were considered different countries by Europeans. By crossing Asia by the land route and contacting Ricci, who had come to China by sea, Bento de Goes proved that Cathay and China were one and the same country. Ricci, *China*, pp. 499–521; full account in Kircher, *China illustra*, pp. 55–9. This fact had been reported earlier by some Europeans such as Rada, in Boxer, *South China*, p. 260, n.1; Carletti, *My Voyage*, p. 156.

[5] This name is used as early as the 13th century by Rubruk (*Journey*, p. 198) and appears several times in the writings of 16th- and 17th-century Europeans. Fróis (*História*, V, pp. 544, 580) maintains that Orancay was a country forming a large bay to the north of Ezo (Hokkaido) and mentions its intervention in Hideyoshi's Korean campaign. Valignano (*Principio*, f. 15) also refers to this large country north of Japan. See also Angelis's description in Cieslik, *Hoku-Hō* , pp. (32) and 101–4. The name actually originates from the Mongol tribe of Urianghit, which is itself derived from *oron*, reindeer. The Koreans used the term to refer to the Manchu Tartars or foreigners in general: Yule, *Hobson-Jobson*, p. 644.

[6] The northernmost of the four main Japanese islands, now called Hokkaido.

the Koreans, a very civilized people and similar to the Chinese in everything. In addition to them, this part includes many different nations of savage and uncultured people. The whole of this Inner Scythia has hitherto been unknown to Europeans, who believed that the region was occupied by the sea.

4. China, the seventh part of Asia, in which are recounted and described its antiquity, names, ancient China, ancient and present boundaries, its divisions, and ancient and modern government

The seventh part of Asia is the kingdom of China, which the ancient Europeans knew as Serica or Seres, meaning the kingdom of silk.[1] It was thus called by the peoples of western Asia who travelled thither overland to trade in silk. It was in China that the use of silk was first invented before anywhere else, for the Chinese have possessed silk for almost 4,000 years and its use has spread from this kingdom throughout the whole world.[2] The country was also known as Sinarum Regio or Siri, derived from the name of one of its ancient monarchs called Qin, or Chin as it is pronounced in Italian, or Shin in Japanese. The people of India, who went by sea to China in ancient times in order to trade, still use this name or Shintan, and it remains to this day in the books of the Chinese themselves.[3] The Malayans pronounce this name as China, and the Portuguese first adopted this in Malacca along with other words, such as 'mandarin' for magistrate, 'dachem' for a balance with a steelyard, and other terms in use to this day.[4]

During the course of this history we must often refer to this kingdom, its provinces, cities, customs, writing, and religion, because the Japanese took the most important of what they possess from this kingdom, and so it as necessary to give more information about this kingdom than about others. But as this may well be done elsewhere, we will mention only briefly here what is sufficient for our purpose.

The true and real China of ancient times was called Jiuzhou, meaning the nine kingdoms or states of the nine rulers who founded the nation long after the Confusion of Tongues, each one of them setting up a kingdom.[5] It was made up of the northern part of modern China that lies north of the river of Nanjing. This river is called Yangzi (or Jiang) meaning River Son of the Ocean on account of its size, for it crosses the whole of China from east to west. Marco Polo, the Venetian, calls it the River Kian.[6] The river separated the northern

---

[1] For example, Pliny, *Natural History*, 6, 20. Strabo (*Geography*, 11, 11, 1, and 15, 1, 34 and 37) makes a vague reference to people called Seres, but was not referring to the Chinese.

[2] See p. 11, n. 1.

[3] 'China' is probably derived from the name of the Qin dynasty of the 3rd century BC. Laufer, 'Name', and Pelliot, 'L'Origine'. Both Carletti (*My Voyage*, p. 162) and Gaspar da Cruz (in Boxer, *South China*, pp. 64–5) make the unlikely suggestion that the name is derived from 'Cochin-China', and not vice-versa. People of ancient India called China Cīnasthāna, and this was transliterated into *Shintan* in Japanese. For early relations between China and India, see Rockhill, 'Notes'; Bagchi, *India and China*; and Liu, *Ancient India*.

[4] 'Mandarin' does not come from *mandar*, to command, as Ricci (*Fonti*, I, p. 55, and *China*, p. 45) suggests, but from the Sanskrit *mantri*, minister of state, whence the Malayan term *mantari*. *Dachem* is derived from *dajing*, hence the Malayan term *daching*: Dalgado, *Glossário*, I, pp. 340–41 and 2, p. 20.

[5] A reference to the Period of the Five Emperors, traditionally 2852–2205 BC. During this legendary period, nine emperors ruled, but five are particularly famous and of these Rodrigues later (pp. 331–2) mentions three by name: Se-Ma, *Mémoires*, I, pp. 25–96; Hirth, *Ancient*, pp. 7–26.

[6] Polo (*Book*, II, 71; Yule, *Book*, II, pp. 170–74) describes the Yangzi as the greatest river in the world, six to ten miles broad, and a hundred days' journey long. *Jiang* means simply The River and this name is still in use. 'Yangzi' is

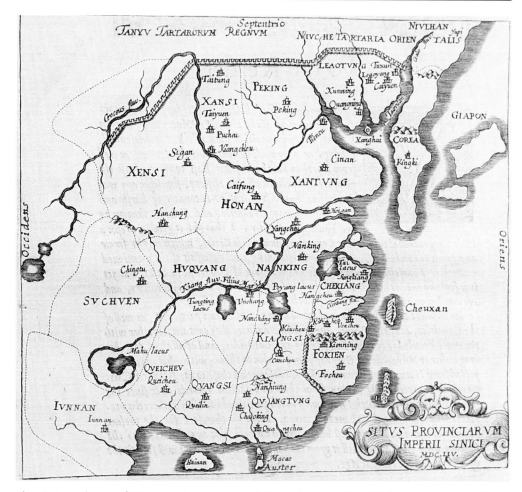

Plate 8: A simple map of China, showing the names of the provinces, the Great Wall and also Korea and Japan. Martini, *Bellum Tartaricum*, 1655.

part of the country from the southern, known as Man or Manzi in ancient Chinese and Manshi in Japanese. Marco Polo calls it Mangi, meaning 'southern barbarians'.[1] In distinction to this, the northern part of China is called Qitan, Kitai, or Katayo after the name of a Tartar who overcame and occupied the region.[2] This part begins in the south at the above-mentioned river at 32°N, and finishes in the north at 42° in the great desert called Shamo where it borders on to Eastern Tartary. A part of the region ends with the sea or bay between Korea and China, and another part of it finishes at 150° of longitude at the River

taken from the ancient Yang kingdom, and does not mean 'Son of the Ocean' as Rodrigues (and Ricci, *China*, p. 311; Carletti, *My Voyage*, p. 163; and Martini, *Bellum Tartaricum*, p. 256) maintains. The error is produced by substituting a different character for the first syllable of the name. The river flows, of course, from west to east: Richard, *Comprehensive Geography*, p. 94.

[1] Polo, *Book*, II, 65 (Yule, *Book*, II, pp. 144–51) and *passim*.

[2] As Rodrigues correctly notes above, p. 23, the name originates from a Tartar tribe and not an individual.

Yalujiang, which separates Korea from China.[1] In the west it is bounded by the desert of Liusha where the Lop Desert is situated at 125° of longitude. The region thus covers 25° of longitude and 10° of latitude.

They ruled within these original boundaries for more than 2,000 years up to 250 years before Christ Our Lord; thereafter the kingdom began to expand and increase until it became the great empire that they possess today.[2] At different times the monarchy subjected various neighbouring countries of barbarians south of the river of Nanjing, incorporating them under the same language, writing, laws, government, dress, and customs, and so now such peoples are all considered Chinese. This happened to the province of Nanjing south of the River Yangzi (or Jiang), Zhejiang, Fujian, Guangdong, Jiangxi, Guangxi, Guizhou, Yunnan, and other places that to this day have their own national language different from genuine Chinese. Up to now the latter language has been used solely by the northern region, which was the real China, embracing the provinces of Beijing, Shandong, Henan, Shanxi, Shaanxi, Sichuan, and Huguang. These provinces made up the real Serica, or China, and to this day they use the indigenous Chinese called Court Language, or the language of magistrates and nobles, because public and judicial matters are conducted in only this language, which is universal throughout the kingdom just as Latin is among us.[3] It is learnt by the people of other provinces that formerly did not belong to China, albeit they have their own local tongue that they use among themselves.

After this kingdom had grown so greatly, its frontiers expanded or contracted under the various monarchies. In this present monarchy of Daming (which the Japanese call Taimei),[4] the whole of China has the same laws, dress, writing, language, and customs. To the south it is bounded partly by the sea and partly inland by the kingdom of Cauchi, or Annam (commonly called Cauchi-China, for it was once a province subject to China), and also by the people of Laos above the kingdom of Siam, and by Burma Tangu, situated above Pegu. Its eastern boundary is formed by the Eoum Sea (Ptolemy calls this Sinus Magnus and it is commonly known as the China Sea)[5] and by the inland sea between China and Korea. It

---

[1] Rodrigues calls the River Yalu, separating Korea from China, 'Alokiam'; Rada's 'Halecan' (in Boxer, *South China*, p. 265) is even more divergent. Both versions presumably originate from the Chinese name of the river, Yalujiang.

[2] A reference to the Qin Dynasty (221–206 BC), during which China was united under one ruler. Its founder was Shihuangdi, who took command of Qin, a region on the northwest frontier, in 246 BC and became de facto ruler of China in 221. After his death in 210, the dynasty collapsed and was succeeded by the Han Dynasty in 206 BC. According to *Breve aparato*, f. 14, the ancient boundaries were kept for about 2,160 years up to 250 BC.

[3] The comparison between Mandarin and Latin is also made by Valignano, *Sumario*, p. 39*, Carletti, *My Voyage*, p. 165, and other writers. Ricci (*Fonti*, I, p. 38, and *China*, p. 29) suggests that this national language originated to save magistrates, who were always strangers in the province in which they held office, from the need to learn the local dialect, for south of the Yangzi basin no less than eight principal dialects were spoken.

[4] Ricci (*Fonti*, I, p. 12, and *China*, p. 6) explains that Daming means 'Great Brilliance'. In *Breve aparato*, f. 13v, Rodrigues reports that Fujian people pronounce the name differently, and as a result Barros (and also Rada, in Boxer, *South China*, p. 260) refers to Taybin or Taben. The Ming Dynasty lasted from 1368 until 1644 when it was succeeded by the Qing. The founder of the dynasty, Hongwu, is mentioned by Carletti (*My Voyage*, p. 160), who correctly gives the date 1368 as the year of his succession.

[5] Ptolemy, *Geographia*, 7, 2 (in Magini, *Geographia*, p. 169). Magini, f. 263, gives a similar description of China's boundaries. Until the middle of the 16th century, European maps of Asia depicted a large gulf to the west of China, named Mare Eoum or, more often than not, Sinus Magnus ('Big Gulf'). Maps showing this imaginary gulf under the two names may be seen in Nordenskiöld, *Facsimile-Atlas*, plates I, XXIX, XXXI and XLV. Thus Rodrigues should say that this sea formed the *western* boundary of China; perhaps he refers to 'its eastern boundary' because the Latin

partly borders on to this kingdom of Korea at the garrison of Liaodong. Its northern frontier faces the Tartars who surround it completely in that part and are separated from China by the famous Wall, which with its loops is 700 leagues in length.[1] To the west lies India extra Gangem, which surrounds it there to the north and south in the provinces of Shanxi, Sichuan, and Yunnan.

The country's biggest distance in latitude is 32½°, beginning in the south at 18½°N at the most southerly point of the island of Hainan and ending in the north at nearly 52°N at the Wall, although even beyond this part it possesses some garrison states and regions belonging to Tartary that they keep to this day.[2] Its greatest longitude is 25°, beginning at the 125th meridian where it borders on to India extra Gangem next to Bengal, and ending at the Oriental Sea on the 150th meridian, which passes through the mouth of the River Yalujiang at the garrison of Liaodong on the boundary between China and Korea.[3] If this great area were formed into a square, it would make a figure of sides 20° or more in length. Such an astonishing size would include in Europe the Iberian Peninsula, France, Italy, nearly all of Upper and Lower Germany, and Greece.[4]

Although a great part of present-day China is washed by the Oriental Sea, it is nevertheless not the most easterly nation of Asia, as geographers have so far maintained. For Korea and Inner Tartary (which is contiguous with New Spain) make up the most easterly lands of all.[5]

The most westerly sea coast of China begins at the boundary of Cauchi, or Hainan,[6] at 22°N where the sea flows in and encircles the land from the south. The coast continues to ascend somewhat towards the north until the mouth of the river of Guangzhou, commonly called Canton, at 23½°N, where the said city of Guangzhoufu is situated. The city of Macao lies at 22⅔°N.[7] From the meridian of Guangzhoufu, the coast continues east-north-east until it reaches the bay of the river of Chincheo, a most ancient place of commerce and

name Mare Eoum means 'Eastern Sea'. But Ortelius's map of Asia (in *Theatrum orbis*) shows the North Pacific as the 'Eous or Oriental Ocean', in which case the ocean would form the eastern boundary of China.

[1] The Great Wall runs westwards from Shanhaiguan (40°N, 120°E) to Jiayuguan (40°N, 98°E). The distance between these two places is 1,145 miles, but increases to about 1,700 miles if all the loops in the Wall are included. If reinforcing and supplementary walls are counted, the total distance would be about 2,500 miles. Shihuangdi (d. 210 BC) built much of the Wall within 20 years: see Geil, *Great Wall*, esp. pp. 326–7; Hayes, *Great Wall*, esp. pp. 9–10; Silverberg, *Great Wall*, pp. 44–9. For map of the cities and posts along the Wall, see Meijer, 'Map', p. 111. The Wall was often mentioned by European writers, including Mendoza ('this superbious and mightie worke', *History*, I, pp. 28–9), and Pinto, *Travels*, Chapter 59; references to ten other works are given in Cooper, 'João Rodrigues', n. 126.

[2] The southern tip of Hainan is at 18°05′N, so Rodrigues's figure for the southern limit of China is accurate enough. The reference to the northern limit at 52° is obviously a mistake for 42°. In *Breve aparato* (ff. 14–14v) he correctly states that China extends from 18½° to 42°N, thus giving a total of 23½°. For a useful survey of early European maps of China, see Szcześniak, 'Seventeenth Century Maps'.

[3] The longitude of China is about 93°E to 130°E. When converted to the Greenwich meridian (see p. 12, n. 5), Rodrigues's figures become about 107° and 132°E. Ricci (*Fonti*, I, pp. 12–13, and *China*, p. 8) gives 112° and 132°E, but admits that, while certain about the latitude, he is not sure of the accuracy of these longitude figures.

[4] The fact that China formed almost a perfect square is also mentioned by Ricci (*Fonti*, I, p. 13). In *Breve aparato*, f. 14v, Rodrigues substitutes Spain for the Iberian Peninsula, thus omitting his native Portugal from the possibly unflattering comparison with China.

[5] Rodrigues notes later (p. 45) that Japan is the furthest country in the East. He is possibly thinking here of mainland Asia, not Asia in general, as was Escalona (in Wyngaert, *Sinica*, III, p. 232): 'China is the last part of the Asian mainland.'

[6] Rodrigues here again makes the mistake of calling Cauchi 'Hainan' instead of Annam. See p. 19, n. 7.

[7] As Rodrigues later mentions (p. 33), the name Canton comes from the local pronunciation of Guangdong, of which it is the capital city. It lies on the Jujiang, or Pearl River, at 23°12′N. An early description of the city is given

navigation for the whole Orient. Here at 25°N is found the port called Quanzhou, which the Venetian Marco Polo calls Zaitun, whence he set sail for India.[1] From here the coast contracts until the river of Fuzhou, or Fuzhoufu, the capital of Fujian province, at 26°N.[2] Then it continues contracting as much as possible northwards until it reaches two capes. The Chinese call the first one Sanmen after a walled fortress of the same name situated there, and Europeans have corrupted the name into Cape Sumbor.[3] The second cape, the most eastern part of China in that region, is called Ningbo Point after a city there that they corruptly call Liampo.[4]

The northern part of the cape forms a famous inlet or bay running from east to west called Qiantang.[5] A great river flows into this bay, at the end of which is situated at 31°N the most illustrious city of Hangzhou, capital of Zhejiang province. This city was formerly the renowned Kinsay or Kinsu, the court of the king of Mangi in the time of the Grand Cham, the king of the Tartars, who conquered it in the year 1278, as the Chinese annals record. Some of its ancient remains stand to this day as we saw with our own eyes, and Marco Polo mentions it in his oriental history.[6] From the mouth of this bay the coast turns northwards up to the mouth of the River Jiang or Yangzijiang, called after Nanjing as it runs alongside the city. Its real name is Yangzijiang, meaning River Son of the Ocean on account of its size as it crosses China from east to west. Marco Polo calls it the River Kian.[7]

The coast continues further northwards up to 34°N, where the mouth of the River

---

by Rada (in Boxer, *South China*, pp. 92–101). In Part 2, Book 1 of the *History* (Ajuda text, f. 183v; Rodrigues, *Nihon*, II, p. 231), not translated here, Rodrigues asserts that both the Apostle St Thomas and the Zen patriarch Bodhidarma (in Japanese, Daruma) entered China through this port. The latter is supposed to have landed at Canton about 520. According to a Chaldean Christian tradition, St Thomas also reached China, but there is no evidence of such an arrival. Mendoza (*History*, I, pp. 37, 53) also asserts that the apostle laboured in China. A popular name for Bodhidarma was Tamo, and this may have led to confusing the two men. The position of Macao is 22°12′N. A useful map of the east coast of China, showing the old Portuguese names, is given in Kammerer, *Découverte*, p. 102.

[1] Two gaps are left in the text, and I have inserted the names Zaitun and Quanzhou. The identification of Chincheo is difficult and the matter is discussed in Boxer, *South China*, pp. 313–26. Rodrigues identifies Chincheo with 'Choancheu' on p. 50, while in *Breve aparato*, f. 9v, he refers to Fujian, 'which we call Chincheo'. Ricci (*Fonti*, I, p. 350, n. 2) seems to favour Zhangzhou. See also Kammerer, *Découverte*, pp. 102–5. There has been much debate about the identity of Polo's Zaitun, but in the light of modern scholarship (Smith, 'Zaitun's Five Centuries'), there can be little doubt that it was Quanzhou (24°50′N), even though Phillips ('Identity' and 'Two Mediaeval') argues for Zhangzhou (24°35′N). For a summary of references to Zaitun, see Arnaiz and van Berchem, '*Mémoire*'. For origin of name, see D'Elia, in Ricci, *Fonti*, I, p. lxii, n. 3.

[2] Fuzhoufu, situated on the Min River, lies at 26°09′N.

[3] Cape Sumbor was often mentioned by European travellers, especially Mendes Pinto, and is depicted on European maps in various positions. According to a Portuguese *roteiro* (in Linschoten, *Discours*, p. 370), the place was 28°15′N and this identifies it with Sanmen Bay (Rodrigues's 'Siumen'). Sumbor was not really a cape but served as a marker, where ships bound for Japan left the Chinese coast and sailed eastwards. Richard, *Comprehensive Geography*, p. 274; Kammerer, *Découverte*, pp. 152–3.

[4] Ningbo, at 29°50′N, was one of the first Chinese cities to be visited by 16th-century Europeans, and Pinto (*Travels*, pp. 127–33) has much to say about the place. See also Kammerer, *Découverte*, pp. 71–82.

[5] A tentative identification of 'Tienkam' in the text. The river Qiantang runs into Hangzhou Bay and the bay was formerly called after this river.

[6] Hangzhou lies at 30°20′N, and Polo (*Book*, II, 76–78; Yule, *Book*, II, pp. 185–218) devotes three chapters to its description. The city was captured by Kublai Khan in 1276, not 1278. For long there was doubt about the identification of Polo's Kinsay, and in fact Rodrigues later (p. 30) seems to identify it with Beijing (as does Mendoza, *History*, I, p. 25). The matter is thoroughly discussed in Moule, *Quinsai*, pp. 3–11.

[7] See p. 24, n. 6.

Huanghe is situated. This means the Yellow River because its waters are always muddy.[1] These are the principal rivers of China and both are mentioned by Ptolemy, who called them Serica and Bautisus.[2] From the mouth of this Yellow River the coast continues up to 36°N and 140°[3] of longitude, where it turns eastwards along the same parallel until reaching 148° of longitude; here it forms a long cape in Shandong province facing Korea at 37½°N. After this cape the coast turns westwards and thus forms another inlying bay, or rather, an inland sea that we call the Beijing Sea;[4] here is to be found Liaodong, whose coast in the north faces the coast of Shandong.

This sea ends at the mouth of the river of Beijing at a place where a fortress called Tianjinwei is situated at 39°N and 143½° of longitude.[5] From there the coast turns towards the east along the same parallel of about 39°N until it reaches the mouth of a mighty river called Yalujiang, which separates China from Korea at 150° longitude in the garrison province of Liaodong. From there the Korean coast descends directly southwards down to 34°N, where the kingdom ends.[6] It then turns eastwards until 154° (the country is thus 4° in width), whence it again ascends directly northwards until 40°N. The coast then continues northeastwards until 42°N, where the kingdom of Korea ends. The coast then carries on in the same northeast direction and ascends to 46° or 47°N, whence it continues eastwards along the same parallel above Japan until reaching 180° longitude, where it is contiguous with New Spain.[7] The island of Ezo lies between Eastern Tartary and Japan. It is inhabited by Tartars, and the Japanese have some ports where they trade with the natives of this island.[8]

The division of the Chinese Empire into provinces

The whole of the Chinese Empire is at present divided into princedoms, provinces, or administrations, some of which are under civil and political government, while others, the garrison provinces, are under military control. Both of these types are divided into smaller states, such as regional kingdoms, and these in turn are split up into cities with their own lands, or into fortresses and walled castles, and in other ways. These are known as *buzheng-*

---

[1] The Yellow River, 2,700 miles long, has changed its course several times; in Rodrigues's time, it flowed into the Yellow Sea at about 34°. Richard, *Comprehensive Geography*, pp. 24–8.

[2] Ptolemy, *Geographia*, 7, 2, and 6, 16 (in Magini, *Geographia*, pp. 170, 158).

[3] The text has 14°, an obvious slip for 140°.

[4] Now called the Gulf of Zhili. Cape Shandong lies at 37°25′N.

[5] The position of Tianjin is 39°10′N, 117°00′E. While Rodrigues's latitude figure is accurate, his longitude, even when converted to the Greenwich meridian, is still 9° too much. Beijing has no sizable river, but presumably Rodrigues (who visited the city several times) is referring to the river in Beijng province.

[6] The southernmost tip of Korea is about 34°30′N.

[7] See p. 12, n. 5.

[8] As Rodrigues implies, Ezo (now Hokkaido) was not then considered an integral part of Japan, and the Japanese were uncertain whether it was an island or part of the Asian mainland. The shogun Ieyasu asked William Adams his views on the matter. In 1618 Angelis, the first European to visit Ezo, wrote that it was joined to Asia and America, and Rodrigues had read Angelis's reports (see p. 75). After another visit in 1621, Angelis realized that Ezo was in fact an island and drew a rough map, making it enormously large. Cieslik, *Hoku-Hō*, pp. (8), (29) and 13. The map is described in Kitagawa, 'Map', pp. 110–14, and Schütte, 'Map of Japan', pp. 73–8. Angelis notes that there were 10,000 Japanese living there. Cieslik, *Hoku-Hō*, pp. (9) and (13). As late as 1652, Sanson d'Abbeville's map (Nordenskiöld, *Periplus*, p. 193) shows Ezo as an enormous country three times the size of China. 'Some ports' refers to Matsumae on the southern tip of the island. The 'Tartars' were the Ainu people, described in *TCJ*, pp. 289–90; Cieslik, *Hokuhō*, pp. (33)-(36). For European maps of the island, Boscaro and Walter, 'Ezo'.

si, or *sheng*, or *dao*, and also *lu*.[1] All the civil administration of the kingdom is distributed within these units.

Two of the provinces are curial as the two courts of Beijing, the northern court, and Nanjing, the southern court, are situated in them; these two provinces are called after the courts.[2] The first one is called Beijing or Beizhili; this means Northern Curial Province because the city of Yingtian-fu, the court where the king of China resides, is situated therein.[3] Its generic name is Jinsu, which in the barbaric tongue of some regions is pronounced as Kinsay, meaning the court where at present the king lives. Marco Polo erroneously translated this name as City of Heaven.[4] At the time when the Grand Cham, the king of the Tartars, conquered China, this city was called Yanjing-lu, meaning the Court Province; Marco Polo calls this in the barbaric tongue Kambalu, changing 'Kim' into 'Kam', and then calling it Kambolu or Kambalu, meaning Court Province.[5] For the past 268 years it has been called Beijing because the court, which was formerly in Nanjing, was transferred thither by the kings of China.[6]

The other curial province is called Nanjing, or Nanzhili, meaning Southern Curial Province, for the city of Shuntian-fu is situated therein. This was the court where the kings of the present Ming dynasty first resided between expelling the Tartars from China and moving to the court of Beijing.[7]

Of the fifteen provinces, six are coastal: Beijing, Shandong, Nanjing, Zhejiang, Fujian, and Guangdong. The other nine are located inland: Henan (in which at one time was the capital of Serica), Shaanxi, where merchants and embassies travelling overland from Persia enter China, Shanxi, Sichuan, Hunan, Jiangxi, Guangxi, Guizhou, and Yunnan.[8]

---

[1] Both the abrupt style and content of this sentence indicate that the text is probably corrupt. Rodrigues elaborates on this matter in *Breve aparato*, f. 14v, where he points out that the provinces were formally called *lu* in the Song Dynasty, 960–1279, but in the Ming dynasty they were known as *sheng*, or *buzheng*. 'Hence the treasurer of each province is also called *buzhengsi*.' For this last office, see p. 38, n. 3.

[2] The number of Chinese provinces varied in history, but from 1428 there were 13 ordinary ones and two metropolitan (or 'curial') ones. As the latter were governed directly by the central administration, the province in which Beijing was located was known as Beizhili (Northern Direct Rule), while the other, containing Nanjing, was called Nanzhihli (Southern Direct Rule). Mendoza (*History*, I, p. 100) makes the same distinction. Further details in Hucker, 'Governmental', p. 7.

[3] Rodrigues should have written Shuntianfu, for Yingtianfu was the former name of Nanjing, not Beijing; he makes the same mistake later in the paragraph when referring to Nanjing. He writes the name correctly on p. 32 and in *Breve aparato*, f. 14v. Richard, *Comprehensive Geography*, p. 71

[4] Rodrigues is obviously in error here because he has already correctly identified Polo's Kinsay with Hangzhou on p. 28; the reference is to Polo, *Book*, II, 76 (Yule, *Book*, II, p. 185). For Polo's translation, City of Heaven, see Moule, *Quinsai*, pp. 10–11. Rada (in Boxer, *South China*, p. 270) also corrects Polo's translation.

[5] Rodrigues's translation of Yanjinglu is sufficiently accurate. The city was captured by Genghis Khan in 1215 and his grandson Kublai made it his capital. Rodrigues errs as regards the meaning of Kambalu, for the name undoubtedly comes from Khanbaliq, the City of the Khan. Polo himself (*Book*, II, 11; Yule, *Book*, I, p. 374), followed by Ricci (*Fonti*, II, p. 26), correctly says that the name means City of the Emperor. Richard, *Comprehensive Geography*, p. 71.

[6] Beijing means Northern Capital. The third Ming emperor, Yong Luo, transferred the court to Beijing in 1421, so Rodrigues's figure of 268 years is too large. He may have had in mind the date 1368, the foundation of the Ming dynasty.

[7] The former name of Nanjing was Yingtianfu, not Shuntianfu (Beijing's former name under the Mongols): see n. 3, above; Hucker, 'Governmental', p. 6; Richard, *Comprehensive Geography*, p. 71. The Yuan (or Mongol) dynasty had its capital in Beijing until its downfall in 1368, whereupon the succeeding Ming dynasty set up its capital in Nanjing. As noted above, the third Ming emperor transferred the capital back to Beijing in 1421 (see n. 6, above).

[8] The listing of the 15 provinces is correct, and their division into six coastal and nine inland provinces is common. Similar lists are found in Magini, *Geographia*, f. 263, and Barros, *Década terceira*, 2, 7 (f. 45). Beijing and

Other smaller states into which these fifteen provinces are divided

Each of these fifteen provinces is divided into other smaller states that really are kingdoms. In olden days people used thus to call those of them which are nowadays known as *fu, funai*, or *fuchū*, meaning a large multitude or assembly, and among them this is the same as a kingdom.[1] Others are called independent *zhou, lingzhou*, or *suozhou*,[2] and this also means kingdom. There are called independent because they govern themselves and are not subject to another state, but rather are direct members of the province, just as are the *fu*. They are also called independent in contrast to other *zhou* that are subject to *fu*, from which they differ only in name and in their slightly lower rank.[3] Thus the total of *fu* in all the fifteen provinces is 162, while the independent *zhou* number 35, making in all 197 *fu* or independent *zhou* kingdoms or states distributed throughout all the fifteen provinces under civil administration.[4]

Among these 162 *fu* or realms throughout China there are eleven *fu* that are not really under either civil or military administration. Instead, they have their own lords and rulers who govern them, but are subject to the viceroy of the province in which they are located. Son succeeds father in the governing of these states, which are called *junmin-fu* (meaning a feudal *fu*), and they are under obligation to go to war whenever necessary and to pay a small due or tribute to the king of China. There are also other minor feudal states belonging to lords, mostly in the provinces bordering India extra Gangem.[5] The *fu* contain other smaller states under them that are also called *zhou*, and these are subject and subordinate to the *fu* and form part of them. Thus the *fu*, as well as the independent and the subordinate *zhou*, have below them other states of even less rank, renown, and territory, and these are called *xian*.[6]

These three types of states — *fu, zhou*, and *xian* — set up three sorts of walled cities as their capitals, where their governors reside and have their palace. These governors are appointed directly by the king and his royal counsellors. The city is called after the palace and bears the same name as the state has. Governors of states of the first rank are called *zhifu, fuli*, or *guanzhifu*, and the cities in which these palaces are situated are also called *fu*. These cities are really one *xian* of the same *fu* or sometimes two combined, just like two wards of the city.

Nanjing were strictly not the names of two provinces, but the names of the two cities situated within Beizhili and Nanzhili (now called Hebei and Jiangsu).

[1] The reference to kingdoms is reminiscent of Ricci's remark (*Fonti*, I, p. 15, and *China*, p. 9) that each of the 15 provinces might well be called a kingdom and was bigger than the whole of Italy. Mendoza (*History*, I, pp. 21–3) and Barros (*Década primeira*, 9, 1 [f. 177v]) make similar statements. *Funai* and *fuchū* are Japanese terms, and are mentioned in a Japanese context later (p. 78). Their inclusion here is explained by reference to *Breve aparato*, f. 14v: the Chinese 'provinces are divided into *fu*, meaning a gathering of many people; in Japan they also use this word *fu, funai*, or *fuchū*.'

[2] The text has *socecheu*, and I presume this means *suozhou*, which may have been a subdivision of a *zhou*, generally translated as subprefecture or department in English. Hucker, 'Governmental', p. 5. Much of Rodrigues's statements about the political organization of China is confirmed by entries in Hucker, *Dictionary*.

[3] Although they were subdivisions of a *fu*, the independent *zhou* (or *zhilizhou*) came under the central administration. Hucker, *Dictionary*, p. 178.

[4] The number of *fu* varied at different times, but Rodrigues's figure of 162 appears accurate. Early European authors give figures from 147 to 160. Ricci (*Fonti*, I, p. 15, and *China*, p. 9) places the figure at 158. According to Hucker ('Governmental', p. 7), there were 159 *fu* in late Ming times.

[5] An amount of autonomy was left to the aboriginal rulers of regions incorporated into China proper. Hucker, 'Governmental', p. 20.

[6] *Xian* is usually translated as county or district. Hucker, *Dictionary*, p. 240.

But such a *xian* is called a *fu* because the palace of the governor of the whole state is situated there. The palace is also called *fu*.[1] Whence it may clearly be seen that a *xian* is properly a city and not a town as some people unaware of this used to call it mistakenly. Throughout the whole of China there are 162 of this type of city called *fu*, for such is the number of states or kingdoms called *fu*.

Cities of the second rank are called *zhou* and their governors are known as *zhizhou*; they are called thus after the *zhou* state, whether independent or subject. In most of these cities may be found the palaces of the governors of these states, and they are also called *zhou*. In all, these cities number 177, that is, 35 of independent *zhou*, and 142 of subject *zhou*.[2]

The cities of the third rank are *xian*, and their governors are called *zhixian*. There are two kinds of these cities. Cities of the first type are known as annexed and are included within the *fu* city, where the palaces of the governors of the whole state are situated. These governors are called *zhifu*, as we have said. There are as many of these as there are *fu* throughout China. But some *fu* are the capitals of provinces, and include within their walls two *xian*, which are like two wards of the city, each of them having the palace of the *zhixian* who governs such a state or its territory. Such are the cities of Beijing's Shuntianfu, Nanjing's Yingtianfu, Hangzhoufu, and Guangzhoufu, and in Fujian, Fuzhoufu, and others that include two *xian*, or wards, within their walls for each of their *xian*, along with the palaces of their *zhixian*.[3] The other type of *xian* are separate cities called outer *xian*, and have their walls and the palace of their *zhixian*. There are in all 1,144 cities called *xian* throughout China.[4] Thus the whole of China has 1,483 walled cities, *fu*, *zhou*, and *xian* under civil administration; this number does not include the walled cities under military administration and their states, and these are separate.

These *xian* states are then divided into smaller units of towns and villages, which are subject to the above-mentioned states. Such are, for example, *du*, a town with its boundary, *li*, *cun*, and *xiang*, villages and places with their boundaries and leaders like judges.[5]

Each of these fifteen provinces has a *fu* city as the capital and metropolis of the whole province, where the magistrates and general governors of the whole state usually reside and have their palaces. Such officials include, for example, the viceroy, a plenipotentiary annual judge from the court, the overseer of the treasury, the supreme judge of criminal cases, the

---

[1] Ricci clarifies this confused explanation: 'The suffix fu is determined not from the size or the population of a city but from the method of its public administration. In fact, the city itself in which the ruler of a whole district lives is known as Hien [*xian*], and it may have its own chief officer called the Cihien [*zhixian*] ... The governor of the district would have no more authority in this particular city than he had in other parts of his district. ... The governor and his Curia adopt the name of the city in which they are located, as for example, in the city of Nancian [Nanchang] the entire district and the governor and his cabinet or council would be known as Nancianfu. ...'

[2] Rodrigues's figure of 177 *zhou* differs considerably from the accounts of contemporaneous authors. Rada (in Boxer, *South China*, p. 268), 235; Ricci (*Fonti*, I, p. 15, and *China*, p. 9), 234 and 247; Escalona (in Wyngaert, *Sinica*, III, pp. 311–12), 245. Hucker ('Governmental', p. 7) gives 240, while Fuchs (*Mongol Atlas*, p. 22), 234 (in 1566) and 247 (in 1579).

[3] For clarification of this somewhat confused explanation of the status of *xian*, see Ricci (*Fonti*, I, p. 64, and *China*, p. 52). Simply, this type of *xian* was not a separate town but only a ward of the *fu* city where the governor of the *fu* resided. If the *fu* happened to be the capital of a province, then the province governor would reside in another city ward called *xian*. All the cities named here in the text are capitals of provinces.

[4] Ricci (*Fonti*, I, p. 15, and *China*, p. 9) gives 1,152 *xian*; *Fonti*, I, p. 15, n. 4, quotes Valignano reporting 1,120, and a 1595 Chinese source listing 1,114. Other European authors provide similar figures. Carletti (*My Voyage*, pp. 154–9) lists the number of *fu*, *zhou*, and *xian* of each province. Hucker ('Governmental', p. 7) gives 1,144; Fuchs (*Mongol Atlas*, p. 22), 1,144 (in 1556) and 1,151 (in 1579).

[5] 'Lyçùm' in the text probably represents two different terms, *li* and *cun*. Rodrigues, *Nihon*, I, p. 138, n. 28.

superintendent and judge of the king's prisoners and of those condemned to his service, the commander of the whole province, in addition to the immediate governors of particular states, as we have said. Thus, for example, Guangdong is the name of a province and its capital is Guangzhou, or Guangzhoufu, which the Portuguese corruptly call Canton, taking the name of the province for that of the capital.[1]

There are thirteen garrison provinces or states along the Great Wall in the north (which, with its loops, is more than 700 leagues long, as is noted in its description) and also along the kingdom's western boundaries. Although in general each of these is nominally included in one of the fifteen civil administrations, nevertheless as far as their territory, administration, land taxes, and the minor states included therein are concerned, they are different from the civil states, nor are they included in them or their small states, but are quite separate by themselves.[2] They too are divided into smaller states, some of which are called *wei* and are walled cities with their lands. There are two types of these: one has its own separate states and walled capital city of these territories, while others, called walled *wei*, are joined to one of the civil cities and are places or stations within the cities like forts or garrisons, with their appointed officers and guards, and other soldiers of lower rank. There are 493 of these separate and incorporated *wei* throughout China. They are divided into other smaller states, called *so*, which are like walled forts with their officers, soldiers, and guards. There are two kinds of these as well. Some are separate by themselves with walls and forts, and others are joined to forts and civil cities, and have their officers and guards stationed in posts within the city. There are 2,503 of these both in the civil and garrison provinces throughout China, and this figure does not include many other garrison posts in which infantry and cavalry troops are always quartered.[3]

Nine of these thirteen garrison provinces are situated along the Great Wall, which begins in the east next to the kingdom of Korea at the mouth of the River Yalujiang in rough mountainous country at 150°E and 39°N.[4] It then ascends northwards with some loops to 41½°N, and thence turns westwards with many great twists until reaching the city of Xuzhou, where there are some gates and a pass in the actual wall. Some 650,000 men are garrisoned along the Wall. The position of the city is 39°N (the same latitude as the place where the Wall begins in the east) and 127° of longitude.[5] The people who come in caravans from Persia and western Asia enter China through these gates. The Wall then turns

---

[1] Both Rada (in Boxer, *South China*, pp. 269–70) and Sande (*De missione*, p. 381) give the same example.

[2] For the separate military organization in China, see Hucker, 'Governmental', p. 60.

[3] The Ming authorities set up these *wei*, or military posts, principally along the coast (against Japanese pirates) and the northwest frontier (against nomadic attacks). A *wei* consisted of a garrison of about 5,600 troops, subdivided into battalions (*qianhu suo*), and companies (*bohu suo*). Hucker, 'Governmental', p. 59; Michael, *Origin*, pp. 29–30. Rodrigues, *Nihon*, I, p. 132, n. 31, quotes 2,593 *wei* from a history of the Ming dynasty, and suggests that Rodrigues's figure of 2,503 may be the copyist's error.

[4] For Martini's account of these nine garrisons along the Wall, see p. 20, n. 1; Ricci (*Mappamundo*, p. 220, n. 274) gives ten. As noted earlier (p. 27, n. 1), the Wall begins in the east at 120°E, about 250 miles west of the mouth of the Yalu River. See Meijer, 'Map', p. 111.

[5] The position of Xuzhou is 39°47'N, 98°00'E. According to Hucker ('Governmental', p. 63, n. 143), there were 553,363 troops on the northern frontier in the late 16th century, so Rodrigues's figures of 650,000 is in the right order of magnitude. Rodrigues's contemporary colleague, Alvaro Semedo, writes (in *History*, p. 97), 'Father *John Rodriguez*, who went very much up and down *China*', said that there were 682,888 soldiers stationed along the Wall. This figure, and another reference to Rodrigues's estimation of China's wealth, do not appear in his *History*, so presumably Semedo is referring to another work, now lost. Further details in Cooper, *Rodrigues the Interpreter*, pp. 332–3.

eastwards at 37°N in very rough mountainous country that partly serves as a wall. It comes to an end at the garrison called Tao-hopien,[1] with 570,000 men in the kingdom.[2] The other four garrisons begin at the end of the Wall and descend southwards. They make up the western boundary of China where it borders on to India extra Gangem, Tibet, Turfan, and Burma Lima in the provinces of Shanxi, Sichuan, and Yunnan.

In addition to the above-mentioned cities and fortresses, there is another type of fortress and walled position belonging to both civil and military administrations. They are called *guanjin* and are the entrance and exit points of the kingdom from one province, city, or state to another. They are really tax or customs stations, where everything passing through is examined and treasury taxes are paid to the king. These places have their own officers and magistrates, and if they are on the frontier they have a garrison. Throughout the realm there are many such passes, and they do not have walls but only gates and guards. On account of the shipping along the rivers, there are custom stations on shore and on a bridge of boats in the river; this opens at a certain hour of the day to inspect the passing ships.[3] There are also other walled places, as we have said. There is yet another sort of walled places that are not proper cities, albeit they are populous, but are rather like merchants' emporia or markets. They are like Indian bazaars and fairs are held in them.

The general administration of the entire kingdom of China, and the particular administration of each province and city

The present political administration in China is very different from the ancient pattern. In olden days the system was monarchical with only one supreme head or emperor, who governed the realm through lords and nobles possessing states and lands. But for the past 250 or 260 years, since the year 1369 up to the present day, the people have been governed by consuls in time of both war and peace. For after the Tartars were driven out, the first king of the present dynasty called Daming and ancestor of the kings now reigning, changed the ancient form of government as far as dignities were concerned.[4] He did away with all the ancient aristocracy and hereditary nobility, and everyone became ordinary people or plebeians, and all the lands reverted to the king. He instituted[5] another form of nobility, to which all the plebeian people (except those guilty of some crimes) could aspire by way of

---

[1] This name is a mystery, for, as Rodrigues has already said (p. 33), the original Wall ends in the west near Xuzhou. Hayes, *Great Wall*, pp. 12–13; Silverberg, *Great Wall*, pp. 49–50. Neither Aurel Stein's detailed description and map of the region (*Innermost Asia*, I, p. 520 and IV, Map 43) nor Meijer, 'Seventeenth Century Maps', p. 111, offer any clue. Rodrigues, *Nihon*, I, p. 132, n. 32, has no solution.

[2] Rodrigues is probably referring to the number of other troops deployed throughout the country, thus making a total of 1,220,000 soldiers. This agrees with Ricci's reference (*China*, p. 9) to 'more than a million soldiers'. Carletti (*My Voyage*, p. 162) gives the total of 1,043,141 soldiers. Exaggerated figures totalling five and six million are given by Rada (in Boxer, *South China*, p. 272) and Mendoza (*History*, I, pp. 90–91).

[3] These pontoon bridges are described by Andre Palmeiro (Macao, 8 January 1630, in Ajuda, 49–V–6, ff. 530v–531), and Pereira and Cruz (in Boxer, *South China*, pp. 33–4, 105). Ricci (*Fonti*, I, p. 343, and *China*, p. 263) also mentions the barrier at Ganzhou.

[4] A reference to Hongwu (1328–99), who ended the Mongol rule of China and founded the Ming dynasty in 1368. Rodrigues provides more information about him later on p. 371. The emperor reformed but did not inaugurate (as Rodrigues implies) the examination system, which had existed for many centuries. Elman, *Cultural History*, pp. 71–88. For an account of this dynamic ruler's reign, see Mote, 'Rise of the Ming dynasty'.

[5] The text reads, 'He abolished another form of nobility', but this is obviously a slip.

letters and sciences. This was done through literary examinations from the degree of baccalaureate to licenciate, and thence to the doctorate, which is the highest rank of nobility among the Chinese at present.[1] These are the men who govern the kingdom's provinces, states, and cities, and are appointed by the king and his royal councils. He established a mixed form of government, partly monarchical and partly republican. The king depended on the assent of his royal counsellors and the supreme senate in many matters, and in accordance with this he made their laws and those of populous nations by which they have been ruled until this day. He did likewise in the military sphere, in which there are the same ranks as there are in letters. Thus any person whosoever can rise through the ranks to the highest dignity of doctor in the profession of arms by military exercises and the composition of literary essays on topics concerning war. These are the officers and generals of the army.[2]

So in imitation of ancient times there are now two sorts of nobility in China. One of them is literary, corresponding to the patrician order, and sees to the civil administration of the kingdom. The other, corresponding to the equestrian or military order, is concerned with the profession of arms and is responsible for the protection and defence of the realm. A man cannot inherit these ranks of nobility simply because he is such-and-such a person, but must either obtain them through his own efforts or else remain a plebeian.[3]

In general all of the Chinese civil administration (to which the military administration is subordinated) is divided into two kinds – the general government of the whole realm and the particular administration of each province. The general government of the whole empire is placed in a supreme senate, six royal councils, a general tribunal or court, and a college of procurators and magistrates of the entire realm. These tribunals are in the court of Beijing, and the same ones, except the supreme senate of the *gelao*, are also in the court of Nanjing.[4]

The first and supreme senate above all the others of the court is the *gelao*; it enjoys the highest rank in China after the king and is second to the king himself in matters concerning government. It is made up of three, four, or even as many as eight members, although only one of them is now the principal and the man who governs. Their office is to be the

---

[1] The early European reports contain many references to the celebrated examination system, for example, Ricci, *Fonti*, I, pp. 44–50, and *China*, pp. 34–41. Adriano de las Cortes (*Viaje*, pp. 219–20) provides an eyewitness account of an examination for 1,000 students in 1625. Teng Ssu-Yu ('Chinese Influence', pp. 275–80) gives an account of European reports on the examination system. Li, *Pratique*, goes into great detail, even reproducing specimen examination papers. Elman, *Cultural History*, studies the social background of the system.

[2] Potential military officers had to pass examinations on the theory and practice of war, but, as Ricci (*Fonti*, I, p. 50, and *China*, pp. 40–41) points out, the military degrees were held in less esteem than were the literary ones. For modern accounts, see Rotours, *Traité*, and Li, *Pratique*.

[3] This was not always true in practice. Cortes (*Viaje*, p. 258) was told that 200 ducats would obtain the post of a mid-ranking official, while 500 or a little more would buy the office of a high official; it was known that the magistrates of the town in which he lived (in 1625) had formerly been merchants and had obtained their posts through bribery. For further instances of bribery, see Rada (in Boxer, *South China*, p. 302) and Valignano (*Historia*, p. 246). But according to Kracke ('Family vs. Merit'), while candidates from well-established families had a better chance in the qualifying examinations, statistics show that a large percentage of officials were drawn from all social classes. Elman, *Cultural History*, provides a lengthy account of the background to the examinations – candidates were known to consult fortune-tellers, cheat, arrange for substitutes, offer bribes, change their names for good luck, and riot after failing four or more times. A photograph of a 'cheating undershirt', on which are written hundreds of characters, is shown in ibid., p. 186.

[4] Ricci (*Fonti*, I, pp. 62–3, and *China*, p. 51) explains that the duplication of government officials in Nanjing was to placate the city's inhabitants when the capital was transferred to Beijing.

direct counsellors of the king, with whom they discuss all the realm's business and dispatches. The king usually follows their advice and orders the particular royal council that the matter concerns to carry it out. For this reason they are greatly feared and respected by all. They do not have a fixed term of office, but when they reach this post they are already very old and thus they quickly die, or with the king's permission they retire to their houses to rest. This senate or government is called *zem* in both Chinese and Japanese, and is called *toshiyorishū* or *rōjū* in one of these two languages.[1]

The second is the Council of State called *libu*. This is the greatest and most eminent of all the other royal councils, and has its own president and his assistants. This council is concerned with the civil administration of the kingdom and the appointment of all the government's officials and magistrates. The second royal council[2] is called *hubu* and is the council of the treasury and the royal revenues of the entire realm. The third, called *libu*,[3] is the council of rites, protocol, and customs of the whole kingdom, and of the ceremonies in the royal household. It deals with ambassadors from both within and outside the kingdom, with the royal mathematicians, and with the ministers of the sects and sacrifices of the kingdom; it also examines the doctrines of them all. The fourth royal council is known as *bingbu* and is the council of war. It is responsible for matters concerning war – officers, soldiers, armies, fleets at sea, the garrisons and fortifications of the whole kingdom and of the Wall. *Xingbu* is the fifth royal council and is the council for crime and punishment throughout the realm. The sixth, *gongbu*, is the council for royal and public works throughout the land, such as the palaces of the king,[4] of those of royal blood, and of magistrates throughout the country, also fortresses, moats, the Great Wall in the north, river dykes to prevent flooding the land, lodgings on the roads for magistrates bound for the court, the walls of the cities, ships for supplies and public service and for magistrates of the realm (for everything goes by water), sea fleets, and inspection of the rivers. It has the responsibility of administering and looking after these and many other similar matters.

The seventh is rather a court or board of justice, called *duchayuan*. In addition to its president and judges, there are thirteen judges who each bear the name or title of one of the thirteen provinces, not including the two curial provinces. These men are like appeal judges, and the affairs of each province are forwarded to its own judge. Every year a judge belonging to this tribunal or court proceeds with authority to each of the thirteen provinces. He refers all the matters to this tribunal, and thence to the pertinent council or thence to the king. Five of these thirteen men are responsible for five wards of the city in which it is distributed, and each one in his ward is like a magistrate from the court. Some are chosen from their number to go with jurisdiction every year to visit the two curial provinces. This board also has the duty of informing the king of its views concerning the administration of the

---

[1] Regarding the *gelao* (the *colao* of European reports), or Grand Secretariat, see Ricci, *Fonti*, I, p. 59, and *China*, pp. 48–9; Carletti, *My Voyage*, p. 168; Hucker, *Dictionary*, pp. 278–9. Various titles of Chinese officials are listed in Mendoza, *History*, I, pp. 100–105; Hakluyt, *Principal Navigations*, VI, pp. 300–304. The meaning of Rodrigues's '*zem*' remains unclear. Rodrigues, *Nihon*, I, p. 137, n. 43, tentatively suggests that it may refer to *dian* (in Japanese, *den*), or 'lord'. *Toxi yorixu yogiu* in the text are the terms *toshiyorishū* and *rōjū*, the supreme council of state in Japan.

[2] Rodrigues probably means to refer to the *libu* as the first, not the second, royal council; he makes this slip by counting the *gelao* as the first, but in fact this board was on a different standing from the other councils. For accounts of these ministries, see Ricci, *Fonti*, I, pp. 57–8, and *China*, pp. 47–8; Carletti, *My Voyage*, pp. 167–8; Hucker, 'Governmental', pp. 31–6.

[3] Thus there were two councils called *libu*, but their names are written with different characters in Chinese.

[4] I have added 'of the king' to make the meaning clearer.

realm and any shortcomings in this field, and of accusing magistrates who do not fulfil the obligation of their office.[1]

Finally, the eighth is a board of six magistrates, each of whom belongs to one of the six royal councils, although they may deal with all of them. These men are like procurators of the realm or of the crown, and general magistrates of the good and evil therein so that they may inform the king of what is happening in the realm and of the observance of laws and customs. They also report on the shortcomings of private people and of all the magistrates of the kingdom right up to those of the supreme senate, and even on matters concerning the king himself and his customs, the government and its supreme court, as well as matters pertaining to the royal household. In addition, they report on the good of the whole country, the observance of the laws and wholesome traditions of their ancient forefathers. They submit these written reports in public memorials. For this office they choose serious men, outstanding in prudence, wisdom, and interior virtue. They must be honest, disinterested men, zealous for the common good of the realm and the people. They are greatly feared and respected by all the magistrates of the kingdom so as to win their favour.[2]

Finally, the ninth is the *tongzhengsi*, the High Secretary of the kingdom.[3]

The particular administration of each province, etc.

The second part of the government is the particular administration of each province. This is divided into the government, or general magistrates, of the entire province, and the government and particular magistrates of each state, for example, *fu*, *zhou*, and *xian*, and towns, villages, and various sorts of other settlements therein. The general magistrates of a province are subject to the royal councils and look after the general administration of the province. They are called *kokushi*.[4] Although they are appointed by the king, the magistrates of each state of the province are subject to those of the province, just as the magistrates of the smaller states are subject to those of the larger one in which they are situated.

First of all we will deal with the general administration of the fifteen provinces, both the curial provinces as well as the others. Their magistrates and courts usually reside in the metropolitan city and capital of the whole province, and these magistrates are divided into six courts. The first and highest official, called *dutang* or *junmen*, is the viceroy of the province and has charge of both the civil and military administration.[5] All the province's

---

[1] This is usually called the Censorate in English and it received its Chinese title in 1380; it had a total of 119 investigating censors organized into circuits (or *dao*): Ricci, *Fonti*, I, p. 59, and *China*, pp. 49–50; Hucker, 'Censorial System', pp. 42–52. There was a list of eight proscriptions (greed, bribery, cruelty, etc.) for which magistrates could be dismissed.

[2] The royal admonitors, or *jianguan*, were bound to denounce the emperor's errors, and Ricci (*Fonti*, I, pp. 60–61, and *China*, pp. 49–50) gives a somewhat idealized account of their activities. In general all the officials were greatly feared and promptly obeyed on account of the severe punishments they could inflict. Cruz (in Boxer, *South China*, pp. 168–74, 179) recounts that prisoners in gaol would queue to hang themselves rather than suffer the bastinado. An early account (1567) of these punishments is given in Escalante, *Discurso*, ff. 79v–84v; first-hand reports are found in Cortes, *Viaje*, pp. 175–8, 179–81, and Galeote Pereira, in Boxer, *South China*, pp. 17–25.

[3] According to Ricci (*China*, p. 545), the office of *tongzhengsi* corresponded to 'what we might call the High Chancellor'.

[4] Probably without realizing it, Rodrigues here slips into Japanese. The term in Japanese means a provincial governor or official; in Chinese it would be *guosi*. In *Vocabulario*, f. 54v, the term is defined as 'viceroy or governor'.

[5] *Dutang* is the Tutam so often found in early European reports about China. The office of *Junmen* was also mentioned by several observers, such as Semedo, *History*, p. 128. For these offices, see Hucker, *Dictionary*, pp. 202, 543.

important cases, whether civil, criminal, or military, of whatever magistrate are referred to him. He has many couriers who continually travel to and from the court, and there are fixed post stations every three leagues. He thus keeps the king informed of what is happening in his province, such as business matters, peace, war, or alarms of war. These dispatches bearing the news come and go in continual succession, and in this way the king always learns quickly what is happening in each province and can decide on everything that has to be done.[1] There are thirty-three of these *dutang*, or viceroys, in the civil and garrison provinces throughout China. When their office comes to an end, they are promoted to judges of the six royal councils, for in China these are senior to provincial viceroys.

The second court of a province is called *chayuan*. This is a judge of the high court with the fullest jurisdiction, and he makes an annual visit to the province; this office lasts just one year. He inquires into all the cases of the province concerning all the magistrates, and informs the king of everything by continual dispatches that come and go by post. In addition to these officials, there are others also called *chayuan* who act as visitors of mercy. With the king's leave, the queen sends them through the provinces every so many years to visit the prisons and inspect the forlorn prisoners who lack the means to free themselves. They have authority to release from prison anyone they think fit, and they set free thousands of such prisoners in all the provinces.[2]

The third court is called *buzhengsi*. This is the superintendent and high treasurer of the exchequer, and he supervises the collection of revenues, taxes, and dues from the entire province. This board attends to every kind of legal action and penalty concerning the royal exchequer, land litigation, etc. It meets public expenses and payments, and finances the navy, barracks, and munitions for them, and everything else concerning the royal treasury.[3] The fourth is called *anchasi*. This is the supreme criminal court and has its corregidors, or circuit judges, and magistrates in districts throughout the whole province.[4] The fifth is called *dusi* and belongs to the military order. This is in charge of the court of the king's perpetual hereditary captives and also of those reduced to the royal service of the province. It also proposes those suitable for military rank and demotes the incompetent, and is concerned with all matters in the province's public council. It has the duty of waging war whenever necessary, and has all the soldiers of the province and those of the sea at its disposal.[5]

Both Escalante, *Discurso*, ff. 71v–73, and Cruz (in Boxer, *South China*, pp. 153–7) write in detail about provincial administration.

[1] Regarding communications, see Pereira and Rada (in Boxer, *South China*, pp. 7, 188–9). Constant communication was maintained between the central government and the provinces, and different speeds were laid down according to the urgency of the dispatches. Details of this transmission system at a somewhat later date are given in Fairbank and Teng, 'Transmission', pp. 21–2.

[2] Marcelo de Ribadeneira (*Historia*, pp. 136–7, 133) describes a *chayuan* court in some detail and also the *misericordia* visits. Semedo (*History*, p. 129) mentions that the 'Queen' was responsible for these visits of mercy. See Hucker, *Dictionary*, p. 105.

[3] The *buzhengsi* was formerly the civil governor of a province, but the title was later applied to a provincial treasurer, whose office was known as *buzhengsi*. According to Hucker ('Governmental', p. 42), the *buzhengsi* was the Provincial Administration Office, handling routine provincial matters. An early account of provincial government is given in Escalante, *Discurso*, ff. 71v–73.

[4] For this court, see Ricci, *Fonti*, I, p. 63, and *China*, p. 51; Mendoza, *History*, I, p. 102; Pereira, in Boxer, *South China*, p. 12. For a modern description, see Hucker, 'Governmental', p. 54.

[5] Also mentioned by Pereira (in Boxer, *South China*, p. 12). Modern account in Hucker ('Governmental', p. 58), who translates *dusi* as Regional Military Commission.

The special administration of the smaller states is in the hands of the particular governor of each state. He governs the people directly and judges their lawsuits; those who wish may appeal to higher officials right up to the viceroy's court. Governors of the first rank are those of the states called *fu*; they are called *zhifu*, or *fuli*, and are superior to the governors of small states within the same *fu*, such as independent *zhou* and *xian*. Each of the *zhifu* has four boards with their different courts. The principal one is the first bench, and the others of the second, third, and fourth are subordinate to the first. The governors of second rank are called *zhizhou* and administer the *zhou* states that come after the above-mentioned ones. The governors of the cities called *xian* are known as *zhixian* and occupy the third place. They also have four collateral boards, just as the others mentioned above.[1] In addition to these three kinds of governors of the particular states, there are various other officials who are subordinate to them.[2]

All the magistrates on each council of the court, the provinces, and smaller states have their own private palace built by itself within a compound with courtyards and gardens. The palaces and tribunals where they and their colleagues hold audiences are situated in these places. They reside here with their wives and children, as well as all the staff, secretaries, and various other officials attached to each particular bench, magistracy, or board.[3] Throughout the whole of China and in the two courts there are 1,721 large palaces or compounds belonging to officials from the royal councils and the *gelao* down to the *zhixian*, or governors of the third rank, in addition to countless other smaller palaces. This does not include the large number of military palaces and courts throughout the kingdom.

The domestic administration of the palaces of the royal family and household and of nobles of royal blood is in the hands of eunuchs. (Nobles of royal blood are called *wangsi*, for they live in their palaces privately in various parts of the kingdom, unable to hold office or take part in the government of the realm.)[4] These eunuchs constitute a republic by themselves with their own leader responsible to the king. They have their own various ranks, courts, and grades distributed among various congregations for different offices, with their own magistrates and special law. In the year 1615 there were 12,000 eunuchs in the royal service within the royal palaces and city of Beijing. This figure does not include the eunuchs in the service of nobles of royal blood throughout the kingdom, those with special duties in various parts of the country, and those in the palaces and court of Nanjing. These are also very numerous.[5]

The ancient and modern administration, and the nobility of China

The nobility of this kingdom under the present monarchy is divided into three classes. The first includes those of royal blood to a certain degree; they are distributed throughout the

[1] Ricci (*Fonti*, I, p. 64, and *China*, p. 52) refers to the four collateral officials, describing them as auditors to help in the administration of justice, and gives their titles.

[2] For these local offices, see Ricci, *Fonti*, I, pp. 63–4, and *China*, p. 52. Modern account in Hucker, 'Governmental', pp. 44–5.

[3] Cruz (in Boxer, *South China*, p. 107) describes the magistrates' residences; a plan of such a residence is given in Cortes, *Viaje*, p. 306.

[4] Ricci (*Fonti*, I, pp. 54–5, 102, and *China*, pp. 43–4, 88) explains that the first Ming emperor introduced this system to prevent royal factions and palace intrigue. Both Ricci and Carletti (*My Voyage*, p. 161) estimate that there were more than 60,000 royal relatives. Hucker ('Governmental', p. 8) is in full agreement: 'the Princes were salaried dignitaries and no more'.

[5] Rodrigues was in the Chinese interior 1613–15, during which he visited Beijing; hence the reference to 1615 here. In his last extant letter (Macao, 5 February 1633, in Rodrigues, 'Rodrigues in China', pp. 237–6), he reports that there were 22 Christian eunuchs at court; Nicolò Longobardo said Mass for them every week and preached in

kingdom without any office, but receive an income from the royal treasury. The second type is of nobles and titled lords of the realm. There are only a few of them now and they enjoy but little esteem. They do not own lands or rents, but are maintained by the royal exchequer, and whenever necessary they serve as officers in the wars. The second[1] class of nobility serves in the royal household, and is responsible for all the posts in the realm, as well as the civilian and military administration. It is divided into two orders. The first is patrician or literary, and is divided into nine grades or courts, and it has its fixed pension and income in accordance with these grades. All the civil administration of the realm is in this class, and promotion to this order is obtained by way of letters and sciences.[2] The second is the equestrian or military order divided into eight classes. It has charge of all the business of war, the protection of the royal person, and the defence of the realm. It has various military ranks, such as that of general and many others.[3]

Ordinary lord and nobles of the kingdom who have some literary degree belong to the third class of nobility. They are promoted to all the offices and boards of the patrician order in keeping with their literary degree and their other talents and qualifications. There are three degrees of letters. The first and lowest is the bachelor's degree. From this they rise to the second degree, the licentiate; they then proceed to the third and highest degree, the doctorate. Nobody can hold the most responsible offices, from *zhifu*, governor of the states and cities of first rank, upwards, without being a doctor.[4]

5. The eighth part of Asia: the principal islands of the Indian and Oriental Sea. The ninth part of Asia: the Islands of Japan

The eighth[5] part of Asia consists of various mighty islands in the Indian and Oriental seas, excluding the islands of Japan, and careful study shows that their combined area equals the size of Europe. First of all, there is New Guinea, which was discovered in the year 1606 from the south and found to be an island, the biggest so far discovered in the world for its latitude begins at the equator and reaches 12°S, while its longitude begins at   ° and ends at   °.[6] In addition to this, there are the islands of the Moluccan archipelago, the Philippines, Borneo, the Javas, and Sumatra (Ptolemy's Golden Chersonese and Marco Polo's

---

their special chapel. According to Rodrigues, there were more than 10,000 eunuchs in the palace and they were divided into 24 congregations. Ricci (*Fonti*, I, pp. 99–100, and *China*, p. 87) and Carletti (*My Voyage*, p. 161) also give their number as more than 10,000; Semedo (*History*, pp. 114–16) provides a detailed account of their internal organization, stating that there were 12,000 eunuchs in the royal palace in 1626.

  [1] A slip for 'third'.

  [2] There were nine grades of officials and each grade was divided into two classes, generally designated by a and b. The Grand Preceptor of the emperor belonged to the highest order, 1a, while a prison warden belonged to the lowest, 9b. Hucker, 'Governmental', pp. 11–12; Marsh, *Mandarins*, pp. 214–28. Officials in Japan were also divided into nine ranks, each grade being subdivided into senior and junior class.

  [3] Ming military officials were graded from 1a to 6b only, and Rodrigues errs in stating that there were eight classes. In later Qing times there were nine classes, from 1a to 9b. Hucker, 'Governmental', p. 19; Marsh, *Mandarins*, pp. 228–35.

  [4] Concerning these academic degrees, see p. 35, n. 1. According to Martini (*Bellum Tartaricum*, p. 268), one of the reasons why the Christian official Ignatius Sun Yuanhua was unpopular at court was because he occupied an office usually reserved for a holder of a doctor's degree, when he himself had only a Master's degree.

  [5] The text here erroneously reads 3ª instead of 8ª.

  [6] The latitude of New Guinea, the largest island in the world after Greenland, extends from 0°19′ to 10°43′S; its longitude (left blank in the text) is from 130°43′ to 150°48′E. Jorge de Meneses was the first European to land

Java the Less, and the ancient Ophir whither sailed King Solomon's ships).[1] There is also the island of Ceylon, Ptolemy's ancient Taprobana, or also Salice or Salandiva, whence it is called Ceylon.[2] Ptolemy declares that there are 1,370 islands before it, and these are now called the Maldive Islands, meaning Thousand Islands.[3] And there are many other islands in the Oriental Sea belonging to Asia.

The ninth and most easterly part of Asia and the limit of the Orient consists of the islands of Japan, which we intend to describe. There is an almost uncountable number of these islands, most of them inhabited, but the principal and main ones in which the rest are included number eight, and they make up a large and powerful kingdom. Up to now there has been little information about these islands because they are so far from Europe,[4] although many people have wished to know in greater detail about this kingdom's affairs and customs on account of their renown, and about the Christian mission that was established therein. For Our Lord passed over many other nearer kingdoms and chose to plant His Holy Law in this one and produce from it the glorious fruit that will be seen later. Before dealing with this kingdom's ecclesiastical history, we will give a very full description of the country, describing its size, position, the names by which it is called by the natives and by foreigners, whence it was peopled, whether there was any news of it in ancient times in Europe as some people maintain, the date when it was first discovered by the Portuguese, and its division into provinces. We shall also deal with many other things concerning the quality of the soil and its produce, and more relevantly, its customs, government, cult, and religion. Finally we will describe the preaching of the Holy Gospel, for such is the purpose of this entire ecclesiastical history of Japan.

---

there (1525), but the first recorded voyage around the southern part of the island was made by Luis Vaez de Torres in 1606: Galvano, *Discoveries*, I, p. 168; Beaglehole, *Exploration*, p. 102.

[1] For earlier references to the Golden Chersonese, Polo's Java the Less, and Ophir, see p. 16, n. 5, and p. 17, n. 2.

[2] Ptolemy, *Geographia*, 7, 4 (in Magini, *Geographia*, p. 173). As ancient geographers exaggerated the size of the island by about fifteen, there was much doubt in the 16th century about the identity of Taprobana, some writers opting for Sumatra, others for Ceylon. The matter was finally solved by Guillaume Delisle, 1675–1726, in the early 18th century in Ceylon's favour. The island took its name from *simhala*, 'Lions Abode': Yule, *Hobson-Jobson*, p. 181.

[3] According to Ptolemy, *Geographia*, 7, 4 (in Magini, *Geographia*, p. 174), there were 1,378 islands there. Rodrigues almost certainly took 'thousand islands' from the erroneous information found in Barros, *Década terceira*, 3, 7 (f. 72v). Other theories concerning the origin of the name are given in Pyrard, *Voyage*, I, p. 95, n. 1, and Yule, *Hobson-Jobson*, pp. 546–7.

[4] Hardly a fair comment as a great deal had been written and published about Japan. For a catalogue of the scores of European works dealing directly or indirectly with Japan and published up to 1633 (the date of Rodrigues's death), see Laures, *Kirishitan Bunko*, pp. 167–239.

CHAPTER 2[1]

[DESCRIPTION, POSITION, AND VARIOUS NAMES OF THE ISLANDS OF JAPAN IN GENERAL]

Although various writers, both Ours and externs, have written descriptions of these islands, they have all been defective because only hearsay information and conjecture were available.[2] But nowadays everything concerning Japan is much better known by intelligent people, its greatest northern and least southern latitudes have been measured with nautical astrolabes, and so on.[3]

The islands of Japan are situated in that part of the ocean dividing the two continents and great regions of the world, Asia on the one side, and New Spain and America (or the New World) on the other. Nature seems to have placed them there in the middle of the sea (which the ancients called Eoum)[4] as an eastern frontier or limit to our world. One of the principal names used by the natives and the Chinese signifies this very fact, for it means Limit, or Boundary, or Beginning, or Kingdom of the Sun,[5] because Japan is the last country in the known Orient. To the west, the Japanese islands face the coast and region of China in which are situated the provinces of Nanjing, Zhejiang, and Fujian. To the east lies New Spain, far nearer than many have hitherto imagined, although admittedly the eastern coast of Asia is much nearer than the New World's coast.[6] The islands are completely surrounded in the north by the coast of Eastern or Inner Tartary, which lies above Japan from west to east until it reaches New Spain. In the south they are washed by the so-called South Sea above the great island of New Guinea and Papua.

---

[1] There is no mention of 'Chapter 2' in the Portuguese text, but this is obviously where the heading should appear.

[2] As noted earlier, 'Ours' refers to fellow Jesuits. Here again Rodrigues is less than fair, for the writings of Fróis, Valignano, Carletti, and others could hardly be said to be based on 'hearsay information and conjecture'. But the statement is reasonably correct if Rodrigues is referring to geographical information about Japan. For a survey of Portuguese cartography of Japan, see Cortesão and Teixeira, *Portugaliae monumenta*, V, pp. 170–78; for European cartography, see Teleki, *Atlas*; Kish, 'Aspects'; Dahlgren, '*Débuts*'.

[3] For example, Valignano mentions (*Principio*, f. 14) a certain Ignacio Moreira who had accompanied him to the Miyako court in 1590. Interested in mapping, Moreira had taken the latitude of many places and inquired about others he could not visit. More about Moreira in Valignano, *Sumario*, pp. 350–51, n. 5; Cortesão and Teixeira, *Portugaliae monumenta*, II, pp. 127–8.

[4] For earlier references to Eoum, see p. 9, n. 1, and p. 26, n. 5.

[5] Nihon, or Nippon, is written with two characters meaning 'sun' and 'origin'.

[6] The relative positions of the east coast of Asia, Japan, and the American coast varied a great deal in European maps. In Magini (*Geographia*, p. 203), Japan is situated equidistant about ½° from the Asian mainland and America, and Ortelius's map (Plate 9) shows approximately the same position. Mercator's map of Asia (*Atlas*, pp. 401–2) is more accurate in placing Japan close to Korea and far from America. In 1601, Valignano (*Principio*, f. 15) reported

Its width begins at the most southerly tip of the kingdom of Satsuma called Bono Misaki (if we may leave aside many notable populated islands lying south of this point) at 30⅓°N, and ends at 42½°N in the kingdom of Ōshū in the duchy of Tsugaru, which faces the Tartar island called Ezo, populated by the Tartars and, in some parts, by the Japanese.[1] Its length begins in the Gotō Islands at 153° of longitude and ends in the east at 168° of longitude on the eastern coast of the large island, which runs from north to south.[2] It is 12½° wide and 15° long, and thus makes up an exceedingly mighty state among the large islands of the world.[3]

The islands of Japan are called by two kinds of names. One sort is used by the natives themselves, while the other is employed by people outside the kingdom. The names used by the inhabitants are again of two kinds. One was applied in their native tongue before they began to use Chinese letters and characters, while the other was employed after they adopted these Chinese letters. These last names are Chinese, somewhat modified according to Japanese pronunciation. Both kinds of names have their own meaning and signification. Some of these are employed solely in books, writings, and solemn speeches, such as sermons, while others are used in ordinary everyday speech all over the kingdom.[4]

The first and most ancient name to be found in their native language was imposed 627 years before Christ Our Lord in the time of their first king, Jimmu Tennō, and is Akitsu-shima or Toyo-akitsu-shima.[5] The second name came a little later and is Toyo-ashihara.[6] Both names are used to this day in books and poetry. The third is Yamato, derived from a kingdom of the same name in Gokinai, where their first kings had their

---

that although some people maintained that Japan and Mexico were only 500 miles apart, sailors had assured him that the true distance was about 1,500 leagues.

[1] Bono Misaki lies at 31°16′N, although Sata Misaki in Kagoshima lies even further south at 31°00′. Oma Saki, at 41°31′N, is the most northerly point of Honshu, the main island. According to Avila Girón (*Relación*, p. 12), Honshu stretched from 34° to 43°N. Moreira (see p. 42, n. 3) calculated the limits of Japan as 30⅔° to about 39°N (Valignano, *Principio*, f. 14). Writing in 1583, Valignano (*Historia*, p. 126) gave the northern figure as 37° or 38°N, but Rodrigues's figure is more accurate.

[2] The Gotō Islands lie at 129°10′E. Todo Saki, at 142°03′E, is about the furthest eastern part of Honshu.

[3] According to Valignano (*Principio*, ff.14–14v), Japan was a large country, and if the northern islands were included, it was as big as Spain, France, and Italy. Modern Japan has an area of 145,800 sq. miles, slightly larger than Finland or Italy, and about the size of the state of Montana in the USA: *KEJ*, IV, p. 2.

[4] For the difference between the Chinese *koe* and the Japanese *yomi* ways of reading written characters, see p. 334, n. 2.

[5] According to 8th-century records, Jimmu, the first emperor of Japan, was born in 711 BC, enthroned 11 February 660, and died at the age of 127 (*Nihongi*) or 137 (*Kojiki*). Rodrigues (*Arte grande*, f. 236) follows the former account, stating that Jimmu was enthroned in 660 BC, reigned for 76 years, and died at the age of 127. Akitsu-shima originally meant Region of Harvests, although it is often rendered as Land of Dragonflies. Jimmu imposed the name in 630 BC. *Toyo* means fertile, fruitful. *Nihongi*, I, pp. 109–37. According to a modern account of Jimmu, 'there is some doubt that he actually existed' and he may have been a composite of several other figures. The dates attributed to him are 'impossibly early', and his story may merely reflect the spread of rice-growing culture from Kyushu to the Kinai region: *KEJ*, IV, p. 57.

After this point, the Portuguese text is corrupt as there follows a jumble of names, which later appear in their proper places. This must have been the copyist's error and I have not included them here

[6] Ashihara means Reed Plain, and is the abbreviated form of Ashihara-no-naka-tsu-kuni. According to the chronology of the ancient records, the name was bestowed before, not after, the name Akitsu-shima. *Nihongi*, I, pp. 40, 134.

court for a long time.[1] The fourth name is Yashima, or Ōyashima-no-kuni, meaning the Eight Great Islands, for the principal islands of Japan containing one or more kingdoms are eight in number, and the countless smaller islands belong to them and are counted in with them.[2]

The first, biggest, and principal of them all is the large island in the middle of which is situated the king's court, and this island contains 49 kingdoms.[3] The second is called Kyushu, or Chikushi, and contains nine kingdoms; it is thither that the Portuguese ships come.[4] The third is called Shikoku and contains four kingdoms.[5] Each of the other five smaller islands – Iki, Tsushima, Oki, Sado, and Awaji – makes up one kingdom. They will be mentioned later in greater detail.

The fifth name of the kingdom is Shinkoku, a name much in use among the people, meaning Kingdom of the Genii or Spirits (called *kami* in their common parlance), for the country belongs to the *kami*. They were greatly worshipped by the Japanese before the sect of the idols was introduced into Japan, because their fables recount that they created the world and everything within it, that land first began to form in Japan at the beginning, and that the kings of Japan are the descendants of the *kami*.[6] Sixthly, the country is also called Fusō, or Yōkoku, meaning Kingdom of the Orient or of the Sun.[7] The inhabitants have many other names used only in poetry, but I do not intend to discuss them here.

Among other names that the Chinese applied to Japan, the most ancient one found in their chronicles and still used in China to this day is Wanu, or Wanuguo, or according to Japanese pronunciation, Wanu, or Wanukoku, meaning servant or slave, or the Kingdom of the Servants or Slaves.[8] The Chinese applied this name to express their contempt and scorn, as they also gave ignominious names to neighbouring countries. Indeed they call all the nations outside China in the four parts of the world 'barbarians', and they give special names to the nations of each part in order to show their low opinion of other countries. For

---

[1] Gokinai is the collective name of the five provinces grouped around the ancient capital of Nara and they were given this name in 716. Jimmu occupied Yamato province, making it his headquarters, and the name then began to be applied to the country as a whole. *Nihongi*, I, p. 13, n. 3.

[2] Yashima means Eight Islands, and Ōyashima-no-kuni means Land of the Eight Great Islands.

[3] A reference to Honshu (or Hondō), the largest of the Japanese islands. In Rodrigues's time, Miyako (now Kyoto) was the capital and the royal court. In a similar passage, Fróis (in *TCJ*, p. 4) gives Honshu no less than 53 kingdoms or provinces.

[4] Kyushu, meaning 'nine provinces', was formerly called Chikushi, or Tsukushi. The port frequented by the Portuguese after 1570 was Nagasaki, although some other Kyushu ports, such as Hirado, had been visited earlier. Boxer, *Great Ship*, pp. 21 *et seq.*

[5] Shikoku means 'four kingdoms'.

[6] The same character can be read as *shin* or *kami*, and so Shinkoku means Land of the Kami (*Vocabulario*, f. 302v). Chamberlain (*Kojiki*, pp. xxiii–xxiv) confesses that *kami* was the most difficult word to translate in the whole of *Kojiki*, for it is a mistake to think of it as a transcendental deity in the Christian sense. The term has the basic meaning of 'upper' or 'above', and thus denotes a superior being, even a rock, tree, or mountain: *Nihongi*, I, p. 3, n. 6; Sansom, *History to 1334*, pp. 25–6; Holtom, 'Meaning'.

[7] Fusō-koku, an ancient name for Japan, means Land of the Protecting Mulberry; it is also listed in *Vocabulario*, f. 111v. Yōkoku means Sunrise Valley. Kaempfer (*Kaempfer's Japan*, p. 40) offers a similar list of names.

[8] The literal meaning of Wanu is not clear, for *wa* can also means dwarf; whatever the meaning, the name was derogatory. Tsunoda, *Japan*, pp. 4, n. 2, 49, 106. Interestingly, the 9th-century author Ibn Khurradadhbih mentions a country named Wākwāk to the east of China, and it has been suggested that this may be a reference to Japan: Schurhammer, 'Descobrimento', pp. 490–94.

this reason the Chinese today call the Koreans, and the Tartars to the north of Japan, Dong-yi; this is Tōi in Japanese and means Eastern Barbarians (eastern, that is, in respect to China).[1] They also call Japan Kishikoku, after the name or family name of one of the first settlers who went from China to populate Japan, as we shall mention hereafter.[2]

Nichi-iki is a dignified name much in use among the Chinese and Japanese in their books and chronicles. The Chinese pronounce this Riyu, and it means Limit of the Sun or of the Orient, where the sun rises and the world begins, for they believe that it begins there. Thus among other names that the Chinese also called India intra Gangem and Upper India (made up of Sogdiana and Bactria, nowadays called Turkestan) – for the Chinese and Japanese knew of the rest of the world only up to this region – is Xiyu; in Japanese this is Sei-iki, or Sai-iki, meaning Western Limit, or the west where the sun hides itself and the world ends. So in the beginning they used to say in Japan that we were people from Sei-iki.[3]

But the best-known name, and at present the ordinary and current one, was given to the country by the kings of China during the Tang, or Datang, dynasty (in Japanese, Tō, or Taitō) nearly a thousand years ago.[4] During this period there was close friendship and much trade between the kings of Japan and China. So to get rid of the ignominious name of the Kingdom of Servants or Slaves, they called the country Nihon, or Nippon, or in native Japanese Hi-no-moto, meaning the Beginning or Origin of the Sun, for *ni* or *nichi* means 'sun' and *hon* means 'origin'.[5] This is because it is the furthest country in the known Orient, and they believed that the sun is born there and that the country marks the limit of the eastern part of the world. The name certainly fits these islands, for not only are they the most easterly known and form the limit of the Orient (which the ancient geographers placed 180° from the prime meridian passing through the Fortunate Isles), but also, as far as India and Europe are concerned, Japan is the true Orient, as we have said, where the sun rises before reaching those countries.[6]

This name of Nihon, or Nippon, is pronounced by the Chinese in their language as Riben, or, in the vulgar tongue of Fujian and Guangdong, as Yatbun, whence the Portuguese, corrupting the name as they so often do with words and proper names of the Orient, obtained the name Japão.[7] After its discovery by the Portuguese, Europeans first called the country the Island of Robbers, because at that time many pirates usually came

---

[1] Rodrigues has already mentioned this name on p. 22. *Vocabulario*, f. 259v: '*Tōi, higashi no ebisu*. Rustic or barbarous people in the East.' Carletti (*My Voyage*, p. 164) echoes Rodrigues's statement about the Chinese view of the outer world, 'They do not think that there is any wisdom outside of their nation, for they believe all the others to be barbarians.' Other Europeans spoke in similar fashion – see also p. 384.

[2] See p. 53.

[3] For a list of Western countries, under the heading '*Xiyu*' in *Mingshi*, a Chinese chronicle published in 1461, see Bretschneider, *Mediaeval Researches*, II, pp. 176 *et seq.*

[4] The Tang dynasty lasted from 618 to 907; Datang means Great Tang.

[5] For Sino-Japanese relations during this period, see Sansom, *History to 1334*, p. 67–81. In 670 the Korean court was informed that Nihon (or Nippon) would be the name for Japan in future, and China began to use the name about this time: *Nihongi*, I, p. 1, n. 1, and II, p. 137, n. 1; Tsunoda, *Japan*, p. 40.

[6] Practically the whole of this sentence and much of the previous one may be found word for word in Lucena, *Historia*, p. 466. Concerning the prime meridian used in Rodrigues's time, see p. 12, n. 5.

[7] For the name Japan, see Yule, *Hobson-Jobson*, pp. 451–2. The first European on record to use this name ('Jampon') was Tomé Pires in *Suma oriental* (1512–15), I, p. 131, while it first appeared on a European map by Giacomo Gastaldi in 1550. Dahlgren, *Débuts*, p. 13.

from Japan with large crews in their fleets to rob and infest the coast of China.[1] The Spaniards called them the Islands of Silver on account of the many silver mines to be found there, and because, apart from this silver, there is no other merchandise that is carried away to other parts in the ships that go thither to trade.[2]

[1] Mercator (*Atlas*, ff. 410, 417), for instance, has two maps with Japan, or at least some of its islands, labeled Ilhas dos Ladrones. See also Linschoten (*Discours*, p. 32), where a 1598 map appears to have north Honshu thus labelled. The pirates in question were the Wakō ('dwarf bandits'), marauding bands of Chinese as well as Japanese who plundered the Chinese coast: *KEJ*, VIII, pp. 220–21; Hazard, 'Formative Years'. For early European references to them, see Valignano, *Sumario*, p. 27, n. 13. For Hideyoshi's anti-pirate decree, see Berry, *Hideyoshi*, pp. 133–4.

[2] Xavier (8 April 1552, in *Epistolae*, II, p. 356) mentions that the Spaniards called Japan the Silver Islands, and Pinto (*Travels*, p. 274) speaks of 'the large number of chests full of silver' brought to their junk for trade at Tanegashima. A map taken from Ortelius ,1589 (reproduced in detail in Cieslik, *Hoku-hō*, p. 12), shows a large island to the north of Japan (more or less corresponding to Hokkaido), labelled the Island of Silver. Both Fróis (Miyako, 20 February 1565, in *Cartas*, I, f. 172) and Avila Girón (in *TCJ*, p. 10) talk of the many silver mines in the country. For a modern account, see Takekoshi, *Economic Aspects*, II, p. 34. The outflow of silver from Japan was considerable. Valignano (*Sumario*, p. 353) reckons that the Portuguese usually received 500,000 ducats of silver bars for the silk they shipped annually from China.

CHAPTER 3

THE ANTIQUITY OF JAPAN, AND THE NATION TO WHICH THE JAPANESE MAY BELONG

It is extremely difficult to learn about the antiquity of these islands and the time when they were first discovered and populated, because the Japanese had no writing with which to record their affairs until the Year of the Lord 285, when they received it from China.[1] So all they possessed was a vague tradition about some more notable events, and during the course of time this was turned into fables. Thus the chronology of the period between the occurrence of these events and their first use of writing remains uncertain. We shall avail ourselves of the information that the Chinese records provide concerning the islands, their antiquity, and their origin. We shall also make use of what the Japanese themselves recorded in their chronicles after they had received the art of writing. To a certain extent the uncertain tradition of the Japanese concerning their antiquity and origin agrees with the Chinese records.[2]

This kingdom's antiquity is certainly very great according to the indications that may be found about this matter. The islands were populated long after the world was peopled by Noah's descendants, but it is not known for certain who were their first settlers, where they came from, or which part of the islands was first populated. For there are so many islands and some of the very large ones are surrounded to the north and west by various neighbouring nations, and so they could have been populated in various places by all these kingdoms. This indeed seems to be what happened, for according to their records and traditions the first settlers were not governed by a single ruler, but were split up under many leaders. They populated various regions and eventually came to be united under only one ruler who was more powerful than the rest. This may be gathered from their chronicles that state that, about the year 87 before the Lord, the tenth king of Japan, Sujin Tennō by name, had overcome the barbarians of four provinces. His descendants later predominated and united the whole kingdom under one ruler alone, and these are the ancestors of the kings who have ruled Japan to this day.[3]

---

[1] The date of the introduction of the Chinese writing system into Japan is traditionally given as 285, when the scholar Wangyin, or Wani, arrived at the Japanese court from Korea and began to teach writing: *Nihongi*, I, p. 262. The year 405 is favoured by modern scholars, such as Sansom (*Japan*, p. 36). Rodrigues is not consistent about the date; he later gives it as 283 (perhaps the copyist's slip?) and also 290 (on pp. 97 and 334). In *Arte grande* (f. 236v), he mentions the year 288.

[2] Tsunoda, *Japan in Chinese Records*, and Wang, *Official Relations between Japan and China*, are useful sources.

[3] According to tradition, Emperor Sujin, the 10th emperor of Japan, was born in 148 BC, ascended the throne in 97 BC and died in 30 BC: *Nihongi*, I, pp. 150–64; *KEJ*, 7, p. 264. There are, however, various inconsistencies in this chronology, as explained by Aston in *Nihongi*, I, p. 164, n. 3. In *Arte grande* (f. 236v), Rodrigues gives the accession date as 97 BC, adding that this emperor reigned for 68 years and died at the age of 120; this agrees with the *Nihongi* account. The reference to the four regions is found in *Nihongi*, I, pp. 159–60, where it is related that the emperor sent

47

The people who began to populate the part of Kyushu that today is the kingdom of Hyūga, one of the nine kingdoms of the second island, are regarded and recognized as the first settlers or founders of the kingdom of Japan. Their first kings and leaders began there, and it was there that they held their court up to the time of the first one to assume the title of king. This was Jimmu Tennō, who began to reign 659 years before Christ Our Lord.[1] There had been twenty-two rulers before him, but they had not enjoyed the title of king.[2]

The first Japanese to write about the antiquity and origin of the kingdom did so long after Chinese writing reached the country. This was also long after the sect of the Indian idols was brought to Japan,[3] as well as the sect of the Chinese astrologers that deals with the creation of the universe and with the genii or ethereal and aquatic spirits, both celestial and terrestrial. Among the Japanese historians, some were astrologers, while others were purely historians.

The first type of historians followed the tradition that they already possessed about the kingdom's antiquity, their kings, and their first ancestors. They wrote about the creation of the universe in the form of various fables involving heavenly and terrestrial spirits and genii, and about natural principles and other things. They described the first man, called Izanami, and the first woman, Izanagi, who are said to have come to Japan before their first king, Jimmu Tennō.[4] They declare that everyone else in Japan has descended from them, and they give names to the first leaders or settlers of Japan, making them out to be the creators of Heaven and Earth, the sun and the moon. They maintain that their kings are descended from them, that Japan is the very first kingdom where the world began, and that these spirits inhabit the land, so Japan was also called Shinkoku, that is, the Kingdom of the Spirits, as we have already mentioned. They recount countless other fables with which, in the fashion of Chinese astrologers,[5] they try to explain the creation of the universe, as will be said in its proper place.

Those who write historically also believe in the same way of creation of the universe by the spirits. They ascribe an infinite number of years to the spirits up to the time of their

---

four generals to subdue savage tribes; in the following year, 87 BC, the generals reported to the throne that the barbarians had been pacified.

[1] In *Arte grande*, f. 236, Rodrigues gives the traditional date of 660 BC for Jimmu's accession. He repeats the date of 659 BC later in this section.

[2] For Jimmu, see p. 43, n. 5. In *Arte grande*, f. 236, Rodrigues gives practically the same dates of his birth, accession, and death as found in *Nihongi*. The reference to the 22 rulers before Jimmu is puzzling. In the beginning there were seven generations of celestial spirits with a total of 11 beings; then followed five generations of terrestrial beings, with Jimmu being born in the fifth generation. In *Arte grande* (f. 236), Rodrigues explains this schematically, clearly showing that there were only 16 rulers before Jimmu.

[3] For Chinese writing, see p. 47, n. 1. The introduction of Buddhism is traditionally dated about 552, when an image of the Buddha and a volume of sutras were sent from Korea to Emperor Kimmei. According to the entry for the 10th month of 552, the king of Korea sent 'a present to the Emperor of an image of Shaka Butsu in gold and copper, several flags and umbrellas, and a number of volumes of sutras': *Nihongi*, II, pp. 65–6; *KEJ*, I, p. 178. Fróis (Nagasaki, 27 August 1585, in *Cartas*, II, f. 155) places the introduction far later, 'about 700 years ago', or the 9th century.

[4] Izanagi in fact was the first man, and Izanami the first woman, and not vice versa. Rodrigues corrects the error in the following paragraph. The same slip was made by Vilela in 1563 (in *TCJ*, pp. 297, 305). As Rodrigues explains (*Arte grande*, f. 236), Izanagi and Izanami belonged to the seventh generation of celestial spirits, and their daughter Amaterasu, the sun goddess, was the first of the terrestrial spirits. They thrust down their jewel-spear from heaven and the drops of water falling therefrom formed the islands of Japan. *Nihongi*, I, pp. 10–12.

[5] The text has 'Prophas medicarias sinenses' here, and I have taken this to mean 'profetas judiciários sinenses'.

first king, referring to the multitude of years as the Great Year, as they call it and which we call the Platonic Year.[1] More will be said later about this in its proper place. Withal they speak in their chronicles about two types of genii or spirits, which they call *kami*. The first kind is of celestial spirits, to whom they ascribe seven rulers or successions called in general Tenjin Shichidai, meaning 'the seven successions of Heavenly spirits'.[2] The last of these seven ages was that of Izanagi, the first man, and Izanami, the first woman, who were the first founders of Japan and of their kings.

The second type is of terrestrial spirits, who were the first to reign over Japan. These were the [...] rulers[3] known as Chijin Godai, meaning 'the five ages of terrestrial *kami*', and succession in government was handed down from father to son.[4] They call all the spirits of both kinds by an honorific name meaning high, sublime, excellent, illustrious, and venerable.[5] Similarly all of them are called by the name of *kami*, meaning genie or spirit. This name *kami* is commonly given to a person after death, just as if we were to talk about the spirit or soul of so-and-so. These are really their *kami* or spirits, and their kings are descended from them, and as such they are venerated.

The last of these is called Hiko-nagisa-take-uguyafuki-aezu-no-mikoto and he had four sons, the youngest of whom succeeded to the throne and was the first to take the title of king. His name was Jimmu Tennō, and he began to reign 659 years before Christ Our Lord. Their chronology begins from his time and does not relate with certainty the years and events before then, except for those twenty-two rulers.[6] If we add their years to the time when this king began to reign, their first origin or that of their king appears extremely ancient and coincides with the time of the kings of Israel or even of the Judges.[7] Although some parts were already populated in the time of these first twenty-two rulers, they were not organized in the form of a nation as their chroniclers imply.

1. The nations that populated the islands of Japan

As regards the places whence Japan was populated, it is quite clear that the country was peopled from various places at different times, because it is certain (and Japanese as well as Chinese and Korean records bear this out) that part of Japan was settled from China and

---

[1] According to *Nihongi*, I, p. 110, more than 1,792,470 years elapsed from the time of the heavenly ancestors down to the reign of Jimmu. The Great Year is mentioned in *Nihongi* (I, p. 111), where it probably refers to the Chinese cycle of 60 years. But as will be seen later (p. 365), Rodrigues is here referring to the Buddhist concept of time.

[2] Rodrigues supplies the names of the seven generations of heavenly spirits in *Arte grande*, f. 236. See also Papinot, *Historical*, pp. 649, 814.

[3] There is a short gap in the text, where presumably 'five' should have been written. Thus, 'These were the five rulers…'.

[4] For the names of these rulers, see *Arte grande*, f. 236; Kaempfer, *Kaempfer's Japan*, pp. 52–3; Papinot, *Historical*, p. 814. According to the ancient records, primogeniture was not recognized. As Rodrigues points out later in this paragraph, Jimmu was the fourth child and had elder brothers. Possibly he was awarded the throne at the age of 15 on account of his 'clear intelligence and resolute will' (*Nihongi*, I, p. 10); for the names of his elder brothers, see *Kojiki*, p. 155.

[5] Probably a reference to the honorific term *mikoto*: *Nihongi*, I, p. 3.

[6] For the full (and long) title of Jimmu's father, see *Kojiki*, p. 153. *Kojiki* records events until AD 628 and *Nihongi* until 697, but neither source can be considered historically accurate, even after Jimmu's time.

[7] According to *Arte grande* (ff. 236, 239), the kings of Israel reigned 1094–620 BC, and Jimmu became emperor in the time of Josias, who reigned (according to Rodrigues's chronology) 673–642 BC.

another part from Korea, a kingdom very close to Japan. It was from Korea that the Japanese received Chinese writing and other things, and they were in contact with that country long before they communicated with China.[1] There are probable conjectures and also records that claim that a part of Japan was peopled from that region which faces Japan in the west, and is now the Chinese province of Zhejiang and the neighbouring province of Fujian. Both of these are now numbered among the fifteen provinces into which the Chinese Empire is divided. Neither of them formerly was part of China, but both were separate nations with their own languages and customs that they preserve to this day. They were later conquered by the Chinese and incorporated into China, as we have already mentioned.[2]

It is more likely that the first settlers, from whom are descended the kings of Japan, came from Zhejiang province. As we shall presently say, they populated the island of Kyushu at the same time as, or even before, the kingdom of Korea peopled that part of Chūgoku that faces Korea. It is also believed likely that a part of Japan (that is, Ōshū, which faces Tartary and the island of Ezo) was peopled by the Tartars.[3]

Let us first of all begin with the most ancient and principal events. The first region in Japan to be populated was that part of the second island, Kyushu, which is now called Hyūga, one of its nine kingdoms or states. It was here that the first rulers resided until the time of the first to call himself king, that is, Jimmu Tennō. Even to this day in the kingdom of Hyūga there are some very large caves cut out of rock, called Udo-no-Iwato, which ancient tradition maintains were the palace in which their first kings or leaders lived from the beginning until the time of Jimmu Tennō.[4] Thence the court was transferred to the kingdom of Yamato in the Gokinai region.[5] Now this part of Kyushu faces the province of Zhejiang and is directly to the east of the city of Ningbofu. Since ancient times navigation has always thrived in this province or land, and people sailing from India intra Gangem to China in ancient times used to come here.[6] The same may be said about Fujian province, in which is situated the city of Guanzhou (commonly called Chincheo), which also faces

---

[1] There were definitely relations between Japan and Korea in the 3rd and 4th centuries, if not earlier. There is a record of the country of 'Nu' (Japan?) sending an embassy to China in AD 27, and 'Wa' at the end of the 2nd century. In the 5th century western Japan was in contact with China, and Japan sent at least 23 embassies to China in the 7th to 9th centuries. *KEJ*, IV, p. 276; I, p. 281; VII, pp. 259–61.

[2] Already mentioned on p. 26. Valignano also believed that the Japanese islands had been populated from China and lists various reasons to support his theory: the proximity of the islands to China; the similarity between Japanese and Chinese physiognomy; the Japanese use of Chinese words and letters (although with different pronunciation); the acceptance of Chinese art and religion, etc: *Principio*, ff. 12–12v.

[3] While there is no actual proof, the geographical positions of Chūgoku and Ōshū make this assertion more than probable.

[4] Udo-no-Iwato simply means the 'Cave of Udo', situated on the southeast coast of Kyushu, about 18 miles south of Miyazaki. The main shrine is set in a large cave in the cliff face. *KEJ*, VIII, p. 125.

[5] The transfer of the court to Yamato is recounted in *Nihongi*, I, pp. 110–15, and is said to have taken place in 667–663 BC. Jimmu officially inaugurated the Japanese empire on 11 February 660 (Ibid., I, p. 132), a date that remains a national holiday in Japan to this day. Sansom (*Japan*, pp. 28–9) dated this migration about the beginning of the Christian era, but later (*History to 1334*, p. 17–21) changed to 'about AD 350'.

[6] Rodrigues states elsewhere (see p. 27, n. 7) that, coming from India, both St Thomas and the Buddhist patriarch Daruma entered China in Guangdong province, and Guangdong and Canton, located in the south of the country, would have been far more convenient ports of call. According to Bagchi (*India and China*, pp. 34, 35, 55, 57, 69) 'Canton was the most important landing place of Buddhist missionaries from India' and various arrivals there are noted throughout the centuries.

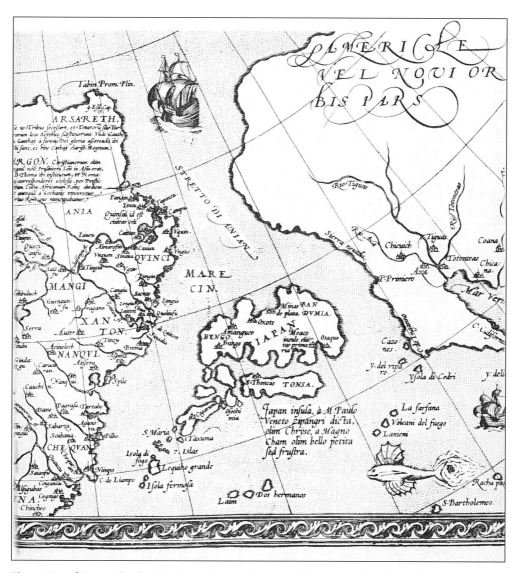

Plate 9: Map of Tartary (detail), in Ortelius, *Theatrum orbis terrarum*. This map was first published in 1570, only seven years before Rodrigues's arrival in Japan; it appeared again in an English edition of the famous atlas as late as 1606. As may be seen, Japan is depicted equidistant between, and close to, China and America. The Anian Strait, mentioned by Rodrigues, is clearly marked.

51

Japan.[1] Thus it is most likely that the earliest inhabitants of Japan who settled in the second island, Kyushu, passed over from these parts.

Perhaps this came about by chance and the people were cast up there by a storm, as still often happens even now, with ships from these parts drifting up to Kantō, the end of Japan, as I myself have seen.[2] But it seems more probable that on account of information received, they deliberately went there to settle or with the plan of discovering and populating new kingdoms. Or it may have come about partly by chance and party by design, on account of the news of these parts received from those who had been thrown up there by accident.

This is shown to be so not only on account of the many ancient things of Japan regarding ancient dress, food (such as the use of *miso*),[3] and other things that are found in the Japanese fashion in that part of Zhejiang, but even more so because all this is in keeping with a story found in both China and Japan. According to this, the descendants of the barbarian kings of Zhejiang province passed over to Japan, and from them was derived one of Japan's names, Kishikoku, as we mentioned earlier.

An ancient Chinese book titled *Rongo* (*Lunyu*, in Chinese) mentions this story in Book 6, Chapter 1.[4] It also appears in an ancient chronicle titled *Shunju*,[5] where it is stated that in ancient times there was a lord of a state or duchy called Shū (Zhou, in Chinese) in that part of China which is now Shanxi province, where people travelling overland from the west enter the country. This duke reigned 1,200 years or more before Christ Our Lord in the time of the Judges of Israel. He had three sons, the eldest and the heir being called Taihaku, or Taibo in Chinese. The name of the second son was Kireki and of the third, Chūyō.[6] Now the father of these three sons wished the second one to succeed him in his estate, but dared not announce this out of consideration for his heir. But learning of this, Taihaku, the eldest son, yielded his rights to his second brother, to whom his father wished to give the duchy. He did this out of love and reverence for his father, wishing to do his will so that he could fulfil his desire. So he left China and went eastwards to a land of barbarians called Jingman, now a part of Nanjing and Zhejiang provinces.[7] There he married the principal barbarian native of the land and raised a family called Go, or Wu in Chinese, and set up the kingdom of Gokoku.

---

[1] For the identification of Chincheo, see p. 28, n. 1. For the importance of Ningbo and Quanzhou in Chinese foreign trade, see Mills, 'Notes', p. 8.

[2] Storms often cast ships on to the shores of Japan, and this is how the first Europeans reached the country (1542/3), as well as William Adams (1600) and Rodrigo de Vivero y Velaso (1609). Rodrigues may have had this last case in mind, for the ship was wrecked off the Kantō coast.

[3] A kind of bean paste. *Vocabulario*, f. 161v: 'A confection of grain, rice, and salt, with which the *shiru* of Japan is seasoned.' Fróis (*Tratado*, p. 178) describes it as 'rice and fermented grain, mixed with salt'.

[4] A reference to the *Analects of Confucius*; in the text, the number of the book and chapter is omitted and I have completed the reference. As Rodrigues says, this story is only mentioned and not recounted in the *Analects*: Legge, *Chinese Classics*, I, p. 207. Rodrigues was familiar with the *Analects*, for he often quotes the work in *Arte grande* (e.g., ff. 3, 9, 16, 24, 87v, 90, 91v, etc) to illustrate points of grammar and syntax.

[5] *Chun Qiu* (or *Shunju* in Japanese), 'Records of Spring and Autumn', a history attributed to Confucius. Rodrigues's reference is found not in the text but in an ancient commentary on it: *Chun Qiu*, Book 12, 7th year, in Legge, *Chinese Classics*, V, p. 812. Rodrigues mentions both *Rongo* and *Shunju* in a list of 'Chinese ethical works', in *Arte breve*, f. 4v.

[6] Duke Danfu is said to have died in 1231 BC, so the reference to 1,200 years is accurate. His first son was certainly Taihaku (Chinese, Taibo), but the second was Chūyō (Yuzhong, or Zhongyong), and the third Kireki (Jili). I have added the name Chūyō in the blank left in the text. Giles, *Biographical Dictionary*, p. 710; Legge, *Chinese Classics*, I, p. 207, n. 1; Hirth, *Ancient Chinese History*, pp. 57–62, 374.

[7] The father wished the *third* son, Kireki, to succeed to the throne so that in turn he would be succeeded by his (Kireki's) son, Wenwang, whose birth had been marked by miracles and wonders. So Taihaku and the elder brother withdrew and left the inheritance to the third brother, Kireki. Se-Ma, *Mémoires*, I, pp. 215–16.

But when the second brother saw that the eldest brother had renounced the estate in his favour, he did not wish to accept. He renounced it in favour of the third brother, and went off to join the eldest brother in the land of the barbarians. The third brother[1] did not think that it would be fitting to accept what his brothers had renounced and did not wish to accept the estate. He left it instead to one of his sons, subsequently known as Bun-Ō, or Wenwang in Chinese, who thus succeeded to the duchy of Zhou. He was a man of much ability and a great philosopher and astrologer. As Bun-Ō was a duke of such prowess and wisdom, he brought under his power the two parts of Serica and with that began the Shū (in Chinese, Zhou) dynasty, calling it after the name of his duchy.[2] He was succeeded by his son, Bu-Ō (in Chinese, Wuwang), who conquered the remaining part of China and became absolute ruler of it all. He was the first monarch of the Zhou dynasty, one of the most famous in China, which began 1,123 years before Christ Our Lord in the time of the priests Samuel and Heli, and lasted 858 years through thirty-seven generations of kings, his descendants.[3] During this period the chief Chinese philosophers flourished, such as Kōshi (in Chinese, Kongzi), founder of the sect of the *literati*, Rōshi (in Chinese, Laozi), and others who will be mentioned in their proper place.[4]

But to return to our account. Taihaku died childless and left as heir to his new estate and family his brother, Kireki, who had left their country with him. He succeeded his brother, and as a sign that he had rejected his Chinese nationality and had joined the barbarian nation, he cut the hair of his head and painted his body with signs in keeping with the country's custom.[5] After his death he was succeeded in the estate by many of his descendants until the family was wiped out by wars in the twenty-fourth generation. They lived in a place that is now the city of Xuzhou in the province of Nanjing, one of the most flourishing in China. They say that some of the descendants of this second brother of Taihaku embarked in the Oriental Sea and went to settle in Japan. The Chinese used to call Japan Kishikoku because Kishi was the name of his ancient family and descendants.[6] They also declare that the Japanese came to cut the *motoi* of the head in imitation of this Kireki, who cut his hair and *motoi* on the death of his brother.[7]

---

[1] I.e., Kireki.

[2] Bun-Ō, or Wenwang (1231–1124 BC), is traditionally credited with the authorship of the famed *Yijing*, or *The Book of Changes*: Hirth, *Ancient Chinese History*, pp. 57–62; Giles, *Biographical Dictionary*, pp. 875–6.

[3] Wuwang (1169–1116 BC) was the first sovereign of the Zhou dynasty (1122–255 BC), which was replaced by the Qin dynasty; it thus lasted 867 years. According to Rodrigues's figures, it must have ended in 265, probably a slip for 255. In *Arte grande*, f. 235, he states that Wuwang began his reign in 1121 BC. The dynasty had 35 rulers in all.

[4] A reference to Confucius and Laozi, founder of Taoism. Rodrigues later deals with these philosophers at greater length on p. 255.

[5] As stated above, it was Chūyō who went into exile with his brother Taihaku, unless Rodrigues is following a totally different version of the story. According to Peter Mundy (*Travels*, III:1, p. 302), 'When a Chinois Forsakes his Country or his Religion, then hee cutteth off his long haire.' Cutting the hair and tattooing the body was performed 'in order to avoid the attacks of serpents and dragons' (Tsunoda, *Japan*, p. 10). Chavannes (in Se-Ma, *Mémoires*, I, p. 216, n. 3) also notes a similar purpose.

[6] Other versions of this story of the family settling in Japan are recounted in Schurhammer, *Shintō*, p. 72, n. 2. The ruling house of Wu had the same name as did the royal house of Zhou, that is, Ki (in Chinese, Ji). The Chinese therefore called Japan the Land of Lord Ki, or Kishikoku. But Kishikoku can also mean the Land of the Princess, and this name may refer to Amaterasu, Empress Jingō, or the queen called Himiko (or Pimiko): Tsunoda, *Japan*, pp. 2–3, and 5, n. 15; Sansom, *Japan*, pp. 29–31. Couto (*Década quinto*, 8, 12; f. 185) also has a vague reference to a Chinese prince who was exiled to Japan and populated the country.

[7] *Vocabulario* , f. 167v: '*Motoyui*. Hair at the back of the head of the Japanese.'

There is a very old temple, venerated throughout Japan, in the kingdom of Ise, and it is dedicated to the first *kami* and lord of Japan. On the front of this temple there is a tablet or inscription on which is written this name. We may see that this is correct because they also say that the inscription runs, *Sanjō* (that is, *mitabi yuzuru*), and this is Kireki's motto, meaning to give away the inheritance three times, although it was something that belonged to him.[1] The sixth descendant was Jimmu Tennō, the first to assume the title of king.[2] Although it is not known in which part of Japan these descendants of Kireki lived, it is most likely, in keeping with what has already been said, that the kings of Japan spring from his descendants. For they went there to live and they dwelt in the above-mentioned part of Hyūga, and on account of their nobility they were received by all as lords and masters. They lived in Hyūga during the reigns of twenty-two lords until the time of the first one to assume the title of king, Jimmu Tennō. He reigned seventy-six years, dying at 127 years of age. In the sixtieth year of his reign he transferred his court from Hyūga to that part of the large island now called Yamato, one of the five kingdoms of Gokinai.[3] The city of Nara, the ancient court of the Japanese kings,[4] is situated here and, as we have said, Japan took the general name of Yamato from this region. These were the first settlers who gave shape to the Japanese nation, and as they were nobler and wiser they eventually subdued all the other inhabited parts of these islands under one ruler. Thus their legends and ancient traditions regard these people who originated in Hyūga as the first progenitors.

It is also certain that people went to these islands from ancient China to populate some parts of them, for this is recounted in the general Chinese records, and is well known in Japan. According to these records, about 250 years before Christ Our Lord (in the time of the Maccabees) a mighty monarch named Shi no Shiko Tei (or Shihuangdi, in Chinese), the first king of the Qin dynasty, reigned in China. He wiped out the descendants of the Zhou dynasty and made himself ruler of China. He was very powerful, and so great was his fame in the Orient that his reputation reached India intra Gangem. He was the first Chinese king to extend the boundaries of ancient Serica by incorporating other neighbouring countries into it. The kingdom or dynasty took the name of Qin from him. This is still used to this day by the Chinese, and the Portuguese follow the example of the Malayans and call the country China.[5] He was a great warrior and very cruel in his government. He wiped out many of the families of the former lords and rulers, and persecuted the Chinese

---

[1] *Mitabi yuzuru* is the Japanese way of reading the two characters *san* and *jō*, and merely means 'to give away three times'. The motto is taken from the *Analects* (8, 1; Legge, *Chinese Classics*, I, p. 207), where it is said of Taihaku that he declined the kingdom three times; according to Legge, this is merely a way of stating that he firmly renounced his inheritance. As regards the inscription at Ise, Rodrigues, *Nihon*, I, p. 169, n. 27, refers to *Baison Saihitsu*, an essay written by Rodrigues's contemporary, the shogunal scholar Hayashi Razan, 1583–1657. This work is found in *Nihon Zuihitsu Taisei*, I, p. 2, and indeed contains much of this material and specifically mentions the inscription at the Inner Shrine at Ise. Although *Baison Saihitsu* confirms Rodrigues's account, it could not have been his source of information as the essay was first published many years after the Jesuit's death.

[2] There seems to be an omission in the text here, for Jimmu was the sixth descendant of Izanagi and Izanami. It was to their daughter, Amaterasu, that the shrine at Ise was dedicated.

[3] According to *Nihongi* (I, pp. 132, 135), Jimmu assumed 'the Imperial Dignity' in 660 BC, and died in 585 at the age of 127, so Rodrigues's figures are correct. Jimmu ordered a palace to be built in Yamato in 662 BC (ibid., I, p. 132). The reference to 'the sixtieth year of his reign' must be mistaken.

[4] Nara was the capital 710–84, when the court was transferred to Nagaoka and then (794) to Miyako.

[5] See p. 24, n. 3 for the origin of the name of China.

astrologers and philosophers, declaring that they were idle people. He prohibited literature and study under pain of death, and to exterminate such things he ordered that all the ancient writings should be burnt and that 460 philosophers of the *literati* sect should be burnt alive in a cave. He also began the famous Wall in the north against the Tartars.[1]

Seeing his cruelty, one of the noble vassals feared that he would order his death, and to escape his wrath he played a trick on him. He deceitfully declared that the inhabitants of some islands in the Oriental Sea (these are now the islands of Japan) lived to an old age for they possessed a medicine that greatly prolonged life, and he offered to go in search of it for the king. As he wished to live a long life, the king believed this tale and ordered him to sail there in ships that he provided for this purpose. The noble embarked for the islands about 220 years before Christ Our Lord, and took with him 1,500 men and 1,500 women in the ships so that they could marry and populate the place. In addition he took with him every kind of craftsman, but he did not take any books – or if he did, they have not been found. He set up on these islands two realms or states, which were called Shinōkoku (in Chinese, Qinwangguo); both were subject to the then-reigning king of Japan, the eighth king after Jimmu. Thus Japan was peopled also in this way by the Chinese themselves.[2]

It is also certain and well known that some private states and coastal regions of Japan were peopled by the Chinese of ancient China. Such, for example, were the Amakusa Islands, whose rulers were Chinese descendants of a king who began the Kan (in Chinese, Han) dynasty. This king overthrew the Qin dynasty and began to reign 205 years before Christ Our Lord, and the dynasty ended in the Year of the Lord 220.[3]

The ruler of Amakusa, Lord Michael, first lord of that island to become Christian, and Lord John, his son who succeeded him, were descended from this Kan monarchy and were proud of the fact. They possessed written records to prove their origin, and their forefathers down to their time kept in touch by letters with their kinsfolk in China. They had come from China on account of persecutions and wars, and had populated these islands that had thitherto been uninhabited or contained people of low culture. They remained in the estate from that time until the war that Taikō waged in Korea, when their lineage and rule of Amakusa came to an end.[4] The same may be said about other ancient families of

---

[1] All these acts are attributed to Shihuangdi (259–210 BC), who by 221 had become virtual ruler of all China. The infamous Burning of the Books to wipe out all memory of the past took place in 213. For biography, see Bodde, *First Unifier.* Also Giles, *Biographical Dictionary*, pp. 252–4; Fitzgerald, *China*, pp. 135–46. The Burning of the Books and the massacre of the scholars are mentioned by Navarrete, *Travels*, II, p. 209, and Sebastiano de Ursis, in D'Elia, *Galileo in China*, p. 64.

[2] There are various versions of this legend, but Rodrigues relates all the essential details. The reference to the 'two realms or states', which Xufu (or Jofuku in Japanese) is supposed to have founded, is a misreading by the copyist. In *Breve aparato*, f. 14, we read: 'He founded in Japan a kingdom or a province, which he also called Qin or Qinguo and the Japanese call Shin or Shinkoku.' Thus he founded only one state in Japan. The expedition is traditionally dated about 219 BC, in the time of the seventh (not eighth) emperor, Kōrei (reigned 290–15 BC). Kaempfer, *History*, I, pp. 131–3; Se-Ma, *Mémoires*, II, p. 151–2; Joly, *Legend*, pp. 240–41; Mackenzie, *Myths*, pp. 106–19.

[3] The founder of the Han dynasty (206 BC–AD 220) was Liubang, or Liuji (247–195 BC), whose title was Gaodi. For details of his reign see Pan Ku, *History*, I, pp. 27–150.

[4] Lord Michael was Amakusa Shizutane, lord of the Amakusa group of islands to the west of Kyushu. Luis de Almeida visited the islands and met him in 1569. In the following year he was baptized with his son John (Amakusa Shizumoto) and died in 1582. He was succeeded by Shizumoto, but after the battle of Sekigahara, 1600, the fief was awarded to Terazawa Hirotaka. Fróis, *História*, II, pp. 222–3; Almeida, 22 October 1569, in *Cartas*, I, f. 280. For Hideyoshi's Korean campaign, see Murdoch, *History 1542 to 1651*, pp. 302–56. I have found no evidence of this family's Chinese origin, but the geographical position of the islands would certainly favour Chinese immigration.

Japanese lords on the island of Kyushu, for example, the Tachibana, Akizuki,[1] and others who are descended from the Chinese.

The tales of Korea and Japan also declare that part of these islands was populated from the kingdom of Korea, called Kore by the natives and Gaoli by the Chinese.[2] This kingdom is so close to Japan that with a favourable wind a ship can sail from it to Japan in less than a day, and on a clear day some parts of it can be seen from the high mountains of Japan. Korea was the first foreign nation with which the Japanese established contact, long before they communicated with China, and with which they waged war. Sometimes they descended on Japan, but the Japanese repulsed them and later conquered them and made them tributaries.[3] Their tales declare that the nobles of that part of Japan called Chūgoku, in which the city of Yamaguchi is situated, spring from a Korean kingdom called Hakusaikoku. The duke of Yamaguchi, Ōuchi Yoshitaka, the seventh successor who was ruling when the Blessed Father Francis Xavier came to that city in 1550, was a descendant from that place, and his lineage finished with him.[4] These people came there in ancient times to populate or conquer these parts, and the island of Tsushima, now part of Japan, in former times belonged to the Koreans.[5]

But it is most probable that the first inhabitants of Japan, which at that time was without form of nationhood or kings, settled in that part of Chūgoku facing Korea, for the kingdom of Korea is about as old as China and is so close to these parts that the crossing may be made on one tide. For this reason the rough tone and the manner of speaking of the Japanese people of that part of Chūgoku are different from those of other parts of Japan and are very similar to the tone of the Koreans. The current native language of Japan has many similarities with the Korean tongue as regards its grammatical construction and parts of speech.[6]

This is borne out by the tales in their fables about the *kami*, for these fables are founded

---

[1] For the Tachibana and Akizuki families, see *Kokushi Daijiten*, IX, pp. 189, 190–92, and I, pp. 87–8. Rodrigues (*Arte grande*, f. 212v) refers to the special status of the Tachibana.

[2] 'Cauly' is mentioned by Marco Polo (*Book*, II, 5; Yule, *Book*, I, p. 343), but he was probably referring to northern Korea. The Japanese word could be used as a term of abuse. In 1613 John Saris had 'boyes, children, and worser sort of idle people' calling after his retinue en route to Edo, 'Coré, Coré, Cocoré Waré [*kokoro warui*], that is to say, You Coreans with false hearts': Farrington, *English Factory*, II, p. 1011.

[3] At their nearest points the distance between the two countries is about 120 miles and contact has continued since early times. According to a legend, Susa-no-o, the unruly brother of Amaterasu, was banished to Silla, a kingdom in east Korea. Later, as Rodrigues mentions, the widow of the Emperor Chūai invaded Korea and received tribute in the year 200, although this incursion probably took place at least 150 years after the traditional date: *Nihongi*, I, pp. 57, 230–32; *Arte grande*, f. 236v. As related on p. 55, a Japanese invasion of Korea was launched in the time of Hideyoshi.

[4] Hakusai, or Kudara, was an ancient kingdom in southwest Korea and was overcome by the Japanese when Chūai's widow invaded the country. When it was vanquished by its neighbouring kingdom of Shiragi in 663, many of its inhabitants emigrated to Japan: Sansom, *Japan*, pp. 33–5. Ōuchi Yoshitaka (1507–51), the seventh successor of Ōuchi Hiroyo (d. 1380) who built the castle at Yamaguchi, committed suicide with his son during a rebellion. He was succeeded by his brother, Yoshinaga (d. 1557), who also ended his life six years later and the family became extinct. The Ōuchi family was said to have been descended from Rim Sŏng, a Korean prince who emigrated to Japan in 611. Xavier met Yoshitaka, who was not amused when Brother Juan Fernández, on Xavier's instructions, read out a condemnation of pederasty, and the audience was abruptly terminated: Fróis, *História*, I, p. 32; Xavier, *Epistolae*, II, p. 261; *KEJ*, VI, p. 135. The Portuguese text has a blank after the name of Yoshitaka and I have added the family name Ōuchi.

[5] Situated between Japan and Korea, Tsushima has long served as a connection between the two countries. The island has belonged to Japan throughout recorded history. In 667, for example, the Japanese built a long stone wall there to guard against possible Chinese invasion: Inoue, 'Century of Reform', p. 210.

[6] Rodrigues notes (*Arte grande*, f. 169v) that Chūgoku people open their mouths too wide while speaking and utter certain high consonants; for example, they pronounce *narumai* as *naruma*. They also use the negative form *zaru*, and say *agezatta*, *mairazatta*, etc. The similarity in the style of farmhouses found in Izumo and Korea is also noted in

on some historical truth. They say that Susa-no-O-no-mikoto was the younger brother of Tenshō Daijin, the principal *kami* of Japan and the first of the terrestrial *kami*. This younger brother wished to seize control and for this reason he was exiled to Hyūga. So he went to the land that is now Izumo, on the north coast of Chūgoku facing Korea. It is said that he found people there already, although he had previously believed that people existed only in Hyūga.[1] These people must have been from Korea for there is no other nearer land. The Chinese chronicles relate that Korea was then populated, for in the year 1130 before Christ Our Lord (in the time of the priest Heli) a king was sent from China to govern Korea and became ruler of the land, for they deprived him of the Chinese kingdom called Jishi.[2]

Finally, it is believed likely that a part of these islands was populated by the eastern Tartars, for example, that part of the large island of Japan in the kingdom of Ōshū that faces the Tartar island called Ezo. This island is only fifteen miles distant from Japan and is separated by a narrow sea strait. Hence the Japanese of these parts are the most rustic of all Japan in their manner and everything else. This island of Ezo is near the continent of Tartary, and the one can be seen from the other. Thus the island could well have been peopled from the continent in ancient times.[3] Even today the Japanese are in contact with the Tartars of the island and trade with them, and the Japanese have some settlements there in which they live.[4] Even after we went to Japan, some Chinese silk and gilt goods came from there, for that part of Tartary is bounded directly by China and Korea.

These, then, are the regions whence it seems that Japan was populated. It is true that the Japanese have been subject to one leader or king after all the rest, with the same language and general customs throughout all the kingdom. Still, it is well known to anyone who has seen all of Japan that each region has many special things similar to those of the parts whence they were peopled, and that there is a difference between some regions and others.[5]

Sansom, *History to 1334*, p. 33. As regards the Korean language, 'the syntax is remarkably similar to that of Japanese, but the phonology and morphology are markedly different.' *KEJ*, IV, p. 289.

[1] Susa-no-o, the unruly younger brother of Amaterasu, or Tenshō Daijin, angered his sister by breaking down the divisions between rice fields and flinging a flayed piebald colt at her, whereupon she retired into a cave, plunging the world into darkness. After she had been lured out, her brother was exiled to Izumo for his gross misconduct. *Nihongi*, I, pp. 40–63.

Although at the end of the 17th century Engelbert Kaempfer (*History*, III, p. 13) condemned Japanese mythology as 'a heap of fabulous and romantick stories of their Gods, demi-gods, and Heroes, inconsistent with reason and common sense,' Rodrigues here shrewdly notes that these fables recount in mythological form historical truth – in this case, the rise and dominance of the Yamato clan. The story of Susa-no-o's exile provided the powerful Izumo clan with an ancient and divine genealogy, yet inferior to that of the dominant Yamato clan, which claimed the Sun Goddess herself as its progenitor. See Sansom, *History to 1334*, pp. 32–3.

[2] This is a puzzling statement and I have been unable to verify it. Rodrigues, *Nihon*, I, p. 175, has a different translation: '… a king was sent from China to rule Korea and separate it from China, and to set up a state called Jishi and be its ruler.' The literal translation of the Portuguese text runs: '… they sent from China a king to govern Korea and be its ruler. For they dispossessed him of the kingdom of China called Jishi'.

[3] Ezo (Hokkaido) is about 180 miles from the Asian mainland, but only 18 miles south of the island of Sakhalin, which Rodrigues presumably believed to be continental. The Tsugaru Strait separating Honshu from Ezo is about 15 miles wide.

[4] For early European references to these settlements, see p. 29, n. 8.

[5] There is still speculation about the origin of the Japanese people, and a summary account is found in Sansom, *History to 1334*, pp. 14–15, where Rodrigues's opinion on this subject is generally confirmed. The three major migration waves were from Siberia in the north, China and Korea in the west, and Okinawa and Ryūkyū in the south. *KEJ*, IV, p. 33.

CHAPTER 4

WHETHER EUROPEANS KNEW ABOUT THESE ISLANDS IN ANCIENT TIMES, AND WHEN THEY WERE FIRST DISCOVERED BY THE PORTUGUESE

Among modern writers there have not been lacking responsible geographers who have held that ancient people knew of the islands of Japan, which, it is said, were the Chryse or the Golden Chersonese, included by Ptolemy in his *Geographia*.[1] They have also maintained that the Ganges, so renowned among ancient people, is the river of Canton, that the island of Sumatra is the Taprobana or Salice of Ptolemy, and that the island of Ceylon, next to Cape Comorin, is the island called Nanigeris by Ptolemy.[2]

This was the view of Gerard Mercator, the dean of contemporary geographers, and he was followed by Abraham Ortelius in his *Theatrum orbis terrarum*, and by Giovanni Antonio Magini in his *Geographia* and commentaries on Ptolemy.[3] This has also been held by other modern authors, who have inclined to this view on account of certain problems noted in Ptolemy's geography of these regions.[4] These are not real problems, however, to those of us who travel in these parts and can compare these regions with what Ptolemy wrote about them. But these authors back in Europe have used surmise and false information in their attempts to guess about things over here in the Orient, so far distant from their eyes. They did not believe what that sober and objective historian João de Barros so accurately described when dealing with these matters.[5] Nor did they heed what has been written so clearly and truthfully after inquiry by other Portuguese authors who have travelled in these parts. Such men have investigated the whole coast of India, its promontories and islands, which Ptolemy described. Whence the authors in Europe are quite clearly deceived by their mistaken guesses and err about the whole coast of India, its islands, capes, promontories, and rivers, which Ptolemy mentions in his *Geographia* when dealing with these regions.[6]

---

[1] Ptolemy, *Geographia*, 7, 2 (in Magini, *Geographia*, p. 170).

[2] There is a blank in the text where Ptolemy's name for Ceylon should have been written, and I have added 'Nanigeris' as the context requires. Ptolemy mentions this name in *Geographia*, 7, 1 (in Magini, *Geographia*, p. 169).

[3] Japan is identified as Ptolemy's Chryse by Mercator (*Atlas*, p. 417), Ortelius (Plate 9), and Magini (*Geographia*, f. 265). Mercator (p. 422) relates that Aristotle, in his *De mundo*, identifies Taprobana with Sumatra, while Ortelius (*Theatrum*, p. 63) and Magini (f. 264) affirm that it is Sumatra. Mercator (pp. 419–20) and Magini (f. 264) identify Ptolemy's Nanigeris with Ceylon. Mercator certainly called Canton's river the Ganges in his 1569 map; for his reasons, see Dahlgren, *Débuts*, pp. 34–5. Gerard Mercator (1512–94), 'the Ptolemy of modern geography', brought out the first part of his famous Atlas in 1585, and was the first to use the term 'atlas' to describe a book of uniformly sized maps: Tooley, *Maps*, pp. 31–2. For earlier references to Ortelius and Magini, see p. 14, nn. 5, 6.

[4] For example, in a map by Antonio de Herrera published as late as 1601, Canton is still depicted on the Ganges: Teleki, *Atlas*, p. 27.

[5] For references to Barros, see p. 14, n. 4.

[6] Ptolemy deals with India in *Geographia*, 7, 1 (in Magini, *Geographia*, pp. 162ff).

Neither Marinus of Tyre nor Ptolemy nor any other ancient author knew anything about Japan, for when they wrote from reports of those who had sailed to China, these islands had neither trade nor contact with China.[1] China is indeed very near to the islands, but they were still very uncivilized, and many coastal areas and regions facing China were not populated until after this time. The Japanese had some contact only with the Koreans, their neighbours, at this time, and even that was tenuous, but it was through the Koreans that they heard of China. According to the Japanese and Chinese records, they made the first contact with China about the Year of the Lord 58.[2] But Marinus of Tyre flourished 60 years and Ptolemy 140 years after Christ Our Lord, so neither could have heard of Japan. Nor could Japan have been the Golden Chersonese, which was so renowned and frequented at that time. Until these islands were first discovered by the Portuguese (as we shall presently describe), no other nation apart from the Chinese and their neighbours, the Koreans, had any information about Japan or any contact with the country. Nor did the Japanese sail further than China and Korea, for their country is situated as a limit or boundary of the Orient here at the end of the world in the midst of this vast and immense Oriental Sea.[3]

For the same reason, before they met the Portuguese the Japanese knew nothing about other nations of the world except for China, Korea, and a small part of Tartary. For the past thousand years, since the sects of the Indian gymnosophists passed over from China and Korea, the Japanese have had for the first time some vague information about the fame of India beyond the China they believed was the whole world.[4] Thus even now when they refer to the whole world, they talk about the kingdoms that they used to believe were the only countries of the world – Japan, China, and India, with Korea and Tartary included within China as its outskirts.[5] But since they met the Portuguese and the Law of God entered the kingdom, the Japanese have learnt about the whole world and now have a very different idea from the concept they have hitherto held.[6]

The shape that Ptolemy erroneously gave to China also clearly shows the falsity of what these authors in Europe have to say. According to Ptolemy, the coast of China ascends to

---

[1] The geographer Marinus of Tyre is known only through references contained in Ptolemy; he was probably contemporary with or slightly earlier than Ptolemy. Early writers tended to place him in the 1st century AD, thus Rodrigues a few lines later refers to AD 60. Little is known about Ptolemy, but it is certain he made observations about 139 and that he was still living in 161, so Rodrigues's statement a few lines later, '140 years after Christ Our Lord', is correct. Bunbury, *History*, II, pp. 519–20, 546–7.

[2] According to 5th-century Chinese sources, in AD 57 an envoy was sent from the Hakata region in Kyushu to the Chinese capital, where Emperor Guangwu (4 BC–AD 57) presented him with a seal. A gold seal was found near Hakata in 1784, but it is now generally believed not to be the seal in question: Tsunoda, *Japan*, pp. 2, 5, nn. 10, 11, 12; Sansom, *History to 1334*, p. 14.

[3] By the mid–16th century, Japanese had in fact reached south-east Asia, and in the following century Yamada Nagamasa (d. 1630) played a significant military role in Siam: *KEJ*, V, p. 378. Japanese trading settlements, called Nihonmachi ('Japanese towns'), were to be found in Burma and Vietnam, while about 3,000 Japanese resided in the Manila area: ibid., VI, p. 183; Sugimoto and Swain, *Science and Culture*, pp. 154–5.

[4] For the introduction of Buddhism from China, via Korea, in 552, see p. 48, n. 3.

[5] Both Fróis (Miyako, 20 February 1565, in *Cartas*, I, f. 172) and Vilela (Sakai, 15 September 1565, in ibid., I, f. 193) mention this threefold division, but the former lists the countries as China, Siam, and Japan. For the inclusion of Siam instead of India, see p. 19, n. 2. See also p. 66, n. 1 for further reference to this concept.

[6] A concrete example of this extended knowledge of world geography is the series of *namban byōbu*, or painted screens executed by Japanese artists using Western painting techniques in the late 16th and early 17th centuries. Among these, several depict world maps according to current Western geographical knowledge.

17°N before turning and descending southwards over the equator to 4°S. The whole of the Oriental Sea is enclosed by Terra Incognita and the great bay that they call Sinus Magnus is thus formed. The land thus descends with the coast 21°, from 17°N to 4°S on the other side of the equator. The land had to ascend the said 21° with the Chinese coast up to 17°N so that the Chinese coast might be certain, as it is in fact, and the capital of China at 35° or 36°N as it was at that time according to their records, and that the Oriental Sea might remain open, as it is in fact. Giovanni Antonio Magini has noted all this very well in his commentary on Ptolemy's *Geographia*.[1]

Whence it is clear that the Golden Chersonese was not the Japanese islands but the island of Sumatra next to Malacca. This is Marco Polo's Java the Less and the Golden Island of Ophir, that is, India, whither sailed King Solomon's ships.[2] Neither is the Ganges the river of Canton, but of Bengal instead; and Ceylon is Ptolemy's Taprobana facing Promontorium Cori, now called Cape Comorin.[3] All this is clearly demonstrated at some length in the *Geographia* of these regions composed of general and particular maps. It was diligently compiled here and for this reason is not yet known in Europe.[4]

It was only after the Year of the Lord 650 that these islands became better known and ships began often sailing to and from China. This was in the dynasty called Tang by the Chinese and Tō by the Japanese.[5] At this time the kings of Japan had a great deal of contact with those of China, and people often went there from Japan. This continued until China was overcome by the Tartars, whom Japan refused to obey, but was resumed after the Tartars were driven out of China in this dynasty of Daming (Taimei in Japanese). Thus every three years ambassadors were sent to China as a sign of recognition.[6]

But this contact was broken about ninety years ago as Japan was embroiled in wars and the people would not obey their own king.[7] Many pirate fleets sailed from Japan to rob and devastate various coastal places of China and even inland areas along the rivers. All this

---

[1] Ptolemy's erroneous concept of East Asia is well illustrated in his reconstructed map of the world in Magini, *Geographia*, f. 26v, or in Plate 7. Ptolemy erred in making the Sinus Magnus, or Great Gulf, run south below the equator, thus giving a west (and not east) coast to what is now known as China. See Bunbury, *History*, II, pp. 599–601.

[2] Rodrigues probably means here 'Ophir, that is, India of the Bible', for although he himself identifies Ophir with Sumatra, he notes, on p. 16, India in general is called Ophir in Scripture. See also p. 16, nn. 5, 6.

[3] For Taprobana, see p. 41, n. 2; for Cape Comorin, see p. 17.

[4] Undoubtedly a reference to the atlas mentioned by Rodrigues in a letter dated 30 November 1627 (Rodrigues, 'Rodrigues in China', pp. 258–7).

[5] The Portuguese text adds here, 'and the kingdom of China, Taitō'. The sense is probably that the Chinese called the dynasty Tang or Datang, and the Japanese, Tō or Taitō. The Tang dynasty lasted 618–907. Why Rodrigues chose the date 650 is not clear, unless the figure is a convenient round number. According to *Nihongi* (II, pp. 165, 166, 242, 245), on which he has based previous information concerning Japan's early history, ambassadors crossed from one country to the other in 630, 632, 653, 654, etc.

[6] The Yuan (or Mongol, or 'Tartar') dynasty lasted 1279–1368. The Mongol rulers were succeeded by the Ming, 1368–1644. It was during the former dynasty that attempts were made to invade Japan, as Rodrigues relates elsewhere. The first Japanese mission, headed by Sorai, to Ming China reached the Chinese court in 1371: Tsunoda, *Japan*, pp. 108 *et seq.*; Wang, *Official Relations*, p. 12.

[7] The reference to 'about ninety years ago' places the break in relations to about 1530, but the official breakdown occurred in 1549. The Ōuchi family at Shimonoseki (see p. 56, n. 4) had a virtual monopoly of trade with China during the Ming dynasty, but this ended with the suicide of Ōuchi Yoshitaka in 1551: *KEJ*, VI, p. 135; Wang, *Official Relations*, pp. 4, 79–81. The 16th century in Japan is known as the Sengoku Jidai, the Period of Civil War, when, as Rodrigues says, 'Japan was embroiled in wars and the people would not obey their own king.' He describes this period in greater detail in Book 1, Chapter 11, below.

made the Chinese greatly hate and fear the Japanese, regarding them as their worst enemies.[1] Whence it can be seen that these islands were not known in ancient times outside China, and it seems that through divine providence God Our Lord arranged that this commerce with the Chinese should cease so that at almost the same time relations with the Portuguese could begin and in this way the Gospel should be carried there and thus enter the kingdom.[2]

The first person to bring to Europe news of these islands was the Venetian Marco Polo in his account of Cathay. He referred to them under the corrupt name of Zipangu. As we have said, the Chinese call them Ribenguo, while the Fujian people know them as Yatbun-guok in their native language, while the Japanese say Nippon-goku or Nihon-goku.[3] But before the Portuguese discovered India and Japan, it was not known for certain in Europe which islands he was talking about. Even now, since Japan has been discovered, many modern authors who write histories remark harshly that Marco Polo was not speaking about Japan; as they do not know the history of these regions, they believe that he was referring to other islands.[4] The Genoese Christopher Columbus offered to King John II of Portugal to go and discover the Zipangu islands.[5]

But it is quite certain that Polo was speaking of Japan, because it may be seen in the Chinese and Japanese records that while the Grand Cham, the king of the Tartars, was ruling China, he ordered in the Year of the Lord 1279 a powerful fleet of 4,000 ships and 200,000 infantry to sail against Japan and subject the country to his rule, for the king of Japan refused to pledge his obedience.[6] Part of this fleet sailed from Korea, which was under

---

[1] For references to piracy, see p. 46, n. 1. Avila Girón (*Relación*, p. 12) mentions this piracy and confirms Rodrigues's observation about the Chinese hatred towards the Japanese: 'they loathe and hate them as their worst enemy'. He says that there was a marble monument in Canton on which was inscribed, 'As long as the sun and moon give light, the Chinese and the Japanese cannot live under the same sky or drink the same water.'

[2] Whether through divine providence or not, it was fortunate for the Portuguese to arrive at a time when the Chinese coveted Japanese silver, and the Japanese coveted Chinese raw silk. As Chinese-Japanese relations were at a low ebb, the Portuguese, with their large commercial vessels, were able to take advantage of the artificial situation and act as middle-men between the two nations. Another factor working to the Europeans' advantage was the favourable values of gold and silver. Mendoza (*History*, I, p. 18) sums up the situation: 'Gold is better cheape there [in China] then it is in Europe, but silver is more woorth.'

[3] Polo, *Book*, III, 2 (Yule, *Book*, II, pp. 253–5). For earlier references to the name of Japan, see p. 45.

[4] But Mercator (*Atlas*, p. 417), Ortelius (*Theatrum*, pp. 62–3), and Magini (*Geographia*, f. 268) all identify Polo's Zipangu with Japan. As stated on p. 45, n. 7, Giacomo Gastaldi seems to have been the first European cartographer to identify Zipangu with Japan in his 1550 map. Dahlgren, *Débuts*, p. 17. As late as the end of the 19th century, George Collingridge (*Early Cartography*, pp. 403–9) still identified Zipangu with Java.

[5] A literal translation of the Portuguese text would run: '… he was referring to other islands, even after Japan was discovered the Genoese Christopher Columbus offered …'. Rodrigues, *Nihon*, I, p. 183, translates the sentence in this way, but 'even after Japan was discovered' must refer to the previous sentence and not to Columbus, who died long before the Europeans reached Japan. Although Columbus did approach John II of Portugal, he broke off nego-tiations with him in 1484 and took his cause to the Spanish court, which eventually patronized him – a fact that the Portuguese Rodrigues fails to mention.

Columbus certainly had Zipangu in mind. On 13 October 1492, he wrote, 'But, to lose no time, I intend to go and see if I can find the Island of Çipango.' In fact he identified Cuba with Zipangu, noting on 23 October 1492, 'I wish to depart today for the Island of Cuba, which I believe should be Çipango': Columbus, *Raccolta*, I, 1, pp. 18, 28. Columbus was familiar with Polo's work and made no less than 366 marginal notes in his 1485 edition of Polo. Ibid., I, 3, pp. 94–100. For a speculative account of Polo's influence on Columbus, see Wagner, 'Marco Polo's Nar-rative'. Rodrigues copied this reference to Columbus from Gonçalves, *Historia*, f. 144v.

[6] Rodrigues evidently took this account directly from Polo (*Book*, III, 2, 3; Yule, *Book*, II, pp. 255–63), who mentions that the Grand Cham (or Kublai Khan, 1215–94) sent the force in 1279, but does not give the size of the invading army. There were two unsuccessful invasions of Japan in 1274 and 1281, and Polo seems to be referring to the second

obedience to him, and another part left from China, sailing from the city of Hangzhou in the Bay of Ningbo facing Japan. This Hangzhou, now the capital of Zhejiang province, was then the court of the king of Manzi, that is, the king of China, and is well known among Europeans under the name of Kinsay, or Kinsu, which was then believed to mean the Court of the King. The city had been overcome by the Tartars, and the king of Manzi, or China, had died only a short time previously.[1]

The whole of this Tartar armada arrived near the city of Hakata in the kingdom of Chikuzen, one of the nine kingdoms of Kyushu island, and there all the fleet was lost in a great storm off the coast of Shimonoseki Peninsula. Many of the Tartars escaped and gave themselves up, but they were given ships in which to return.[2] Even to this day the Tartars' weapons are preserved in the peninsula in a temple of a *kami* as a memorial, and even now this victory is commemorated when the king of Japan is crowned.[3] The Japanese call those Tartars Mokuri, while the Chinese refer to them as Menggu. The Tartars were called Mongug, the name of the tribe from which came the Grand Cham, king of the Tartars.[4]

Now at this time Marco Polo was in Cathay in Kambala, the court of the Tartar king, now called Beijing. He went there from the conquered city of Kinsay (or Hangzhou) after this event in the war.[5] Whence it is clearly shown that he was speaking about Japan. It is true that what he says about this war is correct, but there are many false statements as regards what he wrote from hearsay on other people's reports about the customs and things allegedly existing in the country of Japan. Other statements have some truth. For example, he says that the palaces of the king of Japan were very large and covered with gold plate,

one. Elsewhere (*Arte grande*, ff. 235v, 237v), Rodrigues mentions the invasion, correctly dating it 1281; he also gives the size of the invading army as 4,000 sail and 240,000 soldiers. The same details are given by Francisco Pires (Ajuda, 49–V–3, f. 22), so possibly the reference here to 200,000 troops is a copyist's slip. For modern accounts of the invasions, when the defenders were saved by the famous *kamikaze*, or divine wind (a typhoon), see *KEJ*, V, pp. 243–5 (which gives the 1281 invading force as 4,400 ships and 140,00 troops); Sansom, *History to 1334*, pp. 438–50; Kawazoe, 'Japan and East Asia', pp. 411–23; early Japanese illustrations of the event are found in Smith, *Japanese History*, pp. 107–21.

[1] The 1281 invading fleets sailed from both Korea and China, as Rodrigues correctly states, but according to modern authorities the Chinese base of operations was Quanzhou (or Zaitun), not Hangzhou. From 1127 Hangzhou was the court of the Song dynasty (960–1279). The Mongols captured the city in 1276, and three years later the young Song pretender threw himself into the sea and was drowned. Fitzgerald, *China*, pp. 393–4.

[2] The Portuguese text reads somewhat abruptly here and appears incomplete. Rodrigues later (p. 96) repeats the whole account, and from the second version it may be seen that a couple of lines have been omitted here. For maps of the invasion and fighting, see *KEJ*, V, p. 244; Sansom, *History to 1334*, p. 446.

[3] The temple in question must be Hakozaki Hachiman Shrine, in the modern city of Fukuoka, where many relics of the Mongol invasion are preserved. I have found no reference to the victory in the Japanese coronation ceremony; Rodrigues, *Nihon*, I, p. 183, has nothing to say about the assertion.

[4] For the origin of 'Mongol', see p. 23. Rodrigues has already stated, p. 23, that the Japanese term for Mongol is Mōko. For the alternative version Mokuri, see Rodrigues, *Nihon*, I, p. 184, n. 7.

[5] See the map of Polo's travels at the end of his *Book*, I. He reached the Khan's court in 1275 and sailed from Zaitun in 1292.

As Rodrigues often cites Polo, it may be mentioned here that Frances Woods's book, *Did Marco Polo Reach China?*, throws doubt on his ever reaching Asia. In his review-article, 'Marco Polo Went to China', Igor de Rachewiltz argues against this thesis. In his study of Polo's travels in China and other Asian countries ('Marco Polo and his "Travels"') Peter Jackson concludes, 'The fact that Marco Polo or his co-author or later copyists exaggerated his importance while in China … has long been suspected and can hardly be in doubt. But it does not in itself demonstrate that he was never in China or, worse still, never east of the Crimea.'

because at that time there were some very renowned palaces called Taidairi and their roof tiles and other exterior parts were gilded, and so the Tartars thought that they were made of gold.[1]

The Portuguese were the first Europeans to discover these islands of Japan and to send correct information about them to Europe. After Afonso de Albuquerque captured Malacca in the year 1511, Fernão Pérez d'Andrade led an embassy from King Manoel to the king of China in the year 1518. During his stay there, he heard only of the Luchu Islands, which are a continuation of the Japanese islands and are next to them; they belong to Japan for their kings come from there. He sent a ship of discovery from there under the command of N.[2] But as Antonio Galvão's book, *Various Discoveries*, points out, it was in the year 1542 that the first news of the Japanese islands was obtained.[3] Martim Afonso de Sousa was governing India in this year of 1542 (it was the same year that the Blessed Father Francis Xavier reached Goa by ship),[4] when Antonio de Motta, Francisco Zeimoto, and Antonio Peixoto sailed from Siam to China in a junk.[5] A very great storm arose, which they corruptly call typhoon, from the Chinese word *daifeng* and the Japanese word *taifu*, meaning 'great wind'.[6] After this junk of the three Portuguese had drifted in the sea for twenty-four hours,[7] the ship was stripped of all its rigging, and all hope of safety was lost. It carried them out to sea and thence several days later they reached the islands of Japan.

Up to this time there had been no certain or objective information in the West about these islands, and their discovery was due to Our Lord's great providence as regards the conversion of souls that was later to take place in these islands. God Our Lord permitted that storm so that the islands might be discovered and with them a people so desirous of finding the path of true salvation.

The ship reached port on an island called Tanegashima in the sea of Satsuma, and the Portuguese taught the people how to use arquebuses, and from there their use spread

---

[1] Polo, *Book*, III, 2 (Yule, *Book*, II, pp. 253–4). Rodrigues later mentions more about the emperor's palace, or Taidairi, in Miyako, on p. 173, below.

[2] For the capture of Malacca by Afonso Albuquerque (1453–1515), see Albuquerque, *Commentaries*, III, pp. 101–28; Barros, *Década segunda*, VI, 5 (ff. 143–6). For Andrade's embassy, which reached China in 1517, see Barros, *Década terceira*, II, 6, 8, (ff. 41–4, 48v–53); Castanheda, *Historia*, IV, 28–31 (pp. 60–71); Kammerer, *Découverte*, pp. 14–19. The 'N' in the Portugese text refers to Jorge Mascarenhas, who did not reach Luchu because of adverse weather but traded at Chincheo instead. Barros, *Década terceira*, II, 8 (f. 52); Kammerer, *Découverte*, p. 20.

[3] Galvano, *Discoveries*, pp. 229–30. Schurhammer, 'Descobrimento', argues convincingly that the Portuguese reached the Ryūkyū Islands in 1542 and Japan proper in 1543.

[4] Xavier sailed with Sousa and reached Goa on 6 May 1542 (Xavier, *Epistolae*, I, p. 125). For his optimistic assessment of Sousa, ibid., I, pp. 79–80. Sousa was appointed Viceroy of India in 1542 and governed three years. He died in Lisbon in 1564. Danvers, *Portuguese*, I, pp. 452–67.

[5] Galvano, *Discoveries*, pp. 229–30; Couto, *Década quinta*, VIII, 12 (f. 183). Rodrigues seems to have taken this sentence from Gonçalves, *Historia*, f. 145.

[6] Rodrigues's derivation of 'typhoon' is correct as far as it goes, but see Schlegel, 'Etymology', pp. 581–5. *Vocabulario*, f. 237v: '*Taifū, ōkaze*. Great wind or storm.' For early European accounts of typhoons, see *TCJ*, pp. 12–15. A graphic description of a typhoon is given in the 1605 Jesuit Annual Letter from Japan (Ajuda, 49–IV–59, ff. 282–2v), while Cocks (in Farrington, *English Factory*, II, p. 1515) describes the extensive damage done by another typhoon in Hirado in September 1613.

[7] As Schurhammer points out ('Descobrimento', p. 539, n. 147), Rodrigues did not take this reference to 24 hours from Galvano, but probably copied it from Lucena (*Historia*, pp. 461–2). As Lucena depended on Galvano, the reference to 24 hours was probably his own invention. Neither does Galvano specifically mention a typhoon, although the storm was probably one.

throughout the whole of Japan. The names of the Portuguese who taught the people how to make these guns are still preserved on that island to this day.[1] Fernão Mendes Pinto makes himself out to be one of these three in his book of make-believe and says that he was there on board the junk. But this is untrue, as are many other things in his book, which he seems to have written more for recreation than to tell the truth, for there is no kingdom or event in which he does not pretend to have been present.[2]

After this ship another Portuguese ship sailed to Bungo, as our Brother Paul Yōhōken writes in his *monogatari*, or dialogues, and we personally heard this from him.[3] But the Portuguese could not make themselves understood by the inhabitants of the country as they had no interpreter, and so instead of the language they used weights and scales in their negotiations when they sold various articles. When the then Duke of Bungo, father of Duke Francis who was later converted to the Faith, saw the ship and the riches that it carried, he was moved by greed and wanted to kill the Portuguese and seize the ship. But his son, the prince, went to him and said that he would never agree to such an act as it was against natural reason and the trust due to foreigners who come to trade. It would also be against his kingdom's good name if news of such an action were to be heard in other parts of Japan. His father therefore desisted from his wicked plan and the ship returned in peace.[4] The

---

[1] Pinto declares (*Travels*, pp. 276–8) that 600 arquebuses were made in the five and a half months after his first arrival in Japan, and he was told on his return in 1556 that no less than 30,000 had been produced. What is certainly true is that for a long time these guns were known in Japan as *tanegashima*. But Chinese firearms were not unknown in Japan before the Portuguese arrival. In 1510 a Buddhist monk returning from China presented a gun to Hōjō Uji-tsuna. In *Teppō-ki*, a Japanese account of firearms written between 1596 and 1614, the corrupt names of one, possibly two, of the first Portuguese is recorded (Schurhammer, 'Descobrimento', p. 536), but Rodrigues may be referring here to an oral tradition.

[2] A controversial statement. Fernão Mendes Pinto (1509–83) sailed to the Indies at the age of 28, and for 20 years allegedly led a life of extraordinary adventure. He met Xavier and for a short time was a Jesuit novice. After his return to Portugal in 1558, he wrote his celebrated *Peregrinaçam*, in which he recounts his travels. Pinto's claim (*Travels*, p. 274) to have been one of the first three Portuguese to reach Japan does not lack supporters (e.g., Cortesão, *Monumenta*, V, p. 171; Norton, *Portugueses*, pp. 21–7), but the massive evidence to the contrary produced by Schurhammer ('Descobrimento', pp. 551–77) appears conclusive. For references for and against Pinto's claim, see Boxer, *Christian Century*, pp. 22–4, 453–4, and Kammerer, *Découverte*, pp. 41–7.

Cortesão (*Monumenta*, V, p. 171, nn. 22, 23) brands Rodrigues as 'an enemy of Mendes Pinto, who does not say that the latter was one of the discoverers [of Japan], of course'. Having thus dealt with his critics, Cortesão adds disarmingly, '... Pinto, whose *Peregrination* was written many years after his return from the Far East and therefore subject to failures of memory and accuracy, particularly as regards dates, and exotic names of persons and places...'.

[3] This *monogatari*, or story, was one of a dozen printed by the Jesuit Press in Amakusa and then Nagasaki between 1591 and 1614. Few of these tales have survived, but Doi (*Sprachstudium*, p. 116) lists the titles of a dozen quoted by Rodrigues in *Arte grande*. Among them is *Kurofune monogatari* ('The Tale of the Black [Portuguese] Ship'), quoted twice in *Arte grande* (ff. 11v, 16; possibly also ff. 128, 129), and from the context is probably the tale cited here.

Brother Paul Yōhōken (or Yōhō) was born in Wakasa between 1509 and 1514, was baptized by Vilela at Miyako in 1560, became a Jesuit brother in 1580, and died 16 years later in Nagasaki. Both he and his son Vincent, also a Jesuit brother, wrote Japanese with great elegance: Schütte, *Textus*, pp. 1328–9. According to Fróis (*História*, I, p. 172), Paul did much preparatory work for the compilation of various books published by the Jesuit Press.

[4] This account of the intercession of Duke Francis (Ōtomo Yoshishige) was probably included in *Kurofune mono-gatari*, mentioned in the previous note. Fróis (16 October 1578, in *Cartas*, I, f. 422) gives the same story, relating that the junk in question arrived in 1546 or 1547 carrying six or seven Portuguese traders led by Jorge de Faria Riso. The plan to seize the ship was suggested by its pagan pilot. See also Boxer, *Fidalgos*, p. 30. Ōtomo Yoshishige (1530–87),

Portuguese continued trading from that time until the present, that is, for ninety-one years, from 1542 to the present year of 1633, during which time God continued paving the way for His Holy Law.[1]

There are also some modern theologians who hold that Sacred Scripture speaks literally about these islands of Japan, and they apply to them the contents of Chapter 18 of Isaiah:

> Go, ye swift angels, to a nation rent and torn in pieces; to a terrible people, after which there is no other; to a nation expecting and trodden under foot, whose land the rivers have spoiled.
>
> At that time a present shall be brought to the Lord of Hosts, from a people rent and torn in pieces; from a terrible people, after which there hath been no other; from a nation expecting and trodden under foot, whose land the rivers have spoiled, to the place of the name of the Lord of Hosts, to Mt Sion.[2]

Let us see how the authors explain this text and apply it to Japan. It seems that the 'swift angels' are the preachers, such as the Blessed Father Francis and members of the Society, the apostles of Japan. The description of a people 'rent and torn' by continual internal wars is also fitting, as well as 'a terrible people', a people so eagerly awaiting the things of salvation. A people burned with many errors, destroyed by the torrents of the false doctrines of their idols, which they have embraced so tenaciously. The phrase, 'At that time a present shall be brought to the Lord of Hosts,' etc., is very appropriate, referring to so many souls who have been converted, to so many glorious martyrs who under every sort of torture shed their blood for the Faith of Christ, and to so many glorious confessors, etc.

So it can be said that the prophet was speaking with a prophetic spirit and saw beforehand what was to take place. For at the time when he prophesied, these islands were hardly peopled at all and their first king had not yet been born. And after the land had been populated, it remained in peace for many years under its king, for the wars and disturbances with which it is torn and convulsed began in modern times about 300 years ago and did not exist at the beginning.[3] But when the Law of God reached the country, the land was divided against itself and racked with wars. Before the Law of God came to Japan, the people had

---

son of Yoshinori (d. 1550), met Xavier in 1551, and took the name Francis when baptized in 1578. On his retirement in 1562, he adopted the Buddhist name Sōrin, and many European reports refer to him by this name, which often appears in Fróis, *História*. Valignano, *Sumario*, p. 101, n. 2, and p. 102, for the Ōtomo family tree; portrait of Yoshishige given in Smith, *Japanese History*, p. 159. Rodrigues (*Arte grande*, ff. 211–211v) gives an explanation of the *hōmyō*, or two-syllable name adopted by laymen on retirement, citing Sōrin as an example.

[1] For an account of Japanese-Portuguese trade, see Boxer, *Great Ship*, esp. pp. 21–171, and Boxer, *Christian Century*, pp. 104–21. Presumably 'the present year of 1633' was added when Rodrigues revised the work shortly before his death in that year, as internal evidence shows that he wrote these first two books in 1620–21.

[2] Isaiah, 18, 2 and 7. I have quoted from the Douai Version, which is a literal translation of the Latin Vulgate used here by Rodrigues. He refers to this text again in Part 2, Book 1, Chapter 5 (Ajuda, 49–IV–53, ff. 187v–9v; Rodrigues, *Nihon*, II, p. 289), not translated here. I cannot trace any contemporaneous theologians applying the text to Japan. The great scriptural commentator Cornelius a Lapide, 1567–1637, applied it to Ethiopia (*Opera*, VI, p. 242). Acosta (*Natural*, p. 44) quotes Isaiah 18, 1, saying, 'Many learned Authors hold that al this Chapter is understood of the Indies.' Acosta's chapters 13 and 14 are devoted to identifying Ophir and Tharsis.

[3] In his account of Japanese history in Chapter 11, Rodrigues dates the collapse of central government and the outbreak of civil wars as 1340 (see p. 130), when the shogun Ashikaga Takauji (1305–58) brought about the 60-year schism in imperial rule.

not sailed to other parts and believed that the entire world was divided into three parts, or *sangoku* – Tenjiku, Shintan, and Nippon – that is, India (whence came the sects), China (with which they were in contact and in which were included Korea and Tartary, both subject to China), and in the third place Japan. They did not believe that there was anything else in the world beyond these.[1]

---

[1] *Sangoku* means 'three countries' (see p. 59). For Tenjiku, see p. 17; Shintan, p. 24, n. 3; Nippon (or Nihon), p. 45. *Vocabulario* (f. 218) lists the three countries as China, Siam, and Japan. For the identification of Tenjiku with Siam, see p. 19, n. 2.

CHAPTER 5

A SPECIFIC DESCRIPTION OF SOME OF THE PRINCIPAL ISLANDS OF JAPAN, AND THEIR DIVISION INTO REGIONS

It is generally affirmed that the kingdom of Japan is made up of […] thousand islands, but there are eight principal ones into which the whole realm is divided and from which, as we have said, the kingdom takes its name of Yashima.[1] Three of these eight islands are larger than the others and are the principal ones, and in each one of them there are many kingdoms and states.[2] Each of the other five smaller ones make up one small kingdom. All the other innumerable smaller islands, most of which are inhabited, belong to a state on one of the eight islands and are regarded as part of them. Most of this multitude of small islands are situated in an archipelago or inland sea that lies between the three larger islands and has the general name of Seto-uchi.[3] Among the innumerable small islands belonging to the above-mentioned eight large ones, there are many of moderate size, and these are states of particular lords, such as, for example, Hirado, Gotō, Amakusa, Koshiki, Tanegashima, Yokonoshima, Bizen-no-Kojima, Shōdoshima, Yashima, and many others.[4]

The first island is the largest of the three principal ones. On account of its size it may

---

[1] There is a blank before 'thousand' in the Portuguese text, but Japan is sometimes said to be made up of 4,000 islands. For previous references to Yashima, or 'Eight Islands', as a name for Japan, see p. 44.

[2] Rodrigues would have read a comparison in Lucena, *Historia*, pp. 466–7, where the author notes that just as the British Isles, as well as having two large islands, England and Ireland, has also many other smaller ones, such as the Hebrides and Orkneys, so Japan as well is made up of three big islands and many small ones. The three large islands are now called Honshu, Kyushu, and Shikoku; as already noted, Ezo (Hokkaido) was not then considered an integral part of Japan.

The terms 'kingdoms and states' refer to the various fiefs throughout the country. Although their rulers enjoyed much independence within their domains, they were subservient to the Tokugawa shogunate in Edo, where they were obliged to reside periodically and leave their families as hostages. The term 'kingdom' was therefore not strictly correct, and this is noted by Martinho Hara, or Campo, one of the four delegates to Europe, in his marginal comments to Rodrigues's work *Bispos da Igreja de Japam* (Madrid, Jesuítas 7236, ff. 317–330v), which was to form part of the *History*. Regarding Rodrigues's reference to 'the kingdom of Bungo', Hara observes (f. 318, margin), 'For many reasons I approve of your calling the *yakata* "dukes", but to call the state of Bungo a "kingdom" seems to me to be an inexact European term. For a man is called king inasmuch as he is lord of a kingdom, but however large the states of dukes, they are not called kingdoms but duchies. And so it seems to me better to seek another and more appropriate term.' The Macao copyist seems to have incorporated into the text of the *History* various marginal comments written, perhaps by Hara, in the first person.

[3] Called the Inland Sea in English, the sea is now known as Seto-no-uchi (the Inland Sea of the Channels) in Japanese. About 240 miles long and 40 miles at its widest, the sea is studded with about 300 islands and is renowned for its scenic beauty.

[4] Rodrigues names these islands in anti-clockwise order, beginning with Hirado off the northwest coast of Kyushu and continuing down the west coast to Tanegashima; the last four islands are in the Inland Sea. The last-named island, or bunch of islands, Yashima ('Eight Islands') has the same name as ancient Japan, as mentioned at the beginning of this paragraph.

properly said to be Japan, or Ten'enshi, and also because in the middle of it, as the centre of the kingdom, is situated the Miyako court of the true, proper, and indigenous king and lord of Japan. Its proper name is Tsukushi, but this is not commonly used.[1] Its length begins in the west at 155° of longitude at the most westernly point of the kingdom of Nagato, and then continues eastwards along the parallel of 35°N, finishing at the eastern beach of the kingdom of Hitachi at 168° of longitude. Its latitude begins in the south at 22½°N at Kumano, the most southernly point of the kingdom of Kino in the state of Kinokuni. It ends in the kingdom of Ōshū, the most northernly part of the state of Tsugaru, at 42½°N at Cape Tappizaki, facing the island of Ezo. The island is of considerable size, for it has 13° of longitude and 10° of latitude.[2] These islands are divided into eight provinces or parts, each of which is made up of many kingdoms or states.[3]

The first of these states is in the middle part of the large island and is called by various names according to circumstances. The first name is Kami, which means above, high, head, upper part, and is thus used in contrast to the other parts of the kingdom. Anyone going thence to these other parts is said to be going down to such-and-such a place, but if he goes thither from these places, then he is said to go up to Kami, or Miyako, for the court of the kingdom of Japan is situated there. In common parlance it is known as Miyako, but in Chinese literary language as Kyō, which the Chinese pronounce as Jing. This is the capital, the centre, the middle of the whole kingdom.[4]

Secondly, the region is also called Kinai, or Ki, or Kii, meaning royal province and central kingdom, for the court is located there. It is also known as Gokinai, that is, the five royal central kingdoms, because it is divided into five states. Its third name is Tenka, meaning empire or monarchy of the Japanese domain, because the king's government of the whole of Japan is situated there. Tenka also means the world, or the monarchy of the world; in Chinese, it is Tianxia.[5] Even in present times, now that the military lords have usurped the royal government, he who rules that region is said to rule Tenka and has the command, rule,

---

[1] The largest island is now known as Honshu or Hondo. Rodrigues errs in calling it Tsukushi, as this was the former name of Kyushu, as he correctly states on p. 44, n. 4, and p. 69. The identification of the term 'Ten'enshi' is unclear. Rodrigues, *Nihon*, I, p. 194, n. 3, suggests that it is a slip for Tsukushi, but this seems unlikely in the context. The 'true, proper, and indigenous king and lord of Japan' refers to the emperor, as opposed to the shogun, the de facto ruler residing in Edo.

[2] Honshu extends from 130°53′ to 142°03′E, and 33°28′ to 41°31′N. In the text the position of Kumano is given as 22½°N, but this is an obvious slip for 32½°, otherwise the island would have 20° of latitude and not 10°, as Rodrigues states. Cape Tappizaki is almost the northernmost part of the island, but Oma Saki is 17′ further north. Later, in Book 2, Chapter 14, Rodrigues gives different figures – see p. 383.

[3] There is a gap in the text where the number of provinces should have been given; I have added 'eight', which Rodrigues gives later on p. 79.

[4] For the meaning of the term *kami*, see p. 44, n. 6. Miyako, now called Kyoto, was the capital from 794 to 1868. *Kyō* in Japanese (in Chinese, *jing*) merely means capital; hence Tokyo, Eastern Capital, and Beijing, Northern Capital.

[5] Tenka (written consistently and erroneously as Tença throughout the text) means 'Below Heaven' and reflects a Chinese concept. The term is used extensively in Jesuit accounts, and refers either to the central provinces, or, by extension, to the whole country: *Vocabulario*, f. 254: '*Tenka*. Monarchy or empire.' Rodrigues notes (p. 384) that the Chinese would laugh when they heard the Japanese use the term in reference to Japan. He makes a similar remark in *Arte breve*, f. 83: 'The king of Japan has various names … some mean King, while others mean Emperor or Universal Monarchy (as is the case in China, whence the Japanese have taken these names along with their letters). The kings of Japan use the title of Emperor, but the Chinese laugh about this because the king of Japan is not an emperor.'

and sovereignty of the whole country. Usually he is called the Lord of Tenka, or shogun, or kubō, and he is the commander-in-chief of the kingdom.[1]

The other three parts or regions of this big island also have their own names in respect to this central part. One of them lies to the east of Kami and another to the west. Some three leagues east of the city of Miyako, in the town of Ōtsu on the boundaries of the kingdom of Ōmi and Yamashiro, there are some gates, pass, or customs barrier called Ōsaka-no-seki, and the two principal regions already mentioned begin at this pass. The one that begins to the east of this pass and extends to the end of the island is called Kantō, or Seki-no-higashi, that is, the eastern gate, or the gate towards the east. It is also called Bandō, from the *saka* or ascent towards the east. Hence it is named after the exit or tollgate, because *ban* is *saka*, *kan* is *seki*, *tō* or *dō* is *higashi*, that is, *saka-no-higashi*.[2] Within this Bandō or Kantō there is a part called Tōhasshū. The common people erroneously call this region, or eight kingdoms, Kantō or Bandō (and not Bandeu as in our books), and its name means the Eight Eastern Kingdoms or the Eight Kingdoms of the East, for they are the most easterly of the largest island.[3]

The second region beginning from this barrier or gate stretches to the west as far as Gotō or Satsuma, and is known as Kansai, that is, Seki-no-nishi. The principal part of this region is called Chūgoku and contains sixteen kingdoms. Chūgoku means 'central kingdom' in respect to the second of the three large islands. In relation to this part, this second island is situated to the west and is accordingly known as Saikoku, that is, 'western kingdom'. The city of Yamaguchi, in the kingdom of Suwo, is situated in this Chūgoku. It was the capital of the region and flourished mightily when the Blessed Father Francis arrived in Japan.[4] The third region lies to the north of Kami and is made up of seven kingdoms. It is called Hokkoku, or 'northern kingdom'.[5]

The second of these large islands is in the western sea of Japan and for this reason is called Saikoku, or 'western kingdom'. The island has its own name of Tsukushi and is also known as Kyushu, that is, 'nine kingdoms', for it is divided into that number. Some people have erroneously called it Shimo in the Society's letters and annual reports. This means the lower parts towards the south, or below in relation to the region of Kami, for it is the

---

[1] Valignano (*Principio*, f. 16) makes the same observation: 'He who makes himself king of Gokinai becomes king of Tenka.' The full title of shogun was Sei-i-tai-shōgun, 'Barbarian-Subduing Great General', and the office was created in 720 to drive out the Ebisu, or aborigines, from the centre of the country. In *Arte breve*, f. 82v, Rodrigues erroneously states that the title of shogun dates from 87 BC, but he is referring to the four generals who pacified savage tribes in that year on the emperor's orders (*Nihongi*, I, p. 160). The title was eventually made hereditary and the shogun wrested all effective power from the emperor, as Rodrigues later relates, pp. 130–31. The last shogun, Tokugawa Yoshinobu, ceded authority back to the emperor in 1868. The holder of the office had to belong to the ancient Minamoto clan, so neither Oda Nobunaga nor Toyotomi Hideyoshi could claim the title. Kubō was an honorific title applied to the shogun.

[2] A reference to the barrier at Ōsaka was made as early as the 10th century in the poetry anthology *Kokinshū*. As Rodrigues notes, this barrier was not in the famous city of Osaka, but at a place of the same name (now in Ōtsu, Shiga prefecture). In the Tokugawa age barrier gates, or *sekisho*, controlled inland traffic at strategic places. See Vaporis, *Breaking Barriers*, chapter 3 and 4, for details of examinations, passes, exemptions, etc.

[3] In the maps of Magini (*Geographia*, f. 251v) and Ortelius (Cortazzi, *Isles*, p. 81), the name of the region is written as Bandu; Bandou is also found in Ruiz-de-Medina, *Documentos*, II, p. 184, and Guzman, *Historia*, I, p. 398. Xavier (*Epistolae*, II, pp. 208, 274, 298) writes Bandu, Bandou, and Bando. The Tōhasshū, or Eight Eastern Provinces, were Musashi, Awa, Kazusa, Shimōsa, Shimotsuke, Hitachi, Kozuke, and Sagami. All these provinces lay to the east of the Hakone barrier.

[4] For Xavier's stays in Yamaguchi in 1550 and 1551, see the references in p. 56, n. 4.

[5] The Portuguese text adds at this point, 'porque, Focen, 2° Norte, e focnto, estrella de norte', a corrupt phrase that defies translation. The North Star in Japanese is *hokkyoku-sei*.

most southerly part of Japan. But this is false and incorrect, because not only this region but everywhere in Japan, as we have said, is Shimo in respect to Kami.[1] The latitude and breadth of this second island begins at 30½°N at the most southernly point of Satsuma called Bo-no-Misaki, or Cape of Port Bo. It ends in the kingdom of Buzen at the promontory or cape called Moji facing Shimonseki at 34½°N, where it is separated from the large island by a very narrow strait only as wide as a musket shot. Its longitude begins at 154° and finishes at 155½° in the kingdom of Bungo, where it is separated from the third island by a strait nearly ten miles wide.[2]

The third of the three islands is called Shikoku, that is, 'four kingdoms', because it is divided into this number. It is long and narrow, and lies in an east-northeast direction. Its latitude begins at 32½°N and finishes at 34⅔°N, while its longitude extends from 155⅔° to 161° in the kingdom of Awa, which faces the kingdom of Kinokuni on the big island, from which it is separated by a strait fifteen miles wide.[3]

These three large islands are so located that they form a very great inland sea, with a bay that reaches to the cities of Sakai and Osaka, where the River Yodo flows into it. There is a lake called Ōmi-no-mizumi, or fresh-water sea,[4] in the kingdom of Ōmi, and this river flows from the lake into the inland sea, which is called Seto-uchi. The sea is connected to the ocean by three entrances or straits. The first is a wide strait between the big island and Shikoku, the third island, through which the sea flows up to the town and port of Tomo. The second is the gap between the second island and the third at that part of Bungo that looks on to Tosa. The sea flows through here and again reaches as far as the town of Tomo, and one sea meets the other at this place. Thus a ship sails from Kami with the high tide and there catches the opposite ebb tide of the other sea, and so uses two adjacent tides. The same applies to ships sailing from Saikoku to Kami. The third mouth is the strait between the second island and the large one at Shimonoseki.[5]

Each of the other five smaller islands among the eight that we mentioned contains one kingdom. They are as follows:

1. Sado.
2. Oki, situated in the sea to the north of the big island.
3. Awaji, at the most northernly point of the island of Shikoku in the inland sea that we mentioned.
4. Iki, between Hirado and
5. Tushima.

---

[1] Although possibly correct, Rodrigues is somewhat pedantic for, as he says, most of the early Europeans referred to Kyushu as Shimo; e.g., Valignano, *Principio*, f. 16; Avila Girón, *Relación*, p. 13; Magini, *Geographia*, f. 268. Lourenço Mexia (Funai, 20 October 1580, in *Cartas*, I, f. 460v) elaborates that although Kyushu was generally called Shimo, the Jesuits often meant by Shimo only the parts of the island to which the Portuguese ships came (e.g., Hizen, Amakusa, etc).

[2] Kyushu extends from 31° to 33°57′N and, as regards the mainland, from 129°34′ to 132°E. Bo-no-Misaki (31°16′N) is not quite the southernmost point, but Sata Misaki is. The strait between Honshu and Kyushu is indeed narrow, but it would require a good musket shot to span it. Bungo Channel between Kyushu and Shikoku is about 10 miles wide at its narrowest.

[3] The mainland of the third island, Shikoku, extends from 32°42′ to 34°20′N, and from 132° to 134°40′E. The Kii Channel separating Shikoku from Kyushu is about 20 miles in width.

[4] Usually called Lake Biwa in English because its shape resembles the *biwa* musical instrument. It is the largest lake in Japan. See pp. 89–90.

[5] These three straits are Kii Channel, Bungo Strait, and Shimonoseki Strait.

These last two islands are in the western sea between the second large island and the kingdom of Korea. Tsushima used to belong to Korea and is only fifteen miles distant from it; it is in fact nearer Korea than Japan. It is populated by Japanese with their own ruling *yakata*. It is a goodly duchy, and trade between Japan and Korea is maintained through this island.[1]

Various authors have written about the size and description of Japan. Some make it much longer than it really is, while others make it shorter. All this is due to guesswork and lack of true information, but what we have written is quite certain and true, and most diligently checked. Taikō, also known as Kampaku, ordered in his time that a description should be made of each state and kingdom. Daifu did the same and ordered that each one should make its own. We saw all this, and from that source we have taken many things that are now true.[2]

Beginning at the most southerly point of Satsuma at 30½°N and ending at the northernmost point at 42½°N, the length of this whole kingdom or islands works out at 26°. That is, Kyushu, the second island, has 4° of latitude, and borders the kingdom of Nagato at the beginning of the first island, the largest of them all. The first[3] island has 13° of longitude and this length ends in Kantō. It measures 9° from north to south, beginning at 33½°N in the kingdom of Awa and ending in the north at 42½°N. So in all we make the length of the kingdom 26°, indeed a very large kingdom as we have said.[4]

In the south of Japan there is a string or multitude of islands, islets, and shoals beginning in the sea to the south of Satsuma and almost continuous towards the west from one to another. From Satsuma they go from island to island until the Seven Islands,[5] and from there to the Great Luchu. To the south of this there are many other continuous islands, all of which are called Luchu.[6] I have seen and been on some of them, and on the feast of St Lucy I was on one of them and we called it the island of St Lucy.[7] They have many good qualities, and the same may be said about the trustworthy people who came here. From

---

[1] Tsushima is some 30 miles from Korea and about 48 miles from Kyushu. The term *yakata* originally referred to a palace or mansion, and later by extension to a noble dwelling therein. Pedro Morejon (in *TCJ*, p. 26) describes them as 'senior officers of the shogun's council', who later became absolute lords in their own domains and no longer recognized the shogun's authority. See Valignano, *Sumario*, p. 12, n. 50.

[2] Taikō, or Kampaku, refers to Hideyoshi; for his ambitious land survey beginning in 1582 and continuing to his death in 1598, see Berry, *Hideyoshi*, pp. 111–26. *Daifu* was the title taken by Ieyasu on his retirement from the office of shogun in 1605.

[3] The text erroneously has 'second' written here, when it is obvious that the reference is to Honshu, the first island.

[4] Rodrigues arrives at this figure of 26° by measuring an imaginary line running south-north up Kyushu, then west-east and then south-north through Honshu up to the northern tip of the island; thus, 4 + 13 + 9 = 26. According to Valignano (*Principio*, ff. 12v–14v), the length of the country from the southern tip of Satsuma to the northern tip of Honshu was 400 Portuguese leagues.

[5] The seven islands, or Shichi-tō, are situated between 29° and 30°N, and in a broad sense may be included within the Ryūkyū Chain. For their position, see Chamberlain, 'Luchu Islands', p. 408. They are sometimes called the Linschoten Islands in European maps. Ibid., p. 292.

[6] The Luchu (or Ryūkyū) Islands are a chain formed by three large islands, Okinawa (Great Luchu), Miyako, and Yaeyama, and some 50 smaller islands, stretching 675 miles in an arc between 26° and 28°50′N. In the loose sense, the Luchus embrace all the islands from Japan to Formosa (present-day Taiwan); in the strict sense, they consist of the Great Luchu and its surrounding islands. Chamberlain ('Luchu Islands', pp. 290, 408) divides the chain into six different groups of islands. *KEJ*, VI, p. 357. For early European maps of the islands, see Kreiner, 'European Maps'.

[7] The feast of St Lucy falls on 13 December, but I do not know in which year Rodrigues made this visit. It is also impossible to determine to which island he is referring as the name does not appear in contemporaneous European maps, some of which show islands called St Maria and St Clara, whose feastday is 12 August.

Luchu one goes to the Small Luchu and the island of Formosa, and thence to Manila. The chain then continues with the Moluccan archipelago, the Papuas, New Guinea, Borneo, the Javas, Sumatra, and all the other islands of the southern Indian Sea.[1] Whence we may guess that all this was a continent at the beginning, but was divided into islands by the Flood, with the Japanese islands forming the end and limit, as it were, of all the islands in the Orient.

There are other islands also belonging to those of Japan; they are independent, yet owe allegiance to Japan. Such are, firstly, the islands of the Great Luchu (or Ryūkyū, as the Japanese say), whose kings are said to be originally Japanese from the stock of the family of a commander-in-chief or high constable of Japan called Heike.[2] For the most part the natives use the same Japanese tongue, albeit somewhat debased, the *kana* letters of Japan, Japanese songs and music, and many Japanese customs.[3] They are a hundred leagues to the west of the kingdom of Satsuma and they pay tribute to this kingdom.[4] But they possess many other different things, and at the same time they are in contact with China and owe allegiance to that country, whither they have gone in embassy up to now every three years through Fujian province, which faces them on the west.[5] They are situated at 27°N.

In the Kantō sea in the south there are also some islands of people originally Japanese who have their own ruler, a vassal of Japan. One of these islands is called Miyake-no-shima, and the name of the principal one is Hachijō. Spanish ships pass by it on their way from Manila to New Spain, and the Spaniards call it the Volcanos or Island of Fire, for there is a high mountain there that continually throws up fire and smoke.[6] I was in Suruga in Kantō

---

[1] Avila Girón (*Relación*, p. 13) also mentions this chain of islands, remarking that it is possible to sail from Japan to Manila, and sleep on terra firma every night during the voyage.

[2] A reference to the famous Heike (also known as Taira) clan that wielded much authority until its defeat by the Genji (or Minamoto) family in the 12th century; Rodrigues mentions the rivalry between the two clans on p. 130. According to legend, a member of the Minamoto (and not Heike) clan, Tametomo (1139–70), was the progenitor of the Luchu royal line: Chamberlain, 'Luchu Islands', p. 306.

[3] The Ryūkyū dialects are mutually incomprehensible and, although closely related to the Japanese language, are unintelligible to Japanese on the main islands: *KEJ*, VI, pp. 355–7; Hattori, 'Relationship'. Writing from Ōshima in the Luchu Islands, Richard Wickham (23 December 1614, in Farrington, *English Factory*, I, p. 274) notes that the natives 'speak the Japan toungue, although with difficulty to be understood of the Japons. They wear [their] hare longe, bownd upp like the Chines, with a bodkin thrust through, but it is made up on the right side of theyre heades, & are a very gentle and curteous people'. William Adams sailed twice to the Luchu Islands (1614–15 and 1619) and includes in his log a sketch of a volcano seen on 22 December 1614: Adams, *Log-Book*, pp. 6–8, 59. For an early European account (1512), see Pires, *Suma oriental*, I, pp. 128–31. A catalogue of European references to the islands is given in Schurhammer, 'Descobrimento', pp. 510–19.

[4] Relations between the Japanese and the Luchuans began in the 7th century, and from the 15th century the islanders sent periodic embassies to Japan. In 1609 Shimazu Iehisa (1576–1638) of Satsuma invaded the islands and annexed the Ōshima (or Small Luchu) group: Chamberlain, *Luchu Islands*, pp. 304–16; Totman, *Tokugawa Ieyasu*, pp. 95–7. Writing to Sir Thomas Smythe in October 1614, Richard Wickham notes (Farrington, *English Factory*, I, p. 327): 'A peaceable & quiet people but of late yeares conquered by Ximus [Shimazu] Dono, King of Satchma [Satsuma], soe that now they are governed by the Japon lawes & customes, by which meanes they have lost theyre trade & priviledges in China.' Another account of the Japanese invasion is given by Rodrigues Giram, Nagasaki, 15 March 1610 (JapSin 56, f. 166).

[5] There is a reference to a Chinese army invading the islands as early as 611, and the hapless Luchuans were at times obliged to pay tribute to both Japan and China. On one occasion, envoys sent to Japan pleaded that while Japan was their father, China was their mother: Chamberlain, *Luchu Islands*, pp. 304, 314. Rada reports (in Boxer, *South China*, p. 303) seeing men from the Luchus who had come to China to pay tribute.

[6] These are the seven volcanic islands of Izu, situated off the east coast of Honshu, and while this note was being revised (September 2000) Mt Ōyama on Miyake Island was violently erupting, forcing the evacuation of the local population. Ōshima, nearest the mainland, is about 12 miles east of the Izu Peninsula and 65 miles southwest of Tokyo: *KEJ*, VI, p. 125. The volcanic Mt Mihara on Ōshima still gives off much smoke, while Hachijōjima has two

in the year 1608 when the ruler of the island came there to visit the Shogun.[1] One side of the mountain exploded with the force of the fire, and molten metal flowed from it like iron slag. When this flowed into the sea, it formed quite a large port on this island, which had lacked a port until this time.[2] This island produces a silk with which they weave striped lengths like taffeta, and they bring this to sell in Japan.[3] They exiled thither Bizen-no-Chūnagon, and there he remains. Nobody can go there or leave more than once a year for lack of winds, and it is impossible to row there on account of the strong currents.[4]

To the south of this island, in the South Sea as it is called, there are some islands that the Portuguese called the Islands of Sails. They were later called the Islands of Robbers by the Spaniards, who in their ships passed between them on their way from New Spain to Manila. For their inhabitants are very cunning, subtle, and bold in robbing the Spaniards of various things, such as metal barrel hoops and other things that they hand down to them in exchange for fish, and they make off with what they give them. There are thirteen of these islands, some of them lying north and south, while others are to the south of Japan at the end of the large island at about 167° or 168° of longitude.[5] It is probable that they were populated from Japan, for they continue northwards with the island of Hachijō, which is at 30°N. There does not seem to have been any nearer place than Japan from which they could have been populated, and from which not only people but deer and other animals living there could have passed over. It is impossible to accept the view of some people who say

---

extinct volcanoes that may have been active in the 17th century. Several early European maps (e.g., Ortelius, in Cortazzi, *Islands*, pp. 79, 81, 83, 86, and Mercator, *Atlas*, pp. 417–18) show the 'Islands of Fire' or 'Volcanoes' to the east of Japan. See n. 4, below, for Hachijōjima as a place of exile.

[1] Ieyasu retired from the office of shogun in 1605 in favour of his son Hidetada to keep the office in the Tokugawa family, and in 1607 took up residence in Suruga (now Shizuoka). In 1608 Hidetada visited his father there from 27 September to 12 October, and it may have been at that time that the island ruler and Rodrigues were both at the Suruga court: *Tokugawa Jikki*. I, pp. 465, 468. Most likely, Rodrigues is referring to Ieyasu when he mentions the shogun, for despite his retirement Ieyasu continued to be ruler of Japan in everything but name. Vivero y Velasco (*Relación*, f. 5v) comments that Hidetada did not dare to do anything without consulting his father. For the relations between the father and son, see Totman, *Tokugawa Iyasu*, pp. 92–3, 98.

[2] According to *Tokugawa Jikki*, I, p. 400, there was a volcanic eruption near Hachijōjima on 15 December 1605. In the Portuguese text it is possible to read 1605 as well as 1608 as the last digit is not written clearly. But obviously the eruption had taken place some time before Rodrigues's visit to Suruga in 1608.

[3] Hachijō still produces a special type of cloth called *kihachijō*. *KEJ*, III, p. 74.

[4] A reference to Ukita Hideie (1572–1655), ruler of Bizen and a staunch Toyotomi supporter, who was banished by Ieyasu to Hachijōjima in 1603 and there remained until his death. Chūnagon was originally a court title, and Rodrigues explains (*Arte grande*, f. 209v) that the 20 most noble rulers were not called Kami, but instead added another title to the name of their domain, such as Bizen-no-Chūnagon. In the Portuguese text, the copyist, thinking that Rodrigues was referring to two exiled men, wrote 'Bigeno *and* Chūnangon, and there *they* remain.' Ukita is often mentioned in Jesuit records (e.g., in the 1600 Annual Letter, in Ajuda, 49–IV–59, ff. 8, 44v, 57v, etc.), and his wife was secretly baptized as Maria (ibid., f. 437v). For the life of Ukita, see *KEJ*, VIII, pp. 137–8. Hachijōjima was used as a place of exile, for it was remote, yet near enough to Edo for the Tokugawa authorities to keep an eye on the exiles. For an interesting description by Ernest Satow, who visited the island in 1878, see Murdoch, *History 1542–1641*, p. 432, n. 2; also Caron, *True Description*, pp. 40–41.

[5] These are the Velas, Ladrones, or Marianas Islands (12° to 21°N, 144° to 145°E), discovered by Ferdinand Magellen in 1521. Early accounts are given in Pigafetta, *Magellan's Voyage*, I, pp. 91–9; Markham, *Early Spanish Voyages*, pp. 50–51, 114. Rodrigues seems to have taken his description of the islands from Mendoza (*History*, II, pp. 253–7, first published in 1585), although according to Mendoza there were only seven or eight islands. Mendoza (Ibid., II, pp. 256–7) provides an example of the natives' cunning in stealing iron (which they prized more than gold), adding that they were 'very bolde and subtile in their stealinges, in the which facultie the Egyptians, that are in our Europa, may go to schoole with them for the verie facultie thereof'.

without any foundation that the islands were populated by the Tartars, because they live so far away and Japan lies between Tartary and these islands. The islands are inhabited by white people with pleasing features. Both men and women are very strong, and all of them go about naked without any clothes, although a few women wear deer skins tied around the waist. For weapons they use slings and fire-hardened poles that they throw very skilfully. They eat fish, wild animals, and some vegetables that they sow in the soil.[1]

In the year 1529 various representatives of Emperor Charles V and King John III of Portugal met in the city of Saragossa to discuss the trade and boundary limits concerning the Moluccan islands. They agreed that King John should pay the Emperor 350,000 gold and silver crowns, and in return the Emperor conceded to the King and his successors to the crown of his kingdoms, all right, action, dominion, ownership and possession, or quasi-possession, and all rights of navigation, traffic, and trade in any manner whatsoever, that the Emperor and King of Castile declared that he held and could hold in the Moluccas, its places, lands, and seas. It was further agreed that in whatsoever time the Emperor and his successors returned the said sum, each party would then possess the same rights as before. In order to clarify the division of trade, a line had to be determined from pole to pole by a semicircle extending northeast by east 19° from Molucca, to which number of degrees corresponded about 17° on the equinoctial, amounting to 297½ leagues from Molucca, allowing 17½ leagues to an equinoctial degree. In this northeast by east meridian and direction were situated the Islands of Sails, through which the said line and semicircle passes. As the said islands were more or less the said distance from Molucca, it was nevertheless agreed that the said line be drawn at the said 297½ leagues to the east of Molucca.

All this accords with the letter of the original agreement made at that time, and Diogo do Couto relates this *ad litteram* in his *Década quarta* of the history of India.[2] The above is recorded here as it is highly relevant to the briefs and privileges that the Pope granted to the trade of the Portuguese crown in Oriental India. For it may be seen that Japan falls completely within its area and that the privileges of the kingdom and crown of Portugal still hold good and are valid, in keeping with the agreement made by the kingdom with His Majesty when he assumed possession of the kingdom. Now this Church of Japan was within this possession many years before the Spaniards and other religious arrived there. This is why we mention the matter here.[3]

---

[1] None of the authors cited on p. 73, n. 5, mentions that the islands were populated by Tartars, although Mendoza remarks that the natives bought iron to sell to the Tartars. Along with other writers, Mendoza (*History*, II, p. 254) notes the natives' pleasing features, their white skins, their strength ('bigge as gyants' and capable of lifting two Spaniards off their feet), their nakedness ('yet some of them were woont to weare an aporne [sic] made of a deares skinne before them … for honesties sake'), their slings and fire-hardened staves, their diet of fish and wild animals.

[2] As Rodrigues says, this account is to be found in Couto, *Década quarta*, 7, 1 (ff. 122v–4v), although there are five or six differences or omissions in the wording. For the official text of the part of the treaty quoted by Rodrigues, see Davenport, *European Treaties*, I, p. 173 (English translation, ibid., I, p. 188). For the background of the Treaty of Saragossa, see Davenport, *European Treaties*, I, pp. 146–8; Lach, *Asia*, I, pp. 114–18.

[3] This is the only reference in the *History* to the unhappy Jesuit-Franciscan controversy in Japan. In January 1585 Gregory XIII issued the brief *Ex Pastorali Officio* (text in Magnino, *Pontificia*, I, pp. 26–7), reserving the Japanese mission for the Jesuit order, but the Franciscans in the Philippines had in their favour a brief of Sixtus V, 1586 (Ibid., I, p. 37). The Jesuit case is argued by Valignano in *Sumario*, Chapter 9, pp. 143–9, while Ribadeneira (*Historia*, pp. 331–4) and Alvarez-Taladriz, *San Martín*, present the Franciscan case. As Rodrigues's remarks indicate, the cause of the controversy was partly nationalistic, and in fact some Spanish Jesuits, such as Pedro de Cruz (25 October 1593, in JapSin, 12, ff. 108–11, and 22 February 1599, in ibid., 13, f. 288) favoured the Franciscan cause. For summary of

Ezo, the island of the Tartars, partly belongs to Japan for the Duke of Tsugaru owns a part of it, and also there are two Japanese settlements with their own Japanese ruler who possesses them in subjection to the Duke of Tsugaru. The holy martyrs de Angelis and Diogo Carvalho went there and described the island.[1] It is a large island and according to the description given by the native Tartar inhabitants it is as big as or even bigger than the second of the three big islands of Japan. It lies from east to west and is some fifteen miles distant from Japan. A narrow sea separates it from Tartary, which is visible from the northern part of the island. People go there by sea from various parts of Japan in order to trade, sailing the sea north of Japan from Chūgoku and Hokkoku. Some Christians from Japan have settled on the island, and for this reason Fr Jerónimo de Angelis went there in that year[2] and afterwards Fr Diogo Carvalho. We mention their reports here, for we shall make use of them.

---

this sorry affair, see Cooper, *Rodrigues the Interpreter*, pp. 120–25. In his *Bispos de Igreja do Japão*, Rodrigues argues at some length that Japan fell within the Portuguese zone of influence.

[1] For early European reports about Ezo, present-day Hokkaido, see p. 29, n. 8. Tsugaru was the northernmost part of Honshu and the nearest point to Ezo. Jerónimo de Angelis, 1568–1623, was a Sicilian Jesuit who reached Japan in 1602, entered Ezo in 1618, and died at the stake in Edo. Cieslik, *Hoku-hō*, pp. 4–14, and 'Great Martyrdom', pp. 1–6. Diogo Carvalho, 1577–1624, a Portuguese Jesuit, reached Japan in 1609, was exiled in 1614 but secretly returned two years later, visited Ezo in 1620, and was martyred in freezing water in Sendai. Cieslik, *Hoku-hō*, pp. 14–22. For their accounts of Ezo, see ibid., pp. (3)–(42); partial translation in *TCJ*, pp. 289–90.

[2] By 'that year', Rodrigues must mean 1618.

CHAPTER 6

THE DIVISION OF JAPAN INTO PROVINCES, KINGDOMS, OR STATES, AND SOME OF THE MORE NOTABLE MOUNTAINS, RIVERS, AND LAKES THEREIN

Along with adopting the use of Chinese writing, all these nations grouped around China have also taken over many civil customs, the division in the courts of nobility, the ranks within the royal household; the robes and ceremonies employed by the king and grandees of the kingdom; the way of dividing the land into provinces, kingdoms, and states; the manner of measuring the lands in respect to the rents that are collected therefrom; linear measurements and distances, and many other things of this sort.

Each of the countries adapted these things to its particular kingdom. In all cases the Chinese way in these matters is generally followed, but it is adapted and modified in keeping with the particular kingdom. For example, the Koreans, first of all, imitate the Chinese in everything and have adopted even the literary degrees of baccalaurate, licentiate, and doctorate.[1] This is because they live very close to China and have had a great deal of contact since the most ancient times, and their first kings came from China. The same is true of the inhabitants of the kingdom of Cauchi, or Jiaozhi, which is now called Annam. In former times it used to be a Chinese province, governed by Chinese magistrates just as were the other provinces, Europeans accordingly called the place Cauchi-China, that is, Cauchi of China.[2] This kingdom of Japan is also one of the principal countries to have adopted Chinese writing, civil customs, the partition of the country into provinces, kingdoms, or states, and the division of farmland into yokes and other agricultural measures. All this was taken from China, as their records confirm.[3]

In ancient times the Chinese divided their kingdom in two ways. The first division concerned the civil government and was into provinces, which they call *dao* (in Japanese, *dō*), meaning 'road'. These provinces were then divided into smaller states called *guo*, that is,

---

[1] The Chinese examination system was introduced in Korea about 798, but was not nearly so stringent as that of China, for cheating was both common and easy: Hulbert, 'National Examination', pp. 9–32.

[2] I.e. Cochin-China or Assam in southern Vietnam. In 1400 there was a revolution against the Annam monarchy, which appealed to China for aid; as a result, Ming forces entered the country on 1407 and took Hanoi. Because the Chinese tried to force their language and culture on the people, guerrilla warfare broke out, and in 1428 an independent Annam dynasty was set up. To appease the Chinese, the new king sent ambassadors with tokens of submission and agreed to a nominal dependence on China: D. G. Hall, *History*, pp. 173–4. For the origin of the Chinese name Chiao-chih (a phonetic transcription of a native term), see Aurousseau, 'Sur le nom', pp. 567–9. See also Yule, *Hobson-Jobson*, s.v. Cochin-China.

[3] For the introduction of Chinese writing into Japan, see p. 47, n. 1. Under Emperor Kōtoku (645–54) a reform edict was promulgated in 645–6, basing the administration of the country on Chinese principles and introducing or standardizing units of measurement. *Nihongi*, II, pp. 206–9; Sansom, *History to 1334*, pp. 57–9.

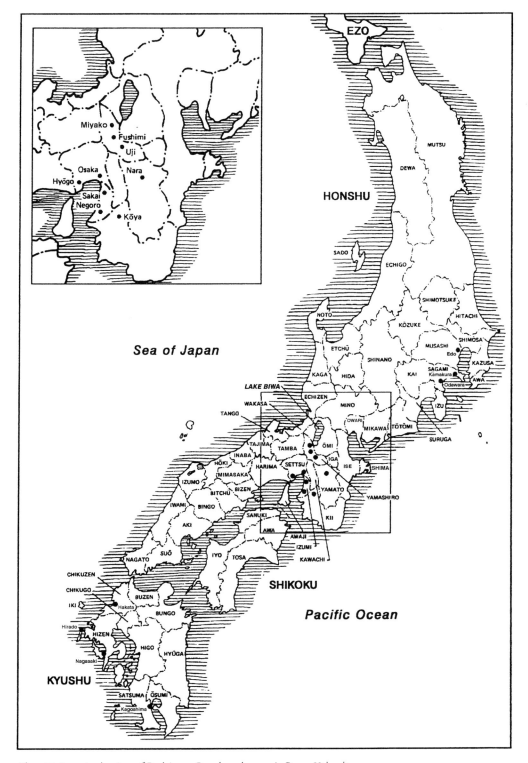

Plate 10: Japan in the time of Rodrigues. Based on the map in Berry, *Hideyoshi.*

'kingdom', or *zhou*, meaning the same, and *fu*, which also signifies the same and means a settlement. Now these *guo*, *zhou*, and *fu* are pronounced by the Japanese *kuni* or *koku* (in common speech, *kuni*), *shū*, and *fu*. Hence the capital of each state is called *funai* or *fuchū*, and in common speech *kō*, which means within or the middle of the state.[1] Then they divided these states or kingdoms into smaller parts, as we shall presently say. These are like regions, districts, and the areas of individual cities and towns. The other partition of the land was made in respect to the rents collected from them. They measured and divided them into certain areas like yokes and other smaller units of fixed measurement in order to know what each land yielded, and how much land each person possessed and ought to pay in rent. The Japanese imitated the Chinese and divided their kingdom in these two ways for the same reasons.

As regards the partition of these islands into kingdoms and provinces, there were in earliest times various estates of individual lords who populated them with their people. But all of them later came under the sway of only one leader or king, who in the course of time divided the whole of the kingdom into parts with boundaries. The first division that we know of was made in the Year of the Lord 590 when their 33rd king, called Sōjun Tennō, divided Japan into eight kingdoms or provinces called *dō*, that is, 'road'.[2] In the Year of the Lord 703 the 42nd king, Mommu Tennō, or Mombu Tennō, later divided the whole of Japan in imitation of China into the eight above-mentioned provinces and these into 66 kingdoms, state, principalities, or tetrarchies. There are now 68 of these states, for they later added the two islands of Iki and Tsushima.[3] Each of these states is called a kingdom and they are really 68 *fu*, as they call them in China. Hence each of these kingdoms of Japan has a metropolis or capital of the whole state called *fuchū* or *funai*, as, for example, the city of Funai in the kingdom of Bungo, for each kingdom has a *funai* or *fuchū* as its capital. The first bishop of Japan took his title from here and called himself Bishop of Funai, as the place possessed the largest gathering of Christians.[4] The same applies to the other kingdoms.

Each of these states or kingdoms has two names, both of which are much in use. One is the ordinary Japanese name found in maps and letters, and we write it in the first place

---

[1] Rodrigues repeats this information in greater detail in *Arte grande*, f. 120. *Vocabulario*, f. 105: '*Fuchū*. Inside the principal city of a particular region or province; the actual city.'

[2] Emperor Sōjun, or Sushun (523–92), ascended the throne in 587; he was the 32nd emperor, or 33rd if Jingō (who was only a regent) is included. During his reign weights and balances were imported from China: *Nihongi*, II, pp. 112–20. As regards the setting up of the eight *dō*, or circuits, Rodrigues adds (in *Arte breve*, f. 92v), 'Some say that this division was made by his predecessor, Yōmei Tennō [540–87].'

[3] Emperor Mommu (683–707) was, as Rodrigues states, the 42nd emperor. By the addition of Jingō as No. 15, the list of emperors in *Arte grande*, f. 236v, differs from modern catalogues. But at the 39th emperor Rodrigues's list comes back into step as he does not mention Kōbun (648–72), who reigned only eight months and was not added to the official list until 1870. By the reform of 645–6 (mentioned on p. 76, n. 3) Japan was divided into 54 provinces, or *kuni*, but under the Taihō Code, 702, there was a further division into provinces under governors (*kami*) and into districts (*gun* or *kōri*). The number of 66 provinces was probably established somewhat later. Sansom, *History to 1334*, pp. 68–9. Early European writers, including Rodrigues himself (in *Arte grande*, f. 210), invariably give the number of provinces as 66: Valignano, *Sumario*, p. 4; Vilela, 15 September 1565, in *Cartas*, I, f. 193; Fróis, in *TCJ*, p. 3.

[4] In 1588 Sixtus V raised the Japanese mission to the status of a diocese, with the bishop's seat at Funai in Bungo. The first three bishops were Sebastião de Morais (1534–89), Pedro Martins (d. 1598), and Luis de Cerqueira (1552–1614); the last-named arrived in Japan with Valignano in 1598 and died in Nagasaki: Rodrigues, *Obispos*, ff. 317–25v; Cieslik, 'Training', pp. 57–8.

below. The second name is Chinese or from Chinese letters, and always has the suffix -shū.[1] This name is always taken by the lord of such a kingdom without his actually owning the land. Or it may be taken by a person who possesses only the title of the said kingdom, as it is the custom of Japan for the Lord of Tenka to bestow the title of a kingdom on some nobles as an honorific name.[2] Each of these states or kingdoms is divided up into even smaller parts called *gun* or *kōri*, which are like regions, and these regions into other smaller parts that are like the areas of towns.[3]

The big island is divided into six provinces and these into fifty-two kingdoms or *fu*. The two islands of Sado and Iki are included in this total, each of them being a kingdom. Kyushu, the second island, makes up one province divided into eleven kingdoms, that is, nine on the actual island plus the two islands of Iki and Tsushima, each making up a state. The third island, Shikoku, is also one province of five kingdoms, four on the island itself plus the island of Awaji, which is a kingdom. There is, therefore, a total of 68 kingdoms called *kuni*, *shū*, or *fu*; *kuni* is really a kingdom, *shū* is an area or circuit, and *fu* is a settlement.

One of the eight provinces is curial and the head of the whole kingdom, for Miyako, or Kyō, the court of the real king, is situated therein. The eight provinces are known by the general name of Gokyō shichidō; this means the five curial or court kingdoms making up the curial province, and the seven circuits or provinces. Six of these seven provinces border directly on to the curial province or one of its five states. The seventh is in the west and is situated in Kyushu, the second island. As it is in the western sea of Japan, it is separate and very remote from the curial province. The eighth province is in the third smaller island called Shikoku.[4]

I. A specific account of the six provinces of the large island, and in the first place the curial province and the names of its states

The first and principal province of the whole realm is the curial province called Kinai, that is, the Home Province, or Kii, Land of the Royal Crown, or Naichi, Within the Court. It is like the centre of the whole kingdom and is the curial province. It is also called Gokinai, that is, Five Kingdoms Within the Curial Province, as it contains that number.[5] Since the

---

[1] In *Arte grande*, f. 207v, Rodrigues explains that each province has two names. The first is the indigenous Japanese name with its *yomi* (now called *kun*) pronunciation (e.g., Yamato-no-kuni), while the second is Chinese, and is formed by taking the first syllable of the name, reading it according to the *koe* (now called *on*) pronunciation, and then adding the suffix -shū (e.g., Washū). For the difference between *koe* and *yomi* pronunciations, see p. 334, n. 2, and the *Advertencias* at the beginning of *Arte grande*, translated in *TCJ*, pp. 172–3.

[2] As Rodrigues points out (*Arte grande*, f. 209v), the names of the 66 provinces were used as honorific titles, although the bearer of such a title might not necessarily own or rule the province in question. The title was made up of the province's name, followed by Kami, or protector, although in three cases, the term Suke was used instead of Kami (e.g., Kōzuke-no-Suke).

[3] *Vocabulario*, ff. 123, 60v: 'Gun. A part or district of a kingdom. …' 'Kōri. A part of a kingdom like a district.' In *Arte grande*, ff. 210–11, Rodrigues lists 619 *gun*. Avila Girón, *Relación*, pp. 270–75, also lists the 66 'kingdoms' and the number of *gun* in each. As regards the 'other smaller parts', Rodrigues notes (*Arte breve*, f. 92v) that *gun* are subdivided into smaller units such as *shō*, *in*, and *ken*.

[4] Rodrigues's thought is expressed in a confused way here. He means that six of the seven non-curial circuits border directly on to the curial province; the seventh, San'kaidō, is in Kyushu and so does not border on it. Although the eighth circuit, Nankaidō, is in Shikoku, it possesses one province on the main island, and in this way borders on the curial province.

[5] The so-called Home Provinces were set up during reforms in the 7th century. Sansom, *History to 1334*, p. 57; map of these provinces in ibid., p. 103.

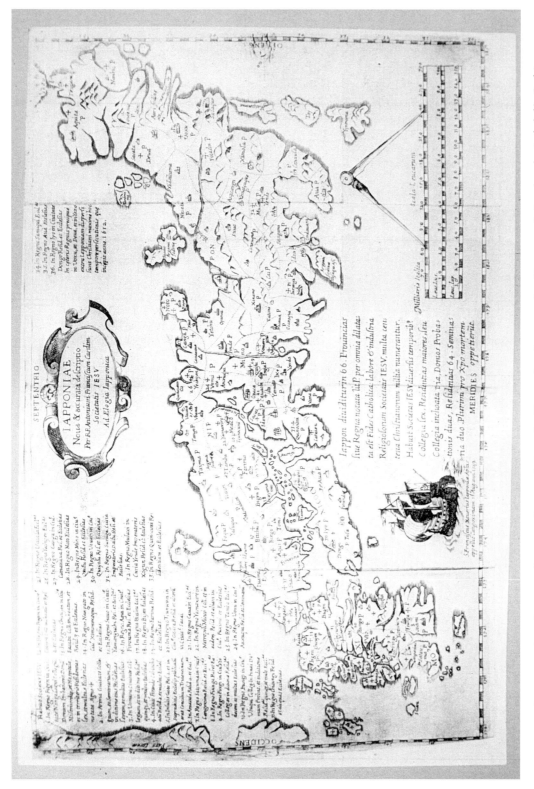

Plate II: Map of Japan in Cardim, *Elogios e Ramalhete*, 1650. Cortesão (in *Portugaliae*, V. pp. 118–19) suggests that this map may be based on that included by Rodrigues in his atlas of Asia (p. xxii). There is certainly a similarity between Cardim's map and Rodrigues's description of Japan, although the former lists sixty-six provinces, but the latter mentions sixty-eight.

80

time of their first king, Jimmu Tennō, the court has usually been located in one of these five kingdoms, apart from times of war and other exceptional circumstances. This is where Jimmu Tennō, their first king, who began his reign 2,280 years ago, transferred the court from the kingdom of Hyūga, where it had thitherto been situated. For 2,220 years the court has remained in one of these five kingdoms throughout the reign of 112 kings of the same lineage and ancestry.[1]

This province is also called Kyōki (or Kinki, which is the same) and means Crown Lands. This is in imitation of the kings of China, where the curial province is called Kinki, for the ancient kings of China used to reserve for the crown an area of thousand Chinese square *li* or *ri* (that would be seventy leagues each side) in the middle of the realm. This used to be called Kinki, meaning Crown Lands, and the kingdom's nobles owned and governed the remaining lands of the realm.[2] In the same way, the kings of Japan reserved for the crown these five kingdoms where the court was located in the middle of the realm. All the other lands were possessed by the nobles, to whom he gave kingdoms along with a hereditary title and lordship, and with a certain tribute that they paid.

The first of the five curial kingdoms is called Yamashiro, or Jōshū, and is divided into eight regions called *gun*. The court of Miyako, or Kyō, is at present within this kingdom, whither it was transferred 825 years ago from the city of Nara in the kingdom of Yamato where it had thitherto been situated.[3] It is located in Otagi, the name of a *gun* or one of the eight regions of this kingdom, in a fresh, spacious plain with excellent waters. It is surrounded on three sides, the east, west, and north, by high mountains containing many large monasteries with sumptuous temples belonging to the priests of the idols. To the northeast there is Hie-no-yama, or Hieizan; it was here that the king who transferred the court from Nara to its present position built a university where there were 3,000 *bō* or formed monasteries with their temples, which Nobunaga burnt down and destroyed.[4] To the north there is a mountain called Kurama, inhabited by bonzes.[5] In the east, Higashiyama is crowded with large and sumptuous monasteries and convents. In the west there is Atagoyama, or

---

[1] As already stated, the traditional date of Jimmu's accession in 660 BC. *Nihongi*, I, p. 132. The reference to '112 kings' is mistaken. In *Arte grande*, ff. 236–8, Rodrigues provides a list of the first 108 emperors up to 1587. If his numbering is continued, then the 109th emperor, Go-Mi-no-o, would have been reigning (1612–29) when the Jesuit wrote his *History*. Vivero y Velasco (*Relación*, f. 71v) is more correct when he refers to 108 generations of kings. Rodrigues's mention of 2,220 years of the court residing in Gokinai shows that there is a 60-year gap in the court's history. This occurred in the Namboku-chō period, 1336–92, when there was a schism at court, and the loyalist centre was moved to Yoshino. But Yoshino is still in Yamato, and therefore the court did not actually leave Gokinai during this period.

[2] Avila Girón (*Relación*, p. 268) also points out that the Gokinai region was formerly governed after the Chinese fashion. Reference to 'the royal domain of a 1,000 *li*' is found in *Shujing*, 4, 3, 4 (Legge, *Chinese Classics*, IV, p. 637), and also in *Great Learning*, 3 (Legge, *Chinese Classics*, I, p. 362), where it is noted that an area of 1,000 square *li* around the capital constituted the royal demesne in the Zhou dynasty. Rodrigues gives the Japanese name for this region; in Chinese it would be Jinji.

[3] Nara was the capital 710–84, when the court was transferred to Nagaoka, and then, in 794, to Miyako, so the reference to 825 years is correct. For the transfer to Miyako, see Sansom, *History to 1334*, pp. 99–101; Ponsonby-Fane, *Kyoto*, pp. 5–14; Toby, 'Why Leave Nara?' Rodrigues gives a full description of Miyako in Chapter 13, below.

[4] The 'king' was the 50th emperor, Kammu (736–805). A temple had been founded on Hieizan in 788 by the monk Dengyō Daishi (767–822), and the monastic complex of Enryakuji, with its 3,000 temples, eventually became the headquarters of the Tendai sect. For its destruction by Nobunaga in 1571, see Fróis in *TCJ*, pp. 98–9.

[5] The term 'bonze' seems to have been first used by Xavier (Kagoshima, 5 November 1549, in *Epistolae*, II, p. 108). It is is derived from the Japanese term *bonsō*, or possibly *bōzu* or *bōsan*, a Buddhist monk or priest: Valignano, *Sumario*, p. 9, n. 33. The term, perhaps now somewhat derogatory, is outdated and no longer in common use.

Atago-san, called after a devil named Atago, whom soldiers worship there in the form of a devil.[1] In this part can also be found the mountain called Nishiyama, at the base of which there are many large monasteries of the idols, with delightful and ingenious gardens and fountains of water all the year around.[2]

Although surrounded by these mountains, the city is nevertheless very open because in some places it is a league in length and to the south there is nothing but a refreshing plain. Nearby flows the great River Yodo on which sail innumerable boats with oars and sails, for it is navigable from the sea up to Toba, a neighbouring place. It flows from Lake Ōmi and enters the sea at the city of Osaka, being called different names, such as Yodogawa and Uji-gawa, in various places.[3]

The second kingdom is called Yamato, or Washū, and is divided into fifteen regions. Here is to be found the city of Nara, Nara no Kyō, or Nanto, the ancient court of the kings of Japan, whence it was transferred to its present location, as has already been said. The city still possesses many relics of its antiquity and nobility.[4] In this kingdom there is a mountain called Yoshino, which is very famous for its temples of the *kami*. It is like the headquarters of this sect and has many great buildings and pleasant gardens, and is a place of much pilgrimage.[5]

The third kingdom is Kawachi, or Kashū, and has fifteen regions. This kingdom is separated from that of Tsu-no-kuni by the River Yodogawa, at the mouth of which is the city of Osaka, which is renowned on two counts. First, on account of Monzeki, the head of the peasants' sect called Ikkōshū. He lived there for a long time, during which he withstood Nobunaga's attacks and overcame various kingdoms with the aid of peasants belonging to the sect. They would kill the lord of the kingdom and hand it over to him, and he is regarded as the living god Amida.[6] The second reason for its fame is that it was subsequently the court of Kampaku, or Taikō, who in the year 1587 exiled the Fathers from

---

[1] Atago is the Shinto protector against fire and is associated with Kagutsuchi, the fire god whose birth killed his mother, Izanami. *Nihongi*, I, p. 21. For European references to Atago, see Shurhammer, *Shintō*, pp. 28–32. Cocks (Edo, 25 October 1618, in *Diary*, II, p. 87) calls Atago the god of darkness or hell, and likens the deity to Pluto. He visited an Atago shrine in Edo, where the god's statue was 'in forme lyke a devill, with a hooked nose and feete lyke a griffon, and riding upon a wild boare'.

[2] The position of these mountains or high hills is shown on a map in Sansom, *History to 1334*, p. 100. Rodrigues later repeats this list of mountains on p. 161 when describing Miyako in Chapter 13.

[3] The course of the Yodo and Uji are seen in Sansom, *History to 1334*, p. 100, while the position of Toba is shown in Sansom, *History, 1334–1615*, p. 42. Vivero y Velasco (*Relación*, f. 18v) also comments on the traffic on this river, likening it to the Guadalquivir in Seville.

[4] The principal relic of Nara's antiquity is the Daibutsu, a bronze statue, 53 feet tall, of Roshana Buddha, cast in the 8th century, although much repaired and renovated since then. For early reports on Nara and its sights, see *TCJ*, pp. 282–3, 333–6.

[5] Yoshino is a mountainous area occupying the southern half of Yamato province. It has many historical associations and has long been the headquarters of the *Yamabushi* monks, for whom see p. 95, n. 2.

[6] The term *monzeki* came into use at the end of the 9th century, and originally referred to a temple where a royal prince resided, but was later applied by extension to the princely abbots themselves. Ikkōshū, or Jōdo Shinshū, is a Buddhist sect founded in Japan by Shinran (1174–1268), and its principal object of worship is Amida Buddha. In 1465 Emperor Go-Tsuchi conferred the title of Monzeki on an Ikkōshū temple, and temples of this sect were later called by this name. The sect's headquarters was at Ishiyama Honganji temple in Osaka, which finally capitulated to Nobunaga in 1580; the abbot mentioned by Rodrigues was Kōsa, who held out for many years against Nobunaga. At one time the sect had at its disposal about 100,000 troops. Ponsonby-Fane, *Kyōto*, pp. 222–4; Sansom, *History, 1334–1615*, pp. 282, 288–90. For early European reports, see Vilela, 17 August 1561, in *Cartas*, I, f . 93; Fróis, *História*, II, p. 249; Ribadeneira, *Historia*, p. 364; *TCJ*, p. 319.

Japan on account of his plan to have himself worshipped after his death, as indeed he did.[1] In the time of Miyoshi Dono, Lord of Tenka, there were many noble Christians in this kingdom. Herein was also located the city and fortress of Iimori, the court of the said Miyoshi Dono, who is mentioned many times in this history.[2]

The fourth kingdom is Izumi, or Senshū, and is divided into three regions. It is a coastal kingdom and situated to the south of Kawachi. On its borders and those of Kawachi is the city of Sakai, renowned for its commerce and the place where the Blessed Father Francis disembarked when he went to the Kami. In ancient times it was governed as a republic, for the citizens of this part of Japan used to be engaged in continual civil war. It now belongs to the Lord of Tenka, who places his governor there.[3]

The fifth kingdom is Tsu-no-kuni, also known as Settsu or Sesshū, and is divided into thirteen regions. It contains the city of Hyōgo, which was briefly the court of the king in the Heike wars. Near this city, or really a continuation of it, is a mountain called Ichi no tani, where Heike fortified himself against Genji and was there defeated by his forces.[4] In this same kingdom is the earldom and fortress of Takatsuki, of which Takayama Darius was the lord. He was succeeded by his son Takayama Ukon Justus, who lost his estate in Taikō's first persecution for refusing to renounce the Faith, and in the time of Daifu was exiled for a second time to Manila for the Faith with his wife and family, thus losing the estate that he owned in Hokkoku. He died in Manila as a result of the trials and hardships he suffered and is regarded as a glorious martyr, as will be related in its proper place.[5]

2. The second province of the large island and the names of each state

The second province of the large island is called Tōkaidō, meaning Eastern Coastal

[1] A reference to Hideyoshi, who completed the magnificent castle at Osaka in 1584; descriptions given in *TCJ*, pp. 135–8, 288. For the text of the expulsion edict, see Boxer, *Christian Century*, pp. 145–8. Hideyoshi wanted to be known after death as Shin-Hachiman, or the New Hachiman, and left orders not to be cremated: Pasio, Nagasaki, 3 October 1598, in JapSin 54, f. 8v; also, Organtino, in Ajuda, 49–IV–57, f. 18, and Fróis in ibid., f. 32v. Vivero y Velasco (in *TCJ*, pp. 340–42) visited Hideyoshi's tomb in 1609 and observed the respect and awe paid to the former ruler.

[2] Miyoshi Chōkei (1523–64) was never actually shogun, or Lord of Tenka, but in his office of *shōbanshū*, or advisor, he in fact controlled the shogun Ashikaga Yoshiteru.

[3] Sakai, in modern-day Osaka Prefecture, was an ancient commercial port frequented by Chinese from the early 15th century. It had an elected government of ten principal merchants and 30 aldermen, and the city's wealth supported a force of soldiers to keep the peace. It had a moat on its north, east, and south sides. It was also a cultural centre, with poetry and the tea ceremony flourishing there: *KEJ*, VI, pp. 375–6. According to Morris ('City of Sakai', p. 23), Sakai was perhaps the most important place in Japan after Miyako at that time. Morejon (*Historia*, f. 5) gives its population as 60,000, while Vivero y Velasco (*Relacion*, f. 18v) quotes 80,000 plus. The city's importance began to wane in the time of Hideyoshi, who favoured Osaka. Vilela, 17 August 1561, in Ruiz-de-Medina, *Documentos*, II, p. 344, and Goa, 6 October 1571, in *Cartas*, I, f. 327; Mexia, 6 January 1584, in ibid., II, f. 124v; Valignano, *Sumario*, p. 128, n. 72.

[4] Hyōgo is now a part of Kobe. Taira Kiyomori (1118–81) rose to pre-eminence in the disturbances of the 12th century and in 1180 moved the court from Miyako to his palace at Fukuwara, now part of Kobe, where it stayed for half a year. As its name implies, Ichi-no-tani is a valley rather than a mountain, and the battle there between the Taira and Minamoto took place in early 1184.

[5] Takayama Hida-no-Kami, governor of Takatsuki, was baptized at Nara in 1563, taking the name Darius. His example was followed by his family, the eldest son, Nagafusa (1553–1615), receiving the name Justus. Justus also had the title Ukon-tayū and is usually called Takayama Ukon in the Jesuit letters. A staunch defender of the missionaries, he was stripped of his fief of Akashi and banished by Hideyoshi in 1587. In 1614 he was exiled from Japan along with the missionaries and died in Manila in February 1615. Ukon was renowned for his skill in the tea ceremony, and knew Rodrigues well. For further references, see p. 289, n. 2, and p. 308, n. 2.

Province or Eastern Coastal Road; it lies along the southern sea and runs eastwards. This province contains fifteen kingdoms or states, and borders on the kingdom of Yamato in Gokinai at its kingdom of Iga. This is the first kingdom of the province and is found at its eastern end, and from there the province continues eastwards along the sea. For this reason it is called the Eastern Coastal Road, although it contains some inland kingdoms as well.[1]

The first kingdom is Iga, or Ishū, and contains four regions. The kingdom borders on to Yamato, one of the five Gokinai kingdoms.

The second is the kingdom of Ise, or Seishū, containing fifteen regions. It is a large coastal kingdom that has the ocean to the south, while in the east its coast runs from north to south, forming a bay or inland sea from north to south called Ise-no-umi. The seas ends in the north at the fortress of Kawana in the same kingdom, where the river enters it ... and also at the place or town called Atsuta-no-miya in the kingdom of Owari.[2] In this kingdom of Ise there is a temple of Japan's principal *kami* called Tenshō Daijin. She was the daughter of the first man and woman who, they say, populated Japan. They declare that she was the first to possess the sovereignty of Japan, and that all the Japanese kings are descended from her. Pilgrims come to this temple from all over Japan and donate much alms.[3]

The third kingdom is Shima, or Shinshū, a small coastal kingdom with three regions.[4]

The fourth is the kingdom of Owari[5] and has eight kingdoms, its capital being the city of Kiyosu. Nobunaga came from this kingdom, and also Kampaku or Taikō (he was first of all called Hashiba Chikuzen Dono), who succeeded Nobunaga as Lord of Tenka.[6] The whole of this kingdom consists of a plain without any mountains or rocks, all of it consisting of paddy fields of rice. The people there are very wise and astute, whence there is a proverb, 'The kingdom of Owari has neither rocks, nor mountains, nor simple, candid men.'[7] It is a maritime kingdom on the Ise inland sea and borders on the kingdom of Mino, often called Mino Owari in letters.[8]

---

[1] The text here is not clear, but Rodrigues is mistaken if he means that Iga is at the eastern end of the Tōkaidō, for this 'kingdom' is at its western end. Tōkaidō is the name not only of this second circuit but also of the most famous road in Japan, the coastal route linking Edo with Miyako. For a map of the Tōkaidō route, and also of the San'yodō and San'indō later described by Rodrigues, see Sansom, *History to 1334*, p. 307.

[2] A gap is left in this sentence, possibly where the name of the river, the Nagara, should have been written. The fortress of Kuwana was built by Oda Nobuo in 1576. Atsuta Shrine in Nagoya is the most sacred Shinto shrine after that of Ise, and contains one of the three sacred treasures – the sword found by Susa-no-o in the tail of the eight-headed dragon. *Nihongi*, I, p. 53; *KEJ*, I, pp. 115–16; Ponsonby-Fane, *Studies*, pp. 429–53.

[3] The Shinto shrines at Ise are set in glorious scenery. The Naikū, or Inner Shrine, is dedicated to Amaterasu, the sun goddess, and contains the divine mirror, another of the three sacred treasures. According to Fróis (*História*, I, p. 191), it was the most frequented pilgrimage site of Japan. Cocks (15 March 1616, in *Diary*, I, p. 121) describes the departure from Hirado of a pilgrimage bound for Ise. Kaempfer (*Kaempfer's Japan*, pp. 117–21) devotes a complete chapter to Ise and its pilgrims.

[4] According to *Arte grande*, f. 210, and *Arte breve*, f. 93, Shima had only two, not three, regions.

[5] Rodrigues omits to say here that the Chinese name is Bishū: *Arte breve*, f. 93.

[6] Toyotomi Hideyoshi (1537–98) was born of peasant stock, but eventually rose to supreme power. As his lowly birth precluded him from becoming shogun, he had to be satisfied with the title of Kampaku, or regent (1585), and Taikō (1592) on his resignation in favour of his adopted son, Hidetsugu. It will be recalled that Rodrigues knew him well and spoke with him on his deathbed in 1598. For contemporaneous European reports about him, see *TCJ*, pp. 111–14; Avila-Girón, *Relación*, pp. 399–404, gives a colourful account of his rise to power. Berry, *Hideyoshi*, and Dening, *Life*, provide biographies. See also *KEJ*, VIII, pp. 94–6; Sansom, *History, 1334–1615*, pp. 311–79.

[7] A reference to the origin of this saying is given in Rodrigues, *Nihon*, I, p. 226, n. 35.

[8] The text is not clear here, although it is true that Mino borders on Owari. If Rodrigues is referring to Jesuit letters here (as Rodrigues, *Nihon*, I, p. 225, states), I do not recall seeing 'Mino-Owari' in any correspondence.

The fifth kingdom, Mikawa, or Sanshū, has eight regions. It borders on the southern sea and also on the Inland Sea in the west. From this kingdom came Lord Matsudaira Ieyasu, who subsequently was Lord of Tenka and known as Daifu. He was a great persecutor of Christians.[1]

The sixth kingdom is Tōtōmi, or Enshū. A coastal kingdom with fourteen regions,[2] it borders on the ocean in the south.

The seventh is Suruga, or Sunshū, with seven regions. Its capital is Fuchū, but it is ordinarily called Suruga, the name of the kingdom; it was here that Daifu had his court and died.[3] In this kingdom there is the highest, loveliest, and most renowned mountain in Japan, and it is called Fuji-san. There are four very famous mountains in Japan and they have been given the general or collective name of Yotsu-no-yama, that is, 'The Four Mountains'. The first is this Fuji in the kingdom of Suruga, the second is Shaka-no-take in the kingdom of Yamato, the third is Shirayama in the kingdom of Kaga in the north, and the fourth is Daisen in the kingdom of Hōki.[4]

Mt Fuji is round in shape, measures about twenty leagues in circumference around its base, and borders on the four surrounding kingdoms of Suruga, Kai, Izu, and Sagami. Its lower regions are covered with grass and hay, while its girdle (or middle regions) is thickly forested and provides valuable cedar wood. There are also many different animals there that are not found elsewhere in Japan. In olden days the Shogun Yoritomo, accompanied by 30,000 hunters, held a famous hunt of wild animals there.[5] The summit of the mountain terminates with three peaks that rise out of the one mountain. The ground is covered with loose dry earth like ash from halfway up the mountain to the summit. The peak is covered with snow all the year around and smoke continually issues from the mouth of a very large pit at the summit.[6]

Many pilgrims come there from all over Japan. The cold is so intense at the summit that it is impossible to ascend except in the summer during the time of the dog-days. Many pilgrims then climb up, spending a day and night in the ascent as the way is very steep. At such times food is sold to the pilgrims along the route. They throw *katana* (or swords),

---

[1] A reference to Tokugawa Ieyasu (1542–1616), whom Rodrigues knew well. Daifu was one of his titles. Winning the battle of Sekigahara in 1600, he established the Tokugawa government that lasted until the arrival of Commodore Matthew Perry in the middle of the19th century. For his life, see *KEJ*, VIII, pp. 49–51, and Totman, *Tokugawa Ieyasu*. Ieyasu expelled the missionaries from Japan in 1614, but showed himself less of a persecutor than his son Hidetada. For first-hand descriptions, see Vivero y Velasco, Saris, and Adams, in *TCJ*, pp. 116, 117–18, 121–3.

[2] 13, according to *Arte grande*, f. 210, but 14 in *Arte breve*, f. 93.

[3] Ieyasu retired to Suruga, now known as Shizuoka, in 1607 and died there nine years later.

[4] There is a blank in the Portuguese text, and I have added 'the kingdom of Yamato'. The heights of the four mountains: Fuji, 12,397 feet; Shaka-no-take, 6,150 feet; Shirayama (or Hakusan), 8,917 feet; and Daisen, 5,653 feet.

[5] A reference to Minamoto Yoritomo (1147–99), who held a famous hunt on the southern base of Mt Fuji in 1193. The Soga brothers took the opportunity to assassinate Kudō Suketsune, who had murdered their father some 16 years earlier. The story of Soga filial piety is famous in Japanese tradition. Fróis (*História*, V, pp. 531–2) mentions this hunt, adding that Hideyoshi held an even bigger one in Owari to eclipse Yoritomo's memory. Such large hunts were also held in the 17th century. Cocks (13 September 1616, in *Diary*, I, p. 175) reports that the shogun had gone hunting that day with 10,000 men. Arthur Hatch mentions (in Farrington, *English Factory*, II, p. 947) smaller hunts.

[6] As regards the 'three peaks', although Fuji appears to be a single cone, it is in fact formed by three separate volcanoes. The depth of the crater is about 820 feet: *KEJ*, II, p. 345. The peak is free from snow in the summer months. The last eruption of Fuji took place in 1707–8, dropping 6 inches of ash on Edo some 62 miles away. The Europeans strangely had little to say about this famous mountain. Valignano (*Principio*, f. 32) mentions it, and Guerreiro (*Relação*, III, pp. 128–9) describes the mountain briefly, but I have not found his source of information.

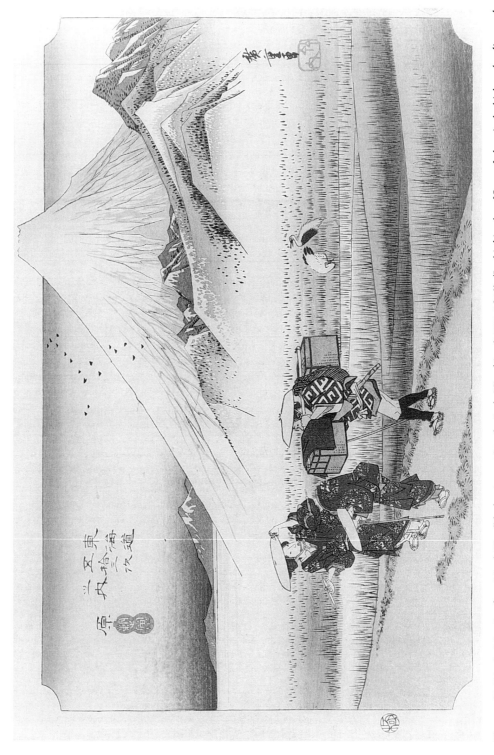

Plate 12: 'Fuji in the Morning from Hara'. Woodblock print, c. 1832, by Ando Hiroshige (1797–1858). 'In this kingdom [Suruga] there is the highest, loveliest, and most renowned mountain in Japan, and it is called Fuji-san. . . . Because of its height the mountain can be seen from afar and looks very beautiful as it is completely round.' pp. 85–7. *Honolulu Academy of Arts. Gift of James A. Michener, 1978 (17,252).*

daggers, and other weapons into that pit or hole as offerings. But the force of the wind and fire that belch out from within it is so strong that it casts the weapons to one side and prevents their falling down inside, and the people in charge of the place gather them up and profit thereby. The descent is made by running down over the loose earth and then reaching the bottom in quick time. As there are so many people, they sometimes fall down on top of each other and some are choked to death. Those who die in this way are accounted blessed, because it is alleged that they afterwards appear in their houses as a sign that they are in a good place.[1] But this is merely something that the devil can do to make people believe in this superstition.

Because of its height the mountain can be seen from afar and looks very beautiful as it is completely round. The clouds are usually halfway up the mountain, and when the peak appears above the clouds it is impossible to persuade oneself that such high land exists, as we ourselves saw many times. Its great height is stressed in a proverb, expressed in a couplet that runs:

> The clouds covering the top of the highest mountains
> Reach only the girdle of Mt Fuji.

Sometimes there is a small white round cloud, rather like a hat or cap, on top of the summit and the people of those parts say that they know from experience that this presages a great wind storm, such as we experienced in that sea with much danger as we were coming from Edo.[2] The southern reaches of the mountain stretch down to the sea. There is a long cave running into one side of the mountain, and nobody knows where it ends. It is called Fuji-no-hito-ana, and they say that there are temples and altars with idols inside.[3]

The eighth kingdom is Kai, or Kōshū, and is divided into four regions. Lord Kai-no-Shingen, a great warrior of Japan, was a native of this kingdom. Such was his devotion to the idols that he vowed to wage war against Nobunaga because he destroyed the idols of Japan, and also to rebuild the universities and temples that he had razed. For greater devotion he lived, dressed, and ate like a bonze, and so he did not marry and had nothing to do with women. He was much addicted to the devil. He died, overcome by Nobunaga, whom he wished to destroy. He left a son, who continued the war against Nobunaga, but he was finally vanquished and his estate confiscated.[4] The southern part of this kingdom borders on Mt Fuji and the mountain can be ascended, as we have noted, only from here.

The ninth kingdom is Izu, or Tōshū, consisting of three regions. This kingdom is a tongue of land surrounded by the sea on three sides. Its most southernly point is a port

---

[1] Thousands of pilgrims and tourists still climb the mountain in July and August, generally making the ascent during the night. *Suna-hashiri*, or 'sand running', is still practised, but is no longer considered dangerous. The last sentence may also be translated: '... because it is alleged that the sign of being in a good place appears in their houses; but...'.

[2] Rodrigues is probably referring here to his return from Edo in 1607.

[3] Of all the *hito-ana* (caves formed by volcanic action), this one to the west of Mt Fuji is the most famous and is associated with the Soga brothers (see p. 85, n. 5, above), although Chamberlain (*Handbook*, p. 170) remarks that it 'is hardly worth turning aside to see.' My chief recollection of this cave, visited on a hot August day, was the abrupt drop in temperature within a few yards of the entrance.

[4] Takeda Harunobu (1521–73) revolted against his father in 1541 and took over Kai province. He shaved his head in 1551 and took the Buddhist name of Shingen. He was killed while besieging the fortress at Noda. His son, Katsuyori, continued his father's struggle against Nobunaga, but after defeat in 1574–5, committed suicide with his son Nobukatsu. *KEJ*, VII, p. 322. Rodrigues's remark about Shingen's celibacy is incorrect.

from which ships embark for the island of Hachijō, which is in the south sea, as already noted. As we ourselves saw, there are many gold and silver mines in this kingdom.[1]

The tenth kingdom is Sagami, or Sōshū. It is divided into four regions[2] and its capital is the city of Odawara. Kamakura, the ancient court of the shogun of Japan, is here in its territory, and to this day contains many relics of its ancient past.[3] It is a coastal kingdom washed by the southern sea.

The eleventh kingdom is Musashi, or Bushū, and is divided into twenty-one regions.[4] Therein is situated the city of Edo, the court of the present shogun, son of Daifu, and now of his grandson.[5] All the nobles of Japan have their palaces in this city where the hostages of each one dwell.[6] it is situated at 35°N at the mouth of a great river that enters the sea there at the end of a bay lying in a north-south direction.[7] There is a large desert or plain called Musashi-no, that is, Musashi Field, in this kingdom, and it is covered with hay and grass without a single grove of trees. There is a proverb about the size of this desert and it runs: 'It is born coming out of the sea, or it emerges from among the grass, and it hides itself and sets in it,' just as in the same way the sun seems to our sight to be born, to set, and hide itself in the sea.[8] There are many mountain pigs or boars in this desert as well as much hunting of innumerable animals, wild ducks that come from Tartary in the winter, many cranes, swans, etc.

In the year 1600 a hunter set up a big rock over a large pit to trap mountain pigs, as is their custom there, and going to see it on the following day he found that it had fallen and the place was full of blood, although there was nothing under the rock. He followed the trail of blood to find out what it was and discovered a large cave. Inside there was a dead monster that was completely covered with hair and had the features of a man. All around the cave there were many bones of animals on which the monster had lived. This had never been

---

[1] The port in question is Shimoda, near the southern tip of the peninsula. Hachijō has already been mentioned on pp. 72–3. For Rodrigues's visit to the Izu mines in 1607, see Cooper, *Rodrigues the Interpreter*, pp. 213, 216.

[2] *Arte grande*, f. 210, lists 8 regions, but *Arte breve*, f. 93, gives only four.

[3] Odawara, a fortress town, was the ninth stage of the Tōkaidō route from Edo to Miyako. Minamoto Yoritomo set up his headquarters in Kamakura, which remained the shogunate capital from 1192 to 1333. Among its relics of the past are the Daibutsu, the large statue of Amida Buddha cast in 1252; Hachiman Shrine, founded on its present site in 1191; and the two great Zen temples, Kenchōji and Engakuji, established in 1253 and 1282.

[4] *Arte grande*, f. 210, gives 24, but *Arte breve*, f. 93, lists 21.

[5] Ieyasu's successor was his son Hidetada (1579–1632), who was shogun 1605–22; he in turn was succeeded by his son Iemitsu (1603–51), shogun 1622–51. The city of Edo, now Tokyo, was founded in 1457 when Ōta Dōkan built a castle there. Realizing its strategic value, Ieyasu made it his administrative headquarters, although Miyako remained the capital until 1869. For the audiences of Vivero y Velasco, Vizcaino, and Cocks with Hidetada, see *TCJ*, pp. 116–17, 118–21, 123–4.

[6] The shogunate obliged nobles to leave hostages in Edo as a guarantee of good behaviour. In 1634 Iemitsu officially introduced the *sankin-kōtai* system, whereby *daimyo* had to reside in Edo at certain times, and to leave hostages, usually their wives and children, when they returned to their fiefs: Tsukahira, *Feudal Control*, especially pp. 28–30. When visiting Hidetada in Edo in 1611, Sebastain Vizcaino (*TCJ*, pp. 118–19) noticed a large group of hostages, whom he reckoned to number more than a thousand. Writing in 1623, Hatch observes (in Farrington, *English Factory*, II, p. 947), 'And each of these severall princes must alwayes bee either himselfe in person, or his brother, eldest sonne, or the chiefe nobleman within his realme, at the Emperour's court … to keepe the severall Kingdomes in quiet and free from tumults, treasons and rebellions.' For other European reports on the subject, see *TCJ*, pp. 81–2.

[7] Situated on the River Sumida, Edo's position was 35°40′N.

[8] The Musashi, or Kantō, Plain, the country's largest flat area, covers 5,000 square miles. In *Arte grande*, p. 109, Rodrigues quotes in Japanese a reference to the plain as an example of *uta* poetry, 'The moon rises from the grass, and sets again in the grass.' For a map of the alluvial plains of Japan, see Sansom, *History to 1334*, p. 8.

seen before. It seems that it went to take the bait of the trap and fell inside. Thanks to its great strength it managed to get out, but was so hurt and injured by the weight that it died.

The twelfth is a coastal kingdom called Awa, or Bōshū, and has four regions. This is a tip of land in the southern sea at 33°N which the ships from New Spain pass when they turn towards Manila.[1] To the east of this tip there are two inhabited islands which ships from Japan that have gone off course have reached and then returned. They say that they are very rich with gold and silver, and the Spaniards call one of them Rich in Gold and the other Rich in Silver.[2] More or less to the south of this point, but a little to the west, are the Islands of Sails, also called the Islands of Robbers, the capital of which is Hachijō-jima. We have already noted that the Spaniards called it the Volcanos as fire is continuously thrown up, etc.[3]

The thirteenth kingdom, Kazusa, or Sōshū, is also coastal and is divided into eleven regions. In the north it borders on Shimōsa.[4]

The fourteenth is Shimōsa, or Sōshū, a coastal kingdom divided into twelve regions. It borders on Kazusa in the north and Musashi in the west.[5]

The fifteenth, Hitachi or Jōshū, the most easterly kingdom of all in that region, is at the end of the large island. In the east it borders on the ocean, in the south on the kingdom of Shimōsa, in the west on the kingdom of Shimotsuke, and in the north on the kingdom of Ōshū. It is divided into eleven regions.

3. Tōsandō, the third province of the large island

The third province of the large island is called Tōsandō, that is, the Eastern Inland Province or Eastern Mountain Road. This province contains eight kingdoms or states, all of them eastern and inland. It borders on Gokinai in the kingdom of Ōmi, the first of its kingdoms, and is contiguous with the kingdom of Yamashiro, in which Miyako is located.

The first is the kingdom of Ōmi, or Gōshū, and is divided into thirteen regions. In the west it has a fresh-water lake or sea called Ōmi-no-mizuumi, the largest of all Japan; this sea lies north-south and its length would be about twenty Japanese leagues, or more than

---

[1] The ship carrying Rodrigo de Vivero y Velasco sank off the coast of Awa in 1609 en route from the Philippines to Mexico. A tall obelisk commemorating his unscheduled landfall dominates the beach in Onjuku, Chiba prefecture.

[2] The first mention of the Islands Rich in Silver and Rich in Gold appears in a letter written by Fray Andrés de Aguirre to the viceroy of Mexico, 1584–5; he tells of a Portuguese ship being blown to these islands, nine days' sailing from Japan: Pacheco, *Colección*, XIII, pp. 545–9; translation in Dahlgren, *Contribution*, pp. 250–52. Vizcaino arrived from Mexico in 1611 to map the east coast of Japan and find the elusive islands (see Vizcaino's *Relación*, and Nuttall's paper on this subject). The Japanese later regarded the English efforts to discover the northwest passage as a pretext for searching for these islands, and Adams was closely questioned about the matter (Cocks, *Diary*, I, p. 177, where Cocks identifies the islands as Formosa). See also Cocks's letter (1 January 1617, in *Diary*, II, p. 283), where he relates that Adams was invited by the Japanese to pilot a ship to look for the islands, 'but Mr. Adames exskewced hym selfe.' As late as 1804–5 a Russian expedition was sent to look for the islands. Dahlgren (*Débuts*, p. 53, and *Contribution*, p. 252) believes that the islands never existed at all, while others have suggested California or Mexico; Chassigneux ('Rica de Oro', p. 70) puts forward a reasonable case for Okinawa. According to Avila Girón (*Relación*, pp. 14–15), the silver and gold islands were Japan itself.

[3] This is mistaken, for Rodrigues has already correctly stated (p. 73) that the Island of Sails (or Robbers) lies to the south of Hachijō, which belongs to the Izu group of islands. But early European maps show the Ladrones (Islands of Robbers) close to the coast of Awa: Mercator, *Atlas*, pp. 417–18; Ortelius, *Theatrum orbis*, ff. 63–4.

[4] The Portuguese text has 'Comas', but a glance at the map shows that Shimōsa is meant.

[5] Shimōsa certainly borders on Musashi in the west, but on Kazusa in the south, not north.

seventeen of our leagues.[1] Many rivers flow into this sea and a copious river flows directly from it. At the beginning of this river, where it flows from the lake, there is a bridge famous throughout Japan. It would be about 200 geometric paces long and is called Seta-no-hashi.[2] The river is called Ujigawa for it passes through the town of Uji, which is about three leagues from its source. From somewhat lower until it flows into the sea at Osaka it is known as the Yodogawa after a fortress of that same name situated a league and a half to the south of Miyako on the way to Osaka. The lake is surrounded on its western side by the mountains Hie-no-yama, at the foot of which on the lakeside is the town of Sakamoto, often mentioned in this account. Then half a league to the south of Sakamoto is the town of Ōtsu, a port with much traffic in this lake, whence goods to be sold are carried to Miyako on carts and animals. Half a league further on is the above-mentioned bridge and next to it on the lakeside there is a fortress called Zeze-no-shiro. On the other side of the lake to the east there is a crag with many settlements. One of them is Azuchiyama, the court of Nobunaga, and is mentioned very often in the course of this history. The lake is navigable and many cargo and passenger boats sail on it, as well as fishing boats for there are various kinds of excellent fish in the lake.[3]

The second kingdom is Mino, or Nōshū, divided into eighteen regions, with the city of Ōgaki as its capital.

The third kingdom is Hida, or Hishū, containing four regions. This kingdom has great mountains of cedar wood that is highly prized for building.[4]

The fourth is the kingdom of Shinano, or Shinshū, with ten regions.

The fifth kingdom is Kōzuke, or Jōshū, divided into fourteen regions. The sixth is the kingdom of Shimotsuke, or Yashū, with nine regions.[5] The university called Ashikaga is found in this kingdom, whither people go from all over Japan to learn every kind of their sciences. There is a superior of the university there.[6]

The seventh is Mutsu, or Ōshū, the largest kingdom of all Japan with 54 regions. This is

---

[1] Lake Biwa, Japan's largest lake, measures 117 miles in circumference and is about 36 miles at its longest. Its total area is 260 sq. miles.

[2] Seta-no-hashi, or the Bridge of Seta, is made up of two bridges meeting on an island in the middle of the river. It has been the scene of many famous historical events, such as Yoshinaka's stand in 1184 during the Gempei War. According to Fróis (*História*, III, pp. 345–6), it was reputed to be the finest bridge in Japan and after the assassination of Nobunaga in 1582, Akechi's advance was delayed by the bridge being cut. Kaempfer passed over the bridge in 1691 and describes it and its legends (*Kaempfer's Japan*, pp. 326–7). Illustration in Skene Smith, *Tokugawa Japan*, p. 54.

[3] The geographical account here is illustrated by the map of Miyako and environs in Sansom, *History, 1334–1615*, p. 42. The magnificent Azuchi Castle was built on the lake's east bank by Nobunaga in 1576, and Fróis has left an excellent eyewitness account (in *TCJ*, pp. 134–5). See also Takayanagi, 'The Glory', for modern commentary. The ruins of the castle can still be visited.

[4] All this region is mountainous and much timber is grown on the lower slopes. Valignano (*Principio*, f. 31) points out correctly that there is no cedar wood in Japan, but there is a similar wood, pleasant smelling and hard, and this is often called cedar by Europeans. In fact the tree is *hinoki* and it belongs to the cypress family: *Vocabulario*, f. 348; Valignano, *Adiciones*, p. 354, n. 22; Geerts, 'Preliminary Catalogue', p. 4.

[5] *Arte grande*, f. 210v, records only five regions, but *Arte breve*, f. 93, gives nine.

[6] Ashikaga Academy, founded in the 9th century and again in the 12th, was richly endowed by the Uesugi family, and for several centuries was the centre of Chinese studies in Japan. It closed down in 1872: *KEJ*, I, p. 99–100. It was the nearest approach to a European university, all the other 'universities' being Buddhist seminaries. Fróis (*História*, I, p. 9) explains the difference. According to Avila Girón (*Relación*, p 260), Ashikaga was the Japanese Paris, Bologna, and Salamanca. When Rodrigues mentions the academy again (Book 2, Chapter 7, p. 348), he adds that the superior was called Gakkō (although the academy itself was called Ashikaga Gakkō), and this is probably the word missing in the text.

the last and most northerly kingdom of Japan. To the east is the eastern sea, while to the north there is a strait fifteen miles wide by which it is separated from the island of Ezo. The kingdom ends at 42½° or 43°N, measured with an astrolabe.[1] There are many gold and silver mines there.[2] It has many great lords who posses the kingdom. The chief ones are: Date Masamune, a great and mighty duke with much territory and revenue;[3] secondly, Hida Dono;[4] thirdly, the *yakata* of Tsugaru, the duke of that state, who has two colonies of Japanese on the island of Ezo.[5] There is a great navigable river in this kingdom. It flows from east to west, and enters the northern sea in the kingdom of Echigo.[6]

The eighth kingdom is Dewa, or Ushū, and is divided into twelve regions. It has many gold and silver mines, and is a coastal kingdom washed in the west by the northern sea.[7]

4. The fourth province of the large island

The fourth province is called Hokurokudō, meaning Northern Province or Northern Road. The northern part of the province is coastal and faces Eastern Tartary. It has many mighty rivers flowing into the northern sea, and there is a great deal of fishing in them for salmon, cod, and sea trout that come to spawn in the rivers.[8] This north sea does not have ebbing and flowing tides, and can be navigated only in the summer for it is too rough to do so in the winter. The ships of that sea have a different shape from other Japanese boats as regards the prow and are like pinnaces. They use oars only according to our fashion on account of that coast's waves.[9] This province has much trade with the island of Ezo in fish and *kombu*,

---

[1] The Tsugaru Strait separates Honshu from Ezo. Carvalho (in Cieslik, *Hoku-hō*, pp. [16]-[17]) reports that the strait is five or six Spanish leagues wide. The northernmost point of Honshu is 41½°N.

[2] Gold was mined at Mutsu as far back as 700: Brown, *Money Economy*, p. 67. One of the reasons why Rodrigues was so familiar with the mines may be that during the persecution many Christians fled from their homes and worked in the mines: Anesaki, 'Kirishitan Missions', pp. 477–9.

[3] Date Masamune (1567–1636), one of the most powerful *daimyo* of the time, fought in the Korean campaigns and later took part in the Osaka siege, 1615. He was not unfriendly towards the missionaries and sent an ambassador to Rome and Madrid in 1613. *KEJ*, II, p. 78.

[4] Gamō Ujisato (1556–95) distinguished himself in battle and married a daughter of Nobunaga. He was later awarded the title of Hide-no-Kami. He was baptized in 1584 and took the name Leo. *KEJ*, III, p. 6.

[5] Tsugaru Tamenobu (d. 1608) sided with Hideyoshi and later with Ieyasu at the time of Sekigahara, 1600. Nobuhira (1586–1631), his son, was baptized in 1596 and helped persecuted Christians, but finally abandoned his religion. Many of the Japanese colonists in Ezo were miners. Carvalho reports (21 October 1620, in Cieslik, *Hoku-hō*, pp. [13]-[14]) that in the previous year more than 50,000 Japanese, among them many Christians, had gone to Ezo to work in the recently discovered gold mines. Carvalho himself went, disguised as a miner, to minister to the Christians.

[6] Probably a reference to the Agano River, which enters the sea near Niigata, in former Echigo province. The river flows from east to west and is certainly navigable, although it can hardly be described as 'great'. Perhaps Rodrigues had in mind the 229–mile Shinano River, although his account does not square with this river. On the map in Cardim (Plate 11), a large unnamed river is shown that agrees with Rodrigues's description.

[7] Carvalho (21 October 1620, in Cieslik, *Hoku-hō*, p. [27]) mentions that he had visited the Christians living in the famous mining town of Inaie in Dewa. The names of other Dewa mines are given in Rodrigues, *Nihon*, I, p. 239, n. 75.

[8] Both Carvalho and Angelis (in Cieslik, *Hoku-hō*, pp. [8] and [18]) mention the large number of salmon and herring caught in Ezo; 3,000 salmon may be caught at one cast of a net, and the fishermen deliberately let some escape so as not to break the net. The fish were not salted, but hung up in the cold air to freeze.

[9] Vizacaino (*Relación*, p. 170), Carvalho and Angelis (Cieslik, *Hoku-hō*, pp. [10], [14], and [30]) all mention the rough seas around the north of Japan, and Angelis specifically refers to the ebbing and flowing of the tides. He also notes that the ships of Ezo are similar to those of Japan and does not speak of the type mentioned by Rodrigues. The Japanese method of rowing is described by Carletti (in *TCJ*, p. 234), who notes that they do not lift the oar out of the water at all, but push it backwards and forwards rapidly. Ralph Coppendale, master of the English ship *Hoseander*, writes (11 September 1615, in Pratt, *History*, II, p. 74) an appreciative account of Japanese rowing.

a very long seaweed a span and a half in width, which the Japanese eat.[1] They also trade in other sea products and *rakko-no-kawa*, or otter skins, for there are many of them on certain islands of Ezo.[2] This is a very cold and snowy region for it faces Tartary, where in the winter there is much hunting of wild duck and many other birds. It is divided into six kingdoms, five of which are on the large island and one on the island of Sado, which is in that sea. Between the kingdoms of Wakasa and Echizen there is a large bay, at the end of which there is a busy port three leagues distant overland from the fresh-water sea or lake of Ōmi.[3] Whence there is easy communication between Miyako and the northern sea by boats sailing along this lake.

The first kingdom is Wakasa, or Jakushū, divided into three regions. To the east lies the above-mentioned bay, while the ocean lies to the north.

The second is the kingdom of Echizen, or Esshū, with twelve regions. It is washed by the sea in the west and north.

The third is the kingdom of Kaga, or Kashū, divided into four regions.

The fourth kingdom is Noto, or Nōshū, with four regions. This kingdom is a long tongue of land, washed by the sea on three sides and pointing to the north and northeast.

The fifth is the kingdom of Etchū, or Esshū, containing four regions.

The sixth[4] is the island of Sado, or Sashū, commonly called Sadoshima, and it contains three regions. This kingdom is an island in the northern sea. It has many rich mines of fine silver, and they are the biggest and principal ones of Japan. There is now also gold mixed with silver.[5]

5. San'indō and San'yōdō, the fifth and sixth provinces of the large island

The part of the large island that we said went under the general name of Chūgoku is divided into these two provinces, the fifth and sixth. This part of Chūgoku is washed by two seas. One of them is the northern sea, while the other is the southern or that inland sea called Seto-uchi, as we have said above. The kingdoms on the north coast make up the fifth

---

[1] Concerning the products of Ezo, Chamberlain (*Handbook*, p. 515) mentions ' … above all *kobu* (or *kombu*), a broad, thick, and very long species of seaweed, which forms a favourite article of diet not only in Japan but in China.' Also *KEJ*, VII, pp. 46–7. Rodrigues refers to *kombu*, or kelp, again when speaking about New Year festivities (p. 194).

[2] The *rakko* is a sea-otter or seal. Angelis (in Cieslik, *Hoku-hō*, pp. [8]-[9], [17] and [38]) explains that it has skin like a marten and fetches high prices. Carvalho also comments on their downy skin. *Vocabulario*, f. 206: 'Rakko. Certain sea animal, with hair that lies in any direction that the hand may stroke it. *Rakko no kawa no yō na hito ga*: a man easily inclined to the opinion of any person on any subject.'

[3] A reference to the port of Tsuruga, lying in a bay of the same name and one of the principal ports of the west coast of Japan.

[4] Hokurokudō had seven 'kingdoms', and not six. Rodrigues correctly notes in *Arte grande*, f. 210v, and *Arte breve*, f. 93v, that the sixth is Echigo, or Esshū, with seven districts.

[5] According to tradition, an Echigo vessel put in at Sado, 22 miles off the coast of Honshu, in 1542 and a member of the crew discovered silver near a village called Sawane. In 1601 a rich vein was found near Aikawa. The average annual production of silver in Sado in the first half of the 17th century was no less than 200 million grammes. In 1604 João Rodrigues Giram (*Carta anua*, pp. 1–2) reported that the peace enjoyed under Tokugawa Ieyasu enabled the Japanese to prosper 'with the many large silver mines that have been discovered in his time and are still being discovered every day, principally in the kingdom of Sado … from which mines he receives every year about one and a half million *reales*.' Gold was found on the island at the beginning of the 17th century, and Sado became one of the principal gold-producing centres of Japan. Between 1618 and 1627, 66–100 tons of gold and silver were produced annually. *KEJ*, VI, pp. 362–3; Brown, *Money Economy*, pp. 59–60, 69. For illustrations of gold mining on Sado, see Skene Smith, *Tokugawa Japan*, p. 190; for illustration of work in the interior of a silver mine, see Smith, *Japanese History*, pp. 192–3. For Japanese mining in general, see *KEJ*, V, pp. 184–5; for the dangers of working in the mines, Totman, *Tokugawa Ieyasu*, pp. 106–7.

province called San'indō, meaning North Mountain Province or the Northern Mountain Road. The kingdoms on the maritime coast of the inland sea of Chūgoku form the sixth province, called San'yōdō, that is, the Province or Road of the Southern Mountains. Each of these provinces has eight kingdoms, making a total of sixteen, which make up the whole of Chūgoku, as has been said before.[1]

San'indō, the fifth province, contains eight kingdoms; seven are on the mainland and one on the island of Oki, which by itself makes up a kingdom.

The first kingdom is Tamba, or Tanshū, divided into six regions. An inland kingdom, it borders on Yamashiro to the east and Tsu-no-kuni to the south, both of which are in Gokinai.

The second is Tango, or Tanshū, with five regions. The northern part is coastal.

The third is Tajima, or Tanshū, containing eight regions. It is coastal in the north.

The fourth is Inaba, or Inshū, with seven regions, also coastal in the north.

The fifth kingdom is Hōki, or Hakushū, with six kingdoms, and is coastal to the north. Mt Daisen, one of the four famous mountains of Japan, is in this kingdom.[2]

The sixth is Izumo, or Unshū, with ten regions, coastal in the north.

The seventh is Iwami, or Sekishū, divided into six regions, coastal in the north. Here are to be found the famous silver mines called Kanayama, although they are not so productive as formerly.[3]

The eighth is the island of Oki, or Onshū, and is composed of three islands, making up one kingdom. It is divided into four regions and is situated in the northern sea.

San'yōdō, the Sixth Province.

The sixth province of San'yōdō contains another eight kingdoms. Most of the islands in the inland sea, which we mentioned, belong to this province or its kingdoms.

The first is the kingdom of Harima, or Banshū, divided into fourteen regions.[4] Its capital is Himeji, of which Hashiba Chikuzen Dono was lord when he succeeded Nobunaga in the command of Tenka and was named Kampaku or Taikō.[5] In this kingdom is the earldom of Akashi, of which Justus Ukon Dono was the lord when he left for Hakata in 1587, exiled for refusing to give up the Faith.[6]

The second kingdom is Mimasaka, or Sakushū, with seven regions.

The third is the kingdom of Bizen, or Bishū, with eleven regions.

The fourth is the kingdom of Bitchū, or Bishū, with nine regions.[7]

The fifth kingdom is Bingo, or Bishū, with fourteen regions. They make the best rush mats, called *tatami*, in this kingdom and they are sent hence to every part of Japan.[8]

---

[1] All this information is correct, although a more literal translation of San'indō would be 'Mountain Shade Road', and of San'yōdō, 'Mountain Sun Road'. The San'indō provinces in general are on the northern and cold side of Japan, facing the Asian mainland, while those of San'yōdō are on the southern side and face the warm Pacific.

[2] For Mt Daisen, see p. 85.

[3] The Ōmori *kanayama*, or 'metal mountain', was opened in Iwami province in 1526 and was the first to be worked in Japan: Brown, *Money Economy*, p. 56. For the history of Iwami silver mines, see Takekoshi, *Economic Aspects*, I, pp. 298–9.

[4] *Arte grande*, f. 210v, lists 12 regions, but the later *Arte breve*, f. 94, gives 14.

[5] A reference to Hideyoshi, who transferred to Himeji Castle shortly before the assassination of Nobunaga in 1582.

[6] For Takayama's loss of Akashi, see p. 83.

[7] *Arte grande*, f. 210v, gives only 5 regions, but *Arte breve*, f. 94, lists nine.

[8] *Tatami* are the thick straw mats with which the floors of Japanese buildings are covered; Fukuyama district in Bingo was renowned for its production of the upper covering of *tatami*. Chamberlain and Aston, *Handbook*, pp. 410–11. Further references to these mats are given on p. 141. Bizen, Bitchū, and Bingo were collectively known as Bishū.

The sixth is Aki, or Geishū, with eight regions. Its capital is now the city of Hiroshima. It has an island called Miyajima where there is a very famous *kami*; it is a place of much pilgrimage and trade.[1]

The seventh kingdom is Suwō, or Bōshū, with six regions. Its capital is the renowned city of Yamaguchi. The great duke of Chūgoku, the *yakata* Yoshitaka, was reigning here when the Blessed Father Francis came to Japan and presented to him the embassy that he led.[2]

The eighth kingdom is Nagato, or Chōshū, and has six kingdoms. This is the last and principal kingdom at the western end of the large island. It is here that the large island is separated from Kyushu, the second island, by a narrow strait at the town or port of Kaminoseki or Shimonoseki, facing the kingdom of Buzen.[3]

6. The seventh province, called Nankaidō

The seventh of the eight provinces into which Japan is divided is called Nankaidō, meaning Southern Coastal Province or Road, for as regards Gokinai it is situated in the south of Japan. It has six kingdoms, the first of which is on the large island and is called Ki-no-kuni, where the province borders on Gokinai. Four of the kingdoms are on Shikoku, the third of the three large islands, and the island of Awaji is a kingdom by itself. This island of Shikoku points east-northeast and is divided into two parts by great mountain chains in the middle. The northern half contains the two kingdoms of Iyo and Sanuki, washed by the inland sea; most of the islands of the inland sea belong to these kingdoms. The southern part is washed by the ocean and contains two kingdoms, one being Awa while the other is Tosa, whence some people used to call this island the Island of Tosa.[4]

The first kingdom is Ki-no-kuni, or Kishū. This is on the large island and borders on Yamato and Izumi in the north, and is divided into seven regions. In the west it is washed by the sea that separates it from Shikoku, the third island, and in the south by the ocean. The most southerly part of the large island is a promontory or cape called Kumano-no-Misaki, situated at $32\frac{1}{2}°$N.[5] The university of Kōya, called Kōyasan, is in this kingdom, and it has big, sumptuous temples and many monasteries. The founder was a bonze named Kōbō, the greatest minister of the devil that ever existed in Japan, and he was buried alive there. This sect is the Shingonshū, and it is a place of great pilgrimage from all over Japan. The whole place is lit with many lamps, and many people ask that their ashes be sent there. This place is quite clearly the mouth of hell on account of the innumerable evils of every

---

[1] The text is corrupt here and a literal translation would read: '… its capital is now the city of Hiroshima, which is situated. It has an island…' Miyajima (or Itsukishima) is an island in the Inland Sea southwest of Hiroshima and one of Japan's three beautiful landscapes, or *sankei*. It is renowned for its Shinto shrine dedicated to the three daughters of Susa-no-o (*Nihongi*, I, p. 35), and records of the shrine date back to 811. References to the shrine taken from the writings of Pinto, Cabral, Vilela, and Rodrigues Giram are given in Schurhammer, *Shintō*, pp. 50–57.

[2] A reference to Ōuchi Yoshitaka (see p. 56, n. 4). Although *Arte grande*, f. 211, correctly supplies the alternative name for Suwō as Boshū, the later *Arte breve*, f. 94, erroneously gives it as Shūshū ('Xûxû'). As Rodrigues gives the correct name here, he seems not to have relied exclusively on *Arte breve* when compiling this list of provinces.

[3] Kaminoseki and Shimonoseki were in fact two different towns situated on either side of Shimonoseki Strait, the former being in Buzen province and the latter in Nagato. Avila Girón (*Relación*, p. 13) separates them by as much as ½°.

[4] For example, Shikoku is called Tosa in Avila Girón, *Relación*, p. 13, and in Linschoten, *Discours*, pp. 377–8. It appears as Tosa in the maps of Mercator, *Atlas*, pp. 417–18; Ortelius, *Theatrum orbis* and *Asiae nova descriptio*, in Cortazzi, *Isles*, pp. 79, 83.

[5] The southernmost point of Ki-no-kuni, or Kii, is actually Shio-no-misaki, at $33°28'$N.

kind that are perpetrated there. Up to the present time it has been a privileged place and asylum for miscreants of every type who took shelter there, shaving their heads and becoming bonzes. But Kampaku, or Taikō, stopped this and ordered those who sheltered there to be put to death, and now the other lords of Tenka do the same.[1] In the same kingdom was a monastery of the Negoro and of those whom they call *yamabushi*, but Nobunaga destroyed this.[2]

The second kingdom is the island of Awaji, situated at the top of Shikoku, the third island, and facing Ki-no-kuni, and is divided into two regions.[3] In the northern part of this island where it faces Akashi in the kingdom of Harima (from which it is separated by a narrow strait called Akashi-no-seto) there is a small island called Iwaya, about which there are many fables in the histories of their *kami*. They say that this was a drop of water that formed on the point of a staff that they plunged down from Heaven into the sea. This congealed into a small island from which began all the rest of the world and thence the land went on spreading. For they believe that in the beginning there was only Heaven and water, without any land.[4]

The third is Awa, or Ashū, one of the four kingdoms of Shikoku, the third island. It has nine regions[5] and is located at the top of the island, separated from the island of Awaji by a very narrow strait. The father of the holy martyr Brother Paul Miki was a native of this kingdom.[6]

[1] Mt Kōya is famous for its Buddhist temples, the first of which was founded in 816 by Kūkai (774–835), better known by his posthumous title Kōbō Daishi, who is said to have entered his tomb alive to await the advent of Miroku, the future Buddha. The place nearly shared the same fate as Hieizan, but Nobunaga spared it at the emperor's request. Hideyoshi modified its rights of sanctuary in 1585. *KEJ*, IV, p. 299; Sansom, *History to 1334*, pp. 119–23, and *History, 1334–1615*, pp. 296–7. Early Jesuit references to Kōya and Kōbō Daishi are given by Vilela, in *TCJ*, pp. 321–2; Fróis, 1 October 1585, in *Cartas*, II, ff. 162–2v, and summarized in *TCJ*, p. 329. Further references are given in Shurhammer, 'Kōbō-Daishi'. The reference to 'innumerable evils' undoubtedly includes pederasty. This practice is often mentioned by the early Europeans, both lay and religious. Vizcaino (*Relación*, p. 187) writes, 'The priests do not have women, but each has a boy with whom he sleeps, and this is general throughout the kingdom.' See also Xavier, *Epistolae*, II, pp. 188–9; Avila Girón, *Relación*, p. 260; Fróis, *Tratado*, p. 140; Valignano, *Sumario*, p. 28, and *Historia*, pp. 138–9. Some of the writers repeated the legend that Kōbō Daishi had introduced the practice into Japan. For this legend, see Schalow, 'Kūkai and the Tradition'.

[2] The monastery at Negoro was founded in 1130 by Kakuhan (1095–1143), posthumously called Kōgyō Daishi, and belonged to the Shingi branch of the Shingon sect. With its armed retainers, or *sōhei*, the foundation became powerful, but was finally destroyed by Hideyoshi in 1585. Sansom, *History, 1334–1615*, pp. 289, 343. Vilela describes the military activities of the monastery in *TCJ*, pp. 322–3, while Fróis (*História*, IV, pp. 172–81) gives an account of the Negoro monks and their defeat. See also Valignano, *Sumario*, p. 13, n. 64. The *yamabushi* or *shugendō* monks belonged to the Tendai and Shingon sects, and were associated with magical practices and divination. The best early account is given by Fróis (in *TCJ*, pp. 324–5). They are also described by Vilela (*Cartas*, I, f. 58v) and Balthasar Gago (Ibid., I, f. 99v). For further references, see Schurhammer, 'Die Yamabushis'. A modern account is given in Renondeau, *Shugendō*.

[3] As Rodrigues correctly states in *Arte grande*, f. 211, and *Arte breve*, f. 94, the alternative name is Tanshū.

[4] Iwaya is certainly at the north of Awaji Island, but is not itself an island. Awaji was formed by the drops of brine dripping from the tip of the spear plunged by Izanagi and Izanami into the water: *Nihongi*, I, pp. 13–15. Vilela (27 April 1563, in *Cartas*, I, f. 139) and Fróis (in *TCJ*, pp. 297–8) both mention this legend.

[5] Five regions, according to *Arte grande*, f. 211, but *Arte breve*, f. 94, gives it nine. There were two provinces named Awa, this one and the one mentioned on p. 89, but their names are written differently in Japanese. Awaji is separated from Shikoku by Naruto Strait, only a mile in width.

[6] Paul Miki (1564/5–97) entered the Society of Jesus in 1586, and was crucified with 25 others at Nagasaki in the presence of Rodrigues: Schütte, *Textus*, p. 1237. A full account of his martyrdom is given in JapSin 52, ff. 290–301. His father, Miki Handayu (or Bundayu), was baptized in 1568: Valignano, *Sumario*, p. 124, n. 54, p. 126, n. 65.

The fourth kingdom is Sanuki, or Sanshū, and has eleven regions. The large productive island of Shōdoshima, situated in the Inland Sea, belongs to this kingdom.

The fifth kingdom is Iyo, or Yoshū. It has fourteen regions and borders on the Inland Sea.

The sixth kingdom is Tosa, or Toshū, with seven regions. European authors erroneously call this third island the Island of Tosa after this kingdom.[1] It is the most southerly and westerly kingdom of the island and faces Bungo.

7. Saikaidō, the eighth province

The eighth province is called Saikaidō, meaning Western Sea Province or Road, for it is situated on the western sea, facing China and very remote from Gokinai. It contains eleven regions, nine on the second island of Kyushu (the island thus takes its name),[2] and two on the two islands of Iki and Tsushima.

The first is Chikuzen, or Chikushū, and is divided into fifteen regions. Its capital is the city of Hakata, situated at the end of a bay, five or six leagues long, which the sea forms there. This city has always been the centre of the trade and commerce that Japan has conducted with China and Korea because it faces these two countries. When in the Year of the Lord 1279 or 1280 the Grand Cham, the Tartar king who overcame China, sent an army of 200,000 men and 4,000 ships against Japan, the fleet arrived at this city. It was lost in a storm at the mouth of this bay at a point called Shika-no-shima, but more than 30,000 Tartars escaped. The Japanese came by sea to kill them, and the Tartars disembarked onto the beach; when the Japanese left their ships and climbed a mountain to seek them out, they boarded the Japanese ships and sailed off with them with their flags to the city. Believing that they were their own troops, the guards of the city and fortress came out to greet them, and thus the Tartars rushed inside the fortress and turned all the inhabitants out. They defended themselves therein for seven months, at the end of which time they emerged on condition that they should be provided with ships. These were given them, and they returned to China. Marco Polo mentions this return in his account of the Orient, in which he calls Japan 'Zipangu', which is Ribenguo, etc.[3]

The second kingdom is Chikugo, or Chikushū, which has ten regions. Its capital is now Yanagawa, situated at the end of the inland sea of Hizen, the mouth of which is between the cape of Shiki on the island of Amakusa and the port of Kuchinotsu. Throughout all Takaku it enters for many leagues between the kingdoms of Hizen, Higo, and Chikugo. This kingdom has a big river called Chikugogawa that flows into the sea at the end of this sea of Hizen between a Hizen port called Terai and a Chikugo port called Enokitsu.[4] There is a very famous mountain in this kingdom where there is a convent of bonzes with many

---

[1] See p. 94.

[2] Kyushu literally means 'nine provinces'.

[3] This account of the 1281 invasion is an expanded version of that given already on pp. 61–2. The tale of the invaders' ruse is taken directly from Marco Polo (*Book*, III, 3; Yule, *Book*, II, pp. 258–63), who says that the Mongols sailed from Japan, disembarked on a small island about four miles away, and it was there that the Japanese forces landed and had their ships stolen. The invaders then sailed to Japan, took the capital, expelled everyone, were besieged for seven months, and finally surrendered on condition that their lives be spared. This fanciful episode is not mentioned in Japanese or Chinese records.

[4] The term Takaku was used in varying senses by the early missionaries, sometimes meaning the southeast of Hizen (and thus including Shimabara Peninsula), or else the possessions of the Arima family. Rodrigues here appears to refer

monasteries of *yamabushi*. The mountain is called Kōra-san, whence came two *yamabushi* who were martyred for the Faith in Yanagawa.[1]

The third kingdom is Buzen, or Hōshū, divided into eight regions. Its capital is now the city and fortress of Kokura, sanctified by the blood of many illustrious martyrs who died there for the Faith.[2] In this kingdom there is a region called Usa where there is a famous temple of a *kami* called Hachiman, who is regarded as the god of war and is greatly venerated by soldiers. He was the sixteenth king of Japan, Ōjin Tennō by name, whose father died in a war while driving out the Koreans who had descended on Japan. Although he was in the womb of his mother, she continued the war against the Koreans and went over to Korea, which she made pay tribute. On her return to Japan, she gave birth to her son in the region of Usa in this kingdom, and attributed the victory to her son in the womb. He was a very capable king and was the first to introduce into Japan the use of Chinese writing about the Year of the Lord 283. After his death he was regarded as the god of war and as such is worshipped. The temple is called Usa-Hachiman, meaning the Hachiman of Usa, for there are other Hachiman with the title of other places.[3]

The fourth kingdom is Bungo, or Hōshū, divided into eight regions. Its capital is Funai, or Fuchū. In this kingdom there is the port of Hiji whither the Portuguese ship went first to trade.[4] A famous Christian *yakata*, Duke Francis, was lord of the kingdom, and he was succeeded by his son, Don Constantine, whom Taikō stripped of the kingdom in the Korean war against China for not arriving in time at a certain important juncture at which the Chinese were victorious.[5] There were many good Christians in this kingdom and many of the lords were fine Christians, so well instructed in the Faith that when they were exiled with their lord to various parts of Japan they spread the Law of God. This kingdom, along

---

in a general way to the north-western part of Kyushu. See Valignano, *Sumario*, p. 82, n. 67. Terai, on the northern side of the Chikugogawa, and Enokitsu, to the south of the river, are now known as Nakita and Okawa respectively.

[1] For *yamabushi*, see p. 95, n. 2. Kōra-san is famous as a centre of religious pilgrimage. A long account of Peter Monjubō and Paul Shōjubō is given by Christovão Fereira in the 1618 Annual letter (30 January 1619, in JapSin 59, ff. 115–16v). The two young *yamabushi* wanted to board a Spanish ship and go to the Philippines. They were cast into prison, where they were baptized in February 1617, and on 26 November were stoned to death by their former brethren.

[2] In 1618, 25 Christians were beheaded at Kokura, another in 1619, and five more crucified there in 1620. Names and dates given in Anesaki, *Concordance*, pp. 37, 38, 40, 41.

[3] Ōjin (201–310) was the 15th emperor, or 16th if his mother Jingō, who was only a regent, is included, as in Rodrigues's list of emperors in *Arte grande*, f. 236v. Emperor Chūai (149–200) was killed while repressing rebels from the south of Kyushu and on his wife's orders was buried secretly. Jingō thereupon inserted a stone in her sash to prevent birth, invaded Korea, and on her victorious return gave birth to Ōjin. *Nihongi*, I, pp. 222–32. Ōjin's reign was in fact peaceful, and his identification with Hachiman, god of war, is attributed to the adoption of that deity as patron of the Minamoto clan. Other famous Hachiman shrines are found in Kamakura and Yamashiro: *KEJ*, VI, p. 76; Ponsonby-Fane, *Studies*, pp. 43–4, 78, 195. For early European references to Hachiman, see Schurhammer, *Shintō*, pp. 74–8. For the introduction of writing into Japan, see p. 47, n. 1.

[4] There is a port called Hiji in Bungo, but I cannot find any reference to Portuguese ships visiting it; in 1558 and 1559 Portuguese ships called at unspecified Bungo ports and may well have put into Hiji: Boxer, *Great Ship*, pp. 24–5. Funai (now Ōita) is on the other side of a large bay from Hiji and Portuguese ships called there in 1556, 1558–9: ibid., pp. 23, 24, and Boxer, *Viagens*, p. 5.

[5] For Duke Francis (Ōtomo Yoshishige), see p. 64, n. 4. His son, Yoshimune (1558–1605) was baptized as Constantine in 1587 and took over the administration of the fief in 1579. When asked during the Korean campaign for help by Konishi Yukinaga, besieged at Pyongyang, he retreated to Seoul instead. As a result he was stripped of his possessions by Hideyoshi in 1593 and banished to Iki. He later returned to Bungo, but was again sent into exile. He often appears in Fróis, *História*, V. See also Guzman, *Historia*, II, p. 521; *KEJ*, VI, p. 132.

with Yamaguchi, Satsuma, and Hirado, were the first Christian centres in Japan, whence the Faith was propagated to other parts.

The fifth is Hizen, or Hishū, with eleven regions and its capital at Saga or Ryūzōji.[1] This is a large kingdom and contains the estates of many lords. Sengan, the grandfather of Don John Arima Dono, was lord of its six western regions, or Nishirokugun. He had many sons, one of whom was placed in the state of Ōmura and was later called Don Bartholomew. Another was placed in the state of Hata, the region being called Kamimatsura; another in the state of Isahaya; and another on the island of Amakusa-no-shiki. He himself remained at Arima and was succeeded as duke of the state by his son who afterwards was known as Don Andrew.[2] He was succeeded in turn by his son, Don John Arima Dono, on whom Pope Sixtus V bestowed the title of king through his ambassador who went to Rome.[3] He was succeeded by his son, Don Michael of Arima, who moved to Hyūga, where he is now exchanging his state.[4] The principal noble family is now the Ryūzōji, to which belonged Lord Takanobu, whom Don John Arima Dono killed in a battle.[5]

Another state of this kingdom is the earldom of Ōmura. Don Bartholomew was lord of this, and the same pope bestowed on him the title of prince through his ambassador.[6] He was succeeded by his son, Don Sancho, who was succeeded in turn by his son, Don Bartholomew, who recently died in the state of Ōmura.[7] The Portuguese who come to Japan

---

[1] According to *Arte grande*, f. 211, the province had 12 regions, but *Arte breve*, f. 94v, gives it eleven. Saga was the residence of the Ryūzōji family. The name Ryūzōji comes from a village in the Saga district and is also the name of a temple: Valignano, *Sumario*, p. 92, n. 93.

[2] Sengan was the Buddhist name taken on his retirement by Arima Haruzumi (1483–1566). His eldest son, Yoshinao (1521–77), was baptized as Andrew in 1576. Sumitada (1533–87), baptized in 1563 as Bartholomew and the first Christian *daimyo*, was adopted into the Ōmura family and succeeded Ōmura Sumiaki. The third son, Naokazu, may have resided in Isahaya, but I can find no record of this; the fourth son, Mori, lived in Hata; the fifth, Morotsune, baptized in 1590, lived in Amakusa. The Arima family tree is given in Valignano, *Sumario*, p. 83, and in Anesaki, *Concordance*, p. 109.

[3] Arima Yoshinao (Andrew) had seven sons, the first of whom Yoshizumi (1550–71) died young and succession went to the second son, Harunobu (1561–1612), baptized as John Protasius. He took part in the Korean campaign, was involved in the *Madre de Deus* affair in 1610, was finally banished, and then executed. While the embassy of the four Japanese boys was in Rome in 1585, a brief was published incorporating the three Christian *daimyo* of Arima, Ōmura, and Bungo into the ranks of Christian princes. Arima's representative was Michael Chijiwa Seiyemon. Valignano, *Sumario*, pp. 83, 87; Boxer, *Affair*, pp. 50–53; concerning the embassy, Guzman, *Historia*, II, pp. 225–95, especially p. 261; Fróis, *Première ambassade*, p. 101; Sande, *De missione*, p. 281; Magnino, *Pontificia*, I, pp. 27–34.

[4] Harunobu's eldest son Naozumi (1585–1641), baptized as Michael, later apostatized, and persecuted Christians. Stripped of his fief on account of his father's disgrace in 1612, he was later granted the fief of Nebeoka in Hyūga. The phrase 'onde agora esta trocandolhe o estado' is rather vague, and may refer either to Naozumi's change of political state or change of religion.

[5] Ryūzōji Takanobu (1529–84) became a monk at an early age, but then left the monastery and spent most of his life fighting to increase his domains. He perished in battle while fighting against Shimazu Iehisa of Satsuma. Fróis often mentions him in his *História*, IV; *KEJ*, VI, p. 359.

[6] As recorded in n. 2, above, Bartholomew was Sumitada, second son of Arima Haruzumi; he was adopted into the Ōmura family and succeeded Ōmura Sumiaki in 1551. He also was incorporated into the company of Christian princes: Guzman, *Historia*, I, pp. 511–13, 516–17, and II, pp. 357–9; Valignano, *Sumario*, p. 75, n. 30, p. 76, n. 31; Ōmura family tree given in ibid., p. 77, and in Anesaki, *Concordance*, p. 144.

[7] Ōmura Yoshiaki (1568–1616), eldest son of Sumitada, was baptized as Sancho in 1570. Having sided against Ieyasu in 1600, he was obliged to retire in favour of his son Sumiyori (1592–1619), baptized as Bartholomew like his grandfather. But Sumiyori fell away from his religion and persecuted Christians: Valignano, *Sumario*, p. 77.

trade at the city of Nagasaki, and Don Bartholomew gave the city and its income to the Society as an inheritance for its upkeep. This arrangement was later confirmed by Arima Dono, who governed that part.[1]

The fourth state is the earldom of the islands of Hirado, where there were exiled Don Jerome Koteda (son of Don Anthony), some of his brothers, Don Thomas (son of Don Jerome) who died a martyr for the Faith in Nagasaki, and other lords of these islands. These lords, together with the people who were exiled with them for the Faith, numbered 700 persons, and together they went forth and left their lands and houses for refusing to deny the Faith.[2] The fifth is the state of the Gotō Islands; there are five main islands, and this gives the state its name.[3] These are the first islands one meets coming from China and make up the westernmost part of Japan. The sixth is the state or earldom of Isahaya, whose lord is now subject to Ryūzōji. The seventh is Karatsu, in the state of Hata, with its own lord directly responsible to Tenka. The eighth is Gotoyama, now subject to Ryūzōji, in the state of Ōmura; it contains a long inland sea called Ehi-umi, while the coast is known as Uchime. The mouth of the sea is very small and next to it is the port of Yokoseura, whither went the Portuguese ship when Don Bartholomew was converted to the Faith.[4] Very good seed-pearls are fished in this sea.

The sixth kingdom is Higo, or Hishū, containing fourteen regions, with its capital now at Kumamoto. It has various principal cities, one of which is Udo, capital of the state of Don Augustine Konishi.[5] Another is Yatsuhiro, where there were many glorious martyrs for the Faith. Here was found an old worked stone with a well-fashioned cross, a relic of some Christians who were formerly there.[6]

Among the fourteen regions of this kingdom there is one called Kuma and its lord is

---

[1] The Portuguese ships first began using the port of Nagasaki in 1570 or 1571, and the town soon became the centre of European trade. Valignano has left a detailed account of how Ōmura Sumitada (Bartholomew) handed Nagasaki over to Jesuit jurisdiction in 1580; four years later Arima Harunobu ceded the neighbouring village of Urakami to the missionaries. When Hideyoshi extended his power over Kyushu in 1587, he abrogated the Jesuits' authority in Nagasaki and placed the town under the direct control of the central government. A wealth of material from European and Japanese sources is given in Valignano, *Sumario*, pp. 68*–81*, 78–80. See also Pacheco, 'Founding', and Boxer, *Christian Century*, pp. 100–102 and *Great Ship*, pp. 33–4.

[2] The Koteda family of Hirado was staunchly Christian, and in 1599 left the island with 800 retainers and took refuge in Nagasaki rather than attend the pagan funeral of the *daimyo* of Hirado, Matsuura Takanobu. Anthony was Koteda Saemon, baptized in 1553 and died in 1581. His son Jerome led the exodus from Hirado in 1599, and his son Thomas suffered martyrdom at Nagasaki in November 1619. Anesaki, *Concordance*, pp. 26, 40, and family tree, p. 130; Valignano, *Sumario*, p. 94, n. 102.

[3] Gotō literally means 'Five Islands'.

[4] The long inland sea is now called Ōmura Bay. Ōmura Sumitada offered the missionaries the port of Yokoseura in 1561 in order to attract foreign trade. As a result, the Portuguese ship went there in the following year and in 1565: Boxer, *Great Ship*, pp. 27–9, and *Viagens*, p. 6.

[5] Udo is mentioned elsewhere (p. 101) in connection with its famous shrine set in a cave. Konishi Yukinaga (d. 1600) served under Hideyoshi and played a major role in the Korean campaign. After Hideyoshi's death, he sided against Ieyasu, fought at Sekigahara, was captured, and decapitated at Miyako on 6 November 1600 after refusing as a Christian to commit *seppuku*. Baptized as Augustine in 1583, he was renowned for his skill in the tea ceremony. Fróis often mentions him in *História*, IV. *KEJ*, IV, p. 270.

[6] For example, six Christians were beheaded at Yatsuhiro in December 1603 and four more were martyred there in January 1609. Anesaki, *Concordance*, pp. 26–8. In Part 2, Book 1 (Ajuda, 49–IV–53, f. 188v, and Rodrigues, *Nihon*, II, pp. 258–60, not translated here), Rodrigues discusses whether Christianity could have reached Japan before the arrival of Xavier in the middle of the 16th century, because about 1590 a stone with a cross worked in relief was discovered in a pagan hermitage in Yatsuhiro.

Sagara Dono.[1] This state is among some mountains and cannot be overcome by force of arms because its entrance is very narrow. It contains its cultivated fields and everything needed for its maintenance. They say that in olden days some lords and nobles took refuge there after escaping from the Heike forces in the wars waged against the followers of Genji, in which Heike was defeated. This happened more than four hundred years ago, but his descendants still survive there in those mountains and are a law unto themselves.[2] The islands of Amakusa, Shiki, and those of Kosura belong to this kingdom. In the region called Aso there is a very great and high mountain, from the summit of which much smoke continuously issues. It often rains ashes on other remote parts more than twenty leagues away in such quantity that they can be gathered in handfuls, as we sometimes saw while at Funai in Bungo.[3] The mountain is called Hiko-san and there are *yamabushi* bonzes there.[4]

The seventh kingdom is Hyūga, or Nisshū, with five regions. It is the eastern kingdom of this second large island and for this reason it is called Hyūga, meaning turned or placed to meet the sun. According to their traditions, this kingdom was the first to begin to be peopled, and their first kings originated and had their court there.[5] In the Year of the Lord 1578 this kingdom was seized by the Duke of Satsuma, who drove out the legitimate lord, Itō Dono, a relative of the *yakata* Francis, Duke of Bungo. He took refuge with Don Francis, begging assistance against the enemy. So Don Francis went there with an army of 50,000 infantry with the intention of making the whole of that kingdom Christian and of governing it by Christian laws in keeping with the directives of the kingdom of Portugal, for this pleased him greatly. To this end he took with him Fr Francisco Cabral,[6] Superior of all Japan, with other Fathers and Brothers of the Society, and we ourselves formed part of that company. But on account of the high and profound ordinances of the Lord and the pride of the Bungo people, who were pagans, God our Lord permitted Satsuma to be victorious, and the Bungo army was defeated at the River Mimigawa. At that time Duke Francis was lord of eight of the eleven kingdoms of Saikaidō.[7]

---

[1] The Sagara family, descended from the Fujiwara clan, was established as local rulers in Higo until the 19th century.

[2] There are still a hundred village communities of *ochiudo* ('fallen people'), such as Shiba (Miyazaki prefecture) and Gokanoshō (Kumamoto prefecture), claiming descent from the fugitive Heike (or Taira) refugees of the 12th century. I can find no such reference to the Kuma region, but the Sagara family was linked with the Minamoto (or Genji) clan and Kuma as far back as 1198: *KEJ*, VI, p. 60; Rodrigues, *Nihon*, I, p. 260, n. 146.

[3] Mt Aso, an active volcano, was located in northeast Higo, bordering on Bungo. Rodrigues studied at Funai (modern-day Oita) in 1581–5. Cooper, *Rodrigues the Interpreter*, p. 66.

[4] Mt Hiko, nearly 4,000 feet high, has been from time immemorial a religious centre dedicated to the eldest son of Amaterasu, the sun goddess; the temples on the mountain are served by *yamabushi* priests. For *yamabushi*, see p. 95, n. 2. Rodrigues here mistakes Hizen for Buzen, for the mountain is located in the latter province, not the former. He also appears to confuse Mt Hiko with the volcanic Mt Aso.

[5] The text is obscure at this point, but Hyūga, formerly Himika, can be translated as 'facing the sun' or 'towards the sun': *Nihongi*, I, p. 196. Rodrigues has already mentioned (p. 48) that Hyūga was the first part of Japan to be populated.

[6] Francisco Cabral (1533–1609) was sent to Japan in 1570 to succeed Torres as superior of the mission. He took a negative view of the Japanese character, and on account of his broken health and disagreement with Valignano over mission policy, returned to India in 1583. Valignano, *Sumario*, p. 112, n. 21; Schütte, *Textus*, p. 1143.

[7] Shimazu Yoshihisa (1533–1611) of Satsuma defeated Itō Yoshisuke (1513–85) and his son Suketaka of Hyūga. The Itō fled to Bungo and appealed for help to Ōtomo Yoshishige, to whom they were related by marriage. Ōtomo drove out the Shimazu forces from Hyūga, but was then defeated in 1578 at Mimigawa, at which Rodrigues was present. The apostate Jesuit Fabian mentions this battle in his anti-Christian tract *Ha-Deus*, 1620, to show that the God of the Christians did not protect his followers. Valignano, *Sumario*, pp. 102–3, and Anesaki, *Concordance*, p. 123 for Itō family tree; for Mimigawa, Frōis, *História*, III, pp. 70–78, and Cooper, *Rodrigues the Interpreter*, pp. 46–50; for Fabian, Elison, *Deus Destroyed*, p. 264.

In this kingdom there is a very large cave or gallery next to the sea, cut out of the living rock like a house. It is called Udo-no-Iwato, and is well known in Japan because according to tradition it was the palace of the first lords and kings of Japan.[1] In those days the first inhabitants dwelled in caves and huts, and it was from here that the first to assume the title of king transferred the court to the kingdom of Yamato in Gokinai.[2]

The eighth kingdom is Ōsumi, or Gūshū, subject to the Duke of Satsuma and divided into eight regions. The island of Tanegashima belongs to this kingdom. This was the first part of Japan to be discovered by the Portuguese for the first time in 1542.[3] It was here that they taught the Japanese to make arquebuses. These have spread thence to all parts of Japan so that now they are as skilful in their use as are the best experts. Books have been written on the various ways of using arquebuses at long and short range, etc.[4]

The ninth kingdom is Satsuma, or Sasshū, divided into fourteen regions. Its capital is the city of Kagoshima, where the Blessed Father Francis disembarked on the feast of the Assumption of Our Lady in the year 1549, when he arrived there from Malacca with Fr Cosme de Torres and Brother Juan Fernández of our Society, and Paul of Holy Faith, a Japanese native of Kagoshima.[5] This kingdom possesses many large islands that lie to the south and continue to the islands of Luchu, or Ryūkyū.

The tenth kingdom is the island of Iki, or Ishū, and contains two regions. It is subject to the count of Hirado.

The eleventh kingdom is the island of Tsushima, or Taishū, with two regions. It faces Korea and is fifteen miles distant from that country and a day's sailing from Japan. The island formerly belonged to Korea and is very mountainous and poor in supplies. Japanese trade with Korea is maintained through this island.[6]

---

[1] For Udo-no-iwato, see p. 50.

[2] Jimmu Tennō. See p. 43, n. 5.

[3] For the 'discovery' of Japan, see p. 63.

[4] A possible reference to *Teppō-ki* ('History of the Gun'), written in 1596–1614 by the monk Dairyuji Fumiyuki of Satsuma: Boxer, *Christian Century*, p. 26; Murdoch, *History, 1542–1651*, p. 42; Schurhammer, 'Descobrimento', pp. 535–8.

[5] For Xavier's arrival at Kagoshima, with Torres and Fernández, see p. 1, n. 1. Paul of Holy Faith was the Christian name of Anjirō, a native of Kagoshima. Having killed a man, he fled to Malacca. Baptized in Goa in May 1548, he returned to Kagoshima with Xavier in 1549 and acted as a somewhat inadequate interpreter. According to one report, he later relapsed into piracy. See his letter, Goa, 29 November 1548, in Ruiz-de-Medina, *Documentos*, I, pp. 38–9, and in Norton, *Portugueses*, pp. 53–6. Xavier, *Epistolae*, I, p. 390, n. 64; Guzman, *Historia*, I, pp. 54–5. In chapters 6 and 7 of Part 2, Book 1, of his *History* (Ajuda, 49–IV–53, and *Nihon*, II, pp. 295–314), not translated here, Rodrigues goes into detail about Yajirō (a more likely form of his name), his reasons for leaving Japan, his baptism by the bishop of Goa, and his return to Japan with Xavier.

[6] Tsushima is situated in the channel between Japan and Korea, being about 50 miles from Korea and the Japanese island of Iki, itself about eight miles from Kyushu. The southern part of the island is mountainous and rises in places to 2,100 feet in height. According to legend, Tsushima was one of the islands created by Izanagi and Izanami. Owing to its midway position, the island long served as a political and military intermediary between Japan and Korea. *Nihongi*, I, p. 14.

CHAPTER 7

THE QUALITY AND CLIMATE OF JAPAN, AND THE FRUITS THAT THE LAND PRODUCES

Although in various parts of the kingdom there are large and spacious plains consisting of sown fields and uncultivated land, the whole of the country of Japan is generally very mountainous with great and high mountain chains and dense forests of trees. Some of the mountains are so lofty that their peaks and summits are hidden in the clouds, which is some cases remain far below the summits. As the country is so mountainous, the land is more barren than fertile, and thus much effort is needed to enrich it so that it may be fruitful every year.[1] The air is extremely healthy and temperate, and thus there are no general diseases, such as the plague, in the kingdom.[2] Hence the ordinary folk, who are not given to luxuries, naturally live to an advanced age in most cases, and old people possess a hearty constitution, strength, and health. But the nobles and rich people, who are inclined to luxuries, fall sick and die younger. The Japanese are very fond of medicines and things that lengthen life, and this is very common throughout Japan.[3]

In our time there was a man in the Hokkoku region who lived seven hundred years, and we saw a reliable Christian who had seen and met him, as well as many other pagans who knew him. They say about this man that he remembered ancient events, such as wars, etc., which he himself had witnessed, and that he recounted details agreeing with written records. He had an ugly face, its flesh like the moss on rocks and not appearing human, and

---

[1] Japan is so hilly that even now only about 18% of the land can be cultivated. Although Valignano and Avila Girón (in *TCJ*, pp. 4, 10) bear out Rodrigues's comments about the barrenness of the land, other European writers, such as Carletti and Alvares (in *TCJ*, pp. 5–7) remark on its fertility. Later, both Rodrigues (pp. 105–6) and Valignano (*Principio*, f. 31) modify their view, pointing out that food shortages were caused by local wars rather than by infertility; this is also the view expressed by Vilela (15 September 1565, in *Cartas*, I, f. 193). Avila Girón (*Relación*, p. 12) also notes that both the land and the women are most fertile. The first few pages of the present chapter are reminiscent of what Guzman (*Historia*, I, pp. 386–7) writes on the same subject, for he mentions, in practically the same order as does Rodrigues, the mountains, the resulting infertility, the healthy climate, heavy snow in places, earthquakes, the natural riches of the land, the crops, fruit, etc.

[2] Writing in 1623 after his short visit to Japan, Arthur Hatch (in Farrington, *English Factory*, II, p. 946) remarks, 'The Climate is temperate and healthie, not much pestred with infectious or obnoxious ayres.' Vizcaino (*Relación*, p. 189) also mentions the rarity of plague, and Mexia (in *TCJ*, p. 241) suggest this is due to the healthy climate and the custom of never drinking cold water. Rodrigues later attributes (p. 277) good health to tea drinking (see p. 277, n. 3, below, for a modern specialist's views on this matter). But infectious diseases were not entirely absent. Cocks (18 June 1615, in *Diary*, I, p. 11) heard that more than 2,000 people had died that year at Nagasaki in a smallpox epidemic, while Carletti (*My Voyage*, pp. 127–8) notes the prevalence of venereal disease.

[3] Ribadeneira (*Historia*, pp. 324–5) states that the Japanese make much use of doctors and medicines, and describes the administration of purges; together with Cocks and Mexia (*TCJ*, pp. 240–41), he also mentions moxa and acupuncture treatment.

his hair was like bird's down. He said that he was already tired of life but was unable to die, and that he sometimes felt like throwing himself off a crag in order to end his life. When asked about his food, he said that a person had once appeared to him in a valley, and had told him always to eat a plant called *kuko*, which grew in the forest, and that he had lived on this and nothing else.[1]

To live such a long time is not contrary to human nature, if we consider what has been recorded of ancient peoples and what was seen a short time ago in Bengal, India, where there was a man who had lived three hundred years and was still very hale and hearty. This case was well known and was authenticated through the efforts of the bishop of Cochin, who ordered witnesses to testify sworn evidence about the man.[2] Also in our time there lived a robust man in the town of Chiriku, in the kingdom of Hizen, who was 130 years old and still played chess.[3] The man mentioned above lived in the time of Taikō, who was greatly interested in this case and ordered the herb which he ate to be planted in Miyako and Osaka; he himself ate it, and it was much in use at the court at that time. They also used it to make wine that prolongs life. We ourselves saw this, and we ate the herb and drank the wine.

The country of Japan is very conducive to a long life for both natives and foreigners, all of whom are very healthy there. The food possesses much strength and energy, and hece a small quantity is very sustaining. The people generally live to over seventy years of age with their powers so unimpaired that from a tender age to the end of their life they never leave aside their weapons.[4]

Although the land is temperate, snow falls everywhere in the winter, and there is a great deal of it particularly in the kingdoms of Hokkoku and the regions of Ōshū facing Ezo. The snow is always accompanied by a northwest wind, which is the coldest wind of all as it blows from Tartary.[5] As this kingdom is made up of islands surrounded by the sea, there are

[1] This tale of the old man of Hokkoku has interesting similarities with the Japanese stories of Wasabioye, who was shipwrecked on the Island of Immortals. He found that the inhabitants were tired of living, would no longer eat mermaid flesh because it prolonged life, but ate goldfish and soot as a poison. Instead of wishing each other health and long life, they wished sickness and speedy death; a sick man was congratulated, a healthy man received sympathy. This story apparently dates from the 18th century, but may well be based on earlier versions. Chamberlain, 'Wasabisuwe'. *Kuko*, defined in *Vocabulario*, f. 63, as 'the name of a tree like a herb', is boxthorn or the Duke of Argyll's tea tree, and is reputed to prolong life.

[2] The fame of this old man of Bengal was widespread and various accounts appear in contemporaneous writings (e.g., Barros, *Década quarta*, 4, 9, f. 522, and Couto, *Década quinta*, 1, 12, ff. 30v–31). The most detailed description appears in Paulo de Trinidade, *Conquista*, II, pp. 66–8, a work written 1630–36. According to this Franciscan author, the man, who had recently died, lived 400 years; he had become a Moor at the age of 100, and had two sons. He attributed his age to the fact that when he was 50 years old he had carried over the Ganges a man whom he later, 1605, identified as St Francis. The Bishop of Cochin, Dom Fray André de S. Maria, held judicial inquiries in 1606, and sent reports of his findings to Madrid and the Archbishop of Lisbon.

[3] Rodrigues, *Nihon*, I, p. 266, n. 3, speculates on the identity of Chiriki. The 'chess' mentioned here was probably the game of *go*, described later on p. 295.

[4] The 'conduciveness to long life' continues to the present time, with more than 11,000 Japanese centenarians living in 1999. In recent years Japan has enjoyed the world's highest rate of life expectancy; in 2000 the rate for women was 84·62 years, for men 77·64. Rodrigues later reports, p. 202, that boys begin girding on a sword at the age of 13 or 15; Torres gives the age as 13, Xavier as 14 (in *TCJ*, pp. 40, 60); Valignano (*Sumario*, p. 13) mentions the age of 12 or 14 years. Vizcaino (*Relación*, p. 186) emphasizes the youthful age at which boys wore a sword by saying that they gird themselves with a weapon 'before they are weaned'.

[5] For reports on the weather, see *TCJ*, pp. 11–15, and Valignano, *Sumario*, p. 4, n. 9. In a contemporary translation, Fróis (in *TCJ*, p. 11) notes, 'In the kingdom of Kaga, as we call it, the inhabitants keep within doors certain

many earthquakes and sometimes these are very strong.[1] These tremors occasionally take place in the sea and cause three successive waves of immense size like great lofty mountains. These waves encircle the Japanese coast in the south and sweep inland, destroying many coastal towns and causing great loss of life to man and beast.[2] The weather often changes and varies with rain, wind, and clouds covering the sky.[3] Ordinarily there are two monsoon winds utilized by ships: the summer south wind, accompanied by heavy rains in May and June (rice is sown at this time and if there is a drought, the land is made barren), and the north wind in the winter, when at a certain fixed time it blows west and northwest. These same monsoons also occur at the same time in China and in almost all of the Orient, although in some places other particular winds sometimes predominate.[4]

1. The produce of the land of Japan

The land of Japan yields every sort of metal and there are many mines producing, for example, a great deal of iron, copper (mixed with silver), lead, tin, and a little mercury.[5] The principal mines are those of silver and may be found throughout the country. Such mines are situated in Kanayama in Chūgoku, in the kingdom of Iwami, on the island of Sado in the northern sea, and in many other places. They say that the method of extracting the silver from the mines is not very ancient and that they began this for the first time in the city of Hakata not many years ago. But now experience has made them very skilful and much silver is used throughout the kingdom.[6] In former times they used a certain copper

---

months of the year, having no way to come forth except they break up the tiles.' Even today in Yamagata some farmhouses have a recessed second floor, or *chishi*, from which the occupants can walk out from the snow burying their houses. The cold was felt even in October in Osaka, for William Eaton wrote (27 October 1614, in Farrington, *English Factory*, I, p. 215) to Cocks in Hirado asking for a fur cap 'for that I am now so extreme cold... that all the clothes I can put on will not kepe me warme, etc.'

[1] Reports on earthquakes are numerous – see *TCJ*, pp. 15–16. Fróis (*História*, IV, pp. 246–8) gives a lengthy account of the 1586 earthquakes ('such a great earthquake that people could not remember having seen or heard, nor even having read in the ancient books') that devastated the Miyako region. For the 1596 earthquake that destroyed Fushimi, see Rodrigues, *Bispos da Igreja*, f. 319v, and Schütte, *Historia inédita*, pp. 303–4; Fróis, *De rebus*, pp. 106–32. For references to Cocks regarding earthquakes, see Pratt, *History*, II, pp. 67–8.

[2] Rodrigues (*Bispos da Igreja*, f. 320, and Schütte, *Historia inédita*, p. 304) describes the tsunami caused by the 1596 earthquake, when three successive waves swept 1.5 leagues inland causing immense damage. Vizcaino (in *TCJ*, pp. 16–17) offers an eyewitness account of a 1611 tsunami and also mentions the three waves.

[3] The variability of the weather is noted by Avila Girón (in *TCJ*, pp. 12–13). Writing at Nagasaki on 21 December, he remarks that the warm south wind made it seem like August; yet only three days previously the northwest wind had brought such bitter cold that he could not keep warm in the house.

[4] A contemporaneous account of the Asian monsoons, which confirms Rodrigues's description, is given in Hakluyt, *Principal Navigations*, VI, pp. 28–34. As regards European shipping, taking advantage of the summer southwest monsoon, Portuguese ships would sail from Macao to Nagasaki in about two weeks, from the end of June to the beginning of August. The return voyage was made in October or November, using the winter northeast monsoon. Boxer, *Affair*, p. 11; Dahlgren, *Contribution*, p. 253.

[5] Cocks (10 December 1614, in Farrington, *English Factory*, I, p. 259) informs Lord Salisbury of the abundance of iron and copper, and the skill of the Japanese in working these metals. Avila Girón (*Relación*, p. 15) also comments on the quantity of copper, iron, lead, and mercury. Information on these metals is given in Geerts, 'Useful Minerals'.

[6] For the Iwami and Sado mines, see p. 92, n. 5, and p. 93, n. 3. About 1530 the *rensuiyō* process of separating silver from copper was introduced in the Iwami mines. Brown, *Money Economy*, pp. 34–5, 56–7; Geerts, 'Useful Minerals', 3, pp. 90–93. Valignano (*Adiciones*, p. 352) comments that if the Japanese learned to extract silver by using mercury and other European techniques, their silver mines would be as rich as those of Peru. The Japanese authorities were anxious to learn European methods, and Vivero y Velasco was asked to provide 50 miners from Mexico

coin, and in their buying and selling they bartered things, such as rice, etc., for others just as we saw in India, and this was the method used in the beginning all over the world.[1]

All the nobles now possess goodly treasures of gold and silver. In the year 1609, while we were at Daifu's court at Suruga, his principal treasurer made a count of all his hoard, and there were 83 million taels (or golden crowns) of silver alone, let alone the great store of gold. This treasure never diminished, but rather increased every year because nothing was withdrawn from it to meet costs and every year many millions were added to it.[2] There are also gold mines. Some of them are in the mountains, where they extract gold mixed with silver and separate it by using mercury. Some of it is extracted from the mines as gold dust, and some is obtained as very thin dust from the mud of the river beds, and this is the best sort of all. The biggest supply of gold is found in the kingdom of Ōshū in Kantō.[3]

The land yields much good rice, and this is the principal food and crop of the whole kingdom. It is sown during the May rains in fields where there is plenty of water and irrigation, and as a result they harvest it in September. There are various kinds and different types of rice. The chief sort is white rice, and here again there are various types and prices; another type is red or reddish in colour, and no matter how much they pound it the rice never becomes white but remains grey in colour.[4] They also grow an abundance of wheat for various purposes, but they do not use it to make bread after our fashion, and in recent years

---

(Relación, f. 14v). A European method of separating silver and copper was introduced about this time: Sugimoto and Swain, *Science and Culture*, p. 183. The abundance of silver is often mentioned: Vilela and Fróis, in *Cartas*, I, ff. 193v, 305 and 172; Saris and Cocks, in Farrington, *English Factory*, I, pp. 211–12, 701–2. According to Ralph Fitch (Hakluyt, *Principal Navigations*, X, p. 198), the Portuguese shipped more than 600,000 crowns of silver annually from Japan; Valignano (*Adiciones*, p. 353) mentions 500,000 ducats.

[1] The first Japanese silver and copper coins were minted in 708. *KEJ*, V, p. 242; Geerts, 'Useful Minerals', 3, p. 3. Rodrigues (*Arte grande*, ff. 218–218v) refers to copper coins called *cash* carried by a cord running through a hole in the middle; he lists the various units of *cash* up to one hundred thousand million. On f. 388, he notes that 1,000 *cash* equaled two crowns, although earlier Fróis (19 September 1577, in *Cartas*, I, f. 388v) had mentioned three crowns. Carletti (*My Voyage*, p. 112) values the *cash* as one-thousandth of a tael, while a century later Kaempfer (*History*, III, p. 56) makes it a farthing. According to Cocks (*Diary*, I, p. I, n.1), the tael was worth five shillings, so the *cash* would have been about 0.06 of a penny. Further information in Mundy, *Travels*, III:1, p. 136, n. 1; p. 137, n. 1; and p. 309, n. 1. The coin, the name of which is derived from the Sanskrit word *karsa*, originated in India: Dalgado, *Glossário*, I, pp. 175–6.

[2] The treasurer in the Tokugawa shogunate was called *kanjō-bugyō*, and Rodrigues must be referring to the first holder of this office, Ōkubo Nagayasu (1545–1613), appointed in 1603. *KEJ*, VI, p. 93. According to Cocks (10 December 1614, in Farrington, *English Factory*, I, p. 259), 'most part of the profitt of the mynes, silver and gould, cometh to the Emperour.' Vizcaino reports (*Relación*, p. 188) that the shogun or lords received 70% of the mines' output, and reckoned Ieyasu's fortune at 23 million, but does not supply any units. Other references to Ieyasu's enormous wealth are given in Rodrigues Giram, *Carta anua*, p. 2; Totman, *Tokugawa Ieyasu*, pp. 105–6.

[3] For the Ōshū, or Mutsu, mines, see p. 91, n. 2. Carvalho (21 October 1620, in *TCJ*, pp. 235–6) remarks that the richest mines were found in Ōshū and describes the method of extracting gold from river beds in Ezo. For a thorough illustrated account of Japanese gold mining, see Geerts, 'Useful Minerals', 4, pp. 89–108. But he notes (p. 98), 'The process of extracting gold from the ore by means of amalgamation with quicksilver is unknown to the Japanese.' Presumably this method, used in Rodrigues's time, had been discontinued when Geerts wrote his paper.

[4] As regards 'red or reddish' rice, in 1697 Hitomi (or Hirano) Hitsudai (d. 1701) published *Honchō Shokkan* (or *Shokukagami*) dealing with food produced in Japan, and in his list of 22 types of rice, he mentions *daitōmai*, popularly called *tōkan*, a coarse, reddish variety, introduced from China and grown throughout Japan: Hitomi, *Honchō Shokkan*, I, p. 46. 'Red rice' may still be obtained today, especially in Kyushu; its manufacturers suggest mixing it with ordinary white rice and adding a little salt and *sake* wine.

merchants have shipped flour to Manila.[1] They also grow barley, and this serves as food for the peasants and poor folk in some barren regions; they cook it like rice and mix a little with it. This happens principally in barren and mountainous places in the Kantō regions and the island of Kyushu, where there is not enough rice. At certain times of the year the peasants and poor folk eat barley, fern roots, and wild acorns in, for example, Bungo, Satsuma, Amakusa, and Gotō.

Some of our first Fathers, noting this and unaware of what happened in other regions, wrote that Japan was very poor and lacking in provisions, and that the people ate only the leaves of radishes and plants, etc.[2] But this is not so in Gokinai and other fertile regions, where there is an abundance of food and provisions. In addition, the continual civil wars waged throughout Japan until Nobunaga's time caused much scarcity, for it was impossible to sow seed and crops were destroyed everywhere. But the shortage of food was not due to the infertility of the land.[3]

They also produce an abundance of every type of vegetable, such as beans, diverse kinds of millet, many various green stuffs, turnips, and large quantities of radishes, which in some regions are so big that four of them make up a reasonable burden for one man, as we ourselves saw.[4]

Much of the fruit is the same as in Europe, for example, different kinds of pears, small apples in the Kami regions, peaches, apricots, and plums. There are only a few grapes because they do not cultivate them and those that do grow are not suitable for wine. In the forests there is a kind of wild black grape that the Japanese do not eat. These are genuine grapes, albeit wild, as regards taste and strength if they are used to make wine. According to the information given from here to Rome, it was decided that Mass could be said with wine made from them in default of wine from Europe, and this indeed has happened.[5]

---

[1] Mention of this trade in wheat to the Philippines is also made in Carletti, *My Voyage*, p. 113; Ribadeneira, *Historia*, p. 322; Alonso Sánchez, in Colin, *Labor*, I, p. 49; and Valignano, *Principio*, f. 32.

[2] Valignano (*Principio*, f. 9v) points out that some of the early reports contained inaccuracies because of the language barrier and the turbulent state of the country discouraged travel. Even before he reached Japan, Vilela wrote from India (24 April 1554, in Ruiz-de-Medina, *Documentos*, I, p. 433) that he had heard that the Japanese ate turnip leaves sprinkled with barley flour because of the barrenness of the country. Later (Hirado, 29 October 1557, in ibid., I, p. 709) he paints a gloomy picture of the missionaries hoarding turnip leaves in case of famine; the commoners' principal food was dried turnip and pumpkin leaves, there was little wheat, and not enough rice for all. Gago (Hirado, 23 September 1555, in ibid., I, p. 556) mentions that Torres, formerly robust, was now old and thin; he ate only a little rice and vegetables as the land was so sterile. At times conditions for the poor could be deplorable. 'In seasons of famine the misery of the farmers was unspeakable' (Murdoch, *History to 1542*, p. 603), and in 1454, 700–800 corpses were collected daily in the streets of Miyako.

[3] Both Valignano and Vilela point out that the food shortages were due to war rather than to barrenness – see p. 102, n. 1.

[4] For lists of Japanese food products, see the accounts of Carletti, Alvares, and Saris in *TCJ*, pp. 5–7, 190. Carletti (*My Voyage*, p. 109) also notes that radishes, or *daikon*, were very large and that three or four made up a load for one man.

[5] Avila Girón (*Relación*, pp. 44–5) approved of *sake*, or Japanese rice wine, and was told by a Fleming that it was better than the beer of his country. He goes on to name various types of *sake* and mentions the conditions for making good-quality wine. Rice wine reminded Mexia (8 October 1581, in *Cartas*, II, f. 17) of beer, and Vivero y Velasco (*Relación*, f. 5) concedes that after grape wine, Japanese wine is the best. Valignano (*Sumario*, p. 42), however, reports that *sake* is harmful to Europeans. Saris (in Farrington, *English Factory*, II, pp. 1014–15) observes: 'other drinkes they have none, but what is distilled out of rice, which is almost as strong as our aquavitae, and in colour like to Canarie wine, and is not deare. Yet when they have drawne off the best and strongest, they wring out of it a smaller and

There are various kinds of melons that are excellent in their different taste and flavours, chiefly in Gokinai; they are different from ours as regards their texture, taste, and piquancy. There are also cucumbers, pumpkins, watermelons, and other fruits that we lack. There are many figs of various sorts and excellent flavour, and they dry like our figs; these dried figs are somewhat similar in appearance and the natural flour they produce, but not in taste and texture. The best are by no means inferior to our good figs and indeed are much better, especially those produced in the kingdom of Mino, which are accordingly called *minogaki* or *edagaki*. This is a choice product, and because of the similarity between this dried fruit and our figs, the first Europeans seem to have called them figs. But in appearance they are more of a kind of pear on account of their shape and the tree on which they grow, for, like pears, they contain pips, but they are hard like stones. While still unripe, they are green in colour, but after ripening they are a reddish yellow.[1]

The country also produces much good sesame oil and this is the type most in use. But oil is also produced from mustard and poppy seeds, as well as a certain kind of oil obtained from the seed or fruit of a tree. The women use this last oil to dye their hair black, in contrast to Europeans who try to make their hair fair, something that they dislike intensely.[2] There is also oil obtained from whales and other fish. There is a great deal of wax for candles, and this is made from the fruit of the tree from which varnish is obtained.[3] Hence many people were mistaken when they wrote that the Japanese had nothing but whale oil and used pieces of pine wood for illumination. They based this observation on what they saw in some of the poor and barren regions and islands that lacked many things, especially in time of war.

The land produces a certain kind of tree from which they obtain excellent varnish, probably the best in the discovered world and better than that of China. The use of this varnish will be described when we deal with the art of varnishing and gilding.[4] The varnish is obtained in the same way as gum is drawn by striking the trunk of the tree, and varnish flows from the incision like gutta or resin from trees. As we have said, they make candles from the wax obtained from the fruit of these trees.[5]

The land produces much hemp and good cotton. The use of the latter has greatly increased since we went to Japan. At that time, and also in ancient times, the cloth most in use was made of woven linen lengths called *nuno* here, and the garment made from these is

---

slighter drinke, serving the poorer sort of people, which through want cannot reach to the better.' The times for drinking hot or cold *sake* are given on p. 251. The problem of supplying Mass wine to the missionaries in Japan was difficult, and Vilela (Hirado, 29 October 1557, in Ruiz-de-Medina, *Documentos*, I, p. 691) reports that they had hidden such wine in the ground in case they were attacked by robbers. The first item on the list of duties (renewed by Valignano in December 1603) of the Jesuit procurator in Macao was the annual supply of 2½ casks of good Mass wine for Japan, to be brought from Portugal or Goa (Ajuda, 49–IV–66, ff 16v, 19).

[1] Avila Girón (*Relación*, p. 14) provides a similar list of fruit. *Edagaki*, or *kushigaki*, may better be described as dried persimmons, although usually called figs by the early Europeans. Fróis recalls that he had been summoned into Nobunaga's presence and 'some very big dried figs from the kingdom of Mino' were served. On the ruler's orders, some were placed into a small box so that Fróis could take them home with him. These Mino 'figs', he writes, were the best in Japan: Fróis, *História*, III, p. 259, and *TCJ*, pp. 96–7.

[2] This dislike of fair hair, shared also by the Chinese (Ricci, *Fonti*, I, p. 88, and *China*, p. 77). is also mentioned by Fróis (*Tratado*, p. 118), and Avila Girón and Carletti (in *TCJ*, pp. 38–9).

[3] The vegetable-wax tree, or *haji*, does in fact belong to the same *Rhus* genus as the lacquer-tree, and the berries of the latter are sometimes used to produce wax for candles. For the preparation and manufacture of this wax, see Gribble, 'Preparation of Vegetable Wax', pp. 94–7.

[4] More about varnishing, or lacquering, is given on p. 326, below.

[5] For the lacquer tree, see *KEJ*, IV, pp. 36–3.

called *nunoko*.[1] Nowadays much good nankeen is woven like cotton and from this they make lengths of cloth. In the early days Portuguese merchants used to bring this to Japan for ordinary people's clothing, but now this trade has ceased. But they bring some black cotton lengths for sale, because the Chinese dye is better than the Japanese.

They also produce much white silk, although it is less fine than the Chinese kind. This is mainly due to the wars when less was used, but now that there is peace and trade has increased, a large amount of more than 1,500 or 2,000 piculs is produced.[2]

There is also much good silk floss. This is very fine stuff and is used in winter for quilts as it is very fine, soft, delicate, and extremely warm. They also make from this a certain kind of hood that they wear on the head in winter and also wrap around the neck, unlike the Tartars, Koreans, and Chinese, who use various animal skins in winter.[3]

They make various kinds of paper from the bark of a certain tree grown for this purpose, for paper is one of the things most used in Japan. Its antiquity is not certain, but it seems that they learnt about it from their neighbours, the Koreans, who make it from the same material. The Koreans received it from the Chinese, who appear to have been the first to invent it in the Orient, or indeed in the whole world, during the monarchy that the Chinese call Han.[4]

In recent years a supply of amber has been found in these islands and according to those who know about it, some of it is of good quality. There may have been some in earlier times as well, but it was not known among them because it was the Portuguese who introduced it to them.

There is also ordinary camphor obtained by boiling wooden splinters from the *kusu* tree. They call this camphor *shōnō* and it is different from the kind that comes from Borneo; the latter is highly prized and expensive, and they call it *ryūnō*.[5] The tree, or rather its wood, is scented and is of almost incorruptible durability, and because of this toughness it is very suitable for ships.

Contrary to what some people (such as the Venetian Marco Polo) have written, the land does not produce any precious stones, neither are their use and worth recognized and valued among them.[6] This applies even to pearls; ordinarily there are none, although they are produced in some places, such as the inland sea of Ōmura, but these are very few and small.

In the forests there are various kinds of timber and wood, and much of it is excellent and highly prized for buildings. They build everything, such as houses, temples, and ships,

---

[1] In the Portuguese text there is a short gap after 'woven linen lengths', but it does not appear to alter the sense. *Vocabulario*, f. 187v; 'Nuno, Cloth made from hemp. Nunoko. Garment made from hemp and silk floss.'

[2] The picul, from the Malay-Javanese term *pikul*, a man's load (Yule, *Hobson-Jobson*, p. 523), was equal to 100 catties, or 133.3 lbs. According to *Arte grande*, f. 219, it was also equal to 1,600 taels weight.

[3] This was the *watabōshi*, or cotton-wool hat, mentioned by Carletti, *My Voyage*, p. 129; Fróis, *Tratado*, pp. 110, 120; *Vocabulario*, f. 268v. Valignano (*Sumario*, p. 234) forbade Jesuits from wearing such caps indoors.

[4] The invention of paper is traditionally ascribed to the eunuch Cai Lun in 105 during the Later Han dynasty. According to *Nihongi*, II, p. 140, paper and ink were introduced into Japan in 610 by a monk sent by the king of Korea. Hunter, *Papermaking*, pp. 155–6; Carter, *Invention*, pp. 4–5; *SCC*, 5:1, p. 40. Rodrigues again deals with paper in Book 2, Chapter 6, p. 343.

[5] The *kusu* tree is the *cinnamomum camphora* and is extremely durable in water. *KEJ*, I, p. 237; Geerts, 'Preliminary Catalogue', p. 10. *Vocabulario*, ff. 211v, 397, distinguishes between *shōnō* and *ryūnō* as inferior and excellent camphor.

[6] In his hearsay report on Japan, Polo (*Book*, III, 2; Yule, *Book*, II, pp. 254–5) writes that the country possesses great quantities of gold, as well as rose-coloured pearls and other precious stones. Rodrigues later mentions (p. 283) the Japanese attitude towards gems.

of wood and not of stone or bricks as we do,[1] except for the walls of fortresses that they build of stone, and the walls surrounding nobles' houses, which they construct of mud. Among the precious woods, the type called *hinoki* and *kayanoki*, a kind of fragrant cedar, is the best and most highly prized.[2] Japan has many dense forests of this, from which they take the wood. As the use of wood is so great, the country is already running short of it, and many mountains that were formerly covered with timber are now as bare as if there had never been a tree growing there.[3]

Throughout the entire kingdom there is much water and excellent springs. Although they do not usually drink it cold, the Japanese nevertheless appreciate the good water for use in their *chanoyu*, as we shall later describe in its proper place.[4] Neither in summer nor in winter do the Japanese usually drink cold water, especially in the western regions of Gokinai. But in the regions of Kantō and eastwards they drink cold water even in winter, although they also make use of hot water. There are many abundant rivers, some of which can be navigated by small vessels; there are also many lakes, some of which are very large. Various kinds of excellent fish are found in both fresh and salt water. In the northern sea there is much salmon that at a certain time of year spawn in the rivers, where the people fish many of them, salting and drying them in the sun.

2. The various types of animals and birds

In Japan there are various kinds of animals, both domestic and wild, such as horses. Some of these fetch a high price, although they are more like ponies than Spanish horses, albeit they are high-spirited and sturdy.[5] They do not use horseshoes but ordinarily do without them, and in stony and rugged places they make use of straw shoes woven to fit the horse's hooves. More will be said elsewhere about the harness, stirrups, and care of these horses.[6] There are many cows used for ploughing, although unlike us they do not harness two together, but instead make use of only one by itself.[7] They sometimes use horses or mares to plough the land. There are neither mules nor asses, although there are many of them in China and Korea, and some were brought thence to Japan during the recent wars. The only domestic animals that they raise are dogs for hunting. They keep hens, ducks, and geese only for recreation and not for eating. For it is the ordinary custom throughout the kingdom not to eat the flesh of domestic animals, such as the pig, hen, and cow, as they regard them as unclean. But with the establishment of trade with the Portuguese, the Japanese

---

[1] This sentence is carelessly written, for Rodrigues obviously did not mean that ships also were built of stone or bricks.

[2] For the *hinoki* tree, see p. 90, n. 4. As *Vocabulario*, f. 348, points out, the tree is more like the cypress than the cedar. *Kayanoki*, or *Torreya nucifera*, cannot be classified as a precious wood. Its twigs were burnt in summer as the smoke drives off mosquitoes.

[3] Such mountains are called *hageyama*, or 'bald mountains'.

[4] A reference to the famous tea ceremony, which Rodrigues describes in great detail below (pp. 282–308).

[5] Avila Girón (*Relación*, p. 22) says that the best of them were fit only to carry firewood. Saris (*TCJ*, pp. 143–4) remarks that they were 'not tall, but of the size of our middling Nags, short and well trust, small headed and very full of mettle, in my opinion, farre excelling the Spanish Jennet in pride and stomacke.' When visiting Edo Castle, Vivero y Velasco noted (*Relación*, f. 9) more than 200 strong horses in good condition, which, if trained in Spain, would have left nothing to be desired. In his audience with Hideyoshi in 1591, Valignano presented the ruler with a fine horse, a second horse having died en route to Japan. Cooper, *Rodrigues the Interpreter*, p. 75.

[6] This is a promise unfulfilled as Rodrigues says nothing more elsewhere on this subject.

[7] It is true that the Japanese plough was usually pulled by only one beast, which was generally an ox, not a cow.

breed these animals at places where the Great Ship[1] and other trading vessels come so that they may sell them. Not only the merchants who come from various places to trade with them, but also many others now eat these things. Even nobles and others do so under the excuse of regarding it as medicine and something new. Thus the practice is no longer considered so loathsome and horrible in the kingdom as it was formerly, when they would strike us in the face as an insult, declaring that we ate cows and domestic animals, and even human flesh.[2]

In the forests there are various animals of the chase, such as wild boar, many deer, hares (but no rabbits), wolves, bears, foxes, tailless monkeys (monkeys with tails come from abroad and are highly prized), and other such animals.[3] There are no tigers or panthers, although there are a lot of them in nearby Korea. There are no poisonous snakes except the viper.

There are many kinds of wild birds, such as pheasant, hens, quails, pigeons, wild doves, and many other types of bird that are excellent to eat, especially many kinds of wild duck and geese, which fill the sky and the fields when flocks of them come from Tartary in the winter.[4] Various kinds of cranes and swans also come at the same time. They are a fine sight to behold, and among the birds that are hunted these are the most prized by the Japanese. The crane occupies the first place, the swan the second, and in third place is the wild duck. In the formal banquets of the nobility in their *chanoyu*, one of these three sorts is always served in order to make the feast more solemn.[5] Indeed, these birds garnished in the Japanese fashion are excellent and very tasty. In certain circumstances it may happen that a fresh crane is worth sixty or seventy crowns, as we ourselves sometimes saw in Taikō's time, while a salted one would be worth ten crowns or sometimes more.

The lords and nobles breed in their houses many kinds of birds of prey, such as falcons, hawks, gerfalcons, and many other types, both big and small, so that they may go hunting with them. They have special houses where the birds are kept on wooden perches, tied by the leg with handsome cords of crimson silk. There are certain men appointed to breed, feed, and clean the birds, and this they do meticulously, as shall be described elsewhere.[6] They are thus much accustomed to hunting with falcons and to giving away as gifts the game they take. They regard this with much esteem and honour, and they observe a special procedure and ceremony when they eat it. The Lord of Tenka holds formal hunts with these birds, and for this reason there are many reserves where nobody may hunt, set traps,

---

[1] The *não*, or carrack, was one of the largest vessels afloat at the time and by the end of the 16th century sometimes had 120,000 cubic feet of cargo space. Boxer, *Great Ship*, p. 13, n. 34, and *Affair*, pp. 84–5.

[2] The Japanese aversion to cow's meat, the rumour that Europeans ate human flesh, and the change in the Japanese attitude since the arrival of the Europeans, are mentioned by many writers. Gago, 23 September, 1555, in Ruiz-de-Medina, *Documentos*, I, p. 556; Vilela, in *Cartas*, I, f. 58; Vivero y Velasco, *Relación*, f. 67v; Ribadeneira, *Historia*, p. 322; Valignano, in *Principio*, ff. 36, 60v, and *Sumario*, pp. 241–4; according to Avila Girón, *Relación*, pp. 15–16, since his arrival in Nagasaki in 1594, the price of cow's meat had risen ten-fold as people began eating it. As late as 1622, Cocks (*Diary*, I, p. 236) notes that he had been given 'halfe a beefe .. But it was kild in the night, for non may be kild heare per themperours command.' Rodrigues again refers to this topic on pp. 262–3.

[3] Several *namban byōbu*, or screens depicting Europeans, show Portuguese merchants processing through Nagasaki and carrying exotic animals in cages as presents. They even brought an elephant (called Don Pedro) as a gift for Hideyoshi in 1597.

[4] On p. 315, Rodrigues mentions that these flocks of geese were often depicted in mural paintings.

[5] The meat dishes at formal banquets are later described in greater detail on p. 262.

[6] The promised description of these men does not in fact appear elsewhere.

or even frighten away the wild birds.[1] The nobles also rear eagles inside a small hut like a cage in certain parts of their palaces. They pluck out their wing and tail feathers for their arrows, as they are excellent for this purpose. As they have no feathers with which to fly, for they are pulled out as soon as they grow, the birds remain there quite tame without escaping.

3. Some marvelous animals in Japan that change into others

In these islands there are some wonderful things outside the ordinary course of nature, for some animals and beasts change into another species without dying or being corrupted, as happens in other natural changes. For as the Philosopher says, 'The generation of one thing is the corruption of another.'[2] But while they are thus still living, they gradually change into another species of animal until they are as perfectly formed in this new species as they had been in their former one. This would seem quite impossible if there were not quite clear experience of this here, for such animals have been seen here before they began to change, others half-changed, while others completely changed. But it is done in such a way that the natives of this land know quite clearly by certain and evident signs which of that species was born quite naturally from its seed just like other animals, and which of them have become members of the species through this change.

Philosophers now seek the cause of all this for they declare that is impossible, especially for animals, to change from one species into another without corrupting and dying, because the corruption and expulsion of the form of one is the generation of another. It seems here that we are bound to admit that the first form corrupted to make way for the second without the actual subject corrupting. This is like the form of the embryo that is animated by the vegetative and sensitive forms, but these give way when the rational soul is infused. It also seems that these animals have a certain disposition and were, so to speak, all ready for the form that was ultimately introduced, although the natural cause that goes with this was not lacking. Nor do these animals finish by chance before they are changed, because all of them are born in the seed of this first species and do not change. Nor is this so only of those that change, for some are born into one species from seed while others are changed into it.

What is certain is that God Our Lord is wonderful in His works of nature and that our weak wit cannot unlock the secrets hidden therein, and this is one of those secrets.

For in these islands there are three sorts of changes from one thing into another.

1. Some land and water animals with feet and paws change into fishes.
2. Other sea things, such as shellfish, change into birds.
3. Animals of one species change into another, and those of another species change into wood or stone.

---

[1] For reports about the size of the shogun's hunts, see p. 85, n. 5. The officials in charge of the falcons and dogs in such hunts were known as *takajo*. Ieyasu was fond of hawking, and two ranking officials were in danger of losing their heads in 1606 for allowing farmers to lay traps in areas where the shogun hunted: Sadler, *Maker*, p. 352. Writing in March 1619 (in Farrington, *English Factory*, I, p. 753), Thomas Wilson mentions the penalties incurred for destroying the protected game.

[2] The Philosopher is Aristotle, and the quotation, given in Latin, is found in *De generatione et corruptione*, I, 3. Rodrigues probably took this quotation from one of the Jesuit textbooks of neo-scholastic philosophy produced at Coimbra University (but widely reprinted in other parts of Europe), such as *Commentarii … in libros de generatione et corruptione*, p. 127. The whole of this section, with its technical terms such as 'species', 'corruption', 'expulsion of the form', etc., is based on scholastic philosophy.

There is, first of all, in some parts of Japan an animal they call *noro*.[1] It has short paws like an otter and very soft fur like yellow silk. It is also found in the Gotō Islands facing China, and the people there regard it as a dainty dish and its skin is highly esteemed and valuable. When it is served in a banquet, they singe the skin and cook it without skinning it, and in this manner they show greater courtesy to the guest and it is more sumptuous.

When these animals are very old, they enter and live in the sea, and there they gradually change into large fish rather like tuna. Fishermen catch these fish, and certain signs tells them which have formerly been land animals and which have naturally been generated from the seed of that species. Sometimes they catch some half-changed; this is well known in those islands and indeed throughout all Japan, for it cannot be doubted as there have often been instances of this.

Among many other examples there is this one. Brother Luis de Almeida,[2] who was later ordained priest in our Society and was a most apostolic man in the work of converting souls among these pagan people, was on the Gotō Islands in the year 1566 when one of these animals, half-converted into a fish, was caught. Parts of it were yet to be changed and belonged quite clearly and distinctly to the original animal. It was presented to the lord of those islands, who then sent it as a gift to Brother Luis de Almeida. When he saw and examined it, he could not deny that it was the above-mentioned land animal, but nor could he deny that it was changing completely into a fish. For the forelegs were already changed into fins, although they still had the tips of the claws and hair. The rear legs were already half-fins, although they still had at the end the toes with their joints and claws. He dissected these half-changed parts and bones, and sent them dried to our Fathers in Rome so that they might there see this wonder of nature.[3]

There is also in these islands of Japan a certain kind of frog, or toad, that changes into mullet fish. Some have been seen half-changed, the head still being that of a frog while the rest has changed into a fish. These very same fish are also sometimes changed.

It is also a proven fact that a certain kind of snake changes into sea octopuses with seven legs or arms; the Japanese know about these and for this reason never eat them. All the genuine and natural octopuses have eight legs or arms, and none of them has seven like this type.

There is also a certain kind of plant root that they eat and call in their language *yamaimo*,[4] meaning forest yam, in contrast to those that they sow in their vegetable gardens. When these have been in water for some time, they change into a certain type of snake, and the people have had examples and experience of this as well.

---

[1] This seems to be an error, for the *noro* is a species of deer, similar to the roebuck and found in northern China and Korea. Perhaps Rodrigues was thinking of the *todo*, or sealion. *Vocabulario*, f. 258v: '*Todo*. A kind of sea animal that has hair and four legs, etc.'

[2] Luis de Almeida (1525–83) was born in Lisbon and went to Japan in 1555 as merchant and surgeon. He made generous financial gifts to the Jesuits for hospital work before he entered the Society as a Brother in 1556. He worked in the Kyushu region until going to Macao for ordination in 1580. He returned to Japan as a priest and died a few years later at Amakusa. Schütte, *Textus*, p. 1124.

[3] Almeida relates (20 October 1566, in *Cartas*, I, ff. 224–4v) a visit to the Gotō Islands and mentions a strange creature, half-animal, half-fish (perhaps a *mairuka*, or *iruka*, a porpoise?). This he dissected, but he says nothing about sending it to Rome. See also Guzman, *Historia*, II, pp. 26–7. The fame of the animal spread, and a reference to it is made on p. 129 in the Coimbra textbook cited on p. 111, n. 2. A century after the event, the animal found its way into Kircher, *China illustrata*, p. 192.

[4] *Vocabulario*, f. 317: '*Yamaimo*. Wild yams.' According to Rodrigues, *Nihon*, I, p. 283, n. 31, there was a widespread belief that *yamaimo* turned into eels.

There is a kind of shellfish with two large shells that are very long at the tips and at the bottom, where they are joined because they open narrow. The people call them *torigai* and they breed in the deep mud of the sea.[1] Some of them change into certain seabirds like ducks; the fish within the shell changes into this bird that they call *chidori*.[2] It has beautiful and elegant feathers of various colours. They are also born from eggs of the same seed just like other birds.

---

[1] The *torigai* is a species of cockle. Alternatively, the *'fororogai'* of the Portuguese text may refer to the *horagai*, a large conch shell used by *yamabushi* monks who 'make a frightful noise blowing upon a trumpet made of a shell' (Kaempfer, *History*, III, p. 52). The previous sentence is a literal translation of a possibly corrupt text.

[2] *Chidori* is generally translated as plover. According to *Vocabulario*, f. 47v, it is a small bird that lives on the beach.

CHAPTER 8

THE MEASUREMENTS OF ROADS, AND THE METHOD OF MEASURING LANDS IN RESPECT TO RENT, AND THE VARIOUS KINDS OF MEASUREMENTS OF THIS KINGDOM

We see that many things in the world are common to all its principal nations, but the how, when, where, and who of their first origin and inventors are not at all clear. This is true of mathematical measurements, the invention of writing, astrology, measurements, the movements of the sun, moon, planets, stars, and the Heavens; the division of the starry sky into signs and constellations (which bring about singular effects in events below when the sun moves among them); the material sphere with its circles, the division of the sky into a dozen equal parts or signs, and all of it into 360°; the solar year divided into 365¼ days, the fours seasons, and a dozen months; the lunar year with 12 or 13 moons, intercalated so as to equal the solar year;[1] the failure of the sun and moon at their appointed eclipses;[2] measurements both of linear and itinerary quantity as well as of area, and also of fluids and liquids, and of weight. All these and other such things are found everywhere in every ancient organized nation, and they are so ancient that nobody can remember their origin. Yet there is so great a similarity among them that if they are all carefully considered everywhere they turn out to be almost the same and can be attributed to the same origin.

We see that authors differ and vary a great deal in establishing the first originators of these things. Some writers attribute their invention to certain people, while others attribute it to others who, they consider, were the first to introduce its use in some treatise or other.[3] But those writers best discourse about such matters who attend to the reference to and antiquity of such things that may be found in Holy Writ. They hold that such things all took their first origin from the first Father, Adam, and the ancient Fathers who lived before the Flood; many arts had this origin as well. They maintain that after the Flood holy Noah taught these things to his sons and descendants before they dispersed throughout the world. Thus they took this knowledge with them when they went to populate various parts of the world and establish new kingdoms, and so there was general conformity everywhere.

Those nations that were most diligent and have suffered fewest changes since their first foundation have preserved these things completely or partially, each nation modifying them

---

[1] Owing to the inaccuracy of the lunar calendar, from time to time it was necessary to add an extra, or intercalary, month (*urū-tsuki*). This problem was removed when the Gregorian calendar was introduced in Japan on 1 January 1873. *KEJ*, I, p. 231; Papinot, *Historical*, p. 836. Further details are given on p. 351, n. 5.

[2] Rodrigues later deals with all these subjects in detail on pp. 372–4.

[3] The Portuguese text reads 'em alguma oração', 'in some speech or treatise', but this is probably a slip for 'em alguma nação', 'in some country'.

for its own use. Thus when the ancients came to describe measurement in general and all its types, they wrote as follows:

> Measurement is defined and described as follows by those who wrote about boundaries: Measurement is whatever is limited by weight, capacity, length, height, breadth, and the mind. The ancients divided the world into areas, areas into provinces, provinces into regions, regions into places, places into territories, territories into fields, fields into *centuriæ*, *centuriæ* into yokes, yokes into *clima*, then *clima* into *actus*, poles, paces, steps, cubits, feet, inches, and a finger's breadth. Such was their ingenuity. The finger's breadth is the smallest unit of rural measurement.[1]

If we have to judge this matter by its antiquity, we clearly find that what we say is quite certain, and the same holds for all these things found in the kingdom of China. For according to their scriptures (and their other writings agree on this point), the nation has existed for more than 3,800 years and is one of the most ancient in the world today, and it has kept intact since its first foundation right up to the present day. It came into being about 4,000 years ago at the time of Babel, for it was founded by the descendants of Noah, who left Babylon in order to populate the world.[2] Among them were nine leaders (according to others there were ten) who founded this famous kingdom with 140 families here at the limit of the Orient.[3] Since its beginning in those ancient times it has possessed all these things mentioned above, and has preserved them to this day. They were taught by their first founders and sages even before the country had the form of an established nation, for from that time their first founders taught the use of writing with figures and hieroglyphics, just as the sons of Seth are said to have written things on columns before the Flood.[4]

They also taught astrology, the movements of the Heavens and planets; the material globe[5] (our authors attribute this to various more modern inventors, but do not agree on the matter), with its equinoctial and ecliptic circles divided into degrees, and with the tropics separated from the equinox, as it is now; the Heavens divided into a dozen equal parts, and distributed through $365°25'$, giving $100'$ to each degree; the solar year of $365\frac{1}{4}$ days, divided into twelve months and four seasons, with the solstices and equinoxes; the lunar year with 354 days divided into twelve moons, and the intercalary year of 383 days divided into thirteen moons; the method of calculating the eclipses of the sun and moon; the starry sky divided up into pictures and constellations, or figures, with the name of each one and of each star.[6]

---

[1] Rodrigues gives this quotation in Latin and must have taken it from a scholastic textbook. The first sentence is merely an introduction to the definition that follows. The complete definition is found in St Isidore of Seville (d. 636), *Etymologiarum*, XV, 15, in Migne, *Patrologia latina*, 82, p. 555. Isidore took the first sentence ('Measurement is whatever … breadth and the mind') from Boethius, *De institutione arithmetica*, p. 373, and then added the descriptive explanation. A *centurium* was a variable unit of land area; a yoke (or *jugerum*, the area ploughed by a yoke of oxen in a day) measured 240 feet x 120 feet; a *clima* equalled 60 sq.ft; an *actus*, 120 feet x 4 feet. Lewis and Short, *Latin Dictionary*, pp. 316, 1016, 354, 25.

[2] The theory that various nations were founded by the dispersion after the Tower of Babel was currently popular. Kaempfer, who lived in Japan 1690–92, rejected on philosophical and religious grounds that the Japanese were descended from the Chinese; instead, he maintains (*History*, I, pp. 135–46) that they were directly descended from the Babylonians, and he ingeniously plots their trans-Asian route to Japan.

[3] For these nine leaders, see p. 24.

[4] For these inscribed columns, see pp. 375–6.

[5] For 'material globe', see p. 11, n. 5.

[6] All this information is repeated in greater detail in Book 2, Chapters 9–13.

They have also possessed since that time linear measurements with all their smaller divisions and substantially the same as the ancient units of Asia and Europe. For example, the point or degree, inch, foot, the small common pace of three feet, the larger pace of five feet, the ell or *covado*, the perch, the celestial and terrestrial degree, as well as other units of liquids and fluids, and also weights and scales. All this is a clear indication that Noah's sons and descendants learned these things from him before the Confusion of Tongues, so that they might take them with them when they parted to populate the world and that there might be conformity among them all. So after the Confusion of Tongues they took all this knowledge with them. Whence it may be inferred that among the descendants of Noah and the nine leaders who peopled China with their 140 families were nobles and clever people, for they had sages who knew all these things and taught them to their nation after it had been founded.

Nor may it be said that each nation invented these things by chance, for it is impossible to have such conformity in these things in such foreign and distant kingdoms, between which there had been no knowledge or communication. This happened in ancient and primitive times when there was no such thing as nationhood in the world. As their records tell us, they did not use fire at that time because it had not been invented. They ate fruit from the trees and clothed themselves with animal skins and the bark of trees, and they lived in caves and tree huts.[1] At that time Earth was still marshy in many places with the waters of the Flood draining off through holes and rivers to the sea. This is a clear argument that all this originated from the same source and was not invented by them in such a short time.

China is a very ancient nation and has possessed all these things since its first beginning. The Koreans and Japanese and other neighbouring peoples have received many of these things from them, such as the method of dividing their kingdom into provinces, and provinces into states, regions, and other smaller divisions. As well as all types of units of both continuous and discrete quantities, and of liquid measures, and also weights and scales.

---

[1] Rodrigues goes into greater detail in Book 2, Chapter 8, mentioning the names of the emperors who introduced fire, cooking, clothing, housing, etc.

CHAPTER 9

[LINEAR MEASUREMENTS]

1. Chinese linear measurements[1]

Just as the Latins and Italians use the mile in their measurements, the Greeks the *stadion*, the Egyptians the sine or degree, the Spaniards, Germans, and French the league, and the Persians the *farsang*,[2] so the Chinese use the *li* and the Japanese the identical *ri*. As far as pronunciation is concerned, it is written with 'l' among the Chinese and with 'r' among the Japanese.[3] As is well known among mathematicians, all these measurements of the various nations are made up of smaller units. In China during the present monarchy called Daming (that is, Great Splendour), various provinces have various larger and smaller linear measures bearing the same name and in common use. This is employed with reference to the land and its use, and they generally call it *chi*, while the Japanese call it *shaku*. Properly speaking, this is their foot or more commonly their ell, and is the smallest of their standard measurements. It is the common unit used by the kingdoms of the Chinese, Koreans, and Japanese.

Among the Chinese this is of two kinds, and the first king of this Daming monarchy revised it.[4] One is large and unusual, and is employed in private use, while the other is smaller by two parts in ten, so that this smaller unit corresponds to eight-tenths of the larger. This is the common and universal unit called *guanchi*, meaning magistrates' measurement, and it is the linear unit used to measure land and everything else. It is universal and common to all, and is used in buildings that have a certain determined measurement. In different Chinese monarchies there has been some variation in this unit, and it has been made smaller or larger for various uses. Yet the linear unit with which the roads and lands are measured and which they have always used in mathematical and celestial matters (such as degrees, and the distances of the sky, and the stars and their size) has always been the same since ancient times. Nor has it undergone any variation in China because otherwise everything would be uncertain and confused, and none of their books says this. Instead, in their printed books dealing with mathematics and astrology they have drawn one of these *chi*, or feet, with its divisions and units of the smaller parts making it up. They call this *tianliang*, meaning celestial measurement.

---

[1] There is no mention of Chapter 9 in the Portuguese text, but it probably was meant to begin here.

[2] The length of the Greek stade varied, but it was commonly about 200 yards; it is sometimes translated as 'furlong'. The Persian *farsang*, or *parasang*, also varied in length, but is generally reckoned as a little below four miles.

[3] The text is corrupt here. A literal translation would run: 'They appear as L. among the Chinese, as R. in their *provinciação*.' This last word is a slip for *pronunciação*, or 'pronunciation'. In *Breve aparato*, f. 14v, and in *Arte breve*, f. 9v, Rodrigues makes the same point about Chinese lacking 'R' and Japanese lacking 'L'. Bartoli (*Cina*, p. 539) goes further and adds that Chinese also lacks 'B' and 'D'.

[4] A reference to Hongwu (1328–99), founder of the Ming dynasty.

This is the common and ancient unit with which they measured the distances in the Heavens and on Earth, and it is an everlasting, invariable measurement, common to all. When they speak about the average height of a man in their books, they give him five feet from feet to shoulders and do not count the head or neck. When a comparison is made, this unit corresponds exactly to our mathematical foot of four mathematical spans. Thus their pace, or so-called ell, equals five of these and is properly a mathematical pace of five feet. These use these to make up their larger units, such as a smaller pace of three feet and a larger one of five, or their ell of ten feet, or their *stade*, which is the largest of their linear units.[1] The actual size of the foot, or *chi*, and its smaller parts is shown in the diagram below. The first and smallest of all their units is the width or thickness of a hair from a horse's tail. Ten of these make one point or degree, and ten points make the width of one of their fingers, and ten fingers make one foot. So their foot has 100 points, just as did the mathematical foot up to the time of Ptolemy, who for the sake of greater convenience reduced it to sixty degrees.

10 hairs together make one *fen*, which is a point or a degree.

10 points make one *cun*, which is like their finger.

10 of these fingers make one *chi*, which is a foot, or common *covado*.[2]

5 feet make one *xun*,[3] which is an ell or geometric pace.

10 feet, or 2 ells, make one *jang*, which is a pole, an ancient measure.

3 feet make one *bu*, a common or small pace.

360 small paces, or 216 geometric ones, or 1,080 feet, make one *li*, the Chinese *stade*.[4]

10 *li* make one *pu*, which is like their league. This is the distance at which guards or messengers are stationed in small houses along the road whenever it is necessary. They raise the beacons there when a message is sent through them to the court.

60 *li*, or 6 *pu*, make one *zhan*, an ordinary day's journey.

300 *li*, according to them, make one *du*, or degree, which, corresponding to Ptolemy's view, equals 60 miles or 21½ leagues. But in fact 17½ leagues (or 243 *li*) make 1 degree.[5]

40 *li* make one league of 3 miles and 24 paces.

50 *li* make one *farsang*, which is a league and a *li*.

Japanese linear measurements[6]

The Japanese use the same linear measurements as do the Chinese, although the names are somewhat different. They have, for example, a long foot and a short foot. The latter is the same as the mathematical foot and the Chinese foot, and is the unit commonly used. Their

---

[1] As Rodrigues points out a few lines later, 'stade' refers to the Chinese *li*.

[2] The *covado*, sometimes translated as 'ell', was a Portuguese linear unit of varying length. According to *Arte grande*, f. 219v, it equalled two spans. As Rodrigues points out, the length of the *chi*, or Chinese foot, varied through the ages. For further details, see Ferguson, 'Chinese Foot Measure', pp. 357–82.

[3] There is a gap in the text where the unit *xun* should have been listed.

[4] Not all of these figures agree with those given in the reference in n. 2, above, but there was a great deal of regional variation. Rodrigues's figures are completely consistent. Barros (*Década terceira*, 2, 7 [f. 45]) notes vaguely that the *li* equals the distance a man's shout can be heard on flat ground on a quiet day, adding that 10 *li* equal one *bu*, slightly more than a Spanish league. He probably took this information from Mendoza (*History*, I, p. 21), who reports that the *li* 'hath so much space as a mans voice in a plaine grounde may bee hearde in a quiet day, halowing or whoping with all the force and strength he may.'

[5] For Ptolemy's erroneous calculation of a degree of longitude, see Bunbury, *History*, II, pp. 563–8.

[6] As mentioned on p. 117, n. 1, there is no mention of Chapter 9 as such in the Portuguese text, and Rodrigues may have meant the chapter to begin at this point.

smallest unit and the base of all the others is called *bu*, and is the same as the Chinese *fen*; the Japanese also call it *fun*, that is, point or degree.

10 *bu* make one *sun*, the distance between the knuckles of the thumb.

10 *sun* make one *shaku*, foot, or ordinary *covado*.

5 *shaku* make one *hiro*, an ell or geometric pace.

2 *hiro*, or 10 *shaku*, make one *jo*, or pole.

6 *shaku* make one *ken*, a unit of six feet for measuring land.

600 *ken*[1] make one *chō*, a kind of Japanese *stade* of 72 paces,

6 *chō* make one Kantō *ri* of 432 paces (or two Chinese *li*).

36 *chō* make one court *ri* of 2,592 paces (or 16 Chinese *li*).

18 *chō* make one maritime Saikoku *ri* (or 6 Chinese *li*, or 1,296 paces).[2]

---

[1] A slip for 60 *ken*, as can be calculated from the data given in the table. Rodrigues provides the correct value of the *chō* in *Arte grande*, f. 220. In some tables the *hiro* is given as equal to the *ken*.

[2] This table is repeated in greater detail in *Arte grande*, f. 219v. Rodrigues goes on to point out there that the *chō* was originally an area equal to 60 x 60 *tatami*, but at that time equalled an area of 60 x 50 *tatami*. In addition to the variations in the length of the *ri* mentioned in the text, Rodrigues adds (in *Arte grande*, f. 219v) that there was also a *ri* equalling 50 *chō*. These variations are confirmed by Nakamura (*East Asia*, p. 81), who cites 17th-century Japanese authors. A useful list of Japanese linear measurements, with their European equivalents, is given in Papinot, *Dictionary*, p. 841.

CHAPTER 10

THE FEATURES, TALENTS AND DISPOSITIONS OF THE JAPANESE

The Japanese are white, although not excessively pale as are the northern nations but just moderately so.[1] They have goodly, somewhat round features, and as regards facial appearance they look like the genuine Chinese of the interior and not like those of Canton.[2] They also resemble the Koreans on account of their dark hair and eyes, and small noses. Thus they greatly wonder at big and long noses, thick beards, light blue or blue eyes, auburn or fair hair, and consider all these things as so many defects. So they do not think very highly of beards, and if a man has a thick one he pulls it out, although the ancient fashion was to allow it to grow naturally but to pull out the hair of the head with instruments. They allow the hair to grow long only at the back and at the temples, leaving the middle and front of the head completely bald. The hair at the temples and back is tied up in a knot most attractively in imitation, they say, of one of their ancient kings who was either bald or shaved that part of the head in this fashion, and the people followed suit so that the king's defect would not be apparent. But it is more likely that it was merely the king's custom that the people followed. It seems that he was king of that part of Zhejiang from whom their kings are said to be descended, as we noted earlier.[3]

This custom continued to be observed later for the sake of fashion, albeit a painful one, as we saw when we went to Japan, for they still plucked out the hair from the head at that time. But from Taikō's time they have shaved the head with a razor in a very handsome way instead of plucking the hair out. Youngsters let the forelock grow very long in front and gracefully toss it back over the shaven part. All this, taken with their apparel, looks very fine indeed.[4]

---

[1] The white complexion of the Japanese is mentioned in Xavier, *Epistolae*, II, p. 277; Ribadeneira, *Historia*, p. 323; Avila and Carletti, in *TCJ*, pp. 38–39; Valignano, *Sumario*, p. 5, and *Historia*, pp. 126–7. Further references to Jesuit sources are given in Valigano, *Sumario*, p. 5, n. 10. The whiteness of the Japanese was a reason advanced for admitting Japanese candidates into the Order. Valignano, *Sumario*, p. 182, #3.

[2] Other writers confirm Rodrigues's observations: Fróis, *Tratado*, p. 98, nn. 3, 4; Carletti and Avila, in *TCJ*, pp. 38–9; Valignano, *Sumario*, p. 36. The difference between the Cantonese and other Chinese is also noted by Linschoten (*Discours*, I, 23 [p. 40]), and by Mendoza (*History*, I, pp. 11, 29–30): 'Those of the province of Canton (which is a hot country) be browne of colour like to the Moores; but those that be further within the countrie be like unto Almaines, Italians and Spanyardes, white and redde, and somewhat swart.'

[3] Apparently a reference to Kireki (pp. 52–3, above) whose descendants are said to have populated Japan. Descriptions of the Japanese hair style are given in Fróis, 20 February 1565, in *Cartas*, I, f. 172; Avila Girón, *Relación*, p. 11; Ribadeneira, *Historia*, p. 324; Carletti, in *TCJ*, p. 38.

[4] Valignano (*Sumario*, p. 19) explains that the Japanese use tweezers to pull out their hair ('with no little pain and tears', as Fróis notes – see n. 3, above). *Vocabulario*, f. 116: 'Kenuki. Little tweezers to pull out hair.' But later, in 1601, Valignano states (*Principio*, f. 37) that Japanese now shaved part of the head instead of plucking out the hairs. See

They also cultivate their beards in various fashions. Some wear only moustaches (and even these are somewhat short and sparse) and shave all the rest. Others grow them according to the fashion that most pleases them. This manner of wearing different types of beard is now fashionable here in the Orient among the Portuguese, Spaniards, and Moors, and they have abandoned the traditional Portuguese beard. The Chinese have not followed their example, for they still prize a beard in its natural state and will never interfere with it.[1]

The Japanese tend to be of medium build and on the short side rather than tall, although they admire well-built men.[2] They have many natural talents and an alert understanding, and experience shows that they are competent in all our moral and speculative sciences and the Chinese language. This can be seen in those who profess their sciences and letters, and in the discerning and subtle questions put by even pagans when they listen to sermons about the mysteries of the Faith preached to the pagans.[3] For in the space of a few years, less than forty in fact, in which this remote nation has began to learn our sciences, many Japanese in our seminaries have become good humanists. Others have studied philosophy and theology with such satisfaction and ability that many of them profess the way of evangelical perfection in religion. Among these are very talented priests, good preachers and casuists.[4] Thus it may be seen that the Japanese in general are very much ruled by natural reason and submit to it, although many do not observe it through weakness. They understand the truth and are converted to the Faith, which they confess, however, very simply.[5]

As the Japanese have been brought up here at the end of the world without knowing or being in contact with anybody save the Chinese and Koreans, they naturally have a high opinion of themselves and of their nation. They accordingly have a haughty and proud spirit, and however much they see or hear about other nations, they always think that their country is the best, especially as regards their weapons and their use in war. They have an

---

also Valignano, *Sumario*, p, 20, n. 99. For an illustrated account of Japanese hairstyles through the ages, see *KEJ*, III, pp. 82–3.

[1] The sparseness of Japanese beards is mentioned by Fróis, *Tratado*, p. 98, and Valignano, *Principio*, f. 37. Avila Girón (*Relación*, p. 17) notes that the Japanese generally wore only a moustache and shaved off the beard, and confirms that there had been a change of fashion among the Europeans in the Far East. In Manila; for example, Europeans wore only a moustache and a mere hint of a beard, so that the time had passed when men could swear 'By the beard of an honorable man.' Chinese beards were equally sparse: Ricci, *Fonti*, I, p. 88, and *China*, p. 77; Alonso Sánchez, in Colin, *Labor*, II, p. 532. Mundy (*Travels*, III:1, p. 262) remarks, 'Some greatt thick beards I have seene, butt very Few.'

[2] Fróis (*Tratado*, p. 98) notes that Japanese tend to be shorter than Europeans. During Valiganano's first meeting with Nobunaga in March 1581, the ruler expressed surprise at his visitor's towering height. Valignano's lofty stature raised comment not only in Japan but also in his native Italy. Fróis, *Miyako*, 14 April 1581, in *Cartas*, II, f. 3v; Schütte, *Valignano's Mission*, I, p. 39, n. 167.

[3] Valignano (*Sumario*, p. 5) notes the speed with which the Japanese pick up European science and disciplines, although later in 1601 (*Principio*, ff. 35r–v), he modifies his earlier enthusiasm. For examples of the intelligent questions put to the missionaries, see Fernández's report in Schurhammer, *Disputationen*, pp. 99–110, parts of which are translated in *TCJ*, pp. 375–6.

[4] The two seminaries at Arima and Azuchi were both founded in 1580, some 40 years before Rodrigues wrote the present account. For the seminaries, see Cielislik, 'Seminario', and Schütte, *Introductio*, pp. 1004–5. Mexia (8 October 1581, in *Cartas*, II, f. 16) praises the Japanese novices for their talent and memory, and compares them favourably with Europeans. Later (6 January 1584, in *Cartas*, II, f. 123v), he notes that within a year of their conversion the Japanese could preach about their religion as if they were born Christians.

[5] Xavier observes (*Epistolae*, II, p. 188) that Japanese lay people (as opposed to the Buddhist monks) were greatly governed by reason. Torres (29 September 1551, in Ruiz-de-Medina, *Documentos*, I, p. 212) compliments the Japanese by declaring that they are governed by reason 'as much as, or even more than, Spaniards.'

第十九章 男子近古の服裝

五つ紋替衿羽織踏込袴

Plate 13: Men's hairstyle. 'They allow the hair to grow long only at the back and at the temples, leaving the middle and front of the head completely bald. The hair at the temples and back is tied up in a knot most attractively.' p. 120.

intrepid and bold spirit, and they believe that nobody in the whole world equals them in this respect and that all are far inferior to them.[1] For regarding military matters they have so far had experience of fighting only among themselves in their own kingdom (for it was involved in continuous civil wars and disturbances) and with the Chinese and Koreans, against whom they have always carried the day with ease.[2] They are so punctilious and meticulous that they do not hesitate to lay down their lives on a single point of honour, and they are equally ready to die for the man whose service and patronage they have entered.[3]

They will not permit insults or calumny, nor will they utter them in a person's presence unless they are determined to die, for they are very long-suffering and secretive in this matter. Hence quarrels are rare because those who begin them must continue to the very end, and they seldom occur without a death as their weapons are at the ready for this purpose.[4] When a man kills another, whether in defence or aggression, justly or otherwise, he seldom escapes. When such an event occurs, a man will cut his own belly before another can disgrace him by killing him, for to kill oneself is regarded as an honourable and courageous course, and is praised by others. This act of killing oneself is attended by much ceremony and solemnity in the presence of many people, who watch to see how he cuts himself. From their pride and meticulousness springs the determination not to show any weakness or cowardice when the authorities execute them (and even women), whatever the manner of their death may be. Instead, they exchange courtesies with the people present, and show great courage and tranquility for they are resolute in dying.[5]

I know a gentleman, the vassal of a lord and the governor of one of his estates, who killed an ambassador sent by the Duke of Satsuma to his lord, merely because this envoy had slighted his master in his presence. As soon as he had killed him, he went to the place where

---

[1] The Japanese tendency to have a high opinion of themselves and look down on foreigners is mentioned by Xavier, in *TCJ*, p. 41; Torres, in Schurhammer, *Disputationen*, p. 94; Fróis, in *TCJ*, p. 42. All of these writers mention the Japanese warlike nature. Fróis suggests that Japanese isolation from the rest of the world was the cause of their haughty attitude towards foreigners.

[2] This last statement needs some qualification, for Japanese forces suffered various reverses in the Korean campaign, 1592–8, although these setbacks were due more to problems of supplies and communications rather than to lack of valour.

[3] The punctilious character of the Japanese is noted by Xavier, *Epistolae*, II, p. 186; Fróis, 20 February 1565, in *Cartas*, I, f. 172v; Ribadeneira, *Historia*, pp. 323–4; Valignano, *Historia*, p. 128. Torres (8 October 1561, in Ruiz-de-Medina, *Documentos*, II, p. 448) compares them with the ancient Romans in this regard. At the same time, Valignano, in *TCJ*, p. 46; Vizcaino, *Relación*, p. 186, and Rodrigues himself (p. 131) note the treachery perpetrated by vassals towards their lords. See also p. 125, n. 2.

[4] Xavier (*Epistolae*, II, pp. 186–7) mentions that the Japanese will not accept insults of any kind, and this is confirmed by Valignano (in *TCJ*, p. 42, and *Sumario*, p. 168).

[5] There are many references to *seppuku*, or *harakiri*, among European writers. Both Vilela (29 October 1557, in Ruiz-de-Medina, *Documentos*, I, pp. 681–2) and Valignano (*Sumario*, pp. 17–19, nn. 85, 87, 89, and in *TCJ*, pp. 161–2) report that the more valiant cut their stomachs in the form of a cross before their seconds strike off their heads; servants would die with their lords in this way, and even small children were known to kill themselves in this fashion. Further comments in Fróis, 19 June 1565, in *Cartas*, I, f. 187; Ribadeneira, *Historia*, p. 324; Vivero y Velasco, *Relación*, f. 75. The custom of *junshi*, or accompanying one's lord to the grave, is mentioned by Cocks (*Diary*, II, p. 202) and Caron (in *TCJ*, pp. 58, 68). The Tokugawa government forbade the practice, but it was not until the 1660s that it managed to end the custom. Sansom, *History 1615–1867*, p. 92. Cocks makes further references to *seppuku* in *Diary*, I, p. 377, and II, pp. 25, 154. A vivid eye-witness account is given in Redesdale, *Tales*, pp. 263–87.

the dead man's companions were staying and told them why he had killed him. He added that he wished to cut his belly in their presence and thereby atone for the ambassador's death in the eyes of the Lord of Satsuma. In this way the death would not cause any strife between his master and the Lord of Satsuma. In the presence of the other party (whom he could have killed had he so wished, because they were in his territory), he gave orders for carpets to be spread in a clean place. Then in a loud voice he told them to watch carefully how he cut himself. He seated himself on a platform on a beach and with his own hand he wrote his will slowly and calmly, asking his lord in this testament to look after his son and household for he was about to die for his honour. When he had finished this, he bade farewell, and ate and drank a little with a cheerful countenance. Then in front of them all he fearlessly cut his belly from top to bottom and then again from side to side, and so he died.[1]

This sort of thing often happens. Gentlemen condemned to death do the same in the presence of the soldiers of the lord who has sentenced them. The same thing happens in castles when the defenders can no longer hold out. First they kill the women and children, and then after setting fire to the castle so that nothing of them will remain, they cut their bellies.

It is also on this account that nobles regard it as correct and brave never to confess any crime, however cruel may be the torture inflicted on them, for they regard this as a weakness and dishonour.[2] This happened only recently to a gentleman whom the Lord of Tenka ordered to be arrested because he was told that the man knew a person whom the Lord feared and was looking for. When asked in court whether he knew of such a person, he answered that he did not. They then threatened him with cruel torture, telling him that these torments would make him confess everything. He replied, 'If you had treated me well and honourably, I would have confessed, had I known him. But now that you have threatened me, do not imagine that an honourable man like myself will confess under your tortures. Do whatever you wish.' They applied exquisite tortures of fire, and pressed him between boards studded with the points of spikes and transfixed him, but despite his certain knowledge he did not confess a single thing before he died.[3]

This is the usual way of this nation, and from this pride originates their custom in war of first shouting out their name when they rush at the enemy so that they may be seen, and their courage and strength may be recognized.[4] They are not content with killing their enemy, but as proof of their courage they must needs cut off his head (although it may cost

---

[1] It is impossible to identify this incident, but Rodrigues, *Nihon*, I, p. 302, n. 5, speculates that it may have occurred about 1583.

[2] An illustrated account of some of the tortures used to wring out confessions is given in Hall, 'Japanese Feudal Laws'. Other punishments are mentioned in *TCJ*, pp. 154–7. According to Caron (*True Description*, p. 50), 'they will die, nay suffer the worst of tortures, rather then discover their complices'.

[3] It is impossible to identify this case with certainty, but a reference in Cocks's diary (I, pp. 176–7) shows a striking similarity. 'September 18 [1616, at Edo]. ... one man was brought in question about Fidaia Samme [Hideyori Sama], as being in the castell [at Osaka] with him to the last hower. This man was racked and tormented very much, to make hym confes where his master was, or whether he were alive or dead; but I canot heare whether he confessed any thing or no.' This case took place 'only recently', some four years before Rodrigues wrote this part of his *History*, and the Lord of Tenka, Shogun Tokugawa Hidetada, was certainly concerned about and looking for Hideyori, son of Hideyoshi, in case he had escaped (as popular rumour believed) from the siege of Osaka Castle in the previous year.

[4] The practice of a noble warrior shouting his name ('name-announcing') and challenging the enemy to single combat in battle was called *nanori*, and is often recorded in chronicles, such as *Taiheiki*, pp. 148, 167, 221, 253–4, 308–9. Rodrigues mentions the custom in *Arte grande*, f. 211, and *Arte breve*, f. 79: 'they also announce themselves in

them their own lives) in order to present it to their commander. This is the usual custom of this kingdom in battle.[1]

They are so crafty in their hearts that nobody can understand them. Whence it is said that they have three hearts: a false one in their mouths for all the world to see, another within their breasts only for their friends, and a third in the depths of their hearts, reserved for themselves alone and never revealed to anybody.[2] As a result, law decays here and everyone acts merely according to the present moment and speaks according to the circumstances and occasion. But they do not use this double-dealing to cheat people in business matters and profits, as do the Chinese in their thieving and other business and trading matters, for in this respect the Japanese are most exact.[3] Instead, they reserve it chiefly for affairs of diplomacy and war, and to prevent themselves from being deceived. In particular, when they wish to kill a person by treachery (a stratagem often employed to avoid many deaths) they put on a great pretence of entertaining him with every sign of love and joy – and then in the middle of it all, off comes his head.[4]

They are very lazy and slothful concerning matters of trade and lack the conscientiousness and zeal of the Chinese. They are given to idleness and merrymaking, at which they spend a great deal of time with banquets, music, comedies, farces, and excellent games that are decent and relaxing.[5] They do not like things that cause worry, sorrow, anguish, and anxiety, and quickly tire of them.[6] They let themselves be overcome with melancholy, to which they are much prone, and many die of it.[7] They do not have any rough, noisy, and loud pastimes except wrestling, which they practise as an exercise and art for war.[8]

They show to foreigners much welcome and kindness, and they are very trusting in allowing them to enter their country. In this respect they are very different from the Chinese and Koreans, who despise foreigners and are very jealous of their kingdom. But they

battle when they come out to challenge the enemy.' Details and purpose of the practice are given in Varley, *Warriors*, pp. 18, 60–62, 173.

[1] Examples of cutting off the head of a vanquished enemy are given in *Taiheiki*, pp. 180, 204, 213, 226–7. Details are found in Varley, *Warriors*, pp. 27–8; illustration in Smith, *Japanese History*, p. 121; copious illustrations of washing, packing, and transporting the severed heads in Sasama, *Nihon Gassen*, pp. 27–9. Sometimes friends removed the head of a fallen warrior to prevent identification of his corpse; Cocks (*Diary*, I, p. 12) mentions this practice.

[2] The custom of not revealing one's innermost heart is also mentioned by Valignano, *Sumario*, pp. 29–30. In an earlier *Sumario*, 1580, he goes into greater detail, declaring that 'those who lightly reveal their mind are looked upon as nitwits, and are contemptuously termed single-hearted men.' Valignano continues that the Japanese are 'the most false and treacherous people of any known in the world'. Translation given in Boxer, *Christian Century*, p. 75.

[3] But Vivero y Velaso (*Relación*, f. 21v) and Avila Girón (*Relación*, pp. 40–41) both mention deception in trade.

[4] Valignano (in *TCJ*, p. 45) makes exactly the same point: the Japanese will laugh and joke familiarly with their enemies, then suddenly draw their swords, kill them with one or two blows, then 'replace their swords quietly and calmly as if nothing had happened, and do not give the slightest indication of passion or anger either by word of mouth or change of expression'. Fróis (*História*, III, p. 237) makes a similar observation.

[5] Valignano (*Sumario*, pp. 31–32) notes with disapproval the time wasted over excessive banqueting and entertainment. The matter is also mentioned by Fróis (20 February 1565, in *Cartas*, I, f. 172v) and Vizcaino (*Relación*, p. 189).

[6] What is more, the Japanese keep their troubles to themselves and appear cheerful in order not to embarrass and burden others with their worries. Valignano, in *TCJ*, p. 43. Cocks gives a concrete example on p. 201, n. 1.

[7] This trait is later mentioned by Rodrigues, p. 283. Perhaps a better description would be fatalism, originating from Buddhist philosophy.

[8] *Luita* in the Portuguese text may refer to some form of wrestling or else perhaps bouts with wooden swords.

are weak and timid, while the Japanese are courageous and intrepid.[1] They wonder at the civil practice of killing tame and domestic animals and things of that sort, for they show much pity and compassion in this respect.[2] But they do not feel this when they kill men in a blood-thirsty way and test their swords on the corpses, and they justify this. Some lords may ask other nobles for some men who have been condemned to death in order to see whether their sword cuts well and whether they can trust it in emergencies. They often sew up bodies after they have been cut up by swords and put together the severed parts so that they may once more cut and see whether their sword passes through a body with one blow. They indulge in this and other types of slaughter. They do not bury the bodies, but leave them in pieces in the fields for the birds and dogs. The delight and pleasure they feel in cutting up human bodies is astonishing, as is also the way that young boys sometimes indulge in this.[3]

Among all the people of this Orient, they are the most inclined to religion and the wor-ship of divine things. This is not only to obtain temporal benefits such as long life, health, wealth, prosperity, children, and other such things for which they ask their false gods, but also even more to obtain with all their hearts salvation in the next life.[4] This they do in their false and erroneous ways. Proof of this may be seen in this kingdom's sumptuous temples, the great respect and reverence shown towards the priests of their idols and teach-ers of salvation, the incredibly severe penances that they undertake, fasting and abstinence from meat and living things, the various vows and alms paid to the idols.[5] Also as proof are the wonderful eremitical lives led by numerous lay people in many parts of the kingdom, where they despise the world and its pomps, and lead a hard life in the wilderness. On hear-ing about the next life from the bonzes in their sermons and other examples, many people kill themselves by cutting their bellies in order to go and enjoy the riches of the life to come which their priests deceitfully preach.[6]

[1] The ease with which Europeans could enter Japan in the 16th century stands in marked contrast to the difficulties experienced by foreigners trying to enter China at the time. Vivero y Velasco (*Relación*, ff. 10–10v) was shown such hos-pitality during his stay, 1609–10, that he declares that, but for his king and religion, he would gladly become Japanese.

[2] Gago (23 September 1555, in Ruiz-de-Medina, *Documentos*, I, p. 556) notes that the Japanese did not breed ani-mals for eating. This is confirmed by many of the references on p. 110, n. 2.

[3] The Europeans often mention and condemn sword testing (*tameshi-giri*) on corpses. Valignano (*Sumario*, p. 31) points out that the custom was not limited to corpses; also Valignano, *Principio*, f. 40v. Cocks, in *TCJ*, p. 160; Car-letti, *Voyage*, pp. 107–8; Hatch, in Farrington, *English Factory*, II, p. 948; Avila Girón, *Relación*, p. 21. Saris (in Farring-ton, *English Factory*, II, p. 1000) goes into detail: after three executions in Hirado, the bodies of the dead men were cut to pieces ('as small as a mans hand') 'to trie the sharpenesse of the cattans [*katana*]'. The remains were then piled up for the testing to continue. The custom was sometimes practised on Christian martyrs, as in the case of Alexis and Dominic, who were executed on 9 February 1624. 'Their heades being off, they hacked the bodies in many peeces to try the edge of their swords': *Palme of Christian Fortitude*, p. 39.

[4] Fróis (in *TCJ*, p. 299) makes the general distinction that people approach the Shinto deities for worldly favours, such as 'health, long life, wealth, children, and victory over their enemies,' while they pray to the Buddhist deities for salvation and forgiveness of sin. The same distinction is made by Vilela (in *TCJ*, p. 300), Ribadeneira (*Historia*, p. 363), and Vivero y Velasco (*Relación*, f. 72v).

[5] Accounts of sumptuous temples and shrines are found in *TCJ*, pp. 302–5, 333–45. As regards penances, see Pedro Alcaçova, or Alcaceva (in *TCJ*, p. 324); Fróis (in *Cartas*, II, ff. 86–7), regarding penances practised by *yama-bushi*. In 1577, an anonymous Jesuit in Hakata (in *Cartas*, I, ff. 402v–3) writes of the penance of standing five days and nights in a cold river as atonement for matricide. Ribadeneira (*Historia*, p. 365) describes people standing naked in mid-winter, having cold water poured over them until they die.

[6] Vilela (in *TCJ*, p. 323) relates that people would kill themselves by deliberately drowning or being buried alive in order to reach Paradise sooner. Other accounts are found in Alcaçova (or Alcaceva), March 1554, in Ruiz-de-Medina, *Documentos*, I, p. 426; an anonymous Jesuit, 1577, in *Cartas*, I, f. 403; Ribadeneira, *Historia*, p. 365.

Nor can the great devotion shown by many people when they invoke their gods be easily described in words. They always have beads in their hands, and some undertake as a daily exercise to invoke certain brief prayers, for example, *Namu Amida Butsu*, ten thousand times. The peasants go along the road loudly singing this same prayer to a certain tone, while others rise at dawn and pray to the idol for a good hour or longer, and beat on a small drum.[1] Another proof is the crowds of people at the temples, especially on certain days and even every day. Also the various long pilgrimages made by men and women throughout Japan to the various celebrated shrines of the idols, begging alms on the way, etc.[2]

But since the Holy Gospel has been introduced into Japan, this devotion and fervour towards the idols have been greatly cooling among the people, for they have been continually hearing about the truth and this is dispelling the darkness. Those who have embraced the truth by the help of divine grace are greatly aided by this natural inclination, and this has been well proved in various places and circumstances. It seems that on account of the good inclination and interest that they have in their hearts for the things of salvation and the other life, Our Lord has had mercy on this nation, and leaving to one side many other nations, He has come to the end of the world searching for them. Indeed, they seem literally to be those people whom Isaiah mentions in Chapter 18: 'Go, ye swift angels to a waiting people, beyond whom there are no others.'[3]

[1] Europeans often mentioned devotion to Amida and the repeated invocation of his name. Xavier, *Epistolae*, II, pp. 256–7, 268–70; Torres, Gago, Fróis, and Ribadeneira, in *TCJ*, pp. 315–16, 317–18, 346–7; Valignano, *Sumario*, pp. 60–61; Cocks, *Diary*, II, p. 88. See also p. 168, below.

[2] Fróis (in *TCJ*, p. 346) reports seeing about 5,000 people at a sermon in Miyako. Mexia (6 January 1584, in *Cartas*, II, f. 125) comments on the crowds of pilgrims, rosary in hand, who flock to Nara as Europeans to Rome. Cocks (26 October 1618, in *Diary*, II, p. 89) reckoned that more than 100,000 people visited the Hachiman Shrine at Edo on the monthly pilgrimage day. See also Ribadeneira, *Historia*, pp. 368–9. For pilgrims to Ise Shrine, see p. 84, above. Nishiyama (*Edo Culture*, pp. 130–41) deals with pilgrimages to various destinations, showing that religion and entertainment at times went hand in hand on such journeys.

[3] Isaiah 18, 2. Rodrigues has already quoted this text on p. 65, above.

CHAPTER 11

THERE IS NO CONTRADICTION, ALTHOUGH THERE MAY APPEAR TO BE, IN THE MANY THINGS WRITTEN ABOUT THE CUSTOMS, GOVERNMENT, NOBILITY, AND WEALTH OF JAPAN; AND THE REASONS THEREOF

Before we come to speak of the general and particular customs of this kingdom, its government, nobility, wealth, buildings, and other relevant matters, we must bear in mind that the members of our Society who came to Japan either before Nobunaga began ruling or in the time of his rule before Taikō, saw what was then happening, and heard and read in their ancient chronicles what had happened in times past. At the same time, they observed what subsequently happened during Taikō's rule, and from that time until the present day they have diligently noted (and also the natives themselves have acknowledged) that there have been three different periods in Japan as regards administration, customs, usages, wealth, and splendour.[1]

Some of our authors have written about the things of the second period, while others have written about those of the third. We must now write about all three periods, and it will be seen that, although there may appear to have been contradiction in many things, this has not really been so in fact, and that this has been due to a change in the kingdom's circumstances and situation. We ourselves saw the second and third stages, and through reading their ancient chronicles and through our experience over many years we know a great deal about the things of the first stage, the true period of this nation. Thus we will be able to recount the truth of what happened.

The first stage of this kingdom was the true and proper age of Japan when the kingdom was governed by the legitimate lord and ruler, and the whole country obeyed the true king. Rites and customs were duly observed, and a distinction was made between the nobles of the patrician order whose office was to govern the country, and the nobles of the military order who, under the patricians' supervision, had the duty of guarding the royal person and defending the realm. There were various noble ranks in the court and offices of the royal household and the different royal councils and other boards governing the kingdom. The king used to send viceroys and governors to the sixty-eight states or kingdoms for a term of three years or more,[2] and he likewise stationed garrisons of officers and soldiers in each

---

[1] Oda Nobunaga can be said to have begun his rule in 1568 when Ashikaga Yoshiaki was appointed shogun under his protection. Taikō, or Toyotomi Hideyoshi, took command from Nobunaga's assassination in 1582 until his own death in 1598 (although see p. 131, n. 5, for greater precision). The Portuguese text of this last sentence is somewhat ambiguous, although the general sense is clear. Portraits of Nobunaga and Hideyoshi are found in Smith, *Japanese History*, pp. 136–7, 171.

[2] See p. 130, n. 4.

kingdom to punish rebels, repress bandits and wicked men, and administer the punishments ordered by the king and the governors. In this age the people and peasants always remained commoners, artisans succeeded their fathers in their trades, and generations of players and actors remained as common and lowly folk.[1] The same was true of butchers, executioners, and those of other base offices, for they could never change their occupation.

Only the sons of lords and nobles of both orders could advance by their services to the various ranks of nobility and offices of the royal household. The king gathered revenues and substantial taxes from the entire kingdom, and the lords possessed the lands and revenues that the king, according to his pleasure, was pleased to grant them for their upkeep. The king's court, with the royal palace and the mansions of the court nobles and lords, flourished exceedingly, while at the same time there also thrived at Kamakura, in the Kantō region, the court of the shogun, or Commander and Constable of the Kingdom, beneath whose command were all the members of the military order.[2] Thus the kingdom was governed in peace and with due order observed among the classes, and there was much wealth, splendour, and nobility throughout the kingdom. In this first epoch, as also in the second, idolatry greatly flourished because it passed over to Japan from China and Korea in this age.[3] In a short time it had spread throughout the whole kingdom with its magnificent temples of idols, large monasteries of monks and nuns, and many universities, some of which consisted of 3,000 monasteries or dwellings with their superiors and disciples.[4]

The first period of 1,960 years lasted from the time of the first king, Jimmu Tennō, and particularly after they made contact with China, whence they obtained their customs and writing, until the Year of the Lord 1340.[5] During this time Japan was most prosperous and flourishing as regards customs, nobility, buildings, and the spendour of royalty and nobility. This may be seen in their chronicles and the vestiges that still remain even to this day, such as the ancient royal palaces (mentioned even by Marco Polo)[6] and the palaces of the

---

[1] For the low status of actors, see p. 296, n. 3.

[2] After successfully overcoming the house of Taira, Minamoto Yoritomo (1147–99) set up his military headquarters in Kamakura to avoid, it is said, the effete atmosphere of the Miyako court. Kamakura continued as the centre of the shogunal government until it was razed by imperial troops in 1333. As regards the various *kuge* ranks, Rodrigues (*Arte breve*, ff. 97–8) provides a detailed account of the six orders of nobility.

[3] For the introduction of Buddhism into Japan in 552, see p. 48, n. 3.

[4] There is a copyist's slip in the Portuguese text where *diversidades* was written instead of *universidades*. Rodrigues has already noted (p. 80) that the monastic establishment of Hieizan, near Miyako, had some 3,000 monasteries or temples. Europeans, especially Xavier, often mention the Japanese 'universities', but this term should not be taken in its European sense. Fróis (*História*, I, p. 9) points out this difference, declaring that the students are usually bonzes or are studying to become one; most of their time, he says, is spent learning Chinese characters, which are almost infinite in number.

[5] If this period of 1,960 years ended in 1340, then it must have begun in 620 BC. As noted on p. 43, n. 5, Jimmu is traditionally believed to have been born in 711 BC, ascended the throne in 660, and died in 584 (or 574). Possibly Rodrigues reached the figure 1,960 by calculating the length of time between 660 BC and 1300, not 1340. Presumably he chose 1340 as a round figure and not as a precise date; a more accurate date would be 1336 when, as Rodrigues explains (in *Arte grande*, f. 238), Emperor Go-Daigo fled from Miyako and Ashikaga Takauji placed Kōmyō on the throne, thus beginning the 60-year division between the northern imperial dynasty (in Miyako) and the southern (at Yoshino).

[6] Polo, *Book*, III, 2 (Yule, *Book*, II, pp. 253–4). Polo never visited Japan and provides only hearsay information.

other great lords and nobles of the realm. At that time the nobles used to proceed to the palace or go to visit other lords in coaches or carriages.[1] None of our authors has so far dealt with this epoch, the proper and natural age of Japan, for they have spoken only of the two succeeding periods.[2] Although this period was always such as we have described, the first organized civil wars began more or less about the Year of the Lord 1130 between two Commanders on account of the rivalry between them. This greatly disturbed the entire kingdom and was, so to speak, the seed of subsequent rebellions.[3] But they never usurped the rule and dominion of the proper king, as happened later.

The second period of this kingdom began in the year 1340, when the Commander and Constable of the Kingdom, the shogun Takauji, and the officers and guards stationed throughout the country, rebelled against the government and taxes of the kingdom, leaving the king and patrician order bereft of government, revenue, and the lands that they guarded.[4] But later these men were moved to greed and quarrelled among themselves, and the whole of Japan was involved in wars. Men killed one another or subjected others to their authority, and each one seized for himself as much as he could. Thus it happened that nearly all the ancient noble families were destroyed, and almost the entire realm was left without central government, except the few kingdoms that still obeyed the shogun in Tenka. In all the other kingdoms the rule of war held sway, and each man did just as he pleased. 'Erat pro ratione voluntas'.[5]

The king and the *kuge*, or members of the patrician order, remained confined to Miyako. They were extremely impoverished and received no revenue for their support, save for the gifts given to them by the shogun and by those who possessed the kingdoms in return for the honours that the king granted them. For although they had usurped the government and the revenues, they always recognized the king as the legitimate ruler. Nor did a shogun dare to assume the title of king, but each one pretended that he governed in the name of the throne, while against his will the king had to confirm the shogun in his office. The royal palaces and those of all the nobles and lords were burnt down and destroyed, and the same

---

[1] See *KEJ*, III, p. 35, for an account of *gissha*, or ox-drawn carriages. A vivid picture of the splendour of court life is seen in *The Tale of Genji*, the great 11th-century account of court culture and intrigue. Background material is given in Morris, *World*. Rodrigues fails to mention that this glittering prosperity was enjoyed by relatively few people and that Miyako was often wracked by crime and violence.

[2] This is not correct, for in 1601 Valignano wrote (*Principio*, ff. 24–25v) a summary of Japanese political history from earliest times to Hideyoshi's rule. Also Pedro Morejon published an account of this first period in his *Historia y Relación* (in *TCJ*, pp. 23–6). As the work was published in Europe in 1621, Morejon must have written the account in Asia before 1620, when Rodrigues began writing his *History*.

[3] A reference to the clash between the Minamoto and Taira clans (*KEJ*, VII, pp. 29–30), although it is difficult to see why Rodrigues chose 1130 as the outbreak of hostilities. In *Arte breve*, f. 85v, he states that the country was at peace until about 1160, when civil war broke out. This is fairly accurate, for the Hōgen war took place in 1156 and the Heiji war in 1159.

[4] For Ashikaga Takauji (1305–58), the first of the long line of Ashikaga shogun, see *KEJ*, I, p. 100. As stated on p. 129, n. 5, the date 1340 should be taken as a general figure. It may be argued that the decline in imperial authority began in the reign of Emperor Shirakawa (r. 1073–86), who, in order to build sumptuous temples, began to sell provincial governorships. The term of office was originally for four years, but was later extended to six years and then for life; finally the office became hereditary.

[5] 'Let my will take the place of reason', in Juvenal, *Satires* 6, 223. Rodrigues again quotes the line in a letter from Macao, 22 January 1616. Rodrigues, 'Rodrigues in China', p. 301.

happened to all the ancient buildings, famous places, and cities.[1] The commoners and peasants rebelled against the taxes, and paid little or practically nothing to those who possessed the lands. They rose up with the officers (or *yakata*, as they were later called)[2] who were garrisoned throughout the kingdoms. As the entire country was in this wretched condition, it remained divided, and each man withdrew into his own fortress in great poverty and misery as there was no trade or communication with other people.

On account of wars, the whole realm was full of robbers and brigands, while on the seas there were countless pirates who continually plundered not only Japan but also the coast of China.[3] Thus it was impossible to travel throughout the country except with the greatest difficulty. Much of the land was not tilled, and when the cultivated parts were sown, they were destroyed and plundered by neighbours and opposing factions. Men killed each other everywhere. Thus the entire kingdom and the nobles were left in the greatest poverty and wretchedness as regards their dignity and everything else, and the only law or authority was military power. Men chastised and killed one another as they saw fit. They banished people and confiscated their possessions in such fashion that treachery was rampant and nobody trusted his neighbour. Often the most influential servants would treacherously murder their own lord and then become lords of the states in their place. If they rose up with other more powerful men, they would kill off all their lord's kindred as a precaution so as to confirm them in the possession of the territory. In this way all the leading noble families came to an end and were destroyed. Some people would rebel and join up with others, but a man could not trust his neighbour and always kept his weapons close at hand. They would enter into league with one party and then desert it for another according as the wind of fortune blew. Thus everything was in complete confusion; everyone remained in his house like a petty ruler and recognized no superior as long as he could defend himself.

This miserable period lasted 245 years from the year 1340 to the year 1585, when Taikō (he was first called Hashiba Chikuzen, and later Kampaku, and finally Taikō)[4] took over the government of Tenka in succession to Nobunaga, thus commencing the third period.[5]

---

[1] The plight of the emperor and his court is well described by Morejon (in *TCJ*, p. 26), who correctly observes that 'the poor *dairi* [emperor] and the *kuge* order were left with nothing but their rank and name and some small revenues in Miyako.' A later historian confirms this decline: 'Hence the net result was that the Imperial Court lost all control not only over the provinces but over the capital itself; that the Shōguns usurped the last shred of central authority possessed by the emperors…'. Murdoch, *History to 1542*, p. 587.

[2] The term *yakata* originally referred to the residence of a noble, but later was applied by extension to the noble himself. Morejon (in *TCJ*, p. 26) specifies that the term refers to the senior officers of the shogun's council. Fróis (*História*, I, pp. 8–9) equates the *yakata* with dukes, as does Rodrigues in his *Bispos da Igreja*, f. 318, with the approval of the Japanese Jesuit Martinho Hara, who writes in the margin, 'You call the *yakata* "dukes", and I approve of this for many reasons.' Further references in Valignano, *Sumario*, p. 12, n. 50.

[3] For Japanese pirates, see pp. 45–6 and 135, n. 1.

[4] For Hideyoshi and his various names and titles, see p. 84.

[5] The period preceding the unification of Japan is aptly called the Period of Civil War, for it was filled with strife between the warring barons. But it was also a period that produced magnificent works of art, such as the ink paintings of Sesshū (1420–1506), Shōkei (mid–15th to early 16th centuries), Sōami (c.1455–1525), Josetsu (early 15th century), etc., and in his determination to contrast this period with the allegedly idyllic first era, Rodrigues presents an account that is exaggerated and simplistic. Elison ('Hideyoshi', p. 229) comments favourably on Rodrigues's choice of 1585 as the date of Hideyoshi's taking over the government, instead of the more usual 1582, after the death of Nobunaga, pointing out that Hideyoshi was not appointed *kampaku* until August 1585. But later in this chapter the text refers to 1582 as the date of his assuming control of Japan.

Japan was in this period when the Blessed Father Francis Xavier entered the country in the Year of he Lord 1549.[1] The following period lasted (and we witnessed this) for thirty-nine years, during which time Taikō finally subdued the whole of Japan. Nobunaga had partially brought about this third period in his time by subduing a large part of the country. Those who wrote about the things of Japan at this time, either at first or second hand, did not know about this nation's past history or true period in any detail. They wrote about what they saw and heard at the time as if it were this kingdom's true and usual state of affairs. They therefore described their customs and everything else in this light, for they believed that Japan had always been thus involved in continuous wars and wretchedness since its first origin, and that it never had any central government except the private law of each individual according to his whim. They further supposed that those in control of the lands were their real and legitimate lords, that the shogun, or *kubō*, was the king of Japan, and that the real king was merely like a priest.[2] Whereas in fact these people were tyrants who had usurped the kingdom by force of arms and had seized control of the territories that they had been guarding.

This third period began partly in the time of Nobunaga, who was the first to begin cutting through the thick forest of wars and discord in Japan. He subdued about half the country, and fear of him made the remaining part ready to obey him in everything.[3] Taikō, his commander-in-chief who succeeded him, completed the subjugation of the entire country, and there was not a single part that did not obey him. When he had brought the entire realm under his sway, his army even crossed over to Korea in order to conquer China.[4] He succeeded to the government of Tenka in the year 1582 and finally managed to subdue the Kantō districts in the year 1588. He had already overcome the island of Kyushu in the year 1587, and had gone there in person to campaign against the Duke of Satsuma.[5] When the war finished in this same year, he exiled the Fathers from Japan.[6] Since then, thirty-two years have passed until the present year of 1620, and during this time Japan has remained united under one ruler.

Nearly everything was destroyed. All the ancient families of the kingdom's lords and nobles were overthrown. Nearly all the sixty-eight kingdoms and the other smaller estates

[1] For Xavier's arrival in Japan, see p. 1, n. 1. The Portuguese text has merely 'when he entered the country', but the reference is obviously to Xavier.

[2] With his usual discernment, Fróis (in *TCJ*, p. 76) points out as early as 1565 that the secluded figure in Miyako had formerly been the emperor but was no longer obeyed, and forty years later this is confirmed by Vivero y Velasco (in *TCJ*, p. 76). Cocks (*Diary*, II, p. 311) stresses the emperor's priest-like status by calling him 'the pope of Japan', while Kaempfer (*History*, I, p. 259) refers to him as the 'Ecclesiastical Hereditary Emperor'. Vizcaino (*Relación*, p. 131) also mentions that the emperor in Miyako was 'like the Supreme Pontiff is among us'. For other references to the emperor, see *TCJ*, pp. 75–7.

[3] Nobunaga is considered to have controlled from one-third to one-half of Japan at the time of his death. *KEJ*, VI, pp. 61–4.

[4] For Hideyoshi's unsuccessful Korean campaigns, 1592–8, see Sansom, *History, 1334–1615*, pp. 352–61; Berry, *Hideyoshi*, pp. 207–17, 232–4.

[5] For the Kantō campaign, which ended with the surrender of Odawara Castle in 1590, see Sansom, *History, 1334–1615*, pp. 324–7; Berry, *Hideyoshi*, pp. 93–6. For Hideyoshi's victory in Kyushu in 1587, by force of arms and diplomacy, Sansom, *History, 1334–1615*, pp. 319–23; Berry, *Hideyoshi*, pp. 87–93. En route to Edo, Cocks (25 August 1616, in *Diary*, I, pp. 165–6) stayed for two days in Odawara and gives a colorful account of Hideyoshi's siege some 26 years earlier. Hōjō Ujimasa finally surrendered the castle on condition that he and his followers should be spared. 'Yet Ticus Samme [Hideyoshi], having hym in his power, made Widen a Dono [Ujimasa] to cut his belly, contrary to promis' – which is substantially correct.

[6] For the 1587 expulsion decree, see the references given on p. 83, n. 1.

of individual nobles contained therein were exchanged and given to new people who had been promoted to become lords and nobles. Many such people sprang from lowly stock, and had risen either by force of arms or because they were related to Taikō, the Lord of Tenka.[1] The laws, administration, customs, culture, trade, wealth, and magnificence were restored throughout the kingdom, and populous cities and other buildings were raised everywhere as a result of trade and peace.[2] Many people became rich, although ordinary folk and peasants were impoverished by the taxes that they were obliged to pay.[3] The lords of the land became very wealthy, storing up much gold and silver. Throughout the kingdom there was a great abundance of money, new mines were opened, and the kingdom was well supplied with everything.

Finally they re-established the ranks and boards of the royal household, especially the order of *kuge* or patricians. The lords of the kingdoms and lands assumed new titles of this order, while the titles of the military order of the *yakata* and others were abolished. The Miyako *kuge* had their revenues increased and their palaces improved. The king himself was provided with adequate sustenance and awarded the respect due to the proper and legitimate lord; his palace was again renovated in a most magnificent and sumptuous manner.[4] But the government still remained in the hands of the Lord of Tenka, who pretends that he governs in the name of the king and that he does everything at his bidding, but this in fact is not true. Finally, the entire kingdom was renewed in every respect. Thus the third period is very different from the second, and in many ways in similar to the first.

Let us sum up briefly by listing what has been renewed and changed in the kingdom.

1. The kingdom was completely united under one sole leader in peace and quiet; until then it had been completely divided.

2. The lords of the patrician order have once again flourished; many have been appointed once more, and new families and houses have been set up. Many ancient families who enjoyed power in the kingdoms have been ended, and with them has disappeared the way of government practiced during the second period. The peasants began to be poor and were persecuted into paying rents and dues.

---

[1] A number of Hideyoshi's close relatives received high offices, but the Toyotomi family ultimately met with little success. His half-brother Hidenaga (1540–91) predeceased him. His first son Tsurumatsu died in infancy, while his adopted nephew, Hidetsugu, was obliged to commit suicide in 1595. Finally Hideyoshi's second son, Hideyori, was killed at Osaka in 1615 at the age of 22. In 1585, Hideyoshi appointed five *bugyō*, or ministers, who, as Murdoch (*History, 1542–1651*, p. 362) points out, were all 'new men'.

[2] Some idea of the restoration of the country may be gained by Fróis's description (in *TCJ*, pp. 135–8) of Osaka Castle, built by Hideyoshi 1583–5. He also constructed Jurakutei (1587) and Fushimi (1593), as well as the Daibutsu statue in Miyako (1588). Further details of his building exploits are in Fróis, *História*, V, Chapter 40, pp. 310–16; Sansom, *History, 1334–1615*, pp. 345–6, 383, n. 1; Berry, *Hideyoshi*, pp. 193–203.

[3] Hideyoshi conducted an ambitious land survey for tax purposes. Berry, *Hideyoshi*, pp. 111–20. He reduced the *tan*, the standard land area, from 1,440 to 1,210 square yards, but levied the same tax on the reduced area. In 1586 he decreed that peasants were to pay two-thirds of their crops in taxation, but in practice this was often reduced to two-fifths. Murdoch, *History, 1543–1651*, p. 337; Sansom, *History, 1334–1615*, p. 319. Avila-Girón (in *TCJ*, p. 57) gives a graphic account of the crushing taxes inflicted on the peasants. Later rates of taxes are provided by Vizcaino, *Relación*, p. 187.

[4] Rodrigues later describes (p. 164) the wretched state of the emperor's palace that, as a young man, he saw on a visit to Miyako in 1577. But once Hideyoshi had undisputed control of the country, he built an imperial palace in Miyako in 1590 and the emperor took up residence in the following year. In 1606 Ieyasu ordered a new imperial palace to be constructed, which Vivero y Velaso (*Relación*, f. 15v) describes as *suntuosísimo*. But however much the emperor's material fortunes increased, he remained practically powerless until the imperial Restoration in 1868. Ponsonby-Fane, *Kyoto*, pp. 253–7; Sansom, *History, 1334–1615*, pp. 340–43.

2.[1] The title of shogun and *yakata* was done away with,[2] and the patrician order was revived.

3. The customs and culture of the court and the construction of sumptuous palaces, richly decorated with costly entrances; and the famous kingdoms, cities, and castles with their walls, moats, and fortified towers of seven or eight storeys, and the fortresses that were formerly built on the top of rugged mountains were then constructed on the plains.[3]

4. The food, luxuries, recreations, and the large volume of trade throughout the entire kingdom.

5. Robes made from an abundance of silk, and new fashions and kinds of every sort of materials; the use of silk among the ordinary people, even the peasants, and the large supply of it now produced in Japan.

6. The use of gunpowder, hitherto unknown, and firearms; they have already begun to use even mortars.[4]

7. The pageantry attending lords accompanied by people, on foot and horseback, attendants, lancers, archers, musketeers – a wonderful sight to behold.[5]

8. The sailing of ships abroad out of the kingdom, and with our rudder and pilot.[6] Formerly they had not gone further abroad than China and Korea, and then only every three years with a limited cargo and number of passengers.

9. The visits they pay each other, bearing expensive gifts of gold and silver, lengths of silk, and silk garments.[7] Before there has been only wretchedness.

10. The large amount of silver now in the whole kingdom and the flow of trade.

11. The buildings of the ordinary people as well as those of quality; the use of tiles, which formerly were used only in temples.[8]

12. The improvements in the royal palaces and those of the *kuge*, and in the revenue paid them so that they may live freely and in luxury, but still lacking administrative power and their ancient splendour.

13. Peace has made the lords very rich, and less warlike and inclined to rebellion.

14. Idolatry flourished greatly in the two former periods and the bonzes received large

---

[1] The Portuguese text mistakenly gives two No. 2 paragraphs.

[2] Yoshiaki, the 15th and last Ashikaga shogun, resigned in 1573, and the title remained in abeyance until Ieyasu, the first Tokugawa shogun, took office in 1603.

[3] This was certainly true, as may be seen by the castles built by Nobunga at Azuchi, by Hideyoshi in Osaka, and by Ieyasu in Edo, all of which were sited on level, or almost level, ground.

[4] For the introduction and spread of European firearms in Japan, see p. 64, n. 1.

[5] Conrad Cramer provides (in Caron, *True Description*, pp. 65–72) a detailed eyewitness description of the magnificent procession in Miyako preceding the meeting of the shogun Iemitsu, the former shogun Hidetada, and Emperor Go-Mino-o on 25 October 1626.

[6] Rodrigues's reference to the Japanese use of 'our rudder' is not clear, but in his letter of October 1611, William Adams (in Farrington, *English Factory*, I, pp. 70–71) mentions that he had built two ships of 80 and 120 tons for Ieyasu, 'being made in all respects as our manner is'. The Japanese were also anxious to hire European pilots, for Cocks (in *Diary*, II, p. 283) reports that Adams had been approached at the Edo court to pilot a ship in search of the Islands of Gold and Silver (see p. 89, n. 2). Boxer (*Great Ship*, p. 76) refers not only to Portuguese pilots on Japanese ships, but notes, 'Portuguese influence is also readily discernible in their sail-plan, navigational charts and sailing-directions'. Further details of Portuguese influence on Japanese navigation are given in Nakayama, *History*, pp. 117–18.

[7] Rodrigues later describes these visits in great detail in chapters 17–21.

[8] Roof tiles were not used exclusively in temples, although it is true that most houses of commoners were thatched.

revenues all over the kingdom. But now it is destroying itself and the lords have taken all the revenues for themselves, with the result that there are no studies or education of subjects, apart from the light of the Holy Gospel manifesting idolatry's falsity and worthlessness.

15. Japan has been completely renovated and is almost a different nation from of old, even as regards ceremonies and customs. Many new ones have been introduced, while many of the ancient ones that took up so much time have been dropped.

Of these three periods, the first was Japan's real and true one. The second was a tyrannical one, contrary to the first. The third in some respects is similar to the first, while in other respects is like the second, for it is tyrannical inasmuch as it usurped the government from the legitimate lord, although it treats him better in every way. We say that it resembles the first period inasmuch as the entire kingdom is under one ruler in peace. It is governed better and with greater justice; they have done away with the oppression of the roads, passes, or ports, and also the sea and land customs barriers that used to exist everywhere in every state. Thieves and brigands have been checked and pirates have been completely put down. They used to collect tribute and money everywhere on the coast near their own base and headquarters, whence they sallied forth in bands.[1] All trade and commerce was freed, and the court and nobility became wealthier. The Lord of Tenka paid honour to the king and again constructed magnificent palaces for him and the *kuge*, granting them revenues for their sustenance. He makes outward show of obeying the king and governing in his name, and pays him solemn visits in carriages and coaches in the ancient fashion. The kingdom's trade and culture thrive, and many of the lords of the realm have been promoted to the patrician rank and its titles. The king now grants these at the request of the Lord of Tenka. To a certain extent the patrician order has been resurrected with its former honours, although these have been given to new people and not to the *kuge*, along with titles such as Kampaku, Daijō Daijin, Udaijin, Sadaijin, Daifu, Dainagon, Chūnagon, Chūshō, Shōshō, Saisho, Jijū, Shodaifu, and others.[2]

Daifu's succession after the death of Taikō brought about some change to this third period. He took the title of *kubō*, or shogun,[3] and partly maintained the equestrian order, of which he is the head. But nobody took his title from this order, and everybody keeps the titles of the patrician order of Taikō's time as regards housing and sustenance, for this is more noble. This Daifu even improved the kingdom and his state as regards housing and sustenance, and before he died he took the *kuge* rank of Daijō Daijin.[4] His son succeeded

---

[1] For earlier references to Japanese pirates, see p. 46, n. 1. For Hideyoshi's anti-piracy decree in 1588, see Berry, *Hideyoshi*, pp. 133–4; Kuno, *Japanese Expansion*, I, pp. 295–7. Murdoch (*History, 1542–1651*, p. 207) remarks that after this decree, the once-dangerous Inland Sea 'became as safe as a ball-room or Scotland Yard itself.' As an early translation of a Jesuit letter (in Purchas, *Purchas*, 1939, p. 45) puts it, 'Taico has settled peace thorow all Japon from Warres, from Robbers by land, and from Rovers by sea, which before continually infested all with Piracies.'

[2] Rodrigues lists most of these court ranks in *Arte grande*, ff. 208–9v, and *Arte breve*, ff. 87v–8v. Many of these titles are mentioned by Valignano in *Principio*, f. 24. The fact that these titles were awarded to 'new men' and not to *kuge* is confirmed by the list of honors showered on men such as Nobunaga, Hideyoshi, and Ieyasu. Ponsonby-Fane, *Kyoto*, pp. 181, 236–7. In his penetrating study of Hideyoshi's quest for legitimization, Elison ('Hideyoshi', p. 228) notes Rodrigues's remarkable understanding of 'the ambivalences of show and reality in the Japanese political arena' when the Jesuit reports how eager the warriors were to acquire the prestige of aristocratic *kuge* titles.

[3] As mentioned on p. 134, n. 2, Ieyasu was appointed shogun in 1603.

[4] The emperor granted Ieyasu the title of Dajō Daijin in the last few months of the ruler's life when it was apparent that he did not have long to live. Cocks (23 August 1615, in *Diary*, I, p. 44) heard the rumour that Ieyasu had asked the emperor for the title ('which, as it should seeme, is as the names of Caeser or Augustus amongst the Emperours of Rome, which is held an honor to all suckceadors)', but incorrectly states that the title in question was Kampaku.

him with the title of shogun and is obliged to take some high *kuge* rank, although in Taikō's time he had the rank of Chūnagon, which he still possesses.[1]

These, then, are the different states of this Japanese nation up to the present time. In recent years many things have been written that appear contradictory, but in fact they are merely changes. We experienced and saw the second and third states for many years, etc.

---

[1] Ieyasu's third son, Hidetada received the title of shogun in 1605, when his father nominally retired to keep the office in the Tokugawa family. Hidetada had been awarded the title of *chūnagon* in 1592. Following his father's example, he chose early retirement in 1623 to ensure that the office remained in the family.

CHAPTER 12

THE METHOD OF JAPANESE BUILDING

After dealing with the material wealth of this kingdom, it is logical to now describe their way of building houses, cities, castles, and all the other edifices, for all this belongs to this kingdom's material side. They are very skilful in their architecture, but we will not speak about this matter here for we will have more to say about it when we deal with their liberal and mechanical arts;[1] here we will deal only with their manner of building houses and laying out cities.

It may be noted in general that when the Japanese and the Chinese come to construct their houses, cities, and castles (especially the larger ones), and when the nobles erect buildings for public functions, they pay much attention to the position of the sites in respect to the four parts of the world, to wit, the front, rear, left-hand, and right-hand sides, for as regards seating arrangements their courtesies and ceremonies depend on this. Among the Chinese, Koreans, and Japanese (for they all follow the Chinese method), the south is the front part, while the rear or back is to the north; the east is on the left-hand, the west is on the right. The left-hand side or part is more honourable than the right.

According to a maxim of their ancient sages, the king, whom they call the Wise,[2] and also those who govern in his name or place, and the lords and nobles, must be seated facing south in public ceremonies. This is the part in front and the highest position. Their back is turned towards the north, which is the part behind and the lowest place. Thus the eastern and nobler direction is to their left, while to their right lies the west, an inferior direction. Hence the middle seat is the noblest of all and is the principal position of the house or place. After this comes the position on the left-hand side, and then in third place the right-hand position; then comes the lowest and opposite position in the south, in which a person faces north and has his back to the south. All this is based on their science and judicial astrology,[3] as will be described in its proper place.

Hence when they come to build their cities, as well as castles, houses, palaces, temples, and all the rest, they pay much attention to these four positions so that everything may be in its proper place and face the right direction in keeping with the degree of honour of the place in question. Thus all the cities, castles, royal palaces and the palaces of the other lords, as well as the residences of the noble and wealthy people must have the front or

---

[1] A literal translation of *artes liberaes e mecánicas*. A freer translation of 'arts and crafts' was rejected as misleading, for Rodrigues later includes football, meat-carving, mathematics, and hunting under *artes liberaes*, and painting, architecture, and metal-work under *artes mecánicas*.

[2] A literal translation of a puzzling phrase.

[3] 'Judicial astrology. The supposed art of foretelling or counselling in human affairs by interpretation of the motions of celestial objects.' *Oxford English Dictionary*, I, p. 136.

forepart facing south as far as the site permits. If the site makes it impossible for the entrance of the outer enclosure to be on the south side, at least the houses within the compound are built with their front facing south and their sides or rear towards the north. Thus royal palaces, or the square enclosure through which they are entered, have four gates: the principal one is in the south, the rear gate in the north, another in the east, while the fourth is in the west. This is also true of cities and castles, for the front or principal part faces south as far as the site permits.

The principal and proper streets are those running north-south, while those running east-west are less important side streets and generally exist only if the site allows. As in China, the cities are square in shape and have as many roads running north-south as there are running east-west, all of a definite and fixed length. Thus these streets cross each other and form perfect squares. The houses, or their fronts, have their main door on the side running north-south. Those that open on to the east-west streets are the side-doors, as we will describe later when speaking about the city of Miyako in particular.[1]

1. Concerning the construction of Japanese houses in detail

We will leave to one side the poverty and wretchedness of the houses and dwellings even of the lords and nobles at the time when the kingdom was involved in continuous wars and everything was laid waste by fire. The lords and nobles ordinarily lived in castles set on high mountains, while other folk dwelt in forests, thick woods, and on mountain tops. The houses of both types of people were of straw or grass for the most part, for it was impossible to live comfortably in the cities and towns except for a few safer places such as Miyako, Sakai, and other places near the castles of the kingdom's powerful lords. But we will describe only the ancient way of building, and this is in fact the present method of constructing used throughout the kingdom.

According to this style, all the houses in the land are built of wood and the architectural art involved in this is as skilful as you will find in any other part of the world. Indeed, in the view of responsible people who have seen various parts of Europe, Japanese construction in wood does not appear to be surpassed or even equalled elsewhere. This is particularly true of the palaces of the powerful lords, the nobles, aristocrats, the wealthy, and those of high birth, as well as of the temples and monasteries.[2] The high quality may be noted in the excellence of construction, the manner of building, and the proportions observed, as well as in the magnificence, neatness, and everything else, as will be said later in a general description. We will not describe here the real king's palace, for we will speak about this later in detail.[3]

We may describe four types of houses in this kingdom:

---

[1] This seems to contradict what Rodrigues has already said about the arrangement of houses. If the houses have the front door on the north-south side, it follows that the principal entrance will face east or west, and not south. Further, if, as he says, there are as many roads running north-south as there are running east-west, it is difficult to understand how the east-west roads 'generally exist only if the site permits'. Rodrigues obviously had Miyako in mind when writing this paragraph, as few Japanese cities were laid out according to this plan.

[2] Fróis (in *TCJ*, pp. 131, 134) writes that he had seen nothing in India or Europe to compare with the grandeur of the castles at Gifu and Azuchi. The skill of Japanese carpenters is highly praised by Avila Girón, *Relación*, p. 30; Vilela, 6 October 1571, in *Cartas*, I, f. 320; and Mexia, 1580, in ibid., I, f. 476v.

[3] Rodrigues later writes about the palace of the Dairi, or emperor, in Chapter 14, but he hardly offers the promised detailed description as that chapter consists of less than 50 words.

I. The houses and palaces of the lords and grandees, the nobility and the wealthy. This is the principal sort about which we will speak.[1]

2. The houses in the streets of the cities and towns. All of these are usually connected with trade and commerce.

3. The houses of the peasants and ordinary folk. These are very mean and abject in every respect, and there is hardly anything to say about them.

4. The monasteries and dwellings of religious, the convents, and the temples belonging to them. Much can also be said about these for, in imitation of China, such buildings are one of the splendours of Japan. But it may well be that we will deal with this fourth class separately when we come to describe Japan's religion and sects, for there are many things in this subject worthy of mention.

Concerning the houses of the lord and nobles, we may consider many things that illustrate the great skill and perfection of the Japanese in this art, the care they exercise in their buildings, and the attention they pay to everything necessary not only for the household but also for visitors and guests. Among other points, we may consider principally the following items.

I. The general manner of building, good or bad building sites in respect to the four directions, construction in accordance with definite and fixed measurements, building materials, and the consideration paid in their buildings to guests and to the household and servants.

2. Everything concerning the parts around the house, the gates and public entrance, and the place[2] where attendants wait.

3. The place within the house where the porters receive messages and take them inside to their master, and these men's work.

4. The entrance to the house's interior through which guests enter its rooms and the reception room.

5. The interior of the house, its decoration, and division.

6. The exterior or public kitchens of the house.

7. The stables, also a public place.

8. The guests' privies and their attendants.

9. The house and place where *cha*[3] is drunk, for everyone has this in his palace.

We shall say something in particular about all these things, although a great deal more could be written.

I.[4] The Japanese method of building in general

There are various considerations to be taken into account concerning the Japanese way of building. First of all, there is the site of the building. It is a widely observed custom in China and other countries that have adopted her customs to pay much attention to a building's site, not so much as to whether it be convenient or not, but whether it be good or bad in respect to the positions and imagined influences of the Heavens; whether, for example, they foretell good or bad fortune, a long or short life, and other things of that sort. There are people, or astrologers, whose office is to predict a site's good or bad fortune as well as to

---

[1] Fróis (*História*, V, pp. 312–16) comments at length on the grandeur of the palaces in Miyako, but lists some of the drawbacks of the city in comparison with its European counterparts.

[2] There is a short gap in the Portuguese text here. Possibly it should read 'the house and place where …'

[3] A reference to tea.

[4] This section is erroneously labelled, as there has already been another No. I section, starting on p. 138.

decide its good or bad days and times, etc. This is very common in China and was also in Japan, but since Nobunaga's time they have paid but scant attention to this, for each man builds in the place assigned to him for the purpose by the Lord of Tenka or on the site that an individual noble grants his subjects near his castle or city. But people who are inclined towards these superstitions concerning the choice of the site of a castle or city have once more begun to pay attention to this matter before they build.[1]

The second consideration, as has already been said, concerns the place where the building's front or the house's principal entrance will be and the direction that it will face, which, as we have noted, is towards the south. This is done regarding the four points of the compass not only on account of their seating arrangements, but also as it is cool in summer because of the south wind that then blows, while in winter it is warm because of the north wind.[2]

The third point to be taken into account is that in all their buildings they show great consideration towards their guests and their attendants, the reception rooms fitted out for them, the house's domestic service in regard to the guests, and the public offices in which everything necessary is prepared for the guests and their natural needs that do not brook delay. This is all done for the use of the guests and their retinue whenever it may be necessary so that they do not absent themselves for this reason, and do not meet servants when they go along [to the privy], and also on account of the place's cleanliness, for the Japanese greatly insist on this in everything.[3]

The fourth thing is that all Japanese buildings are constructed of wood and that they do not build houses of stone, brick, or plaster. The walls are covered with mud, mixed with straw to strengthen it so that it sticks and does not fall. The ancient Jews seem to have used this method, for the Prophet says that they smeared the walls with mud without straw and mixture.[4] It seems that they do not build with stone or brick because of the many earthquakes that occur, or perhaps because it is more difficult. Also a wooden building constructed in their way can be transferred elsewhere. They do this every day, moving not only houses but also cities and populous towns, as we ourselves saw many times. This could not be done if they built with stone, brick, or mud.[5]

---

[1] A reference to the pseudo-science of geomancy, called *tsuchi-uranai* ('land divination') in Japanese and *fengshui* ('wind and water') in Chinese (this is quite distinct from the Middle Eastern and European system of divination called geomancy). Ricci (*Fonti*, I, p. 96, and *China*, p. 85) also mentions the practice, which is still observed today. For detailed accounts of geomancy, in which a balance between the opposing forces of nature is sought, see Eitel, *Feng-shui*; *SCC*, II, pp. 359–63; March, 'Appreciation'.

[2] Ricci (*Fonti*, I, p. 72, and *China*, p. 60) also mentions this orientation of buildings towards the south. The word *quanto* in the Portuguese text is probably a slip for *cuente*, 'warm'. But the sentence is not clear as it stands. Rodrigues presumably means that the southern side is warm in winter because it is protected from the cold north wind. Japanese and Chinese seating arrangements were perhaps originally due more to this climatic consideration rather than to any abstract reasons.

[3] The Portuguese text of this sentence is tortuous and confused, but the general meaning is clear.

[4] Ezechiel, 13, 10. Rodrigues seems to mean that the Jews used to mix straw into their building clay (Exodus, 5, 7–18). As an exception, the false prophets mentioned in Ezechiel's text would not use straw and so the walls thus built would fall down.

[5] Vilela (15 September 1565, in *Cartas*, I, f. 193v) gives the same reason, as also does Mexia (6 January 1584, in ibid., II, f. 123). Vilela points out that the advantage of wooden buildings in earthquakes is offset by their vulnerability to fire. Another reason for using wood in building was, of course, the plentiful supply of timber. It was usual to dismantle buildings before removal, but Rodrigues later specifically states, p. 323, that only the roof was dismantled. Transfer of wooden buildings is also mentioned by Avila-Girón, *Relación*, p. 30, and Fróis, *História*, III, p.

All the houses of the nobles are built of various kinds of precious wood. The most usual is very fine cedar, esteemed for its quality and polish.[1] All the pillars are made of this cedar or of another kind of wood that is even more valuable. The common folk use pine and other inferior wood, although ordinary people of quality construct at least the reception quarters for guests with cedar wood.

Fifthly, every kind of house and dwelling, both the complete house in general as well as its rooms and apartments, is constructed according to certain excellent measurements and proportions as regards length and breadth, and also the height of the walls. This is because all the houses are matted or carpeted with a certain kind of estrades like thick mats of a standard size as regards their length and width, the width being half the length.[2] Each fits in with the others so that there is never any empty space between them. In this way a very large room can be carpeted with them and appears to be carpeted with squares, for each mat has a hem of coloured cloth or silk around its edges that makes it very attractive.[3] The rooms are furnished thus because it is their usual custom to sit upon these mats, and indeed this is the usual fashion of the whole of Asia for they do not use chairs in their houses. China is an exception, although in ancient times they too used this method, as may be seen in their books and chronicles, and at the time when they began to use chairs in their rooms and other places.[4]

In the sixth place, the roofs of the houses, palaces, temples, and other buildings always slope towards the entrance and the house's place of honour, as also is the case in China and Korea. On no account will the top of a room be situated in a place where there is no sloping roof. Even if there is such a roof, as in the case of a four-sided roof, the entrance and the top of a room will always lie in the breadth of a house and not in its length. This is quite contrary to our fashion, as, for instance, in one of our churches where the sanctuary is at the top of the church and the sloping roofs along its two sides. In contrast, their principal part would be located at our southern side-door (if such a door existed there), while their place of honour would be at our northern side-door. Finally, whatever the house's site, its place of honour and entrance are always below the sloping roofs of the breadth, and not the length, of the building.[5]

---

258. Almeida (17 November 1563, in *Cartas*, I, f. 125v) reports that backsliders expelled from Christian communities would take their houses with them. Fróis (*História*, IV, p. 35) notes that a church was transferred four leagues from Okayama to Osaka in 1582.

[1] A reference to *hinoki*; see p. 90, n. 4.

[2] Rodrigues later gives the *tatami* measurements as 6½ feet by 3 feet (pp. 150, 235), and also as 8 spans by 4, and three fingers thick (p. 322). See also Avila Girón, *Relación*, p. 27 (8 spans by 4); Carletti, in *TCJ*, p. 217 (4 ells by 2); Valignano, *Sumario*, p. 6, n. 19. See also Morse, *Japanese Homes*, pp. 26, 111, 123, for different patterns for laying out these mats.

[3] Avila Girón (*Relación*, pp. 27–8) also comments on the neatness of *tatami*, and mentions their cloth borders and their price; he remarks that the mats fitted so closely that they seem to have been born in that position. See also Vilela, 15 September 1565, in *Cartas*, I, f. 193v. *Vocabulario*, f. 395, gives: '*Shiki-awase*. The joining of one *tatami* with another.'

[4] According to tradition, the *huchuang*, a large folding camp stool, was introduced into China from the West during the reign of Emperor Ling Ti (168–87), and a back was added to the chair in the 12th century. Ricci (*Fonti*, I, p. 35, and *China*, p. 25) mentions that the use of chairs was wholly unknown in the nations surrounding China, admitting that he is at a loss to explain why. As Rodrigues later points out (p. 214), the introduction of the chair into China brought about a change in social customs. Fitzgerald, *Barbarian Beds*, pp. 1, 2–4, 16–17; Stone, *Chair*, pp. 11–12.

[5] Morse, *Japanese Homes*, does not mention the direction of the roof, but a glance at his illustrations shows that Rodrigues's comments, especially this last sentence, are generally true. An exception is noted in Paine and Soper, *Art and Architecture*, p. 260. Illustrations of different types of roof are supplied in Rodrigues, *Nihon*, I, p. 329. Valignano

2. The enclosures or walls within which they build, and the doorways and vestibules of the entrance to the houses

The second thing to be noted about Japanese buildings is the compound or wall, within which they build their houses, with their entrances through doorways and vestibules inside the compound. The Japanese lords and grandees, noble and wealthy people (but not merchants and traders who live together in the streets of the cities and towns with their shops in the street) are wont to build their houses within a surrounding plastered wall that is rather like a mud wall of a house. This serves as a wall and protection for the whole house. Usually these compounds are guarded along the four greater or lesser walls according to the means of the person who dwells therein. For in various ways it surprises the nobles and lords to have the doors and windows of our houses and palaces opening directly on to the street. The Chinese do the same after their fashion.

Instead, they dwell inside these enclosures and walls, and the houses therein are separated from the street gates set in these walls through which people enter inside. They build everything within this compound – the houses and offices for both guests and the household, the women's quarters in the innermost part of the house, and the quarters of the domestic staff and other servants.

The palaces of the Japanese lords, nobles, and people of quality have, in accordance with their dignity, two gates or entrances in these walls. One of them is a public and common one for the guests and visitors who arrive.

The buildings in these palaces and houses of the nobles are fashioned with rich workmanship and skill, and have large gates that are opened when a noble or person of importance arrives. At the sides of these gates there are small doors that are usually used by outsiders to enter and leave when they come to the houses of these lords. The houses of nobles and well-born people have in due proportion the same arrangement; there is one entrance for outsiders that leads directly to the guest houses, while there is another gate in the same wall for the householders and staff. Household members enter and leave through this gate, and it is also used for domestic goods, such as food and any other things brought in on carts or pack-animals. The horses of the lord of the house also enter and leave through here when he goes out riding. This is because this gate leads to the public kitchen of the house and the horse stables, about which we will speak later.

This is the general custom of the entire kingdom among the nobles and the houses that are not shops or commercial offices. The shops cannot boast of such excellence, although in these as well, especially in Miyako and large cities such as Sakai and others, they have a closed entrance set in the street façade. This has its neat path, and those who come as guests enter here; they are received in clean houses reserved for this purpose even though the site may be small and narrow. For it is not usual for a guest to use the service entrance and thus see the house's interior and its less clean places.

It was through these gates of the guests that coaches or carriages used to enter the court in ancient times when formal visits were made. They would draw up by the house's verandas at a special place constructed for this purpose and called *kuruma-yose*, and the guest would alight from the carriage on to the veranda of the room, as we shall say later. Even though these visits in carriages or coaches are not now usually paid, this place mentioned above is

---

(*Cerimoniale*, p. 278) ordered that in Jesuit houses the European custom of siting the chapel along the length, and not the width, of the building should be observed. In other respects, the chapels were to follow Japanese custom.

still constructed in the palaces of the lords and nobles as a decoration and a relic of ancient times. It is also constructed out of reverence towards the Lord of Tenka so that he may be received in his coach when he wishes to go to a lord's palace for a banquet.[1] Even now it is his custom to go many times, although without a coach. As these gateways are at the front of the house or palace, they thus stand immediately on the street. Many of them are of great value as regards their beauty and craftsmanship. They are constructed with every kind of woodwork and metalwork richly done out with gold, silver, black copper, and wood even more precious than cedar. We saw such gateways that cost more than three or four thousands crowns.[2] They employ porters and guards who are always on duty there.

These gates open on to the first courtyard, which leads to the inner vestibule of the house. Here are stationed people who receive and deliver all the messages that arrive. On one side of this first courtyard there is another gate in the wall by which guests enter the second courtyard, which is even neater and more interior. This leads up to the front of the house, where the guests are received and enter the house's verandas and rooms.

In the first courtyard there are special places where minor attendants, such as footmen, grooms, and other servants await their master's return, for they may not accompany him inside unless they are pages, squires, and other noble attendants.

The length of many of these compounds, especially those of the great lords in Miyako (when Taikō's palace was there in Fushimi), Osaka, and Edo, is 150 geometric paces (with five feet to each pace), and this makes a circumference of 600 paces – a large area, indeed, and all of it full of houses.[3] Others would be half this in length, and this is the least size in the houses of the lords. We shall later speak more in detail about the other things in these compounds. On three sides of many of these palaces (that is, not including the front where, as we said, the gateways are located), there are long houses instead of walls, and these are as long as the side of the compound. All of these houses have two or more storeys and are occupied by the lords' retainers, chiefly their soldiers and other guards.[4]

3. The composition of the houses in particular and their parts; and firstly the inner vestibule where messages are received

There is a great deal to note and learn about the composition of the houses and their parts that are suited for all their requirements. The whole construction may be divided in general into the outer part reserved for guests, and the inner part where the lord usually has his

---

[1] According to Caron (*True Description*, p. 31), these formal banquets were sometimes arranged three years in advance to allow time for proper preparation. The shogun used these extravagant occasions to weaken nobles financially and thus reduce their military potential.

[2] While describing his visit to Edo in 1610, Vivero y Velasco (in *TCJ*, p. 285) noted the elaborate mansion gateways, some of which cost more than 20,000 ducats. The style and size of these gateways indicated the rank of the mansion's owner. For illustrations and plans of these structures, see Coaldrake, 'Edo Architecture', pp. 261–84, and *Architecture and Authority*, Chapter 8.

[3] Hideyoshi built his magnificent palace/castle at Fushimi, about five miles south of Miyako, between 1592 and 1594, employing a labour force of 20,000–30,000 men. It was there that Rodrigues visited him two weeks before the ruler's death in 1598. According to Ponsonby-Fane (*Kyoto*, pp. 313–21), the area of the enceinte was 7 x 8 *chō*, or 840 x 960 yards. Rodrigues's measurements are therefore only approximate. Brief history of the magnificent building in *KEJ*, II, p. 375. Details of its construction and size in Berry, *Hideyoshi*, pp. 228–9. A stylized illustration of the building, found in a screen depicting Miyako, is given in *Kokushi Daijiten*, XII, p. 159.

[4] These *nagaya* ('long buildings') were, as Rodrigues notes, usually occupied by guards. A photograph of such a building in Edo in the 1860s is shown in *Monumenta Nipponica*, 49 (1994), p. 283.

quarters and lives informally and keeps his wardrobe. This is where the women live and no man, except the lord himself, enters and all the servants are women.[1] There is also much to be said about the division of the rooms and chambers; the interior decoration of these houses; the immediate entrances to the guests' quarters where they are received; the public kitchen and the inner one; the public stable; the privies for the guests; the place where *cha* is drunk; and finally the inner vestibule where porters are on duty and messages are received. We will first of all describe here the vestibule and will then later deal with the others things in due order.

We have already dealt with the surrounding wall and the gates through which people enter the house or palace and the other buildings mentioned. After entering through the main gate, a person first comes to the vestibule at the end of the first courtyard; they call this the *sōshadokoro* and the officials here the *sōshaban*.[2] The vestibule is composed of clean and goodly rooms where guests, visitors, and honourable people who bring messages wait while the porters take the messages in to the lord, or inform him who has come to visit him. They have various outer and inner rooms there, and these are used in accordance with the visitor's dignity.[3] These porters' room is also here. These officials are people of quality with the rank of equerries, and they take it in turns to be always on duty there both day and night. Their task is to receive all the messages from outside, concerning both visits and other matters, and take them inside when the lord is in the house. When he is not at home, or when he is busy and pretends to be absent (as they often do), the porters have books in which they record the messages, the names of the persons who sent them, and the names of the men who brought them.

The same thing happens on the festivals in the year when it is customary to visit each other, even though they do not see the host. The porters write down the name of the persons who sent greetings or came to pay a visit on that day. When the Japanese are ill, they usually do not see anybody; on such occasions the officials record all the visits paid during the sickness so that when the lord recovers he may know who came to visit him. This is done so that he may afterwards thank and fulfil his obligation towards those people who paid a visit either in his absence, or on a festival, or while he was ill.

In addition, it is customary in Japan on these visits or at other times to send gifts of cloth, robes, silk, gold, silver, and food such as birds or animals caught in hunting, esteemed fish, fruit, wine, and many other things. It is the duty of these men to record in the books all the gifts brought from outside for the lord in his absence. Even if the lord is at home, the officials receive all these things so that they may later show them to him. After he has seen them, they are handed over to the person in charge of such things, such as the keeper of the lord's wardrobe or the steward of the household. The porters write this down, firstly as a record of the gifts presented so that their master may later thank the donor or

---

[1] In his instructions on the need for adaptation to the Japanese way of life, Valignano (*Cerimoniale*, p. 272) suggests that this division should also be observed in Jesuit houses. There should be public rooms for guests, while other interior rooms should not be accessible to outsiders.

[2] According to Tsukahira, *Feudal Control*, p. 191, the *sōshaban* were masters of ceremony and etiquette in the shogun's court, but from Rodrigues's account (and also in Rodrigues, *Nihon*, I, p. 337, n. 18) they also functioned in the mansions of the nobles. For Valignano's rules about the duties of the porters in Jesuit houses, see *Cerimoniale*, pp. 146, 300.

[3] Valignano (*Cerimoniale*, p. 276) laid down that all Jesuit houses should have a vestibule where messages could be received and visitors' retinues entertained. In the larger cities, where there was a greater likelihood of visits from lords and *yakata*, there should be special interior rooms for the reception and entertainment of their retinues.

repay him with an equivalent gift in return; and secondly, so that nothing may be lost when these things are handed over and received, as happens in large houses. Thus when the lord later reads the list, he may know in detail what has been given him. For this reason the porters are obliged to receive the gifts and to account for them. They hand them over to the man in charge of keeping them and receive a receipt certifying what was handed in and who brought them.[1]

Near this vestibule and the place where they receive visitors is a house with its office and officials who are responsible for keeping there a supply of hot fresh water and ground *cha*. Thus they can provide *cha* to the guests who are with their master, and this is in keeping with the general custom throughout the kingdom. They also serve *cha* to the guests waiting in the outer rooms and to people of quality who come on business.[2] It is the duty of the younger pages who serve in the lord's presence to take this *cha* to the guests.

In the houses of public figures involved in business or various transactions, these porters receive no little profit from people who come on business in order that they may hand in their messages or inform the lord of their business at a favourable time, or else tell them when the lord will have time so that they may ask for an audience. If the gifts of those who come from afar are of things that will not go bad, they leave them in the hands of these porters to save having to take them away and then bringing them back once more; then they return when the lord is at home in order to present them to him personally. But if the gifts, such as fruit and other ripe things, are perishable, they leave them with the porters to present to the lord on his return before they are spoiled. Everyone who has business to transact in these houses regards it as important to know these porters and be their friends.

In the house of the *kubō*, or the Lord of Tenka, these *sōshaban* are great territorial lords and vassals who take on the duty in rotation. Their office is to present ambassadors and the person, or his gift, in a formal ceremony; that is, they publicly welcome them in an outer room and convey the messages or business matters that arrive.[3] On the day that falls to each one, nobody else may make the presentation, for that would be usurping another's office.

4. The immediate entrance to the guests' quarters

We have already dealt above with the gate on the street. Further in, after the first courtyard, there is another very fine one where the guests enter, accompanied by their pages, squires, and shoe-boy, and proceed to the entrance of the corridor next to the room. Some of the other servants remain in the street, while the rest stay in the first courtyard. The lord wears footwear made of glove-leather, silk, or a certain neat woven fabric; these are like stockings and are worn in the matted rooms as we described above.[4] This is the usual footwear of the kingdom both inside and outside the house, for sandals are used only for stepping on the ground.

[1] Ricci (*Fonti*, I, p. 74, and *China*, p. 62) notes that the porters in Chinese mansions also compiled lists of donors and gifts to show to their masters later.

[2] Valignano (*Cerimoniale*, p. 278) also ordered that there should be a tea room near the entrance of Jesuit houses so that visitors could be entertained with *cha*.

[3] The Portuguese text is unclear at this point. When describing his audience with Hidetada in Edo, Vivero y Velasco (in *TCJ*, p. 116) makes express mention of these numerous gentlemen-in-waiting, who conducted him to the shogun's presence.

[4] These are *tabi*, later described on p. 186.

It is the general custom throughout the kingdom for any person of quality, from the highest ranking to the lowest, to be accompanied by a lad who takes his sandals at the entrance of the rooms in houses. The boy also carries clogs in case of mud and an umbrella against the sun or rain. He gives his master the sandals on his coming out of the house or room when he has to tread on the ground. If the owner of the house or room comes out to meet his guest in one of the courtyards or sometimes in the street, he too is accompanied by a lad with the same duty of seeing to the sandals. This is a very base office, and the pages who are honourable and have the rank of squires will on no account ever take or present the sandals to the lord with their own hands, even if he is waiting for the lad to come. For each of the pages has his own shoe-boy to serve him when he enters the room in the company of his lord or with a message.[1]

As we have said in regard to the exterior or front of these houses, all of them usually face south, and in front of the rooms there are corridors or verandas made of such spotless cedar wood that it looks like a mirror.[2] From here the guests enter directly into the matted rooms where they are received, and they exchange compliments as they enter. The guest always stays on the eastern part or left-hand side of the centre of the top of the room for this is the most honoured position, while the host remains on the western or right-hand side. The serving staff coming from the interior of the house go to this place as well, and it is their custom to come from the side that is in front of the guest.[3] The corridors and verandas are as long as the actual guest-house and cross with other passages leading into the interior of the house. They have sliding doors that are put to one side on the guest's arrival. When it rains, they are generally closed, because from the middle to the top they consist either of panes made of white oysters or of a certain fine paper, and these take the place of windows because of their brightness.[4] The guest room also has sliding doors, and in this way the whole house lies open.

In front of this room and corridor there is a courtyard containing a garden with trees and various flowers arranged naturally with much skill, proportion, and charm, along with other artificial things that imitate nature. Flowers are found there according to season. These gardens are very pleasant to behold as one stands there looking at the many different things in them, for in this matter they go to much trouble and seek trees, plants, and rare stones in remote parts for the garden. There are craftsmen who make their living by constructing and arranging such gardens in keeping with their rules for laying out the different kinds. They

---

[1] Valignano (*Cerimoniale*, pp. 138, 140–42) makes a similar observation. He warns Jesuits that they should not touch the shoe or umbrella of a guest, for this was the office of the *komono*, or lowly page, and ordinary servants would refuse to do this job even for their king. When priests made a journey, they should be accompanied by a Brother or catechist, and, if possible, two boys to take care of their shoes.

[2] The high polish of Japanese wood often produced this comparison. For example, Almeida (in Boxer, *Christian Century*, p. 55) in his description of Tamon Castle, and Fróis (in *TCJ*, p. 133) in his account of Gifu Castle.

[3] As Rodrigues later observes (p. 233), the serving staff enter the room from the opposite side as a safety precaution for the guests.

[4] There are two types of sliding doors. *Shōji* are found between a room and the veranda, while *fusuma* form the partitions between rooms. See Fróis, *Tratado*, p. 220; Morse, *Japanese Homes*, pp. 126–33. Valignano (*Cerimioniale*, p. 274) ruled that in Jesuit houses, the rooms, or at least the guest room, should be equipped with these sliding doors so that one large chamber might be made out of several smaller rooms when required. As regards windows made of oyster shells, Kaempfer (*Kaempfer's Japan*, p. 228) reports that merchants from the Ryukyus would bring to Satsuma transparent shells 'used to make windows, to slide across in winter against the rain,' but this practice does not appear to have been widespread. The Chinese certainly employed highly polished translucent shells in their buildings. Mundy

sometimes completely imitate nature and this is their custom. Much could be said about these gardens, for they are one of the most excellent things in Japan, but this must wait until another place where it will be more relevant. It should only be remarked here that the custom of having these gardens is very common in China. Thus there is not a single room, however interior it may be, which does not have its garden in front, and its quality will depend on the requirements of the place. It will contain various kinds of flowers to which these nations are much attached, for the people are wont to divert themselves in peace and quiet more often inside the house than outside.[1]

5. The interior of the house and its divisions

We now come to the plan of the houses and their divisions for various purposes. But it would be extremely tedious to describe the great variety of places within some of the palaces, especially those of the Lord of Tenka and the other great lords of the kingdom. There are the chambers and antechambers, the offices, and the corridors and passages running from one palace to another. Each has its own private garden and the necessary light. The palaces are built with great style and craftsmanship, and they are connected to each other by various passages and corridors in such wise that a person is always sheltered from the sun and rain as he passes quite a long distance through the different linked houses, as if he were going through only one house. So if anyone not knowing the entrances and exits were by himself, he would lose his way and be unable to find the exit and would return to the place where he started. As we often saw, it is necessary to have competent guides in such houses.[2] So I repeat, it would be very lengthy to describe all this, and I will therefore speak only about the way the houses are generally divided into an outer part for guests and an inner part for the owners and their womenfolk. I will also describe these houses' interior decoration.

The chief division within the houses and palaces of the lords is between the exterior part for guests and the interior part where the owner of the house resides. This interior part has two sections. The first is the inner residence of the lord of the house and has various rooms. This is where he usually stays, lives informally, eats, sleeps, and has his wardrobe, his treasure of gold and silver, weapons, and various other articles that the Japanese value highly. Pages and chamberlains wait upon him here, and household members and his friends may come as far as this part. He can divert himself in various ways here with gardens, birds and falcons for hunting; there is a special house for business and study, and others for private enjoyment. These rooms are next to those wherein the guests are received and are joined to them by passages and corridors. There is also a private kitchen here for his own

---

(*Travels*, III:1, pp. 193, 219) speaks of a Chinese pagoda having walls made of oyster shells and also a town built of the same material.

[1] Descriptions of fine gardens have been left by Fróis and Avila Girón, in *TCJ*, pp. 280–82, 133, 222; Vilela, 15 September 1565 and 6 October 1571, in *Cartas*, I, ff. 196, 320. Valignano (*Cerimoniale*, p. 276) stipulated that Jesuit houses should have 'a well-made and neat *niwa* [garden]' in front of the veranda. Fróis (*Tratado*, p. 258) verifies Rodrigues's observation, noting that whereas Europeans enjoyed themselves by strolling through the streets and squares, the Japanese relaxed at home and used the streets only for getting from one place to another.

[2] Exactly the same point is made by Pasio (Nagasaki, 3 October 1598, in JapSin 54, f. 11) when describing Rodrigues's visit to the dying Hideyoshi at Fushimi in 1598. 'The Father [Rodrigues] went, and says that before reaching the room in which Taikō was lying, he passed through so many rooms, chambers, corridors, and verandas, that had he not had a guide when he left, he would not have been able to find the way.' See also Cooper, *Rodrigues the Interpreter*, p. 186.

needs, and clean places like chimneys where he personally comes to prepare prized delicacies such as crane, wild duck, swan, and other esteemed game. All this has been taken by his falcons or those of his friends who have sent it to him, for this is highly thought of among them.[1] He may prepare prized fish such as salmon and other kinds.

All of this is carved by stewards in his presence. Carving is one of the liberal arts of Japan and there are people very skilled at it. While they cut up the crane before making the dishes, they do not touch anything with their hands, and this has to be seen to be appreciated. For this purpose they have a variety of extremely clean, suitable instruments, such as very sharp knives and cleavers made of highly rated iron, and forks or similar instruments made of iron or wood with an iron tip, with which they hold the meat while they carve. They carve these things on tables or a certain kind of thick bench made for the purpose. The skill, cleanliness, and rules observed in all of this are beyond description, and it is a palace duty performed in the lord's presence.

These lords have their own cooks, and also a chef or head cook. He is a gentleman who arranges everything prepared for the lord and the guests. Above all, he spares no pains in observing cleanliness in preparing the things, which he seasons after their fashion, and in the instruments with which he cooks and offers the food, such as the pots, plates, ladles, serving trays, and other instruments with which they serve at table in their manner.[2] This place is called *ryōri no ma*, that is, the room of the dishes or where the cooking is done. Here also they warm themselves in winter at a wood fire that is made there. In the middle of the room there is a chimney through which rise the flames and smoke. Next to it is the inner kitchen and other necessary offices. At night there are songs and merrymaking, and places for acting in the inner rooms.

The other part of the house's interior is the most private of all, and is where the women and their ladies-in-waiting dwell. They have their own private rooms in keeping with their rank, for there are various ranks between the serving ladies and the mistress of the house. No man whatsoever, not even pages, may enter this inner part of the house, except the actual lord of the house. These rooms are next to his inner room where he sleeps and has his wardrobe. All the waiting from here to the interior is performed by women. Mature ladies are appointed as porters and they come to this place to receive messages that pages carry from the lord. Any man entering the place would be immediately punished with death for the Japanese are very jealous. The Chinese and Koreans are even more so and their women are kept even more withdrawn from dealing with men than are Japanese women.[3]

[1] The 'clean places like chimneys' are the ovens or cooking-ranges, called *kamado*. As an example of a lord giving away the game killed in a hunt, Cocks (29 October 1618, in *Diary*, II, p. 91) records: 'The Emperor [Hidetada] went this day a fowling, and with his owne handes kild 5 elkes (or wild swans) which coming out to send them abroad to his brothers and frendes (after his retorne to his pallace or castell) ...' See also p. 211, n. 2, for another example.

[2] Another European much impressed by the cleanliness of the Japanese kitchen was Avila Girón, who describes (in *TCJ*, p. 222) in some detail the kitchen he visited in an Arima mansion. Nishiyama (*Edo Culture*, pp. 146–55) deals with culinary arts in some detail: 'Guests at banquets derived great pleasure from watching a chef give a brilliant, virtuoso performance with the cutting knife.' He mentions that there were 55 ways of carving a trout, as well as many ways of preparing wild goose, crane, and pheasant 'on a large ... cutting board used for the cutting ritual.' Contemporaneous illustrations of chefs at work in Smith, *Japanese History*, pp. 132–3.

[3] Avila Girón (*Relación*, pp. 18, 269) confirms this arrangement when speaking about the management of the emperor's palace. All the waiting inside the palace is done by boys, aged from eight to twelve years, and by maids. A husband would kill his wife if he found her alone speaking to a man; no witnesses were needed, and quite rightly so, for, as Avila Girón points out, what further witnesses does a husband need when he finds another man with his wife

The second part of the house is made up of the outer reception rooms for guests and places for public ceremonies and gatherings of visitors; it has various rooms, all of them provided with suitable corridors for servants to use.[1] Some rooms are for eating in, while others are more secluded and are used for conversation and business. Others are for sleeping in whenever it happens to be necessary, as it often does, and here they have silken beds, after their fashion, reserved for guests.[2]

On one side of the courtyard or patio in front of the principal room is an excellently fashioned wooden stage on which they produce plays, comedies, farces, and other things involving their music, and in this way they entertain guests, who watch the acting from the room.[3] To one side of these stages there are houses where members of the cast put on their costumes, and there is a path along which they come out on to the stage, acting as they come.[4] When such plays are performed, it is usual for the guests to send gifts of silver, silk robes, or other valuable things to the actors at the end of each piece as a sign of their appreciation of the play or farce,[5] or the musical instrument played by a person famous for his skill, for they earn their living in this way. The author comes with the others to the middle of the courtyard to receive the present; he bears it away with great reverence and signs of gratitude, and if it is a robe he carries it on his back. When plays are put on in a formal way, many people from outside are permitted to enter. The nobles are seated on the verandas and in the rooms, while the common folk sit on mats on the ground of the courtyard.[6]

Both in the interior part of these houses and in the section for guests there are several things worth describing, for the Japanese take great pains over such things in the interior of their houses. The first is that they have various divisions of rooms and chambers. These have sliding doors made of panels lined with thick paper on lathes painted, as we shall presently describe, like the walls of the house. Thus there are many different rooms, but they can turn them into only one when they wish by putting the doors together or pulling them apart.[7] It is wonderful to see each door with its fittings of copper richly worked and

---

in his house? Various salutary stories on this theme are recounted by Caron (*True Description*, pp. 32, 38), who adds that if the husband is absent, then his father, brother, son or servant may kill the offender.

[1] 'Serviço de caminho' in this sentence is puzzling, but is probably a slip for 'caminho de serviço', and I have translated it in this way.

[2] The 'beds, after their fashion' were *futon*, or mattresses, laid on the floor.

[3] Noh plays were sometimes performed in a noble's mansion, but Rodrigues seems to be describing the popular kabuki form of drama. Cocks often mentions kabuki actors and dancers: 'Ther came a company of players (or *caboques*) with apes and babons sent from the *tono* (or king) to play at our house, unto whome were geven iii *taies* in small plate' (11 July 1618, in *Diary*, II, p. 53). Towards the end of his life, Hideyoshi took an interest in noh and performed before the emperor. Elison, 'Hideyoshi', pp. 242–5; Berry, *Hideyoshi*, p 230–32. Theatrical performances were also popular in China: Ricci, *Fonti*, I, p. 33, and *China*, p. 23; Ribadeneira, *Historia*, p. 112.

[4] The raised *hanamichi*, 'flower path', along which the principal actors make their formal entrance and exit through the audience, is still a prominent feature of the kabuki theatre today.

[5] This was a long-standing custom, for we read in *Taiheiki*, p. 131, that in the 14th century Hōjō Takatoki invited actors and dancers to perform in Kamakura. The noble audience was so pleased with their performance that 'the lords bestowed gold and silver and precious stones upon them, and fine garments of damask and brocade.'

[6] On 31 October 1613, Cocks attended a theatrical evening at the Hirado *daimyo*'s mansion. He notes that the nobles took part in the play, and that all the local people, including those living in villages outside Hirado, were invited to attend. Farrington, *English Factory*, II, p. 1529.

[7] For these sliding doors, see p. 146, n. 4.

embellished with gold and silver, and with a place of the same fashion by which a person can pull the door without touching the painting with his hands.[1]

Thus there are rooms, principally in the palace of the Lord of Tenka, which are divided up in this way into various rooms under one roof and are so large that they have a thousand mats. This is equal to a floor area of 500 squares with sides 6½ mathematical feet long, for these mats are 6½ feet long and just over 3 feet wide. The shape of the mats is well proportioned, as anyone knowing about these things will understand. Sometimes, when the Lord of Tenka holds public ceremonies with the kingdom's lords, this room is made into only one apartment. We saw this sometimes in Taikō's palace at Osaka and in the shogun's in Edo, and its special name is *senjōjiki*, meaning the room of a thousands mats or estrades.[2] The palaces of the other lords and the mansions of nobles and aristocrats are also divided up, in due proportion, into room in this fashion.

The second point to notice is the walls and their interior decoration. The walls are made of kneaded clay plastered over a neat cane framework. The spaces between the columns are skilfully covered with many layers of fine clay, which binds together by being mixed with things like straw cut into small pieces and boiled. The final coat is applied on top with fine lime, which the plasterers use there so that the entire surface of the wall appears unbroken without any sign of joints, just like a mirror.[3]

The inner surface of these walls is lined with paintings executed on many layers of paper like thick parchment, and is excellently painted with trees, rivers, springs, animals, birds, lakes, seas, ships, human figures, and scenes from ancient legends, some of them including soldiers, according to individual taste. Or the four seasons of the year may be represented, each one depicted by whatever blooms in that particular season. In the part representing spring there will be various kinds of flowers that bloom therein, mist, clouds, and other things proper to that time of year. For summer there will be other flowers that bloom in that season and green fruit about to ripen. The autumn scene will depict ripe fruit, the leaves of the trees losing their colour and falling, and fields of ripe rice being harvested. In winter there will be dry leafless trees, for their vitality leaves the branches and gathers in the roots. There will also be snow, and birds of that season, such as wild duck, cranes, swans, and others, flying in flocks from Tartary with their guide in front, and other birds moving through the fields.[4]

---

[1] The device for pulling open or shut the *fusuma* is called *hikite*, usually consisting of a small metal plate inserted in the panel at about the same position as a door handle. They are often of artistic beauty and skill, and several fine examples are illustrated in Morse, *Japanese Homes*, pp. 129–31.

[2] In an early English translation of Jesuit letters, we read: 'Hee [Hideyoshi] caused at Ozaca a Hall to bee erected, with a thousand Tatami (very elegant Mats) the timber costly, the gilding incredible', but on 4 September 1596 the building was destroyed by a severe earthquake (Purchas, *Purchas*, pp. 44, 46). There was also a thousand-mat chamber in Fushimi palace. Ponsonby-Fane, *Kyoto*, p. 319. When Kaempfer had an audience with the shogun in Edo in 1691, he noted that the palace hall was called 'Sen Sio Siki' [*Senjōshiki*], but this is erroneously translated as 'the hall of a hundred mats' (Kaempfer, *History*, III, p. 88).

[3] The technique of plastering seems to have changed little through the centuries. According to Morse (*Japanese Homes*, pp. 31–2), writing in 1885, the first layer (*shita-nuri*) was composed of mud mixed with chopped straw; the second (*chū-nuri*) of rough lime and mud; the third and last (*uwa-nuri*) of lime and coloured clay.

[4] A similar list of artistic themes in paintings is given by Vilela (6 October 1571, in *Cartas*, I, ff. 320v–321), and Avila Girón (*Relación*, p. 28). When Cocks visited Edo Castle on 1 September 1616 for an audience with Hidetada (*Diary*, I, pp. 168–70), he noted, 'The Emperours pallis is a huge thing, all the rums being gilded with gould, both over head and upon the walls, except som mixture of paynting amongst of lyons, tigers, onces [jaguars], panthers, eagles, and other beastes and fowles, very lyvely drawne and more esteem [than] the gilding.' The building of palaces

Everything is done to imitate nature so that you seem to be looking at these very things.[1] They do not fancy artificial and imaginary paintings, such as ornamental designs with artificial fancywork and flourishes; instead, their painting must be a realistic depiction of natural things or scenes, or else legends. Each of these rooms is variously decorated with different paintings. In one they paint a hunt with hawks that looks so real that it leaves nothing to be desired; in another, a scene from nature; in another, there will be a legend; in another, a war, either on land or on sea; in another, other different things, as we have said.[2] In the houses of the lords and nobles these paintings and the doors of the rooms have a background richly painted in gold, and on this gold they paint the picture in various suitable colours. But there are others that are not gilded, but are executed on a white background and painted with black water-colours, and they are unique in this.[3] They are fond of melancholy subjects and colours rather than happy ones, and always seek contemplation and nostalgia in everything.

They finish these paintings with delicate black varnished laths. The end of the laths that terminate in the columns are laminated with gilt or copper plates. The best kind are made of black copper inlaid with gold of excellent workmanship; this is very expensive and more highly admired among them than if it were made of silver and gold. Some crosses fashioned in this style have gone to Europe.

Thus the inner surface of the walls is excellently decorated with a variety of paintings, and there is always someone admiring them and enjoying the sight of their great variety and beauty, for they are painted by famous artists for whom the Japanese have a high regard. They are most accomplished in painting birds, flowers, trees, and the things of nature, and they excel in this.

The third thing about which they take much care in the houses is the neatness with which they carpet them with these estrades or clean mats, finely woven of rushes that are sown and cultivated for the purpose. The mats have a border around their sides, as we have said, and are made by skilled craftsmen who earn their living doing only this. The mats are joined and united together as if there were only one, and are laid down in different ways so that they present a pleasing symmetrical appearance.[4] Because of these mats or estrades

---

by Nobunaga, Hideyoshi, and Ieyasu gave rise to the Era of Great Decorators (Warner, *Enduring Art*, p. 64), who lavishly decorated the interior of palace chambers with paintings depicting, as Rodrigues notes, scenes from nature and legends. Many illustrated examples of mural paintings depicting the items listed in this paragraph are found in Takeda, *Kanō Eitoku*.

[1] The realism of Japanese painting was also noted by Vilela (in *TCJ*, p. 255) when describing a screen seen in Miyako. The painting was so realistic 'that the spectator seemed to be looking at the actual thing which was thus portrayed.' The snow depicted in one of the screens 'appeared no less real than the snow which falls in its proper season.'

[2] The halls and chambers of palaces and temples were often called after the theme of their painted decoration. For example, the Chrysanthemum Chamber, the Stork Chamber, and the Wild Geese Chamber in Nishi-Honganji temple in Kyoto.

[3] The traditional use of ink monochrome was largely superseded by a dazzling display of gold leaf and bright colours, necessary for large-scale paintings in somewhat dim interiors. Paine and Soper, *Art and Architecture*, pp. 92–3.

[4] For earlier references to *tatami* mats, see pp. 141, 150. The various patterns in which they may be laid is shown in Morse, *Japanese Homes*, pp. 122–3; the corners of four mats are never allowed to come together. Writing about Edo Castle, Cocks notes (1 September 1616, in *Diary*, I, p. 169), 'I forgot to note downe that all the rowmes in his pallis under foote are covered with mattes edged with damask or cloth of gould, and lye so close joyned on to an other that yow canot put the point of a knife betwixt them.'

(which are three fingers thick), all the houses are built according to certain measurements. Indeed it is a joy to see such rooms and their neatness.

When it becomes cold in winter they have a kind of deep sunken grate in one of the rooms where they converse with guests and visitors. They kindle a slow charcoal fire inside this grate, the top of which lies level with the mats. On top they place a kind of square table over which they spread a long cloth or quilt of soft silk, which keeps the heat in and makes it like a gentle stove. They then put their hands, and sometimes their feet, underneath this quilt, and thus warm themselves as they lean against the square table and converse. They have these stoves in the winter in the inner part of the house as well so that they may warm themselves.[1]

The fourth thing to be noted is the interior ceiling of the roof above the rooms. They go to great trouble over this, and even an inferior one is made of delicate and precious white wood. They are divided into squares by laths, and in the ends and corners of the squares they are covered with plates of the type mentioned above. Other ceilings, especially in the palaces of the Lord of Tenka and other nobles, are of rich workmanship, decorated with gold and various paintings.[2] I will give only one example of a room of a thousand mats that the shogun has in his palace in the city of Edo. I have seen this room and so can give a true account of it.

In this room the matted area below equals that of the ceiling in the roof above. This is a flat surface of 500 squares with sides of 6½ feet in length, so that the area of each of these squares comes to 54 square mathematical feet. This makes a total of 27,000 square mathematical feet in the ceiling and each of these costs ten crowns, for the work is of the richest kind and intermixed with gold, and is the finest in Japan. So the whole ceiling would cost 270,000 crowns, and if this grandeur is found in only one public room, how many other houses must there be in the whole palace?[3]

Indeed, unless you have seen this, it is impossible to describe adequately or imagine the reality of it all. For the interior alone of such houses is quite immense. There are corridors running on either side of the rooms. Then courtyards and gardens provide brightness and light right up to the very interior of the house where the women and palace ladies dwell, not to mention the various buildings and offices are either side. It is, as they say, a labyrinth.[4]

6. The public kitchens in the palaces of the lords and other noble people

The palaces of the nobles and the houses of the lords and gentry have their public kitchens

---

[1] The *kotatsu*, still in use today, although now usually heated by electricity. A somewhat similar arrangement for airing bedclothes is shown in Morse, *Japanese Homes*, p. 213.

[2] Rodrigues's description of the ceilings is illustrated in photographs of the Audience Hall from Fushimi Palace and the Reception Hall of Nijō Castle, in Warner, *Enduring Art*, plate 55, and Boger, *Traditional Arts*, pp. 192–3.

[3] Either Rodrigues's mathematics is at fault or there is a copyist's error here. A square of side 6½' would have an area of 42¼ sq.ft, not 54. The total area of 500 such squares would be 21,125 sq.ft. At 10 crowns a square, the ceiling would cost 211,250 crowns. But this error does not invalidate what Rodrigues says about the high cost of such ceilings.

[4] Fróis (in *TCJ*, p. 132) makes the same comment when describing the interior of Gifu Castle: 'The halls and compartments within are like the labyrinth of Crete and are deliberately constructed thus with no little ingenuity.' This complex layout made an armed intrusion into the building more difficult.

(public, that is, as far as the guests are concerned) as part of their adornment and splendour. They are indeed worth seeing for their craftsmanship, size, cleanliness, and the necessary instruments, with their public cooks as well as the serving staff. In Japan this is a dignified and honourable occupation, and all the nobles value it highly. The work entails cutting and seasoning the dishes by themselves without their head cook or prefect of the kitchen. The stoves of these kitchens are fitted with their chimneys so that there is no smoke at all in the kitchen, nor can one … the place where the fire is burning.[1] They keep there large and small pots over the stoves with their well-made lids, and there is extreme neatness all around. These kitchens are built with marvelously thick columns and great timbers, and have their courtyard and patio in front of them. Part of the kitchen inside is level and part has a high matted floor. Next to it there are many rooms, neat and painted as we have said, and here the pages, equerries, and other dignified people engaged in honourable service come to eat. The head cook, who is like a majordomo, supervises all this.

There are other places where they prepare the food for the lord and the guests, and other offices, all of them with passages and corridors or covered verandas through which the servants make their way to the outer rooms.

There is much cleanliness in the cooking in these kitchens with their washbasins and everything else so that none of the food is touched by hand except when it is washed. They have special people who cut up fish and the flesh of birds and animals of the chase. While still raw and not yet cooked or dressed, all the food is cut up on spotless thick tables with iron forks, knives, and cleavers, and nothing is touched with the hands. As has already been said, they sometimes cut the meat in the presence of the lord and his guests when it is of high quality and caught by falcons during the hunt. They are so skilful at this carving that it is astonishing to see them at work.

On no account do the Japanese eat with their hands or touch the food directly. Instead, they use two sticks, a span and a half in length and as thick as the end of a silver fork. They are made of fine, smooth, white wood, and take the place of forks. The people are very skilled at eating with them with much delicacy and grace. The wooden sticks are new, and the gentry and guests use them only once. They are changed many times while they are eating, and so there is no need for napkins as they do not touch anything with their hands and all the food arrives at the table already cut up, as we have said. They are greatly astonished at eating with the hands and wiping them on napkins, which then remain covered with food stains, and this causes them both nausea and disgust. This way of eating with these sticks is common to China, Korea, Cauchi, Luchu, and Japan.[2]

As well as these public kitchens, which many people go to see, there are also inner ones, as said above. All the other houses of honourable people, even those of well-to-do city people, have their clean kitchen for guests in addition to the kitchen that serves the house, and orderliness is observed there in due proportion.

---

[1] There seems to be an omission in this sentence in the Portuguese text.

[2] An early European reference to chopsticks is made by Pires (*Suma oriental*, I, p. 116), who reached Canton in 1517; later Europeans often mentioned them. Carletti (in *TCJ*, pp. 193–4) and Avila Girón (*Relación*, pp. 43–4) both correctly report that they are called *hashi* in Japanese. The latter admired the dexterity of the Japanese and notes that even a four-year-old can remove the bones of a sardine with them. Pinto (in *TCJ*, pp. 195–6) reports that the courtiers of Bungo laughed and jeered at him and his companions for eating with their fingers. See also Fróis, *Tratado*, p. 170, and Valignano, *Sumario*, p. 41, on this point. The Europeans' eating habits and lack of bathing were in stark contrast to the Japanese way of life.

7. The horse stables in the lords' houses

One of the parts of the houses and palaces of the lords is the public stables. These are next to their palace within its enclosure.[1]

8. The washrooms for the guests

All the houses of the nobles and gentry have bathrooms for guests. These places are very clean and are provided with hot and cold water because it is a general custom in Japan to wash the body at least once or twice a day.[2] These extremely clean washrooms or baths have matted places where the guests undress for the bath. They put their clothes in a place where there are white perfumed robes of fine linen hanging up, and they use these to dry the body after bathing. Clean new loincloths are available, and they put them on when they wash and bathe themselves in order not to wet their silk ones, which they wear instead of under-drawers. There are also perfume pans there; these give a sweet smell so that the guests can scent themselves after the bath.

Their baths consist primarily of a sudatorium made of precious scented wood or other medicinal wood, with a small door that they shut behind them when they enter. The bath is heated by the steam of boiling water; this steam enters at a certain place and is turned into hot dew. In this way it gently softens the body, and brings out and expels all the adhering dirt and sweat that are thereby loosened and detached. On leaving the sudatorium, the guests enter a very clean room opposite, where the floor is made of precious wood and slopes slightly so that the water may run away. Here there are found clean vessels of hot purified water and others of cold, so that everyone can adjust the temperature of the water more or less as he pleases. As they bathe there, all the dirt that comes to the surface in the sudatorium is washed away leaving the body very clean.

Pages are in attendance there and look after the operation. If a guest is embarrassed by the pages of the house, then he is attended by his own pages; otherwise, those of the house attend there and prepare all that is required. Some people do not like going into the suda-torium and so only bathe themselves with warm water in order to wash away the sweat and refresh themselves. They say that this way of bathing greatly refreshes the body in very hot weather and warms it in winter. When many guests go into the sudatorium or bathe together, they observe great courtesies and compliments towards each other.

This custom of taking a bath is universal throughout all Asia, as is well known from the chronicles. But the Japanese seem to excel everyone else in this regard, not only in the fre-quency with which they bathe every day, but even more in the cleanliness and dignity observed in that place, and in their use of precious and medicinal wood in the construction thereof.[3]

---

[1] This meagre account of Japanese stables can be supplemented by fuller descriptions in Avila Girón, *Relación*, p. 30; Vivero y Velasco, in *TCJ*, p. 141, who visited Edo Castle's stables in 1609; Fróis, in *TCJ*, p. 135, concerning Azuchi Castle's stables. See also Fróis, in *TCJ*, p. 281, and *Tratado*, p. 200.

[2] Jorge Alvares (in *TCJ*, p. 238) comments that the Japanese wash twice a day and show little modesty when doing so.

[3] Although Rodrigues appears to regard these bathing habits with approval, Valignano (*Sumario*, p. 231, n. 8) prohibited the *furo*, or Japanese bath, in Jesuit houses on account of excessive indulgence and the expense of the fire-wood. The missionaries were limited to one bath a fortnight in winter and one a week in summer. A later Visitor, Francisco Pasio (JapSin, 57, f. 249) banned Jesuits from using the bath in 1612, except in case of illness. Cocks mentions the 'fro' several times and once invited guests to bathe, 'whome (as I think) I entertayned to content' (*Diary*, I, p. 44). Fróis comments on Japanese washing habits in *Tratado*, pp. 110, 114, 120.

9. The house called *Suki*,[1] where they give *cha* to the guests to drink

We do not intend to describe here the ceremonies observed when they are invited to drink *cha*, nor the various admired pieces that they use, nor the end or purpose of *cha* (which of all secular things is the one most admired by the Japanese), nor its antiquity and the relatively recent time when this custom began.[2] Instead, we will describe only the construction and fabric of these places, for they are a relevant and necessary part of the lords' palaces and the houses of the nobles and gentry.

Among this kingdom's social customs, that of meeting to drink *cha* is the chief and most esteemed among the Japanese, and is the one in which they most show their excellence. So they spare no pains in the construction of the place where they give *cha* to their guests. This is a special building, with a path or entrance leading to it and with various other things suitable to the purpose of the custom. In general this purpose is the quiet and restful contemplation of the things of nature in the wilderness and desert. Hence all the material of this place is entirely accommodated to this end and to eremitical solitude in the form of rude huts made quite naturally with rough wood and bark from the forest. It is as if they had been formed by Nature or in the usual style of those people who dwell in woods or the wilderness. In everything in these houses they imitate nature and its simplicity, but with as much proportion and measurement as Nature herself observes in the things that she naturally creates.

Thus this *suki*, as they call it, is a sort of rustic recreation for the nobles as they entertain a friend with eating and drinking *cha* in their house or hut in the wilderness. They may thus contemplate the path, the wood through which they enter, and everything artlessly formed there by nature with proportion and grace, as well as the house or hut itself and the serving utensils therein, as if it were a recluse's hermitage in the wilderness. They do not indulge in conversation there apart from what is fitting to the place, but contemplate instead the form, proportion, and quality of all the rustic things to be found there.

Thus fashionable, finely wrought, and elegant things, such as those belonging to the court and not to mountains and the wilderness, are most unsuitable for this building, the eating and drinking utensils therein, and everything else. Instead, they use rough things, twisted artlessly and naturally.[3] As the Japanese lords, nobles, gentry, the wealthy and ordinary people of quality exercise their skill in this, they all almost necessarily have one of these buildings attached to their palace or house, so that they can privately entertain their friends and acquaintances there without any ostentation. However noble he may be, the host generally serves at table, makes the *cha* with his own hands, and offers it to the guest after he has eaten there. This way of entertaining is the greatest honour that can be paid to a guest. Hence a lower-ranking person can also invite lords and nobles to drink *cha* in his own *suki* place. The lord will accept with great courtesy and affability, and behave on this occasion as an equal and not as a superior and noble, even though the host is his own vassal.[4] For this is a rustic relaxation and pleasure.

---

[1] As Rodrigues later notes (p. 156), the actual house was called *sukiya*; the *cha* drunk therein was, of course, tea.

[2] All this, and much more, is described in detail in chapters 32–5.

[3] This admirable account sums up the ideal of *fūryū*, the cult of elegance, refinement, and taste. Much of what Rodrigues says here is echoed by Soper (Paine and Soper, *Art and Architecture*, pp. 263–4), when, writing more than 300 years later, he mentions 'simplicity and apparent artlessness', 'delight in natural materials and colours, pleasure in bareness and simplicity, insistence on proximity to nature', and 'The materials are those offered by nature, the same that grow in the garden outside or in near-by woods.'

[4] On a practical note, this enabled a noble to converse privately on business matters with a wealthy merchant.

Various things are considered in the construction. The first is the site, which must be next to the palace or house and within the same compound. The second is the entrance and path where the guests enter on their way to the *sukiya*.[1] As far as the site permits, this entrance must be in a solitary and quiet place, set away from the street and the ordinary business of the house. The entrance gate is a small, narrow, and low door, through which a person can enter only by stooping.[2] Inside this entrance or door there are wooden seats like benches at the sides, and here the invited guests sit down and wait while everything is being prepared within.[3] Near this spot to one side there are some toilets, very rough but spotlessly clean, with a pool of water and stepping-stones. There is also a certain kind of coarse sand there with a wooden shovel, and everything is freshly sprinkled with water. There is nothing more, such as scented eaglewood or aloes, for there is no filth there as it is merely a formality of the place. Hence nobody goes there unless his need is so urgent that he cannot wait, and then servants are there to clean the place so that it looks just as it was. These toilets have a rustic gate with a bolt inside and windows of latticewood roughly woven from reeds.[4]

Further on there is a wood of trees, partly natural if they were already growing there, partly transplanted thither with great skill. They choose trees that have the best shapes and branches, and the most natural and elegant artlessness. Such trees are mainly pines interspersed with others in such a way that there does not seem to be any artificiality about them, and they appear to have grown there naturally and haphazardly.[5] A long narrow path runs through the middle of this wood, and it is paved with stepping-stones over which the guest passes.[6] The path leads to the house or hut where the guest is received. Just before reaching there, he comes to a rough rock erected halfway along the path to one side. This has a pool of clean water in the middle and a container at its base, so that he may draw water there and wash his hands. If it is winter, there is warm water inside.[7]

When the guest reaches the house, he finds on one side a small covered cupboard where he leaves his dagger and fan, for they do not enter the house with these things.[8] There are also some hats roughly made of bamboo bark,[9] which the guests use to shelter from the

---

[1] That is, 'the *suki* house', or tea house.

[2] For an account of the various types of gates leading to the tea house, their technical names, and traditional measurements, see Rodrigues, *Arte del cha*, p. 83, n. 201.

[3] One of the purposes of this *machiai*, or waiting-arbour (illustration in Sadler, *Cha-no-yu*, p. 23), was to determine who was the senior guest, if this had not been made clear in the invitation. Strictly speaking, the rite was performed for only one guest, with a few other people present. Ibid., p. 48. See also Rodrigues, *Arte del cha*, p. 83, n. 202.

[4] According to Sadler (*Cha-no-yu*, pp. 32–5), some tea-houses were equipped with two privies, or *setsuin*. The *kafuku setsuin* was intended for actual use, while the *kazari setsuin* was for exhibition purposes only. For a wealth of information on these *setsuin* (derived from the name of the 9th-century Chinese monk who obtained enlightenment by cleaning the monastery privies), see Rodrigues, *Arte del cha*, p. 84, n. 203.

[5] The various arrangements of the 'sad pines and trees', as Ribadeneira (*Historia*, p. 373) not ineptly calls them, are described in Sadler, *Cha-no-yu*, pp. 27–9. Fróis (*Tratado*, pp. 228–30) notes that the Japanese hang weights on the trees in order to twist the natural shape of the branches.

[6] There is an omission in the Portuguese text here. A literal translation runs: '... through the middle of the wood; they are separated from one another, and the guest passes over them.' For the various patterns of stepping-stones used in these paths, see Sadler, *Cha-no-yu*, p. 28.

[7] A reference to the *chōzu-bachi*, or water basin, described, with illustrations, in Sadler, *Cha-no-yu*, pp. 29–32.

[8] Alternatively the guests would leave their swords in a rack, called *katana-kake*, outside the house. Rodrigues, *Arte del cha*, p. 89, n. 207.

[9] These large circular hats are known variously as *take-no-kawagasa*, *roji-gasa*, *sukiya-gasa*, etc. Rodrigues, *Arte del cha*, p. 90, n. 208.

rain or sun when they go to wash their hands at the above-mentioned place or walk through the wood contemplating the form of things therein.

The *cha* house is usually very small of three or four mats, sometimes of only one and a half, according to each person's preference.[1] The wood is rough and still has its bark as if it had come straight from the forest. Sometimes the wood is very old and worn, and only where it joins other pieces of wood is it skilfully worked. Below the above-mentioned cupboard there is a small door in the corner of the hut where guests enter inside. It is of a height and breadth that will fit a person who is seated or squatting.[2] Light enters the little house through windows in various places; these are also rough and woven of reeds. The exterior of the house is completely and skilfully thatched, while the interior roof or ceiling is also made of hay or coarse woven reeds like a mat, and is smoke-dried to show its age and solitary poverty. In the place of honour there is a kind of recess let into the wall with a step at the bottom. Here they hang an ancient picture or an old maxim written in ancient letters by an admired writer, or place a flower in a vase, so that the guest may contemplate it as he enters.[3]

When someone enters the house and comes along the path, he is alone or with a companion. The host goes to the first small gate to receive them, puts his head outside, thanks them for coming and bids them enter, and then retires straight away by another path leading inside. There is also in the house a grate with an iron pot full of boiling water; below it there is special clean ash and a certain kind of charcoal burning. Everything is neat and excellently proportioned. The guest or guests quietly contemplate each of these things without speaking loudly or making a noise.

When the host thinks that they have seen everything, he comes into the hut through an inner door that is so low and narrow that he has to bend down to enter. He there thanks the guest for deigning to come, and the guest thanks him for having so honoured him with an invitation. Thus they speak in low voices about some goodly and wholesome topics until the host thinks that it is time to eat. He goes inside and brings out a table, which is a tray with tall legs and made of lacquered or white wood, carrying two dishes. He places it in front of the guest, who takes it and lifts it above his head. Then there is brought a little rice in a spotless moist *goki*, or vessel.[4] The host places in front of the guest a bowl of rice and the wine, and he again retires and leaves him to eat what he pleases. There are also other ceremonies in this.

When the guest has finished eating, the host tells him that it is time to drink *cha*. The guest goes out into the wood through which he entered and washes his hands. The host closes the door of the house and sweeps everything carefully, replacing the painting or flower with another of the season. When everything is ready, he opens the door and the guest again enters. He then contemplates the flower once more until the time comes to

---

[1] The number of mats, ranging from the standard 4½ down to only 1½, and their arrangement are given in Sadler, *Cha-no-yu*, p. 11.

[2] The *nijiriguchi*, or 'crawling-in entrance', its origin, standard dimensions, and development, are described in Rodrigues, *Arte del cha*, p. 91, n. 210, and Kumakara, 'Sen no Rikyū', pp. 50–55.

[3] The recess, or *tokonoma*, is later described on p. 231. Suitable flower arrangements within the *tokonoma* are given in Sadler, *Cha-no-yu*, pp. 57–9.

[4] Avila Girón (*Relación*, p. 43) correctly explains that the *goki* is the largest of the four bowls used in a meal and contains the rice. The Portuguese text says that the bowl is *orvalhado*, or dew-covered, besprinkled; I have translated this as 'moist'.

drink the *cha* with all its ceremonies.[1] When everything is finished, he goes back and leaves by the first gate near the entrance to the wood, and there he awaits the host outside. The latter puts his head out of the gate, and they thank each other for the *cha* and the visit. They later exchange compliments either personally or in writing.

Next to this small *cha* house is the kitchen and place where everything needed is prepared for the guest,[2] while adjoining it is a house or inner room where the owner of the house generally studies and converses informally. After they have drunk *cha*, he sometimes brings a guest here to talk with him informally. There are valuable articles and various things to see in this room or place. He has a small bell there which he uses to summon the pages. Sometimes when the *cha* is ready or when it is time to drink it, he rings the bell so that the guest who is walking around contemplating in the wood may hear the signal and enter the little house.[3]

---

[1] The Portuguese text has 'contemplar o racho' here. This may be the copyist's error for 'contemplar a rosa', as translated here. Or it may mean, 'Meanwhile he once more contemplates…'.

[2] The kitchen is called *mizuya*, or 'water house'. For an illustrated description, see Sadler, *Cha-no-yu*, pp. 25–7.

[3] The bell is called *dora*, *yobigane*, or *sho*, and is generally rung five or seven times. Rodrigues, *Arte del cha*, p. 95, n. 218. Much of this description of the *sukiya* is repeated in chapters 33 and 34. The *sukiya* was not exclusively reserved for tea-drinking, but was also used for any suitable manner of relaxation. Nor should the way of tea described here be confused with the more formal *chanoyu* ceremony as practised today.

CHAPTER 13

THE CITY OF MIYAKO IN PARTICULAR

Some of our authors have described in their books this city, which in the vulgar tongue is called Miyako and in the literary language Kyō or Kyōto.[1] In China it is known as Jing or Jingdu, meaning the court of the true king. They have also described its position and its size in both ancient and modern times. Some authors write from hearsay, while others wrote from what they personally saw and investigated.[2] What we ourselves have to say here about the city and royal palace is certain and accurate, for we have carefully read about its ancient history in their books on this subject, and we have seen the vestiges remaining to this day, and the names of the streets and districts included within its limits. We also know very well the state of the city when the Blessed Father Francis went there in the year 1550.[3] The city was later destroyed on the death of the *kubō* and remained in a wretched state until Taikō governed Tenka. It was then greatly enlarged and began to resemble its ancient condition. We saw not only all these states, but also the change that took place after Taikō in the time of Daifu.[4]

We shall first of all describe the city and its ancient and modern site, and afterwards the royal palaces that are or were in the city and those that the Lords of Tenka have or had there.

The noble and populous city of Miyako, the capital of all Japan and the court of its kings, is situated in the kingdom of Yamashiro, one of the five Gokinai kingdoms in the region called Kinki.[5] Its position is 35°15′N in latitude and 162° in longitude in respect to the meridian passing through the Canary Islands between Tenerife and the Great Canary.[6]

---

[1] The Chinese character for 'capital' can be read in Japanese as either *miyako* or *kyō*, while Kyōto means 'capital city'. See p. 68, n. 4.

[2] A compilation of eyewitness accounts of Miyako by early Jesuits is given in Schurhammer, '*Stadtbild Kyōtos*'; see also *TCJ*, pp. 275–82. This chapter of the *History*, translated into Spanish with copious notes, appears in Alvarez-Taladriz, 'Miyako Visto por un Europeo'.

[3] Xavier actually went to Miyako in January 1551 and stayed in the capital only eleven days; on 29 January 1552, he noted that although the city had once been large, 'because of the wars it is now sadly destroyed'. Schurhammer, *Francis Xavier*, IV, p. 211; for his Kyoto visit, ibid., IV, pp. 193–200. Later, in Part 2 of the *History*, not translated here, Rodrigues describes in some detail Xavier's heroic journey in winter from Yamaguchi to Miyako, and his unsuccessful quest to see the emperor. Ajuda, 49–IV–53, ff. 222v–5v; Rodrigues, *Nihon*, II, pp. 430–45.

[4] The *kubō* in question was the shogun Ashikaga Yoshiteru (1536–1565). Taikō was Hideyoshi, Daifu was Ieyasu.

[5] I have added the name Kinki in a short gap in the Portuguese text. Rodrigues has already mentioned Kinki and Gokinai on pp. 79, 80.

[6] The city's precise position is 35°00′N, 135°45′E; the latter figure adjusted to the Canary Islands meridian would be about 152°E. For the Canary Islands meridian, see p. 12, n. 5.

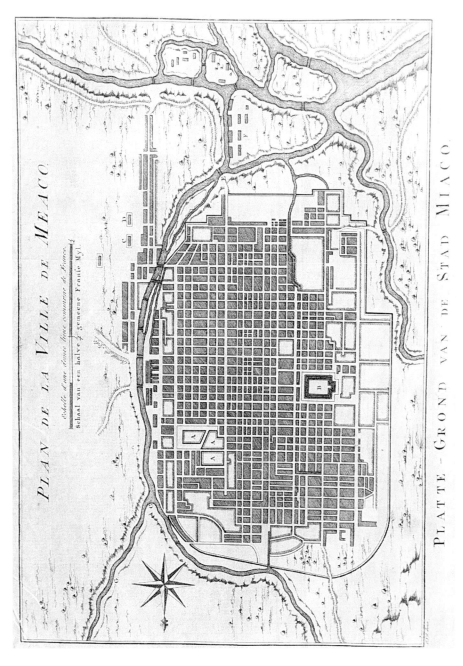

PLAN DE LA VILLE DE MEACO.

Echelle d'une demie lieue commune de France.

Schaal van een halve ½ gemeene Franse Myl.

PLATTE - GROND VAN DE STAD MIACO.

Plate 14: Plan of Miyako, in Prévost, *Historische Beschryving der Reizen*, vol. 17, Amsterdam, 1758. A = imperial palace compound, B = Nijō Castle. The plan is based on a large map attributed to Hayashi Yoshinaga, c. 1686, brought back to Europe by Engelbert Kaempfer in 1692, and now held in the British Library. *Private collection.*

The city 'was laid out in a square . . . and was about a square league in area. It was divided into thirty-eight main streets running north-south and the same number running east-west.' p. 161.

160

It is located in the middle of spacious plains surrounded on three sides by high mountains, which, however, are not close enough to cast their shadow on it.[1] Mt Higashi lies to the east, Hie-no-yama (or Hieizan) to the northeast, Kitayama and Kuruma to the north, Nishiyama and Atago-san to the west, while the whole of the southern side remains open.[2] All of these mountains are adorned with various monasteries and universities[3] with magnificent temples and their delightful gardens. As these mountains are covered with snow in the winter, they make the city a very cold place. The actual site of the city is not quite flat, but slopes almost imperceptibly from south to north.[4] It is a very pleasant spot and its many abundant springs provide excellent water; the streams running down from the hills irrigate the region and make it cool in summer. So on summer mornings there is a great deal of mist until the heat of the risen sun disperses it.

The city was built on this site about the Year of the Lord 800 when the king transferred the court from Nara, where it had been situated, to this place near the university of Hie-no-yama, the foot of which is about three short leagues from the city. This university had been founded shortly before with 3,000 monasteries of priests who worshipped the idols of the Tendai sect.[5]

This was the size of the actual city in ancient times when the real kings reigned, all apart from the suburbs on its four sides that formed yet another city. It was laid out in a square, each side being 2,764 geometric paces in length; as one of these paces is five feet long, the city was about a square league in area. It was divided into 38 main streets running north-south and the same number running east-west. Each of these streets was 78 geometric paces distant from the next, and they crossed each other to form a total of 1,444 blocks of 78 geometric paces in length.[6] Each of these blocks was made up of the inhabitants' houses, with their backs to each other east and west and their principal gateways on the north-south street. At the junction of any two of these streets there were four gates, each one closing the entrance of a street, and this arrangement still holds good to this day. This makes a total of 5,300 gates, because the entrances of the streets running lengthwise or breadthwise next to the city walls or moat have only one gate, for they do not cross another road there. All these gates are closed every night for the sake of security. Each has a small door with a guard always on duty at night with a fire burning, and when a person on some business passes through, he is identified. If there is a theft or brawl in the street either day or night, then the gates and

---

[1] The highest of the mountains mentioned here is just over 3,000 feet, so the reference to 'high mountains' may give a wrong impression.

[2] A map showing the regions around Miyako is given in Sansom, *History to 1334*, p. 100.

[3] As noted earlier, these 'universities' were large monastic complexes rather than the academic centres found in Europe.

[4] The site of the city makes it clear that the ground slopes *upwards* from south to north.

[5] In 784 the court transferred from Nara to Nagaoka, but then moved again in 794 to Miyako. Possible reasons for this costly operation are given in Toby, 'Why Leave Nara?'. Saichō, or Dengyō Daishi (767–822), founded a temple on Mt Hiei in 788, thus protecting the city from the malign influences from the northeast. In time the number of temples there grew to about 3,000 and Hieizan became the headquarters of the Tendai sect. The complex was destroyed by Nobunaga in 1571. For references, see p. 80, n. 4.

[6] These figures as they stand cannot be correct. They would be consistent, however, if there were 2,964 geometric paces to the city's length, and not, as the text gives, 2,764. There were two types of road: the ōji, 80 feet wide, and the kōji, 40 feet wide, and as a rule three kōji ran parallel between two ōji. Ponsonby-Fane, *Kyoto*, pp. 14–18. See Plate 14.

doors are shut so that the rascals may not escape. These doors are kept by the people of the same street. either by taking it in turns or by jointly hiring some people to attend there.[1]

On the eastern side of the upper part of the city stood the royal palace (as it still does today) within a large square enclosure. The palace of the *kuge*, or nobles of the patrician order, surrounded it, while the members of the royal guard were stationed in barracks and designated places.[2] In Rokuhara, an ample plain outside the city to the east and southeast, stood the palace of the *kubō*, the Commander and Lord High Constable of the kingdom, and those of the other officers and nobles of the military order under his command.[3] So the city, with the royal palace, the palaces of the patricians, together with the suburbs and the palaces of the *kubō* and other officers belonging to the military order, was enormous in size, to say nothing of the many large and magnificent monasteries with their temples. Many of these, or at least their ruins, still survive to this day.

There were two ways of dividing the city and they still partly hold good today. The first was made by dividing the city into its four principal parts; the western part, called Nishi-no-kyō; the eastern, Higashi-no-kyō; the northern, Kamigyō (the royal palace is just above the centre of this part); and the southern part, Shimogyō, extending from the centre of the city downwards. It is as if we were to speak about Upper, Lower, Eastern, and Western Miyako.[4]

The second way is made by dividing the city into seven districts, each of which contains four roads running from west to east, and measures 312 geometric paces from north to south and 2,764 paces from east to west.[5] Each of the wards beginning with Kamigyō towards the south, has its own name.[6] The first is called Ichijō, the second Nijō, the third Sanjō, the fourth Shijō, the fifth Gojō, the sixth Rokujō, and the seventh Kujō.[7] In each of these wards were situated the palaces of one of the six great lords of the kingdom, the counsellors of the king, rather like the *gelao* of China.[8] There is a saying about the number of

---

[1] From the figures given, there must have been a total of either 5,628 or 5,624 gates. For references to these street gates, see Fróis, Carletti, and Vivero y Velasco in *TCJ*, pp. 281, 152–3; Avila Girón, *Relación*, p. 31.

[2] The Taidairi, or Greater Palace Enclosure, was located in the exact centre of the northern part of the city, but the *dairi* or *kōkyō*, the actual imperial palace, stood in the north and east of the enclosure. Maps and plans are given in McCullough, 'The Capital', pp. 110–14. The *kōkyō* was built in 793 and Emperor Kammu took up residence in the following year. Ponsonby-Fane, *Kyoto*, pp. 59, 77.

[3] There had been a small estate belonging to the Taira family in Rokuhara, southeast of Miyako. Kiyomori developed the site and it became the Taira headquarters; it later was the Miyako headquarters of the Kamakura shogunate (1192–1333). Ponsonby-Fane, *Kyoto*, pp. 149–53.

[4] The city's original division was between *ukyō* (the right side, that is, right in relation to the *Taidairi*), the western half, and *sakyō*, the eastern half. The division, mentioned later by Rodrigues on p. 164, between *kamikyō*, upper Miyako, and *shimokyō*, lower Miyako, was introduced only in the 16th century. Ponsonby-Fane, *Kyoto*, pp. 15, 241–2.

[5] If, as Rodrigues states, the city was laid out in the form of a square, it is difficult to understand how there could have been seven wards with these measurements. In fact, the city was laid out in the form of a rectangle, measuring about 3.3 miles from north to south, and about 2.8 miles from east to west, with a total area of about 9.24 sq. miles. In addition, its western part never thrived and was eventually abandoned. Ponsonby-Fane, *Kyoto*, p. 16; Sansom, *Japan*, p. 194; McCullough, 'The Capital', p. 102, and plan of the city, p. 104.

[6] As its name suggests, Kamigyō was the northernmost ward. The Portuguese text here is rather vague, but presumably Rodrigues means that the wards begin with Kamigyō (in the north) and continue down to the south of the city. There are at present nine wards in the city, the northernmost still being called Kamigyō.

[7] These are in fact the names of the long streets running east-west; Kujō means ninth street, not seventh. There are still nine parallel avenues running east-west; the seventh is Shichijō, the eighth Hachijō, and the ninth Kujō.

[8] For the Chinese *gelao*, see pp. 35–6. The 'six great lords' probably refers to the *go-sekke*, the five branches of the Fujiwara family, from which the *kampaku* were to be chosen; the total is brought up to six by including the Sanjō family. Four of these six families bear the names of districts in Kyoto (Ichijijō, Nijō, Kujō and Sanjō).

households in the city of Miyako in ancient times, and it runs: 'Kyō kuman hassengen, Shi-rakawa jūman hassengen', meaning, Miyako has 98,000 houses or hearths, and Shirakawa has 108,000 hearths; this gives a total of more than 206,000.[1] This Shirakawa is a contin-uation of the actual city with a river running through the middle from the foot of Mt Hie-no-yama to the northwest.[2]

In the time of the civil wars and strife between the families of Heike and Genji (two commanders, one from the western kingdoms of central Japan and the other from the other half among the eastern kingdoms),[3] the city was destroyed and the royal palace burnt down. But after Genji was victorious, he rebuilt the palace and the city was restored to its former condition.[4] After this the royal palace was twice again destroyed by fire that came from the sacrifice offered in the palace to the idols and the devil himself, whom they wor-ship for the peace and prosperity of the king.[5] The palace was rebuilt sumptuously, and the Venetian, Marco Polo, mentions this last one, for it was standing when the Grand Cham held sway over China. He sent a large army to conquer Japan in the Year of the Lord 1278,[6] and in connection with this, Polo, who was in China at that time, says: The king of Japan has a sumptuous palace covered with plates of gold just as we cover them with lead and copper; the floors of the houses and rooms are also covered with small gold plates.[7] In this our author and his informants were mistaken, because the Japanese chronicles describing the royal palace (called Taidairi, that is, the great royal palace) say nothing about this nor was it ever like this. But the king and other Japanese nobles do decorate the outside of their palace roofs with gold, and they shine magnificently from afar and appear to be of gold,

[1] Before going to Miyako, Xavier (5 November 1549, in *Epistolae*, II, 207 and 209) was told that there were 90,000 or 96,000 houses in the capital. After his visit, he wrote that, of the 180,000 houses in former times, more than 100,000 still existed (29 January 1552, in ibid., II, p. 262). See also Vilela (6 October 1571, in *Cartas*, I, f. 319v), who heard that the city had formerly a population of more than 300,000, but at the time of his writ-ing this number had been reduced to 60,000. Avila Girón (*Relación*, p. 271) gives a population of over 130,000, corrected in the margin by Pedro Morejon to 90,000. In 1610 Vivero y Velasco (in *TCJ*, pp. 279–80) was informed that the city had a population of more than 80,000, while between 300,000 and 400,000 lived in the vicinity. He states, probably correctly, that there was no more populous city in the world. According to a 1624 census, Miyako had a population of 410,000, although in Hideyoshi's time, before the exodus to Edo when the Tokugawa established their headquarters there, its population may well have been about 500,000. Ponsonby-Fane, *Kyoto*, p. 243.

[2] The small Shirakawa river rises east of the old capital, passes through Shirakawa itself, and then enters the Kamogawa, the main river running through Miyako. In time much of the area east of the Kamogawa came to be known as Shirakawa.

[3] See p. 130, n. 3.

[4] A reference to the Heiji Uprising, 1159, when Minamoto Yoshitomo of the Genji clan rose up against Taira Kiyomori of the Heike, overpowered Emperor Go-Shirakawa, and burned down his Miyako palace. In the subse-quent fighting, Yoshitomo was killed and his troops defeated. Sansom, *History to 1334*, pp. 256–8. But the Genji family ultimately triumphed, and Minamoto Yoritomo (1147–99) became the first permanent shogun. He rebuilt the imperial palace, and Emperor Go-Toba took up residence there in 1189.

[5] The wooden palace suffered much from fire, earthquake, and war, and was repeatedly destroyed; it is impossible to identify the two particular instances mentioned here by Rodrigues. Ponsonby-Fane (*Kyoto*, pp. 78–80) lists the dates of 14 fires, 960–1082, which razed the palace. As regards 'the sacrifice offered in the palace to the idols and the devil himself', see p. 173, n. 1, below.

[6] Rodrigues has already twice mentioned this attempted Mongol invasion of Japan (pp. 61–2, 96). As stated on p. 61, n. 6, there were two such invasion attempts in 1274 and 1281, but here he is undoubtedly referring to the second.

[7] Polo, *Book*, III, 2 (Yule, *Book*, II, pp. 253–4).

and indeed we saw many of them; and the ceilings and the interior walls are richly gilded.[1] So the person who informed our author about this must have believed that they were plates of gold.

Fifty-five years later, in the Year of the Lord 1334, the *kubō*, or commander and head of the equestrian order, and all the officers, or *yakata*, seized the government and revenues of the kingdom, and displaced the king and the members of the patrician order who ruled the kingdom. He allowed the king to live privately in the court with the *kuge* and obliged him to confirm him in his office, thus indicating that he ruled in his place.[2] From that time until now, or 286 years so far, the country has not obeyed the king and has been racked by war. During this time the royal palace and those of the other lords were burnt down and the city was largely destroyed, and so the king and *kuge* were reduced to a wretched state. But as the *kubō* resided there, and he and other officers had their palaces there, the city once again prospered to a certain extent, and reached the condition in which Blessed Father Francis found it in the Year of the Lord 1550.[3] This state continued until the death of the *kubō* who was then governing Tenka. One of his officers, named Miyoshi Dono, treacherously killed him and burnt down the palaces of the *kubō* and of the other officers and lords, his subordinates.[4] A large part of the city was destroyed and remained in a wretched state as regards houses, their number, and everything else.

We came to Japan twenty-six years after the Blessed Father left Japan for India, and we saw all this.[5] The city was divided into two wards, Kamigyō and Shimogyō, and these were located next to each other in the centre. There was only one of the original thirty-eight north-south streets and very few of the transverse streets. The palaces of the king and *kuge* were wretched and made of old pine wood, while the walls were constructed of pine planks. The outward life of the *kuge* was extremely wretched and poor. The walls surrounding the king's palace were made of wood covered with reeds and clay, and were very old and dilapidated. Everything was left open and abandoned without any guards, and anyone who so desired could enter the courtyards right up to the royal palace without anyone stopping him, as we ourselves did to look around.

For 240 years, from the time this uprising against the king and *kuge* began until Nobunaga took over Tenka,[6] the king and his family maintained themselves mainly on anything the *kubō* might give them in exchange for a writ or charter confirming his successor to

---

[1] When describing the splendour of Osaka Castle, Fróis (in *TCJ*, p. 135) mentions that Hideyoshi had the donjon done out in gold and blue so that it might be seen from afar. The gables of Azuchi Castle were also gilded, and both castles contained richly gilded chambers. Caron (*True Description*, p. 20), describing the nobles' mansions within the enclosure of Edo Castle, reports that they were 'all almost gilt, so that this goodly Edifice appears at a distance not unlike a Mountain of Gold.'

[2] Ashikaga Takauji (1305–58) captured Kamakura in 1333 and overthrew the Hōjō family. Declaring himself shogun in 1338, he advanced on Miyako and set up a rival emperor, thus beginning the 60-year era of northern and southern courts at Miyako and Yoshino. Sansom, *History, 1334–1615*, chapters 3 and 4.

[3] For Xavier's visit to Miyako in early 1551, see p. 159, n. 3.

[4] Yoshiteru (1536–65), 13th Ashikaga shogun, was attacked by rivals and committed suicide in Nijō Castle in Miyako. Fróis (in *TCJ*, pp. 109–11) had an audience with him at New Year 1565, and left his impressions. He also describes in great detail Yoshiteru's death on Trinity Sunday of that year (*Historia*, II, pp. 92–8). 'Miyoshi Dono' refers to Miyoshi Chōkei.

[5] That is, 1577, as Xavier left Japan in mid-November 1551 and reached Goa in mid-February 1552. Xavier, *Epistolae*, II, pp. 238, 274.

[6] That is, from 1334 to 1573, when Nobunaga deposed the 15th and last Ashikaga shogun, Yoshiaki.

the *kubō*'s office and granting him some honourable title. Secondly, on what they received from the territorial lords for granting them warrants of nobility with the name of a title belonging to the offices of the royal household. Thirdly, on what they received from the bonzes for granting them scholarly ranks and honours, and for confirming and approving the affairs of the sects. The king depended on all these and other similar fees. Neither the *kubō* nor anyone else could possess any rank unless it were confirmed by royal patent, and so although they seized the government of the kingdom and the revenues, they never assumed the title of king but only that of commander.[1] The *kuge* also live on other similar payments, travelling on behalf of the king with patents to award a rank to a lord. He would treat them well because, although poor, they belonged to the patrician order, and everyone always esteemed and revered them in everything concerning honours. This wretched state lasted until Nobunaga took over Tenka and wished to build a palace in Miyako where the *kubō*'s palace had originally stood. Nobunaga began to take the king and *kuge* into greater account, but nothing was achieved by the time of his death.[2]

Taikō, or Kampaku, succeeded Nobunaga, and he ennobled and enlarged the city, for he first of all made much of the king and the *kuge*. He built the king a famous palace gilded both inside and out like the ancient palaces; it was set in a square compound with lovely gates on the four sides.[3] He donated the revenues from around Miyako for the upkeep of the royal person and family, the staff, and the guards both inside and outside the palace. He ordered palaces to be built for the *kuge* around the Dairi with enough revenue for the upkeep of each one. He thus relieved them from their former wretchedness in which they had lived, and each one enjoyed the rank and office that he possessed inside the palace of the royal household.[4]

The royal palace was situated in the eastern part of Kamigyō, and in front of it to the west he build a very large fortress with stone walls and a broad moat. Inside this he constructed such a beautiful palace that people said they had never been anything so splendid in Japan in the past nor would there be in the future, as indeed so far there has not. He called it Juraku, meaning the assembly of delights, or paradise.[5] He ordered all the lords of Japan to build their palaces next to Juraku, and they did this to the best of their ability. A very broad and straight road ran from Juraku to the royal palace, and both sides of this road were occupied by the palaces of the territorial lords. The outer walls of these were covered with gilt tiles, and had wooden beams and rafters richly plated with sheets worked in copper

---

[1] Both Vivero y Velasco (*Relación*, f. 15v) and Ribadeneira (*Historia*, p. 323) confirm Rodrigues's account that the emperor was administratively powerless, but retained the right to grant ranks and titles. Thus Ieyasu went to Miyako in 1603 to receive from him the rank of shogun, and on his retirement in 1605 his son, Hidetada, proceeded to the capital to be invested by the court. Shortly before his death in 1616, Ieyasu received the title Dajō Daijin. Totman, *Tokugawa Ieyasu*, pp. 86–8, 91–2, 187–8.

[2] Not completely accurate, for Nobunaga began clearing the city and had a new palace built for the emperor there in 1571. Ponsonby-Fane, *Kyoto*, pp. 180, 253.

[3] Emperor Go-Yōzei moved into the new palace built by Hideyoshi in January 1591, although construction work was not completely finished until several months later. Ponsonby-Fane, *Kyoto*, p. 253.

[4] Fróis, who knew the city well, records that Hideyoshi made 'another new Miyako' with such beautiful palaces that Nobunaga's Azuchi Castle and his own Osaka Castle, admittedly great works, could not compare with what he constructed in the capital. Fróis, *História*, V, p. 37.

[5] The magnificent castle-palace of Jurakutei was completed in October 1587 and Hideyoshi transferred his residence there from Osaka. For a detailed description of the building, with map and plan, see Ponsonby-Fane, *Kyoto*, pp. 261–71; Berry, *Hideyoshi*, pp. 194–6. Its depiction in a screen painting is shown in Rodrigues, *This Island*, p. 199;

and gold. In the front of the compounds there were most splendid and costly gates. In accordance with the old custom, Kampaku used the road to pay solemn visits to the king in his palace, and this he sometimes did and we were present. On these occasions he would drive in a coach or carriage, accompanied by all the lords of the realm, each one displaying the insignia of his office. The king also used the road to go to Juraku when he visited to divert himself.[1] There were more than 380 palaces of the principal lords alone.

It was in this Juraku castle and palace that Taikō received an embassy that the viceroy of India, Dom Duarte de Meneses, had sent with rich presents. The ambassador was Fr Visitor Alexandro Valignano, and he was accompanied by many Portuguese and the four Japanese nobles, dressed in our fashion, who had been to Rome.[2] The reception was one of the most solemn events of Japan at that time, for the principal *kuge* and grandees of the kingdom were present. He ordered that the whole city should line the route of the ambassador, who was carried in a litter while the Portuguese and the Japanese nobles rode on fine, richly caparisoned horses.[3]

The city was greatly ennobled and enlarged by these buildings and business, and many of the old north-south and transverse roads were once again populated. He ordered all the inhabitants of the city to make the front of their houses two-storyed and use precious cedar wood, and they all immediately did so. So the whole city with its wide and spacious streets was extremely beautiful. He ordered the construction of broad, high earthworks with their moats around the city in the place of walls, and had them all planted with large thick bamboo transplanted from different places. They grew entangled together and thus formed a thick bamboo wall. The earthworks to the north and south are two leagues long and one and a half wide.[4]

There had been many monasteries with their temples of idols inside the ancient city, and he ordered that they all be assembled in a long road around the city just within the earthworks; they are there now in the eastern part and greatly embellish the city.[5] Each one has

---

Hirai, *Feudal Architecture*, figures 4 and 40. Fróis (*História*, V, pp. 310–16) devotes an entire chapter to the new palaces of Miyako, and compares them favourably with similar buildings in Europe.

[1] The road was called Gokōmachi-dōri, and Rodrigues perhaps has in mind Emperor Go-Yōzei's visit to Jurakutei in May 1588, when Hideyoshi escorted the emperor in a magnificent procession, with 6,000 troops lining the one-mile route. As no such visit by an emperor had taken place for more than a century, Maeda Munehisa (whom Rodrigues knew well – see p. 167, n. 1) was commissioned to plan the protocol. The visit lasted four days, with banquets, a poetry party, and lavish gift-giving. Ponsonby-Fane, *Kyoto*, pp. 263–5; Berry, *Hideyoshi*, pp. 184–6; Elison, 'Hideyoshi', pp. 234–5.

[2] In 1582 four Japanese boys, representing three Christian *daimyo*, set out for Europe to deliver messages to the pope in Rome. On their return in 1590, they accompanied Valignano to the audience with Hideyoshi. A useful summary account of their remarkable European tour may be found in Lach, *Asia*, I, pp. 688–706; for their day-to-day activities in Europe, see Fróis, *Première Ambassade*.

[3] Rodrigues was present as interpreter at this audience on 3 March 1591. Fróis (*História*, V, pp. 298–309) describes the event in great detail. An account in English is found in Cooper, *Rodrigues the Interpreter*, pp. 75–81.

[4] This earthen rampart, called Ō-doi, was built around the city under the supervision of Maeda Munehisa in five months in 1591. With a circumference of about 14 miles, it was, as Rodrigues observes, planted with bamboo and had seven or ten openings. Ponsonby-Fane, *Kyoto*, pp. 243–53. Citing contemporaneous reports, Berry (*Hideyoshi*, pp. 198–9) describes the rampart and discusses its purpose, noting that as a defence measure, the wall was 'little more than a weak line of resistance.'

[5] Hideyoshi's policy was to congregate the temples, with some exceptions, in three separate districts of the capital – Teramachi, Ankyō-in, and west of Ōmiya. Ponsonby-Fane, *Kyoto*, p. 240. According to an early English version of the Jesuit reports, 'He [Hideyoshi] tooke from the Bonzi their Lands: and after that, making ditches round about Miyako, has forced them all to dwell together neere the said ditches; which reducing their discrepant Sects to an unformed Chaos together, made many of them forsake their profession' (Purchas, *Purchas*, 1939, pp. 38–9). Berry (*Hideyoshi*, p. 200) suggests the reasons behind this massive relocation.

its enclosure, walls, gates, and beautiful neat courtyards in the entrance, while further inside in front of the temple there are other cloisters and gardens of various esteemed flowers and trees, laid out in their fashion. But even though the city has so increased in the number of houses of its citizens and inhabitants, it nevertheless has not reached the former number of hearths. For in the house of the viceroy, Gen'i Hōin, who then governed the city and was our friend, we saw the list of houses.[1] There were 60,000 households or hearths belonging to citizens and ordinary people alone, and a large number of them have many rented houses that count as only one, and this does not include many free or privileged houses there.[2] In addition to the royal palace, the *kuge* palaces and the Juraku fortress (which in itself was a considerable city), there were 380 palaces belonging to the principal lords, as we said, and on the road around the earthworks there were 370 monasteries with their temples, many of which were very large convents. There were also the city's suburbs and many other splendid monasteries and universities outside the city.

When Taikō later wished to perform *inkyo*,[3] he renounced the government of Tenka in favour of a nephew, for he did not have a son at the time. He made him like a king by investing him with the rank and office of Kampaku, and handed over Juraku to him for his residence as well as some kingdoms with their revenues for the maintenance of him and his dependants.[4] He built for himself the city and fortress of Fushimi, and it was here that the lords of Japan built their own palaces lavishly and handed those in Miyako to the new kampaku's followers. Fushimi is two leagues from Miyako, and the intervening distance is completely taken up by the houses of the Miyako people, so that the two cities are just like one.[5] The nephew was later accused, albeit falsely, of treason against his uncle, and Taikō ordered him and some of his nobles to cut their bellies.[6] He then destroyed Juraku, and the whole of

---

[1] Maeda Munehisa (1539–1602) was formerly a monk on Hieizan, and his religious name was Gen'i, with Hōin as a clerical title. In 1584 he was appointed *shoshidai*, or governor of Miyako, and entrusted with the rebuilding of the capital. According to Jesuit accounts, 'Ghenifoin' was friendly to the Christians and his two sons were baptized in 1595. He greatly helped Rodrigues in the aftermath of Valignano's embassy in 1591. According to Fróis (*História*, V, pp. 367–9), he had the reputation of being 'an upright man of much prudence and truth'. Ponsonby-Fane, *Kyoto*, pp. 238, 258–60; *Kokushi Daijiten*, 13, pp. 9–10.

[2] For the population of Miyako, see p. 163, n. 1.

[3] *Inkyo* (lit. 'living in the shade') means retirement from active life and transfer of estates and responsibilities to an heir. Valignano (in *TCJ*, p. 84) points out the disadvantage of young men sometimes receiving authority too early and misusing it. But often enough the retirement was a matter of political and social convenience, and little, if any, authority was transferred. Ponsonby-Fane, *Imperial House*, pp. 238–9; Valignano, *Sumario*, p. 315, n. 7; Avila-Girón, *Relación*, p. 33.

[4] In early 1592 Hideyoshi resigned the office of Kampaku in favour of his nephew Hidetsugu (1568–95), whom he had adopted as heir in 1591, and himself took the title of Taikō. As Rodrigues notes, Hidetsugu was also given Jurakutei palace for his residence. Rodrigues met the young man at Valignano's audience with Hideyoshi in 1591. Cooper, *Rodrigues the Interpreter*, p. 76–7; Berry, *Hideyoshi*, pp. 218–19; *KEJ*, VIII, p. 94.

[5] Fushimi was situated strategically between Miyako and Osaka, and Hideyoshi's magnificent palace was completed in 1594; it was there that Rodrigues visited the dying ruler four years later. Ieyasu lived there for a time, but the palace ('a very gallant, beautifull thing', according to Cocks writing in March 1620), was finally demolished in 1620. Farrington, *English Factory*, I, p. 779; Ponsonby-Fane, *Kyoto*, pp. 313–21.

[6] In 1592, Yodogimi, Hideyoshi's secondary wife, bore him a son, Hideyori, although according to Fróis and others (Valiganano, *Adiciones*, p. 365, n. 42), Hideyoshi was incapable of siring children. In the following year Hideyoshi urged Hidetsugu to adopt the child and take part in the Korean campaign. His dissolute nephew prevaricated and may have entered into intrigue against his uncle. In 1595 he was banished to Kōya, where he duly committed suicide on 20 August. To eliminate any possible rivals, Hideyoshi had his nephew's infant sons and more

the site was used for houses of the citizens and merchants. The number of houses thereby increased and the city became very prosperous.

The city of Miyako is extremely clean, and in each of its broad streets is to be found water from excellent springs and streams flowing along the middle. The streets are swept and sprinkled with water twice a day and are thus kept very clean and fresh, for each man looks after the part in front of his own house. As the ground slopes, there is no mud, and when it rains the water dries up in no time. The inhabitants' houses lining the streets are usually offices, shops, and workshops of various crafts, and the people have their living quarters and guest rooms inside. Some streets are very long and wide, and on either side have arcades under which people walk to avoid the rain or sun, or to look in the shops. In these streets they sell only rolls and articles of silk for the entire kingdom. These arcades have curtains hanging up to protect the shops from dust, to keep them clean, and to provide light. Each house has a curtain hanging in front of the door in the arcade, and it bears a painted device of an animal, tree, plant, flower, bird, mathematical figures, numbers, and a thousand and one other things serving as a nickname or emblem of the family and house. Even though they may live in another street or place, all the members of such a family display the same device, as if we were to speak of the house of the tiger, the crane, the pine, the circle, the square, and so on.[1] In Miyako there is a register of more than 5,000 looms that weave various lengths of silk and almost all are to be found in one ward.[2] Women usually serve in the shops and sell cloth and other wares, while their menfolk go out either on business or to amuse themselves in various places. They say that this custom is designed to keep the peace and avoid brawls in the shops, for the men are very high-spirited, and the women, being women, take care to disregard what they say.

The people and residents of Miyako are very even-tempered, courteous, and hospitable. They are well-dressed, exuberant, and are much given to continual recreation, amusements, and pastimes, such as going on picnics in the countryside to enjoy the sight of the flowers and gardens. They invite each other to banquets, comedies, plays, farces, and various other songs performed according to their fashion. They often go on pilgrimages and have much devotion for their temples. There are usually so many men and women going to pray there and hear sermons that it seems like a jubilee.[3] Their speech is the best and most eloquent of the whole kingdom because of the presence there of the court and *kuge*, among whom the language is best preserved.[4]

On going out of the city at any point, you find the loveliest and most delightful countryside of all Japan, and there are refreshing woods and groves around about. Every day

---

than 30 of his household publicly executed in Miyako. Details in Ponsonby-Fane, *Kyoto*, pp. 266–7; Berry, *Hideyoshi*, pp. 219–20. The indefatigable Fróis wrote a treatise on Hidetsugu's death, and an Italian translation was published in Rome and Naples in 1598. Laures, *Kirishitan Bunko*, p. 191.

[1] Even today shops in Japan have their own distinguishing *mon*, or emblem, prominently displayed in advertisements. For a contemporaneous illustration of a Miyako street scene that bears out several points of Rodrigues's description, see Smith, *Japanese History*, pp. 168–9.

[2] Nishijin, the silk-weaving ward, was located in the northwest of the city. In the first part of the 17th century, there were, as Rodrigues notes, about 5,000 looms in Miyako. Ponsonby-Fane, *Kyoto*, pp. 408–9.

[3] The devotion of the Miyako populace is also noted by Fróis (in *TCJ*, pp. 346–7) when describing a sermon in Chion-in temple.

[4] Rodrigues (*Arte grande*, f. 84) insists on this point: accepted and approved Japanese is that spoken by the *kuge* of Miyako. It is pure and elegant Japanese, unlike the improper and barbarous form employed elsewhere. As noted in the prologue of *Vocabulario*, the dictionary makes a clear distinction between words used only in the Miyako area and those peculiar to Kyushu.

crowds of people from the city enjoy themselves there with banquets in a kind of enclosure they put up to obtain some privacy.[1] The people of the city are very fond of this nation's poetry, for in its own way it is very excellent and subtle.[2] In these parts there are also many great monasteries with beautiful and refreshing gardens. They highly esteem flowers and cultivate them in this region, and when these flowers are in bloom, a person will send a branch of them to another person's tent, even though they may not be acquainted. This is an even more common practice among acquaintances, who will send a poem about the flower and place written on a long, narrow piece of paper, excellently decorated with gold, silver, and various flowers, hanging from the branch rather like a flag and made for this purpose.[3] The people in the other tent reply with another poem about the same subject.

At certain places along the road at the entrances to the city there are gated wooden enclosures in which are held continuous performances of comedies, farces, and other plays recounting ancient legends to a certain singing and tone accompanied by musical instruments, and these provide much recreation for the Japanese. The gates are always kept closed, and everyone who enters pays a certain sum. The actors earn their living with the money thus collected, because a goodly number of people attend each performance. When the play is over, they leave and others enter, and there begins another play or drama, in which the actors wear rich silk costumes suited to each character. At the end of every play they put on an amusing farce, at which their actors are extremely skilful.[4]

The city is provided with abundant provisions, such as much game, wild birds, and a lot of various kinds of excellent fresh fish from the rivers and lakes; also sea fish, especially in the winter when it is brought from the sea in the north, about nine leagues away, and from the sea in the south, some dozen leagues distant. There are many different kinds of vegetables and fruit according to season, and groups of two hundred or more carriers bring these at dawn from nearby places and farms. In addition to the markets where every kind of food is on sale, men walk through the city selling their wares and crying out in a loud voice to buy such-and-such a thing. All over the city there are also many inns and taverns providing food for non-residents, and there are public baths where a man blows a horn and invites people to the baths, for the Japanese are much given to this. There are many other trades and it would take too long to describe them. Anyone who has seen the city will know that our account has indeed been very brief.[5]

It is possible for boats to navigate along a big river from the coastal city of Osaka

---

[1] People on picnics often erected screens or curtains for privacy rather than a roofed tent. Illustrated examples are seen in Rodrigues, *This Island*, p. 201, and in the paintings of 'Cherry Viewing Party' and 'Maple Viewing Party', in Jacobson, *Art of Japanese Screen Paintings*, pp. 64–6. See Plate 15.

[2] An excellent account of Japanese poetry, with examples taken from early anthologies, is found in *Arte grande*, ff. 181–4; English translation in Rodrigues, 'Muse'.

[3] The card attached to the flowers is a *tanzaku*. Ribadeneira (in *TCJ*, p. 358) also gives a pleasing picture of picnics in the countryside and poems on the beauty of nature. For illustrations of such scenes, see Smith, *Japanese History*, pp. 208–9.

[4] The 'amusing farce' is a *kyōgen*, a short slapstick comedy aimed at reducing and contrasting the dramatic tension of the serious noh plays. As regards the entrance fee, Cocks (14 March 1617, in *Diary*, I, p. 241) notes: 'A common kabuki or Japon play was sent out and alowed for 7 daies space, at 2 condrins each one that entered, etc.' For illustrations of such enclosures for plays and puppets, see Smith, *Japanese History*, pp. 166–7; Rodrigues, *This Island*, p. 202. For European criticisms of Japanese music and singing, see *TCJ*, pp. 256–7; Valignano, *Sumario*, p. 53, n. 73.

[5] A similar description of Edo is given by Vivero y Velasco (in *TCJ*, pp. 284–5), who visited the city in 1609. He too mentions the abundance of game, fish, and vegetables, the food markets, the various trades, and the street sellers.

Plate 15: 'Flower viewing', hand-scroll in gold and colours on paper, early 1690s. 'On going out of the city [Miyako] at any point, you find the loveliest and most delightful countryside of all Japan, and there are refreshing woods and groves around about. Every day crowds of people from the city enjoy themselves there with banquets in a kind of enclosure they put up to obtain some privacy'. pp. 168–9. *Honolulu Academy of Arts. Gift of Mr Robert Allerton, 1960 (2733·1)*

right up to the vicinity of Miyako.[1] There are many of these boats, and they are very smart and carry provisions and every other kind of goods. There is also a big service of packhorses (instead of mules) and many carts drawn by oxen also ply. The carriages and coaches of the Lord of Tenka (and formerly also those of the *kuge* and other nobles of the kingdom) are used in public and formal visits. These are drawn by large black oxen that are bigger than ordinary ones and are of a certain kind that came from abroad in ancient times. Their horns are gilded, and on their hooves they wear shoes of crimson silk thread, and there is the public office of grooms. Nowadays only the Lord of Tenka uses these in public ceremonies when he formally visits the king, as we witnessed several times.[2]

When Daifu took over Tenka on the death of Taikō, he built a palace in the western part of the city practically on the central north-south avenue as a residence for himself when in Miyako. The Shogun, his son who succeeded him, now lives there. It has its walls and large moats, and some of his gentlemen's palaces are built around it.[3] In addition to the royal palace built by Taikō, Daifu constructed another one for the king. It is very grand and sumptuous, and is admirable as regards craftsmanship, beauty, size, and magnificence, and has excellent walls and gateways.[4] The king now reigning lives in this palace, while the king who performed *inkyo* dwells in the other.[5] Thus the king is now regarded as the legitimate and true lord, although he is not accorded administrative power or total obedience in any literal sense. The marriage of the Shogun's daughter with the Prince is now being negotiated so that they may be related and everything done to perpetuate his family in the office of shogun.[6] For this reason, the devil instigated him into persecuting the Christians, for he believed that they might topple him from the government as they were very united among themselves and subject to the Church's commands.

This must suffice for now about this city, and everything else may be understood from what has been said. Nowadays throughout the kingdom there are lovely cities that formerly did not exist in the time of the wars; everything at that time was laid waste and people lived in castles on mountain tops. But each territorial lord now builds a city

---

[1] The River Yodo – see p. 82.

[2] Carriages drawn by oxen are often mentioned in classical court literature, such as *The Tale of Genji*, in which there is the well-known chapter 'The Carriage Dispute'. For information on the inconvenience and discomfort of these slow-moving vehicles, see Morris, *World*, pp. 35–7.

[3] This was Nijō Castle, built by Ieyasu in 1602–3; full description in Ponsonby-Fane, *Kyoto*, pp. 271–9. The son who succeeded Ieyasu was Hidetada.

[4] Although Nobunaga built an imperial palace in Miyako in 1571 and Hideyoshi another in 1591, Ieyasu constructed a third one, into which the emperor formally moved at the beginning of 1611. Ponsonby-Fane, *Imperial Family*, pp. 253–6. This largesse was prompted not so much by reverence towards the throne as by the rulers' desire to legitimize and promote their political authority.

[5] The emperor reigning in 1620, when Rodrigues wrote this passage, was Go-Mino-o. His predecessor, Go-Yōzei, lived in retirement from 1611 until he died in 1617, and presumably Rodrigues had not heard of his death. Strictly speaking, emperors did not perform *inkyo*, but abdication, or *jōi*, while retiring ministers of the third rank or above performed *nyūdō*; only less exalted persons performed *inkyo*. Ponsonby-Fane, *Imperial House*, p. 238.

[6] In 1620 Shogun Hidetada's daughter was married to Emperor Go-Mino-o, who had succeeded to the throne in 1611 at the age of 17. The marriage was forced on the young emperor when he showed himself unwilling to submit docilely to the dictates of the Tokugawa shogunate. On his abdication in 1629, he was succeeded by his daughter, Empress Myōshō, whose mother was, of course, a Tokugawa.

in his domain, along with a fortress and a palace in which he resides. This is surrounded by the beautiful houses and their compounds built by the nobles and officers who owe him allegiance. But it is usually the merchants and tradesmen who most concern the city.[1]

---

[1] Some idea of the splendour of Miyako in its heyday can be gained from numerous *rakuchū rakugai* ('scenes in and around the capital') screens depicting the city's palaces, temples, and houses from a quasi-aerial view. Doi, *Kanō Eitoku*, pp. 32, 34–5, 56–7; Murase, *Byōbu*, pp. 110–17.

CHAPTER 14

THE ANCIENT ROYAL PALACE CALLED TAIDAIRI

The Taidairi was burnt down twice in the time of the 77th king by the fire that came from the stove of the *higoma* where the *kitō* was performed. It was burnt down the third time in the time of Heike, and the fourth time in the time of Shogun Takauji, and Marco Polo refers to this palace, etc.[1]

[1] As stated on p. 162, n. 2, the Taidairi was the Greater Palace Enclosure, in which was situated the *dairi*, or *kōkyō*, the actual imperial palace. The *higoma*, or *goma*, was a sacred fire, in which fragrant wood and perfume were burnt in front of a statue by Buddhist priests to mark some special event, such as victory or peace. *Vocabulario*, f. 121: 'Goma. Certain ceremony that the Shingonshū [monks] perform to supplicate the devil. As, *goma wo taku*, To perform this ceremony, throwing into the fire sesame oil, & laurel bark, etc.' *Kitō* were the prayers recited on such occasions. According to Rodrigues's list in *Arte grande*, f. 237v, the 77th emperor was Go-Shirakawa (r. 1156–58), but I can find no reference to the palace being razed during his short reign (see p. 163, n. 5). 'The time of Heike' refers to the 12th century, and Rodrigues may have had in mind the disastrous fire of 1175, mentioned in Kamo no Chōmei, *Hōjōki* [*Ten Foot Square Hut*], p. 2, and *Heike*, p. 56. Ashikaga Takauji (see p. 164, n. 2) was shogun 1338–58. The imperial palace was razed in 1336 when he captured Miyako and the emperor Go-Daigo fled to Enryakuji temple. Ponsonby-Fane, *Kyoto*, p. 166. For references to Polo, see p. 163, n. 7.

As may be noted, this brief chapter is practically identical with a passage on p. 163.

CHAPTER 15

THE CUSTOMS AND MANNERS OF THE JAPANESE IN GENERAL

The manners, courtesy, and ancient customs of the Japanese have their origin and foundation for the most part in Chinese manners and ancient customs, for the Japanese and other nations near China (principally those that use Chinese writing) have received their best things from that source. All recognize China as superior in the excellence of these things and regard the country as teacher and lord in everything. So they try to adapt themselves to the Chinese model by imitating their customs, rites, manners, and administration as much as they can and as far as their way of life allows. Hence all the nations, especially the Japanese and Koreans, have many customs similar to those of ancient China, and this will be seen later when we speak about this matter in detail. But the Chinese completely lacked true interior virtue, and there was nothing in their books and the writings of the ancient sages about salvation in the next life, the basis on which all human life should be founded. Instead, they dealt only with the things of the present life.[1] From the time when the sects of the Indian idols arrived in China, Korea, and Japan until the present day, they have learnt through these sects that there is another life and salvation, but they have erroneously taught these things. The indigenous Chinese sects, that is, those of the *literati* and the Chinese magicians, as well as the sects of the Japanese spirits and genii, have nothing to say about these things.[2]

Thus all these nations and their social customs and etiquette are founded on pure fiction and merely exterior hypocrisy, for they show publicly what they do not possess in their hearts. So all their ceremonies, compliments, and manners are dressed up in this exterior hypocrisy, and as they spend the best part of their lives engaged in these long-winded things it would be tiresome to describe it all here. As the Japanese are naturally mettlesome, they are very punctilious among themselves in the observance of their ceremonies and customs, and do not depart from them one little bit. But as these were so long drawn out, they left no time for other important affairs. Hence since the time of Nobunaga and Taikō until the present, many of these ancient ceremonies have been curtailed, while others have been done away with completely. Others have been changed and shortened, and so are more suitable as they do not take up so much time. Their banquets are now much better than in the past, when they were usually mere ostentation and practically everything was a public display of things after the Chinese fashion. Food was not eaten for its own sake, but merely as

---

[1] The *locus classicus* is found in the *Analects of Confucius*, 11, 11 (Legge, *Chinese Classics*, I, pp. 240–41). In answer to his question concerning the spirits of the dead, the Master tells Jilu, 'While you do not know life, how can you know about death?' See also *Analects*, 5, 12 (Legge, *Chinese Classics*, I, p. 177).

[2] That is, Buddhism teaches about salvation, but Confucianism, Taoism, and Shinto have little or nothing to say on this matter. Fróis, Ribadeira, and Vilela all note that the Japanese prayed to the Buddhist deities for salvation, but to the Shinto gods for wealth and material gain (see p. 126, n. 4).

a preparation for drinking wine, and this drinking was the purpose and principal feature of their feasts.

The Chinese have two kinds of manners, and the Japanese imitate these after their own fashion. One is moral and pertains to the virtue and good moral customs on which the government of their nation is founded. The other is pure civility, courtesy, and exterior custom that promote the good political customs and breeding of the kingdom. Strictly speaking, these are voluntary and are to be found in each nation and kingdom in a form adapted to its way of life.

As regards the first kind, it must be noted that the Chinese and other nations that imitate them did not have any knowledge of God, His Providence, and the other divine attributes that they could imitate after their fashion. Instead, they knew of only three principal things in the world among all the other things of the universe: Heaven, which contains the air; Earth, which contains the water and everything else within it; and Man, the head of all the other heads. The Chinese call this *sancai* and the Japanese, *sansai*. It is as if we were to call these things the three supreme or paramount things constituting the universe.

The three branches of science that are dealt with in their books and the sect of the Chinese *literati* are made up in keeping with these three things: the science of Heaven, the science of Earth, and the science of Man, that is, moral science. These three things are expressed respectively by the three terms *tiandao*, *tudao*, and *rendao*, and in Japanese *tendō*, *chidō*, and *jindō*. All their physical or natural science is included within the first two, while moral science is included in the third.

The science of Heaven deals with the first principle of the universe's production, general things, the elements or elementary qualities of which things are composed in conformity to them, the generation and corruption of things, the sky, sun, moon, stars, and planets, their nature and influence on the things below, the planets' movements and revolutions, divination or horoscopes that depend on the stars and planets, every man's fate according to the hour, day, and month of his birth, and various other natural things related to or depending on the things of above and the region of air.

The science of the things of Earth deals with the variety caused therein by the four seasons of the year, its qualities and properties, and is causality. In these seasons Earth as the universal mother receives its power from Heaven, the common father of all, and produces the fruits and other various things found therein, and nurtures and supports them. It also deals with the climacterics, and good and bad places in which to dwell, build, and bury the dead according to their relation to the four directions with good or bad fortune.

Human or moral science deals with Man inasmuch as he is a political and social animal who lives in community, imitates the order, mind, and qualities of Heaven and Earth as of common and universal parents, and observes the five moral virtues common to all men. In Chinese these five virtues, or *wuchang*, are called *ren*, *yi*, *li*, *zhi*, and *xin*, while the Japanese refer to them as *gojō* and call them *jin*, *gi*, *rei*, *chi*, and *shin*. The first is compassion, observance, benevolence, love, and kindness, for it embraces all these virtues. The second is justice, fairness, equity, and integrity. The third is reverence, courtesy, and politeness. The fourth is wisdom. The fifth is loyalty and truthfulness in social matters and agreements.[1]

---

[1] For these Five Constant Virtues in Chinese classical literature, see *Shujing*, 2, 1, 19 (Legge, *Chinese Classics*, III, p. 44). *Vocabulario*, f. 121: 'Gojō. Five moral and social virtues, which the Chinese and Japanese practise.' Semedo, *History*, p. 149, describes these virtues at some length.

All the other moral virtues may be reduced to these five, which are like categories. They do not form acquired habits, but are rather the qualities of the five elements that they believe make up a man. Each of these virtues produces in a man exterior acts of virtue corresponding to all these qualities.

The people of the entire nation are also divided into five classes of related persons on whom the practice of these virtues is incumbent. The first is a lord and his noble vassal; the second, a father and his son; the third, a husband and his wife; the fourth, older and younger brothers, gentry and plebeians, old folk and young; and the fifth, companions and equals. Each member of these groups must observe the obligation that falls on him in respect to his correlative. For example, the prince must show justice and fairness towards his vassals, while the vassals, loyalty towards the prince; love between father and son; between husband and wife, there is a difference and distinction in duties, for the husband sees to external affairs while the wife looks after the household;[1] among the elderly, the order of seating and places, and due courtesy; among companions and equals, sincerity and trust.[2]

It also deals with the good ordering of the individual, the family, the nation, and the universal monarchy, all being directed towards others as to an end. They have various instructions, moral precepts, and laws usually founded on the natural law, along with the various examples of men of ancient times whom they consider virtuous and wise.

This category also includes the liberal arts, weapons, and everything else connected to the ordering of the individual, the family, and the nation. In addition, it includes religion and worship with various rites and sacrifices to heaven and earth, the planets, stars, elements, parts of the earth, their genii and spirits, also to the genii of the mountains, rivers, the dead, the tutelary spirits of places, and some men of ancient times who were famous in some field or other, and finally to various things they consider lucky or unfortunate. This will be described at some length when we discuss their religion and worship.

The second category embraces civility, courtesy, compliments, and the exterior social customs of the kingdom, such as Japanese dress and the times when it is changed, the manner of visiting people, the gifts usually brought on these visits, the courtesy and respect observed inside the house by a lord towards a vassal and servant, a noble towards a plebeian, and between equals; also the manner of entertaining and the ceremonies therein, and various other things of this sort. Thus in these matters, just as in the manners of the first moral category, the Japanese imitated the ancient Chinese as much as they could, for they originally came from China, as has already been said, and everyone considered that they were inspired by all the good behaviour and government that ought to be imitated. We intend to devote several chapters to this second category as it is an interesting topic and well illustrates these people's quality for they attached much importance to it.

Just as there are two different sorts of families or orders of nobility and rank in this kingdom, that is, apart from the royal household, the patrician order of the kingdom's grandees called *kuge*, and the equestrian and military family or order, so also there are two types of social customs and ceremonies. The first pertains to the royal household and the

---

[1] There is a gap in the Portuguese text here. It reads: '… the husband […] and the wife the interior of the house'.

[2] The Five Human Relations, known as *wulun* in Chinese and *gorin* in Japanese, are mentioned by Semedo (*History*, p. 149), and also Ricci (*Fonti*, I, p. 120, and *China*, p. 97), who correctly attributes them to Confucian teaching. The apostate Japanese Jesuit Fabian refers to them in his anti-Christian tract (Elison, *Deus Destroyed*, pp. 282–3), alleging that devotion to the Christian God may sometimes clash with feudal loyalty.

patrician order, in which there are different offices of the royal household. One of them is the master of palace rites and ceremonies; he deals with ambassadors[1] and teaches the way to be followed in the royal services and audiences. The other type belongs to the equestrian order whose head is the *kubō* or shogun; there are also special officials in his household who teach this order's courtesies and ceremonies. These ceremonies and courtesies are the ordinary and common ones observed throughout the kingdom, and we shall now speak especially about them here.

It may be noted for this purpose that in the *kubō*'s household there are, among various others, two offices handed down from father to son. One is the office of master of ceremonies, courtesies, and social customs of the kingdom, such as dress, the way of visiting, and the presents given on these visits, the manner of receiving and taking leave of guests, the entertainment provided, the manner of holding feasts, and other things concerning the rites and ceremonies of the kingdom and people.[2] This office is held by the family of Ise-no-Kami Dono, and the family possesses copious books dealing in detail with the subject of their customs and the way of observing them. Some of the things that we have written here have been taken from their books.[3] The other office was that of the master of weapons, the art of horse-riding, and other liberal arts and customs of the whole kingdom. This office runs in the family of Ogasawara Dono, from whose books material has been taken to serve our purpose.[4]

[1] Not, of course, ambassadors from foreign countries, but representatives of the shogun.

[2] In *Arte breve*, ff. 82v–91, Rodrigues supplies an incredibly detailed account not only of the *kuge* and *buke*, but of the emperor's names, the nobility in general, the six orders of nobility, the scores of ranks in the civil service, not to mention the names of the governing tribunals in China.

[3] Fróis (*História*, I, pp. 162–3, 230–31) refers to Ise-no-Kami Sadataka (d. 1562) as 'the court master of ceremonies', who was helpful towards the missionaries. Rodrigues (*Arte grande*, f. 189v) remarks that the Ise family was an authority on the various styles of letter-writing. For the cooperation of Ise Mitsutada in the compilation of a manual of etiquette, see n. 4, below. Further references in *Vocabulario*, f. 101; Rodrigues, *Arte del cha*, p. 53, n. 145; Rodrigues, *Nihon*, I, p. 400, n. 5. Mexia (6 January 1584, in *Cartas*, II, f. 124) notes that there were many books of ceremonies and etiquette; seven or eight rules were for only drinking a little water and more than thirty in the use of the fan. Valignano (*Sumario*, pp. 54–5) also comments on 'the infinite number' of books dealing with etiquette.

[4] The Ogasawara family was descended from Takeda Yoshikiyo (d. 1163). While Ogasawara Nagahide, famous for his skill in riding and archery, was instructing the Ashikaga shogun Yoshimitsu (1358–1408), he was asked to compile with Ise Mitsutada a code of ceremonial, later known as the Ogasawara-ryū, to which Rodrigues refers. *Kokushi Daijiten*, II, pp. 733–4, 757–8; Rodrigues, *Arte del cha*, p. 53, n. 145. In *Arte breve*, f. 75, Rodrigues mentions other relevant works; '*Buke no Reigi Hatto*, that is, laws and customs of the military order; *Kyūba no Michi no Narai*, dealing with weapons and riding; and *Shitsukegata no Koto*, that is, social customs, rites, and ceremonies of the kingdom.' See the illustrations on pp. 212, 221 taken from an Ogasawara manual.

CHAPTER 16

THE DRESS AND GARMENTS OF THE JAPANESE

There are three orders of notable people in this kingdom and they will be described in their proper place. One of them consists of the gentlemen of the patrician order called *kuge*, and they attend to the government of the realm and the office of the royal household and family; it is for this reason that they are called the house or family of the lords and grandees of the realm, because the term *kuge* means this. The head of this order is Sesshō and Kampaku.[1] Another order is that of the gentlemen belonging to the equestrian or military order called *buke*, meaning 'military family'; their office is to guard the royal person and defend the realm. The head of this order is the shogun or *kubō*, the High Constable or Commander of the Kingdom, and he participates in the court of both orders, patrician and military.[2] The third is of those belonging to the religious and ecclesiastical state.

Hence there are also three certain and fixed sorts of dress and public clothing. The first is worn by the *kuge* and is called *shōzoku*; it is similar to the ancient dress of Chinese lords, and they wear this in public ceremonies and when they appear before the king. Each one wears the robe appropriate to his rank and court as they appear in the king's lists. The other type belongs to the religious state and is also special and determined; they wear it when they appear in public or are engaged in ecclesiastical matters, and it is also called *shōzoku*.[3] Both sorts will be described when we come to speak about the patrician order and the religious state. The third type of dress pertains to the military order and properly belongs to the house of the *kubō*; it is worn in public ceremonies and is called *shitaku*.[4] This is the dress

---

[1] The two characters forming the word *kuge* mean 'prince family'. *Sesshō* was formerly used for a member of the royal family acting as regent for an emperor in his minority. But in 866 Fujiwara Yoshifusa was appointed regent during the minority of Emperor Seiwa (851–81), and the custom was continued thereafter. When the emperor came of age, the regent would be appointed *kampaku* (imperial regent for an adult emperor) and continue the administration under the sovereign's authority. In time, the two titles became distinct. The title of *kampaku* always ran in the Fujiwara family (with the exception of Hideyoshi) down to the 19th century, although by the 16th century the holder of the title possessed little authority outside the capital. *KEJ*, VII, p. 69.

[2] The office of *Sei-i-tai shōgun* was created in 720 when an army was mobilized to repulse the Ebisu, the forefathers of the Ainu, in northern Japan. The title was originally awarded to a different commander for a new expedition, but was eventually bestowed on Minamoto Yoritomo for life. Since then the title was reserved for the Minamoto family, and hence neither Nobunaga nor Hideyoshi occupied the office. In time the power of the shogun became absolute, although in theory the emperor could refuse investiture of a new candidate. The office was finally abolished in 1868 when political power was restored to the emperor.

[3] *Shōzoku* is usually translated as 'ceremonial dress'. *Vocabulario*, f. 313: '*Shōzoku*. Robes or clothes used in festivals, etc.' For an illustrated account of Japanese clothing through the ages, see *KEJ*, I, pp. 329–33.

[4] *Vocabulario*, f. 307: '*Shitaku*. To clothe or robe oneself to go out or for any other purpose.'

in ordinary social use within the kingdom, worn on visits, in public, and at official functions. This type should be understood when we speak about the ordinary dress and costume of the kingdom, because everybody usually wears this sort, and this is true even of the *kuge* and religious when not involved in public ceremonies related to their offices.

The garments of the Japanese in general do not have many styles and devices, but are standardized and fixed without much variation. They are all cut in only one plain style, and this is true of the dress of both men and women, laymen and religious. This applies to lined or padded garments as well as unlined, to silk ones as well as those woven of cotton or linen. Among these garments there are some that are the ordinary dress worn by everybody in the kingdom both in public and in private, and this is properly a garment or dress. Another type is, properly speaking, formal dress used when appearing in public before a lord, guests, and people of standing; there is, for instance, a certain kind of [...] and a humeral overgarment that is thrown over the shoulders.[1] The rest is ordinary and common, such as the sash, underdrawers, stockings, shoes or sandals, cap, and gloves, and we will describe each of these things in detail.

1. The principal garment, called *Kirumono*

The principal robe invariably worn by the nobility and ordinary folk, both men and women, throughout this kingdom is called *kirumono* or kimono.[2] It is a long garment after the fashion of a nightgown; it used to reach down to the middle of the leg or shin, but nowadays it is considered more formal and fashionable to wear it long down to the ankles. The wide sleeves are like those of the Portuguese *sainhos*,[3] covering the elbow and leaving the rest of the arm bare; this has been a most ancient fashion of China since the time of Qin, or Shin, and it seems to be on account of weapons. But they now use in China the same sleeves but very much longer, for the part that hangs over the hands is just as long as the part stretching from the shoulders to the fingertips, although Chinese solders in war use jerkins with tight sleeves after our fashion.

They put it on like a *cabaia*[4] and fold one side over the other, the left being wrapped over the right, thus forming a [...], and this is true also in China.[5] Although these robes are all

---

[1] A reference to the *hakama*, or ceremonial trousers, is probably missing here in the Portuguese text. The humeral overgarment was the *kataginu*.

[2] The word is derived from *kiru*, to wear, and *mono*, thing. A description of this robe is given in Carletti (in *TCJ*, pp. 208–9); Fróis (*Tratado*, pp. 110–16, 122–4) often mentions this robe while comparing Japanese and European dress. Cocks employs the older form of the word, *kirumono*, when referring to the robe; for example (12 February 1621, in *Diary*, II, p. 139), 'I silk *kerremon*' and 'I damask *kerremon*.' Hatch mentions (in Farrington, *English Factory*, II, p. 948) 'kerrimoones, or coats'. The earliest extant European depiction of the robe is the drawing by Peter Mundy (in his *Travels*, III:1, facing p. 270), who while in Canton in 1637 drew a Japanese 'with his Cotan [*katana*] by his side, and Dagger or Cuttbelly'.

[3] The *sainho*, a woman's robe, was a smaller version of the *saio*, an ample, loose-fitting gown with a collar, generally made of thick material and often worn by soldiers. *Grande enciclopédia*, XXVI, pp. 626, 637–8. Barbosa (*Book*, I, p. 113) describes the costume of the women of Gujarat as a *sainho*.

[4] The *cabaia*, from the Arabic *qabā*, was a long tunic worn particularly by wealthy Muslims in India. Dalgado, *Glossário*, I, pp. 158–9; Yule, *Hobson-Jobson*, pp. 105–6.

[5] There is a gap in the Portuguese text here, but the missing word is certainly *seio*, bosom, as Rodrigues (p. 185) later repeats the phrase when mentioning that the handkerchief was kept in the bosom. Both Fróis (*Tratado*, p. 104) and Avila Girón (*Relación*, p. 25) note that the kimono is wrapped around the body left over right, the former pointing out that this is the opposite to the European fashion.

the same as regards style, there are three different kinds as regards decoration. Some are padded with flock-silk and are worn by the nobles in the winter, while those of the common folk are padded with cotton-waste; those made of silk are called *kosode*, and those woven of linen or cotton, *nunoko*. Others are lined only for use in the spring and autumn when it is a little cold, and these are called *awase*. Finally there is the unlined robe, called *katabira*, which is worn in the summer and when it is hot.[1]

In olden days these robes, whether padded or merely lined, used to have a kind of collar or hem of some richer material, usually silk, called *eri*.[2] This used to serve as a decoration for noble and aristocratic people because silk was both rare and costly in those days. Whence comes their proverb, *Eri wo miru*, that is, 'to look at the collar of a robe', meaning to show partiality towards people. On account of this shortage of silk they used to adorn their linen or pongee (or *tsumugi*)[3] robes by inserting strips of silk, or some other material richer than the robe's fabric, into the sleeves at the shoulders, rather like a border. This was most fashionable and is called *kosode*, that is, 'short sleeves', and thus silk robes are now called *kosode*.

The outer surface of the robe's material, whether it be silk, hemp, or linen, is generally painted handsomely with flowers in various colours, although some of the silk robes have a striped pattern, others are dyed with one colour, others with two. The Japanese are extremely skilful in this matter of painting their robes of silk and other fabrics; they intermingle gold among the flowers painted in diverse ways, and they are especially clever in the use of crimsons and, even more, violets.[4] The robes of both the men and women are of the same style and fashion, although the women's are very long and reach right down, and they wear underneath a white petticoat from the waist downwards.

The *katabira* is generally made of very fine linen, somewhat like a veil, but there are silken ones called *susushi*.[5] These unlined linen garments are worn in summer; they are either white or else fashionably painted with various flowers, or they may be of only one colour with just a little floral decoration. The usual ones are white, blue, green, cinnamon, or other similar colours. Now these summer robes are very thin and transparent, and, unlike all the Chinese, the Japanese do not wear drawers or underbreeches but only a loincloth or *langhoti* underneath, like that worn by the Kanarins;[6] this is merely a sash, silk for the nobles and linen for ordinary people. Thus the garment is far from modest and in this respect the Japanese are not at all bashful by nature, for such in their custom. Thus in their wrestling bouts and in other activities that require the body to be naked or nude, both nobles and commoners feel no shame in appearing stripped to these loincloths; this seems to be the

---

[1] These names of Japanese garments are all listed in *Vocabulario*, ff. 15v, 42, 59, 187v. Fróis (*Tratado*, p. 100) quotes the Japanese saying 'Natsu katabira, aki awase, fuyu kimono' ('In summer the *katabira*, in autumn the *awase*, in winter the kimono'). Rodrigues later (p. 188) goes into greater detail concerning the seasons for wearing the different types of robe. Vilela (15 September 1565, in *Cartas*, I, f. 193v) also distinguishes between summer and winter dress.

[2] *Vocabulario*, f. 321v: '*Eri*. A strip of cloth which the Japanese place in their garment from the collar down towards the front.' Today *eri* means merely a collar.

[3] *Vocabularuio*, f. 248: '*Tsumugi*. Length of cloth woven from Japanese floss.'

[4] Fróis (*Tratado*, p. 100) also mentions that robes of men, except monks, were coloured. Rodrigues later (p. 328) describes the Japanese technique of dyeing. Suitable matching of colours was considered extremely important among the nobility, and more than sixty shades of colour were recognized.

[5] *Vocabulario*, f. 232v: '*Susushi*, Certain type of raw stiff silk.' A description of the *katabira* is given in Nishigōri, *Kokon*, pp. 131–2.

[6] *Langhoti*, a Hindi word, sometimes appears as langooty, lungooty, langoty, or langotee in English accounts. For various references, see Dalgado, *Glossário*, I, pp. 509–10.

ancient usage before drawers were devised. The more noble people use this *katabira* as an undershirt below their other clothes on account of sweat, but this is not at all usual and people generally wear these robes next to the skin. The lining of the nobles' silken robes is always made of very soft and smooth silk. As the robes are very ample and have wide sleeves, people can insert their hands inside with the greatest of ease and wipe away body sweat with a handkerchief.

The use of silk in olden days and even up to the time when we went to Japan was rare, and because of its scarcity and dearth the ordinary people did not use it, nor indeed did the gentry, and the lords but seldom. Usually the people wore garments made from linen, and the nobles and gentry also wore this with a silken collar or with some silken strips in the sleeves as we have said. But the nobles had a silken robe to be worn in public at formal ceremonies, banquets, and visits. But since the time of Taikō there has been a general peace throughout the kingdom, and trade has so increased that the whole nation wears silk robes; even peasants and their wives have silk sashes and the better-off among them have silken robes.[1]

The women of the gentry and above, and even ordinary people, wear the *katabira* over their heads instead of cloaks. When they go to a church or temple, or appear in public, they wear these *katabira* or cloaks so that they may not be seen.[2] This is especially true of noblewomen who are not usually seen by men even in their homes, not even by the male servants, as has already been said. When in mourning for their dead, the Japanese wear white clothing; this is a Chinese custom that the Japanese and Koreans have adopted.[3]

They gird themselves by wearing a sash over their robes. The sash is a long silk band that they wind around their waist twice and fasten with a bow, leaving the two long ends of the sash hanging down. The common folk who cannot afford better use painted sashes made of hemp or linen, but the most usual kind is made of silk; poor people possess at least one silk sash even though their garments may be of linen or cotton. Women wear the same sashes, except that they are rather like broad bands, while those of the men are round and stuffed within. In olden days and up to the time when we went to Japan, and even long afterwards, women of quality used to wear sashes a hand or more in width. It was thought fitting to wear them very loose, and they always placed both their hands inside the sashes in the same way as the men do in order to stop them slipping down to their feet.[4] Nowadays all the women tie their sashes in the same way as the men do, for there has been much reform in the kingdom as regards ancient customs, many of which have been cast aside and replaced by more reasonable ones.

[1] As early as 1565 Vilela (in *Cartas*, I, f. 193v) reported that nearly all the Japanese wore silk. The use of silk robes by missionaries became an issue, and in 1570 the newly arrived superior, Francisco Cabral, forbade the practice. Valignano, *Sumario*, pp. 231–2, nn. 9, 10, 11.

[2] Women's use of *katabira* as cloaks is also mentioned by Avila Girón (*Relación*, pp. 25–6), and Vilela (in *Cartas*, I, f. 193v).

[3] A practice often mentioned by the Europeans; for example, Fróis, *Tratado*, p. 108; Valignano, *Sumario*, p. 34; Carletti, *My Voyage*, p. 126; Ricci, *Fonti*, I, p. 83, and *China*, p. 72.

[4] Carletti (*My Voyage*, p. 125) reports that noblewomen wore their sash very loosely; Avila Girón (in *TCJ*, p. 208) confirms this and points out the difference between the sashes of men and women. But Valignano (in *TCJ*, p. 240) observes that pregnant women wore their sash so tightly that their figure was less bulky than before; he marvels that they did not kill both themselves and the unborn child, but was assured that the custom results in an easier childbirth. Fróis (*Tratado*, pp. 122, 128) confirms this practice. For a general account of the *obi*, or sash, see Nishigōri, *Kokon*, pp. 136–9.

Up to a certain age, children wear a robe that is fastened from behind by two ribbons sewn on either side. But when they reach a certain age and their childhood comes to an end, they throw away these ribbons and gird themselves with an ordinary sash as a sign that they are now men and can carry a sword.[1] For the Japanese carry both the long and the short sword at the side by inserting it between the sash and the robe. They carry the dagger in the same way, as they do not use swordbelts for their swords and daggers (which they call *katana* and *wakisashi*), but carry them in their sashes. They use swordbelts only for a certain kind of broadsword, called *tachi*. In addition to these belts, they gird themselves with their usual sash, to which the belt is attached.[2]

2. The *Hakama* and *Kataginu* (which are their formal trousers and humeral overgarment) and their *Dōbuko*, or robe, etc.

The ordinary Japanese trousers are a certain kind of drawers, wide at the bottom and open on both sides from the top down to the knee. One part is in front without any opening but with ribbons attached by which it is tied, while another is behind, also with ribbons attached for tying and girding the garment. This rear part has a small thin triangular board covered with the same material; the two lower corners are long and sharp, while the one above is short and blunt. This is called *koshi*, meaning 'thighs', because it falls behind over the thighs.[3]

The invention of trousers seems to have come from that part of China facing Japan called Zhejiang and Fujian, from which we have already said that Japan was populated. They belong to that nation, and we saw them as we passed overland through those parts and took note of them as we had already seen them in Japan. The Japanese properly use them as official or formal dress, and they are not the normal attire of the nation. They are worn when people appear in public, when they receive guests, and when they are on duty or appear before lords, when they go out visiting, etc. It is considered impolite to come to welcome a guest and not to wear these trousers but only the attire mentioned above. They put them on over all the other clothes, and the ends of the sash hang down inside the trousers and appear at the side openings that we mentioned. When they buckle on a broadsword, it sticks out of the opening on the left; the same applies to the dagger, for both are girded together on the left-hand side. In keeping with their custom these formal trousers must necessarily be made of woven linen, painted with various kinds of flowers and attractive pictures suitable for such a garment, with some flowers, rings, and other special fashionable emblems in the above-mentioned *koshi* at the back.[4] These trousers are also made of glove-leather for journeys, riding, or wearing inside the house in winter. Other people, especially noble youths, have them made of silk, but only to wear in the house and not specifically for official use.

---

[1] For reports on the age when a child begins carrying a sword, see p. 103, n. 4. Rodrigues later (p. 202) describes the entry of a boy into adulthood.

[2] The best European description of Japanese weapons is given by Avila Girón (in *TCJ*, pp. 141–2), although he does not mention the *tachi*, or long sword. Illustrations and technical terms of weapons and armour are found in Sasama, *Nihon Gassen*.

[3] The *hakama*, also worn by women, was a kind of divided or pleated skirt. For a detailed account of the different types of this garment, see Nishigōri, *Kokon*, pp. 112–17.

[4] The family crest was also worn on other parts of the clothing, for example, on the *kataginu*. For an illustrated account of such crests, see *KEJ*, II, p. 42.

In addition to these trousers, they have others of the same style and pattern, but so wide at the feet that after they put them on they extend two or three spans beyond the foot. These are used in the public service of the Lord of Tenka, or *kubō*, and all the other territorial lords at certain festivals throughout the year, at banquets with important guests, and when on duty in the public ceremonies that take place before them, chiefly in the presence of the many grandees, such as *yakata*, and in the houses of the nobles. Those on duty there wear these trousers with their feet hidden within, and the trouser legs trail along two or three spans after the foot; they must accordingly exercise diligence lest they trip over. This is done, in addition to other things, out of pomp and because it is the custom of the kingdom. The people on duty in public and solemn ceremonies in the presence of the grandees go in their bare feet without wearing stockings or anything else, and they cover their feet with these trousers out of respect. In ordinary and common service the servants wear ordinary trousers that reach to above the ankle, and also stockings made of glove-leather or their kind of cloth, and this is quite usual. Those who attend the palace of the Lord of Tenka, or the *kubō*, in some serving capacity, even if they be territorial lords, take with them these long trousers for what is to follow. For this reason they are called *nagabakama*.[1]

In addition to these formal trousers, they also have an overgarment, which has to be worn with trousers, whether the ordinary sort or the long kind. This is also a formal costume and is called *kataginu*, meaning 'veil over the shoulders'.[2] This reaches down only to the sash where its ends remain tucked into the trousers. It is a fine veil made of linen or silk, painted just like the trousers, or sometimes of only one colour with a flower, or with attractively painted stripes. It is open in front and at the sides, and behind it covers the back and both shoulders completely; it is stiff for it is pleated to get this effect. On no account is this worn without trousers, although they ordinarily wear trousers without this garment inside the house. When all the gentry and higher-ranking people go to the palace of the Lord of Tenka, the *kubō*, and the other lords, and on visits and in public, they must necessarily wear trousers and this humeral veil. For this reason they say, 'kataginu hakama,' meaning two things that necessarily go together.[3] So the kingdom's proper dress for all people who have a horse and have not shaved their beard, that is, people involved in public affairs, is this above-mentioned costume: these trousers, the overgarment, the footwear consisting of sandals and stockings made of glove-leather or of a certain kind of other cloth, and the sash. Everything else is variable and at choice, and not necessary in the public and official usage of this nation.

Usually they do not wear a hat, beret, or hood on their heads, but go bareheaded with their hair tied up as we have said earlier. Indeed, in official dealings it is discourteous to have the head covered, and anybody who is ill and must needs cover his head begs leave to

---

[1] The shorter trousers were called *hanbakama*. Vivero y Velasco remarks (*Relación*, f. 12v) on the *nagabakama* worn by the Surugu nobles and trailing more than two spans behind them. *Vocabulario*, f. 190v: 'Kemawashi, su, aita [the different parts of the verb]. To manage skilfully with the feet the *hakama* that drag behind while one walks in a room.' The original purpose of this ungainly garment may well have been to discourage sword fighting, which would be virtually impossible while wearing these trailing trousers. See Plate 16.

[2] *Vocabulario*, f. 42: 'Kataginu. A kind of light, short garment without sleeves, which men wear over the other clothes.'

[3] As Rodrigues says, the *kataginu* was a stiff sleeveless robe worn over the shoulders and tucked in at the waist; its colour and pattern were the same as those of the *hakama*. See Plate 16.

do so to avoid being rude.[1] This is the proper and usual way in Japan, and if the contrary is practised by some people, or if it is read about, it is, you must know, only among friends and members of the household in their private and informal dealings, or among ordinary people who have neither the means nor the dignity to do as we have described.

They have a kind of dressing gown or robe or loose upper garment called *dōbuku*. This is of the same cut and fashion as the robes mentioned above, but shorter and with a piece less.[2] It has a collar of silk or of some other richer fabric. This originated in China for use in the house in cold weather. It was first used in Japan as a robe worn over the weapons when soldiers went off to war; it later came into common use. Nobles wear it indoors or when hunting or riding on a journey, but not in public ceremonies, nor with important guests, but rather with friends and family members. Its use has become popular since Taikō's time, because before then it did not exist, except, as I said, in time of war. Nowadays shaven people also wear it, even in public or in place of the *koromo*, as shall later be said.[3]

Those who have performed *inkyo* and have shaved themselves do not wear trousers and *kataginu* in public and on visits, and neither do religious, for this is a secular and official dress. Instead they wear the kimono or the robe mentioned above, as well as a loose, unlined overgarment or fine black or grey linen veil, with long sleeves down to the knees; this is a sign of their having left the world and become a bonze. This robe is called a *koromo*, but it differs from the overgarment, or *koromo*, of real religious or bonzes. Nowadays since the time of Taikō these shaven men use the *dōbuku* instead of the *koromo*. Although in public and formal ceremonies, in *cha* meetings, and at other times they wear not the *dōbuku* but the *koromo*, which takes the place of the *hakama* and *kataginu*.[4] On such occasions their head and beard are freshly shaven, for it would be discourteous to present themselves with the hair growing, unless it were the result of illness or some other justifying reason. These shaven men also use in the winter the *watabōshi*,[5] a scarf padded with silk flock that they tie on the head, or else padded caps (but these are not padded in the summer); but at public ceremonies and visits they do not wear anything on the head. If they cover their head, it is at the host's behest, or after they themselves have asked leave for both of them to do so.

In the bosom formed by the two sides of the robe, as mentioned above, they carry a handkerchief to wipe away sweat, as well as a supply of sheets of soft, clean paper to use to blow their nose or spit when they are in carpeted rooms. This paper is used throughout the whole kingdom, and nobody – the gentry and ordinary people, women and children – fails to carry this in the bosom. These are used as handkerchiefs when they blow their nose and

---

[1] Various types of men's headgear, mostly those used in court and Shinto ceremonies, are featured in paintings, but Rodrigues is correct in saying that men in general wore no hat.

[2] There is a blank in the manuscript at this point.

[3] Valignano (*Sumario*, p. 232) describes the *dōbuko* as a kind of coat with sleeves, while Cocks (3 February 1621, in *Diary*, II, p. 135) talks of 'a silk coate or doboque, an upper garment or Japon cloake.' According to Avila Girón (*Relación*, p. 26), it was worn over other clothes and reached down to the knees; it was not worn inside the houses except by guests. If a man did not wish to wear it while on a journey, his page carried it folded up, and on arrival at his destination the man would put it on.

[4] The *koromo*, or *hōe*, is an ample robe with wide sleeves, worn by Buddhist monks; the *hōe*, literally 'robe of the law', was the official sacerdotal robe. See *Vocabulario*, f. 59.

[5] For references to the *watabōshi*, see p. 108, n. 3.

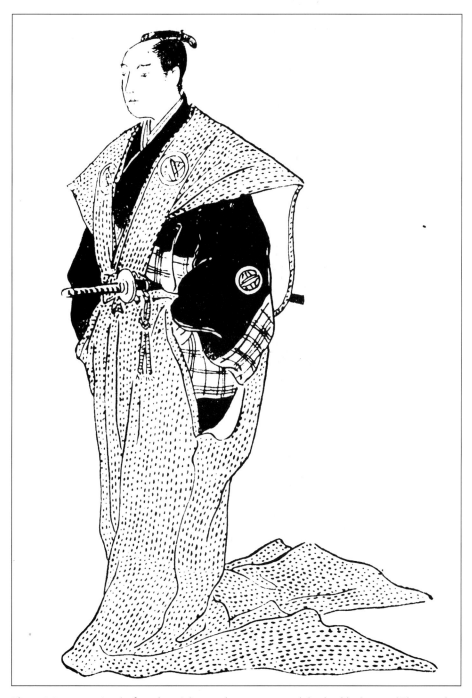

Plate 16: A man wearing the formal *nagabakama*, or long trousers, and the shoulder *kataginu*. 'Those on duty there [in palaces] wear these trousers with their feet hidden within, and the trouser legs trail along two or three spans after the foot; they must accordingly exercise diligence lest they trip over . . . they also have an overgarment . . . called *kataginu*, meaning "veil over the shoulders".' p. 183. Nishigōri, *Kokon Fukusō*.

185

for other purposes. Nobles and the gentry observe great cleanliness by immediately throwing away the sheet of paper after they have blown their nose. For this reason there is a great abundance of this paper throughout the kingdom.[1]

Throughout the land people wore sandals woven of rice-straw with a thong in the front to fix between the big toe. For journeys and in time of war the ordinary folk and soldiers wore straw half-sandals that covered half the foot but not the heel. This type of sandal, which they call *ashinaka*, or 'middle foot', was in use up to the time when we went to Japan. But ever since the time of Taikō it has been greatly improved, for it is now made of bamboo bark and also of straw as we have said, and covers the entire sole of the foot.[2] These straw sandals are the original native footwear of Japan. Religious people have bigger and better sandals made of fine rush-matting and with leather soles. They also wear clogs for walking in the mud and rain.[3] But every type of footwear has the above-mentioned thong between the big toe.

They wear on their legs stockings made of glove-leather or a kind of cloth, with the big toe separated from the other four so as to leave a gap between the toes, and thus they can wear their sandals. The stockings reach halfway up the leg, and the nobles tie them with silk ribbons (ordinary people make do with other ribbons) that are attached to the stockings for that purpose.[4] On a journey or in time of war they use a kind of leggings that they tie on their legs from ankle to knee.[5]

The Japanese observe certain courtesies regarding their footwear, that is, their sandals and clogs. A man wearing clogs may not greet or pass in front of another man wearing sandals, if he is an honourable person or an equal, without removing the clogs and putting on sandals like the other person. If the man wearing clogs is of lowly stock, he takes them off and stands with his feet on the ground while the other person passes, or else he passes with his bare feet. When an honourable person passes on the road a man who is seated, he will greet him by making the gesture of removing his sandals; the seated person, however, will bid him keep them on and will stand up as he passes. If he is riding on horseback, he will dismount and then, after walking past a little way, will remount. If the person passing is of lowly rank, he takes off his sandals and silently passes barefoot, bowing a little as he passes in front as a sign of respect.[6]

---

[1] Speaking about the Japanese in Macao, Mundy observes (*Travels*, III:1, pp. 294–5), 'They blow their Noses with a certaine sofft and tough kind off paper which they carry aboutt them in small peeces, which having used, they Fling away as a Filthy thing, keeping handkercheifes of lynnen to wype their Faces and hands.' Valignano laid down (*Sumario*, p. 236) that there should be an amply supply of *hanagami*, or paper tissues, in Jesuit houses. These are mentioned in *Vocabulario*, f.78v, and Fróis, *Tratado*, p. 106. Mexia notes (6 January 1584, in *Cartas*, II, f. 124) that it was impolite to spit in Japanese gardens and verandas, and handkerchiefs had to be used.

[2] Fróis (*Tratado*, p. 114) remarks that these half-shoes were the ordinary footwear, but were not worn by women, monks, and the elderly. *Vocabulario*, f. 197: '*Sekida*. Sandals made from bamboo bark.' Avila Girón (*Relación*, pp. 24–5) goes into some detail when describing footwear, mentioning by name the different types.

[3] The usual wooden clogs are called *geta*; high clogs for walking through mud are *ashida*.

[4] Mundy (*Travels*, III:1, p. 294) describes these socks, or *tabi*, as 'buskins like Mittens, in 2 parts, one For their great toe and the other For the rest'. Avila Girón (*Relación*, p. 23) goes into detail, describing how they were decorated; he adds that the silk ribbons were 2½ spans long, and that skins were imported from Siam, Manila, and Cambodia for this purpose. *Vocabulario*, f. 121, adds: '*Gomen*. A certain soft skin of a red colour from which they make women's Tabi, or gloves.' Carletti (*My Voyage*, p. 123) refers to 'cloth slippers or half-boots of goatskin.' The type of *tabi* to be worn by Jesuits was laid down by Valignano (*Sumario*, pp. 233–4). Nowadays *tabi* do not reach much above the ankles.

[5] *Vocabulario*, f. 194: '*Kyahan*. Like stockings stretching from the knees to near the ankles, and used on journeys.'

[6] Carletti (*My Voyage*, p. 124) relates that their shoes are easily removed and that the Japanese take them off in the street whenever they meet a person of any standing. Alvares (in *TCJ*, p. 56) makes the same comment.

Thus some have mistakenly written that the Japanese take off their sandals among themselves as a sign of respect just as we take off our hats.[1] But there is no such custom among the gentry. Also when a lowly person or a servant is speaking with a noble who is standing, he takes off his sandals, or he pushes them halfway off his feet, while he is speaking or delivering a message. If the person is very noble, he will kneel down, but he will only bow somewhat to a man of lesser rank.

They also wear long leather gloves that reach to the elbow or the middle of the arm, covering that part of the arm that protrudes from the sleeve. But they wear these only when they are riding or hunting with falcons or using a bow; for this last activity they wear a special glove for drawing the bowstring.[2] But they do not wear gloves in public, but when it is cold they put their arms and hands up their wide sleeves. But as this is a grave discourtesy and impertinence in the presence of the gentry, a lord will do this only in front of his servants. On no account whatsoever may a servant do this in the presence of his master, nor may anyone, however noble he may be, do it during a public ceremony, nor in the presence of guests or people of consequence, unless he be among friends in private. All the noble and aristocratic ladies, and maids in the service of the lords, wear silk gloves covering the back of the hands and all of the arm protruding from the sleeve; the fingers and palm of the hand, however, remain outside the glove, which is hooked around the thumb.[3]

As we have said, the men wear their hair tied up behind with half the head shaven like a tonsure in a very attractive and comely fashion.[4] The noble women and ladies tie their hair behind and let it hang down their back over their dress. The longer their hair is, the more dignified it is, and so some find it necessary to insert wigs into their hair.[5] Their hair must be black; on no account may it be fair, and for this purpose they dye it after their manner.[6] Palace ladies, noblewomen, and all ordinary women observe the ancient custom of plucking out the hair of the eyebrows and thus the face remains without any hair at all, except for the eyelashes. This is considered very fashionable, but in reality it is an abuse and against the decoration that Nature herself places on the human face. When the nobles and people belonging to the palace make up their face, they use a sort of bright black dye to paint their eyebrows delicately just above the position of their natural ones.[7] In like manner it is the custom of many nobles, both women and boys, to make their teeth as black as pitch with a

---

[1] The custom is mentioned by Valignano, *Sumario*, p. 36; Ribadeneira, *Historia*, p. 324; Linschoten, *Discours*, I, 26 (p. 45).

[2] Ordinary gloves are called *tebukuro*, while those used in archery are *yagake*. *Vocabulario*, f. 326, gives the word *yugake* for a glove.

[3] According to Fróis (*Tratado*, p. 124), women's gloves were like small silk sleeves reaching to the elbow; as Rodrigues says, the fingers were left uncovered.

[4] For earlier references to men's hair styles, see p. 120.

[5] In classical Japanese literature, reference is often made to the beauty of noblewomen's long hair. In *The Tale of Genji*, Lady Ochiba's hair was six feet in length, while in her diary, Lady Murasaki expresses admiration for Lady Dainagon whose flowing hair was as much as 3 inches longer than her height. Morris, *World*, p. 203. Fróis (*Tratado*, p. 120) remarks that the hair of some court ladies swept for three ells on the floor behind them. For illustrations of women's hairstyles, see *KEJ*, III, pp. 82–3. Paintings of Heian court life invariably show the hair of noble ladies trailing behind them. For example, Doi, *Kanō Eitoku*, p. 77.

[6] The Japanese aversion to fair hair has already been mentioned on p. 120. Fróis (*Tratado*, pp. 120–22) notes that even 60-year-old women did not have a single grey hair in their head because they used oil on their hair.

[7] Fróis (*Tratado*, p. 120) also mentions this practice. In court circles eyebrows were shaved and artificial ones painted with a black preparation called *haizumi*; instead of eyebrows, patches called *motomayu* were sometimes painted

certain dye made of iron and vinegar. This was very common when we arrived in Japan, but the practice has now been given up completely by men and largely by women, who now leave their teeth in their natural condition. This custom really sprang to the eye, but they regarded it as fashionable. The dye would so adhere to the teeth that it would never come off, except with great effort.[1]

3. The times of the year when the Japanese change their costume

The Japanese and Chinese make their principal visits in the four seasons of the year, that is, in spring, summer, autumn, and winter. At certain fixed conjunctions of these seasons and in keeping with the weather and tradition, they change their costume for another suited to the season; this costume will be more or less padded in keeping with the season's natural temperature. When they go to visit a noble or an equal, they regard it as only polite and good breeding to wear the robe that is used in that season, even though they may wear it on top of another garment, which they put on underneath on account of ill-health.

In the summer, which according to their reckoning begins on the fifth day of the fifth moon, which falls in June, they wear an unlined robe, or *katabira*, until the last day of the eighth moon, or September, making four months in all. From the first day of the ninth moon, they wear the *awase*, or robe with only a lining. From the ninth day of the ninth moon until the last day of the third moon of the following year (that is, from October to March, including part of October, the whole of winter, and part of spring, which begins on 5 February), they use padded robes. From the first day of the fourth moon until the fifth day of the fifth moon, falling in June, when they begin wearing unlined robes, they use the *awase* once more, or the silk robe with only a lining. They are most punctilious in the observance of these ceremonies.[2]

Pictures of Japanese dress that we have described

We will include here various pictures of Japanese dress, beginning from infancy or childhood, with their explanations.[3]

    1. Pictures of secular dress of various men.

    2. Of ordinary women and of noble ladies and those of the palace.

    3. Of kings, *kuge*, etc.

---

high up on the forehead. Illustration in Nishigōri, *Kokon*, p. 207. As late as March 1868, Sir Harry Parkes and Algernon Mitford (later, Lord Redesdale) noted that the youthful Emperor Meiji had high artificial eyebrows painted on his forehead. Casal, *Japanese Cosmetics*, pp. 14–17; Redesdale, *Memoirs*, II, p. 460.

[1] The custom of dyeing the teeth black was known as *nesshi*, but was not found in China. At one time it may have served as a sign of a wife's fidelity, but it was also practised by men at court. In 1868 Mitford observed that Emperor Meiji had black teeth, as well as rouged cheeks and lips painted with red and gold. Casal, *Japanese Cosmetics*, pp. 17–25; Redesdale, *Memoirs*, II, p. 460 (and the footnote in ibid., II, pp. 438–9, for the alleged origin of the custom). Not surprisingly, the early Europeans often referred to teeth-blackening: Valignano, *Sumario*, p. 36; Fróis, *Tratado*, p. 122; Avila Girón, *Relación*, p. 17; Carletti, in *TCJ*, p. 38.

[2] Exactly the same list is given in *Ogasawara*, f. 8. *Koromogae*, or robe changing, is also noted by Mexia (6 January 1584, in *Cartas*, II, f. 123) and Fróis (*Tratado*, p. 100), but neither go into such detail as does Rodrigues.

[3] Unfortunately these illustrations are not included in the Portuguese text. As noted above (p. 179, n. 2), the earliest extant European drawing of Japanese dress was made by Peter Mundy. Engelbert Kaempfer, in Japan 1690–92, provides various sketches in his work. The illustrations appearing in Montanus's celebrated *Atlas Japanensis*, 1670, are inaccurate and based on hearsay.

CHAPTER 17

THE JAPANESE MANNER OF PAYING VISITS, AND THE REGULAR TIMES AND OCCASIONS FOR THIS

The Japanese, as well as the Chinese, are very punctilious when they pay each other visits at certain times of the year, at festivals, and on various occasions. These visits are the usual custom unless there be enmity between people, for failure to visit on certain occasions is a sign of enmity or lack of friendship. It is the usual and ordinary custom for the person paying the visit to take with him a gift; and on these visits a certain manner is observed both by the person paying the visit and by his host. The visits are made personally by a man who is in or near the estate of a person who is to be visited, unless he is unwell or prevented from making them, and not by message or letter. If the person lives afar off, it is customary to pay these visits by means of a squire or a person of rank belonging to the household, along with a message and without a letter, or also with a letter and a gift, or also by a lad with a letter and a gift. When a squire or person of standing does this, the person who receives him will pay him honour and invite him to eat and to the *sakazuki* on account of his rank.[1] He will then convey to his lord the welcome that the other extended to him and everything given to him so that his master may do the same as the other. It is also a necessary custom to repay the visits and the gifts to each other, except in the case of a noble or person involved in business who cannot repay so many.

The usual way in which the Japanese pay visits to each other is as follows, although some long-winded parts have been done away with and others amended since Nobunaga's time. First of all, when a noble person is going to visit another noble, he always sends ahead to warn him by dispatching a message through a member of his household so that he may inform him of his visit. If he is going at midday, he sends the message in the morning, and if he intends to go in the afternoon, he informs him at midday. This is done so that the host may prepare the house in which he is to receive him, as well as the other things needed when he receives him. Then when he is on the point of setting out, he sends his gift on ahead so that it arrives just a little before him, although some people carry the present with them, and then finally the person paying the visit sets out. When the guest is with the host in the room, the latter has the gift presented in front of the guest so that he may thank him for it. When the guest arrives at the street gate, he waits at a little distance from it so that he cannot see what is happening inside nor can he be seen by the people within. He sends word of his arrival inside and enters once he receives an answer. The host goes out into the street or to the inner courtyard to greet him in accordance with his rank and dignity, and they pay each other the due courtesies that are described when we speak about the manner of receiving guests.

---

[1] Rodrigues later (pp. 238 *et seq.*) goes into detail when describing the rite of *sakazuki*.

The times appointed to pay visits are chiefly their New Year, the third day of the third month, the fourth month, the fifth day of the fifth month, the sixth, seventh, and eighth months, the ninth day of the ninth month, the tenth and eleventh months, and the end of the year.[1] All these times are festive for the Japanese and it is then that they make their visits. When these visits are paid, they observe certain determined courtesies as they greet the guests and entertain them in their houses. In addition to these festivals, there are also other occasions when they are wont to visit certain persons, and we will speak specifically about all this. They normally pay these visits either in the morning, at midday, in the afternoon, or finally at any time whatsoever if the visit does not involve any business but is merely to fulfill an obligation. Some people go to fulfill their obligation of visiting a person when they know that he is not at home. In this way they pretend that they have gone to see him and leave a message saying that they have called. If they meet the person while they are on their way to visit him, they there and then wish him a happy New Year (if it be the season for this), and tell him that they were on their way to see him at his house. He replies, 'I receive your visit here,' or 'Your Honour's visit may be counted as paid.' Then they bid each other farewell and depart. If they are bearing a gift for him, they summon their servant who is carrying it and tell him to present it or to inform a servant of the person so that he may receive it. He immediately goes and tells his master, who is already on his way after the farewell. He returns and expresses his thanks, and tells one of his servants to take it and carry it to his house. But the donor then says that his own servant will take it to his house for him.

1. The festival of the New Year, its ceremonies, and the manner of paying visits at that time

All these Far Eastern nations, such as principally the Chinese, Japanese, Koreans, the natives of Luchu and Cauchi, and other, celebrate the New Year in a grand way with various ceremonies and superstitions that they observe at this time.[2] First of all, they make great preparations of provisions for banquets, both for guests and members of the household. However poor he may be, everyone has new clothes made. They clean their houses both inside and out, decorate them as best they can, and put down new mats. They clean out the kitchen, wash everything, and shut up the pots. They do not kindle the kitchen fire that night nor do they go to sleep. Instead, they all make merry and hold certain ceremonies with lighted lamps in honour of the god or spirit of the hearth, and other spirits or lares of the household; then they relight the fire with other ceremonies. They decorate the street door with a certain kind of tree (such as the pine, which they call *matsu*) that denotes good fortune and longevity, and also with bitter oranges called *daidai*. They arrange these things together, and then say 'Matsudai', meaning 'for ever or for many years.'[3] At the foot of the

---

[1] The festival on the third day of the third month was called Jōmi; the fifth day of the fifth month, Tango; the ninth day of the ninth month, Chōyō; the end of the year, Ōmisoka. The festival in the seventh month is either Bon or Tanabata. *Vocabulario*, ff. 24v, 51, 161v, 229v, 240, 250v. See *KEJ*, II, p. 262, and Casal, *Five Sacred Festivals*, for these festivals. Rodrigues goes into greater detail below.

[2] Descriptions of the Chinese New Year are given in Mendoza, *History*, I, pp. 139–40; Cruz, in Boxer, *South China*, p. 143; Ricci, *Fonti*, I, p. 87, and *China*, pp. 76–7.

[3] *Matsudai* literally means future ages or generations; see *Vocabulario*, ff. 153 and (for *daidai*) 69v. Avila Girón (*Relación*, p. 37) also mentions the custom, still observed, of placing pine branches at the door in the New Year. Cocks reports (15 January 1618, in *Diary*, II, p. 5): 'Taffi Dono sent us 2 pine trees to set at our dore on the new years of Japon, being Shonguach [Shōgatsu], which begyneth on Sattarday next, being the 17th currant.'

pine or other trees they place chopped kindling wood that they burn on the fifteenth of the month, when they make bonfires in the streets in memory of a certain festival of the idols.[1] In front of the door they hang a certain straw rope, which also has a superstitious meaning.[2]

During this first and principal month of the year, there are seven days that are especially noted and celebrated. These are the first three days of the month (that is, the first day and its two octave days; these are official holidays and by tradition people do not work then), the fifth day, the seventh, the fifteenth, and finally the twentieth, and on this last day they conclude their feasting and merrymaking.[3] On these above-mentioned days wealthy people of means try to change their clothes, putting on a new robe of different material every time they go out. Poor people unable to do this much try to change their clothes at least on some days. The bonzes do not change their robes, although they try to go about in clean and new apparel.

Their principal aim in celebrating and paying visits is to enjoy themselves, feasting and starting off the New Year well. The main thing is for everybody to exchange greetings and pay visits, especially on these more solemn days. It is enough to visit each other only once, and on these visits and meetings they say, 'Gyokei senshū banzai', that is, 'May your pleasures and joys last a thousand autumns and ten thousand years.' This is their way of saying, 'For thousands of years.'[4] They also use other expression suited for this season of the New Year.

As these New Year visits are so customary with everybody visiting everybody else at the same time, it is not possible to greet everyone in person, and so they do not enter a house to give their New Year greetings. Instead, when they come to the door of a house, they convey their greetings to somebody of the household who is always stationed there just for that purpose. For it is the custom of the gentry to post near the porch a responsible man provided with paper and ink, and in the name of his master when he is absent this man receives the visitors' New Year greetings and other messages along with their gifts. He enters in his book the name of the visitor and the gift that he brought, and every day he reports to his master their names and shows him the gifts that they have presented.[5] This official tells such visitors that he will take great care to inform his master as soon as he

---

[1] *Vocabulario*, f. 215v: '*Sagichō*. Pagan ceremony performed at Shōgatsu. They make a fire in front of the house, and burn various things in it.' Cocks notes (30 January 1618, in *Diary*, II, p. 11), ' This day ended the Japon feast of 15 [days], and they took downe the trees sett up first day, and set their faggotes with rise and wyne, as yearly they do on this day.'

[2] *Vocabulario*, f. 301v: '*Shime*, or *shimenawa*. Rope in front of an idol, from which hang some papers and other things.' This straw rope, from which often hang printed prayers and petitions, may still be seen at Shinto shrines.

[3] According to *Ogasawara*, f. 8, the five principal days of the New Year were the 1st, 2nd, 3rd, 7th and 15th. Rodrigues's phrase 'the first day and its two octave days' refers to the first three days of the year. The Japanese observed the lunar calendar until 1873 and so their New Year did not coincide with the beginning of the European year, usually occurring between 14 January and 13 February. Avila Girón states (*Relación*, p. 264) that the New Year festival ran from the first day of the February moon until the full moon; this is confirmed by Pereira (in Boxer, *South China*, p. 17) and Ricci (*Fonti*, I, pp. 79–80, and *China*, p. 68). Ribadeneira (*Historia*, pp. 371–2) reports that wealthy people celebrate the New Year for two weeks, but the poor observe only three days. When visiting, people presented gifts of rice-cakes (*mochi*), which he likens to the *turrón* of Alicante.

[4] *Vocabulario*, ff. 119, 296v: '*Gyokei*. Term with which festival greetings, congratulations, etc., are given.' '*Senshū*. Term with which the Japanese greet each other at Shōgatsu and other festivals, as if to say, May you live a thousand years.'

[5] The Europeans entered into the spirit of New Year and also sent gifts to their patrons and friends. For example, Cocks (12–15 February 1621, in *Diary*, II, pp. 139–40) lists the gifts given and received at the English factory in Hirado for the New Year, which fell on 12 February that year. The presents included kimono, fish, Spanish wine, and *sake*.

returns home that His Honour has paid a visit. For although his master may well be at home, he is said to be out in order to show greater respect to the visitors. They know this very well for they do the same in their own homes.[1] So the visitors say that they do not wish to come in and go only as far as the door, although as a compliment they are invited to enter. Sometimes his master may tell this official that should such-and-such persons come, then he should let him know. So when they arrive, he bids them enter and asks them to wait while he informs his master. He also does this when he sees that the visitors who come to convey their New Year greetings are persons of quality whom his master would wish to see. So he asks them to wait and goes to inform his master, who then bids them enter and entertains them.

During these days the only visitors who freely enter and gather together to celebrate the New Year are members of the family and close relatives. On these visits they need not send a message ahead to say they are coming, because as these are the appointed days everything is already prepared and ready for them. Nor is it necessary to take gifts to everybody but only to some three or four principal people of the region and to close friends, as a sign of respect and affection.

The bonzes do not normally convey New Year greetings to layfolk, nor do they visit their houses on these appointed days, but rather on some other day, for example, the fourth, sixth, or any of the other days until the fifteenth or twentieth of the month (especially if they come from afar), or finally on any day whatsoever of the entire first month. For they regard it as an ill-omen for the bonzes to enter their homes at the time of the festive New Year, which the people wish to begin well so that they may live many long years. But it is the bonzes' office to teach the way to the next world, but the people have no desire to go there too quickly, nor do they wish to speak with the bonzes for their talk is about the things of death. Many people are so superstitious that during these days they will not use certain words that either signify death or have a similar pronunciation, and they also observe other superstitions. There are people who are so superstitious and given to omens that they will never in their lives on any account pronounce the syllable *shi* in whatever word it may occur, for although it may have another meaning it sounds like the word 'death'.[2] Should any misfortune befall them at this time in the beginning of the year, they deeply grieve and regard it as an ill-omen. If somebody happens to die at this time, especially the first three days of the year, they try to conceal the matter. After the festival of the New Year, the things of salvation are not discussed for two weeks so that they do not recall sad things such as death.[3]

People of quality who come a long way to convey their New Year greetings or who send a message or letter (as those who live afar generally do) fulfil their obligation by visiting or writing during the whole of the first month or even throughout the entire second month. On such visits they first of all convey their New Year greetings and then turn to business matters, or in their letter they first of all offer their greetings and then deal with business.[4]

---

[1] *Vocabulario*, f. 40v: '*Karikoto*. Lies, as when somebody says that the lord or *tono* sends such a thing, without it being so. Thus, *karikoto wo iu*, to tell these lies.'

[2] Rodrigues explains in *Arte grande*, f. 214v: '*Shi*, meaning four, is not used with some words because it is the same as the word *shi*, meaning death or to die. ... Therefore in its place they use the *yomi* term, *yo*.' He then gives examples of this custom: the fourth day of the month is *yokka*, not *shi-nichi*; four years is *yonen* and not *shi-nen*. Even today some Japanese hotels do not list a fourth floor.

[3] Almeida (20 October 1566, in *Cartas*, I, f. 214v) also reports that sermons were not preached for two weeks after the New Year so that people might not be reminded of death.

[4] The Portuguese text of this sentence is probably corrupt, but the sense remains clear.

Women usually do not go out to convey their New Year greetings except after the first two weeks, unless it be to the lord or master, because of the large crowds of men at these times. They usually send word ahead a day before they intend to go, and they do not leave their greetings at the door as do the menfolk, but enter inside the house and celebrate the festival together. Men do not normally go to wish a woman a happy New Year, except in the case of relatives or perhaps a noble and related widow. Men convey their New Year greetings among themselves, and the women do the same in their own circles.

At the New Year the lord of the territory is visited by all, from the noble vassals with their gifts to the bonzes of his region. The peasants living on rented land belonging directly to the lord bring him firewood, vegetables, and other produce according to the land. The other lesser nobles are visited by their subjects and the peasants of their lands in due proportion.[1] On this day and festival of the New Year it is usual to show all possible honour and courtesy to each one in keeping with his station and rank, even between a lord and his vassal. It is also ordinary people's custom to pay these visits with greetings or, if the other person has brought one, with a gift. But the nobles are not obliged to thank everyone who comes with greetings and presents when they do not actually meet them. But if they should meet some people to whom they wish to show more than usual honour, they will thank them.

---

[1] According to Fróis (in *TCJ*, pp. 109–11), nobles would visit their territorial lord from the 9th to the 15th or 20th day of the first month. It was also usual for nobles and high-ranking monks to have an audience with the shogun at the New Year, and Fróis and Vilela took the opportunity of visiting Ashikaga Yoshiteru at Miyako during New Year 1565. Fróis, *TCJ*, pp. 109–11. Ribadeneira (*Historia*, p. 371) confirms Rodrigues's account of these visits.

CHAPTER 18

THE CEREMONIES AND ENTERTAINMENT PROVIDED FOR GUESTS WHO VISIT THE MASTER OF THE HOUSE AT NEW YEAR

There are various ceremonies and entertainment for the guests and people when they meet the master of the house for the first time in the New Year. First of all, everything required on such occasions, such as food, drink, and the utensils with which they are served, is prepared beforehand.[1] The guest enters the formal matted chamber and is seated in his place in the manner described elsewhere.[2] At the top of the matted room there is placed a large pot rather like a water-basin for washing the hands, and this is full of very white uncooked pounded rice. On top of this are placed dry cuttlefish and pieces of a certain seaweed obtained from the island of Ezo, where it grows in the sea there. This is called *kombu* and is like a long belt, a good span in width and five, six or more ells long. The pot also contains peeled chestnuts and a bitter orange. Thus there are five things in all, an uneven number and to their way of thinking a perfect one. The names of these things indicate a good omen.[3]

When all the guests and host are in the room and are sitting back on their feet with their knees pointing forwards (they call this *kashikomatte*, and it is a very respectful position),[4] a serving page enters, takes this dish, and offers it to all present. Everyone takes one or two grains with two fingers of his right hand and puts them in his mouth, or at least pretends to put them there without actually doing so. When all have done this, the page returns the dish to its original position, and there it always stays during the first two weeks of the New Year and is not taken away. On the morning of the fifteenth day, the rice is made into a soup and eaten.

After this ceremony, three tables or trays are brought out one after the other, and on each of them there is a cup on a salver and wine in a tankard. This wine ceremony is the usual and best sign of affection among them, and to this end delicacies and various appetizing things are produced to persuade the guests to drink the wine. These things are brought out in the following way.

A page comes in with a cup that at this season is usually made of clay with the texture and colour of a tile, and it is placed on its tray or salver. The latter are of various kinds, and

---

[1] As Avila Girón (*Relación*, p. 37) points out, the New Year is a general holiday when there is no buying or selling, and anyone not obtaining beforehand everything necessary will not be able to buy it later during the festival.

[2] For the guest's place in the room, see p. 235.

[3] For an earlier reference to *kombu* (or kelp), see pp. 91–2. According to Ogasawara ceremonial, pounded rice, chestnuts (*kachi-kuri*), and *kombu* were served at the New Year, and from the names of these three items it was possible to form the phrase 'utte katte yorokobu', meaning to rejoice after pounding and defeating the enemy. Rodrigues, *Nihon*, I, p. 432, n. 2. For an exhaustive list of European references to the New Year celebrations, see Valignano, *Adiciones*, pp. 358–62.

[4] *Vocabulario*, f. 44v: '*Kashikomari, u, atta* [the parts of the verb *kashikomu*]. To be on one's knees. ... *Kashikomatte iru*. To be reverently in front of someone, with the hands on the floor, etc.'

have tall or short legs as the rank of the host and guest requires. He places it at the top of the room about four spans in front of the pot containing the five things mentioned above. Then they bring out some tables, each of which bears dishes proper to the season, and place them in front of the guests. A page then comes in with a jug of cold wine in his hands, and stations himself at the entrance of the room on his knees (*kashikomatte*). Then all are seated, crossing the legs according to their fashion without the feet being visible. They pick up the *hashi* with their right hand, the plate of delicacies with their left, and take a small portion from it (meantime they pretend to take a piece without actually doing so). Then they replace the plate along with the *hashi* on the tray in front of them. The page with the jug then rises to his feet.

Then out of courtesy and respect the host and the principal guest send the cup to each other with their usual compliments so that the other may take it and drink it first.[1] In this season of the New Year it is customary for the host to drink first, as the guest says to him, 'Drink, Your Honour, as it is the custom of the New Year.' To which he replies , 'I will do as Your Honour commands.' Then he drinks, taking the wine in the cup three times[2] in succession, and then raising it to his mouth again he makes as if to drink another time without actually taking anything. The page rises and goes to put more wine in the jug (or makes as if to do so) even though it is full, and for this purpose there is another page in sight at the veranda door at the entrance to the room with another jug. While the page goes to pour wine into the jug, the person who has drunk remains with the cup in his right hand. Without lowering it, he keep his arm extended and resting with the elbow on the thigh of his right leg, while his left hand rests on his left thigh. When the page returns, he receives wine for the third time and does not make a second bow towards the guest as is done in an ordinary drinking session. Instead, the host drains the cup over the delicacies in front of him, and sends it to the guest without any further compliment. The guest raises the cup above his head up to his forehead, and in the same way takes the wine twice in succession, and before the second time[3] the host, and the page who supplies the jug with wine. He performs the same ceremony as the first time. The guest receives the wine for the third time, and after he has drunk, the host asks him to send him the cup from which he has drunk, for he wishes to raise it above his head. The guest drains it and places it on the tray, and the host lifts it up. If there are other guests, he pays his compliments to the next one before he takes the wine, and performs towards him the same courtesies as he did towards the first one. But the page does not go to replenish the jug as he did the first time so as not to unduly delay in these courtesies.

After he has drunk, the host sends the cup to the second guest, and when he has taken the wine twice, the page goes to replenish the jug out of courtesy, as in the first case. This is done for each of the guests who are present. If the guests are just ordinary people, the host orders the pot to be replenished when the guest in the first place drinks, and then afterwards each of the other guests takes the wine three times in the manner described above.

When this first formal ceremony of the New Year is over, a second similar table is produced with a broth made of the flesh of the crane, which among them is the most highly

---

[1] The Portuguese text of these last sentences appears to be corrupt, but the general sense is clear.

[2] From what follows, this seems to be a slip for 'twice'.

[3] Probably a slip for 'third time'. As can be seen, the rest of this sentence is obviously corrupt. Rodrigues presumably means that the guest pretends to drink a third time, the page goes to refill the wine jug and returns, pours out more wine, and the guest then drinks for a third time.

esteemed bird. Or it may be of another prized bird, such as swan, wild duck, and others. After the pages have placed this second table in front of the guests, they take away the first one inside. Sometimes to pay greater honour to his guest, the table will be taken away inside by the host himself or by one of his sons or a well-born lad instead of the page. The guest lifts up the first table with both hands to make room for the second, and after it has been placed in position he will touch it with his hand, and thus show greater courtesy. But if this is done by only an ordinary page, he will let him put down the table and take away the other without making any move to help. After the table comes a page with the flask of warm wine, and this is put in the first place. Then everyone begins to eat the meat and to drink the broth, sipping it if they so desire. They help themselves to pieces of the other delicacies that have arrived on the table. The cup passes around once more with the same ceremonies as before, and compliments are exchanged, as before, between the guests in the first place. But now it is the guest who is the first to take the wine, after exchanging compliments with the others. Thus the wine passes around everyone just as it did the first time.

After everybody has drunk, but before the second tables are cleared away, another cup is produced and placed at the top of the room, and then follows the third course. This consists of another broth made of something else with two dishes, and is passed around, as has been described in the previous courses, with the same ceremony. But this time the host starts off the drinking as if he is obliging his guests to drink, and this is the sign that he wishes them to relax.

When these three courses and the wine have been finished, the guests bid farewell and return home. But if in addition to this entertainment there is to be a banquet, as there often is, then the banquet courses continue in the manner described when we talk about banquets. When the banquet is concluded, *cha* is provided and they drink this with their accustomed ceremonies.

These are the ceremonies performed formally for important guests, although there are others less formal and solemn in keeping with the host's dignity, means, and arrangements. But each one does his best to perform this completely or in part, for this is the way of honouring guests at this season.

All the territorial lords perform these ceremonies at this season for their vassals, servants, and even senior peasants, giving them the *sakazuki* in the clay cup, mentioned above, as a sign of benevolence. They entertain the principal vassals and show them great affection. As regards the peasants, the lord drinks first and sends them the clay cup from which he has drunk, and the peasant raises it above his head. The peasant is, as it were, lying bowed to the ground on the mat or veranda, and after drinking he carries the cup away in his bosom without returning it to the lord.

CHAPTER 19

THE OTHER FESTIVALS HELD DURING THE YEAR WHEN THEY
ALSO PAY VISITS

There are four most solemn festivals throughout the year and they are called *gosekku*, that is, 'five festivals',[1] although in fact there are only four of them because they count the New Year festival and that of the old year as two.[2] The festivals are first, *Shōgatsu*; second, *Sangatsu sannichi*, that is, the third day of the third moon; third, *Gogatsu gonichi*, the fifth day of the fifth moon; fourth, *Kugatsu kunichi*, the ninth day of the ninth moon; and fifth, *Shōgatsu* of the following year. But there are other festivals in between these, and it will be better to talk about them all in the order of the months, omitting Shōgatsu, which we have already described.

After Shōgatsu, or the New Year, they celebrate the second festival, which occurs on the third day of the third moon.[3] It is the custom on this day to indulge in much revelry out of doors. On this particular day there is an extraordinarily high tide, the highest on any day of the year, and they go to gather shellfish and make merry on the beaches, while people living inland make merry in the countryside. They make certain cakes of rice and green herbs on this day, and these cakes are green in colour. They eat these first of all in the morning as a special treat, and they entertain their relatives and friends who come to visit them by serving these cakes on a paper plate; on top they put some peach blossoms, for these cakes are proper to this particular day.[4] They entertain their guests with these cakes and serve them in place of *sakana* with cold wine. According to their own ancient custom, wine is served cold from this day until the ninth day of the ninth month, although this is no longer

---

[1] There is a blank in the manuscript at this point, and I have added 'festivals', although *gosekku* literally means 'five seasonal offerings'. *Vocabulario*, f. 122: '*Gosekku*. Five times when there is an obligation of paying a visit and respects to the lord of the territory in five months of the year, i.e., at the beginning of the year in the first month, the third day of the third month, the fifth day of the fifth month, the seventh day of the seventh month, and the ninth month.' A similar explanation is given in *Arte grande*, f. 229v. See *KEJ*, VII, p. 5, and p. 190, n. 1, above, for other references.

[2] This explanation is mistaken for there are certainly five festivals, and in the following list Rodrigues (or the copyist) omits Tanabata, a Chinese festival first celebrated in Japan in the eighth century and observed on the seventh day of the seventh month. This festival is correctly listed in *Arte grande*, f. 229v, and *Vocabulario*, f. 122.

[3] This festival, originally called Jōshi no sekku and held on the third day of the third month, is now known as Hina-matsuri, or Dolls Festival (3 March), when sets of traditional dolls are displayed in homes. Hence the festival is also called Girls Festival, although the dolls originally used were merely made of paper, charged with the sins of its owner, and then thrown away into a river, along with the sins, according to Shinto belief. Further details in Casal, *Five Sacred Festivals*, pp. 36–60; *KEJ*, II, pp. 127–8.

[4] The day is also known as the Peach Festival, for the peach trees were in bloom at that time when the lunar calendar was in use.

observed. They cut up very fine a few peach blossoms and throw them on top of this cold wine. This has its origin in the story of one of their ancient hermits who lived on the dew that formed on peach blossoms, as if this were a most nourishing thing.[1] There are far fewer visits paid among the nobles on this day than among the common and ordinary people, and among relatives and friends.

The third festival takes place on the first day of the fourth moon, on which day nothing festive is done except to put on lined robes, called *awase*, in the place of garments padded with silk or cotton floss, worn from the ninth day of the ninth moon until this day.[2] Their custom is to celebrate this changing of garments with wine, but they do not pay visits.

The fourth festival is the fifth day of the fifth month, on which day they cook rice, wrapped up in the leaves of certain plants or the leaves of Kan, in the steam of hot water.[3] This is eaten to celebrate the festival, and they send it out as a gift, still wrapped in the leaves in which it was cooked. They entertain their guests with this rice and fill a tray with the bundles. A page takes it around the guests, each of whom takes only one with his right hand and raises it above his head if the person carrying them around is of noble birth. They unwrap them and begin to eat them at the narrowest end, and then the wine circulates around all the guests with due ceremony. This festival was also instituted in memory of a great sage, a confidant of an ancient king of China, who threw himself into the sea for a certain reason on the fifth day of this fifth month.[4] Others, however, attribute this festival to a certain noble damsel, the daughter of a king, who threw herself into the sea.[5] On this day in both China and Japan there is a great rowing race with the boats side by side, and there are various amusements in the sea.[6] The Japanese also pay visits to one another on this day,

---

[1] Possibly a reference to the mysterious Western Queen, who dwells in the Kunlun mountains. In her palace garden grow peach trees that bloom every 3,000 years; it then takes a further 3,000 years for the fruit to ripen. Those fortunate enough to taste this fruit will enjoy immortality. Werner, *Dictionary*, pp. 163–4; Giles, *Biographical Dictionary*, p. 272.

[2] Hence this day is called *Ikō*, 'garment change'.

[3] This festival, formerly known as Tango no sekku and held on the fifth day of the fifth month, is now generally called Kodomo no hi, 'Children's Day' (5 May). Tiers of dolls depicting military figures are displayed in homes and carp kites are flown. A speciality of the day is *kawashi-mochi*, or rice dumplings wrapped in oak leaves, or *chimaki*, steamed rice wrapped in bamboo leaves. The copyist left a blank after the word 'Kan' in the text; possibly *kashiwa*, or oak, is intended; the 'certain plants' may refer to the iris. *Vocabulario*, f. 48: '*Chimaki*. Cooked rice wrapped in bamboo leaves, or leaves of other plants, etc.' Ribadeneira (*Historia*, pp. 372–3) has left a detailed description of the festival, in which young boys dressed up as warriors and wore paper armour. Further information on this festival is found in Casal, *Five Sacred Festivals*, pp. 61–78.

[4] A reference to Quyuan, also known as Quping (332–295 BC), the chief minister of Prince Huai of Chu. The prince ignored his advice not to wage war against the Qin state and was captured in an ambush. His son and successor, Prince Xiang, showed his disfavour towards Quyuan, who threw himself into the Milo River on the fifth day of the fifth moon. Giles, *Biographical Dictionary*, pp. 200–201.

[5] This reference is too vague to identify with any certainty.

[6] In China the Dragon Boat Festival is held on this day to commemorate the search for the body of Quyuan (see n. 4, above). For details and illustrations, see Mackenzie, *Myths*, pp. 40, 268–9; Gray, *China*, I, pp. 258–60. In Japan the festival is called Peiron, and is held in mid-June at Nagasaki, when boats rowed by 30–40 men to the beat of a drum, compete in racing. Paske-Smith, *Western Barbarians*, pp. 298–300; *KEJ*, VI, p. 171. Cocks (28 May 1617, in *Diary*, I, pp. 256–7) gives an eyewitness account of the race, in which the rowers kept in time 'with stroke of drum and bras bason', and offers two explanations of the festival's origin. Kaempfer (*History*, III, p. 236) attempts to explain the meaning of the name Peiron.

and they change their dress and wear unlined garments from this day until the last day of the eighth moon, which is also a festival.[1]

The fifth festival falls on the first day of the sixth moon, when in the morning they are wont to eat rice cakes baked like biscuits and mixed with garlic and raw beans; they eat only a very little of this and drink water on top of it. This is a ceremony that everyone performs in his house and not in the presence of guests, nor are visits paid on this day on account of the festival.

The sixth festival falls on the fourteenth and fifteenth days of the seventh moon when they celebrate the feast of their dead, for the ignorant people believe that the departed have permission on these days to return to this life. Afterwards they give this food to the poor. They kindle many fires in the woods and on the roads, and in cities such as Miyako all the streets are lit with lanterns of fine workmanship and decoration, with which (they say) to light the route of the departed souls.[2] This error was common throughout all the pagan part of the world. On this day they cook a kind of rice, called *pulau* in India, in the steam of hot water, and they put it on green lotus leaves, the symbol of man's soul and heart in the sect of the idols.[3] They offer this to the departed souls, and they also eat it with their hands without chopsticks, because it is hard and made like a ball. They add a certain kind of salted fish to it.[4] It is customary on these days to visit relatives and hold banquets for them.

The seventh festival falls on the ninth day of the ninth month, when they start wearing padded garments, and from then on they drink warm wine in keeping with the ancient custom of Japan. On this day they cut up some white daisies and drop them into the wine flasks. They strew these daisies first of all on the *sakana* tray and then on top of them they place the *sakana* that is served to the guests.[5]

The eighth[6] festival takes place on the first day of the tenth moon, when they begin to wear robes.[7] They make two kinds of cakes, one of rice and the other of beans, and they entertain their guests with them.

[1] Rodrigues has already mentioned the dates for changing clothes on p. 188, above.

[2] This is the famous Bon festival, inaugurated in Japan by Empress Suiko in 606 and still celebrated today in midsummer. *KEJ*, I, p. 160. *Vocabulario*, f. 24v: 'Bon. Pagan festival of the dead, celebrated on the 14th or 15th of the seventh moon, when they light candles at dusk for three days.' Mention of the festival is also made in *Arte grande*, f. 229v. Vilela (17 August 1561, in *TCJ*, pp. 359–60) describes the festival in some detail, while Cocks (27 August 1615, in *Diary*, I, p. 46) notes, 'This day at night all the streetes were hanged with lantarnes, and all the pagons vizeted all their *futtaquis* [*hotoke*] and places of buriall with lantarns and lampes, inviting their dead frendes to com and eate with them. …' Fróis (*História*, III, pp. 261–2) recounts how Nobunaga lit up Azuchi Castle with coloured lanterns in 1581 to celebrate the festival. Further references are given in Avila Girón, *Relación*, p. 264, and Ribadeneira, *Historia*, p. 373.

[3] *Pulau*, or *pilau*, is a meat and rice dish of India and Persia. Dalgado, *Glossário*, II, p. 210. Two special dishes of this festival are *okuri-dango* (farewell riceballs), which are cooked for the dead, and *hasumeshi* (lotus rice). The lotus is used as a symbol in Buddhism, for although its roots grow in mud, its flowers are always pure and clean.

[4] Another Bon speciality is *sashi-saba*, salted mackerel strung on bamboo canes. Visser, *Ancient Buddhism*, I, p. 91. For Bon in general, ibid., I, pp. 88–91.

[5] The festival, known as Chōyō-no-sekku, or more popularly Kiku-no-sekku, the Chrysanthemum Festival, was held on the ninth day of the ninth month. In former times the chrysanthemum was often called daisy in English. Writing in Edo on 17 October 1618, Cocks (*Diary*, II, p. 85) records: 'This day was the great feast of Shecco [*sekku*], all the Japon kinges (or *tono*) viseting themperour [the shogun] with presentes. Soe we could doe nothing at Cort.' Details about the festival in Casal, *Five Sacred Festivals*, pp. 95–105.

[6] The text erroneously reads 'fourth' here.

[7] The text seems to be in error here, for Rodrigues has already correctly noted (p. 188) that padded robes are worn from the ninth day of the ninth month.

The ninth and last festival occurs on the twenty-ninth or thirtieth day of the twelfth moon, the last day of the year. It is the general custom at this time to go visiting and to offer congratulations for the past year. This festival is called *Seibo*, meaning 'the end of the year'.[1]

---

[1] *Vocabulario*, f. 293v: '*Seibo*. Last day of the year.' Cocks (11 February 1621, in *Diary*, II, p. 139) notes at the end of the Japanese year, 'Divers neighbors sent wyne and fish for presentes.'

CHAPTER 20

OTHER OCCASIONS ON WHICH THEY ARE ACCUSTOMED TO VISITING CERTAIN PERSONS

In addition to the general visits mentioned above, when everyone visits everyone else at the same time, there are also other special visits paid on certain occasions, and we will list some of the principal ones.

One of them takes place when congratulations are offered for some success or happy event; another is when sympathy is offered for a sad and unfortunate happening.[1] For it is a very common custom among the Japanese, Chinese, and Koreans to offer congratulations for happy events and sympathy on sad occasions. Such visitors always or usually take along a gift. But this is not necessary nor is it given when sympathy is offered for a sad event, except in the case of the death of parents or children, and this is also very common in China. The gift goes to help the banquet given to the bonzes who come to conduct the obsequies to Amida, and it may consist of casks of wine and things to eat. In China they also give money for the entertainment of the guests who come to offer their sympathy, and also for the perfume and lamps placed around the corpse, which is placed inside a coffin of precious and incorruptible wood. In China each guest bows towards the corpse in the coffin and performs a certain kind of adoration. He casts perfume into the incense burner there as if he were to incense the body, and wails there in front of the corpse in a falsetto voice. As a token of his sorrow, the guest brings something signifying mourning, such as a cap of unbleached linen, because the colour of mourning in China, Japan, and Korea is white.[2]

But let us first begin with the happy events. When a noble gets married, a person under some obligation to him pays a visit one or two days before the wedding. It is usual to send some suitable gift, such as a roll of silk or other material, to the woman, and the same to the husband. Or it may be enough to send some casks of wine with some things to eat; a male and female bird are also sent.[3] If a bonze is invited to the banquet, he attends without any obligation of bringing anything, except that three days later he will visit the couple.

---

[1] When Cocks visited the *daimyo* of Hirado on 3 October 1613 to offer sympathy for the destruction of his mansion by fire on the previous day, the noble assured him in typically Japanese fashion that 'the losse he had sustained was nothing'. Farrington, *English Factory*, II, p. 1519. Valignano (*Historia*, p. 150) confirms that the Japanese do not burden others with their troubles.

[2] A detailed description of Chinese funeral rites is given in Ricci, *Fonti*, I, pp. 83–5, and *China*, pp. 72–3; see also Mendoza, *History*, I, pp. 59–60; Cruz, in Boxer, *South China*, pp. 146–7. More modern accounts are found in Groot, *Religious System*, I–III; Gray, *China*, I, pp. 284–93. For references to white as the colour of mourning, see p. 181, n. 3. In a letter (Macao, 22 January 1616, in Rodrigues, 'Rodrigues in China', pp. 308–7), Rodrigues expresses deep misgivings about the Jesuits in China using incense and perfume at funerals, a 'superstitious ceremony', as he calls it. He says that he has written treatises on the subject, but these are no longer extant

[3] There is a gap in the text after 'a male and female', but Rodrigues seems to be referring to a bird.

When the wife of an acquaintance gives birth to a child, congratulations are sent to the parents, and casks of wine and food are brought as gifts. A person of standing is sent to visit the father also, and if he is not at home, the person takes a letter. In the same way, when a lord or noble person adopts somebody (for this is as highly esteemed as if a son had been born again to him), they pay a personal visit or, if he is absent, they send a man with a letter. If the person who has adopted somebody is very noble, they are also wont to congratulate the true father of the adopted son. The latter then drops his surname or family name, and assumes the name of his adoptive father.

Young children up to five or six years of age wear two ribbons sewn on to the front hem of their robe on either side, and they tie them at the back with a bow in place of a sash. When the child reaches this age and is no longer an infant, they ask a person to act as a sort of godfather. He sends the child a silk sash, with which a man is accustomed to gird himself, in keeping with his rank. Subsequently the father goes to visit him, accompanied by the child wearing this sash already girded about him with the bow in front, as is the custom to wear it. The godfather also goes to visit them in their house. Sometimes they also ask the godfather to untie with his own hands the babyish ribbons. He unties them, and then girds the boy with the sash he sent him and ties the bow in front.[1]

Childhood lasts until the age of thirteen or fifteen years when adolescence begins. When they reach this age, they have the custom of changing their childish name and adopting a man's name.[2] They gird themselves with a sword and dagger, and cut the hair of their head a little and make it somewhat shorter, for until this time they have worn their hair long like a woman. When the eldest son of a noble changes his name, it is customary to visit and congratulate him; if he is away, they send around a man with a letter. When a person changes his name, he has a sponsor who gives him the name that he wishes to take. If he leaves the choice to the sponsor, he writes down three names on a paper, and the godson then chooses from them the one he most likes, and the sponsor gives his approval. Or else the godson produces a name that he wants or is common to his family, and the sponsor confirms it as if he himself had given it to him, and he calls him by this name. As a sign of rejoicing, he entertains him with wine and food, and gives his godson something as a gift, or he sends somebody to his house with casks of wine and food.

In the same way, when a lord or his son receive some honourable rank or title of an office in the royal household, it is customary to pay him a visit; if he is away, then this is done by a man bearing a letter. Those who shave their head and leave all public business behind them take the name of a bonze, and choose as their sponsor a person who cuts a lock of their hair with a pair of scissors or only places the cutting edge of the scissors upon their hair. They then have it shaven, and wine is given to drink.[3]

---

[1] This ceremony was called *obi-toki*.

[2] *Vocabulario*, f. 116: 'Genbuku. To give a man's name to children and to gird them with a *katana* for the first time.' Rodrigues speaks at length (in *Arte grande*, f. 207) about boys' names, and lists the ten types of name that nobles bore in succession from infancy to after death. Ricci (*Fonti*, I, pp. 90–91, and *China*, pp. 78–9) describes the various names used in China. References to the age at which Japanese boys began wearing a sword are given on p. 103, n. 4.

[3] In *Arte grande*, ff. 211v–212, Rodrigues explains in detail that men who retire and shave their heads adopt a monastic name, or *hōmyō*, consisting of two syllables, e.g., Toin, Sōrin, Sōka, etc. In addition, some also adopt another name called a *saimin*.

The ceremonial and public cutting of hair is still practised today by sumo wrestlers on their retirement in a public rite called *danpatsu-shiki*.

When a noble receives an increase in revenue or when some notable event occurs, it is customary for people under obligation to him to pay a visit. Also when a noble has the lord of the same territory or a great noble as his guest, at his departure best wishes are sent, along with thanks for the trouble taken in entertaining him. Similarly when a noble finishes building some large house or any other building, a man is sent to visit him. And when the lord of the land builds a castle in some place, the same is done when the work is about halfway finished.[1] When there has been exceptionally heavy rain, much snow, a great wind storm, or thunder, etc., it is the custom to pay a visit to nobles once the storm is over. They send him a message saying how happy we are that everything has ended safely.[2]

It is also a general custom the day before a noble or even an equal leaves on a long journey to visit him at his home with a present (which they call *hanamuke*);[3] if he is not at home, they do this through a messenger and a letter. On the very day when he returns, we send a man to welcome him, and on the following day we go personally to welcome him back.[4] Similarly when a man goes off to war, they visit him with a gift. While he is away, they send their greetings to him through a messenger from time to time,[5] or congratulate him when he performs some outstanding exploit or defeats his enemies. If his wife is in the region, they go to pay her a visit, congratulating her as well on his glory. When somebody performs *inkyo* and hands over his house to his eldest son, it is customary to pay a visit to the father without a gift and to the son with a gift, congratulating him on his acquisition of the house and estate.

When a person of quality falls sick, it is customary to pay him a visit,[6] although it is not usual for the visitors to see him because he will be in the interior of the house where his women live and where there are household things that they do not wish to be seen. An exception is made for a relative or an old and close friend. Instead, a man is appointed to receive the visits. If the illness was serious, the patient is again visited after his recovery and congratulated. The man who was ill then returns these visits and thanks them for the affection they showed him during his illness. When people learn that an absent person is ill, they send a man to visit him with a letter. When an important person dies, it is the custom to offer condolences personally to the wife, husband, or son if they are in the same region. If we wish to express more sympathy, a message is sent four or five days later to console them and urge them to be resigned. If the bereaved are absent, a messenger is sent with a consoling letter of a certain kind and form, accompanied by other ceremonies.[7]

---

[1] Thus Rodrigues Giram notes from Nagasaki (14 March 1609, in JapSin 56, f. 1v) that on completing his new castle at Suruga, Ieyasu was visited by nobles bearing gifts and congratulations. The castle/palace was burnt down shortly afterwards.

[2] The change to the first-person plural here and in the following passage is found in the Portuguese text. This may indicate that the Macao copyist has incorporated marginal notes written by Martinho Hara – see p. 67, n. 2.

[3] *Vocabulario*, f. 78v: '*Hanamuke*. Gift given to a person going on a long journey.' The term is derived from the old custom of friends going to see a traveller off and turning his horse's head in the direction of his destination; thus, *uma no hanamuke*, 'turning the horse's nose'.

[4] Again, the use of the first-person plural here may indicate the inclusion of a marginal note written by Martinho Hara.

[5] This is called *jinchū-mimai*, an inquiry about a man away at war.

[6] A visit to inquire about a sick person is called *byōki-mimai*.

[7] A letter of condolence is called a *kuyami-jō*.

CHAPTER 21

THE GIFTS THAT ARE GIVEN, AND THE MANNER IN WHICH THEY ARE OFFERED AND RECEIVED

Now that we have spoken of their visits, which are usually accompanied by gifts, we will here deal with gifts in general and their way of giving and receiving them. After that we will speak of the manner of entertaining a guest, the courtesies they observe among themselves, and other things concerning this matter. But it has already been noted that the Japanese usually follow the ancient Chinese rites, ceremonies, and customs, and in everything concerning visits and gifts they imitate these after their own fashion. It will therefore be best to speak briefly in the first place about the manner observed by the Chinese in these matters so that the reader may better understand the Japanese way.

1. The Chinese manner of giving presents
Ever since ancient times it has been a very common and ordinary custom in the kingdom of China for the people to pay visits on one another and take gifts along with them. These visits are made personally at certain times of the year and also on various occasions, so much so that they seem to follow completely that precept, 'Thou shalt not appear empty-handed, etc.,'[1] for the visits are usually accompanied by a gift as a token of love, friendship, and benevolence. The visits are paid at the festivals throughout the year, at other times to mark a happy event, or on a wedding, or on account of some business that a person is negotiating with somebody so that he may win his goodwill and thus be favoured in the matter. There are various other obligations and occasions when subjects offer gifts to superiors, students to their teachers, etc.

The Chinese have two kinds of presents. Some, such as various articles and other costly things, are purely complimentary and for display, and as a token of reverence and friendship. But these gifts are not accepted because the nature of the gift shows that it is purely complimentary. Hence there are merchants' shops that hire out such things for this purpose, and people pay so much for a certain article and later return it. But there are other gifts that are tokens of true love and friendship from the heart, and these, or at least part of them, are usually accepted, as will be said later. By the nature of the gift they can tell whether it is purely complimentary and not to be accepted, or whether it genuinely comes from the heart and so may be received.

As regards the way of decorating these gifts that are to be presented (for their entire significance lies in their outward appearance), costly things are always wrapped in white paper

---

[1] The quotation, given in Latin, is taken from Deuteronomy 16, 16; Exodus, 23, 15 and 34, 20; and Wisdom 35, 6, all of which similar texts can be translated as 'Thou shalt not appear empty-handed.'

and then fastened along their length and breadth by a strip of red paper, either with or without an inscription; this is a form of decoration and courtesy. All these gifts, and all the others, even those merely of food, are presented on trays or small tables suited for this purpose, and these are used like salvers. Whether these gifts are presented personally or vicariously, they are accompanied by a visiting card, at the end of which is written the name of the person paying the visit and sending the gift, along with some humble and reverent phrase called *pai* or *paizhuang* (in Japanese, *hai* or *haijō*), meaning adoration or reverence. The rest of the card is left blank. According to their greater or less respect, these visiting cards are of three types. One of them is folded into six, each fold being a hand's width or more in breadth, and a span and a hand's width in length. This is because their way of writing runs from top to bottom and from the right-hand side to the left. This is called *taitiezi*, that is, 'big letter'. Another card consists of two folds and is the medium type. The third consists of only one fold and is the inferior type. Along with any of these cards is always included separately a paper on which is written a list of the things sent as gifts.[1]

It is the usual custom in China for a person not to accept a gift that is sent if he does not wish to do so, and this is mostly done when the present is purely complimentary. In this case, nothing of the gift, or only a small part of it, is taken. The usual custom is to take from the present some small thing that one likes; this is done as a sign of friendship and so as not to have to repay the gift with another of equal value, as is the custom.

The Chinese give their gifts in the following manner. When the man paying the visit goes personally, he presents the visiting card, and after paying his compliments in the guestroom and performing his bows and courtesies after their fashion (as will be described later), he gives the inventory of his gift to the host. He scans this list and then says, 'I cannot bring myself to accept such a great gift. I will take only this and this from it.' With that, he declines the rest, although the donor may insist. Sometimes on the guest's insistence, he may accept everything when the two are close friends. But when the visit is paid merely by a letter brought by one of his men, he writes a courtesy letter saying that he has taken such-and-such a thing and that he is returning the rest, because he dare not take everything as it was such a great gift. But when the present is given by a friend and comes from the heart, and consists of ordinary things to eat, such as fruit, etc., he will accept it all just as it is sent to him, for it would be rude not to take it. When a person declines to accept a present and also the visiting card, this is a sign of enmity and that he wishes to have nothing to do with the donor.

It is also the general custom for a person to repay the visit in the same way as he himself was visited and also repay the gift with another equal in value to the one sent him, along with the same type of card that he himself received. Thus the Chinese evaluate the things that are given, and if they consist of things from another region whose value is unknown, then they will make inquiries about their worth so that they can make exact repayment. In fact there is nothing admirable about this, as it is merely a form of trading and not of love and affection. This repaying of the gift is observed when the donor is not subject to the recipient nor under any particular obligation to him, for in this case there is no obligation to repay with another gift. Even if there are no such obligations, the gifts that are sent at weddings, as congratulations for some happy event, for promotion to some office or literary degree, or from an inferior to a superior, from students to their teachers, and those sent

---

[1] Ricci (*Fonti*, I, p. 73, and *China*, pp. 61–2) describes these cards in detail and confirms Rodrigues's account.

when a father or mother dies, etc., are not repaid by another gift, but by some general entertainment provided for those who pay a visit.

It is also a general custom always to give a little silver or some copper coins to the servant who brings the present. The money is carefully wrapped in paper and fastened on top with a strip of red paper, with a label saying how much is given. For whether he went with his master or whether he went alone, the man who carried the present would take it ill if he were to return empty-handed. When he goes by himself, he later shows his master how much he received, so that he may know how much honour they paid to his servant out of respect towards himself, and so he can pay the same amount to the other man's servant when he comes to his house. When they send presents and visit another outside their region, it is not customary to decline the gifts. Instead they accept them and send the return gift by the same servant who brought them.

This, then, is in brief the general Chinese manner, and it is substantially the same as the ancient usage that holds in Japan, except for some points they have adapted to their country as we will soon see, as well as other things that have been changed and reformed since the time of Nobunaga and Taikō.

2. The manner in which the Japanese give presents

To some extent it is an even more common custom to take a gift along when paying a visit in Japan than in China, so we will now speak about Japanese gifts in general. As a gift is a token of love and friendship, it is not a restricted thing that must necessarily be sent, nor is it something that must accompany another thing without fail so that when a person sends this thing he must always send that. An exception is made when he sends wine, for this must always be accompanied by something to eat, called *sakana*, because when wine is drunk, it is accompanied by food that whets a person's thirst. Or instead of *sakana*, if there is none available, ancient custom dictates that they send as a courtesy certain shellfish, wrapped in paper, or dry squid, bonito fish, or something of the sort, along with the wine. But at the present time wine is also sent without *sakana*, especially if it is a highly prized wine, although there is nothing determined or fixed concerning the quality of the things sent as gifts.

There is nothing in common use that may not be sent as a gift, and this applies to food as well as to everything else, such as cloth, silk robes, sashes, fans, costly dishes, silver, etc. On festivals and days of rejoicing, however, it is usual to send wine and *sakana* as a festive gift, although other presents may also be sent. As regards the wine presented as a gift, Ours who wrote in former times did not explain the matter at all well. They said in their letters that a person would bring as a present so many hogsheads of wine, when they should have said barrels or small casks of wine. Each one of these holds three or four *canadas* of wine, and the larger ones contain an *almude*.[1]

Up to the time of Nobunaga and Taikō, while Japan suffered from extreme poverty and wretchedness on account of wars and uprisings, all this giving of gifts was done merely as a compliment with things of little value and sometimes even dissemblingly. For in place of a roll of silk, they used to give a piece less than an ell in length, rolled up and stuffed with paper and decorated on the outside. It had the appearance of a large roll, although the small

---

[1] The *canada* and *almude* are Portuguese liquid measures, containing about 1.4 and 20 litres respectively. Both units varied considerably in former times.

piece was very coarse and bad. Instead of offering fans on festival days, the ordinary people would give sham ones that were of no use whatsoever except as a compliment. So on account of poverty, gifts were of little or no value. Usually the gifts were of tankards of wine, or very small barrels or casks,[1] or of food obtained from the land or hunting, or fish from the rivers and sea.

But since the time of Nobunaga the kingdom has enjoyed peace, the lords and city dwellers have become wealthy, and commerce has increased. It is impossible to describe the lengths to which this practice of giving costly presents has gone among the nobles. They give each other gold, silver, rich lengths of silk of various kinds, weapons, and silk robes. Many of these things are given at one time, and many other costly things pass between aristocratic people and, according to their means, ordinary folk. It is a general custom of the country for bonzes to give gifts to the lords, and if this usual obligation had not been waived, it would have been a great burden on religious and preachers of the Gospel who had houses in the territory of the lords, especially the pagan ones, for among their vassals there were Christians whom they tended and others whom they converted.[2] The same happens in China.

There is no determined and fixed number of things to be sent as gifts, but when giving some things that are similar, they send a pair, such as two lengths of silk, two barrels of wine, two fishes, two birds male and female, etc. But when large presents contain more than two things of the same kind, such as lengths of silk, etc., then an odd number (one, three, five, seven, nine) is highly considered among them for certain astrological reasons that will be explained elsewhere. Even numbers, except for a pair, are not used, especially the number four because it signifies death and is regarded as a portent.[3]

3. The manner of preparing and presenting the gifts

The Japanese as well as the Chinese pay much attention to the exterior decoration of their gifts[4] and the way of presenting them, and they observe several considerations concerning this, the most important of which are three in number. These are the way the gift is wrapped; the salver or tray on which it is offered; and finally the place in the room where it is received and put. This is in order to show greater honour to the donor in keeping with the quality of the gift. They exercise a great deal of care and exterior hypocrisy in this

---

[1] There is a short gap in the text at this point, followed by the word *ostentação*; possibly the text should read '… out of ostentation'. Avila Girón (*Relación*, p. 48) writes that a visitor might bring two flasks of wine, containing about three pints, some fruit, or perhaps *mochi* (rice-balls), as a gift. He adds that it would be impolite to decline such a present.

[2] Fróis (10 August 1577, in *Cartas*, I, ff. 397–7v) wrote to Valignano before the Visitor's arrival in Japan, suggesting a long list of suitable gifts that he might bring to Japan. He points out that such gifts were essential. 'If you go to speak with a lord thirty times in one year, then you must take a gift on all thirty occasions.' Although, as Rodrigues notes, missionaries may have been officially exempt from giving presents to territorial lords, Valignano (*Sumario*, p. 310) laments the high cost of such gifts, but he observes that no business can be conducted without them. He lays down (*Cerimoniale*, pp. 256–68) detailed instructions, stipulating how, when, where, what and to whom gifts should and should not be given. Further references to such gifts are given in Valignano, *Sumario*, pp. 518–24, 660–61. Avila Girón (*Relación*, p. 35) also notes the necessity of gifts: 'They certainly confirm the saying, "Gifts take away sorrow."' It was not possible, he says, to visit an important man without a present, and it had to be shown first before business could begin. See also Boxer, *Christian Century*, pp. 113–14.

[3] For avoidance of the word *shi*, see p. 192, n. 2.

[4] The care with which gifts are wrapped and the different forms of wrapping are still meticulously observed today.

matter, as we noted about their customs and courtesies, and on no account are gifts usually offered without this display.

As regards the first point, it is the general custom to wrap the things to be presented in a certain sort of good folded paper if they are of value, such as gold, silver, eaglewood, aloes, various perfumes, lengths of silk, fans, sashes, and many other things of various kinds. All of this is so necessary that according to authentic Japanese custom it is considered rude and mean to offer such things without wrapping and adorning them with their paper as is befitting. There are various graceful ways and manners of folding this paper, and they learn this art and its rules from their books of etiquette. The paper is folded in accordance with the things offered as gifts, for this wrapping paper with which the gifts are decorated is folded in a certain way. For example, the paper in which is presented perfume is folded in its own particular way, and so on for all the other things. This folded paper in which the gift comes is fastened on the outside with coloured paper string tied with pretty bows. They do not wrap things to eat with this paper, but there are some things that are finely sprinkled on top with gold and silver as decoration out of respect for the recipient. This happens especially in banquets either in the house or out in the open, when a person sends along with the gift a salver made of cedarwood, on which is placed a gilt or silver-plated clay cup so that they may drink from it at the end of the banquet. This salver is very large and is like a small light tray. It is made according to a certain form and fashion, and imitates some natural thing, such as a stony or sandy inlet of a river or sea, or a wood or a cliff, in the middle.[1] It is prettily decorated with artificial flowers of silk or other material that are very like natural ones. This nation has a particular skill in making such things with silk, paper, or precious wood cut as finely as the thinnest paper, and they are wonderful to behold.

As regards the second point, it is a general custom in China and Japan, as we have already noted, not to offer these gifts with the hand for this would be discourteous; instead, all gifts are presented upon trays. In China these are lacquered, but in Japan they are made for the purpose by craftsmen who earn their living thereby and always have some ready-made in their shops because they are used a great deal. Otherwise they can be made very quickly if they are of a certain shape, as these craftsmen are most skilled at this and the trays are very cheap. The trays remain with their presents and are not returned to their donor, and they are used only that one time. This is certainly something most cultured, courteous, and worthy of praise after their fashion. Sometimes when gifts are offered on varnished trays of very fine wood of which there are not so many examples, the trays are given back to the person who brought them. When somebody goes or sends a present outside his region, he takes with him the above-mentioned wooden trays if there is none to be obtained in that place, as sometimes indeed happens. Wine that is offered in barrels or small wooden caskets (these have their staves running from top to bottom; one of its ends or lids is at the bottom, while the bung is in the other end at the top) is not placed on these trays, but is presented without them and tied with special string in a certain way.

The third point concerns the place in the guests' reception room where these things are presented. Now there are two sorts of gifts. One kind is of precious things such as gold, silver, lengths of silk, robes, etc., and these are placed on their long-legged trays in the middle at the top of the room. Other gifts consisting of raw food are placed on the veranda

---

[1] These exquisite stands are *suhamadai*; Rodrigues later describes them in greater detail on pp. 241, 250.

at the entrance of the room; such gifts may be of game, salted birds, deer, boars, big game, and other large things, and things that drip and smell.

The interior of all these rooms is neatly carpeted or matted, and it is on this that the people sit. There is an order in which to present the things that are offered, for they have rules even about this. The precious things occupy the first place in the room, while the things connected with the elements are placed in the following order. In the first place, the things of the air, such as birds; in the second, mountain game; in the third, fish; and finally barrels of wine at the end. When this is offered along with other things, it is put in the position of the fish, after the mountain game; if somebody brings fish and vegetables, the fish is put in the first place.

4. The manner of offering and receiving a gift

When someone pays a visit personally or sends a person with a present, the way of offering the gift is not to give it immediately to the host. But when a person takes a present and pays a noble a visit, he first of all informs the porter of his arrival through one of his servants or the servant who carries the gift. This official is charged with receiving guests before they meet the host and with taking messages and delivering them to his master. The gift is handed to the master together with its list of content. This list is usually made when the things that have been brought are of five or more kinds, and on the list are written the things and the name of the person who sent them.

The folded paper on which this list is written is of a certain kind and shape in keeping with the genuine custom. But this is also done even when the contents are not varied, when they send a horse together with a sword, or a sword and, instead of a horse, several thousand copper coins strung through the middle as its equivalent price; then without fail a list is sent of the horse and the sword, or of the sword and the copper coins.[1] The servant who brings the present hands the list and gift to the above-mentioned porter who takes in messages. He in turn shows only the list to his master, and tells him what the guest has brought so that at his convenience he may thank him for the gifts thus received in keeping with their value. They are put beforehand in their place within the room or at the entrance on the veranda before the guest enters.

After this, the host receives the guest, obliging him to enter the room as will be later described. Even though the gifts are actually present there, the host must not look at them as he passes by, but pretending not to see them, he continues exchanging compliments with the guest until they both enter and are seated in their places. Otherwise he would appear to esteem the gift more than the visitor who brought it. Then after the host and the guest have paid their courtesies and compliments, the man who receives messages and gifts in the front hall shows the present to his master, saying in the presence of the guest; 'Mr So-and-So brought these things as a gift for Your Honour,' mentioning the donor's name. At this the host pays his respects and bowing to the guest thanks him. Then the messenger carries the gift inside. He does the same for each present if the guests are numerous, and mentions each donor by name when he shows the present, so that the host may bow and offer

---

[1] In *Arte grande*, ff. 205–6v, Rodrigues mentions these lists, which were called, depending on the circumstances, *mokuroku*, *origami*, or *chūmon*. When a sword and horse are sent along with the copper coins, the list is called *tachi-mokuroku*. If a horse is sent, its colouring and markings are given in the list; as a sign of respect towards a noble recipient, the honorific prefix *on-* should be used: *on-uma*, honourable horse; *on-tachi*, honourable sword. Rodrigues provides several specimen lists. For the copper coins, see p. 105, n. 1.

his thanks. They take great care about this, because guests are deeply upset when they sometimes bring things of great value and the host does not know which of them presented such a gift. In order to show greater honour to a guest who is a lord or noble, his gift is left at the top of the room until he leaves.

When the present is merely delivered by a messenger, he hands the list and the gift, and also the letter if there is one, to the said porter, who shows his master the inventory of the gift. Afterwards the master sees the messenger and the gift he has brought, and on the back of the same list he certifies that he has received everything included in the list. At the end he writes the era, month, and day, and finally he signs it. He then returns the paper to the messenger so that he can prove his honesty, and gives him a written or verbal reply to the letter, if he brought one. If a gift with its list arrives for the master of the house when he is away and the messenger has left by the time he returns home, he is obliged to write a letter of thanks to the person who sent the gift without saying anything particular in it. He also writes on the back of the list that he has received everything (as has been said above), and sends the letter with this list.

When messengers come from afar to pay a visit on behalf of some lord, especially if they bring a gift with them, it is customary to give them something to repay them for the pains of the long journey. There is no longer any obligation to give anything to the other messengers, although according to ancient custom (which still holds in China) this was given for the sake of their master, in addition to the entertainment provided.[1] The servant must tell his master what was given him so that he may know the esteem in which he is held and that he may likewise treat the servants of the man to whom he sent the gift. Also when congratulations are conveyed to a noble on his wedding or on his increasing his revenues, etc., something is given to the man who bears the message, and the same happens when congratulations are sent on a joyful event. Also, when a gentleman sends to another a gift of a horse with a lad, the bridle is always given back to the groom who brought the horse, together with a thousand cash or copper coins, worth two crowns, and they call this the bridle money.[2] If the horse comes without a harness,[3] as sometimes happens, then nothing is sent back, but only a thousand cash is given to the man who brought it by the reins, for such a man is not a messenger but a squire.

5. The manner of offering some particular things

There are some special things that have their own particular way of being presented, and a different way of giving them into the hands of others and of receiving and accepting them. A special elegance and conformity to natural reason are to be found in this matter.

When the flowers of plants are to be offered, the Japanese usually singe the end of the stalks with fire so that the moisture may not seep away; they wrap and tie the ends with folded paper of a certain kind. But they do not do this to the stalks of tree blossom. But when they carry both kinds along the road, the bottom of the bouquet is carried upwards with the flowers hanging down so that the movement of the air may not break the long stems of the flowers. But when the flowers are shown or offered, they are held with the bottom of the bouquet below and the flowers on top. The flowers are given and received

---

[1] The text appears to have some words missing in this sentence, but the general meaning remains clear.
[2] *Dachin* means the fee for hiring a packhorse, and also, by extension, a tip or gift.
[3] The text reads, 'If the horse comes *with* a harness', but the context seems to require a negative.

with the right hand supported by the left out of politeness. Both the Japanese and Chinese highly esteem various kinds of flowers and roses,[1] and various elegant poems have been written about them. Vegetables are presented on their trays with their leaves pointing towards the recipient and the roots towards the donor. Melons are offered with the head towards the recipient and the foot towards the donor.

Small birds, such as thrushes, quails, etc., are not presented on trays but are strung by their wings on a stick split from top to bottom, with their necks hanging down one after another. Large birds, such as duck, wild fowl, etc., are presented lying on their backs on trays with their breasts uppermost, their wings open, their legs drawn and extended, and their necks turned or twisted to the left. When these are offered, their heads are always pointing to the recipient or the top of the room.[2]

As regards wild game, an entire deer or boar that has been sent is not placed on the veranda, but those who bring it on a pole[3] wait with it outside in the courtyard in front of the veranda and room, and the master of the house views it from there. But if they bring a quarter, it comes on its tray, and when it is offered, the hoof points towards the person who presents or delivers it. When many hares or similar animals are offered, they come on a tray; some are placed on their backs,[4] others resting with their left side uppermost, and only the last one points with its belly towards the penultimate one and rests with its right side uppermost. They are always offered with their heads towards the recipient. Fish are offered on a tray with their head toward the recipient and the left side uppermost. The last one has its belly towards the end in the last place and the right side uppermost.

As regards the manner of offering and giving a letter, it may be noted that according to the genuine Japanese usage, it is very impolite to carry a letter to a noble in the hand and not enclosed in a box. These boxes are made of a special shape and fashion for this purpose,[5] for the Japanese take great pains in sending their letters to nobles with much courtesy and respect.[6] This custom has its origin in China, for the Chinese carry their visiting cards in a suitable box or case made for the purpose, although when they deliver it they take it out of the box and present it, wrapped in a paper envelope with a red strip on top.[7] But the Japanese hand over their letters still placed in the same box, and for this purpose they have various boxes or cases made. Some are gilded after their fashion with golden flowers on an exquisite black laquer background, with silver flowers inserted in various places,

---

[1] 'Roses' should be taken in a general sense, as the cultivation of this flower (as opposed to wild roses) was begun only in recent times in Japan. *KEJ*, VI, p. 339.

[2] An example of a gift of birds is provided by Fróis (Miyako, 14 April 1581, in *Cartas*, II, f. 4), who records that after Valignano's meeting with Nobunaga in the previous month, the ruler presented him with ten ducks ('the biggest we've ever seen here'), which had just arrived from a *daimyo*. Totman (in *Tokugawa Ieyasu*, p. 100) mentions Ieyasu's presenting to friends the catch of his hawking expeditions.

[3] Rodrigues uses here (and also on p. 345) the word *ninga*, meaning a yoke or pole for carrying loads. The term is probably derived from the Malayan word *pungah*, a load-carrier. Dalgado, *Glossário*, II, pp. 213–14.

[4] The Portuguese text literally translates as 'some are placed behind', but Rodrigues seems to mean 'on their backs'; this is more in keeping with Ogasawara etiquette.

[5] Called *fubako* in Japanese, and mentioned in *Vocabulario*, f. 104v. See also Fróis, *Tratado*, p. 216.

[6] Rodrigues was certainly knowledgeable about the etiquette involved when sending letters to nobles. In his *Arte grande*, ff. 189–206v, he goes into immense detail describing the different sorts of letters written to the shogun, nobles, Zen monks, and women, as well as the correct forms of salutation, addressing, conclusion, and dating. As he aptly observes, 'A large part of the breeding and courtesy of Japan is to be found in letters and their style.'

[7] For Ricci's description of these cards, see p. 205, n. 1.

Plate 17: 'Receiving Gifts', an illustration from *Ogasaware Shoreitaizen*. 'Large birds, such as duck, wild fowl, etc., are presented lying on their backs on trays with their breasts uppermost.' p. 211. Rodrigues, *This Island of Japon*.

with silver or gilt handles and cords of crimson silk thread. Others are adorned only with exquisite black laquer that gives them a smooth appearance. And finally others are newly made of white cedar wood, and are used only for this particular occasion. They put their letters inside these boxes. If the box is one of the first two sorts, then it is returned with the reply inside it. But if it is of the third kind, then, according to genuine Japanese usage, the reply is put into another new box, because they write on the wood the address of the person to whom the letter is sent. They have special ceremonies for giving and receiving these letters in the boxes, and also for opening and closing them again. When the letter comes from a noble or a person's own lord, courtesy demands that after reading it the recipient raises it above his head with both hands by the part bearing the sender's signature, for this is an act of veneration towards his signature.

In general, things that are given and taken with the hand are received in the same hand as gave or offered them: if it was the right hand, then the right hand, and if the left, then the left. For there are special things that are offered and given with the right hand, and other things with the left. There are various kinds of many other things that are given as gifts in special ways, such as the way of offering and receiving a horse, a bow and arrow, a sword in its scabbard or unsheathed, and many other things, and they pride themselves more than any other nation in not deviating from convention. This also applies to their way of viewing various precious things that are shown them. Thus they do not seem to possess anything, no matter how small it may be, which does not have its own rules and points of honour, etc.[1]

In their books of etiquette and ceremonies a great deal is written concerning good manners and the way in which servants and subjects must courteously serve their lords. They also deal with other details that they would regard as discourteous in the actions, exterior movement, and posture of the body. Hence they also give instructions and good advice to young boys so that they may become accustomed to speaking of weighty topics[2] from childhood and not of baseless trifles, and that they may be prudent in their dealings with their superiors and keep good company.[3] For a man and his customs may be known from the good companions with whom he mixes. To this end they have a very apt proverb that runs: 'Sono kimi wo shirazuba, sono shi wo miyo', that is, 'If you do not know what kind of man is the lord, see what kind of man the vassal is.' This is as if we were to say, 'The vassal's customs indicate the type of lord he serves.'[4]

---

[1] According to Valignano (*Principio*, f. 39), everything in Japan has its own special way of being done – eating, receiving guests, using weapons, riding, writing letters, etc. He also comments (*Sumario*, p. 42) on the number of rules concerning eating. See also the references to this subject on p. 177, n. 3.

[2] There is a gap in the Portuguese text where another adjective describing 'topics' should have been written.

[3] Valignano (in *TCJ*, p. 45) was much impressed by the maturity of Japanese children; they used elegant language among themselves and did not fight like European lads; their incredible gravity made them appear like solemn men instead of children. Caron (*True Description*, p. 49) observes that their discourses and answers savour of a riper age.

[4] This saying also appears in a work published by the Jesuit Press at Amakusa in 1593, and originates in *Kongzi jiayu*, 'School Sayings of Confucius'. Rodrigues, *Nihon*, I, p. 466, n. 19.

CHAPTER 22

THE COURTESIES, BOWS, AND OBEISANCES IN USE AMONG
THE CHINESE, FROM WHICH THE JAPANESE HAVE TAKEN MOST
OF THEIR ETIQUETTE

The principal feature of the social customs and exterior ceremonies consists of the courtesies, bows, and obeisances in use among the Japanese. Like the Japanese themselves, they trace back their origin to those of ancient China, albeit at present for various reasons they are dissimilar in many respects. But both the one type and the other differ in part from our European usage, for neither Japanese nor Chinese etiquette is concerned with the feet or the hat, but is expressed in another manner, as we shall presently say. In order, then, that the reader may better understand these things of Japan and the conformity between them and those of China, we shall first of all say a brief word about the etiquette of ancient China (whence that of Japan takes its origin) and the etiquette that is practised there at present.

To this end you must know that in ancient times before the Han dynasty (which the Japanese call Kan)[1] the Chinese wore robes with short sleeves reaching down past the middle of the arm, and these sleeves were as wide as those that the Japanese still wear at the present time. They subsequently lengthened them so much that the part trailing over the tip of the hand is almost longer than the part covering the whole of the arm. The sleeves thus are very long and resemble those of the borachio or the *sainho* of ancient Portugal.[2] In the same way. the Chinese in ancient times did not use chairs or high tables as they do now, but instead sat down on the floor of the matted and carpeted rooms, after the fashion of the Japanese, the whole of Asia, and the Moors. Thus, the courtesies and obeisances performed within their houses in that epoch were different in style from those of the present day. While seated on the floor, they used to perform their etiquette in various ways. They later began to use high chairs, and now they perform their etiquette standing just inside the room at its entrance. Thus when they changed various things concerning their customs (such as being seated and eating high up) and their robes, they also altered some courtesies and bows, adapting them to the fashion that they subsequently followed. They partially changed their dress and way of sitting, and with it they altered their etiquette and manner of kneeling.[3]

As may be seen in their ancient books, there were three ways of sitting down in ancient China before they began using chairs. They call the first manner *guizuo* (in Japanese, *hiza wo*

---

[1] The Han dynasty lasted from 206 BC to AD 221.

[2] 'Borachio' is an obsolete English rendering of the Spanish *borracha*, a large leather bag or bottle used for carrying wine or water. Presumably this container (or its spout) had somewhat the same shape as a kimono sleeve, although the comparison seems far-fetched. *Oxford English Dictionary*, I, p. 261–2. For the garment called *sainho*, see p. 179, n. 3.

[3] The change in Chinese social customs affected by the introduction of the chair is discussed in Fitzgerald, *Barbarian Beds*, pp. 2–4. In Chapter 12 of his *History*, Semedo deals with Chinese courtesies at some length.

tatsuru), and this is to sit on the calves of the legs and feet, with the knees pointing forward. This was their proper way of kneeling, and the Japanese employ this method today.[1] In addition, they also used to kneel in our fashion, and they call this *qiqilai* (in Japanese, *taka hiza wo tatsuru*). This can be done in two ways, one with both knees and the other with only one.[2] The second method is called *panzu* (the Japanese say, *hiza[3] wo kumu*), and this is to rest oneself on the carpet just as one wishes, crossing one leg over the other. This was their usual way of seating themselves on the mats as they pleased without any formality, just as is generally done in Japan today. In China this method is used by bonzes when they settle down to meditate on the points of their sects, and also by some lay people in certain circumstances. The third method is called *dunzuo* (in Japanese, *kashikomaru*), which is sitting in a squatting position. In keeping with these three ways of sitting, the ancient Chinese paid their compliments and made their obeisances. To this day these are retained in Japan, for the Japanese have preserved the ancient Chinese fashion.

The Chinese etiquette, bow, and obeisance in general use at present throughout the entire kingdom are made up of many parts. Some of them are the formal obeisance and bow, while others form or contribute to a more profound etiquette. Of these, there are seven principal ones employed in their etiquette.

1. A deep inclination of the body and head forwards.

2. Entwining the arms and placing one hand above the other within the long wide sleeves of the formal robe. With his hands thus bent, a person bows down to the ground and shakes his hands. This moving the hands and bowing is called *zuoyi*, and is their ordinary way of bowing among themselves.[4]

3. Kneeling down with both knees on the ground.

4. Striking the head lightly against the ground or carpet, placing the head next to the ground and touching it.

5. Raising and shaking the hands thus entwined up and down when people meet, for this is a method of greeting.

6. Pointing with the hands entwined within the sleeves, shaking them towards a certain place. This is the polite way of pointing somewhere or persuading someone to go thither.

7. Putting something in the hand of another person with both hands or with one hand assisted and supported by the other. This is the polite way of placing a thing into another person's hand.

The Japanese make use of the second method.[5]

All these actions are to be found in Chinese etiquette. Many of them are performed

---

[1] Valignano (*Sumario*, p. 43) mentions this Japanese way of sitting on the matted floor, adding, 'For them it is restful, but for us great fatigue and hardship until we gradually become used to it with the passing of time.'

[2] The copyist repeated the second part of this sentence at the end of the previous sentence; for the sake of clarity, I have omitted the first, and erroneous, insertion from the translation.

[3] The Portuguese text here reads *fixi*, which I take to be the copyist's slip for *fiza* (*hiza*), meaning 'knee'. From the context, it seems unlikely that this reference is to *hiji*, 'elbow'.

[4] Ricci (*Fonti*, I, p. 72, and *China*, p. 60) describes this form of salutation, calling it *zoye* [*zuoyi*]. He adds that people greeting each other in this way would repeat *Zin, zin* [*Qing, qing*], which he says is a respectful interjection. Other accounts are given in Mendoza, *History*, I, pp. 141–2; Cruz, in Boxer, *South China*, pp. 138–40. For a sketch of the 'salutation off a Chinois', see Mundy, *Travels*, III:1, pp. 270, 295–6.

[5] Rodrigues must surely mean 'the first method' here as the Japanese certainly do not make use of the second. Rodrigues, *Nihon*, I, p. 470, translates, 'The Japanese use the latter method.' Later, p. 222, he notes that a Japanese servant's most profound courtesy towards his master *corresponds* to a Chinese kneeling down and striking his head

together as a deep bow, while others are made individually for some things, depending on the persons who pay the compliment and those who receive it.

In general there are two kinds of bows and courtesies among the Chinese within their houses and reception rooms, and even outside. The first is called the Great Courtesy,[1] and this is the biggest and most profound of them all, and consists of four things. The first is called *zuoyi* and is a deep forward inclination of the head and body, with the hands entwined within the long sleeves of the formal robe. The hands remain covered and are lowered towards the ground, and are shaken by drawing them up and then stretching them downwards; this is their usual obeisance. The second comes after this obeisance, and the person kneels down with both knees on the mat, carpet, or ground. The third then takes place when the person thus kneeling bows his head down to the floor, striking it lightly on the carpet up to three times. The fourth is to rise to one's feet and then repeat the first bow, *zuoyi*, which then concludes this kind of Great Courtesy. This Great Courtesy is made four times in succession, and all these actions are included four times when it is done correctly with all the ceremonies.

This kind of obeisance is mainly performed when they worship their false gods in front of an altar or statue in a temple. Christians also do it when they worship God and statues of the saints. Secondly, vassals, grandees of the kingdom, magistrates, and nobles do it to the king when they visit him and withdraw from his presence. The king is seated on his royal throne or in a chair at the top of the room. Thirdly, children perform it before their father and mother on festival days and on their parents' birthdays, for the Chinese pay much regard to this. Fourthly, subjects do it to lords and magistrates when they meet them for the first time, and also on festival days and days of precept. Fifthly, students perform it towards their teachers on big festival days. Sixthly, people who go to visit (or, as they say, wail over) a dead person (a very common custom in China) perform this obeisance and homage towards the corpse. The body is placed in a coffin or casket of precious wood, which serves as a tomb or sepulchre after their fashion. It is kept in the house many days, sometimes months or even years, as shall be described later. When they make this obeisance, they place scent at the same time in the perfume pan that is set there. The dead man's son or closest relative places himself on the guest's right, for the left side is more honourable. He makes the same obeisance along with the guest, as if in this way to repay him.[2]

When all these Great Courtesies are performed, the person who receives them is seated in a chair at the top of the room, for he is the superior. But when his sons are married, the father receives these courtesies standing up, as also do teachers in the same way when their students are dignified people; lords do the same towards their honourable retainers. When students, servants, or subjects are very dignified, their teachers and lords do not stand in front of them at the top of the room, but to one side, so as to show that they make more account of them.

---

against the floor. If, in the present instance, he were to write, 'The Japanese usage *corresponds* to the second method,' then the statement would not be inaccurate.

[1] Ricci (*Fonti*, I, p. 72, and *China*, pp. 60–61) supplies a similar description of this rite.

[2] For Chinese funeral rites, see p. 201, n. 2. Ricci (*Fonti*, I, p. 84, and *China*, p. 73) confirms Rodrigues's account, adding that the coffins were sealed with pitch, and instances of keeping a parent's body in the house for three or four years were known. Cortes, *Viaje*, p. 188, mentions even ten years in the case of nobles. Mendoza (*History*, I, pp. 59–60) notes that coffins were usually displayed for fifteen days for visitors to pay their respects. See also Cruz, in Boxer, *South China*, pp. 146–7.

The second type of courtesy mentioned above is the ordinary and common bow, called *zuoyi*, which they make towards each other. They perform this towards guests in their houses and to each one individually as a sign of greater respect. The guest remains on the left of the host, and they both make the same courtesy together as they face the top of the room, which ordinarily lies towards the north. After performing this courtesy, the guest goes to the right of the host in order to pay this courtesy to him. With the host now on his left, they both together repeat the same courtesy or obeisance, and this is done to honour the host. When this is performed, there is much disputing on both sides as to who will occupy the lowest place.

Sometimes when there are many guests, in order to shorten these ceremonies that are performed individually for each one, all the guests place themselves in due order on the left of the host and make the *zuoyi* together with him. Then all of them turn about and from the other side, on the right hand of the host, they pay their courtesies as described above. After this they sit down, each one receiving the place he merits according to their rules. The most honourable places are given to the oldest guests, even though they be less noble. Students concede the higher place to their former teachers, even though they may be dignified magistrates or even some of the greatest men of the realm, and their teacher a plebeian and ordinary person. They are extremely particular about this matter of seating arrangements, and the host always takes the lowest place for himself.

When acquaintances walking along the road meet each other, they perform *zuoyi*, just as they do within their houses, or only with their arms bent at their sides and lifted up. If they are travelling in a litter or in an open palanquin and thus can be seen, as soon as they spy each other from afar, they begin to greet each other in the same manner by raising their hands and arms upwards until they pass each other. If the persons travelling in a litter or on horseback are or were students or in any way subjects, they get off and wait on foot, and when they meet they make their obeisance or *zuoyi*. The teacher will get out of the litter and receive the salutation outside of it. When ordinary people meet an acquaintance, they greet each other with both their hands, placing one on top of the other and shaking them up and down. When a man receives a guest, or, if the guest is a dignified and noble person, goes out of the gate to receive him, they perform the *zuoyi* there to each other. When they enter the room, they do it again as mentioned above, and they repeat it once more in the same way when they bid farewell. The host accompanies the guest to the door where they part, and the guest remains on foot until the host turns his back or disappears. But if the guest goes on horseback or in a litter, there are certain ceremonies when he departs. The guest conceals himself until he is in the litter or on the horse, and then he salutes him there and says farewell, and through a servant sends after him a complimentary message, which he gives to one of his pages to deliver.[1]

The lowly servants of nobles and special officials who are destined for lifelong service, always stand in each court on both sides of the magistrates, some behind and others in front, and servants stand behind their lord. Both kinds have their sleeves and hands hanging down the length of their bodies out of respect towards the magistrates and lords. When

---

[1] Ricci (*Fonti*, I, pp. 76–9, and *China*, p. 64) also describes the formalities observed by the host and guests during a visit. This sentence should surely begin, 'The *host* conceals himself until he is in the litter …'. This is borne out by Ricci's account; he adds that the host sends a servant after the guests to bid them a further farewell and they in turn return the compliment through their servants.

they offer anything to the magistrate or lord, they kneel down and present it with both hands, and the same thing happens when they receive anything from the lord. In the same way, when they speak or deliver a message or reply to the magistrates and nobles, they kneel in front of the person while they speak, and then they rise and retire once more to the side. And when the thing is [   ],[1] they place only one knee on the ground.[2] The servants of people of good breeding and the *literati* generally do not do this.

After the guests have been welcomed at a banquet with due courtesies, the time comes for the meal to begin. Before they sit down to eat, the Chinese have various ceremonies, of which the principal and most esteemed one is to lay down a carpet inside the room at the entrance. They begin with the wine and the *hashi* with which they eat. These are like table utensils with which they begin to eat, and the table is decorated with various things that are not eaten.[3] The host takes up a cup and the salver on which it stands, and summons a page who is there with a vessel of wine, and from this he fills up the cup and holds it in his hand. The principal guest then comes up and positions himself on the carpet to the right of the host, and both of them make a *zuoyi* together. Then the host, accompanied by the guest, carries the cup full of wine to the place at table where the guest is to be seated. He places the cup upon the table, and after this, the host himself asks for some *hashi* (these are certain sticks with which they eat and use instead of forks). He carries them in the same way to the table and places them next to the cup of wine, with the guest accompanying him as he did the first time when he carried the cup. The same is done for each of the guests, and at the end, when everybody's cup and *hashi* are on the table in the appointed place, the principal guest takes a cup with its salver and fills it with wine. Then he makes the above-mentioned obeisance on the carpet, and accompanied by the host and all the guests he takes the cup and places it on the table at the appointed place, and then also carries the *hashi* with the same accompaniment.[4] By now serving the host, they repay in this way the compliment that the host paid by serving them. Then they all sit down at the table.

This is now the current method of beginning a banquet and corresponds to the custom in Japan of the host's bringing the tray of food and placing it with its *hashi* and other things in front of the guest, the cup of wine being already placed on a salver at the top of the room as a sign of feasting. It appears that when the Chinese used to eat in ancient times, seated on the floor upon the mats or carpets, each guest had his own low table, and this is the same method now in use in Japan, as shall be seen later.

When they are seated in the chairs, it is given to the guests, who take it with both hands; sometimes they rise to their feet out of respect in order to take it.[5] Thus seated, they take

---

[1] A blank in the Portuguese text.

[2] For a description of court procedure in an actual case, see Ricci, *Fonti*, I, pp. 204–6, and *China*, pp. 162–4. For an early European sketch of a Chinese magistrate presiding in court, see Mundy, *Travels*, III:1, p. 256.

[3] This is a fairly close rendering of a somewhat confused sentence in the original text. The general sense seems to be that the first things to be used in a banquet are wine and chopsticks. During his many years spent in China, Rodrigues had ample opportunity of attending banquets. In a letter from Canton, December 1615 (Rodrigues, 'Rodrigues in China', p. 318), he describes a banquet of thirteen courses.

[4] The second part of this sentence remains rather vague in the Portuguese text, but the translation seems to fit the context. Rodrigues, *Nihon*, I, p. 476, gives two versions in the Japanese translation, neither of which completely agrees with my rendering.

[5] The Portuguese text does not make clear what is given, but presumably it is the cup.

the porcelain cup of *cha* in both hands, and they all make a *zuoyi* together with the host, bowing and lowering their hands with the *cha*. When they receive wine in their cup, they do the same before they drink it, just as is done in Japan. They raise the *cha* or wine or cup above the head or up to the forehead (this is a sign of respect that the Japanese make when they receive something), just as we do when wine is spilt.[1]

---

[1] 'Ao modo que entre nôs sobeja', a puzzling concluding phrase. My translation agrees fundamentally with the version in Rodrigues, *Nihon*, I, p. 447.

CHAPTER 23

THE COURTESIES AND CEREMONIES OF THE JAPANESE IN GENERAL

The courtesies described above are those in current use among the Chinese. If we carefully examine them, they are seen to be essentially the same as the ancient usage that the Japanese employ to this day. But they have been changed to a certain extent, because the ancient Chinese robe and the way of sitting on the floor and eating from trays have also changed. They now use robes with short sleeves, sit on high chairs, and eat from tables as described above. Nowadays only one table is used in place of the many trays employed in former times. Even now the Chinese place the cup of wine on their salvers, just as do the Japanese. So everything follows the same fashion and for the most part the Japanese imitate the Chinese, as has already been said. This is also true as regards the three ancient Chinese ways of sitting on carpets or mats, for the Japanese have preserved them unchanged to this day. That is, kneeling down and sitting back on the legs and feet, sitting cross-legged, and finally placing oneself in a squatting position, as has already been said.

1. The various kinds of obeisance and signs of courtesy and good breeding

Among the Japanese there are various kinds of courtesies, obeisances, and signs of good breeding and upbringing, which we list here in general so that when we hear of some of them mentioned or hear about them being performed, we will know what they are and the esteem that they imply. First, let us say a few words in general. Just as in Japan there are four kinds of persons between whom there are various relationships, so also there are three[1] sorts of bows, obeisance, and courtesies performed within the house or room. The first is the respect shown by a servant towards his master; the second, that of people of mean birth towards a noble, or of inferiors towards a superior; the third, between equals; the fourth, the etiquette of bonzes or clerics towards the laity.[2] These bonzes are the spiritual instructors of the laity concerning the things of salvation, and also their masters in the teaching of secular learning.

The first and most profound courtesy is shown by a servant towards his master and is performed in the following manner. The lord is seated at the top of the room with his legs crossed in the way described above when we were speaking about ancient China. The servant enters the room, kneels down according to their fashion, and sits back on his legs and feet with his knees bent and pointing forward. He bows and makes a deep obeisance until his forehead touches the floor. He also places the palms of both hands on the floor and

---

[1] An obvious slip for 'four'.
[2] But on p. 175, Rodrigues has already mentioned the *gorin*, or *five* human relationships.

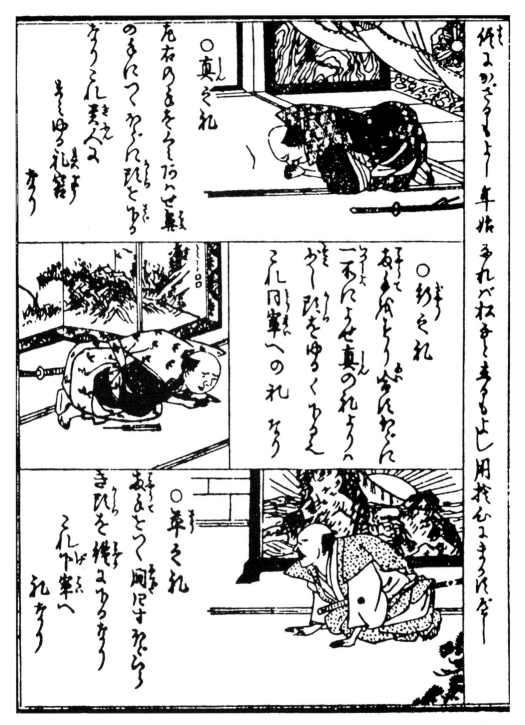

Plate 18: 'The Three Types of Obeisance', an illustration in *Ogasawara Shoreitaizen*. 'There are three sorts of bows, obeisance, and courtesies performed within the house or room.' p. 220. Rodrigues, *This Island of Japon*.

stretches his arms a little, in such a way that if he were to raise his eyes while in this position, he would not be able to see his master at all, as may be seen in the diagram of this which we include.[1]

This obeisance corresponds to that now in use among the Chinese, when a person kneels down and strikes his head against the floor, with his hands arched on the floor. When there are many servants together who have to perform this obeisance and form of worship towards their lord, one makes his obeisance and goes out of the room, and then another comes in and does the same. This is done mainly at the great festivals and times of much rejoicing when they go to visit their lords. It can happen that, according to the place and the occasion, many people together make this obeisance to the lord simultaneously. When this is done outdoors, the lord remains standing; in Japan this gives more honour and dignity to the lord than it does in China, where to remain standing at such a time would be to pay greater honour to the person making the obeisance. Among the servants there are also many nobles and others of medium or low rank, and according to their rank they bow low to a greater or lesser extent. Here, then, is the difference: the Chinese do this standing for some, and seated for others.

The second obeisance is made by an inferior towards a person superior in rank or dignity, or by a person of mean birth towards one of high. This is done with the recipient being seated, as we noted, while the person performing the obeisance kneels in the manner above described, places the palms of his hands on the floor in front of his knees, or with only the left hand on the floor and his right hand on his thigh, bending his head and body so much that, if he were to look at the person to whom he is making the obeisance, he would be able to see only his eyes. But if the person making the obeisance is of mean birth and the other is a noble, he will perform the first type of obeisance.

The third type takes place among equals and is common among ordinary people, both honourable persons and those of mean birth. This is done by both persons kneeling down with their hands and bodies towards each other in such a way that if one of them, while thus bowed down, were to look towards the other he could see his sash. This type of bowing corresponds to the *zuoyi* of China, which we said was their ordinary obeisance.[2]

The fourth type is performed by the bonzes towards their lay guests inside the house. The profoundest obeisance that the bonzes make has several degrees and is done within the house. They kneel down, sit back on their feet and legs, and bow down,[3] placing the left hand on the matted floor and the right hand upon the thigh and next to the right knee. They make this obeisance to guests of great nobility and to the lords of the lands and estates in which they themselves dwell. When dealing with noble people of lesser rank, they place their hands on their thighs or join both their hands in front, one on top of the other, and then make a moderate bow with their body and head. Layfolk reply to this with a deep bow of the first two types mentioned above, because the bonzes are, so to speak, their spiritual guides and their teachers in letters and the humanities. The lords and nobles make

---

[1] The diagram is unfortunately not included in the Lisbon manuscript.

[2] In *Ogasawara*, ff. 8v–9, three types of obeisance are illustrated (see Plate 18), and they are called the *shin*, *gyō*, and *sō* types, corresponding to the three styles of writing (see pp. 336–7). In the first kind, the man is kneeling and bowing low, with both hands in front, one on top of the other; in the second, the hands are placed flat on the floor, side by side; in the third, the bow is less profound and the hands, still flat on the floor, are about a foot apart.

[3] There is a gap in the Portuguese text here; the sentence should probably read, '... and bow down their bodies', or something similar.

use of this type of courtesy and obeisance of the bonzes when they greet visitors of lesser nobility and people of medium rank whom they wish to honour.

These, then, are the ordinary reverences in current use throughout the kingdom. In addition, there are various other kinds used in different circumstances in keeping with good breeding and respect and as a sign of courtesy. We will list them here in their order so that when they are mentioned elsewhere, the reader will know the courtesy that they signify.

The first is performed when a man is standing outdoors. He bends his body slightly and places his hands on his thighs between his knees and his sash. The reverence is performed in the street or road by a bonze or a person of great nobility as a compliment to another of lesser rank. The same bow is made when a person of lesser dignity passes in front of people of noble and gentle birth who happen to be present. He remains there, bowing profoundly with his hands clasped decently in front.[1] This same bow of the body is always made when a person passes another along the road and greets him with words. If the other should be a noble, the person passes him, bowing his body and not saying a word. This is a sign of great respect and is called *mokurei* (in Chinese, *muli*), that is, silent courtesy with the eyes.[2] People also use this reverence, bowing the head and body forwards and holding the hands in front of them, when they greet each other as they travel on foot or horseback.

The second type is made by a person placing himself in a squatting position, or almost so, with both hands, or one hand, hanging at his side and his fingertips touching the ground, or squatting on his left knee with his left hand on the ground. This is the most profound reverence paid by a vassal to his lord or prince when speaking to him outdoors, or giving or receiving a message or something else. People of low birth do the same towards the nobility. When servants of low or medium rank and young lads speak to their lord who is standing outside in the street or road, or when they give him a message or reply, or receive from him a message for someone else, or offer or receive something from the lord's hand, or when the lord speaks to them, they squat down with their hands on the ground or joined in front of them, one on top of the other. This reverence corresponds to kneeling down in China, as already described, and to our custom of kneeling on the ground.

When the lord is waiting on foot, or is otherwise occupied, all the servants of low or middle rank remain squatting while the lord is thus standing. When there are two or more lords present, their servants squat as long as they remain standing. If he is an important person such as a prince, the shogun or Lord of Tenka, everyone, however noble he may be, does the same as a sign of fear and reverence, for such a person calls them all *tu* and some of them *vos*.[3] When respected servants of rank and officers speak with their lord while he is standing, they usually bow their body and head deeply and join their hands in front.

The third type is the reverence of the hands, and this corresponds to the Chinese reverence with the hands and arms entwined within the long sleeves of the formal robe. First of

[1] The last two sentences in the Portuguese text are not at all clear, but their general meaning is apparent.

[2] The meaning here presents a problem, because there are two Japanese words pronounced *mokurei*, one meaning 'eye courtesy' and the other 'silent courtesy'. The former is pronounced *muli* in Chinese, the latter, *moli*. Although 'moly' is given in the text, Rodrigues is probably referring to *muli*, for he later (p. 225) repeats the Japanese term, saying that it means 'courtesy of the eyes'. But *Vocabulario*, f. 164, gives: 'Mokurei. Kotaba nashi no rei bakari suru. To bow outwardly without saying anything.' Valignano (*Cerimoniale*, p. 192) mentions this word, spelling it as *mokutei*, saying that it is a silent compliment.

[3] That is, he addresses them using informal language. Fróis (*História*, IV, pp. 98, 369, 371) relates that Hideyoshi used the Japanese equivalent of the *tu* form when talking to nobles.

all, raising and stretching the completely open right hand, as if in blessing, is a sign of greeting or farewell, and a sign of confirming a thing as if it were for that purpose. When a person points out the way or the entrance of a house or some object or seat or invites some-one to a higher place, etc., it is the usual courtesy to stretch the arm and open hand with the palm uppermost, and point towards the place that he wishes to indicate, etc. This must be done with the hand that is on the side of the person whom I am persuading or to whom I am pointing something out. For example, if the person is on my left, I stretch out my left hand, but if on my right, I use my right hand.[1]

When offering and giving something to a person of dignity, the usual courtesy is to do so with only one hand, supported by the other. The recipient does the same, taking the object with the same hand as it is given. When giving or receiving something, the Chinese use both hands, or only one hand supported by the other. But there are other things in Japan that are also received and given with both hands. When a person receives something in his hand from a noble, or a letter from the Lord of Tenka, or his own lord, or a cup from which another person has drunk, or things to eat, etc., the usual courtesy and reverence is to raise the thing with both hands up to the head to the level of the forehead. This is a sign of great esteem and reverence.[2]

The fourth kind is performed when a person is moving indoors or anywhere outside and by chance touches with his feet something belonging to another person, such as a sword, a fan, the hem of a robe, etc. He then touches the same object with his right hand or makes to touch it, and then lifts his hand to his head, level with his forehead, as a sign that he places the object on his head, and that it was all an accident and not done out of contempt. For it is the height of rudeness among the Japanese to point out something with the foot. It is also the greatest insult and offence to strike a person or his things with the foot, however lowly he may be. Even though the person who does this is a great lord of a kingdom or estate and the person thus touched is his lowly servant or lad, he will kill him for doing so. It is as if he were to kick him, the most disgraceful thing among them, or step on his feet. Even in our times it often happened that lowly servants and the lads who look after the lord's shoes or sandals (and they are the meanest of all) have killed great lords who have touched them with their foot in scorn or anger. But if it were done accidentally and the apology, mentioned above, is offered, nothing comes of the matter.[3]

---

[1] The change to the first person singular is found in the Portuguese text, and may indicate the insertion of a marginal note written by a Japanese, perhaps Martinho Hara. See p. 67, n. 2.

[2] *Vocabulario*, f. 49v: '*Chôdai. Itadaki, u.* Raising something above the head with reverence.' Valignano (*Cerimonale*, p. 190) instructs Jesuits to preserve this custom with respect to the *sakazuki*. During his visit to the Suruga court, Vivero y Velasco (*Relación*, f. 13v) records that he was toasted by Honda Masazumi, who raised the salver and cup of wine above his head as a sign of honour.

[3] Gago (10 December 1562, in Ruiz-de-Medina, *Documentos*, II, p. 608) notes that if a person accidentally brushes against somebody's sword or scabbard, he should touch the relevant place with his hand and then raise the hand to his head once or twice to show that the incident was not intentional. An incident in which the sword scabbards of two samurai brushed against each other was so serious that it had its own technical term, *saya-ate*, and could result in a duel to death. Valignano (*Cerimoniale*, pp. 244–6) warns Jesuits never to touch or point to anything with the foot, as this is a great insult. This is borne out by Fróis (*História*, III, p. 339), who suggests that Nobunaga's kicking Akechi Mitsuhide was the remote cause of the ruler's assassination. This sensitiveness was not limited to Japanese. Francisco Manríques de Lara, bishop of Salamanca, related that he had seen the young soldier Iñigo de Loyola draw his sword after being jostled in the streets of Pamplona, and 'he would have killed some of them or would have been killed himself', had he not been restrained. *Monumenta Ignatiana*, p. 566.

CHAPTER 24

THE COURTESIES PAID BY THE JAPANESE WHEN THEY MEET ON THE ROAD

Having given a general description of the various kinds of courtesies that the Japanese practise both inside and outside of the house, we will now speak more in detail. In this chapter we will first of all deal with the courtesies performed in the street when they meet each other on foot, on horseback, or in a litter.[1] These are three usual ways of travelling, and there is no particular courtesy to be paid when going by boat. Later on, when we deal with the way of receiving, entertaining, and bidding farewell to a guest, we will describe in detail how these courtesies are performed within the house.

1. When a person is travelling on foot

It has already been mentioned above that the Japanese regard the left-hand side as more noble and honourable than the right, and this is also observed in the courtesies paid when they meet a person on the road.[2] When a man is going along the road and meets a person worthy of respect, he always steps aside to the right, thus making room for him to pass on his left. But if that part is muddy or the road is very bad, he steps aside to the left. The same is done when a person is riding on horseback or in a litter. If the person to whom the courtesy is paid does the same in order to honour the other man, insists that he passes first, offers him his compliments more than once, points out the road with his hand, and does not want to pass first, then the man passes. The same is observed when riding on horseback.

These are the greetings exchanged when a man meets an unknown person on the road. He says to him, 'A prosperous journey!'[3] and out of courtesy inclines his head and body somewhat, and the other person does likewise. But if the other party is, or appears to be, noble and worthy of esteem, he passes by, somewhat bowing out of courtesy and not saying a single word. They call this 'courtesy of the eyes'. When they meet acquaintances, they say

---

[1] Japanese litters were formerly called *kago*, but the larger and more comfortable *norimono* (*Vocabulario*, f. 186) was later introduced. Avila Girón (*Relación*, p. 265) gives an account of the litters used by senior Buddhist monks. In 1613 Saris (in Farrington, *English Factory*, II, p. 1015) had 'Six men appointed to carrie my pallankin in plaine and even ground. But where the countrey grew hilly, ten men were allowed me thereto.' Other references to the type of litter called *koshi* are given in Valignano, *Sumario*, p. 262, n. 47. Valignano (ibid., p. 298) laid down that Jesuits were not generally to use litters. Cocks often refers (e.g., *Diary*, II, p. 77) to the bearers of litters as *rockshackes* (*rokushaku* – see *Vocabulario*, f. 212). Illustrations in Kaemmerer, *Trade*, pp. 102–3.

[2] See p. 137. Vivero y Velasco (*Relación*, ff. 4v, 72) explains that the left-hand side is more honourable because the sword is carried on the left, and anyone trusted on that side must be a good friend. Similarly, going in front of somebody is considered complimentary as it shows implicit trust in that person.

[3] The salutation in Portuguese, *Hide embora*, is not easy to translate adequately.

anything they like to them. To a person carrying an object or a weight on his back, they only say, 'You are bearing a great load.' They call this *goshinrō*.[1] Raising and stretching the nearest hand, a person says the same to people who are working at a distance from the road, ploughing, reaping, or cultivating the fields. They greet people travelling along another road nearby by raising only the hand, or by raising the right hand and opening the fan carried therein. This is also done when two ships meet at sea. This is a very common way of silently greeting people at a distance.

When a person walking on foot meets someone on horseback whom he does not know, or even a person whom he does know, he does not stare at him because this is equivalent to telling him to dismount. Instead, when he sees him, he looks the other way as if he has not noticed him. Still, if he sees that the rider wishes to dismount according to custom, he says to him, 'Your Honour, please pass on your horse.' If despite this he dismounts, the man thanks him and begs him to remount immediately. They bow towards each other and the rider walks a little way out of respect before he gets on his horse again. If a man goes in front of a noble person walking on foot, or if he wishes to go quicker and overtake him from behind, he must pay a compliment to such a person as he does this, so that he may not seem to take the better place and have the other follow behind him. If he meets a person of mean birth, he does not pay him any compliments, whether he is travelling on foot or horseback.

When a man wearing clogs meets a noble who is not wearing them and he speaks to him, he asks his lad for his sandals and wears them while he is talking. If he does not have sandals with him and cannot take off his clogs because of the mud, he removes his toes or the part containing the big toe from the straps of the clogs, for this is equivalent to taking off the shoes. He says, 'Pardon me, Your Honour, because I am high up.' While speaking, he bows slightly, and if he is carrying a sunshade in his hand, he puts it slightly to one side as a sign of respect while he is talking to the person.[2]

When passing between some people or in front of a person or in front of people seated within or outside a house by the wayside, a man bows and says, 'Pardon me, Your Honours.' This is not done if they are of low birth. If the person or persons in front of whom the man passes are of great nobility and rank, he comes up in front of him or them, drops to a squatting position, or almost so, and pauses a little while, placing the tips of his hands on the ground. He then rises to his feet and, bowing his body, passes along without saying a word.

When a man travelling along a road meets a lord's falconer bearing a hawk on his arm, he steps aside so that the falconer may pass him on his right, for he carries the hawk on his left arm. When he arrives in front of the falconer, he pauses briefly and looks at the bird, without praising it or saying a word, and then continues on his way. If he is travelling by horse, he dismounts when he is near at hand. These courtesies are observed out of respect for the lord owning the hawk. If they are not duly performed, the man carrying the hawk has authority to rebuke the rider who does not dismount from his horse. Sometimes the men accompanying the lord's hawk may forcibly oblige the rider to dismount.[3]

---

[1] *Go-shinrō*, literally, 'honourable hardship'.

[2] The Portuguese text has 'sombreiro de mão do sol'; this seems to refer to the *sashikasa*, listed in *Vocabulario*, f. 221, as 'A hand umbrella for sun and rain.'

[3] The overbearing attitude of falconers and their attendants is mentioned in Sadler, *Maker*, p. 356.

2. When travelling on horseback

When a noble lends one of his valuable horses to another person to ride, the man will praise the animal as soon as he sees it, and will declare that it is a very fine beast if the noble is actually present when he comes to mount. Before getting on the horse, he turns towards the noble and pays his respects by bowing and placing his hands on his thighs or clasping them in front on him. After he has thus bade farewell, he mounts the horse.

When a man on horseback sees a noble or honourable person coming on foot, he must dismount even if he does not know the person. This happens especially if the person is carrying aloft a lance, the usual ensign of nobles in Japan, because the lance is proper to such a person with two or three servants.[1] Even if he does not carry a lance, the rider must still dismount at a greater or lesser distance according to the person's rank and the respect that the rider wishes to show him. The closer he dismounts, the less courtesy is shown. Usually he dismounts about fifteen paces away. The person on foot thanks him for the courtesy thus shown and begs him mount directly he has gone a little way past him. If the person on foot is very noble, the rider continues walking for a while before remounting so as to show greater respect, and the noble sends one of his servants to ask him to mount forthwith. The reason for dismounting is because the man on horseback is in a higher and more exalted position than the man walking on foot. To a certain extent he looks down on him and is, as it were, his superior, while the man on foot is in a low and inferior position.

When a man is riding a horse quickly, sees a person of rank travelling in front on foot, and must overtake him, he sends him a message asking permission to pass. When the man on foot turns around, the rider dismounts, offers his compliments as he passes, and then remounts. If the other man is also riding on horseback, all the rider does is ask permission. As they pass each other, they pay their compliments while still on horseback by bowing the body and head, and drawing up their hands in front of the saddle pommel. As they pass each other, he tries to pull over to the right, thus leaving the left-hand side for the other rider.

When a rider on horseback meets some closed litters in which people are travelling, he always dismounts and withdraws to the right. When he meets another rider, who also wishes to pass, at the entrance to a bridge or some other narrow place, he withdraws to the right, and once or twice tries to persuade the other to pass. If the other declines, the rider will show him the courtesy mentioned above and then pass. In the same way, when a rider is fording a river and meets another man on horseback in the middle, he passes and bows as has already been said. If a person of rank is crossing the river on foot and is met in the middle by a man on horseback, the rider will dismount after he has crossed the river and will there pay his respects.

There are certain places where a rider on horseback must necessarily dismount as he passes in front, in order to show respect for those who dwell there. This is principally observed in front of the main gate of the wall around the royal palace, and the palace of the Lord of Tenka and the *kubō*, etc. The same holds true in China where a person may not pass, even in a litter, in front of the main gate of the wall around the royal palace without

---

[1] Avila Girón (in *TCJ*, p. 142) states that the pike (or glaive) called *naginata* was a sign of rank and permission was needed to bear it. When Saris (in Farrington, *English Factory*, II, p. 1015) was carried to Suruga in a litter, 'According to the custome of the countrey' he had a man 'appointed me to runne with a pike before mee' as a sign of honour. Likewise, Cocks (4 October 1618, in *Diary*, II, p. 82) records: 'And sowne after we met on of the King of Hirado's-gentlemen sent to meete me, with pikes carrid before hyme. ...' Kaempfer (*History*, II. p. 335) gives illustrations of four types of 'pikes of state', carried in the great *daimyo* processions to and from Edo.

dismounting. This gate is situated in the south, for usually there are four gates set in the four directions, north, south, east, and west.[1] This happens when people pass in front of the castles of the *yakata*, or dukes of the kingdom. They dismount on reaching the building, and after they have passed, they once more get on their horses.[2]

The same happens when a man passes near a place where they are shooting at a target with bows and arrows, or guns. He must also dismount until he has passed the target under pain of sometimes being shot at. This has actually happened, for the people who indulge in this exercise are usually nobles. Finally (omitting many other courtesies that they pay when riding on horseback), when a person goes on a horse to visit a noble, the further he dismounts from the door, the greater respect and courtesy he shows him. This is done so that he may not be seen from within the house coming on horseback. The same is observed by a person coming in a litter to pay a visit.

---

[1] Ricci (*Fonti*, I, p. 81, and *China*, p. 69) confirms that there were four main entrances to the royal palace in Beijing, corresponding to the four points of the compass. As regards the gates of the Miyako palace, *Vocabulario*, f. 201, gives: '*Kyūgū*, or *kyūmon*. The nine gates situated around the palace of the Dairi.'

[2] *Vocabulario*, f. 115: '*Geba*. To get off one's horse in front of a person out of respect or in front of a temple out of courtesy.' Even today some temples have ancient *geba* stone markers at their entrance.

CHAPTER 25

THE MANNER OF RECEIVING A GUEST IN THE HOUSE, AND THE HOSPITALITY AND BANQUET GIVEN HIM UNTIL HE DEPARTS

Before the arrival of the sects of the Indian idols, which erroneously deal with the things of salvation, the Chinese, Japanese, Koreans, and other heathen nations of this Orient knew nothing of the next life and the ultimate end of man. Their knowledge was limited to the present life, at the end of which they believed that everything comes to an end. They thus placed all their happiness and ultimate end in corporeal pleasures and recreations, and all their efforts were directed to the end of serving their bellies.[1] Hence they seem to have attached the greatest importance to the business of entertaining and banqueting each other, diverting themselves with various revelries during the banquets and with their devices to encourage people to eat and drink. From this it follows that among their various occupations the lengthiest one, which takes up the greater part of the time throughout their whole life, is this business of entertaining, feasting, and entertaining each other.[2]

Thus it would be possible to compose a lengthy book about what has been written on this subject. But we shall mention only some of the principal points, and this will enable the reader to realize how much is involved in this matter. In this way, he will form some idea of the subject and the great obstacles that it raised against the law of God, which was to be preached to these people. For long practice had already converted this into second nature and into thick brambles of vices and sins that spring up with such great fierceness from this business of eating and drinking. All of this had to be overcome by the power of Holy Scripture.

First of all, we will deal with the house where the guests are received and banqueted, because this has the first place. Secondly, the manner of receiving a guest up to the time he reaches the room. Thirdly, the manner of entering the room and the courtesies exchanged after they are seated. Fourthly, the manner of entertaining them with wine, and also with *sakana* to encourage them to drink; this is the principal entertainment and courtesy for the guest. Sixthly, how they entertain some guests in particular, and how they bid farewell to a guest.

1. The room in which the guests are received and the eating arrangements therein

In the section dealing with the building methods of the Japanese, we have already spoken

---

[1] An oblique reference to Romans 16,18, where St Paul warns against those who do not serve the Lord but their own belly.

[2] In his list of the five defects of the Japanese, Valignano (*Sumario*, pp. 31–3) puts in the last place their inclination to drinking and feasting, 'in which they spend so much time that they pass the whole night therein.'

about the construction of the rooms, their entrances, divisions, decoration, the interior of the verandas, the corridors, the gardens of trees and flowers set before them, and other similar matters.[1] In this chapter, we will touch on only two things used for the entertainment provided for the guest and the respect shown towards his person. The first consists of the preparations that are made, the cleanliness not only inside the room itself but also in the street, the entrance, and the inner courtyards, and also some special things that are placed therein according to the custom of the country. The second is the arrangement of the seating in positions of greater or lesser honour, so that each person may be given his proper place.

As regards the first point, the preparations to be made and the welcome to be shown depend on knowing the rank of the guest who is going to be received. But we will speak briefly about the main things observed in receiving a noble person, and from this it will easily be seen what must be done for those of less dignity and authority. The Japanese pay great attention to exterior cleanliness, and they exercise much care in this matter not only inside the houses and rooms but also outside in the street, in the porches, in the exterior courtyards, and in the inner patios of the houses within their compounds.[2] This is not only so when they receive guests, for as an ordinary matter of course they keep everything, including out-of-the-way places, so clean and tidy within and without the house that should a guest arrive unexpectedly, they can welcome him in a way befitting his person, however noble he may be. Thus in the houses of the lords, nobles, the wealthy, and gentry, there are special people whose office is to keep clean the road in front of the house, the entrances and gates of the compound, the courtyards, gardens, the privies for the guests and the others for their servants, and the special places with pots to urinate into so as to prevent soiling anywhere. Thus everything is kept clean and decent. There is a special public place where they hang up a supply of street brooms and other implements necessary for cleanliness, as well as one to root out weeds that spring up in the courtyards and paths. All these places are invariably kept so clean and neat that they are a joy to behold. When people come on horseback and some manure is dropped on the road, it is immediately removed and the place cleaned.

The entrance of the house and the paths within the compound and courtyards which lead up to the rooms are all paved and sprinkled with coarse sand. They are slightly sloping so that water will run away and no mud will form. The stones paving the paths are so extremely clean that even when it has rained a person can walk over them without dampening his sandals. For this reason, when a guest comes to visit another person, his shoe-boy brings an extra pair of clean new sandals, which the guest puts on at the beginning of these paths so as not to dirty the stones with his old sandals that have mud stuck to their soles. Similarly the host does the same when he comes out to greet the guests.

Just as there are these people who see to cleanliness outside, so there are others of greater dignity and rank who look after the interior of the rooms and corridors with even greater care. They sweep and dust them every day and clean away the spider webs spun during the night. Then with damp cloths they wipe away the dust and stains from the floorboards of the verandas and the wooden columns. These are usually made of fine cedarwood, and as a result of this care they are as clean and bright as a spotless mirror, and at times you can see

---

[1] That is, Chapter 12.

[2] Mexia (6 January 1584, in *Cartas*, II, f. 124) remarks that the cleanliness of the Japanese cannot be imagined, for any breach in this regard is considered a major crime. Nobunaga condemned a maidservant to death for not sweeping away some orange peel in a room.

your face in them, as we sometimes noticed.[1] When it is very warm, or after a meal, they sometimes sit on these verandas to refresh themselves. Some of the verandas are also matted, especially in the winter on account of the cold. In an out-of-the-way place in these corridors near the rooms, there are very clean wash-places provided with clean, fresh water so that guests may wash their hands whenever they please, for this is a very frequent custom among them.

In addition to this ordinary cleanliness observed in the houses and palaces, the cleaning is renewed with special care when they are going to receive a guest in the house. They sweep the street in front of the house once more, as well as the entrances, paths, and courtyards, and they sprinkle water everywhere, even on the walls, in order to lay the dust and freshen these places. Thus when the guest passes through everywhere is dewy and very fresh. The rooms, verandas, and corridors are also swept again. Rooms that are not gilded or painted by a famous artist, as is their custom, are adorned for greater decoration with a frame of byōbu, which either run along the walls or else take the place of walls. Each set of these contains six or eight panels, gilded or painted by an artist of note.[2]

At the top of the room there is a kind of alcove set into the wall and its lower part is like a step, beginning[3] about a span and a half from the mats. The height and width of this alcove are in proportion to the room, and it may sometimes be a dozen feet wide and proportionately high. On the step at the bottom of the alcove they place an old vase of copper, earthenware, or some other material, on a salver or tray. Seasonable flowers are placed into this vase, and this is maintained throughout all four seasons of the year for they use the flowers that bloom in each of them. There are many rules about putting the flowers into the vase, and there are private persons who learn these rules from books and practise the art with teachers, making it their best endeavour to imitate nature and its lack of artificiality in everything. One flower will perhaps lean over this way, another that way, while others are set among other plants that grow near them in their natural setting. Some of the flowers will be in full bloom, others only half-open, still others merely in bud, but each flower is put into a place where it seems naturally to belong. They avoid anything smacking of the artificiality with which we are wont to make up large bouquets of flowers, bunched together to obtain a beautiful but unnatural effect. The Japanese and Chinese take great delight in contemplating these natural things and their simplicity, and they do their best to imitate them artificially. The same applies to their paintings and their gardens, and the trees and the flowers planted therein.[4]

In the middle of the same alcove they hang a renowned and admired painting by an outstanding artist of olden times, or else a scroll bearing their hieroglyphic letters written by

---

[1] For the shining quality of polished wood, see p. 146, above.

[2] *Vocabulario*, f. 23: '*Byōbu*. A kind of thick panels that stand by themselves. Used by the Japanese to decorate their houses and keep out draughts.' Appreciative descriptions of *byōbu* (hence the Portuguese word *biombo*, screen) are given by Carletti, in *TCJ*, p. 219; Fróis, 12 July 1569, in *Cartas*, I, f. 272v, and Vilela, 6 October 1571, in ibid., I, ff. 320v–321. Saris (in Farrington, *English Factory*, II, p. 1023), 'beobs or large pictures to hang a chamber with'. Mundy (*Travels*, III:1, p. 255) remarks, 'Beeombos are certaine skreenes of 8 or 9 Foote Deepe, made into sundry leaves. ... They make a Most Delightsome shew, beeing painted with variety off curious lively colleurs intermingled with gold, containing stories, beasts, birds, Fishes, Forrests, Flowers, Fruites, etts.' Valignano (*Cerimoniale*, p. 65) forbade Jesuits to keep *byōbu* in their rooms as ornaments, but in 1612 Pasio (JapSin 57, f. 249v) allowed *nimai*, or two-panel screens, to hide the bed; they were not to be made of paper because of the risk of fire.

[3] There is a short gap here in the Portuguese text.

[4] This may well be the earliest European account of Japanese flower arrangement, now called *ikebana*. The alcove set in the wall is the *tokonoma*.

an esteemed calligrapher of bygone days, for indeed their writing is more a kind of painting than script.[1] Some of these ancient paintings and scrolls are worth thousands of crowns while others are valued at many hundreds, and it is quite beyond belief how they are prized and regarded as wealth and gems.[2]

They provide the guests with very clean privies set apart from the room in an unfrequented place. The path thither is paved with large stones spaced out and set in place like stepping-stones, and the guests can pass over them with all cleanliness even though it is raining. Or instead of being paved with these stones, the path may be strewn with pebbles. New clogs are placed there for use in wet weather and also new slippers for the guest's use, as the shoe-boy does not come to this place but only the pages. The interior of the privy is kept extremely clean, and a perfume pan and freshly cut paper are placed there for this purpose. The place is always free from any bad smell, for when the guests depart the man in charge there cleans the privy if necessary and strews sand so that it is left as if it had never been used. A ewer of water and other things needed for washing the hands are found nearby, for it is an invariable custom of both nobles and commoners to wash their hands every time after using the privy for their major and minor necessities. In the case of persons of great nobility, however, a page gives them water, a towel, and their type of pitcher and basin after they have mounted the veranda of the room so that they may wash their hands.

It may often happen that a guest staying in the house of a person receives some letters or business matters that require an immediate answer, and for this purpose their kind of writing instruments are needed. It is usual to find in a prominent place in the room an extremely beautiful box, decorated with gold and silver flowers upon very delicate black laquer and richly ornamented. Within are contained all the instruments needed for writing and signing a letter.[3] It is divided into five compartments and in the middle is the inkwell. This is a special stone, about a span in length and a half-span in breadth. It is slightly hollowed out and has an elevated rim around the sides. At the top of it there is a deeper well skilfully carved out in which the water collects. This water is used to grind the ink in the other part of the stone, for the ink is a stick made from the vapour of sesame oil. In the compartments there is a small gilded copper pot containing water to pour into the inkwell, and small brushes made of the fine hair from the paunch of rabbits and other animals.[4] There is also the ink stick, as well as a knife, instead of scissors, for cutting purposes, a punch for sealing, and everything else necessary. On a salver near this box there will be two or three types of paper. Letters are written on one kind of paper and enclosed in another kind, for this is their method of closing letters, and they use flour or rice glue instead of sealing-wax.

---

[1] Acosta (*Natural and Moral History*, p. 402) notes about Chinese script, 'the writing in China is no other thing but a manner of painting or ciphring.' Rodrigues later has much to say about Japanese styles of writing in Book 2, chapters 4 and 5.

[2] A reference to the *kakemono*, or scroll, hanging in the *tokonoma*. Valignano (*Sumario*, p. 47) states that a small painting of a bird or a tree, executed by a famous artist of former times, could be bought and sold for 3,000, 4,000, or even 10,000 ducats.

[3] For illustrations of the *suzuribako* (writing-box) and *bundai* (writing desk), see Ogasawara, f. 11v.

[4] *Vocabulario*, f. 233: '*Suzuri*. Inkstand of Japan.' Also, f. 191: '*Kenchi. Suzuri no ide*. Depression in the Chinese stone inkwell, with water to mix the ink.' Further references to ink-stones and ink-sticks are given in Carletti, *My Voyage*, p. 164, and Fróis, *Tratado*, p. 214. A modern account on this subject is found in Gulik, *Mi Fu on Ink-Stones*. The *fude*, or brush, is described by Fitch (in Hakluyt, *Principal Navigations*, V, p. 499) as 'a fine pensill made of dogs or cats haire.' Fróis, *Tratado*, pp. 214, 218, also mentions the brush. Cortes (*Viaje*, pp. 216–7) gives an account of Chinese ink, brushes, and paper.

As often happens, and indeed it is quite usual, the guests may arrive at night, most of which they spend eating and drinking. So they prepare lamps and candlesticks in certain special places, as well as lanterns along the paths and at the entrances and exits.[1] To warm the guests in winter, they set up a very clean and handsome copper brazier with lion's feet, in which they burn charcoal made from a certain tree. This ignites very quickly, but lasts a long time and does not throw out sparks.[2] They also use a kind of small stove in the middle of the room and cover it with a high table and a quilt of soft, fine silk that retains the heat. The guests come and recline there, warming their hands and even the feet inside by the very mild and gentle fire, which is very different from the brazier. They throw into it various excellent perfumes, such as aloes, eaglewood, or their own preparations, for the Japanese and Chinese are extremely fond of delicate scents and perfumes.[3]

As regards the seating within the room, it has already been noted that, when it comes to their buildings and seating arrangements, on account of their astrology the Chinese and Japanese pay great attention to the position of the places with respect to the heavens. They regard facing the south, which is the front, as the principal position, and after this comes the eastern position on the left, then the western position on the right; finally, facing north and looking towards the back is the lowliest place. Hence the top of the room is the middle part situated on the northern side, and here is to be found the above-mentioned alcove or place for flowers. This part faces the south, while behind it lies the north; the left-hand side is more important and honourable than the right, for it lies to the east where the sun rises and whence comes all wholesome influence. The lowliest part, which serves as the entrance to the room, is to the south and faces the north. All their houses are built so that the top and entrance of the room are always below the slope of the roof.

Usually the guests are never seated in the middle of the upper part of the room, except the king when he meets grandees or goes out in public, or the ruler of Tenka, or *kubō*, or a territorial lord with respect to his subjects, or some great lord whose dignity demands that place of honour, and also the bonzes in respect to both ordinary and well-born people for they are their teachers. But generally they sit on the left of the upper part of the room in a higher or lower position according to their rank, while the host is seated on the right-hand side. If there are many guests who are also on the right-hand side, the host himself always takes the last and lowest place. Thus their houses and rooms are planned so that the entrance through which the guests enter lies conveniently on the left-hand side, and the serving, which comes from within the house, is on the right-hand side where the host is placed. This is because the serving is done from the lowliest side, and besides, it is more polite, as a safeguard, to serve from in front of the guest than from behind him. This also leads to greater convenience, for the waiters can quietly ask the host anything necessary.[4] On some occasions the host will show greater hospitality by rising and retiring inside the house where the preparations are being made so as to arrange things personally. Sometimes,

---

[1] For illustrations of Japanese lamps, lanterns, and candlesticks, see Morse, *Japanese Homes*, pp. 219–25.

[2] The *hibachi*, illustrated in Morse, *Japanese Homes*, pp. 214–19.

[3] The *kotatsu* – see p. 152.

[4] In this rather unclear account, Rodrigues seems to mean that important guests sit facing south, but ordinary visitors face west, while the host sits facing east. The guests enter from the eastern side, while the servants come in from the west. Valignano (*Cerimoniale*, p. 184) stresses that the entrance of the waiters and pages should be on the side where the host sits. Traditionally the safest position in the room was to sit with one's back to the northern wall, as that side with the *tokonoma* generally did not have any doors.

indeed, in accordance with his rank, he may bring out the first table for the principal guest and thus pay him greater honour. Although the serving comes from the right-hand side, everything comes in by the southern and lowliest part of the room. The servants and pages do not remain in the actual room, but kneel down and sit back on their feet on the veranda, where they wait to serve the guests. They sit down directly on the mats, as has been said.

2. The way of welcoming a guest up to the time he enters the room

First of all, the guest may have come a long way from outside the territory. In which case, as soon as the host learns that he has reached the place but has not yet arrived at his lodgings, he sends a person of quality to welcome him and commiserate with him on the hardship suffered on the journey. If the guest is a woman, the message is given to the chief person of her retinue. If the guest goes to the lodgings and postpones his visit to the following day, a servant of rank is sent around bearing a gift, usually of firewood, vegetables, food such as fish and wild game, and wine, all in sufficient quantity to last him two or three days. This is because he is new to the district and so cannot suddenly send out to buy such things. But should he be an important person and lord, only wood is sent to his kitchen, because such people always take with them their kitchen and its staff, their kind of tableware, and every-thing else needed. If the person whom such people are going to visit is also an important man, there are various formalities involved in all this, because they proceed in their litters with great pomp with their caparisoned horses by them and accompanied by a large retinue of their retainers both on horseback and on foot, and by ranks of lancers, archers, and mus-keteers marching there in front. The lord of the territory will have had convenient lodgings prepared in the city for the guest and his servants, and he sends some of the nobles of his house, such as his son, brother, a relative, etc., accompanied by a large retinue, to meet the guest on the way and bid him welcome. Such visits involve much pageantry and grandeur, for the Japanese lords pride themselves in this.[1] But we will not speak about this now, but only about the ordinary visits of nobles and people of quality.

On learning that the guest is coming to his house, the host or another person, according to the guest's dignity, goes out to greet him, dressed in trousers and a *kataginu*, a formal robe. A person who has already renounced his property and has shaven his head goes out wearing a long robe and over this a loose upper-coat, made of a fine black veil, after the fashion of a bonze, or else another upper-garment. He has freshly shaved his head and chin, for all this is to honour and make much of the person to be entertained. For some people he will go to the street entrance of the compound or to the street itself; for other people, only as far as the inner courtyard; and for others as far as the veranda in accordance with the rank and nobility of the guest.[2] As soon as they meet, they pay each other their proper respects with the bows and obeisances due to the person. The first to speak is the host as he welcomes the guest and thanks him for coming. Then in a pleasant and courteous way he stands on the right-hand side of the guest and insists that he goes first through the street door. As they exchange compliments, he points out with his hand the path and the place

---

[1] The pageantry and splendour of such retinues are graphically described by Kaempfer (*Kaempfer's Japan*, pp. 271–3). For illustrations, see Skene Smith, *Tokugawa Japan*, p. 64.

[2] Valignano (*Cerimoniale*, pp. 184–6) notes that when a *yakata* or other ranking noble visits a Jesuit house, the missionaries should go out into the garden to receive him. He adds (ibid., p. 210) that the *daimyo* of Bungo, Ōtomo Yoshishige, would never go to the garden to greet guests, unless they were the shogun's envoys.

where he must enter. This is repeated at any narrow place or slope, at every door, and on entering the room. The number of times the host must thus insist depends on the guest's rank. For some guests it is done three times, for others twice, while for others only once.

All the houses, even those of only one storey, have a veranda, and when they reach there and come to the entrance of the room, the host gestures with his hand to the guest that he should enter first. When after being thus urged two or three times the guest declines to go ahead, the host then enters in front. At the same time they pay each other their due respects and courtesies, bowing with their hands on their thighs, or with the knee and left hand on the floor, as has already been described. When entering a room or passing any place, they step off with their left foot first, but on leaving they start with either foot. When they have entered the room and the guest is there inside, he is given a suitable place. If he is nobler than the host and of very high rank and station, this will be at the top of the room. A guest of great nobility can go up to the third mat from the entrance towards the top of the room. When they are both of equal status, they are seated about two mats from the entrance. In all cases the host remains a little below the guest in order to pay him honour, with the result that they are not placed one in front of the other. Each of the room's mats is six and a half feet in length and half as wide.

If, as ordinarily happens, the guest places himself below his due place, the host gestures him with his hand as often as three times to go higher; if he declines, the host goes up a little in order to make him do so. Then courtesy obliges the guest to go up just a little, but he goes only in front of the place whither the host has gone. After remaining there a little time, the host then returns to a place lower than that of the guest, as has been said.

When both are seated by kneeling back on their legs and feet, the guest bows to the host, who then responds with one of the three bows, mentioned above, in keeping with the dignity of each one. When the bowing has been completed, the host speaks to the guest, welcoming and thanking him for the visit and the inconvenience experienced on the way thither. After this, the man whose office is to receive messages and gifts, shows, as has been said, the guest's present, which has already been put in a suitable place. Then the host bows to the guest, and the guest responds with another bow, and the host thanks him for the gift he has brought. However good the present may be, the guest will belittle it, declaring that it is useless and that it is but a mere token of his goodwill and respect.[1] After they have been sitting in this kneeling position for a little while, the host and guest seat themselves as they please and cross their legs. But their feet must always remain hidden in their trousers, which are very wide at the bottom and rather like a robe. They then talk on any subject they wish.

---

[1] Even today a Japanese presenting a gift will say politely, 'This is a very poor thing.' If the present consists of food, then, 'This is not at all tasty.' See also pp. 258, 268, 304, for other examples of the Japanese custom of disparaging their own gifts.

CHAPTER 26

THE MANNER OF ENTERTAINING THE GUEST WITH WINE AND *SAKANA*, WHICH IS THE FIRST AND PRINCIPAL COURTESY PAID TO A GUEST ON THESE VISITS

As the end of this pagan people is to serve their bellies in feasting and drunkenness[1] chiefly with wine, all the banquets, revelries, and recreations are aimed at persuading them by various means to drink too much wine until they end up drunk and many of them completely lose their senses. The Chinese and Japanese do not consider drunkenness in banquets and revelries as something wrong, although they will not countenance violent intoxication, but this is rare among the nobles.[2] But because they have the habit of drinking a great deal and Japanese wine by its very nature is not very strong, the people become so accustomed to it that, however much they drink, they do not usually lose their senses. Nor do they become so excited that they forget themselves and neglect any matters that may crop up.

Many of them are so strong in this regard that, although they become merry with the excessive amount of wine that they are made to drink, they maintain as much control of themselves as they had at the start. Indeed, in order to honour and favour the host who is holding the banquet and to show appreciation of his hospitality towards them, even those who do not normally drink exert themselves to do so. There are many among them who humour their host in these gatherings by pretending to drink, while there are others who drink a great deal if they suspect that something is wrong.[3] But they do this in such a way as always to retain full possession of their faculties. To show more gratitude towards the host and to excuse themselves from drinking many times in the middle of the feast, or because of the strength of the wine, they say, 'I am completely tipsy and cannot manage any more (as if owning themselves to be vanquished), nor am I capable of returning home.'

Thus on the day after the banquet they tardily send a message of thanks for the feast and wine, saying that from the time they returned home up to the time of writing they had been

---

[1] A reference to Romans 13, 13. Rodrigues quotes the last four words in Latin.

[2] Fróis (*Tratado*, p. 178) notes, 'In Europe it is a great disgrace to get drunk. But it is esteemed in Japan. When you ask, "How is the lord?", they answer, "He is drunk."' According to Caron (*True Description*, p. 47), a Japanese overdrinking at a banquet retires and sleeps off the effects of the wine, but Arthur Hatch (in Farrington, *English Factory*, II, p. 948) observes that the Japanese drink a great deal at a banquet, 'and being moved to anger or wrath in the heate of their drinke, you may as soone perswade tygers to patience and quietnesse as them.' This is borne out by Ribadeneira (*Historia*, p. 372), who notes that many drinking bouts were held at the New Year. The excessive *sake* would make the drinkers' faces flushed and loosen their tongues. Sometimes a young man would show off in his drinking and walk around like a mad man with a drawn sword, waving it around and injuring people unless they got out of his way.

[3] '... se tem algua sospeita de mal ...' A puzzling phrase, which according to Rodrigues, *Nihon*, I, p. 506, refers to illness.

intoxicated and incapable on account of the amount they had drunk. This is to show how great was the welcome and affection that the host had shown them. It was for his sake that they forced themselves to drink so as to afford him pleasure, and belatedly complied with their obligation of writing to him. In this way, they show that they honour and respect the host, and thank him for his hospitality and the expensive preparations made for their sake. For according to the type of banquet, these preparations are made many days beforehand, and the host sends off to remote parts in search of tasty things for the *sakana* in order to persuade the guests to drink. The host feels that the expense and preparations are well repaid when the guests drink a great deal and become noisy, and in their conversation praise their manly and strong spirit. However many times they are challenged by others, those who have drunk a lot keep up with all of them in their drinking without any agitation or falling behind. They prize themselves on this ability, and they consider it important not to show any weakness in this matter, nor allow themselves to be beaten by another who challenges them to a drinking match, just as if they were fighting a battle or duel.

It is also astonishing to note the various devices and means that the devil has taught them to encourage much wine drinking, and those who usually drink next to nothing are often obliged to partake. There are cases in which such people cannot avoid doing so nor will any excuse be accepted, and so they are obliged to drink even when it is injurious to their health. They not only concoct a thousand kinds of tasty *sakana* (these are appetising things to eat that encourage a man to drink) as incentives, but they also sometimes summon women dancers, singers, and other types of depraved people who, when they drink, challenge whomsoever they wish to partake as well. They take the cup from which they have drunk and give it to a person, and pride prevents his refusing to accept it and drink from it. Matters sometimes reach such a pass that the wine stirs them up and makes them all so noisy that some of them challenge others to drink wine from basins and other large vessels instead of cups. When they find themselves in such a predicament, many get up on the plea of some necessity and secretly have recourse to their jugs that they have ready there for this purpose, only to return straight away in order to continue.[1] So the purpose and result of the expense, preparations, and other things are to be found in wine, and they certainly overlook the countless disorders resulting from this excess.

They give away important secrets, and without realizing they reveal things that they would not want said.[2] In such cases some of them kill their rowdy enemies *inter epulas* for no other course remains to them, just as Absolem killed his brother,[3] Judith killed Holofernes,[4] and other people recorded in Holy Scripture. Secular literature also mentions other similar cases. There are also many other innumerable vices resulting from drunkenness. This vice of excessive drink and drunkenness is very common throughout almost all

[1] Casal (*Notes*, pp. 35, 54, 65) mentions large and deep bowls for heavy drinking of *sake*. An extant bowl, dating from the 13th century, has a diameter of 17 inches and a depth of 4.5 inches. The *leiteiras*, or jugs, to which the guests might have secret recourse, were the *haisen*, receptacles containing tepid water to rinse the cups (Casal, *Notes*, p. 26). Presumably Rodrigues means that guests might surreptitiously empty their cups into this container. Alternatively, they might vomit into the *haisen*, but this could hardly have been done secretly. Frói (*Tratado*, p. 176) also comments on the pressure to make guests drink too much; some of the diners become drunk, while others throw up.

[2] There was a precautionary maxim, 'Kabe ni mimi, tokkuri ni kuchi', 'Walls have ears, and wine flasks have mouths'.

[3] For the murder of Amnon by his brother Absalom's servants during a feast, see 2 Samuel 13, 28–9.

[4] Judith, 13, 1–8. Judith killed the Assyrian general Holophernes while he was in a drunken stupor.

of Asia, and even the Moors do not refrain from this, however much they are forbidden to drink by their false prophet.

Among the Japanese about whom we have been speaking, the first and chief courtesy and token of interior love and friendship is the *sakazuki*.[1] This is to entertain with wine, and two or three persons drink in turns from the same cup as a sign of uniting their hearts into one or their two souls into one. They use this entertainment with both people drinking wine from the same cup first of all as a token of friendship and courtesy. Hence if a person does not wish to accept the cup from which the other has drunk, it is taken as a sign of enmity and of his not wishing to be friendly.[2] On the other hand, this is done when two enemies are reconciled. Both drink from the same cup from which one of them has drunk, and they pass it to each other as a sign of reconciliation and union of hearts.[3] Secondly, it is performed when they make a conspiracy, alliance, or promise that must be fulfilled at all costs. They also do this when they take oaths of loyalty to each other, sometimes mixing in the wine some drops of blood that both draw by pricking their finger, and then both drink the wine mixed with blood.[4]

Thirdly, it is a sign of great pleasure in their festivals and merrymaking, and a token of welcome on every occasion and in every circumstance. Fourthly, at a farewell before a long absence. Fifthly, at the hour of death, whether it be natural or violent, when they cut their bellies, bidding farewell to their relatives and friends, and even to those who are to cut their belly in some place at the same time.[5] This happens often enough when they are surrounded by their foes. They kill their women and children, and then cut their bellies after bidding farewell by passing the *sakazuki* around to each other. Also in various other circumstances when they are obliged to cut their bellies.[6] Finally, they invariably use wine in all human agreements and alliances. The Chinese do the same, eating and drinking first of all, and when they are warmed by the wine, they deal with business. They seem to do this on purpose in order to avoid deceit, for the wine does not allow any dissembling because it makes them blurt out everything hidden in their hearts and speak their minds without any duplicity.

---

[1] The rite of *sakazuki* is described in some detail by Avila Girón (*Relación*, pp. 45–8), who includes a diagram of a shallow bowl (rather than a cup) called *sakazuki*. For these bowls, see p. 239, n. 3. Valignano (*Cerimoniale*, pp. 214–32, 250–56, and *Sumario*, pp. 191–3, nn. 11–14) also deals with the subject and the etiquette involved. For a detailed account of *sakazuki* bowls, see Casal, *Notes*.

[2] Brother Lourenço (2 June 1560, in Ruiz-de-Medina, *Documentos*, II, p. 270) records that when the shogun Ashikaga Yoshiteru received Gaspar Vilela in audience at Miyako in 1560, he gave the priest the cup from which he himself had drunk and invited him to drink from it, 'and this is a sign of friendship.' The audience is also related in Fróis, *História*, I, p. 161.

[3] Also mentioned by Fróis, *Tratado*, p. 264.

[4] Vilela (29 October 1557, in Ruiz-de-Medina, *Documentos*, I, p. 688) mentions another method of swearing loyalty. The man stands in front of a heathen statue, draws blood from his arm, writes (with his blood?) some mysterious characters on paper, burns the paper, and drinks the ashes (in wine?). Rodrigues deals with written oaths at some length in *Arte grande*, ff. 202v–204v. Further references are given in Valignano, *Sumario*, p. 26, n. 9.

[5] An indirect reference to collective punishment, widely practised in Japan. Caron (*True Description*, pp. 39–40) relates the horrendous story of a government official found guilty of overtaxing local people. Messengers were sent out with orders for him, his uncle, three brothers, and three sons (all living in different parts of the country) to commit *seppuku* at the same time on the 8th day of the eighth month.

[6] For example, before the fall of Kamakura in 1333, various defeated warriors drank wine before committing ritual suicide. *Taiheiki*, p. 310. This custom was observed by the Augustin friar Hernando Ayala and the Dominican friar Alonso Navarrete at the hour of their martyrdom near Nagasaki on 1 June 1617. Just before their death, they 'brought wine reserved for Mass and poured it into cups, and lifting them up high (for this is the courteous custom of Japan), each gave a cup to his executioner to drink'. Sicardo, *Christiandad*, p. 149.

1. The various types of entertaining guests with drink, and the kinds of cups or goblets employed

As this custom of entertaining guests with drink is so general among the Chinese and Japanese, we must first of all examine their various ways of doing so on occasions of greater or less solemnity and magnificence, and also the kinds of cups and goblets used in their celebrated etiquette and rites. To this end it may be remarked in general that among both the Chinese and Japanese there are two ways of entertaining visiting guests with wine. The first is the usual and ordinary entertainment with wine as a token of courtesy, urbanity, and honour paid to the guest, and as a sign of good feeling, welcome, and friendship. This is performed without a banquet, but with only wine, accompanied by something to eat. This is done for every kind of guest, both nobles and even people of mean sort, when they pay a formal visit. When, however, they are very friendly and often meet together, this ceremony of wine is not necessary, but instead they entertain with *cha*. This is a certain kind of leaf from a bush, and in Japan it is ground into powder and dissolved in hot water; in China, it is boiled in hot water and served as a drink, but we will speak about this elsewhere.[1] The second type of entertainment with wine is festive and solemn, and takes place in formal visits, banquets, revelries, recreations, and public and solemn events, in order to show honour, courtesy, and respect towards the guests.

These two types are distinguished only by the exterior and extraordinary solemnity, adornment, and magnificence, in the one sort, of the cups or goblets and the salvers on which they are placed, and the various kinds of accompanying *sakana*. While in the other sort, there is neither formality nor pomp, but only a common cup of wine on an ordinary salver along with ordinary *sakana*, and this is the usual and ordinary Japanese etiquette, as we have said. Both types of drinking are invariably accompanied by different things to eat, cut up and prepared in small pieces so that they may be given with some *hashi* into the hand of the guest as a sign of courtesy so that he may drink the wine that he receives. They also provide other dainty morsels that have the same appetising effect. Served with various broths and sauces, they bring on thirst, and show courtesy and respect towards the guest. All this in general is called *sakana*.[2]

Just as in general there are two ways of entertaining a person with drink, that is, the ordinary and the solemn ways, so also there are various kinds of goblets or cups from which the wine is drunk. These are placed on salvers, and it is in these salvers that most of the solemnity of the rite resides. As regards the material of the cups, goblets, and the salvers on which they are placed in Japan, there are again two sorts. The ordinary and common cups and salvers are painted with a very delicate varnish, adorned with wonderfully and richly gilded flowers. Some of the ordinary salvers are also flat and painted with delicate black varnish, others with red, purple, and green. And in the middle of the salver there is a deep well in which they pour the wine after they have drunk from the cup so as not to soil the mats, and they place the goblet or cup over the top of this well.[3]

The second type of cup is the formal and festive one, and these are made of mere baked

---

[1] Rodrigues describes tea, or *cha*, in great detail in Chapters 32–4.

[2] For further information on *sakana*, see Avila Girón, *Relación*, p. 47; Valignano, *Cerimoniale*, pp. 226–30; Fróis, *Tratado*, p. 178.

[3] The *sakazuki* were generally more like shallow dishes than cups or goblets, and part of the ideograph with which the word is written in Japanese signifies 'plate'. Usually these dishes were lacquered red, while the stand on which

clay of the colour of a tile, without any handiwork or decoration at all. The most formal ones are gilded with gold both inside and out. Cups of lower quality are all silver-plated, while those of the basest sort are made of earthenware, as above, but without any such ornamentation, consisting of only pure clay. The salvers on which they are placed are made of fine cedarwood in various fashions and shapes according to the rank of the guests. Such clay goblets or cups are used only once, and the guest, the host, and others who are present drink from them until the end of a toast. When it is concluded, they must begin another toast again and a new clay cup of the same kind is brought in, so they are never used more than once. This type of cup is for the use of great nobles and lords, and for feasts and merrymaking. This kind of earthenware is used for certain delicacies by the king himself,[1] the great nobles belonging to the patrician order, and other territorial lords in accordance with their ancient customs and ceremonies, when they could use other ware made of precious materials such as gold and silver, for the land possesses a plentiful supply of these.

The Chinese also use cups and salvers in their banquets and feasts just as do the Japanese, but they differ in many ways. First of all, as the Chinese are so given to wine, banquets, and feasting (for this is their paradise in this life), they pay much attention to the drinking cups and their salvers, and esteem them as jewels. For this reason they make them from various precious materials. Their king, the great lords, and the important magistrates use cups made of alabaster, or of a certain precious stone that they highly prize and import from abroad. Others are made of gold, silver, or unicorn or rhinoceros horn, others of red sandalwood, others of the very large and beautiful beaks of certain birds that are found in China, others of very fine red scented wood with delicate work on the outside while the inside, where the wine is poured, is overlaid with silver. Others are made of various kinds of materials admired by them, and finally, there are others of porcelain, and these are the meanest of them all.

As regards their size, the Chinese cups are much smaller than the Japanese ones, for the latter are usually big, while the Chinese ones are so small that many of them put together would not make up a good swig of wine.[2] They thus linger a long time in their drinking, chatting, and relaxing until they become quite noisy with the succession of so many rounds. In addition, the Japanese all drink from only one cup, sending it around from one to another as a sign of true friendship. But however many people may be present, the Chinese all have their own cup with its salver, and each one drinks from his own cup and does not send it to another, for this would be discourteous among them. If another person arrives, they produce a new and clean cup for him, or they order a cup from which somebody else has drunk to be washed so that he may use it. Thirdly, the actual etiquette of drinking is somewhat different. Finally, they always end the banquet, feasting, and winedrinking with the drink of *cha*, which is sometimes served while they are drinking wine because it greatly keeps down the fumes.[3] But the Japanese also serve *cha* while they are drinking and after the wine, just as the Chinese do.

---

they were carried was generally black and had perforations to drain off excess wine. For illustrations of choice items, see Casal, *Notes*, pp. 12–30.

[1] Torres (in *TCJ*, p. 75) was only one among various Europeans who retold rumours about the secluded emperor, including the fact that he always used earthenware dishes and never set foot on the ground. Kaempfer (*Kaempfer's Japan*, p. 89) has much to say on the subject. His account is defended in Blacker, 'Forgotten Practices'.

[2] Ricci (*Fonti*, I, p. 76, and *China*, p. 64) asserts that their cups did not hold more wine than would a nutshell.

[3] Rodrigues later (p. 277) mentions that tea 'checks the fumes of excessive wine that rise to the head' in his list of its beneficial effects.

Then the Japanese use five kinds of cups when they entertain guests with wine. The first is the ordinary type of varnished cup, gilded or plain, with which they receive their ordinary guests, as well as other nobler guests with whom they are on intimate terms. This kind of cup or goblet is placed on its varnished salver, which is either gilded or plain, and of some little height. In the middle of it there is a receptacle into which courtesy demands that the cup be emptied after a person has drunk from it before he sends it to another person to drink from. This kind of entertaining with drink has its own special etiquette to be observed, and we will say something about this later.

The second type is like a cup of simple earthenware without any handiwork or decoration, but left in its natural state and with the colour of the very clay from which it is made. This unpainted cup is placed on its square cedar salver, which rests on four high legs. This kind of cup is used in the reception of a noble when he visits another person of rank for the first time, or on solemn festivals, such as the New Year, and other occasions. The cup must always be new and not old or used, and many are on sale for these and other uses. They are so cheap that they are worth hardly anything at all. They are used only for ancient ceremonies in which their etiquette and courtesy are observed. The courtesies that are here performed are the same as those of the ordinary cup. But as this sort of new clay cup is dry and therefore sticks a good deal to the lips, people who are not careful sometimes find themselves in trouble because they cannot easily unstick them. Before they drink, they first of all must moisten their lips so that they will not stick to the clay when they drink. Whence may be seen the power of the ancient customs and notions of countries that could well use precious and convenient things that do not have such drawbacks. Instead, they leave them aside in favour of those of little worth, whose use presents such difficulties.

The third sort of cup is the same as the previous earthenware type and differs only in the shape of the cedar salver on which it is placed. These salvers are square trays of a span or more in height, their sides projecting upwards and taking the place of legs. They are entirely enclosed on all four sides from top to bottom, and the actual tray is contained inside and is surrounded by handiwork in the actual wood itself. They use this type of cup on their salvers when they receive all their guests who belong to the patrician order, or *kuge*, or other very noble lords. Noble ladies also make use of this. The courtesies and compliments observed as they take and send the cup to the others are the same.

The fourth kind is the same earthenware cup completely gilded or silvered, or half-gilded and half-silvered, both inside and out. This type also differs from the previous kinds as regards the salver on which it is placed, for this is made of a board of fine cedar supported by three legs a span in height. Its shape is in imitation of a jagged seashore with its entrances and exits like the bays and capes of a shore. It is painted entirely blue, or the colour of the sea, and decorated with various paintings of flowers or small trees, especially the pine that grows along the coast. When they paint these trees, they imitate and copy their natural colour. Everything is executed very naturally on the actual cedarwood with exquisite perfection and delicacy.[1] On top of this they place the earthenware cup, as we have said. They are accustomed to using this kind of cup on picnics or at banquets. After the host has wined and dined the guests, they celebrate by drinking from this sort of cup and salver before returning home. It serves, as it were, as the end of the celebration or banquet in order to send the guests off to their homes. The courtesies observed are the same as with the other cups.

---

[1] For the *suhamadai* stand, see p. 208, n. 1, and p. 250.

The fifth type is the cup that the lords use at the end of formal banquets or entertainments in order to persuade guests to drink more when they wish to return home. The salver on which they place the cup is the same as the fourth type, which depicts the seashore and is painted and decorated as already described. They place on this salver in due order three gilded and silvered earthenware cups, and for this reason they are called *mitsuboshi*, meaning 'three stars'.[1] One is a large cup and is placed at the foot of the trees and flowers, the next largest one is placed after it, and then the third and smallest is put next to this. If the middle one is gilded, then the two on either side are silvered, and vice versa. The courtesies and compliments are the same as before, and when they are concluded the person who is to begin drinking first makes the accustomed bow, if he is the host, to the guest. He then takes the large cup, has wine poured in, drinks, and puts it back in its place without draining it. Then he successively takes the second cup, receives the wine, drinks, and replaces it. Finally, he takes the third and smallest cup, and having drunk a little of the wine, he places the cup on the mat below. He bows to the guest as if to invite him. He takes the cup again and receives, or pretends to receive, a little more wine, drinks it, and puts the cup back in its place. He drinks from all three cups so as to oblige the guest to do likewise. The cups on their salver are carried to the guest and placed in front of him by a page, who carries the wine in his other hand.

The guest bows, takes the first and largest cup, and raising it to his head up to the level of his forehead, he receives and drinks the wine. In the same way, he takes the second cup and drinks from it. At this moment the host rises, and goes and puts a little *sakana* into his hand with some *hashi*. When the guest has eaten this, he once more takes some wine, drinks, and puts the cup back into its place. Then he drinks from the third cup and replaces it. If there are many guests, everybody does the same in due order. When all the honourable people in the room have drunk in their due order, the salver with the cups is placed in the centre of the room a little above the entrance, and there the other people of lesser rank, down to those on the veranda, come and all drink from the three cups. The last to come and drink takes the place of the host, for it falls to him to end the wine session by drinking last. When this person has finished drinking from the first cup, he places it on the mat below by his side. After he has drunk from the second, he places this on top of the first cup. Having drunk from the third, he puts it on top of the second cup. He then places all three cups in the palm of his left hand, and then after he has put the salver on top of them with his right hand, they are taken inside. With this, the wine session is ended.

The sixth and last type of cup used when inviting people to drink is called *itsutsuboshi*,[2] because they put five cups on a cedar salver, which is like the salver already described in the third type. The five earthenware cups or vessels, partly gilded and partly silvered, are placed together. This type of cup is used only by the *kuge* of the patrician order at the end of their festivities and banquets, as has already been said in the fifth example. The courtesies are the same as those observed with the three cups mentioned above. Having bowed, the first man drinks from all five cups, beginning with the middle one and then from those on the four sides according to a fixed order that they observe.[3] The session is ended in the same way as before. As these cups are made of clay that has been badly baked, they are sometimes softened by the wine. So the rim can come off in the hand of the man about to drink the

---

[1] *Vocabulario*, f. 162: '*Mitsuboshi no dai*. Large wooden stand in which are placed three *sakazuki*.'
[2] The term means 'five stars'.
[3] The order observed in drinking wine from the three and five *sakazuki* is illustrated in Rodrigues, *Nihon*, I, p. 518.

wine that he has received and some is spilt. Then the person who is drinking smiles and says, 'Pardon me.' With the paper that they always carry in the bosom in place of a handkerchief, he cleans up the spilt wine, and in the meanwhile another clay cup is produced.

2. Their way of entertaining with wine and the courtesies observed among them

There are many things involved in this common and universal ceremony of entertaining guests with wine. The Japanese – the host, as well as the guests and the pages who serve on these occasions – carry out the ceremony with much dignity, care, and tranquillity, and without any hurrying that might result in the wine being spilt, or the cup or *sakana* slipping from the hand, or some other mishap occurring. For this is the principal and most solemn of all the courtesies that they practise to honour and entertain a guest, whatever his rank may be.

Let us begin with the pages who wait on these and similar occasions. Always honourable young lads and boys of gentle birth, they are clad in fine robes and look very neat as regards their hair, its cleanliness and elegance, as well as their spotless silk robes of various colours and patterns. They wear these robes both summer and winter, and change them according to the four seasons of the year. They carry their ornamental daggers in their sash on the left-hand side, and they also gird their swords in it. They wear their ceremonial trousers and upper jacket, both of fine veil-like material, which we described in the chapter dealing with Japanese dress. At ordinary banquets and ceremonies these formal trousers reach down to above the ankle. On their feet they wear stockings of soft glove-leather or of some other material of pleasing colour, and they are fastened by silk ribbons.[1]

Should, however, the host be a great lord and the gathering to eat, or only to drink wine, is on one of their solemn festivals, such as the beginning of the New Year or any other, the pages wear long trousers like drawers. These are so wide at the bottom that their bare feet are hidden within the trouser legs, which extend more or less two spans past the feet. This looks much better and more solemn when it is seen rather than when merely described, because they show great skill and grace in this, especially when they are serving in the presence of the governor of Tenka, the *kubō*, or another great lord of the patrician order, or *kuge*, or a *yakata*, or a great landed duke.[2]

In the ordinary service of such people, for example, when they eat in public with the pomp that their rank demands or when they receive a lord, those who serve always use these long formal trousers. They always take them with them along with other robes in light leather boxes, which a lad in their employ carries. The pages accompany the lord wheresoever he may go, for they are of noble and gentle birth. Many of them are sons of gentlemen and officers in the service of the great lords, and they serve them in this way. This kind of service of the great landed lords is by no means something abject among the Japanese (neither, for that matter, is it among Europeans) as it is among the Chinese. Such pages have their own revenues, servants, and an excellent house for themselves, and Japanese lords and nobles of high birth take great pains to be served in these social affairs by noble pages of gentle birth.

The pages will never, even to save their lives, perform some lowly service, such as hand sandals, slippers, or clogs to the lord for him to put on, or carry his sunshade, or hold the

---

[1] The ceremonial trousers were *hakama*; the upper jacket, *kataginu*; the stockings, *tabi*. See pp. 183, nn. 1, 2, and 186, n. 4.

[2] For the graceful handling of these trailing trousers, see the reference to *Vocabulario* on p. 183, n. 1.

horse's reins while his lord mounts, or other things of such sort. These are performed among them by young lads, lackeys, people of mean birth, and others, who on no account may wait at table or enter the room of the guests and serve. Thus sometimes the host himself, his sons, brothers, and relatives of rank will wait on the guests, and in this matter of serving the guests at table within the room the Japanese are far better than the Chinese. In China there is no pomp or dignity in the waiting at table and in the serving of guests (even of the greatest and highest magistrates of the realm) at banquets, entertainments, and solemn functions. Nor is this performed by well-clad people of good birth, but by lads and lowly people who are clothed in plain black cotton dress and who also perform lowly offices.

Indeed, in the light of the great reputation of Chinese culture and the very civilized ceremonies they hold among themselves, this is a great defect and impairs all other public matters, for the nobility and breeding of servants who wait in public is a great adornment to a kingdom. The Japanese pay much attention to this point, as indeed do Europeans as well.[1] In addition to accompanying their lords on horseback or on foot (depending on their rank) and delivering messages concerning visits and other things to lords and nobles, the pages' work in Japan also involves waiting on the lords and guests at table, bringing out and removing the tables and dishes, giving wine to the guests, placing the drinking cups and *sakana* on their salvers in the room, and removing them in due course, as well as performing other public, dignified, and fitting services between the gates and the interior of the rooms. The Japanese pay such regard to this that the books dealing with their ceremonies and etiquette teach the manner of serving and the ceremonies that must be observed in this matter. They include various instructions about the dignity, modesty, and composure of the people who are serving, the difference between good breeding and bad, and the proper way of serving guests.[2]

When a guest is invited to drink wine only to pay him honour and courtesy, this is what the serving pages have to do first of all. At the proper time, when the host and guest are talking in the room after they have paid their compliments to each other there in the way already described, a page enters bearing a cup upon a salver. He goes to the top of the room and places the cup in the middle, a little beyond the guest who is seated in the first place but somewhat closer to him as a sign of honour. The cup or goblet is empty and is always brought standing the right way up so that wine may be poured in. This is a way of forcing and obliging the guest not to leave, because the host wishes to entertain him with wine. This is also done at the conclusion of a banquet when they have eaten and drunk much, so that the guests may not depart.

Thus they are put under an obligation by this cup being placed there, because it would be impolite to leave while it is still there as it would be equivalent to scorning the host's invitation to drink wine, for he wishes to honour and entertain them. Thus if one of those invited has important business, he asks the host for permission to leave, while the other guests remain. Or else he begs that the cup placed there may be taken back inside for he wishes to go and attend to something urgent. For while the cup remains there, they may not leave or say goodbye without permission unless the cup is first withdrawn inside.

[1] Valignano (*Cerimoniale*, p. 152) confirms this point, laying down that Jesuit catechists, or *dōjuku*, and servants must wear clean clothes at festivals and put on different clothing when they go out of the house, 'because in Japan a person's reputation depends no less on his servants' dress and behaviour than of those of the lords themselves.'

[2] Rodrigues may well have in mind here illustrated manuals based on the teachings of the Ogasawara school of etiquette (see plates 17 and 18). Reference to similar books is made on p. 177, nn. 3, 4. Even today bookstores are amply stocked with books dealing with etiquette observed in every aspect of Japanese life and culture.

After putting the cup in the room, the same or another page enters with a jug of wine in his hand, and kneeling down he sits back on his legs just inside the entrance and looks towards the host. The host signals to him to carry the cup on the salver and also the wine to the guest. He rises and places it in front of the guest, who bows and declines to take the wine, and sends the cup back by the page to the host so that he may drink first, as their etiquette demands. In general the etiquette observed by the host in sending the cup of wine for the guest to drink first is as follows. He sends the wine as many as three times to a person of great nobility before he himself begins to drink; to those of lesser rank, he sends it twice, while to others he sends it but once.[1] He does not send it at all to people of lowly birth, such as peasants and artisans, for it is enough to compliment them by word.

There are three ways of performing this etiquette of sending the cup and wine to the guest. The first takes place when the guest is a very noble personage. After the page returns from the guest and places the cup and salver in front of the host,[2] the host looks towards the page and humbly bows low. Then without signalling with the head or pointing with the hand, he tells him to carry it back. If the guest is of lesser rank, the host looks towards him, nods his head but does not point thither with his hand, and tells the page to take him the cup and wine. If the people are of middle rank and not very noble, he signals with his hand and points to the person to whom he is sending the wine, and tells the page to take it to him.

After this etiquette of sending the cup and wine three times, twice, or once has been performed and the guest has insisted that the host should be the first to drink, the host looks towards the guest with a dignified but cheerful expression on his face before he touches the cup with his hand, and gives him one of the three bows mentioned above according to his rank. He then says, 'As Your Honour has commanded, so I obey.' He takes the cup with his right hand and then, holding it in both hands, he receives the wine. When this has been done, he places the cup with the wine on the mat at his side, saying, '*Saraba*,' that is, 'As Your Honour thus commands me, so I will drink.'[3] He then takes the cup with the wine and drinks. He repeats this, taking the wine again (or making as if to take it), and drinks once more. Their etiquette and politeness require that both the guest and the host always take the wine twice. Out of courtesy he empties the cup in order to send it to the guest, and when the latter is very noble, he puts the empty cup on the mat next to the salver as a sign of greater reverence, and the page places it there on the salver. When the guest is of lesser nobility, the host places the cup on the salver without putting it on the mat.

The page carries the cup and wine to the guest and places it in front of him. The guest takes the cup with his right hand and, holding it with both hands, lifts it to his head to the level of his forehead. He then puts it to his lips as if to kiss it, although this is not done

---

[1] Writing in 1623 about his visit to Japan, Arthur Hatch (in *TCJ*, p. 192) observes: 'They use to give and receive the emptie Cup at one the others hands, and before the Master of the house begins to drinke, hee will proffer the Cup to every one of his Guests, making shew to have them to begin though it bee farre from his intention.' More specifically, Valignano (*Cerimoniale*, p. 190) lays down that missionaries should offer wine three times to important guests. If they accept it, well and good. But if after the third offer they again decline, then the priest is to take the cup, raise it to his head, and drink first.

[2] There is a short gap in the Portuguese text at this point.

[3] A more literal translation of *saraba* would be, 'In that case.' The term is a contracted form of *sore saraba*, 'If that is so.'

when the cup is carried from a woman.[1] This is like someone drinking the dregs of the host's drink. After he has received a full cup and has drunk for the first time, the host begs him to drink again. If he declines, the host rises and gives him some *sakana*, as we shall say later. He receives this on the fingers of the right hand, and when he has eaten it, he once more takes wine in order to drink some after the *sakana*. When this has been drunk and the cup emptied, he places the cup on the mat next to the salver or on the salver itself, depending on the host's rank.

The page carries it to the host, who takes it, raises it to his head, and touches it to his lips. The guest then bows to him, to which the host responds with another bow, receives wine, and drinks. Before the guest repeats the process, he goes and gives him some *sakana* as well in order to honour him. When he has eaten this, he receives more wine and drinks, or makes as if to take the cup and drink, and then emptying the cup, he asks the guest whether he wishes to drink any more. When he declines, the host finishes the wine, places the cup on the salver, tells the page to take it inside and to bring *cha*, a certain kind of brew with which they divert themselves while conversing.

If there are many guests of noble birth, the host does the same for each one of them as he does for the first, as regards giving and receiving the cup and *sakana*. It is always the host, however, who concludes it all and finishes the wine. When there are many guests together, it is usual for the host to perform this etiquette in the manner described to each of the two or three most distinguished guests. Then he sends the cup to the person next in rank, and this man pays his compliments to the next, and so they all mutually toast each other until all have drunk. When the last one has drunk, the host receives the cup to finish and conclude this ceremony and courtesy, for it is the custom for the host to bring this to an end and be the last to finish. Before raising the cup to his head, he turns to the guest at the top of the room and asks him if the wine should go around again. He and all the other guests then tell him to finish it. The host then bows to all of them and they reply with another bow. He then raises the cup to his head, and, taking the wine once and then a second time, he brings the session to a close.

But if the guests are lowly people, such as peasants working on the land (they are called *hyakushō*), and persons and artisans of mean condition, the room in which they are received and in which the host meets them can be the same and common for all, although there are special rooms adorned with costly decoration for persons of great nobility. This does not redound to the honour of such lowly guests, but is in keeping with the propriety and stature of the host. The lords thus meet with their servants in the same guest room at public ceremonies and festivals. With people of this sort, the host who is noble sits in the most distinguished place high up at the top of the room or else in the middle. He honours women, even the lowly ones, and thus usually makes them enter the room and does not allow them to stay outside on the veranda.

The ordinary way of entertaining such people does not involve any compliments, nor is the cup sent around at all. Instead, the host takes the cup in his hand, and looking towards the guest, he says to him a word of compliment, takes the wine, and drinks. He then repeats this by taking a little wine (or making as if to take it), drinking again or putting the cup to

---

[1] Avila Girón (*Relación*, p. 48) adds further details in the case of a woman. 'If the *sakazuki* comes to me from a noble lady, I must accept it with much politeness, raise it above my head but not kiss it, for this would be very rude. Nor will a woman, however lowly she may be, kiss it or take it with both hands.'

his mouth. He then empties the cup and sends it to the guest. The peasant raises it and performs the usual etiquette and ceremonies, receiving wine a first and then a second time. They are not generally accustomed to give *sakana* to this sort of person, or perhaps a servant of the house or the page who pours the wine may offer it. When he has drunk, the host does not take the cup again and drink from it, but instead the page takes it away inside. If the guest is a person to whom the host wishes to show greater favour and honour, he commands one of his servants, if he is present, to take it and finish it. Otherwise the same serving page gives the jug to the guest, receives wine twice, and then takes the cup and wine away inside.

There are various ways of entertaining with wine when a large number of lowly people gather together. This happens at festivals and the New Year, when all the peasants come to visit their lords and landlords with gifts of produce of the land, such as firewood and wild game; fishermen bring fish and shellfish, while artisans present vessels containing their produce, etc. The first way is for the lord or noble person at the top of the room to bow to all of them with the word *Saraba*. He receives wine twice and drinks a little, and then the page takes the same cup and carries it to the middle of the room. Then all the guests come in due order to drink twice from the cup, each one raising it before he drinks. At the end it is not necessary for the host to finish it, for it is enough for a servant to do this, as we have already said.

The second method is to note the number of guests and pile as many clay cups, one on top of the other, on a cedar tray. They carry them thus and place them next to the host, who is seated at the top of the room. Then another cup on a salver is produced. The host takes it and saying a word of compliment to all, he takes a little wine, drinks from it, and pours the rest into one of the cups from which the guests are to drink. Then all come up one after another to drink until they finish. When all have drunk, each one takes the cup from which he has drunk and keeps it for himself.[1]

This is the usual etiquette for entertaining guests with wine during the visits of honourable and noble people and of ordinary and lowly folk. We will speak later about the way of persuading people to drink during banquets and about the various ceremonies performed in these, when we come to deal with their way of entertaining guests.

There is one further point concerning the ordinary etiquette of entertaining a guest with wine and *sakana*. If, in addition to what has been described, the host wishes to extend a great welcome to a guest, then it is usual to serve a certain kind of fish or meat broth or sauce called *soimono*.[2] After this, he will once more resume the entertainment with wine and *sakana*, because every time this *soimono* is produced for the guest, wine is invariably drunk and *sakana* taken. As regards this point, it may be noted that in these entertainments of the Japanese there are two kinds of this sauce, or *soimono*. One is used in these ordinary visits that we have hitherto been describing and is served to the guest as an act of courtesy and greater welcome, but this sauce is not usual today. It is accompanied by various things, which are

---

[1] Fróis (in *TCJ*, p. 137) relates that Hideyoshi followed a similar procedure when showing some Jesuits around Osaka Castle in 1586. 'Hideyoshi sat down and ordered the *sakazuki* to be brought in. He took it with his own hands and gave it to Fr Coelho. Then asking for two more *sakazuki*, he took a little wine from each of them; he made them pour what was left into cups, saying that this was just the same as giving the *sakazuki* to each person individually, for this was the custom of Japan. He urged us all to drink and thus it went around all the Fathers and Brothers.' Fróis (*História*, V, p. 304) also mentions that Hideyoshi honoured Valignano with *sakazuki* during the audience in 1591, at which Rodrigues was present as interpreter.

[2] *Vocabulario*, f. 378: '*Soimono. Sakana* that is served to honour guests. It is cooked with a broth or sauce, so that wine may be drunk afterwards.'

often brought out one after another in order to make the guests drink more wine and thus entertain them, because every time this sauce is produced, wine is invariably drunk.

We will talk about this later when dealing with banquets, but here will describe only the first kind. This is placed on a table of cedarwood with high legs and sometimes on as many as three tables. On the first they place the *hashi* with which to eat, and a fish broth or sauce in a plain clay dish. On the other two tables, they place other sauces made from the meat of birds and deer, or from mushrooms, truffles, and other things that bring on a thirst. These sauces in a formal *soimono* are brought out in clay dishes, but in the ordinary kind they can also be served in their kind of varnished bowls or dishes from which they eat.

This sauce is usually given to the guests after they have finished with the wine and *sakana*, but before the host has concluded the wine session. When everything is about to end, another page comes out again with another cup on its salver, goes to the top of the room where the first cup is, and places it there in token and sign of the sauce that is to come. When they have finished with the wine, the first cup and the *sakana* are cleared away, and the *soimono* is brought out on the tables and placed in front of the guests and host. Another tray bearing fresh *sakana* is brought out and placed where the first one was. Then a page comes out with a jug of wine and takes up the same position as in the beginning. Then everyone takes the *hashi* in the right hand, the dish of sauce in the left, and begins to eat two or three mouthfuls of fish or meat. Then they sip the broth quietly without any audible noise, because it is not polite to sip noisily. When this is finished, they place the *hashi* and sauce dish on the table, and then, kneeling down and sitting back on their feet, as has been said, they all begin once more the ordinary etiquette of the cup and *sakana* until the host finishes and ends with the wine, as has been described above. When this *soimono* ceremony has been concluded, it is not usual for the guests to delay and talk in the room, but beginning with the guest who is in the first and highest place, they rise to their feet. The host rises last so as not to appear to say to the guests that it is time to go.

CHAPTER 27

THE MANNER OF GIVING AND TAKING THE *SAKANA* FOR NOBLE, COMMON, AND LOWLY PEOPLE

Whenever a person of standing goes to pay a formal visit on another, it is not enough to entertain him with wine alone, but it is necessary to serve along with it something to eat that may persuade the guest to drink. This is also a token of courtesy and welcome that they make towards the guest. Now although the Japanese call every kind of food, such as fish and meat, *sakana*,[1] strictly speaking this term should be applied only to appetizing things to eat accompanying the wine, and are put into the guest's hand with some *hashi* so that he may drink after eating them. Thus, just as the cup on its salver is placed in the room to oblige the guest to drink from it whenever necessary, so also in due course they place a salver (sometimes two or more) by itself with some *hashi* and some things to eat, cut into pieces or morsels. These *hashi* are used in serving the *sakana* that is given to the guest, for in no circumstances is it given with the hands. To welcome and honour the guest, there must be at least two or three different things to eat, each type separated from the others and set apart on the same salver. They generally consist of dry or dried-up things that cannot soil the guest's hands when he takes them.

When the cup on its salver is brought into the room, this *sakana* follows straight after it and is put in a suitable place near the cup in the direction of the host, who has to give it to the guest when he drinks. This is done when the guest had already drunk once and the host begs him drink again before receiving the *sakana*. For after he has taken the *sakana*, he is obliged to drink once more. If, as is the custom, the guest declines to take the wine a second time, the host rises, and proceeding quietly and slowly, he kneels after their fashion in front of the tray of *sakana*. He takes the salver with his right hand, and out of reverence puts it somewhat towards the place where the guest is seated so that it is near him. The nearer he places it, the greater honour he pays the guest. Then he takes up the *hashi* that are on the same tray and uses them to pick up a morsel of whatever is on the tray. Leaving the cup from which he has drunk on the mat on one side, the guest rises from his place and goes to receive the *sakana* with great politeness. He stretches out his right arm, supporting it with his left hand. Then bowing as a sign of respect, the host places the *sakana* upon the fingers of the palm of his hand. When the guest has received this, he lifts it above his head, bows to the host,[2] puts it in his mouth, eats it, and then each one returns to his place.

The guest takes the wine once more and drinks it to follow the *sakana*. He then empties the cup and sends it to the host, who receives it back with the courtesies already described.

---

[1] The primary meaning of the term *sakana* today is 'fish', while the secondary meaning is 'an accompaniment of *sake*'. The two words are written with different Chinese characters. See p. 239, n. 2.

[2] The text here has 'to the guest', but from the context this must be a slip.

But before he drinks the wine a second time, the guest rises from his place and goes to give him the *sakana* in the way described above. If there are many honoured guests, the host does the same for each of them, or else the guests help themselves to the wine and give the *sakana* to each other until they finish, and then the host brings the wine to an end, as has already been said. When the guest is a woman, men do not usually serve her the *sakana* on account of modesty and respect. Instead, custom demands that one of the women of rank who is present gives it to her. When women pay visits to men, the *sakana* is brought into the room more as a decoration than to be served. The women do not rise from their places on the occasions when it is served to them, but it is brought to them where they are seated.

They decorate these trays in various ways suitable to the *sakana*, using flowers and green branches of trees or plants, and other skilful embellishments with artificial flowers and trees. They thus imitate some natural scene, such as a tree in a craggy place or something else.[1] When they serve and accept *sakana*, they observe various ceremonies, points of honour, etiquette, and innumerable compliments that would be tiresome to recount. Then just as there are various sorts of cups and salvers with which they honour and entertain their guests and persuade them to drink much wine, so, in addition to the ordinary sort that we have been describing, they serve various kinds of *sakana* on their salvers. These salvers are fashioned in various shapes and are highly decorated with dew-like gold and silver on top, and with various artificial flowers and trees that look very natural, for they are most skilful at this. These are employed principally at banquets and entertainments to honour and entertain the guests, so that the various different and tasty *sakana* may encourage them to drink a great deal of wine until they all end up tipsy and are unable to return home except in the litters that they commonly use. They consider this ceremony of wine and *sakana* as the greatest token of affection.

---

[1] The *suhamadai* — see p. 208, n. 1.

CHAPTER 28

THE WARM AND COLD WINE SERVED ON THESE VISITS, AND HOW THE JAPANESE MAKE IT

It would be as well to say something at this point about the wine served at these visits and banquets, and which the Japanese commonly use in their kingdom. First of all, let us say something about the wine served at every kind of entertainment with drink, and about its common use throughout the kingdom. In keeping with the true and ancient custom of Japan, warm wine is always drunk from the ninth day of the ninth moon to the third day of the third moon (that is, from September until March), except for the first wine that is brought out on New Year visits, as mentioned earlier.[1] Cold wine should be drunk for the rest of the year, although nowadays this is neither usual nor definite because everyone now usually drinks warm wine all the year around. The Chinese also observe this custom, for in their feasts, entertainments, and ordinary meals they always drink warm wine throughout the year.

Neither in China nor in Japan and the Orient are there any vines, still less any wine made from grapes. Instead, throughout the kingdom all their ordinary wine is made from rice.[2] The rice is cooked in steam, and is mixed with a certain kind of yeast made from the same rice. They put a certain amount of rice and a fixed amount of water into some wooden vats or big martaban casks,[3] where it ferments for several days until it is changed into wine. They then put this into hempen sacks and squeeze it in something like a press into a large tub, while the crushed rice remains in the sacks. It is drawn off from the tub into vessels, and they now have a goodly stomachic wine.[4] Like grape wine, it intoxicates if drunk in quantity, and they remain drunk for a long time because it does not settle in the stomach so quickly as does grape wine. Although it has a goodly taste, its effects are different from those of the true wine of the grape, which remains so close to the blood.[5]

The rice wine made in China and Japan is of various kinds and flavours just as in Europe, because there are various ways of producing it as they use different water (and this is important) in various places throughout the kingdom. Just as among us there are different qualities and types of wine according to the grapes and the places where they are produced, so also among them there are various kinds of wine according to the places.[6] There are also

---

[1] Rodrigues has noted on p. 195 that cold wine is drunk at New Year.

[2] For early references to *sake* wine, see p. 106, n. 5, above.

[3] Martaban (mortivan, mortaban, or Pegu) jars were named after a city in Burma, famous for the production of glazed pottery. *Oxford English Dictionary*, I, p. 704. Barbosa (*Book*, II, pp. 158–9) gives an account of the place and specifically mentions the jars produced there.

[4] For a description of *sake* production that bears out Rodrigues's account, see Casal, *Notes*, pp. 70–71; for the history of *sake*, ibid., pp. 2–9.

[5] A literal translation of '*que he tão chegado ao sangue*'.

[6] Called *jizake*, or 'local *sake*'.

different flavours according to the preparation of the materials from which the wine is made, for example, from white ground rice or from unground rice. It also depends on the seasoning and mixing that each person uses with the same ingredients.[1] They always try to produce the best and most celebrated wine at their banquets and entertainments, and send for wine beforehand from remote places famous for their produce. To show greater hospitality they are wont to entertain their guests with wines from various famous places that everyone rates highly. Just as we have wine cellars, so also they have ones containing big barrels of astonishing size, and these are so high that they climb up them on ladders to draw the wine off from the top.[2] So much wine is drunk in China, Korea, and Japan that they say that more than one-third of the rice grown in Japan is used in making wine. This is why they do not have so much rice as the people's staple diet. There would certainly be enough if they did not use it to make wine, vinegar, *miso*, and other various things in which rice is used up.[3]

---

[1] Avila Girón (*Relación*, p. 45) gives a detailed list of the various types of *sake*. The best type, he says, is called *morohaku*, and this is also mentioned by Cocks (*Diary*, II, p. 47), 'a barrill morofack'. According to Avila Girón, the quality of the wine depends greatly on the seasoning and dehusking of the rice; only a little water should be used, not brackish and not drawn from a well. He also refers to other types, such as *migawa* and *onomichi*, named after the places of their manufacture.

[2] Fróis (*Tratado*, p. 262) mentions another way of preserving *sake*: 'The Japanese keep their wine in jars that have large sealed mouths and are buried in the ground up to their mouths.'

[3] Rodrigues has already pointed out on p. 106 that although Japan produced much rice, the peasants in some regions had to subsist on barley; for such folk, rice was a luxury. The brewing of *sake* was sometimes restricted by the Tokugawa authorities when there had been a poor rice crop. Casal, *Notes*, p. 43.

CHAPTER 29

THE BANQUETS HELD BY THE JAPANESE,[1] AND HOW THEY ENTERTAIN THEIR GUESTS AT THEM

As has been noted already, eating and drinking in these nations (especially among the Chinese, Koreans, and Japanese), serving their bellies and giving themselves over to corporeal pleasures, is their god, their heaven and bliss. It is also the ultimate purpose of their efforts in the present life, for they know nothing about the future and eternal life, and they believe that everything ends with the present one.[2] They call and consider a man happy and blessed who has the wherewithal to occupy himself in these things and thus enjoys greater corporeal pleasures. For this reason, they occupy themselves in continual banquets, treating each other to various entertainments and recreations. These are so long drawn out and involve so many excessive methods and devices to induce nature to enjoy the delights and pleasures of eating and drinking that they cannot be easily described in words.

Thus we shall touch on only some of the principal features so that the description of these may form some idea of all the rest. The genuine manner of banqueting among the Japanese, as described in the books of rites and customs, corresponds to the ancient Chinese way. As this to some extent forms the basis of the modern way, we shall briefly describe in the first place the Chinese way of holding banquets so that the reader may better understand thereby the Japanese method.

1. The way in which the Chinese hold a banquet for their guests

The Chinese are greatly given to pleasure and joy in the treatment and service of their own persons. They squander much of their substance and nearly all their lives (we are speaking now of those who have the means to do so) in eating and drinking. The most important things are banquets, at which they spend days and nights not only in their houses but also in the countryside, in their country estates and orchards, where they have pleasant and delightful villas and fish ponds. The nobles and court eunuchs in China have many of these country villas. The monasteries of the idols, which are usually outside the populated parts, are likewise situated in delightful woods, where there are tables and other things set out and prepared for this purpose. Their monasteries are used to this end, and the same is true for the Japanese. Banquets are also held by the rivers and lakes that irrigate the whole of

---

[1] Probably the copyist's slip as this chapter deals exclusively with Chinese banquets and topics. The following chapter describes Japanese banquets.

[2] An unfounded and inconsistent statement. Here, as elsewhere, Rodrigues perhaps has the Zen sect in mind, but ignores the teaching of the popular Amida sects regarding the future life. He has already pointed out (p. 126) that the faithful pray to the Buddhist deities for salvation and that some of them even commit suicide to reach paradise more quickly.

China. Also on boats, which they have painted and decorated for this purpose, with cabins, rooms, kitchens, and everything else necessary. They travel in these boats, seated in their chairs on either side of a long table as they pass through beautiful places and enjoy the fine view.

They include in their banquets all kinds of instrumental music, acrobats, clowns or buffoons, and every other kind of entertainment that can cause them pleasure.[1] They use high tables made of scented and precious wood as well as various other kinds, and they are so varnished that you seem to be looking into a mirror. They also use various sorts of splendid chairs provided with backs so that the body can rest, and the nobles sit on chairs covered on top with silk cloth. They make use of delicate porcelain, which is highly valued everywhere, and they drink from many kinds of vessels made of gold, silver, alabaster, and other metals skilfully worked, and delicately varnished cups of various colours. They are all decorated with golden flowers, and some have various figures in mother-of-pearl intermingled with the gold. They eat with a certain kind of fork consisting of two slender sticks made of ivory, black or red scented sandalwood, and other wood. The tips with which they eat are overlaid with silver, and on no account do the hands touch the food, except when they eat fruit.

There is an abundance of various delicious fruits in addition to many that we ourselves grow. There are innumerable animals and birds, both wild and tame, as well as fish from the sea and rivers, for the whole kingdom is watered by navigable rivers. Hence in their banquets there are countless dishes of meat and fish that do not seem to have been brought into this world except to afford pleasure to the body.

This is in accordance with the teaching of their ancient sages who placed the ultimate end of man in corporeal pleasure and the absence of all pain and sickness of body and soul, living to an old age on account of a certain elixir of life, and enjoying a wealth of riches and an abundance of silver acquired through alchemy, which they believe they know how to practise. These indeed were true epicureans, for they held the same view as those sages, although those of over here lived many centuries before those of Europe.[2] Among the ancient Chinese philosophers in this kingdom there were three celebrated theories concerning the ultimate end of man. All three placed this end in the body and in the present life, because they believed that everything ended with death. Of these, some placed the end of man in the common good without any distinction or respect for persons. They maintained that the ultimate end consisted in all men loving everyone else equally without any distinction for father and mother, lord and vassal, husband and wife, thus destroying all civil and political order. Their ancient philosopher Mozi held this view and explained that as all men were of the same mass and material, and were bound to return to it at death, as members thereof they ought to love each other equally.[3]

Others, on the contrary, placed the ultimate end in the good of the individual, because a

---

[1] At the banquet attended by Rodrigues in Canton, the guests were treated to juggling with lighted torches and skilful bird imitations. Rodrigues, 'Rodrigues in China', p. 318. Semedo (*History*, Chapter 13) has much to say about Chinese banquets.

[2] The Portuguese text is vague, but the meaning is clear. Rodrigues, *Nihon*, I, p. 537, has Rodrigues saying that the European epicureans lived centuries before the Chinese sages. In fact he means that, although the Chinese sages lived centuries before the time of Epicurus and his school, they were nevertheless genuine epicureans in spirit. He later repeats, on p. 358, that the Chinese sages lived 'long before … the Greek philosophers'. See also p. 10.

[3] A Chinese philosopher who lived between 480–381 BC. His teaching differed radically from Confucian theory on various points. As Rodrigues observes, he is best known for his teaching of *jianai*, or universal love. Creel, *Chinese Thought*,

man has nothing more than the present life, and a short one at that. They said that the ultimate end was universal, and was to be found in total pleasure of body and spirit, and in the absence of all sorrow and sickness of body and soul. They denied the obligation of human compliments and civility, which cause only trouble and disgust. So they placed the ultimate end in a long life and an abundance of riches, acquired by their supposed elixir of life and the art of alchemy. They declared that a man should direct all his efforts to this end of personal advantage, and that nothing should be done for the common good or out of love for another. A man should not even pull up a blade of grass if it is not for his own benefit. This theory was held by Yangzhu and Laozi, or Rōshi as the Japanese call him, who were ancient philosophers and flourished in the time of the kings of Juda.[1]

Others were wiser and relied more on natural reason, placing the ultimate end in the common good of the state. They held that this was based on natural reason that enjoined on a person the good government of his family. This was conducive to the good government of the kingdom or of a particular province, and ultimately to the good and peaceful government of the world, or Tenka as they say. This produced a peaceful, quiet, and prosperous state both of the nation and of private individuals. As a result, the people living therein could continue their family and lineage from one generation to the next, and so on down through their descendants. They censured celibacy and permitted concubines at will in addition to the real and legitimate wife, because, like the Jews, they held that it was the greatest joy to have many children and the greatest misery (as well as disobedience towards their ancestors) to be sterile and barren, for then the lineage of their forefathers and the descent of their family in the direct line came to an end. This theory was held by the ancient philosopher and teacher of their kingdom, Confucius, or Kōshi as they call him in Japan. He was the founder of the sect of the Chinese *literati*, and the kingdom is at present governed in accordance with his doctrine.[2]

The fourth is a foreign theory and is the doctrine of Shakia, or Shaka in Japanese, the founder of the Indian gymnosophist philosophers, whose teaching entered China sixty-seven years after Christ our Lord, and flourished and spread very widely there.[3] He placed

---

pp. 60–80; Fung, *History*, I, pp. 76–105. Ricci (*Fonti*, I, p. 116, and *China*, p. 95) mentions a certain school that taught a type of pantheism. 'From this unity of substance they reason to the love that should unite the individual constituents.'

[1] Laozi was born in 604 BC (Rodrigues gives this date in *Arte grande*, f. 235v, although he might have been expected to have written the traditional date of 1321 BC). As Rodrigues later notes (p. 370), legend held that he remained in his mother's womb for 81 years. Popularly regarded as the founder of Taoism, he was the author of the famous text *Daodejing*. About the seventh century AD, Taoism began to adopt the practice of alchemy and elixir-hunting. Giles, *Chinese*, pp. 416–28; Creel, *Chinese Thought*, pp. 109–26; and Fung, *History*, I, pp. 170–91, esp. p. 134, n. 2.

Yangzhu lived in the fourth century BC and taught an ethical egoism. Mencius reported about him, 'He would not pluck out a single hair of his body to benefit the empire' (Legge, *Chinese Classics*, II, pp. 464–5), although he probably meant that he would not do this to *gain* the empire. Giles, *Chinese*, p. 899; Creel, *Chinese Thought*, p. 83, 107–9; and Fung, *History*, I, pp. 133–43.

[2] For the biography and teaching of Confucius, the Latinized name of Kong Fuzi, 'Philosopher Kong', 551–479 BC, see Legge, *Chinese Classics*, I, pp. 56–111; Creel, *Chinese Thought*, pp. 39–59; and Fung, *History*, I, pp. 43–75. In his *Arte grande*, f. 235v, Rodrigues mentions that Confucius was born in 551 BC and died at the age of 73. Ricci (*Fonti*, I, pp. 115–20, and *China*, pp. 94–98) provides a full account of Confucianism, mentioning, with Rodrigues, that it reprehends celibacy.

[3] A reference to Buddhism, founded by Śākya Muni; see p. 19, above. According to tradition, Emperor Mingdi (reigned 58–76) sent ambassadors to the West as a result of a puzzling dream. In the year 67 they returned with the Indian monks Kasyapa Matanga and Gobharna, who introduced Buddhism into China, although it is possible that the religion entered the country as early as 217 BC. Edkins, *Chinese Buddhism*, p. 88. Rodrigues (in *Arte grande*, f. 235v)

the ultimate end in peace of soul, obtained by the mortification of the passions and pleasures through the contemplation of the vanity and deception of temporal things. A man must withdraw from them as from vain, false, and fickle things that rob the soul of peace, and devote himself to the solitude of a hermitage, renouncing father, mother, wife, children, and everything else in the world. The Chinese, both the *literati* as well as the rest of the people, not only have scant sympathy for this opinion, but greatly detest it.[1]

Although the kingdom is governed according to the third teaching, that of Kōshi, yet in fact the people subscribe to the second or epicurean teaching, giving themselves over to every pleasure and delight, and they all regard this as their final end and happiness. As a result, everyone indulges in an excess of eating and drinking according to his means.

But to return to our subject. The Chinese have three types of banquet. One is the common, ordinary banquet among friends and relatives; the second is the solemn, public banquet among nobles and lords. The third is not a formal banquet at all, but they call it a box or tray banquet, for the tray is covered with various kinds of appetizing things that encourage wine drinking. In Japan this would be properly called wine and *sakana*.

The ordinary Chinese banquet is held for one or a few guests who can fit around one table. All of them sit around it on their chairs, and if there are many guests they use a long table or one made up of many joined together. They sit facing each other on both sides of the table. They do not use tablecloths but eat from the table, for it is made of precious wood or else varnished. Nearly all the food is put straight onto the table; it is cold and cut into many pieces arranged one on top of another on their plates like a pyramid. Pork is the ordinary and common dish, and in this alone are they distinguished from the Jews, because they have many similarities in everything else.

As regards the seating, it is the general custom for the oldest guest to sit at the top out of respect for his years even though he may be of lower rank than the others, for they are very punctilious in the matter of age. The host who gives the banquet is the exception to this rule, because he always sits in the lowest place of all. We will presently describe below the manner in which they begin to sit down and eat in both this kind of banquet as well as the public, solemn one, and also in the closed-box type. When they eat in these and other banquets it is considered bad manners to sit close to the table and bend over it, and so they do not draw close to it. Whence they have a proverb that runs, 'Junzi li tai sanchi', or, as they say in Japan, 'Kunshi wa dai wo sarukoto san shaku nari', that is, 'A man ought to keep three of their *covados*, or three spans, away from the table.'[2] In the same way, the host may wish to honour a guest at table or during a visit by giving him the top seat, although he is not obviously senior to the rest. After he has declined a little, he is obliged to accept, and when everyone has sat down, he bows from his chair and says, 'I have usurped this place which was not mine.' (The Japanese say in similar circumstances, 'I am too high,' or 'This place is too high for me.') The others then reply, 'It is the proper place for Your Honour.'

They do not take up the *hashi* to eat nor drink from the cup, which is already there with

---

assigns the introduction of Buddhism into China to AD 72. Ricci (*Fonti*, I, p. 121, and *China*, p. 98) gives 65 as the date, while Semedo (*History*, p. 89) opts for 63.

  [1] Ricci (*Fonti*, I, pp. 121–6, and *China*, pp. 98–101) offers a general account of Chinese Buddhism, and attributes its unpopularity among the Chinese to the fact that it runs contrary to the Confucian ideal of filial piety and obedience. It should be recalled that the 16th-century Europeans witnessed Buddhism in both China and Japan in a period of decline.

  [2] I have been unable to trace this saying. Rodrigues, *Nihon*, I, p. 541, offers no help in this matter.

Plate 19: Chinese gentry at a banquet. An illustration in Adriano de las Cortes, SJ (1578–1629), *Viaje de la China.* 'The ordinary Chinese banquet is held for one or a few guests who can fit around one table. All of them sit around it on their chairs . . . facing each other on both sides of the table.' p. 256. The British Library, Sloane MSS 1005, f. 157.

the wine, nor put the *hashi* down on the table, before the host or oldest person at table first takes them up or puts them down. While they pay him this compliment by not putting the *hashi* down, they keep them in their hand, even when they are not eating. When they take wine, they must not drink it all and drain the cup unless the host bids them do so. Nor when they have the cup in their hand and are about to drink may they look at the wine inside the cup. Instead, they should gaze at the others as if they were noting what the rest are doing so that they may follow suit. When they are about to eat, they do not plunge the *hashi* into the dish in order to take some food, but do this together with the other companion or companions who are eating from the same plate. They always take the portions that are placed below, in the middle, or at the sides, and not the pieces on the top, nor the best morsels. For it is the custom at these tables where many eat together and there are many dishes, for all to take the same things from the same plate or dish with the *hashi* that they have already put in their mouths. Sometimes they choose a choice piece or portion, and place it with these *hashi* near a guest so that he may eat it. This is something indeed contrary to all cleanliness among us and nauseating, but it causes hardly any qualms among them.[1]

When the tables are set apart and each person eats by himself at a table, as they do at solemn banquets, they look and see the dish that the principal guest or host is eating, and then they all eat the same at their own tables. The bones or pips that they eat must be taken from the mouth inconspicuously and deposited under the table. When they eat rice, they must eat everything, even the smallest grains, in the bowl. When they finish eating the first bowl of rice, they must not take another without the host inviting them to do so, and they therefore must proceed slowly so as not to finish before him.

In the middle of the meal the guest must decline when they wish to pour more wine in his cup. If the host offers him more to drink, he accepts the wine and then for a little while he must again decline once or twice, declaring that he has already drunk a great deal. In the same way, when he sees that the banquet is coming to an end, he must rise to his feet as if he wishes to leave and cannot eat any more, first saying to the host, 'I wish to inform you that I am leaving.' Then as the host begs him to stay a little longer, he sits down again. When the host disparages the dishes and declares that they are few and bad, they must praise them greatly and say that they are many and good, because the food is belittled for this very reason. It is very common in Japan to disparage the things they give to one another, as well as banquets, however good and splendid they may be.[2]

To mark the end of the meal, they pour the water of boiled *cha* into the rice bowl and after rinsing it they drink this washing swill. The Japanese do the same with hot water.[3] This custom does not sound very well to European ears, although they display their special elegance in this, as if someone were to say that such was the banquet that he even cleaned the bowls without leaving anything. On the morning of the day following the meal they send a letter of thanks to the host, and if he is an important man, they go in person to thank him with a courtesy letter.

---

[1] Rodrigues fails to note the general custom of reversing the *hashi* on these occasions so that the donor offers food with the blunt, unused, ends. It is surely ironic for a European of those times to refer to Chinese eating habits as 'nauseous'.

[2] For donors disparaging their gifts, see p. 235, n. 1, above.

[3] Fróis (*Tratado*, pp. 176–8) also notes this custom.

This in brief is the general custom of China regarding banquets, and they are substantially the same in nearly all respects as the banquets held by the Japanese. It is also very common among the Chinese to buy a banquet prepared at an inn, where they sell whatever is wanted according to the desired price and food. The host knows the number of the various meat and fish dishes required, and so he sends word to the innkeeper that he wants a banquet with such-and-such things at a certain price.

The second kind is the public and solemn banquets of the nobles and people of good birth, or a formal one held in honour of a lord or magistrate. In these banquets each person has his own individual table at which he eats by himself. In the middle at the top of the room is the table of the noble person, and of others if they are of equal rank, while the other tables are placed down the two sides of the room. They adorn these tables with various things placed on them, such as pyramids of cut and arranged things; these are not eaten but are merely for decoration. They also have pyramids of fruit in wire frameworks made for this purpose, pyramids of sugar in the form of a loaf, and various hollow figures of lions and other animals made from the same material. Many of the dishes are served together and the same is given to each guest. Other dishes are served hot and well spiced according to their fashion. None of the things placed on the table is taken away until the end of the banquet. The more meat and fish broths with different seasonings there are, the more solemn is the banquet. These so-called broths are not merely broths, but consist of meat cut up into pieces together with the broth. Strictly speaking, they are food together with a broth, and this is what the Japanese call *shiru*. In these solemn banquets it is usual to perform various ceremonies and courtesies. After the guests have been greeted with the usual courtesies, and wish to enter and eat, they observe the ceremonies and courtesies described earlier in Chapter 22, where we dealt with the courtesies of Japan and China, and the reader will find them there.[1]

To entertain the guests at these banquets there are plays and performances with music and instruments as we have said, although the same is true even in the ordinary banquets held on rivers or in the fields. During the plays they put in the hands of the guests, especially the principal one, the script of the piece that is being enacted and they sing as they read out the plot.[2] These are also available if they wish to have performed a particular play that would give them pleasure to see, for they have many of these printed scripts, dealing with ancient matters and stories of various themes of the world.[3]

The aim of a box or covered-tray banquet is to entertain a person at home, in the open air, in a boat on the river, or in the house of the guest himself, whither they sometimes

---

[1] Ricci (*Fonti*, I, pp. 76–8, and *China*, pp. 64–8) gives a detailed description of Chinese banquets and confirms Rodrigues's account on many points. Rada (in Boxer, *South China*, pp. 287–90) also provides an eyewitness account of banquets held in Fuzhou. Other reports are found in Cruz (in ibid., pp. 141–2), and Mendoza, *History*, I, p. 138. In a letter written in 1615, Rodrigues relates that he attended a banquet in Canton, at which he was guest of honour. Rodrigues, 'Rodrigues in China', pp. 319–18.

[2] Even today, experienced members of an audience at a traditional noh play may be seen more intent on reading the text than viewing the stage.

[3] In the letter cited in n. 1, above, Rodrigues relates that in the Canton banquet, the guests were entertained by singing and an orchestra of six instruments, followed by juggling with lighted torches and bird imitations. According to Ricci (*Fonti*, I, p. 33 and *China*, pp. 23–4), troupes of actors were hired to entertain guests. They often presented the host with a volume of plays, leaving him to choose which should be performed. Such banquets might last as long as ten hours. Rada (in Boxer, *South China*, p. 289) reports seeing a play and a tumbling act during a banquet. Cocks (9 January 1617, in *Diary*, I, p. 228) writes that the Chinese merchant Li Dan 'envited the king [the *daimyo* of Hirado] and the nobles to dyner, and feasted them both day and night with a China play'.

order the food to be brought along with wine so that they may thus make merry and discuss some business. For business is generally done after eating and drinking when the heart is more joyful and relaxed, and as a result they discuss such matters with a better will. Inside the trays there are normally fifteen small bowls duly arranged in three rows of five along the length of the tray and in three along the breadth, and the food can be served in these bowls. Or else there are as many kinds of different things arranged and cut into portions so that they may be easily eaten. They include their various kinds of sweetmeats and sometimes two portions of the same thing. As has been said above, this is equivalent to the wine and various appetizing *sakana* to persuade them to drink.

CHAPTER 30

THE BANQUETS OF THE JAPANESE, AND FIRSTLY THE DIFFERENT KINDS OF BANQUETS

The Japanese hold five sorts of banquets. The first is the ordinary, common one and has been held since the reign of Nobunaga and Taikō, in whose time practically everything was reformed.[1] The second is called the banquet of three tables, for they provide that number of formal tables or trays for each individual guest. The third is a more solemn kind and is called the banquet of five tables or trays. The fourth is the most solemn and formal of all, and seven tables are provided for each guest. Properly speaking, this type is for persons of great nobility when they invite guests also of similar rank as a sign of hospitality and of their respect towards them. The fifth is a private meal as regards its form and ceremonies, and its purpose is to invite a person to drink *cha* with much solemnity. This last is something of the greatest excellency, honour, and respect among the Japanese, and they spend much of their wealth buying very expensive utensils that they highly esteem. Some of them are worth more than 20,000 crowns and are used when a person is invited to drink *cha* in a special house built for this purpose, as we shall presently say below.

In general the banquets held in Japan up to the time of Nobunaga and Taikō belonged to the second, third, and fourth categories, and each one had a certain number of tables and dishes that were limited and fixed as regards the number and quality of the things offered. In these banquets many of the dishes were served on plates in the form of pyramids neatly arranged with their corners as in the Chinese fashion, and it was from China that they derived their origin. But they served only for decoration and were there to be looked at and not eaten.[2] Special people prepared these banquets, and we ourselves had experience of them some years after our arrival in Japan. All the dishes used in them were of earthenware (we mentioned this above when speaking about wine cups), but this was more for the sake of ancient ceremony than through lack of better ware. The tables, trays, and salvers used at these banquets and also at those of the present day are all of new cedar, and the wood is left in its natural state. They are extremely clean and have legs about a span in height, and are used on only that one occasion. They were wont to hold these banquets more as a rite to

---

[1] The military 'new men', such as Nobunaga, Hideyoshi, Ieyasu, and even Hidetada, were known for their preference for plain food, and Rodrigues is perhaps implying that their taste may have had a general influence throughout the country. Nishiyama, *Edo Culture*, pp. 144–6. For Ieyasu's preference in this regard, see Totman, *Tokugawa Ieyasu*, p. 108.

[2] In his description of the banquet given in 1591 by Hideyoshi for Valignano, accompanied by Rodrigues, Fróis (*História*, V, pp. 306–7) reports that each guest had three tables, or trays, placed before him, and later five more were brought out. 'Everybody ate very little and drank even less, so that it seemed that they were seated at table as a compliment and not to eat; although as regards the dishes and service, there was the greatest possible solemnity that could be provided in Japan.'

Plate 20: A display of formal banquet dishes. 'In these banquets many of the dishes were served on plates in the form of pyramids neatly arranged. ... In the third and most solemn banquet ... there are thirty-two dishes, among which are included eight *shiru*, that is, five of fish, one of shellfish, and two of meat.' pp. 261, 263. Rodrigues, *This Island of Japon*.

show honour and regard towards the person of the guest than to enjoy eating tasty dishes. Hence the more entertainment provided in these banquets, the more formalities were there in drinking wine. They provided various appetizing *sakana* that gave a thirst, as well as other entertainments of instrumental music, plays, and other things that were interspersed throughout the banquet.

The food was cold and insipid as it was cut up in portions and brought in on tables, and the only hot thing one could enjoy was the *shiru*, or broth. These were the principal dishes of the banquets and the rest were merely additional, for they were made of things highly prized by them, and even now this is true of modern banquets. The more solemn the banquet among the Japanese, and also in China, the greater number of different broths and *shiru* provided for each guest. Each of these is made from different things. Some are made from fish of high quality, others from the meat of prized birds, such as the crane, which ranks in the first place, the swan in the second, and wild duck in the third. This is still true even today, for on no account will they use anything but wild game, and never the domestic animals and birds that they rear. They will not eat the latter and in this they differ from the Chinese, who esteem the flesh of the ass more than that of the horse, the latter more than the cow. They have an even higher regard for pork, lard, and bacon, as well as domestic duck, hens, and geese, while lowly persons eat dogmeat and other things.[1]

In keeping with their customs the Japanese abominate all this, for on no account whatsoever will they eat ass, horse, cow, much less pig (except boars), duck, or hens, and they are naturally adverse to lard. They eat only wild game at banquets and their ordinary meals, for they regard a man who slaughters an animal reared in his house as cruel and unclean. On the other hand, they do not show this compassion towards human beings, because they kill them with greater ease and enjoyment than they would an animal.[2] This is despite the fact that some people, especially the traders who have had dealings with the Portuguese since their arrival in Japan, now eat cow, pig, and hens, but such things are not eaten at solemn banquets or, for that matter, throughout the entire kingdom. Although these *shiru* are called broth in China as well as in Japan, they are in fact fish or meat dishes with their sauce, seasoned together with different spices, and not broth just by itself.

In the banquets of three tables, which is the least of these three types, there are twenty dishes, and they include four *shiru*, one of them consisting of the meat of a swan or wild duck, and this is the principal dish of the banquet. The other four[3] are fish dishes. Each of them is of some prized fish, and one is of various dry shellfish, for this is served in all three types of banquet.

In the second type of banquet with five tables they serve twenty-six dishes, among which are included six *shiru*, four of them of fish. Among these dishes, in this and in the following kind of banquet, one is always of whale meat, another of dry shellfish, and one of meat, as above.

In the third and most solemn banquet of six tables or trays, there are thirty-two dishes, among which are included eight *shiru*, that is, five of fish, one of shellfish, and two of meat. One of these is of crane, the most prized bird of Japan, and this is the principal dish of the banquet, all the rest being merely in addition.[4] In winter these cranes and innumerable wild duck, swans, and many other sorts of birds that they hunt, come from Tartary on account of the great cold and snow there. The second *shiru* is of swan, and these two dishes of crane and swan, the most highly esteemed food in Japan, constitute the solemnity of this banquet. In winter they are eaten unsalted, but at other times when they return to Tartary, they are served salted. Sometimes fresh birds are so valuable that I saw cranes bought for sixty taels and swans for ten, but salted cranes fetched only ten, and swans sold for four. Many of these salted birds are imported into Japan from Korea.

In addition to these solemn banquets before Taikō became Lord of Japan, there were other ordinary ones in the kingdom that were held among friends and intimates, even those who were nobles and lords. This was at a time when Japan was wracked by wars and each lord was by himself in his own domain, while the entire kingdom was plunged in great poverty and wretchedness. In keeping with the times, these banquets too were very poor

---

[1] The Portuguese text is not clear at this point, but the context seems to require this translation.

[2] There is a short gap in the Portuguese text in this sentence, but the general sense remains clear. Rodrigues's sentiment is echoed by Carletti (in *TCJ*, p. 156), who declares that the Japanese have no more scruple in crucifying a person than in killing a fly. For references to the Japanese aversion to eating domestic animals, see p. 110, n. 2.

[3] Presumably a slip for 'three'.

[4] See Plate 20 for the arrangement of dishes; also, Rodrigues, *Nihon*, I, p. 548. As Rodrigues mentions, some of the dishes are piled in the form of cubes, others in the form of pyramids. In *Ogasawara*, f. 23, four diagrams are given, showing the order and position of the dishes in banquets where one, two, three, or four tables are used.

affairs and no more than a mere compliment and token of friendship. Indeed, the principal part of their ordinary banquets[1] consisted of only the wine and *sakana*. Mention is made of these banquets in old letters as if they alone comprised the solemnity of the banquets of the kingdom.

The fourth kind of banquet is the first in the list that we placed at the beginning of this chapter. This is the modern banquet that has been held since the time of Nobunaga and Taikō up to the present day and is now general throughout the kingdom. Since that time many things have been reformed, many of their ancient customs changed, and everything superfluous and time-consuming thrown out. In the same way, matters concerning their banquets and even ordinary meals have been greatly improved. First of all, let us speak about the tables, trays, and other wooden utensils. These are either made of the same fine cedarwood, so highly esteemed in Japan, or they use tables varnished black so delicately that they look like smooth ivory or a mirror into which one is looking. These are either left like this or are gilded after their fashion. Then there are the rice bowls and the serving trays with gold and silver flowers and branches inlaid among the gilt. Such things are found not only among the nobles and grandees, but also among the wealthy and well-born people of the kingdom. They also abolished, or do not now hold, banquets of five or seven tables, but ordinarily use three. They likewise did away with the earthenware vessels of such ancient tradition, except in certain festivals of the year when they are used ceremoniously for some things, chiefly as cups from which to drink wine. They now use varnished ware instead, as we have said. These are not harmed by water, nor can damp or grease penetrate them because they are almost like glass, and nothing sticks to them when they are washed. Or else they use delicate ware from China or other glazed ware made in Japan itself.

As regards the actual food, they did away with the dishes placed there merely for ornament and to be looked at, and also the cold dishes. In their place they substituted well-seasoned hot food brought to the table at the proper time, and is substantial and of high quality. This was done after the fashion of their *chanoyu*, which they greatly imitate in this matter. They also omitted the multitude of broths, or *shiru*, and now provide only two or perhaps three. These will include on the first table a light one of herbs and tasty vegetables along with the rice, and they start with this. Another will be of some prized bird and this is the principal dish of the banquet. The third will be of another substantial and esteemed thing. They drink often and intermittently while they are eating. The wine is produced in the first banquets almost at the end. So food at banquets nowadays and at ordinary meals gives pleasure and enjoyment, all apart from the wine, and it is not only for the sake of ceremony and courtesy and merely to look at, as in former times.

---

[1] The text has 'music' here instead of 'banquets', but this must be the copyist's slip.

CHAPTER 31

THEIR MANNER OF INVITING GUESTS TO BANQUETS

The Japanese are wont to invite guests to a banquet either on account of some obligation existing among them in certain circumstances, or spontaneously as a token of love and friendship in order to entertain them. In the first place, when a noble or man of standing comes a long way from outside the territory to visit another person, or, as often happens, sends another person in his stead, the host has an obligation to invite either him or the person sent in his place to a banquet in his house. If the guest is to stay in his house, then the host must also invite his retinue. Above all, he must take great care of the guest's horse if it is a valuable one, for the lords esteem this highly. But if before going to the house that he comes to visit he takes lodgings in the territory, then there is the obligation of entertaining only him, although entertaining his retinue is a favour paid to one's lord. The invitation is not issued when the guest comes to the host's house to pay his visit, but when some time has elapsed after he has returned to his lodgings. A person is then sent to invite him to the banquet and tells him the day and whether it is in the morning or the afternoon. This is done for every kind of banquet so that the guest may prepare himself and know when he has to go.

It is the custom to invite other people of lesser rank either personally or by a message or letter. When many are invited together, a list of people is drawn up and a page goes around with it to all of them. Although the names of the principal guests appear in the first place,[1] there is written at the top the phrase, 'The list is not compiled in order.' This is the same as saying, 'The people in this list are not named in order but haphazardly, merely as they came to mind.' Then nobody will be upset by being preceded by another. This is done by list not only to help the messenger's memory and to know who has accepted and who has declined, but also so that each person may know who has been invited and whether there is among them someone whom he dislikes and does not get on with. For they will necessarily have to compliment and converse with each other there, and toast each other with wine and accept the cups from which they have drunk. Those who accept the invitation place a mark against their name, while those who decline leave it blank without a mark. These excuse themselves by sending word through the messenger, saying either that they have already promised someone else to go to his banquet or that they have urgent business on hand.[2]

Before they go to the banquet, the guests neatly robe themselves in a new formal dress of

---

[1] There is a short gap in this sentence in the Portuguese text.

[2] For the somewhat more formal invitation card sent out before a banquet in China, see Ricci, *Fonti*, I, pp. 76–7, and *China*, p. 65.

silk, trousers, and *kataginu* (this is an over-garment covering the shoulders and has already been mentioned).[1] They also freshly shave the front part of the head, as we have said.[2] Some wear the robes of a shaven monk, and in addition to the fine black dress and veil-like over-garment of a shaven man, they also freshly shave the head and chin. It would be impolite to go with the hair growing as this is a sign of mourning or illness, so they shave out of respect for the host.

Everything in the house is made ready, and all the food is duly prepared. Then if the guests are nobles, a messenger of rank is sent to their homes and informs them that it is now time for them to pay them the favour of coming. When they arrive, the host goes out to meet them in the manner already described when we spoke about visits.[3] While they exchange their due courtesies, the host leads them to the guestroom, where he leaves them after paying some compliments and enters further inside to arrange the banquet. He leaves there, however, someone to converse with them quietly until the tables are brought out. Courtesy and respect for his guests demand this, and it is regarded as careless and a poor reception if he stays there talking.

When the invited guests are of less honourable rank, it is not customary for them to wait to be summoned to the house, for it is considered impolite for such people to wait until they are called. Instead, they anticipate the summons and thus show their appreciation of the favour the host has paid them by his invitation. When such guests arrive, neither the host nor anyone else need go out to greet them. After they have entered the room, they wait on the veranda out of respect for the host. To show them greater hospitality, he sends out a messenger to converse with them while he is occupied in arranging the banquet.

When it is time, he comes out and pays his compliments to them, and makes the more honourable guests sit down in their places in the room. While they are doing this, the guests exchange many compliments among themselves and with the host. The host also sits down, and although he is head of the house, he usually takes the lowest place, unless he is an important person to whom respect is due. But before they sit down and begin to eat, all of them place their swords at one side of the room and retain only the daggers in their sashes, for they never part with these. Although they are accustomed to washing their hands very often, they do not do so before meals because they do not touch any of the food with their hands while eating. If they come by horse, however, water is provided on the veranda for their hands.

When they are all in their places, a drinking cup on a salver is produced before the tables are brought out and is placed at the top of the room, as was said earlier when we spoke about visits.[4] This is like a token of the meal that is to follow, because it is used in due course when they come to pay the courtesies that are customary when drinking wine. The principal tables or eating trays then begin to appear, and they all kneel with their knees pointing forwards. The serving pages enter and, beginning with the guests at the top of the room, they place the main table in front of each one. If the host's son brings a table to the principal guest at the top of the room so as to honour him, the guest must ask his father at

---

[1] See pp. 182–3.
[2] See p. 120.
[3] See p. 234.
[4] See pp. 244–5.

least twice to make him also sit down at table. If the host does not wish to comply with this request, the guest pretends not to notice.

As we have said, nowadays at banquets they usually place three principal tables in front of each guest. All the tables are generally of white cedarwood, square in shape and with legs a span in height. The table placed in the centre is the highest and has another table on either side. The covered bowl of rice is placed on the middle table in the left-hand corner nearest the guest, while the bowl of *shiru*, also covered, is in the right-hand corner, and the salt-cellar stands next to them.[1] There is food, either fresh fish or bird, on a plate in each of the two corners and in the middle. The second table after this is placed on the right-hand side and bears the principal *shiru*, as has been described, and two dishes. The third table is placed on the left with another *shiru* and two other dishes, one of which will be their highly esteemed raw fish cut up into small pieces. Along with it there will be a dish containing a tart sauce or one that burns like mustard, and this takes away the rawness of the fish. For it is the general custom throughout the kingdom to eat a certain kind of esteemed fish raw. This may sound horrible to someone who hears about it from afar and is not accustomed to it. But anyone who becomes used to eating this fish with its appropriate sauce enjoys it and does not find it horrible at all.[2]

When the tables have been put into position, they all sit down on their own accord and cross their legs, while their feet remain decently covered by their robes or trousers so that they are not seen. When they have gracefully and neatly uncovered the rice, the *shiru*, and everything else that comes covered, they first of all pick up the *hashi* in their right hand, the rice-bowl in their left, and begin to eat the rice. They keep the body erect and do not bend over. They eat two morsels one after the other, and then putting the rice back in its place, they take up the bowl of *shiru*, eat two mouthfuls from this, and drink a little broth. They then eat another mouthful of rice, and then something from the dish in the middle or from the corner on the right of the *shiru*. After this, they once more eat rice and *shiru*, and then something from the dish in the other corner.[3] They follow this order twice when they begin to eat, and then they eat whatever they please from the other tables on either side, beginning with the *shiru* on the right. This is the principal dish of the banquet, for it always consists of some precious thing such as crane, swan, wild duck, etc.

Meanwhile, the servers bring out in due order bowls of other food on fine salvers that have no legs, and the guests begin eating from these as well. Now the principal dishes are the rice and *shiru*, but for the sake of courtesy only a little is placed in the bowls. So a page usually comes with a tray of rice and a clean lacquered spoon, and goes around offering the rice to the guests. He puts the rice into the bowl with the spoon and each guest receives as

---

[1] A possible, but admittedly unlikely, translation of the phrase 'tudo cuberto em saleiro alli junto'. Rodrigues, *Nihon*, I, p. 557, has in Japanese, 'with lids in the shape of salt-cellars.' Avila Girón (in *TCJ*, pp. 194–5) also mentions that the rice is placed on the left, the *shiru* on the right; he adds a description of the low tables and various bowls used at meals.

[2] Fróis (*Tratado*, p. 172) remarks on the Japanese preference for raw, rather than cooked, fish. According to Mexia (Macao, 6 January 1584, in *Cartas*, II, ff. 123–3v), eating raw fish, or *sashimi*, was a great torment for the Europeans, although the Japanese enjoyed it greatly. They were edified, he writes, at seeing us eat it, for they observed that people who did such violence to themselves in their efforts of adaptation must indeed be holy men. In fact, as long as *sashimi* is eaten with the 'tart sauce' mentioned by Rodrigues, it is by no means unacceptable to the Western palate.

[3] According to Avila Girón (in *TCJ*, p. 195), the diners first took three morsels of rice, then the *shiru*; then two morsels of rice and then *shiru*; finally, one morsel of rice, then *shiru*, and after that anything they pleased.

much as he pleases. Other pages come with salvers to remove the bowls of *shiru* and replace them with others, with each person asking for the one he likes best. If the host's son or a person of rank helps to serve the *shiru* and rice, they observe certain ceremonies and courtesies towards him by bowing their body and head.

The host is wont to show great hospitality and regard towards his guests by providing them with, among other dishes, a bird taken by his hawk, and this is esteemed very highly. This is served roasted and is eaten not with *hashi* but with two fingers of the hands with the other three fingers closed in the palm. Before they begin to eat it, they raise it above the head to the level of their forehead as a sign of respect towards the hawk's owner, and then they eat it all without leaving a scrap. When it is served in a broth, it is eaten with *hashi* so as not to soil the hands. It is also the custom to feast the guests with birds prized in the four seasons of the year, and they serve them at formal banquets in the appropriate season as a treat. In spring and summer it is the lark; in autumn, the bird called *shigi*, a very tasty bird of the same colour as the lark and with a very long beak;[1] in winter, the pheasant and wild fowl.[2]

The guest must praise the food, especially some good dish or seasoning, once or even twice, and thank the host for the hospitality and diligence involved therein. The host, however, must always disparage, declaring that it was no good at all, and that there was nothing worthy of Their Honours, etc.[3]

Each dish has a fixed and suitable place on the table, and a dish in one place is never placed in another. They eat the food from its place with their *hashi* without picking up the bowl in their hand, except when it contains broth or sauce, which they sip. When all the guests have eaten the rice, *shiru*, and also the dishes they desire, and do not want anything more, they take from the large table a little broth of *shiru* made from herbs, or from another table a morsel of something highly prized, such as crane, swan, duck, etc. They drop it on the rice remaining in the bowl, mix it all together, and this marks the end of the eating.[4]

1. The wine and hot water served in the banquet, and the fruit and *cha* at the end thereof

According to ancient custom, the wine is generally brought out at the end of the meal when they have finished eating both the rice, *shiru*, and the dishes that they fancied. The host and guests exchange drinking compliments with the cup that was placed on its salver at the top of the room at the beginning of the meal before they began to eat. The wine must be warm or cold according to season, as was noted above when describing visits, although nowadays it is always served warm at a suitable temperature at banquets. For they believe from experience that warming the wine improves its quality, goodness, and taste, and they consider it more nourishing. But at modern banquets they are now accustomed to drink intermittently while they are eating, and each person drinks from his own private cup. The wine circulates three or four times, and at the end of the banquet they perform their ceremonies with the cup that was placed in the room. Sometimes the wine stirs them up so much that there is a great deal of intemperance at this conclusion.

When all have eaten and drunk intermittently, as we have said, and with their *hashi* in

---

[1] *Vocabulario*, f. 301: '*Shigi*. A bird thus called, having long legs and beak.' The reference is to the snipe or long-bill.

[2] *Galhina do matto* – literally, wild chicken.

[3] Yet another instance of the Japanese custom of disparaging their gifts. See p. 235, n. 1.

[4] The last line of the Portuguese text ends abruptly and obviously has a part missing. At the beginning of the previous sentence, the text runs, 'When all the *banquets* have eaten the rice, …'

their hands look as if they wish to finish and rest, the domestic steward in charge of the meal then orders a page to enter the room with a vessel of wine. The page places himself on his knees after their fashion and looks towards the host. When this page appears, they all put down their *hashi*, place them on the table, and sit in their kneeling position, as has been described. The host orders the wine page to take the cup with the salver that was at the top of the room, and only the host performs the customary courtesies of offering it to the guests before drinking, as we have mentioned when speaking about the ordinary method of entertaining guests with wine. All the others drink in succession from the cup, but are not obliged to make these courtesies, except when he meets them for the first time. In that case the host raises the cup towards each guest individually, as this is a courtesy due in token of friendship. When the cup has circulated around all the guests once, one of the last guests to drink offers his own cup again to the guest sitting at the top of the room and thus renews the drinking. They invite each other to drink as the wine passes among them and this arouses them. All this is a compliment paid to the host. As a token of love and confidence, the guests are also accustomed to exchange among themselves the cups from which they have drunk, and taking the cup of another person, they raise it and drink from it. When a guest asks another for his cup so that he may raise it and drink from it, the other must always show reluctance before handing it to him.

When the banquet is very solemn with much adornment and pomp, the wine is brought out three times at intervals, and each time they produce a new cup with *sakana* on its decorated and finely made salver, as has already been said. This is done in the following way. After they have paid their compliments with the first cup that was in the room and most of them have drunk from it, out comes another fresh cup on its salver, and is put in the room in the place where the first one stood. The cup from which they have just drunk is taken away after the host has lifted it up to conclude the round. They then converse a little with the host. The *sakana* is not produced, and they go on drinking from the second cup with fewer formalities than with the first. If it was a guest who began the drinking from the first cup, then they oblige the host to start the second. In the same way, when everyone has drunk, the second cup is taken inside and they again converse for a little while, and then continue drinking from the third cup. This is also put in the room in the same place of honour as the other two cups when they are just finishing the second one. The cup is placed there at this point to oblige the guests to remain seated, for it is not the custom to rise from their place to leave while a new cup is there without having drunk from it. Thus this anticipates any request from the guests to depart or not drink more wine.

Sometimes as a great favour the host may have his small son serve wine to the guests. In this case, after the father has finished paying his compliments with the cup, the guest at the top of the room does him a favour by giving the cup to his son in the following way. The lad takes his father's cup to the guest, who raises it and takes a little wine. Then looking at the boy, the guest places the cup on the mat next to himself and bowing his body[1] pays him his due courtesies. He next takes a little wine, drinks it, empties the cup, and places it on the mat in front of the boy. Then the guest himself takes the jug from his hand and acts as

---

[1] The text is corrupt here. If *e não* is a slip for *e mão*, the translation reads: 'He pays the boy due compliments with his body and hand.' Alternatively, a clause beginning 'and he does not…' (*e não*) has been omitted in the text.

cup-bearer.[1] After the boy has drunk, the guest returns the jug to him and, raising the cup from which the lad has drunk, he once more drinks from it. This ceremony affords the guest a way of repaying the boy for acting as cup-bearer. Sometimes the host also rises from his place, takes the jug from the person who is serving, and then goes and gives wine to the guest. The guest pays his compliments and, after drinking a little, places the cup on the mat, bows reverently, and entreats the host to return to his place. When the host declines to do so, the guest finishes drinking the wine in the cup, and thanks him for the honour paid him by rising up to serve.

When they have finished drinking the wine and the cups have been collected, the host tells the guests, who until then have been sitting on their knees, that they may be at their ease, and they then sit cross-legged. Then, to mark the end of the meal, hot water is brought in and poured into the rice bowls of all the guests, although in China *cha* is used instead. They sip this quietly and unhurriedly. Any rice remaining in the bowl is mixed with this warm water, and they drink all this swill. If the water is very hot, they do not blow on it (nor, for that matter, do they blow on the *shiru*), and for this reason they usually take only a little so that it may cool quickly. After everyone has drunk the hot water, they put the *hashi* back in their place on the large table.

It is customary at banquets to provide some fruit as dessert, and there are always seven, five, or at least three kinds of different things. These are served on a white cedar tray supported on tall legs, and on top are brought all the different kinds of fruit placed in separate piles. Along with these is provided a toothpick, well made, wide at the base, and almost a span in length. In addition to this ordinary fruit, they serve in due season various fruit such as melons, pears, and certain things like apples. These are yellow in colour and quite excellent, and there are various kinds and flavours. Europeans have mistakenly called them figs, because when they are dried they look somewhat like dried figs.[2] Other various fresh fruit are served on their trays or large plates. Their various kinds of excellent melons are served in a large basin of water, and they greatly cool down the wine that the guests have drunk.[3]

When all the guests have finished with the hot water, the waiters come and remove the side tables, beginning with the one on the right. Then when they come to remove the large table in the middle, they bring the tray of fruit and leave it in front of the person who is to eat it, and carry inside the middle table last of all. When the tray of fruit arrives, everyone takes the toothpick and breaks off a piece of wood about the breadth of a hand in length. This is done out of respect and courtesy, because it is rude to use a long toothpick. Before eating the fruit, they turn aside and pick their teeth, and out of courtesy they place their left hand over their upper lip and clean their teeth under this hand. It is very impolite to clean the teeth without hiding or covering the mouth with the left hand or a fan.[4]

When the guests have finished eating the fruit, the servants remove the trays and take them inside, and everyone goes out on the veranda overlooking the garden of flowers and trees in front of the room. Before washing their hands, they once more clean their teeth

---

[1] The 'jug' has the form of a kettle and is called *chōshi* in Japanese. As illustration of the correct manner of holding this vessel is given in Rodrigues, *This Island*, p. 150.

[2] A reference to *kaki*, usually translated loosely as 'persimmon'. See p. 107, n. 1.

[3] Fróis (*Tratado*, p. 172) has some observations on the way the Japanese eat melons.

[4] Fróis (*Tratado*, p. 178) and Avila Girón (*Relación*, p. 20) comment on the length of Japanese toothpicks, both saying that they were sometimes more than a span long.

with their left hand, covering their mouth with their right.[1] They then go to wash their hands in a secluded place, where they find the water for their hands neatly prepared. For the very noble guests the water is brought to the room with a towel and a varnished basin and pitcher, richly gilded after their fashion. In winter all the guests are provided with hot water for their hands.

[1] Thus the Portuguese text, although it is probable that the left and right hands have been confused here, perhaps by the copyist.

271

CHAPTER 32

THEIR MANNER OF ENTERTAINING WITH THE DRINK OF *CHA*, AND A DESCRIPTION OF *CHA* AND OF THIS CEREMONY SO HIGHLY ESTEEMED BY THE JAPANESE

The custom of drinking *cha* among the Chinese and Japanese is common throughout the whole kingdom and is one of the principal courtesies with which a guest is entertained. Indeed, it is the first and most usual thing with which they begin to entertain and divert a guest and, finally, with which they bid farewell to him. In addition, it is a very common drink for everyone and is used on account of its inherent good effects, as will be mentioned later.[1]

The first thing with which they usually entertain a guest in the above-mentioned nations is *cha*, and it is offered not only once but many times when it is not served solemnly, as the Japanese are accustomed to do. They pay their compliments and courtesies with it and thus entertain the guests, and while they are conversing it is often produced to raise their spirits and pass the time with this wholesome diversion. Its use throughout China and Japan is so common that in China they always keep it prepared and hot (as thus it is drunk) for ordinary guests, while for nobles they make tea especially in a very short time.[2] In the same way the Japanese always keep hot water ready in a special place to entertain their guests at whatever time they may arrive.

Although these nations have placed much of their elegance and etiquette in this *cha* and it is a very famous drink, it has so far been but poorly described and understood. So we shall deal with this subject sufficiently for the reader to understand what sort of thing it is, its wholesome properties, and the way in which they entertain with it in general, as well as another special way practised by the Japanese with *cha*. They attach the greatest importance to this and regard it as the supreme way of honoring and entertaining a guest however noble he may be, even the Lord of Tenka himself. They make great account of this and so highly esteem it that they regard this, rather than gold, silver, and precious stones, as their principal treasures and precious jewels, as we will say hereafter.

This celebrated and famous *cha*, then, is a small tree, or rather bush, which some have mistakenly believed to be the sumach shrub. It is the same size as and somewhat similar to the myrtle bush, and bears leaves all the year around without shedding them, although they are slightly bigger and are green on both sides.[3] Its new leaves, which are used in the drink,

---

[1] A summary of practically all the European accounts of tea – its cultivation, price, drink, and *chanoyu* – is found in Cooper, 'Early Europeans'. In addition, Alvarez-Taladriz supplies an enormous amount of reference material in his Spanish translation of these chapters on tea, in Rodrigues, *Arte del Cha*.

[2] For brief accounts of tea-drinking in China, see Ricci, *Fonti*, I, p. 26, and *China*, pp. 16–7; Cruz and Rada, in Boxer, *South China*, pp. 140, 287.

[3] Cortes (*Viaje*, p. 164) agrees that the tea bush, if not the same as the sumach of Spain, is very similar to it. For a description of the bush, see Gribble, 'Preparation of Japanese Tea', p. 5.

are extremely soft, tender, and delicate, and frost may easily make them wither away. So much damage can be done in this way that in the town of Uji,[1] where the best tea is produced, all the plantations and fields in which this *cha* is grown are covered over with awnings or mats made of rice straw or thatch.[2] They are thus protected from damage by frost from February onwards until the end of March, when the new leaf begins to bud. They spend a great deal of money on this for the sake of the profit that is to be obtained, as we shall say, for the trade in *cha* is very great.

The fruit produced by this bush is like a cypress nut, and it opens and contains pips from which the plant begins and is sown.[3] The good and highly esteemed *cha* used for the drink is tended with much care in plantations and orchards, and is sown and transplanted separately. The wild *cha* bush that grows naturally is quite useless because it is very tough and bitter. Although it is grown throughout nearly all the kingdom in both China and Japan, the excellent and highly esteemed *cha* of the nobles, the wealthy, and gentry, is cultivated in a few particular places in certain parts of some Chinese and Japanese provinces or kingdoms. It is from here that it originates and is distributed throughout the country. This is the *cha* used for important guests, in the houses of the lords and in the *chanoyu* ceremony. No value is attached to the inferior type used by commoners throughout the kingdom, not does this sort appear in formal etiquette. In China the most excellent *cha* of all is to be found only in the state and city of Hangzhou[4] in Nanjing province, whence it is taken to the king and nobles, and in the state and city of Jianning-fu in Fujian province.[5] In Japan the best is grown only in the town called Uji, three leagues from the court of Miyako, whence it is taken to all parts of the kingdom. The *cha* leaves used in the drink are the soft new ones and the first to sprout in the spring in March, when they are picked. Just as in our vineyards, so too this crop is brought in by large numbers of people, who can distinguish the good new leaf that is to be picked from the old and inferior one that is left.[6]

Now this is the way of preparing the *cha* leaf in China and Japan to make it fit for serving as a drink.[7] When the new leaf has been gathered in, they first of all cook it in the steam of a certain solution made up water, wine,[8] and other ingredients until it is sufficiently softened. They have set up some wooden stoves or grates like deep trays or lidless boxes, eight

---

[1] From time immemorial, Uji, about 10 miles southeast of Miyako, has been the centre of production of the finest tea; its plantations date from the end of the 12th century.

[2] An illustration of such awnings, called *oishita*, and of other stages in tea production, is given in Rodrigues, *Nihon*, I, pp. 566–7, although according to the explanation (p. 569, n. 3) the screens were erected to protect the bushes from the sun.

[3] For an illustrated description of the tea plant, see Kaempfer, *History*, III, pp. 216–24.

[4] There is a gap in the Portuguese text and I have added 'Hangzhou'. Hangzhou, actually in Zhejiang province, was for long a centre of the tea trade. Richard, *Comprehensive Geography*, pp. 232, 395.

[5] Jianning-fu is still a tea centre. Richard, *Comprehensive Geography*, p. 225.

[6] According to Kaempfer (*History*, III, pp. 224–5), the leaves must be carefully picked and not torn off in handfuls. Skilful pickers collect as many as 9 or 10 catties a day, but casual labourers only about three. Gribble ('Preparation of Japanese Tea', pp. 7–8) notes that most of the picking is done by women, who collect on average about 3½ lbs of leaves a day.

[7] Owing to the copyist's error, the whole of this paragraph, with some variations, is repeated in the Portuguese text, from the beginning of the paragraph down to the words '... thick paper made for this purpose.' I have translated the second version, which seems to fit into the following text better.

[8] Both Rodrigues, *Nihon*, I, p. 571, n. 6, and Alvarez-Taladriz (in Rodrigues, *Arte del cha*, p. 5, n. 18) remark that there is no knowledge today of wine ever being used in the preparation of tea.

spans or more in length and half that in width. They pour very clean, fine, and sifted ash into these, and place lighted charcoal inside and cover it with the ash. In this way they produce a slow, gentle fire that slowly roasts but does not scorch. Above these stoves they construct cane grills, which do not receive much heat, and they cover them with a certain thick paper made for this purpose. On top of this they pour the *cha*, already cooked as we have said, and there it roasts gently.

There are three persons on either side of each stove and with their hands they continually move the *cha* together with the paper so that it may all be roasted evenly and not scorched. As it is new, the leaf remains intact and curled up like a hawk's talons, and they call it precisely this on account of the likeness.[1] This is the usual way pf roasting it in China and Japan. But as in Japan they drink the actual *cha* ground into powder, while the Chinese cook the leaf in hot water and drink the mixture containing all the goodness of the *cha*, the Japanese pay much attention not only to the taste and flavour but also to the colour of the *cha*.[2] They see to it that, after the leaf has been roasted and ground, its colour is as green when they pour it into the hot water as when it was growing on the tree or even greener, and indeed this is the case.

Some years ago they sought from experience another method that is now in use and is as follows. They pass the *cha* leaf through the same solution, soften it, and extract its natural bitterness and sourness without losing its colour. They then roast it as before. The leaves of this sort remain flat and open, and after roasting they look extremely green and attractive when held up to the light.

These stoves are found in very large rooms, and there is a house with more than 170 of them in various rooms that open on to each other, where more than a thousand people roast the *cha*; there are others with fewer people. This town would have fifteen or twenty principal houses making *cha* and employing more than five or six thousand people.[3] Some pick and collect the *cha* leaf, others do the roasting, and the rest perform various other tasks. The roasting is done in such a way that they all keep in time. They pour the leaves in at the same time and a signal is given for them all to stop together, for the master of the house is there to see whether the leaf has been sufficiently roasted or not.[4]

When this *cha* has been roasted, the leaves are selected by other people who divide them into their grades and qualities. There are usually four sorts or kinds of *cha* according to their delicacy. The first and most excellent is the first leaf taken from the best bud and is called *gokujō*, that is, 'best tea'. The second one after this is called *betsugi*; the third, *goku sosori*; the fourth, *betsugi sosori*. There are other grades of inferior *cha* below these, but no importance is attached to them nor are they esteemed. For some years they have placed in the first grade a *cha* that is of even higher quality. They have not given it a name but call it *shirabukuro*, meaning 'white paper bag', because it is packed in small white paper bags without any label

---

[1] *Taka-no-tsune*, literally, 'hawk's talons'. This and other types of tea are listed in Sadler, *Cha-no-yu*, p. 6. Kaempfer (*History*, III, pp. 229–33) goes into much detail about the roasting of tea leaves, stating that some producers would repeat the process as often as five or six times.

[2] Ricci (*Fonti*, I, p. 26, and *China*, p. 17) also points out the difference in brewing tea in Japan and China.

[3] For the names of the some of the principal tea producers in Uji in the Tokugawa period, see Rodrigues, *Nihon*, I, p. 572, n. 10.

[4] An illustrated account of the whole process is given in Gribble, 'Preparation of Japanese Tea', pp. 7–15, where it may be seen that by 1885 the process had changed little since Rodrigues's time. For the somewhat different Chinese method of processing the leaves, see Ball, *Account*, pp. 103–53.

at all. The *goku* and *betsugi* grades are also packed in the same small bags, but they are tightly tied up at the mouth with a label bearing the name of the *cha*.[1]

As regards the quantity of the *cha* produced in this town and distributed throughout Japan to nobles, the lords, and the wealthy, they commonly say that it would weigh in all some 300 piculs, each picul equaling 100 catties or 120 of our *arrateis*.[2] A catty weighs 80 ounces, with eight mace to the ounce.[3] So 300 piculs are equal to 36,000 *arrateis*, and this would be 1,125 *arrobas* and 281 quintals.[4] This is quite certain, for seven or eight thousand clay caddies are assembled there from all over Japan and they hold three or four catties each.

In this town there are fifteen to twenty leading concerns in whose houses the kingdom's principal *cha* is made. Each of the lords, nobles, and those who perform the *cha* ceremony has his custom here in one of the houses, whence he obtains the *cha* that he needs. To this end he sends his precious caddies there in due time for them to be filled with *cha*. The ordinary price of *cha* is as follows. First-quality *goku* costs six silver taels a catty; *betsugi*, four taels; *goku sosori*, two; and finally, *betsugi sosori*, one. *Cha* of lesser quality costs five, four, three, two, and even one *mace*, but the landed lords and important people who perform the *cha* ceremony make no account of this type.[5] In order to receive good choice *cha* of the best quality, they pay for it in another prestigious way. That is, for each caddy of three or four catties, they pay a bar of gold (equivalent to sixty taels), a hundred or two hundred loads of charcoal, some silk robes, and other gifts, so that a catty comes to be worth more than twenty taels.

In addition to this quantity of *cha* and caddies, there is another goodly *cha* produced in the villages in the neighbourhood of the town. They make an enormous number of new caddies there, fill them with this *cha*, and sell them throughout Japan. The gentry of the kingdom buy this *cha* for ordinary use at two or three silver taels a caddy. Thus the *cha* trade of this town is greater than can be easily imagined.

It is true that the *cha* producers have to meet heavy expenses, for each must pay his hired workers at harvest time, buy charcoal, entertain decently in his house his clients or their agents who come to collect the *cha* in due season, weigh it, and pack it in caddies, and other similar expenses. They nevertheless manage to make a good profit. The Lord of Tenka, or

---

[1] Notes and references to the various grades of tea are provided in Rodrigues, *Nihon*, I, p. 573, nn. 12–16. *Vocabulario* lists them on ff. 21, 120v, 334, 354.

[2] As stated on p. 108, n. 2, the picul was equal to 100 catties, or 133.3 lbs. The *arratel*, therefore, was equal to about one pound weight.

[3] This must be erroneous, for it would mean that a catty equals 640 mace. But in *Arte grande* (ff. 217v, 218v), Rodrigues gives 10 mace to the tael, and then 20 taels 6 mace to the catty of *cha*.

[4] The Portuguese text has 3,600 *arrateis*, but this is an obvious slip for 36,000. The number of arrobas and quintals is left blank in the text, and I have filled in the appropriate figures. As regards the number of arrobas and quintals, Rodrigues, *Nihon*, I, p. 573, correctly gives the figures 1,125 and 281; Alvarez-Taladriz (in Rodrigues, *Arte del cha*, p. 7) has 1,500 and 375; Abranches Pinto (in Rodrigues, *Historia*, I, p. 443) suggests 375 and 1,500. The quintal equalled 100, sometimes 112, lbs, but the value of all these units varied according to time and region.

[5] As regards the price of tea, Almeida (in *TCJ*, p. 263) says that the best quality costs 9 or 10 ducats a pound. Avila Girón (Cooper, 'Early Europeans', p. 111) gives the price of one catty as one *real*, although the best in Miyako would fetch two or three taels. Ricci (*Fonti*, I, p. 26, and *China*, p. 17) states that whereas in China the best tea sold for three gold pieces a pound, in Japan the same amount would be priced at 10 or 12 gold pieces. Writing some 70 years later, Kaempfer (*History*, III, p. 227) gives the price for a catty of best tea as one tael or a little more, while the poorest type would sell at three silver mace a catty.

shogun, patronizes the leading house, which enjoys the best reputation for *cha* production, and he grants it the revenues of many good lands as well as other favours and privileges.[1]

After the *cha* has been thus prepared and graded, they pour it into jars until there is none left. Then each merchant notifies his customers the day on which they can come or send someone to collect the *cha* in their caddies. This they do with great solemnity, bringing their gifts personally if they happen to be in Miyako at the time, or else sending their agents, who have already been stationed there for this very purpose. But nobody does this until the *cha* of the Lord of Tenka and his family has been collected so that thereby they may show him their respect, and this is the ordinary law.[2] When the *cha* is being made, they always stock various kinds of esteemed river and sea fish and other kinds of prized wild fowl, and entertain all their customers with this on the day when they, or their agents, receive the *cha*. They give them the same *cha* to drink so that they can note the flavour, colour, and quality of the *cha* they are receiving.

Before they pour the *cha* in, they first of all heat the caddy both inside and out to a certain temperature so as to expel any dampness. Then before it cools and while the warm, pure, and dry air remains within in good proportion, they pour the *cha* inside and close the top with its lid made of a certain light, damp-proof wood[3] and with many paper wrappings arranged decoratively on top. They then put on it the seal and name of the house that made the *cha*, and place the caddy into a clean bag made of a very delicate raw hemp with silken cords. It is put thus wrapped inside a box made of a certain light wood that does not admit humidity, and then this itself is placed in another larger box, which is then closed and sealed. The caddies thus packed are carried to certain high mountains famous for their coolness, where there is no trace of humidity.[4] They are entrusted to the bonzes who live in monasteries there, and they store them in a cool place so that the *cha* may be safely preserved there from all harm during the hottest days of summer and not lose its green colour. In the ninth month of October, when it begins to get cold, the owners send for it to entertain their guests with the new *cha* in a special place with great solemnity. This is done to much applause in the form of a banquet on the day when they first open the caddy of new *cha*, and this honour is paid to a guest who is an old friend or to the lord of the territory. They pay the rent of the mountain house to the bonzes who looked after the caddy. But instead of sending the caddies to the mountains, other people dig a deep, dry well and hang it in its box down there in the air, so that the place's coolness may preserve the taste and colour of the *cha*.

1. The qualities of *cha*

We will leave to one side the etiquette and elegance connected with *cha*, for this will be

---

[1] According to Rodrigues, *Nihon*, I, p. 576, n. 19, and Alvarez-Taladriz (in Rodrigues, *Arte del cha*, p. 8, n. 34), the houses of Kambayashi and Mori enjoyed the highest reputation in Uji.

[2] The extraordinary precautions taken when picking the tea destined for the shogun and his family are described in Kaempfer, *History*, III, pp. 228–9. The pickers must abstain from fish and unclean food, bathe two or three times a day, and wear gloves. The tea was then sent to Edo with an escort of nearly 200 people and might cost as much as 100 taels a catty. When the tea procession, or *Uji-chatsubo-dōchū*, was on its way to Edo, commoners prostrated themselves, nobles dismounted from their litters, and even imperial messengers yielded way. Sadler, *Cha-no-yu*, pp. 60–64.

[3] Paulownia wood. Rodrigues, *Arte del cha*, p. 9, n. 37.

[4] The mountain in question was usually Atago-san (3,031 feet in height), mentioned earlier on pp. 80–82. Later the custom was transferred to Tanimura in Kai province. After 1738 the tea for the shogun was stored in Edo Castle. Rodrigues, *Nihon*, I, p. 578, n. 21.

described later. Both the Chinese and Japanese list various properties, natural powers, and benefits of *cha*, and indeed the experience of those who drink it shows that it has a great many, and is very conducive to good health.[1]

Its first and principal property is that it greatly helps to digest food and brings relief to the chest stuffed with too much food. It helps to digest and make the food descend, and this greatly eases the stomach. It therefore is naturally better to drink it on top of strong and solid victuals so that their toughness gives it something to work on, rather than on top of soft and weak foods, because it quickens the digestion. Hence it is usually very suitable and convenient for Europeans, who on account of the solid food they eat are more robust than the people of these nations over here. For this reason, when they formally invite guests to drink *cha* at a banquet, as shall be described hereafter, the food eaten on such occasions of honour is much more solid, substantial, rich, and of higher quality than at other solemn or informal banquets.

The second quality is that it greatly drives away sleep, much reduces and disperses the vapours of the head, checks the fumes of excessive wine that rise to the head, and thus also relieves headaches. It is very helpful to those suffering from migraine and pains in the stomach, the back, and the joints. So it is useful to people who study or have to conduct or discuss business at night as it helps them to keep awake. It is therefore used a great deal by those who work at night, but they do not drink it so strong or so much as in a banquet. Anyone wishing to sleep at night does not drink good and somewhat strong *cha* after supper because he will not be able to sleep a wink. On the contrary, he will remain only too wide-awake, and his head will be so light, quick, and discursive without any pain or discomfort that he may fear that his brain is turned, although there is no danger of this.[2]

Thirdly, *cha* is naturally weak and is inclined more to cold than to heat. Hence it is refreshing and brings down the temperature in a fever. As a cordial it eases the heart and relieves melancholy. The scent of excellent *cha* is most pleasing, and when a lot of it is drunk very strong, it leaves in the throat a very mellow taste that lasts quite a long time. Because of its cold nature, it is included among the antidotes against poison.

Fourthly, it greatly helps to evacuate all superfluous material through the urine. People who drink a lot of it urinate very often, not indeed in a painful way but rather as a relief. It has various other advantageous properties. Both China and Japan are densely populated and the people, especially in China, are greatly crowded together. Yet there is usually no plague in these two kingdoms as in Europe and other places, and pestilence is very rare. Many people maintain that this results from *cha*, which evacuates all superfluous matter that causes evil humours.[3] They drink *cha* continuously both day and night, and never touch

---

[1] According to Carletti (in *TCJ*, p. 199), tea drinking relieves stomach weakness, assists digestion, and impedes fumes from rising to the head. He errs, however, in declaring that 'drinking it after supper brings on sleep.'

[2] Zen monks are said to have drunk tea to help them keep awake during their *zazen* meditation. Kaempfer (*History*, III, pp. 218–21) repeats the legend that the first tea plant sprang up in the place where the Zen patriarch Daruma cut off his eyebrows and threw them on the ground as a penance for falling asleep during meditation. Tea is said to have been introduced into Japan by the monk Dengyō Daishi (see p. 81, n. 4) in 805, although the Zen monk Eisai (1141–1215) is also credited with its introduction and the composition of *Kissa Yōjōki*, a treatise extolling the virtues of tea.

[3] This is confirmed by a modern specialist, William H. McNeill, author of *Plagues and Peoples*, who suggests that boiling the water for tea greatly helped to check infectious disease and led to significant increases in population in both China and Japan. McNeil, 'Historical Significance', pp. 259–61.

cold water, for hot *cha* is their ordinary drink[1] summer and winter, and normally they always drink it at the end of meals. Unlike water, it does not upset the stomach but rather settles it. It is also a singular remedy against phlegm because it is desiccative by nature.

In the fifth place, it is very good against the pain caused by the stone and strangury, because it causes much frequent urination and purges anything superfluous; thus it does not let any material from which the stone can form collect inside. For this reason the stone is extremely rare among the Chinese and Japanese, and indeed only the name of this ailment exists among them.[2]

In the sixth and last place, they say that it is good for chastity and continence because it has the quality of restraining and cooling the kidneys. It purifies and purges them through the urine of any superfluous food not needed for the body's nutrition. Hence in Japan there is a famous story about this in a collection of tales and it concerns a bonze and a rustic peasant.[3] They say that there was once an important bonze going on a journey with his servants. He put up in a country hamlet and spent the night in the house of a local unmarried peasant. That night after supper the bonze said to the householder that while he was lodging there he wished to treat him to the most precious *cha* in existence, for he was carrying some with him. He added that this was an excellent medicine for continence and chastity. As he lived in the mountains and did not know about good *cha*, the yokel replied, 'Pardon me in your kindness, but do not give me this medicine. For I am a poor man and am kept busy working on the land all day, and so I need a wife to look after the house during the day and take care of it, and to cook me a meal when I return from the fields, and to wash my dirty clothing.' For he thought that drinking *cha* would make him completely impotent and thus he would not be able to have a wife.

But people declare that *cha* has indeed this property, as well as others in addition to those mentioned above.[4]

2. The way in which the Chinese and Japanese prepare the *cha* and give it to guests to drink

The way they nowadays prepare the *cha* in Japan and give it to guests to drink is different from the method employed in China.[5] For the Chinese do not drink the actual *cha* as do the Japanese, but boil clean water in a clean earthenware container, which is used only for this purpose so that it may not smell of anything else. They then pour the hot water from this kettle into another clay pot. This is a very smooth, clean, and delicate container they

---

[1] There is a gap in the text here, but the context demands something such as the noun 'drink'.

[2] Semedo (*History*, p. 19) and Ricci (*Fonti*, I, p.76, and *China*, pp. 64–5) also attribute freedom from the stone among the Chinese to their habit of drinking warm tea. Kaempfer (*History*, III, pp. 240–42) agrees, declaring that he has never met a tea drinker suffering from gout or the stone. But, he adds, tea can hinder the effect of other medicines, and should not be drunk by those suffering from colic or inflammation of the eyes.

[3] This tale is based on the story *Senseibō no Koto* in *Shasekishū*, a 13th-century collection of uplifting tales attributed to Mujū Hōshi. See *Shasekishū*, pp. 326–34. The incident mentioned by Rodrigues, however, is found in an appendix, pp. 500–501.

[4] Of 'The Ten Virtues of Tea' listed by the monk Myōe (1173–1232), Rodrigues here refers to only four (aids digestion, drives away sleep, conducive to health, and aids continence). He does not mention other classical qualities, such as conducive to filial piety and a peaceful death, nor that tea 'has the blessing of the deities'. Sadler, *Cha-no-yu*, p. 94.

[5] See p. 274.

keep for this purpose, and has a lid made of the same material. They are of various delight-ful shapes and fashions, and like a jar they have a lip and handles. They also have other con-tainers of the same type but made of tin. They pour a little, about half a handful, of the roasted *cha* leaves into this hot water in the container. The Chinese do not keep this *cha* in caddies but in clay pots, and these keep it dry.

The action of the hot water soon brings out the goodness and strength of the *cha*, and the water is coloured a clear, bright, golden, yellow like pale wine. They then pour it into delicate porcelain cups suitable for this purpose. Some of these cups are overlaid inside with silver, while others have their edge or rim covered with silver or copper. They place as many of these porcelain cups on a tray or small table as there are guests (including in this number the host, who always drinks with them), and offer them thus to the guests so that they may drink. The Chinese do not observe any particular ceremony in this, nor do they drink in a special place reserved for entertaining with *cha*, but use the ordinary and usual room where they receive their guests. The Chinese are accustomed to dropping into these porcelain cups small pieces of various kinds of different sweetmeats and peeled fruits, such as apricot and almond (of which there is an abundance in China), as well as various other things kept in the house for this purpose. They send abroad for such things when they are not available in the kingdom. A small silver or bronze spoon is put inside each porcelain cup so that they may eat the sweet or fruit that is in the *cha*.[1]

As they take the *cha*, they observe their etiquette and bowing among themselves, just as they do when they receive wine. They are seated in their chairs, but courtesy demands that they all rise to their feet when they receive the porcelain cup of *cha*. Thus they take it together from the tray at the same time, and after drinking they all replace the cups together on the same tray. Good manners require that they all rise to take the *cha* at least the first time they drink, but afterwards each guest can take the *cha* seated in his place, observing great politeness towards the others. When a person in China invites important guests to drink *cha* formally, it is brought out three times in succession. Each time there is a new or different sweet or fruit in the *cha* for the guests' greater entertainment and honour.

Thus the first thing with which the Chinese entertain a guest is *cha*, and this is the stan-dard and current custom when a guest arrives. It is also usual to drink it after eating to mark the end of both ordinary meals and also feasts. They keep it ready-made and prepared from morning to afternoon in certain large tin urns, padded with cotton and placed in closed boxes with only the lip protruding by which they pour out the *cha*. In this way the *cha* is kept hot all day, and guests need never go without. When they go out in the countryside, they take this *cha* thus prepared for themselves and for their guests, if there are any. But this kind of *cha* is not so good and tasty, because it loses its heat and tastes as if it has been boiled up again. So they usually serve this *cha* to less important guests, members of the household, and people who arrive suddenly and leave quickly. But for other guests[2] they make and prepare an expensive *cha* in the earthenware or tin pots that we mentioned, and they do this very quickly.

---

[1] Ricci (*Fonti*, I, p. 75, and *China*, pp. 63–4) also mentions these fruits dropped into tea and says that they are eaten with a silver spoon. He adds that on formal occasions the tea may be served three or four times, and that a dif-ferent fruit is added on each occasion. Alonso Sanches (in Colin, *Labor*, I, p. 531) remarks that small spoons are provided with the drink 'to take out the three or four dried plums or prunes therein'. The custom was not unknown in Japan. William Eaton (Hirado, 8 September 1619, in Farrington, *English Factory*, I, p. 761) asks Cocks at Osaka to obtain some licorice for him, or else 'a kind of leafe that they use to put in chaw' that had the same flavour as licorice.

[2] There is a short gap in the Portuguese text here, where the word 'guests' or some similar term should be.

In ancient times the Japanese used to drink *cha* prepared in the same way as in China, whence this drink was introduced. Even now it is drunk in some parts of Japan by peasants and lowly people, and is known as *senjicha*, that is, 'boiled *cha*'.[1] But as time passed they began to drink the actual *cha*, grinding first of all the dry or roasted leaf into green powder like fine flour in small, black stone mortars. These are extremely well fashioned and are made for this purpose, and are called *cha-usu*, that is, '*cha* mortar'. They then pour this green powder thus ground into a finely varnished small box,[2] or into certain small earthenware caddies that serve the same purpose, and take the powder out with a cane spoon[3] used for this purpose. They ladle out one or two spoonfuls of this powder into a porcelain cup, and then pour in boiling water that they always keep ready for this. They mix it delicately and subtly with a small cane brush,[4] which they have at hand for this purpose. This dissolves the powder and any lumps, and the result looks like green water, the same colour in fact as the *cha* powder. In this way the actual *cha* is drunk and as such brings about its natural effects, mentioned above, with greater strength and efficacy than does boiled *cha*. But *cha* boiled in the Chinese way seems naturally more wholesome and suitable as an ordinary and frequent drink. For when it is merely lightly boiled in hot water, only the goodness and substance of the *cha* come out, and everything else, such as the useless dregs and sediment, is left behind. Thus it is possible to drink this kind more often than the other. Hence when making the ordinary and frequent drink, the Japanese are wont to pour in such a small quantity of the ground *cha* powder that it merely tinges the hot water a very clear green colour, like slightly cloudy water.

As this use of *cha* is so common and ordinary throughout the Japanese kingdom, the gentry, all the nobles, lords, and monasteries of bonzes have in their houses a special place where there is a stove with a charcoal fire always burning. There will also be a cast-iron kettle[5] in which there is always very clean hot water for *cha*, vessels[6] of cold water to cool it, porcelain cups[7] with their salvers for drinking, and all the other things needed to prepare the *cha*. These include the box or caddy of *cha* powder, the cane spoon, the cane brush for mixing, the mortar to grind the *cha*, and a table or cupboard to store all this. There is a special person who is present there all the time and has the office of preparing *cha* for guests. In the house of the *kubō* and lords all this is found in a special room with their officials who prepare and look after the place. In the *kubō*'s house, there are some shaven men or bonzes called *dōbō* who have this as their special duty.[8]

---

[1] When the *cha* leaves are infused with water, the drink is called *hacha* or *sencha*. When the powdered leaf is mixed with hot water, the drink is then called *matcha*. Sadler, *Cha-no-yu*, p. 5.

[2] The *chaire*, illustrated in Sadler, *Cha-no-yu*, p. 68. Many of the utensils mentioned in this account are described in Valignano, *Sumario*, pp. 44–5. Photographs of various sets of utensils are given in Boger, *Traditional Arts*, pp. 217–19.

[3] The *chashaku*.

[4] The *chasen*.

[5] The *kama*, illustrated in Sadler, *Cha-no-yu*, p. 17.

[6] The *mizusashi*. Sadler, *Cha-no-yu*, p. 18.

[7] The *chawan*, illustrated in Sadler, *Cha-no-yu*, pp. 72–3.

[8] *Vocabulario*, f. 72: '*Dōbō*. Certain shaven men who serve in the palaces of a leading *yakata* or lord.' In his list of the officials in the house of the kubō, Rodrigues mentions (*Arte breve*, f. 87) the *dōbōshu*, described as 'shaven men engaged in domestic service like pages.' Among the rules, promulgated in 1592, of the Jesuit mission, a section is devoted to the office of the *chanoyu-sha*, usually a lay catechist living in the Jesuit house. He must have two or three days' supply of tea powder always in stock; he must not allow anyone to play *go* or *shogi* in the tea room; nobody may sleep in the room without leave of the guest-master, etc. Then follows a minimal list of the 34 tea utensils that each house must have. Cooper, 'Early Europeans', pp. 106–9. See also Valignano, *Cerimoniale*, pp. 160–62.

This, then, is the ordinary and usual Japanese way that has lasted until the present and will continue to last. This is how they usually entertain their guests with *cha* always kept ready for ordinary use, instead of with cold water, which they seldom drink. But in addition to this ordinary way, they have introduced another particular method by which they entertain some guests with special welcome and favour. This used to be called *chanoyu*, but is now known as *suki*, and we will speak about it in the next chapter. This has not replaced the ordinary and common way, above described, throughout the kingdom, because it is very special and not for every class of person.

CHAPTER 33

THE GENERAL WAY IN WHICH THE JAPANESE ENTERTAIN
WITH *CHA*

The custom of drinking *cha* is common to both the Chinese and Japanese. It is with *cha* that they entertain their guests during visits, and by giving them *cha* to drink many times they divert them while they are talking and conversing. *Cha* is drunk when the guest comes to leave and also brings their banquets to an end. It is, in fact, the ordinary drink throughout the kingdom and takes the place of cold water on account of its good qualities, as we have said. But in addition to this ordinary way of drinking *cha*, the Japanese have another special manner, which the Chinese lack, whereby they entertain guests of whatever quality and rank, even the Lord of Tenka himself. In this way, ordinary people of inferior rank yet of gentle birth, who practise this manner of *cha*, may invite any lord or noble to it, and he may not decline on account of the person who invites him unless he has some prior engagement. For in this manner of entertainment and etiquette, no attention is paid to rank either by the host or by the guest, for both nobles and people of lesser standing who practise this art are regarded as equals whilst engaged in it. Hence lords and nobles invite people who are not of their rank to come and drink *cha*, and they themselves are invited by such people.

This type of banquet, then, consists of inviting each other to drink only *cha*, for the banquet itself and the food serve only as a preparation for the *cha*. Far from being excessive and abundant, the banquet is very sober and moderate. Each guest eats and drinks soberly as much as he pleases without having to be persuaded. Nor do the guests converse among themselves while eating, but they say in a low voice only what is necessary. Great modest and tranquility are observed in everything.

Hence this manner of entertainment and courtesy is in a different category from ordinary social dealings and conversation. Indeed, in some ways it is contrary to it as there is neither pomp nor splendour involved. It is a secluded and solitary exercise in imitation of solitary hermits who retire from worldly, social dealings, and go to live in thatched huts and give themselves over to the contemplation of the things of nature. So this gathering for *cha* and conversation is not intended for lengthy talk among themselves, but rather to contemplate within their souls with all peace and modesty the things they see there (without their praising the host for them) and thus through their own efforts to understand the mysteries locked therein. In keeping with this, everything used in this ceremony is as rustic, rough, completely unrefined, and simple as nature made it, after the style of a solitary and rustic hermitage. Thus the house and the path leading to it, as well as all the utensils used therein, are all of this kind.

So they do not make use of spacious rooms and richly decorated apartments for this gathering as they do in ordinary social usage, nor do they use costly and delicate china dishes or other rich and choice utensils. Instead the desired effect is obtained by a small cottage, thatched with straw and weeds, situated within the compound of, and next to, the houses in which they dwell. This is fashioned from timber as rough as it came from the forest, with one old piece of wood merely fastened to another. This is done in imitation of an old desert hermitage or cell, worn out with age and constructed roughly and rustically from things obtained from the surrounding wilderness and left in their natural state. There is neither artistry nor elegance at all, but only natural negligence and age.

The vessels and dishes used in this gathering are not of gold, silver, or any other precious material, nor are they richly and finely wrought. Instead they are made of clay or iron without any polish, embellishment, or anything that might incite the appetite to desire them for their beauty or lustre. In keeping with their naturally melancholy disposition and character, and also with the purpose for which they collect these things, the Japanese find such mystery in these *cha* utensils that they attribute to them, as well as to their ancient swords and daggers, the value and esteem that other people place in precious stones, pearls, and old medallions. In fact the Japanese regard them as their gems and medallions, as we shall say hereafter.[1] Above all else, they pay more attention to the cleanliness of everything, however small it may be, in this rustic and ancient setting than can be easily imagined. As they greatly value and enjoy this kind of gathering to drink *cha*, they spend large sums of money in building such a house, rough though it may be, and in buying the things needed for this way of drinking the *cha* served therein. Thus there are utensils, albeit of earthenware, that come to be worth ten, twenty, or thirty thousand crowns or even more; this is something that will appear as madness and barbarity to other nations that come to hear of it.[2] We will here describe briefly how this practice began in Japan, and why it is now so highly esteemed by the Japanese throughout the whole kingdom.

1. The origin of this *cha* meeting, and why the vessels used therein have reached such a price

The Japanese are in general of a melancholy disposition and nature. Moved by this natural inclination, they take much delight and pleasure in lonely and nostalgic places, such as woods with shady groves, cliffs and rocky places, solitary birds, torrents of fresh water flowing down from rocks, and in every kind of solitary thing imbued with a natural artlessness and quality. All this fills their souls with this inclination and melancholy, producing a certain nostalgia.

Hence they are much inclined towards a solitary and eremitical life, far removed from all worldly affairs and tumult. Thus in olden days many solitary hermits devoted themselves to contempt of the world and its vanities. They gave themselves over to a solitary and contemplative life, believing that in this way they purified their souls and obtained salvation in their false sects. Thence arose their custom of *inkyo*; that is, during their lifetime they hand over their house, estate, and public affairs to their heirs, and take a house for themselves

---

[1] The same observation is made by Almeida (in *TCJ*, p. 262) and Vivero y Velasco (*Relación*, f. 72v). According to Valignano (*Sumario*, pp. 45, 49), the Japanese point out that such costly items at least serve a useful purpose, which is more than can be said for diamonds and rubies.

[2] Almeida (in *TCJ*, pp. 263–4) saw a kettle costing 600 ducats (although it was worth more), a tripod bought for 1,030 ducats, and then mentions a caddy in Miyako reputedly worth 30,000 ducats. Ōtomo Yoshishige, *daimyo* of Bungo, showed Valignano a caddy bought for about 14,000 ducats, 'for which in all truth I would not have given more than one or two farthings' (Valignano, *Sumario*, p. 45).

where they lead a quiet and peaceful life, withdrawn from all worldly business and disturbance. They shave their head and beard, and exchange their secular robes for religious and sober dress. They are called *nyūdō* or *zenmon*, which is a certain kind of religious state of bonzes and is the first rank of those who begin to devote themselves to the things of salvation and religious cult.[1] The beginning and origin of this *cha* meeting and the various ceremonies performed therein are founded on this natural disposition.

In connection with this, you must know that among the *kubō* who governed in Miyako there was one who flourished in the years of the Lord 1443 to 1474.[2] In keeping with the custom of Japan he performed *inkyo*; this meant renouncing his house and estate in favour of his eldest son, withdrawing from public life and affairs, and devoting himself to a quiet and retired life. He chose Higashiyama as his place of retirement. Situated in the eastern vicinity of the city of Miyako, it contains many splendid monasteries of bonzes with their temples. He built his palace and houses there in the shady woods and retired thither, adapting himself to a solitary and retired life. There he led a quiet life withdrawn from the affairs of court, and he is known as Higashiyama Dono, after the name of the place.[3]

This *kubō* had a great natural liking for *cha* and had search made for the very best kind so that it could be prepared not only for his own use but also for him to entertain, as is the custom, the court grandees and gentlemen and other lords who came to visit him. As his principal recreation and pastime he had built next to his palace a small house that was even more secluded, and this was used only for keeping the utensils needed for preparing and drinking *cha*.[4] These included a copper stove and its cast-iron kettle of a certain fashion and shape for the hot *cha* water; the vessel of cold water to pour in and replenish the kettle when it became empty, and also to cool the hot water; a little container for the *cha* ground into powder and its small spoon with which it is put into the porcelain cup when the drink is being prepared; a small delicate cane brush to mix and dissolve the *cha* in the hot water; and various porcelain cups, with their salvers, from which they drink the *cha*. There was a box containing charcoal made from a certain kind of tree, and with this they replenish the fire in the stove that heats the kettle of water, as only charcoal is used in the fire.[5] There was

---

[1] For *inkyo*, see p. 167, n. 3, above; for *nyūdō*, see p. 170, n. 5, above. *Zenmon* literally means 'Zen gate'. The mood of this custom is well described by Sadler (*Cha-no-yu*, pp. 79–82), who notes that often enough the religious overtones of the retired state of life were replaced by a spirit of dilettantism; freed from social obligations, a man could devote himself to the aesthetically pleasing cult of *suki*.

[2] Ashikaga Yoshimasa (1436–90), the eighth Ashikaga shogun. I have supplied the dates of his rule, which are missing in the Portuguese text. His term of office was marked by continual civil strife and the ten-year Ōnin War. His son, in whose favour he retired, was Yoshihisa (1465–89).

[3] As pointed out in the Introduction (p. xxxviii), Rodrigues's lyrical description of Yoshimasa's 'solitary and retired life' in Higashiyama is far from accurate.

[4] A reference to the famous Ginkaku (Silver Pavilion), built by Yoshimasa in 1479 in the grounds of his palace at Higashiyama in Miyako. After his death the estate was converted into a temple, and is now called Ginkakuji, one of the outstanding cultural sites of modern Kyoto. Rodrigues's generally favourable account obscures the fact that Yoshimasa was an incompetent effete ruler who helped to ruin the country's shaky economy by his excesses. ('While Kyoto burned, Yoshimasa pursued his interests in poetry, painting, and the tea ceremony.' *KEJ*, I, p. 101, and III, p. 132.) His leading a 'solitary and retired life' hardly describes the retired shogun's existence, 'surrounded by bonzes, poets, actors, etc., continuing to exhaust the treasury by his prodigality' (Papinot, *Historical*, p. 32). In fact, Yoshimasa's tea-room and utensils were ornate, and it was only later that the keynote of simplicity was introduced by the tea master Sen no Rikyū (1520–91), whom Rodrigues met on at least one occasion. Sansom, *Japan*, pp. 401–3; Sadler, *Cha-no-yu*, pp. 83–4, 94–7; Cooper, 'Early Europeans', p. 120.

[5] For the types of charcoal and its container (*sumitori*), see Rodrigues, *Arte del cha*, p. 67, nn. 174–6.

everything else needed for him to drink *cha* there, and to entertain privately visiting nobles in his capacity as a retired and solitary person who had left behind the world and all social dealings.

This small house was constructed of drab materials in keeping with the rustic and solitary life that he was leading. Nevertheless, the workmanship was first-class and it was kept extremely clean. It was square in shape, its sides a dozen spans in length, and it was laid with four and a half mats, one mat being eight spans in length and four wide.[1] The utensils and vessels that we mentioned were also fashioned to the same end. They did not present a beautiful appearance or any curious feature as regards their material, but all of them were made of clay, iron, or bronze.

But as such plainness might well have appeared somewhat unfitting for his dignity, he did two things. First, most of these utensils, instruments, and vessels came from foreign kingdoms and were not made in Japan. Second, each had such proportion, size, shape, etc., that it seemed to have been deliberately made as a *cha* vessel for that particular house and not for any other purpose, although in fact the artisans who made them in their countries had no such intention in mind. Similarly the material was excellent of its kind and the craftsmen were also skilful in their art. As he was a mighty lord and, in addition, naturally had a good eye and judgement for recognising the properties of both natural and artificial things, he had a search made throughout Japan and also abroad for many such foreign pieces. These suited his plan and that house so well that they seemed to be made for the place. Thus he not only removed any reproof that people might make against him, but also caused admiration and applause in those who saw and reflected on them. In addition to the intrinsic qualities that these pieces contained, as we have noted, he observed a special order in using them in that house and a particular proportion in setting them in their places within the table-like cupboard[2] where they were kept. For many pieces were used, one after the other, is preparing and drinking *cha*, and as a result this order, and no other, seemed to be the most suitable for these utensils.

He made a kind of niche or vase alcove in the place of honour of the small house, just as we described elsewhere when speaking of the guest house.[3] To decorate this recess he hung on the wall a fine panel bearing a painting or some of the hieroglyphic letters, and he also placed therein a vase containing various flowers. All this was inside the *cha* house, but in keeping with the requirement of the house he did not hang coloured paintings, however good they might have been, but pictures executed in black water-ink by distinguished painters of ancient China, who depicted their theme better with black ink than did other artists with all their colours.[4]

He used to take noble guests, to whom he wished to show special welcome and favour, to this *cha* hut, and there prepare the *cha* with his own hands and give it to the guests. He would drink with them, and show them the various items obtained from foreign kingdoms and the order that he observed in using them. Thus this goodly pastime won the approval of all who witnessed it, especially those who had performed *inkyo* and were freed from

[1] Ginkaku has in its grounds a small companion hall, Tōgudō (or Tokyūdō), containing the 4½-mat tea room, called Dōjinsai. Murai, 'Development', pp. 23–4; Paine, *Art and Architecture*, p. 260. The plan of the room is given in Sadler, *Cha-no-yu*, p. 95; photograph of exterior in Boger, *Traditional Arts*, p. 210. For plan of a 4½-mat room, see Sadler, *Cha-no-yu*, p. 11.

[2] For illustrations of the *todana* for storing tea utensils, see Sadler, *Cha-no-yu*, p. 8, and Rodrigues, *Nihon*, I, p. 595.

[3] An earlier reference to the alcove in a guest house is found on p. 231, above.

[4] Rodrigues later mentions these ink paintings in greater detail on p. 321.

public life, and they began to imitate him. Each of them built a similar house especially for *cha* in his own home, and likewise sought and tried to collect the vessels and utensils necessary and suitable for it. As most of the people who imitated him could not recognize the correct measurements, proportions, and forms right away, they were obliged to show him the items they had found in order to know what he thought of them and be guided by him, for they looked on him as the teacher and originator of that ceremony. Noble and important lords would also have such a house built and equipped with everything required, and when they were tolerably well versed in the procedure and had sufficient confidence they would ask him to do them the favour of coming to see the house, and would entertain him with *cha* therein with much taste and simplicity. They did this not only to please Higashiyama Dono but also to win his approval and carry this honour before the other lords.

Even during Higashiyama Dono's lifetime, this way of entertaining with *cha* in that house spread in this way among cultured people of leisure both in court circles and other parts of Japan. This was true not only of the nobles but also the ordinary people, mainly in the two cities of Miyako and Sakai, where there were many rich merchants and citizens who had performed *inkyo* in favour of their sons and were leading quiet lives, as we have said. It was not difficult to introduce this method with ease, for the custom of entertaining guests with *cha* was extremely ancient in Japan. So people could not reject this modern way when they saw that it was developing the ancient usage into a new manner of entertaining guests, a new culture, a new etiquette, and a very wholesome pastime suitable for a gathering to drink *cha*. So they easily became addicted to this, and its principal innovator was this Higashiyama Dono, a person highly respected and esteemed by all. This, then, is what was called then and subsequently *chanoyu*, and those who performed it *chanoyu-sha*, the house *chanoyu-zashiki*,[1] and the vessels and utensils *chanoyu-dōgu*.

Hence it came about that *chanoyu* items began to have great value among those who practised the ceremony. For with the passing of time the number of such things decreased, while the number of people searching for them increased. Items that could be becomingly and suitably used in the ceremony were foreign and rare. Thus the wealthy did not consider the cost when they found a good piece, and people possessing such an item so highly prized it that they would not part with it at any price. When after a great deal of persuasion they gave it to someone, it would be for a very high price, greatly exceeding its intrinsic value when the item, and not the longing of the person who desired it, is considered. For what was bought and sold in such transactions was the artistic taste of both parties and not the item itself. After passing several times from one hand to another at this price, it would then retain this high esteem and price. Other pieces of the same kind would command the same price and value. Then on account of the price for which some items of this kind were sold, pieces of another kind used in *chanoyu* began to be highly priced as well, although they had thitherto never been bought. The greater or lesser price that could be given for them was decided by their perfection in comparison with other items already purchased. If the urge or necessity of the person wishing to buy them was very great, or if there were many people wishing to buy them because the items were foreign and unobtainable in the kingdom, then they were sold for much more than their estimated price, and ever afterwards such an item would always remain at the same price.

---

[1] Initially the term *chanoyu* appears to have referred to the place where the tea was drunk. *Vocabulario*, f. 79v; Valignano, *Sumario*, p. 43; Avila-Girón, *Relación*, p. 29. Later the word came to mean the actual ritual.

It is true, however, that some of these items were later much reduced in price because of some defect discovered in them, or because they were no longer suitable for the modern way as the ceremony later went on partially changing and improving. There were some items, on the other hand, that continued to be used in the ceremony and their price rose, either because they were rare and there was only a limited number of them, or because they were the very best examples, or because they had belonged to persons of great authority in this art. In this last category are included the items that Higashiyama Dono used. They were bought after his death for a great price, and today they are highly regarded by those who profess this art.[1]

Among the very valuable *chanoyu* items that are always used and are inseparable from this art, the first place is taken by those called *katatsuki*.[2] These are small foreign clay caddies, glazed on the outside, the largest being half a span in height and less than a span in circumference. In the second place come those called *matsubo*, which are caddies of the same clay and are also foreign, and are used to preserve the *cha* leaf; they contain three, four, five, or even six catties of *cha*.[3] In the third place are the ancient cast-iron kettles of a certain special shape, in which they warm the water for *cha*. In the fourth place are the ancient foreign earthenware and porcelain cups from which they drink *cha*. In the fifth place, the panels of paintings and Chinese letters executed by certain painters and calligraphers. In the sixth place, the vases made of copper, clay, and other materials, in which they place flowers and roses for decoration.[4] In the seventh place, certain vessels used for the charcoal; these are made of metal, earthenware, or various other materials, while some consist of large gourds cut through the middle.

All these items are esteemed and have high value. Among them the small caddies, the kettles, and the large caddies of *cha* are always esteemed and fetch a very high price. Among these the large caddies used to preserve the *cha* leaf have a very high value because of the following reason. In addition to being rare and limited in number, they possess the special property of preserving the *cha* leaf from one year to another with such constancy that it always seems to be as fresh, even at the end of the year, as when it was poured in. They also improve it by the flavour, sweetness, and mildness that they impart to it.[5] Caddies of other kinds do not possess this property. Although they indeed preserve the *cha*, they make it so sharp and bitter without any sweetness at all that it is impossible to drink. In addition, these large clay caddies are of such exterior workmanship, shape, glaze, and proportion that they compare well with all the other items of *chanoyu*. This is the general and almost principal condition sought for in all the *chanoyu* items. Among these caddies there are some better

---

[1] The caddy worth 30,000 ducats mentioned by Almeida on p. 283, n. 2, was the famous Tsukumo-nasu, or Tsukumo-gami, belonging to Matsunaga Hisahide but formerly part of Higashiyama Dono's collection. Fróis, *História*, II, p. 41; Valignano, *Sumario*, p. 45, n. 121. Reference to other Higashiyama pieces, some dating from the 13th century, is made in Sansom, *Japan*, pp. 401–2.

[2] An illustration of a *katatsuki*, or 'shouldered', caddy is given in Sadler, *Cha-no-yu*, p. 68.

[3] Kaempfer (*History*, III, p. 234) mentions that the *matsubo* caddies were brought up from the seabed by divers and imported from China. According to common belief, the quality of the tea improved while stored in these jars, and the longer it was kept therein the better.

[4] As regards 'roses', see p. 211, n. 1, above.

[5] A reference to the jars called Ruson-tsubo, imported from the Philippines. When Carletti (*My Voyage*, pp. 99–100, 101–2) arrived at Nagasaki in June 1597, his ship was searched for these jars as Hideyoshi wished to own all of them. The jars fetched 10,000 scudos each and were reputed to preserve the *cha* leaf for 20 years. According to Fróis (20 October 1595, in JapSin 52, ff. 90v–91), their price was 8,000 crowns. Further details about these jars in Valignano, *Sumario*, p. 44, n. 117; Rodrigues, *Arte del cha*, p. 35, n. 101.

than others and therefore differently priced, although they are all more or less the same as regards preserving the *cha*.

2. The modern and current way of *chanoyu* called *suki*, and its general origin and purpose

As time passed, there were many people throughout the kingdom, but especially in Miyako and Sakai, who devoted themselves to this pastime and took great pains therein so that they won the acclaim of the world in this art. As such they were regarded and esteemed by all. They continued to improve this way of *chanoyu* more and more, and partly changed Higashiyama Dono's ancient method by reducing some less essential things and then adding others that they believed were opportune and in keeping with the purpose of the exercise. In this way they established another way called *suki* and this is now in current use. Its teachers are known as *suki-sha*, the house where they entertain with *cha* as *suki-ya*, and the items used therein as *suki-dōgu*. Now this word comes from the verb *suku*, which means to desire, to have an affection and inclination for something that pleases.[1] Those who practised *chanoyu* were also greatly versed in the subject, and when they changed something or added something new, they did not explain in words the reason for such a change and addition. For it is a rule of this art that its experts do not explain the reason and cause of the things they do in this matter by words but by deeds only, for they leave everything to the consideration and reasoning of their pupils. In this way, the pupils may come to understand the reason through their own efforts by watching what the teacher does.

This is how the masters of the Zen sects teach their doctrine, and the followers of this art imitate them and say that they are doing this only out of *suki*, that is, because it seems good to them and pleases them; from this they came to be called *suki-sha*.[2] This way of speaking is ordinary and common in Japan, for when a person does something peculiar and does not want to give any explanation for it, he says that it is *suki*, that it is his desire, that it pleases him, and thus appears good to him and gives him pleasure.

This art of *suki*, then, is a kind of solitary religion instituted by those who were supreme therein to encourage good customs and moderation in everything concerning the devotees of this art. This is in imitation of the solitary philosophers of the Zen sects who dwell in their retreats in the wilderness. Their vocation is not to philosophise with the help of books and treatises written by illustrious masters and philosophers as do members of the other sects of the Indian gymnosophists. Instead, they give themselves up to contemplating the things of nature, despising and abandoning worldly things. They mortify their passions by certain enigmatic and figurative meditations and considerations that guide them on

---

[1] *Arte grande*, f. 101, defines the verb *suku* as, 'To be inclined towards, or have an affection for, something or be pleasing. E.g., *cha, sake ni suku.*' See also *Vocabulario*, f. 231v; Murai, 'Development', p. 22. The first to employ the term *suki-ya* was Sen no Rikyū, who laid down the basic pattern still followed today. Rodrigues, *Arte del cha*, p. 38, n. 104. *Suki* has basically a far wider meaning, such as 'artistic taste', 'elegant pursuits', 'refined arts', etc. For its development from its Heian meaning of 'a passion for and a commitment to amorous dalliance' to its later meaning of 'single-mindedness and dedication', see Pandey, 'Suki and Religious Awakening', pp. 300–303.

[2] Zen masters traditionally taught by example and not by words. This method is illustrated by Huairang's polishing a tile, Nanquan's killing a cat, and Juzhi's cutting off a finger. Independence from words and writings is expressed by Bodhidharma's famous verse, 'A special tradition outside the scriptures; No dependence on words and letters; Direct pointing at the soul of man…'. Dumoulin, *History*, pp. 67, 98, 99, 101.

their way at the beginning.[1] Thus, from what they see in things themselves they attain by their own efforts to a knowledge of the First Cause. Their soul and intellect put aside everything evil and imperfect until they reach the natural perfection and being of the First Cause.

So the vocation of these philosophers is not to contend or dispute with arguments, but leave everything to the contemplation of each one so that by himself he may attain the goal by using these principles, and thus they do not teach disciples. So those belonging to the sect are of a resolute and determined character, without any slackness, indolence, mediocrity, or effeminacy. As regards the care of their own persons, they do without many things that they regard as superfluous and unnecessary. They believe that the chief thing in keeping with a hermitage is frugality and moderation, with much quietness, peace of mind, and exterior modesty, or, to describe it better, complete hypocrisy, after the fashion of the Stoics, who maintained that perfect men neither felt nor had any passions.

Those who practise *chanoyu* try to imitate these solitary philosophers and hence all the pagan followers of this art belong to the Zen sect, or else join it even though their forefathers have hitherto belonged to another sect. Although they imitate the Zen sect in this art, they do not practise any superstition, cult, or special ceremony related to religion.[2] For they have taken none of this from the sect, but imitate it merely as regards its eremitical seclusion and withdrawal from all dealings in social matters, its resolution and mental alertness in everything, and its lack of tepidity, sluggishness, softness, and effeminacy. They imitate them as well in the contemplation of the things of nature, not as regards its end (that is, the knowledge of the being and perfection of the First Cause through exterior things), but only in the natural part that they see exteriorly in them. For this moves and inclines the spirit to solitude, nostalgia, and withdrawal from worldly, ostentatious activity and business.

Apart from some general principles, they do not teach anything by word but rather by deed, and they leave everything else to the contemplation of each individual, until he understands the purpose and essentials of the art through his own efforts. He adapts anything merely incidental as he believes fit and suitable, provided it does not go against the general rules of *suki*. The purpose of this art of *cha*, then, is courtesy, good breeding, modesty, and moderation in exterior actions, peace and quiet of body and soul, exterior humility, without any pride, arrogance, fleeing from all exterior ostentation, pomp, display, and splendour of social life. Instead, sincerity without any deceit as befits a hermit in the wilderness, honest and decent attire, with certain order, neatness, and plainness in everything in use and in the house, in keeping with such a calling. For everyone highly regards those who profess this art, and they have a reputation among the people for being men of wholesome customs, and they are esteemed and revered as such. They therefore gather in the said house to drink

---

[1] A reference to *kōan*, or irrational riddles used in the quest for *satori*, or enlightenment. For reports and examples, see *TCJ*, pp. 319–21; Cooper, 'Early Jesuits', pp. 266–9; Fróis, *História*, I, pp. 171, 176 ('1,600 koan'). For references to Zen meditation, see Valignano, *Sumario*, p. 62, n. 18. Despite his adverse comments about Buddhism, Rodrigues obviously admired the Zen sect and saw in its influence the inspiration of much of Japanese art.

[2] Rodrigues stresses that the *pagan* enthusiasts of tea belonged to the Zen sect, for there was a number of eminent Christian devotees. At one time, five out of the seven principal disciples of Sen no Rikyū were Christians – Takayama Ukon, Gamō Ujisato, Seta Kamon, Oda Yūraku, and Shibayama Kenmotsu. To these may be added the names of Konishi Yukinaga, Kuroda Yoshitaka, and Diego Hibiya. Dumoulin, *History*, pp. 218–23. Tea bowls of this period bearing the Christian cross are still extant; illustrations are given in Cooper, *Southern Barbarians*, pp. 198–9. The fact that *Vocabulario* lists some 150 tea terms illustrates the pastime's importance in the missionaries' view. Cooper, 'Early Europeans', p. 109.

tea in order to perform these things concerning solitude, withdrawal, and contemplation of the utensils and everything in the house. This moves them to nostalgia and a withdrawal from public life in some way, and to moderation in their exterior actions. This gathering and the other ceremonies carried out in an unpolished and rough way therein serve as an exercise of these things and as a setting for drinking *cha*. For this is the pastime of the hermitage and takes the place of the wine-drinking of solemn social gatherings.[1]

This new way of *chanoyu*, which is called *suki*, originated in the famous and wealthy city of Sakai, the biggest and busiest trade centre of all Japan. Up to the time of Nobunaga and Taikō it used to be governed like a republic and for many years did not recognize any outside authority. For it was a very strong place and was like the court of Japan, containing wealthy and well-to-do citizens and noble people who retired there from various places on account of the vicissitudes of war.[2] Those of the city who had the means devoted themselves to *chanoyu* in a grand manner, and because of the trade that the city conducted all over Japan and even outside the kingdom, the best *chanoyu* pieces, after those of Higashiyama Dono, were to be found there.[3] As a result of the continual practice of *chanoyu* among its citizens, Sakai produced the most eminent people versed in this art, and they formed the *suki* now in fashion by changing some of the less essential things of *chanoyu*.[4] For example, they built the hut on a smaller scale than before because they were cramped by the place's straitness, for the city is situated on a hot dry plain on the seacoast, or rather, in a sandy plain surrounded to the west by a rough coast. There are no refreshing fountains and groves of trees nearby, nor lonely and nostalgic places in keeping with *suki*, as there are in the city of Miyako.

Because many people dwell in the moats and near the city,[5] the sites of the houses were for the most part so cramped (formerly, that is, because they have been recently rebuilt after the great fire)[6] that the inhabitants could not have there either gardens or refreshing villas with groves where they could recreate and build houses in which to invite guests to *cha*. As a result of this cramped position it was impossible for all the people who practised *chanoyu* (and these made up the larger and better part of the city) to build their *chanoyu*

[1] In an appreciative evaluation of the tea ceremony, Sansom (*Japan*, pp. 400–401) mentions, with Rodrigues, 'a calm withdrawal from worldly cares and a serene enjoyment of beauty'. But he rightly warns that 'it is a cult which lapses with dangerous ease into … a mock simplicity'.

[2] For early European references to Sakai ('the Venice of Japan', according to Fróis, *História*, I, p. 234), see p. 83, n. 3, above. Nobunaga placed a governor there in 1577, and the city's importance began to wane under Hideyoshi, who favoured Osaka. For Sakai and tea, see Kumakura, 'Sen no Rikyū', p. 33.

[3] For instance, the collection of the Sakai merchant Diego Hibiya, who personally showed Almeida the tripod that had cost him 1,030 ducats. Almeida, in *TCJ*, p. 264. Fróis, *História*, II, pp. 40–41. For an example of a Sakai merchant, Imai Sōkyū (1520–93), who profitably combined tea and business, see Watsky, 'Commerce'.

[4] For example, the tea men Imai Sōkyū, Diego Hibiya, and Sen no Rikyū were all born in Sakai.

[5] A literal translation of a possibly corrupt sentence. But Vilela (September, 1562, in Ruiz-de-Medina, Documentos, II, p. 509) notes that Sakai had strategic value, for the sea lay to the west and the city was surrounded by deep moats in the other three directions. The sense of the sentence may be: Because of the many inhabitants dwelling in and around the city and because of the many moats (or canals), building land was scarce. Under the pretext of land shortage, Hideyoshi ordered one of the largest canals to be filled in, thus greatly reducing the city's defence and commerce. Rodrigues, *Arte del cha*, p. 42, n. 113.

[6] Osaka and Sakai were razed during the siege of Osaka Castle in 1615. Cocks (25 February 1616, *Diary*, II, p. 275) reports, 'And Osakay and Sackay, two great citties burned to the ground, not soe much as one howse being saved.' His other references to the city's destruction are given in Farrington, *English Factory*, I, pp. 252, 377, 387. See also Morejon, *Historia*, ff. 5–5v. It is possible to read 'guerra universal' in the unclear text instead of 'queima universal'. Thus Rodrigues, *Nihon*, I, p. 606, has 'great war' instead of 'great fire'.

house in the fashion laid down by Higashiyama Dono. Also on account of other relevant considerations certain Sakai men versed in *chanoyu* built the *cha* house in another way. It was smaller and set among some small trees planted for the purpose, and it represented, as far as the limited site allowed, the style of lonely houses found in the countryside, or like the cells of solitaries who dwell in hermitages far removed from people and give themselves over to the contemplation of the things of nature and its First Cause. These are wont to be very nostalgic places for the Japanese and, in keeping with their temperament, not a little attractive, especially for those engaged in the business and bustle of courts and populous cities. In the same way we see that Europeans enjoy the sight of cattle, and the pastoral and rustic life of the countryside on account of its peace and calm.[1] In order that the furnishings might be in keeping with the smaller hut, they did away with many of the utensils and items required by *chanoyu*, together with the order and arrangement of these things, and in everything they did what seemed most fitting and appropriate for their purpose.

So they entertained each other with *cha* in these small huts within the city itself and in this way they made up for the lack of refreshing and lonely places around the city. Indeed, to a certain extent this way was better than real solitude because they obtained and enjoyed it in the middle of the city itself. They called this in their language *shichū no sankyo*, meaning a lonely hermitage found in the middle of the public square.[2] This manner that they introduced came to please all those who performed *chanoyu* more than *chanoyu* itself. They all practised the new way not only in Sakai but also in other parts, for they abandoned the old way of Higashiyama Dono as experience showed that the new manner possesses all the qualities of the old, but does not need so many rare and expensive items. Above all, the new method has many other things that the old lacked and is more within everyone's reach.

But because of what it imitated, this *suki* could not but be an imitation of poverty and lack of things, and this by its nature is unpleasant and despicable in men's opinion. To avoid this drawback, then, they laid down two things in their *suki*, just as Higashiyama Dono had taken care about his authority and propriety in *chanoyu*. The first of these was extreme cleanliness. The second was for each person to try to obtain, according to his means, some good items, both foreign and Japanese, or at least one, without giving any regard for their price and sparing no effort. For they declare that nobody can truthfully say that he is a *suki* man, that is, fond of something, or practise an art (for this word means this as well) if he allows himself to be overcome by difficulties and does not do everything possible, with the result that he fails to obtain what he so greatly desires.

Thus it happened that, once this *suki* began, the prices of famous items came to rise very steeply and were far higher than at the beginning, and each day they continue to rise even more. This is why those who devote themselves to *suki* are so resolute in what they do and steadfast in what they learn to be good and honest. For such people regard as a particular disgrace any weakness and lack of firmness (even in matters that have nothing to do with *suki*) and any haggling over the price of suitable items that a person desires.[3] Thus they

---

[1] This observation has special relevance as a number of *namban byōbu* screens (painted by Japanese artists in semi-Western style) depict European pastoral scenes.

[2] The phrase literally means, 'mountain dwelling in the midst of a city.' *Vocabulario*, f .300, renders the phrase as 'To be a hermit in the middle of the square or market or among people, and remaining religious and recollected.' See Murai, 'Development', p. 26.

[3] Akimoto Suketomo (or Suzutomo) (1717–75) refused to look at a tea item bought at great expense after he learnt that his page, on his own initiative, had obtained a reduction in price. Sadler, *Cha-no-yu*, pp. 216–17.

consider *suki* as a very wealthy poverty and a very poor wealth, because the things used therein are very poor in appearance but very rich in price, for there are items worth more than twenty, thirty, or forty thousand taels. The *suki-sha* make it their best endeavour to practise this in everything else that they use in the *cha* house. For example, they see to it that these things are always more valuable than they look, or at least that they do not outwardly show their excellence, and that they do not have any glitter, lustre, or contrivance but must be entirely natural, unadorned, and simple. They abhor in the *suki-ya* all gilded things that look like gold but are not, although various kinds of gilded things are used a great deal in social and public life. Rather, it is more in keeping with *suki* to have gold looking as if it were bronze or brass as its poor appearance harmonizes with the house, although in fact it is intrinsically valuable and precious. The same applies to all the other things. The more precious they are in themselves and the less they show it, the more suitable they are.[1]

Hence they have come to detest in *suki* any kind of contrivance and elegance, any pretence, hypocrisy, and outward embellishment, which they call *keihaku* in their language.[2] For example, many hypocritical phrases of flattering compliments, praise and adulation towards superiors; a person's desire to show himself as a greater expert in everything that he does than his strength or ability warrant, and other things of this sort. Instead, their ideal is to promise little but accomplish much, to praise sparingly but serve much; not to show off their talents and powers; always to use moderation in everything; to take care that their customs,[3] and even the manual things they use, be substantial and solid without any deceit; finally, to desire to err by default rather than by excess.

3. The great expense involved in *suki*, and the people who mainly practise it

Now it may seem to somebody hearing about it from afar and not seeing it with his own eyes that the poverty thus described is a barbarity in people of such honourable excellence, and that it just does not make sense. For everything used in *suki* is rough and mean; for example, the house made of rough and old wood covered with straw and old reeds; clay caddies and vessels badly made with an artlessness and naturalness that seem to make them more ugly; clay cups to drink from; a clay stove; an old iron kettle or pot; a path paved with rough stones; a basin made of the same material with water for the hands; wild fruitless trees, and a wood with the ground covered with moss and decrepitude; and many other things, all of them rough with no visible trace of splendour that might delight and please the senses.

For this reason it will not be out of place to say something about the great expenses occurred in *suki* and the reason why only lords, and very wealthy and well-to-do people, can practise it in its fulness. For you must know that *suki* is practised generally throughout the kingdom by all those who devote themselves to it in some way or other, even though poorly. For instead of the rich and expensive items we mentioned, they use other native ones that are similar as regards form but not as regards price and esteem in the genuine *suki*. This

---

[1] Speaking of the canons of taste in Japanese art, Sansom (*Japan*, p. 399) echoes Rodrigues's account. 'Beauty must not be displayed and underlined, but must lie modestly beneath the surface of things, to be summoned forth by the trained taste of the connoisseur.'

[2] *Vocabulario*, f. 190: '*Keihaku*. Flattery, or shallow deeds and words, by which a person tries to please others.'

[3] *Seus costumes* can also be translated as 'their garments', as in Rodrigues, *Nihon*, I, p. 610.

way is called *wabizuki*, and it is a kind of poor *suki* that imitates, insofar as possible, the purpose of the genuine *suki*.[1] But not every sort of person can perform the true and genuine
suki, because it involves a great deal of expense in various things, and so wealth and ample
means are necessary for this.

In the first place, the people who practise this *suki* are usually rulers, lords of territories
and vassals, and rich and landed nobles because, firstly, as has been mentioned, in addition to
the very costly caddy, or even caddies, in which the *cha* leaf is preserved and which they all
possess, they must also have some other esteemed item, foreign or Japanese, to use[2] in the *cha*
meting within the said house. This would include, for example, the small caddies in which to
keep the ground *cha*, or a prized kettle, or a panel bearing a picture or some famous letters.
These form, so to speak, the basis of the *suki* that they practise and, as has been said, they
cost a great deal of money. Some people even have many of them for different occasions.[3]

Secondly, the house itself is small and a dozen spans square. The largest has four-and-a-
half mats laid down, while others, eight spans in length, have three mats, and there are even
smaller ones of one-and-a-half mats. They are made of rough wood, have clay and wattle walls,
and are thatched on the outside. The inside of the roof is made of old reeds smoke-dried with
age. Although, however, it might seem that the construction of such a place would cost nothing, it is incredible how many hundreds of crowns are spent only on the construction, on the
suitable materials for which they search in different places with much labour and expense, and
on working and adjusting the wood with incredible skill by special carpenters who do only
this kind of work. They spend so much time, even months, in perfecting only the house,[4]
laying down the mats, coating the walls with clay, and fastening the reed latticework with
osiers, that indeed a beautiful wooden house could be built and completely finished much
more quickly. This, then, is the small house of those people who perform the art properly.

Thirdly, nor do they spend a trifle on the hut's own special offices, such as the kitchen
and others, and on the excellent utensils reserved for this place alone, and the greatest
cleanliness is observed in everything.

Fourthly, they spend much money on the white cedar tables that are normally used when
they eat. They are used only once and are always changed.[5] It may happen that for much of
the year gatherings for *cha* are held twice daily in the same house. There is also the tableware
that is changed at each step and appears with various devices. Although very rough, it is
also costly and is good for nothing when it is left.

Fifthly, there is the expense of laying out the wood and the path leading to the hut, for
they search in remote areas for a special type of tree of certain fashion and shape to plant
there, for any tree whatsoever will not serve. This costs a great deal of money until the trees
take root, and the wood looks as if it sprang up there quite naturally.[6] The stones with
which they pave the path make up one of the main expenses. They are of a certain special

---

[1] 'Vigizuky' is written in the Portuguese text, but this is probably an error for *wabizuki*, *wabi* being the root of
wabishii, wretched, miserable. *Vocabulario*, f. 266v: '*Wabizuki*. An inclination towards *chanoyu* with few items, or within
poor walls, etc.' As Rodrigues notes later, genuine *suki* is called *honzuki*.

[2] There is a short gap in the Portuguese text as this point, and I have added 'to use' to complete the sense.

[3] The text has here 'para diversos vazos', 'for different vessels', but *vazos* must be a slip for *casas*, houses, or *vezes*,
occasions. I have chosen the latter meaning.

[4] Another gap here in the text, but the sense remains clear.

[5] Another gap in the text; to complete the sense, I have added the words 'are changed'.

[6] See p. 156.

kind and are sought for in distant places. Although rough and unworked, they look as if they appeared there quite naturally and have a certain grace, attractiveness, and simplicity about them. They buy choice stones at a high price, and among them there will be a special one containing a pool of water within a cavity and well in the rough stone for washing the hands. Suitable ones are found only seldom and are worth a great deal.[1] Also to be considered is the construction of the street gate through which they enter the wood, for although this is very small, it is very costly. Also some wooden benches placed inside where the guests sit down and converse in a low voice after they have entered and closed the street gate.[2] From there they proceed along the path through the wood and contemplate the nostalgic things therein. Then there are some very clean privies made of a reed framework, and these are constructed in a special laborious way at great expense.[3]

Sixthly, the banquets before the *cha* consist of a few but excellent and substantial dishes of costly things that they greatly esteem. Sometimes a fresh crane is served in the *shiru* and will cost up to sixty crowns. Then they serve other prized and expensive birds, the best and choicest fish, and various other things. Thus they spend much money on these banquets,[4] which are held often for the greater part of the year, for there are also the cooks and the special utensils only for this and set apart from the everyday kind. They take great care as to the cleanliness of all the utensils thus used and the way of preparing the banquet.

Seventhly and finally, there is the expense of the very *cha* leaf itself, for this costs relatively a great deal as it is of excellent and best quality, because they cannot serve ordinary or mediocre *cha* in this *suki* house. Each person fills up four or five caddies with this *cha*, and every one of these costs up to more than sixty crowns. In addition, there are the charcoal, the silk robes, and other gifts that they send to the people who make the *cha*, as has been mentioned, as well as other expenses over and above these.

So this poverty is really very rich and wealthy, and is not so unseemly as it appears at first sight. Indeed, it is so rich that it is beyond poor people, and it is so poor that even the rich and mighty can keep it up only with difficulty. Although this house is both solitary and rough, it nevertheless is accompanied by luxurious and spacious palaces adorned with gold and fine cedar wood. The *cha* house is built by itself next to them and communicates with them from the inside. We have already described above their construction and workmanship when we spoke about the Japanese method of building.[5]

4. The heads and teachers of *suki* called *suki-no-oshō*

Among those who practise the genuine *suki*, there is always one who surpasses all others in every respect and as such is recognized and esteemed. The teacher and head of this religion or art is commonly called *suki-no-oshō*, in imitation of the Zenshū (which this art imitates) whose head or teacher is called by this style or name, just as we would use the title 'Doctor'.[6] You must know in this regard that all the liberal and mechanical arts usually have

---

[1] See p. 156.

[2] For the purpose of the *machiai*, or waiting arbour, see p. 156, n. 3.

[3] For the *setsuin*, or privy, see p. 156, n. 4.

[4] The text has here *bosques*, woods, an obvious slip for *banquetes*, banquets.

[5] See pp. 155–8, although Rodrigues has not much to say about the construction and workmanship of the *cha* house in this section.

[6] *Vocabulario*, f. 286v: 'Oshō. Certain rank of bonzes.' In its list of Zen ranks, *Arte breve*, f. 96, has: 'Oshō, or Chōrō. The highest rank, divided into *Seitō* and *Tōdo*. Are like doctors or teachers.'

a teacher or head who surpasses the rest in that field, and everyone acknowledges him as such and submits to his teaching in it. Some of them are promoted and chosen by the king, who invests them with their authority. Others are recognized as such by their superiority over everyone else in a particular art, and are esteemed by the entire kingdom.

The head of the poets in every kind of Japanese verse comes first of all in this first category.[1] There are others in the game of chess[2] and in another similar game of 360 squares on a board with the same number of counters or pieces, half of them white and the other half black. It consists of certain kinds of battles and of surrounding the enemy, and is a very social and common game much esteemed by the Chinese and Japanese nobles.[3] The same also applies to *suki*, which we are describing, for it too has its head and teacher. This is also true of the game of football; the balls are inflated and are the size of a man's head. The nobles and *kuge* play this a great deal, and many of them gather[4] in a circle wearing on the right foot a certain shoe with a blunt point.[5] It is a fine sight to see them kick forward the point of the foot and hit the ball upwards, and then do various tricks and clever feats with it without letting it touch the ground. Among the *kuge* there is a noble family that is the head of this art, for it belongs to the royal household and palace.[6] The same applies to archery, riding, and various other liberal arts.

But if these offices are not hereditary in a family and do not belong perpetually to the royal household or the *kubō*'s household, then the masters are chosen by election, and in their lifetime they select the best of their disciples and instruct them so that they may succeed them. They teach them the principal rules and secrets of their art and issue them with a patent confirming their succession therein, just as the ancient philosophers used to do in the succession of their academies.[7] The same also applies in the mechanical arts, in which someone is always chosen as the one natural master of the art by election, approbation, or

[1] Rodrigues notes (*Arte grande*, f. 183v), 'In Miyako there is a general master of poetry who is called *renga-no-oshō*; when he dies, another is chosen in his place.' He gives an excellent account of Japanese poetry in *Arte grande*, ff. 181–4, translated in Rodrigues, 'Muse'.

[2] A reference to the game of *shogi*, mentioned in various places in *Vocabulario*, f. 310v, for example, '*Shogi-daoshi*. A chess piece overthrowing its neighbour and then another, and thus all the remaining standing pieces.' Ricci (*Fonti*, I, p. 92, and *China*, p. 81) mentions this game and points out its similarities with and differences from European chess.

[3] *Vocabulario*, ff. 119v, 393v: '*Go*. A certain game played with many pieces. *Go wo utsu*. To play this game.' '*Shichō*. As, *Shichō ni kakaru*. To place a piece in such a position while playing *go* that it cannot escape.' *Go* was introduced from China in the 8th century, and is mentioned in Heian-period literature. Ricci (*Fonti*, I, pp. 92–3 and *China*, p. 81) notes that Chinese magistrates would often spend most of the day playing this game. 'Each one endeavors to drive his opponent's pieces to the middle of the board and in so doing to win over spaces, and the one who accumulates the greater number of vacant spaces wins the game.' Carletti (*My Voyage*, p. 179) also comments on the amount of time spent playing the game. The Jesuit Visitor Passio (JapSin 57, f. 249) laid down in 1612 that Japanese priests and Brothers were not to play *go*, *shogi*, or any other similar game within the house or with the laity outside.

[4] The Portuguese text here has clearly *imitandose*, but this must be a slip for *juntandose*.

[5] *Vocabulario*, f. 34v: '*Kamogutsu*. High shoes for playing ball with the feet, after the Japanese fashion.'

[6] On p. 312 Rodrigues mentions again the ancient game of *kemari*, performed in the open by 6–8 players standing in a circle. The ball, or *mari*, was stuffed and shaped like a dumbbell, as may be seen in Kaemmerer, *Trade*, pp. 88–9. The game was a court pastime, and the family mentioned by Rodrigues was the Asukai, descendants of Asukai Masatsune (1170–1221), who established the family tradition of *kemari*. In 905 a record was set in the presence of the emperor by courtiers kicking the ball 260 times without letting it touch the ground. The players wore elaborate costumes and often carried fans. *KEJ*, I, pp. 106–7, and IV, p. 191; Morris, *World*, pp. 152–3; McCullough, 'Aristocratic Culture', pp. 404–5. See Plate 22.

[7] Presumably a reference to the academy established by Plato in the 4th century BC. The directors were called *diadochi*, or successors. *Oxford Classical Dictionary*, p. 2.

hereditary succession. Sometimes, indeed, there are some nominated as such by themselves without anyone awarding it to them, and they are called *Tenka-ichi*,[1] that is, the leading person of the kingdom in such an art, or *kashira*, that is, 'head'. If this occurs by inheritance and there are many in the same society, then he is called *wakashira*, that is, head of a society or brotherhood. Such people are wont to place a notice or inscription above the door of their house, for example, *fude Tenka-ichi*, that is, the best manufacturer of writing brushes in the kingdom, etc. This also applies to sword-masters who possess sufficient self-confidence to call themselves unique in their art. In the court of Miyako, the capital of Tenka, they set up a written board at, for example, the entrance of a gate in the main public square or street of the city where everyone passes by. It reads,

> So-and-so of such-and-such a place, the most skilled swordsman in all Japan, or Tenka, lives in such-and-such a street or house. Anyone denying this or desiring to challenge him and test him with either real or practice swords, should go and seek him out.[2]

When this has been published and nobody searches him out to challenge him, his claim is confirmed because there was no-one in the capital of Tenka who dared to contradict him.

All players, actors, and those who profess the art of music and of playing instruments have their head who succeeds by inheritance, for this is an office, albeit lowly and base, in the *kubō*'s house. All these musicians and players of instruments, even though they may be unique, are nevertheless subordinate to the heads of the actors.[3] The same is true of the other mechanical arts.

The Japanese also practise the art of recognizing the grades and qualities of perfume and scented things, especially aloeswood and eaglewood. They do this skilfully by means of a slow fire and discern various differences and degrees in the same kind of perfume.[4] In our time there was one of these experts in Miyako whom we knew very well because he was a Christian, and he was called by his name of Bannai. In addition to being able to distinguish various scents, he could correctly recall having smelled the perfume of a particular wood many years previously, and he had samples of more than twenty different sorts of aloeswood.[5] This art and its principles seemed like magic and was most extraordinary, and had we not seen it we would not have believed it possible.

There are also certain experts whose office is to recognize by their rules and marks the swords, daggers, and other iron weapons made by ancient and famous craftsmen. Such

---

[1] Rodrigues provides a list of such titles in *Arte grande*, f. 95: 'Nippon-ichi, Tenka-ichi, Tenka-dai-ichi, Tenka-busō: Supreme or unique in the whole kingdom.'

[2] The challenge to fight with real blades was not an idle boast, as historical records attest. *Vocabulario*, f. 305v: 'Shiraha. Cutting edge of katanas. Shiraha de mairiau. A term used in sword fighting with which a man shows that he wishes to meet his opponent with real naked swords.'

[3] A host of words and phrases, culled from *Vocabulario*, relating to actors and acting is given in Rodrigues, *Arte del cha*, p. 55, n. 150. The most relevant reference is found on f. 219v: 'Sarugaku. People who perform comic plays; the head one among them is called *tayū*.' In *Arte grande*, f. 225v, Rodrigues lists the *shichi-kojiki*, or seven lowest classes of society, three places of which are occupied by actors, dancers, and singers.

[4] *Kōdō*, the art of blending perfumes and incense, is often mentioned in classical literature. See Morris, *World*, pp. 191–3. For the incense ceremony, see Morita, *Book of Incense*, and *KEJ*, III, pp. 284–5.

[5] Sorori Jinzaemon, best known as Bannai, was born in Izumi and manufactured sword scabbards in Sakai, but was also famous for his skill in poetry, *chanoyu*, and incense blending. A favourite of Hideyoshi, he was the author of the celebrated remark concerning the ruler's alleged likeness to a monkey. He died on 26 October 1603. Rodrigues appears to be the only person to record that he was a Christian. Rodrigues, *Arte del cha*, p. 57, n. 154; *Kokushi Daijiten*, VIII, p. 672.

weapons command a high price and esteem among the Japanese, not only on account of their age and the smith who made them, but also much more because they are excellent weapons that can cut anything without notching or blunting the cutting edge. Nor do they rust like modern weapons because they are made of extremely pure iron and steel. Some of the blades cost two, three, four, and five thousand crowns, and the very best one even ten thousand.[1] We saw this sword in the hand of Taikō, who had bought it from the *yakata* of Bungo for 10,000 crowns. It was called *honebami*, that is, devourer of bones, for even when it touched them lightly it cut them like lopped turnips.[2] This is a highly esteemed and important art among the Japanese, and even the noble lords devote themselves to it so that they may not be deceived when they deal with such valuable things. For some of these blades bear the mark of the craftsman who made them, but there are many false and counterfeit ones. Others do not bear any mark, but there are infallible rules by which it is possible to distinguish the genuine blades from the false ones, the old from the new, and those people who are skilled in this matter are so expert that they never make a mistake.

In the time of the present Shogun, the son of Daifu[3] (both cruel persecutors of the law of God), there lived in Miyako a Christian whose family name was Takeya, and his forefathers were skilled in this art. The Shogun summoned him and laid before him a hundred different swords for him to identify. He drew them out one by one from their scabbards, and without looking at any marks but only the blade, he identified each one without a single mistake. The Shogun was full of astonishment at such a rare feat and wanted to present him immediately with a royal patent, as is the custom, and raise him to the supreme rank of *Tenka-ichi* of his art in Japan, and this carries with it many great advantages and much honour. This happened during the present persecution against the Christians, and the Shogun was not aware that he was a Christian. So this good man then told the Shogun that he was a Christian and that he was informing him of this in case it was an impediment against his receiving the rank that he wished to bestow on him. The Shogun pondered for a little while, and then replied that it did not matter and that he should go ahead and accept the rank. He seems to have answered thus as he did not wish to lose a man so outstanding in this art. In this matter the good Christian deserves the highest praise for his confession of faith, preferring to lose his life and honour rather than the Faith, and also for his skill in not making a single mistake with the hundred swords.[4]

---

[1] Valignano (*Sumario*, p. 48) mentions that good swords could fetch between 3,000 and 6,000 ducats, while Vivero y Velaso (*Relación*, f. 72v) goes as high as 100,000 ducats, adding that a first-class blade could cleave from top to bottom a man sitting cross-legged. According to Avila Girón (*Relación*, p. 272), the best blades were made in Bizen. In 1611 Hideyori presented to the emperor a sword and dagger worth 100 bars of gold. Vilela (15 September 1565, in *Cartas*, I, f. 193v) mentions prices ranging from 1,000 to 4,000 crowns.

[2] Valigano (*Sumario*, p. 48) was shown this famous sword in 1580 (or 1581) by Ōtomo Yoshishige of Bungo, and noted that it had been bought for 4,500 ducats, although it carried no decoration. Hideyoshi acquired the sword in 1585. For a complete history of this sword, made by the 13th-century master Yoshimitsu, see Valignano, *Sumario*, pp. 127*–128*.

[3] That is, Tokugawa Hidetada, son of Ieyasu.

[4] The Takeya was an outstanding Christian family that gave several martyrs for the faith. Cosmas Takeya was crucified (in Rodrigues's presence) at Nagasaki in February 1597, and other members of the family were martyred in 1623 and 1632. The Takeya mentioned here cannot be identified with certainty. Rodrigues, *Arte del cha*, p. 59, n. 159; Valignano, *Sumario*, p. 127, n. 69.

In order to reach this rank and excel everyone else, this teacher and head of *suki*, whom we are describing, must have many natural gifts and abilities suited to the office, because there are many highly talented lords, nobles, and wealthy people who practise *suki*. First of all, he must possess in his person and in his deeds the abilities and good customs, mentioned above, of those who profess this art, and he must possess them to a higher degree than other people and must be acknowledged as such. Secondly, he must be of a resolute, firm spirit, withdrawn from trifles and a multitude of things, after the fashion of a contemplative hermit in the desert. Thirdly, he must have great discernment and an eye for proportion in the appearance of things, and he should know how each thing suits the place, the time, and other special circumstances, for the same thing may be fitting at one time but not at another.[1] He must also possess knowledge of the natural proportions of these natural and artificial things in various degrees, and by his long experience of them he should know about their hidden qualities. Fourthly, according to the time and circumstances, he must be able to invent incidental features that are in keeping with *suki*'s purpose, and to reject other things hitherto used. Thus there is always variety and change in these incidental things so that they may not become tedious and the spirit may be renewed.

Everything artificial, refined, and pretty must be avoided, for anything not made according to nature causes tedium and boredom in the long run. For if you plant two trees of the same size and shape, one in front of the other, they will end by causing tedium and boredom; the same applies to other things as well. But lack of artificiality and a note of naturalness (for example, in a complete tree made up of various disordered branches pointing this way and that, just as nature directed them) is never boring, because experience shows that there is always something new to be found therein. But this cannot be said of artificial things, which look well only at first sight and in time cause boredom and disgust.

In the fifth place, he must have a genuine knowledge of ancient and precious items necessary for *suki*, such as large and small caddies, kettles, porcelain cups, and paintings, and must never make a mistake about them, however similar they may be. He must also know which are the best and finest examples among such items and the good and bad points of each one, and be able to approve some and reject others unerringly. It falls to him to put a price on such items and to grade them according to their greater or less conformity with the purpose of *suki*. In fact their assessment in these matters is generally based on what is suitable and what these things inherently possess for such a purpose. Hence they have often passed judgement on things that, unknown to them, have been approved by former masters, and experts in this art have later said the same, approving and condemning the same good and bad features. Whence it may be clearly understood that among these experts there are secret rules and knowledge that ordinary people do not know about, for they all independently make the same judgement.

It falls to their lot to be able to change the shape of the house, enlarging or reducing it as the site demands. Finally, on account of their great practice, discretion, and experience regarding the correct proportions of things as they strike the eye, they alone have buildings, utensils, and vessels made for the common use and service without a trace of mediocrity or

---

[1] For an example of this principle, see Sadler, *Cha-no-yu*, p. 140, where a master tells his pupil, 'Mere imitation without regard for what is harmonious is quite contrary to the spirit of *cha-no-yu*.'

effeminacy about them. Hence anything they make, however new it may be, will always look well, not only on account of the high opinion and esteem that people have of their knowledge, but also because of the pleasing natural proportions that its parts bear to one another, just as a tree possesses the same proportions in its disordered parts pointing in different directions.

CHAPTER 34

HOW GUESTS ARE ESPECIALLY ENTERTAINED WITH *CHA* IN THE *SUKI* HOUSE

As the entertainment with *cha* in the *suki* house and all its ceremonies are special and different in form from the ordinary way, we will describe in this chapter enough to understand the procedure observed therein. For nowadays it involves the greatest perfection, and the Lord of Tenka and lords, as well as all kinds of nobles and wealthy persons with the necessary means, make great account of it in Japan. Those who do not have the wherewithal to do so much perform it with the *wabizuki* as best they can.

Although they entertain with *cha* with all the required formality the whole year around, they hold these gatherings chiefly from October onwards when their ninth moon or month occurs. For just as we open and try wines and entertain our friends about the feast of St Martin in November,[1] so from October onwards the Japanese send for their caddies of *cha*. These have been stored on the high cool mountains so that the *cha* may pass the hottest summer days there and thus retain its strength and bright green colour, for this is one of the desirable things in *cha*. They open the mouth of the caddy for the first time with great celebrations, and they call this *kuchigiri*, that is, to cut or open the mouth of the *cha* caddy.[2]

From then onwards they begin to entertain with greater zeal their friends and acquaintances, the persons whom they wish to honour or to whom they wish to show their *suki*, and especially people who are famous in this art. Because the *cha* house is small and there is no room for many people to assemble together therein, they invite only one, two, or even three, and at most four persons.

They send them a brief and polite letter saying that they wish to entertain them with *cha* (they call this *kai*, that is, to gather together for this purpose),[3] and that it would be a great honour for them if they deigned to come. They inform them of the day and the hour, because it is held either in the morning, or at midday, or in the afternoon.[4] The person thus invited replies in the same manner, thanking the host for his kindness in inviting him to *cha* and saying that he will come without fail. Before he attends this gathering, he goes in person to thank the host for having invited him to drink *cha*, but if he is very noble in rank he does this by letter.

---

[1] 11 November.

[2] *Vocabulario*, f. 62v.'*Kuchikiri*. To open a caddy of *cha* for the first time.'

[3] *Vocabulario*, f. 203v. '*Kai*. Chanoyu meeting. As, *Myōchō kai wo mōsōzu*. I invite you to *chanoyu* tomorrow morning. ¶ Item, A gathering and entertainment for many people. As, *Uta no kai, tsuzumi no kai*. A meeting for writing poems, a meeting for those who play the small drum.'

[4] For the traditional times of the day to hold the tea ceremony, see Sadler, *Cha-no-yu*, pp. 42–6.

At the appointed hour on the day each guest robes himself neatly and becomingly.[1] Lay people shave a part of the head, while bonzes and those who have performed *inkyo* shave the head and chin. Wearing new stockings, they proceed to the private gate and entrance to the woods. Outside, in front of this gate, there is a swept terrace that, together with the walls, has been recently sprinkled with water for the sake of freshness. The gate is so small and low that a person can enter only by stooping down. In front of the gate there is a rough, clean stone where the guest changes his sandals before entering the wood, and puts on new clean ones so as not to soil the path stones for they are sprinkled with water and are very clean.

Up to this point the gate has been locked from within, but now comes the master of the house, opens it, and thrusting only his head outside bids the guests welcome. He closes the gate without locking it and then retires inside his house by another special path, reserved for his use, through the wood; he neither enters nor leaves the little *cha* house. Once he has withdrawn, the guests open the gate, enter, and then lock it again from the inside. They sit there in an arbour for a short while, relaxing and gazing at the wood.[2] Then as they walk along the path through the wood up to the *cha* house, they quietly contemplate everything there – the wood itself, individual trees in their natural state and setting, the paving stones, and the rough stone trough for washing the hands. There is crystal-clear water there that they take with a vessel and pour it on their hands, and the guests may wash their hands there if they so wish. In winter hot water is available there on account of the cold. They now approach the closed door of the small house. This is set somewhat above the ground and is just large enough for a person to pass through provided he stoops.[3] They remove their fans and daggers from their sashes, and deposit them in a kind of cupboard placed there outside for this purpose.[4] Then they open the door and, leaving their sandals there, they all go inside, observing in the meanwhile due etiquette as to who shall enter first. The host is not present, and the place is empty except for some *cha* utensils.

Then without saying a word, they begin to contemplate everything there. Each guest first of all goes by himself to the *toko*[5] in the middle in order to look at the flowers placed there in an old copper or clay vase or in an old basket of a special shape. After that, he looks at the hanging panel of a painting or letters, and considers this or the meaning of the writing. Then he goes to see the stove, the kettle, and the arrangement of the burning charcoal, and the certain kind of fine ash, so neatly and tastefully laid out that it leaves nothing to be desired.[6] He next looks at all the other things there, one by one, and then inspects the very house itself – the windows made of reeds tied with osiers; the roof overhead made of old reeds, smoke-dried but very neat and clean; the twisted timber of the house; and everything else in the hermitage. Finally he goes and sits down silently in his place.

When everyone has finished his inspection and has squatted on his knees, the host opens an inner door, enters the little house, and thanks his guests for having come to his retreat,

---

[1] A description of the quiet and unostentatious clothing worn at such gatherings is given in Sadler, *Cha-no-yu*, pp. 46–7.

[2] For this waiting-arbour, see p. 156, n. 3, above.

[3] For references to the *nijiriguchi*, or 'crawling-in entrance', see p. 157, n. 2.

[4] For the *katana-kake*, see p. 156, n. 8, above.

[5] Or more usually now called *tokonoma*, 'the place of the bed', as bedding used to be stored in this recess. See p. 157.

[6] When Almeida (in *TCJ*, p. 263) attended a *cha* meeting, he noted: 'A pleasingly wrought kettle rested on a handsome tripod, and the ashes on which the live coals lay looked like ground eggshells.' Even today in country houses it is still possible to see exquisite patterns traced out daily on the smooth surface of the ash in the *irori*, or sunken hearth.

Plate 21: Tea house in the grounds of the Nezu Institute of Fine Arts, Tokyo. 'Then as they walk along the path through the wood up to the *cha* house, they quietly contemplate everything there – the wood itself, individual trees in their natural state and setting, the paving stones. ... They now approach the closed door of the small house. This is set somewhat above the ground and is just large enough for a person to pass through provided he stoops.' p. 301.

while they return him thanks for having invited them. They then converse gravely and modestly on wholesome topics for a short time, until the host rises and fetches the charcoal and the ash in special containers along with a suitable copper spoon. He takes the kettle from the stove, places it on one side, and begins to put on more charcoal. All draw near to watch him put on the charcoal for this is done in a special way. Only a little is used and each piece is laid next to another, and fine ash is poured around to obtain a pleasing effect. The charcoal is made from a certain wood that immediately kindles and does not throw out sparks. It is round in shape, as it was naturally thus before it was skilfully cut up with a saw, burnt, and made into charcoal. He next replaces the kettle and again pours water into it on top of the hot water so that it may come to the boil. A small quantity of delicate perfume prepared for the purpose is placed in the ash, and although it does not burn, the heat of the fire makes it give off a pleasant smell in the house.[1]

When this has been done, he takes the vessels inside, sweeps a little with a large feather,[2] then returns to the house and tells the guests that it is now time to eat in order to drink the *cha*. He goes inside and with his own hands brings out the tables and, beginning with the senior guest, he puts one in front of each person. The table is most neatly arranged and set out with rice, vegetable *shiru*, and two wholesome dishes. Then he brings the second table with *shiru* made of some prized bird or fish and other food. The quantity of the food is such that it can be eaten without any superfluity; hence there are not many dishes, but only two or three. A bowl of rice is at hand for each guest to take what he requires. The host then retires inside, closes the door, and leaves the guests to eat. This they do in deep silence and do not say a word, except to ask in a low voice for something needed. From time to time the host comes out to see if they want more *shiru*, and he goes and fetches it for them. Then in due course he brings out a glazed jug with a spout containing hot wine, and also cups for each one. He places it in front of the guests for each one to take and drink what he will, and does not press them to drink more. When everyone has declined, he collects the wine, takes away the second course of *shiru*, and then, in conclusion, brings hot water and each guest takes as much as he wants.

When this has been done, he takes the tables one by one inside and then brings out a small quantity of some suitable fruit as dessert on a separate plate for each guest, and then retires inside. When they have eaten the fruit, the guests collect the salvers and place them aside near the service door. They then leave the house, close the door, and go into the wood to wash their hands and mouths in preparation for drinking *cha*. As soon as they have gone out, the host locks the door from the inside, sweeps the little house with his own hands, changes the flowers and puts in fresh ones of another sort. When all is ready, he opens the door slightly and retires, thus giving the guests to understand that they may enter.

After they have washed their hands and mouths, the guests enter the house again and once more, just as before, they inspect everything placed there, including the utensils for serving *cha*. Then in deep silence each one sits down again in his place. The host now appears and asks if they wish to drink *cha*? They thank him and say that they do. He comes out with the necessary vessels, and should he own a small valuable caddy he brings the ground *cha* inside it, enclosed within a silken bag. Then in their presence he takes off the

---

[1] Extensive notes on the type of charcoal used, its preparation, and the perfume added are given in Rodrigues, *Arte del cha*, pp. 67–8, nn. 176–8.

[2] Called *haboki*. For its size, texture, and use, see Rodrigues, *Arte del cha*, p. 68, n. 179.

bag, puts down the small caddy, and washes and cleans the cups. He then puts the *cha* into the cup with a cane spoon. Having poured in a spoonful of the powder, he says, 'Your Honours had better drink this *cha* weak, for it is very poor stuff.'[1] But the guests beg him to make it stronger for they know that it is excellent when drunk thus. So he puts in as much *cha* as is needed, and with a suitable jug he draws off hot water from the kettle and, while it is still very hot, he pours it on top of the powder. He next stirs it with a small cane brush and places the cup on the mat in front of the guests. They then pay each other compliments as to who shall be the first to drink. The senior guest begins first and takes three sips before handing it to the second guest, and thus the *cha* goes around until they have finished drinking. Sometimes when a new caddy is opened for the first time, the host asks them to allow him to try the *cha* in order to see what it is like.[2]

---

[1] *Vocabulario*, f. 274v: '*Unkyaku*. Poor *cha*. Thus, *Unkyaku wo mōsōzu*. I wish to entertain you with poor *cha*.' The term literally means 'movement of clouds'. This is another instance of the Japanese custom of depreciating their own gifts – see p. 235, n. 1.

[2] Rodrigues is here describing a form of tea gathering that was practised before the more formal type of *chanoyu*, as known today, was developed by Sen no Rikyū. For this earlier version, see Murai, 'Development', and Ludwig, 'Before Rikyū'.

CHAPTER 35

THE END TO WHICH THEY ASPIRE IN *SUKI*, AND THE BENEFITS RESULTING THEREFROM

As we mentioned earlier, there are two kinds of *suki*. The first is called *hon-no-suki*, and this is the genuine and proper kind in which there must always be some costly item as the basis of the *suki*. But, as we have said,[1] not every class of person can practise this way because of the heavy and excessive expenses involved. The other sort of *suki* is called *wabizuki*, and many people, even commoners of limited means, practise this. This is a poor *suki*, and in place of costly utensils they use similar cheap ones, thus trying after their fashion to imitate the genuine article and its purpose. But this manner of *suki* is very useful and serves a practical purpose, because entertaining a person in this way does not involve so much expense as in the formal gatherings; it is moderate and does not have too much wine, *sakana*, and various exquisite dishes. A guest of whatever rank is entertained soberly, honourably, and becomingly at *suki* with less expense and without any pomp or ostentation, but with greater love and courtesy than is to be found in *suki*. But both types of *suki* have the same purpose and benefits, because they both imitate the same thing and have the same end.

Now you must know that the whole complex of things involved in *suki* – the house, the path through the wood, the meal, the utensils, etc. – must be such that it is adapted and geared to what *suki* professes, that is, the solitude and rustic poverty of a hermit. Hence the house, the path leading thereto, the meal, the utensils, and the robes worn when entering the house, must all be fitting and suitable for this. They therefore must not be glossy things of rich appearance, nor anything of rare and excellent workmanship. Instead everything should be natural, comely, lonely, nostalgic, and agreeable. Nature has endowed natural things with an elegance and grace that move the beholder to loneliness and nostalgia, and the discernment of these qualities is one of the main features of *suki*. In the same way, they imitate the members of the Zenshū, even in the style of writing that they use in their letters. The writing must be different from the usual style, yet attractive and interesting, rather like a scholar's hurried writing. The letters should be short and to the point, and not contain many unnecessary compliments.[2]

In addition to this general conformity and proportion, there is another special relation between the various parts. For instance, if the house is of a certain size, then the *toko* (the

---

[1] See pp. 292–4.

[2] *Vocabulario*, f. 140v: '*Zenpitsu. Zen no fude*. A certain kind of letters or characters that the Zenshū bonzes like to imitate, resembling the letters of China.' But even ordinary Japanese epistles were brief and to the point. Fróis (*Tratado*, p. 216) reports: 'Our epistles cannot express ideas without a lot of writing, whereas those of Japan are extremely brief and compendious.' Fróis's own letters and writings are a good case in point.

vase place), the stove, the kettle, and the other utensils that go with these, must be mutually proportionate in size so that they harmonize with one another. The same applies to the parts of the house itself, such as the inner service-door, the windows, etc., and also to the planting of the wild trees in the wood and along the path. Attention is paid to the length and width of the whole site. In keeping with this, they work out the best proportion as regards the size and number of the trees, their relation with one another, their position, and distance between each one. In all this, they bear in mind what Nature herself would do if she were to plant these trees there with natural grace and artlessness.

From this practice of observing the relations and proportions of these things both among themselves and with the whole, the *suki-sha* attain a higher degree of knowledge of things. This knowledge has to do with certain more subtle and hidden qualities in them, all apart from their general aptitude and suitability for *suki*. If this is lacking, there is no means of discerning the other hidden qualities in things, such as *yowai* (feeble, weak, slack); *tsuyoi* (strong, stable); *katai* (too strong – this is a defect); *sunei* (active, alert); *nurui* (tepid, feeble, lifeless); *iyashii* (lowly, base, mean); *kedakai* (distinguished, dignified), etc.[1] There are other such inherent natural qualities in relation to other things, place, and purpose.

Thus they distinguish genuine *sunei* (a quality very much in keeping with *suki*) from *iyashii*, which is a defect; *tsuyoi* from *katai*; and *nurui* or *yowai* from *jinjōna*[2] or *kedakai*, and so distinguish the subtle natural qualities possessed by both natural and artificial things. Not everyone is capable of such discernment. In addition, they distinguish the genuinely good from the defect that appears with it. Such a defect is a genuine defect in some things, while in other cases it is merely a blemish as regards the purpose of *suki*, but not as regards other purposes.

The *suki-sha* also pay attention to the proportion and suitability that things ought to have according to various times and people. For example, as regards the time of the *cha* meeting,[3] whether it be spring, summer, autumn, or winter, whether in the morning, afternoon, or at night.[4] They also take into account who is invited and who invites. In this way everything may be performed in keeping with natural reason and suitability. So the principal science of *suki* lies in this ability to recognize the natural proportion and suitability of things. This is what those who practise the art look for among themselves, observing whether a person succeeds or not, and how far advanced he is in this knowledge. They appraise him by what he does in the performance of *suki*, and this is mainly discovered in the gatherings that he holds, in his serving *cha*, and in all the attendant circumstances. For it is here in this performance that a man shows what he knows and understands.

This, then, is the real reason why they regard the entertainment and the serving of *cha* as so important in *suki*, because each person thus shows how advanced he is in this art. The guests take careful note of everything the host does, and afterwards they say among themselves that the *suki* of so-and-so is *nurui*, or *sunei*, *taketa*, *shoshin*, *jinjōna*, or *niawanai*, etc.,[5] because he displays all that he understands about this art in the meal, the preparation of the

---

[1] All these Japanese terms are found in *Vocabulario* (ff. 325, 151v, 42, 379v, 188, 138, 193). The list given in the text illustrates Rodrigues's grasp of the Japanese language and its subtle nuances.

[2] *Vocabulario*, f. 142v: 'Jinjōna. A politic, serious, modest thing.' The term now means 'ordinary, common, usual'.

[3] There is a short gap in the Portuguese text at this point.

[4] The type of *suki* and the food provided thereat varied somewhat according to the season, the time of day, and the weather. Details are given in Sadler, *Cha-no-yu*, pp. 43–6.

[5] *Vocabulario*, ff. 241, 313, 182: '*Take, uru, eta*. To raise oneself on high. ... *Taketa hito*. A man of great knowledge. ... *Gakumon no taketa hito*. A great scholar.' '*Shoshin*, Something new, or an apprentice in an art or office. ... *Shoshin na koto wo*

house, and the utensils. For in the wood and the path he shows what he understands about the natural proportions of trees and the wood so that they may look agreeable, and also in the suitable stones for the path and in their position, and thus in everything else both inside and outside the house. Hence it is quite certain that not everyone who devotes himself to *suki* and practises the art is a genuine *suki-sha*. For it is not easy to arrive at a genuine knowledge of such proportions and suitability; this is chiefly because the masters of this art do not teach by word but by performance, as we have said earlier. Thus many people do no more than copy the masters without understanding the reason for what they do. Even among those who reach this knowledge there are higher and lower grades, and also various opinions. But in fact, as this is a genuine science, anything that an expert in the art does according to its rules is approved by others. They appreciate it when they see it, even though they may not know who has done it.

So *suki* has three principal and essential features, and all the rest is incidental and variable. The first is the extreme cleanliness in everything, not only in what can be seen outwardly in the *suki* meetings and gatherings, but also in those things that are not seen. These include, for example, the *suki* kitchen, the preparation of the dishes, and the utensils that they use therein without touching any of the food with their hands except when they are washing it. Everything is done there with as much cleanliness and delicacy as if they were doing it publicly in front of the guests themselves.

The second is the rustic solitude and poverty, and the withdrawal from a multitude of superfluous things of every kind. The third and principal feature is the knowledge and science of natural proportion and suitability, and the hidden and subtle qualities inherent in natural and artificial things, which are in keeping with the purpose of *suki*. The genuine and discerning *suki-sha* extend this knowledge and science to other secular things, both artificial and moral, concerning honest and suitable customs, and apply it according to the end and purpose of each of these things.

First of all as regards customs, this has led them to reform many ancient social customs, which were once observed at court but have now been found inconvenient and not to the purpose. The same has happened in their etiquette, letter-writing, and dealings among friends. From this also followed the reform of people as regards good breeding, modesty, exterior humility, wholesome and earnest conversation, and the avoidance of exterior hypocrisy and a host of superfluous and unnecessary things employed merely out of ostentation. It has resulted with everyone living within his means and not beyond them and what is fitting. Hence a person is observed and rebuked by others when he exceeds them. The great nobles can thus mix with the lesser gentry when they are invited to deal with people of inferior rank at *suki* in this restrained fashion without any pomp or state. They do not lessen their dignity thereby, for this is a kind of rustic relaxation in the countryside.

They also extend this knowledge to artificial and secular things, whence they have suitably improved some offensive and defensive weapons. It is a great help when applied to the proportions of buildings, houses, courtyards, stairs, and everything else of this kind, as well as clothing, footwear, and having vessels and utensils made suitable for their intended purpose. They thus improved many kinds of things with much profit and advantage, especially in the reform of solemn and public feasts. According to ancient usage, these involved a

---

iu. To say things that show little experience or knowledge.' '*Ni ai* … To fit or be convenient.' (*Niawanai* is the negative form of this last term.)

great deal of expense and labour, although there was hardly anything to eat.[1] Everything was cold and tasteless, and was served merely for the sake of ceremony in order to drink wine after the banquet. But now these have been completely changed, for they are less expensive and have hot, tasty, well-seasoned, and good dishes, and they drink while they eat just as we do. There are many other benefits that have resulted therefrom and still continue to appear in the kingdom every day.

For example, Takayama Justus was unique in this art in Japan and as such was highly esteemed.[2] He was very famous for his Christianity and was twice exiled with loss of his property for love of the Faith. The second exile was to the Philippines, where he died as a result of hardship, and it is believed that he did not lack the crown of martyrdom. He was wont to remark, as we several times heard him, that he found *suki* a great help towards virtue and recollection for those who practised it and really understood its purpose. Thus he used to say that in order to commend himself to God he would retire to that small house with a statue, and there according to the custom that he had formed he found peace and recollection in order to commend himself to God.

This is enough about *suki* to understand why the Japanese think so highly of it and how the kingdom has benefited from the advantages resulting therefrom in customs and other features of social life.

---

[1] For the formal banquet, conducted in profound silence, given by Hideyoshi on the occasion of Valiganano's audience at Jurakutei in 1591, see p. 261, n. 2.

[2] For Takayama Ukon, see p. 83. As mentioned on p. 289, n. 2, at one time Ukon was one of the 'seven wise men of tea', or seven illustrious disciples of the master Sen no Rikyū. In early 1591, Ukon attended Rikyū's tea gatherings three times (once as the sole guest), only a few weeks before the master's enforced suicide in April. Rodrigues, *Arte del cha*, p. 78, n. 199.

BOOK 2

Wherein Are Described the Liberal and Mechanical Arts of Japan, their Letters or Characters, their Antiquity, and Japanese Language and Poetry.

CHAPTER 1

THE LIBERAL AND MECHANICAL ARTS OF JAPAN IN GENERAL
AND THEIR DIVISION

As the Japanese are so ingenious and industrious, and are given to exterior religious observance and magnificence, they possess almost every kind of liberal and mechanical art necessary for social life among people in a well-ordered society. Thus not only do all the liberal arts flourish greatly in this kingdom, but also the mechanical ones. Among the other nations of these parts the Japanese are naturally very skilful and accomplished in this regard. We are not speaking here about those who are engaged in such things professionally, for every kind of Japanese, even nobles and gentlemen, are naturally very clever with their hands in imitating natural things without having to learn the art. They do not use a multitude of tools, but only a kind of small iron knife, and with this they make anything they wish out of both wood and paper. This knife is used as scissors to cut things, and as a chisel and adze and everything else in order to cut and fashion the material to the desired shape in the way they wish. Whoever sees this cannot help but admire it, for their skill and perfection leave nothing to be desired.

In dealing in general with their liberal arts, the Japanese divide them into two principal sciences in which all the others are included as subsidiary members. They call this *bunbu-nidō*[1] in their language, meaning the two arts of science or letters, and of weapons or military matters. They say that both of these are as necessary to the nation as are the two wheels of a cart to move or the two wings of a bird to fly. If one of the pair is missing, then it is not possible to move. For a nation, therefore, to be preserved in peace and tranquility, it is first of all necessary to have wise and prudent persons who with just and suitable laws will govern it with all justice and equity, rewarding the good people with honours, favours, and offices in the nation, and punishing the wicked and rebellious with penalties, exile, and, when it is deserved, death. But brave and bold persons, skilful in the use of weapons are also needed, and they will prudently and expediently defend the kingdom from its enemies, guard the royal person, and punish rebels. Thus, to say that a man is perfect in his nation means that he possesses the two arts of science and weapons, and consequently all the other liberal arts of his country, for they are included in these two categories as integral parts. All the political and military government by which the kingdom[2] is ruled is based on these two arts.

---

[1] Also known as *bunbu-ryōdō*, which has the same literal meaning, that is, the two paths of literature and weapons. In *Breve aparato*, f. 15, Rodrigues correctly notes that the expression is *wenwu erdao* in Chinese.

[2] There is a short gap in the text here. The literal translation is: '... in which the kingdom ... of these two arts.'

Plate 22: Nobles playing *kemari* football. Colour on paper. The ball is shown halfway out of the upper frame. Three of the four traditional marker trees (pine, cherry, willow, and maple) are shown. 'The game of ball with the tip of the foot. This is a game of the royal palace and played among the kingdom's grandees called *kuge*.' p. 313. *Private collection.*

But descending to greater detail, they list their more important liberal arts in two groups, signified by the words *gei* and *nō*.[1] The first one, *gei*, means the liberal art that a person pursues as a profession and for this reason it is less honourable. Those who pursue them, or most of those who practise the art as a profession by which they earn their living, are held in low esteem. The lords, nobles, and gentry learn and perform them for recreation, but this is not disreputable. They list seven of these arts.[2]

1. Writing, or being a scribe.
2. Music, after the fashion of plays and comedies.
3. Playing small musical instruments, rather like kettledrums or tabors.[3]
4. Reciting stories to a particular tone and tune, along with a certain dance;[4] they derive much pleasure from this.
5. Wrestling.[5] This is very common among them, and young nobles engage in it as an exercise of war.
6. The art of fencing.
7. Speaking or debating as a profession.

The second word, *nō*, means the liberal arts, or the skill and ability in them, and this in itself is honourable, esteemed, and practised by grandees, nobles, and gentlemen of both the patrician and military orders. They list ten of these.[6] Some of them pertain to the office of families in the royal household and are therefore noble, while others belong to the household of the *kubō*, the High Constable and Commander of the Kingdom, and are therefore highly regarded by the nobles and gentry. They are as follows.

1. The art of shooting with bow and arrow, a military and very noble exercise among them.[7] This is the principal military art in the whole of Asia and in China, and among the Tartars and Koreans.

2. The game of ball with the tip of the foot.[8] This is a game of the royal palace and played among the kingdom's grandees called *kuge*. Thence it has spread to the ordinary people and even to the bonzes, their religious.

3. Carving, a very common and noble office among them.[9]

---

[1] *Gei* may be translated as art, craft, accomplishment; hence, *geisha*, an accomplished person. *Nō* means talent, ability, skill; the same character is used for noh drama. *Vocabulario*, ff. 184v, 185: '*Nō*. Arts, skills, or abilities. *Item*, drama. *Nō wo suru*: To act or perform a drama or tragedy, etc.' '*Nōgei*, or *Geinō*: arts or skills.'

[2] *Vocabulario*, f. 393v: '*Shichigei*. The seven arts or skills.' Rodrigues mentions (*Arte breve*, f. 4) this term without further elaboration, adding that all missionaries should be familiar with the concept.

[3] *Vocabulario*, f. 251v: '*Tsuzumi*. Small drum or tambourine.' Cocks (in Farrington, *English Factory*, II, p. 1529) accurately, if quaintly, describes this instrument: 'Their Musique is little Tabers, made great at both ends, and smal in the middest, like to an Houre-glasse, they beating on the end with one hand, and straine the cords which goe about it, with the other, which maketh it to sound great or small as they list, according their voices with it, one playing on a Phife or Flute; but all harsh, and not pleasant to our hearing.' Illustration in *KEJ*, VIII, p. 119.

[4] Chanting a section from a noh play, with musical accompaniment and dance, was, and still is, a common practice, especially for amateur performers.

[5] A reference to sumo wrestling, immensely popular in Japan today. *Vocabulario*, ff. 231, 379v: '*Sumō*. Wrestling.' '*Sumō-tori*. A wrestler.'

[6] *Vocabulario*, f. 146v: '*Jūnō*. The ten arts. Thus, *Jūnō shichigei no tasshita hito*. A man highly skilled in all the arts.'

[7] Known as *kyūdō* or *kyūjutsu*. A list of relevant words beginning with *yumi-* (bow) is given in *Vocabulario*, ff. 326–6v, 401v.

[8] See p. 295 for the elegant pastime of *kemari*.

[9] The Portuguese verb used here, *trinchar*, refers to carving meat. Rodrigues has already noted (pp. 148, 153) that much attention was paid to this when preparing banquets.

4. The art of horse-riding.[1]

5. The art of good breeding and social customs of the kingdom. There are various books written about this, and there is a noble family in the *kubō*'s household that provides masters of this art and ceremonies.[2]

6. Arithmetic.[3]

7. The art of hunting and shooting, practised by all the lords, even the Lord of Tenka.[4]

8. A certain kind of poetry that many people jointly compose on a theme or verse, each one composing his verse in keeping with the previous verse that it follows. Among the nobles this is a very common art and requires great understanding and judgement.[5]

9. Playing musical instruments used by the nobles, such as flutes and others.[6]

10. The game on a board, or chess, of which they have two kinds. There is another of 360 pieces, half of them white and half of them black, with a board of the same number of squares. This is a very common game among the nobles in China and Japan, for it is a certain kind of battle that requires great judgement.[7]

These are the principal arts to which the nobles attach importance and which they practise and are proud of their skill in them. In addition, there are still others belonging to particular families who possess them as an office in the royal household. These are not learnt by the nobles, as it does not serve their purpose, but only by those who profess them. They include mathematics and astrology that the royal mathematicians practise, and also the art of prognosticating by the stars and signs in the Heavens and the conjunctions of the planets among them. And also by the birth and hours[8] of each person, that is, by the hour, day, month, and sign in which he was born. This also belongs to a particular office and family of the royal household, and it has spread thence to others throughout the kingdom.

We will speak in detail about some of the principal liberal and mechanical arts because they contain things that are well worth knowing. First of all, we shall speak about the mechanical arts, and then the liberal ones.

---

[1] *Vocabulario*, ff. 272v–3v, lists more than a score of words and phrases connected with horses (*uma*), and riding (*umanori*).

[2] A reference to the Ise family. See p. 177, n. 3.

[3] '*Arismetria*' in the Portuguese text, where it is erroneously listed as the seventh, instead of the sixth, item.

[4] Various hunting terms (such as *karibito*, hunter, and *kariginu*, hunting robes, etc.) are given in *Vocabulario*, f. 40v. See pp. 85, 110, for references to hunting.

[5] A reference to *renga*, or linked verse. Elsewhere (*Arte grande*, ff. 183v–184; Rodrigues, 'Muse Described', pp. 74–5), Rodrigues explains at some length the practice of *renga*, noting that its form is the same as that of the *uta* as regards feet and syllables (5, 7, 5, 7, 7), but differs as regards the number of verses, which can go up to a hundred (*hyakuin*) or even a thousand (*senku*). Many people take part in composing the series, each adding in turn a verse bearing some relation to the previous one.

[6] *Vocabulario*, f. 133: '*Fue*. A flute. As, *fue wo fuku*. To play the flute.'

[7] For an earlier reference to the game of *go*, see p. 295.

[8] There is a short gap in the text at this point. Rodrigues later describes in detail both Japanese and Chinese astrology on pp. 396–400.

CHAPTER 2

SOME MECHANICAL ARTS OF JAPAN, AND FIRSTLY THEIR PICTURES

Among their other mechanical arts, the principal one is the art of painting. They are very skilful at painting the things of nature, and copying them as best they can with great exactness. In these paintings they devise many things that are fancied and conceived in the imagination rather than found in nature, such as various imaginary flowers and figures cleverly entwined and intermingled, and other things of that sort. In keeping with their melancholy temperament, they are usually inclined towards lonely and poignant pictures, such as those portraying the four seasons of the year.

They assign a particular colour to each of the seasons and depict various suitable things that grow or are found in them. For example, they associate white with winter on account of the snow, frost, and chill of that season, and also on account of the different kinds of wild birds, such as wild ducks, swans, cranes, and many others, which come flying in flocks from Tartary at that time. The colour green is associated with spring because plants, vegetables, and various kinds of flowers in the trees and fields are in bud, and also because of the mist that falls then. Red depicts summer on account of the great heat, the fruit ripening on the trees and everything in bloom. Blue is the colour for autumn, when the fruit is ripe and the trees shed their leaves as they lose their vitality and draw in their roots. Hence it is said that this vitality is produced in the spring, flourishes and comes to fruition in the summer, withdraws in the autumn, and is hidden in the winter when the trees are leafless and as if withered.[1]

Such pictures, painted successively in the rooms or on decorative panels, are very pleasing and moving as they so vividly depict the things of nature that flourish in the different seasons. They are also very skilful at painting realistically all kinds of trees, plants, flowers, birds, and animals, as well as shady woods, mountains, and water tumbling down from rocky crags. They also depict hermitages of recluses dwelling in the wilderness, as well as valleys, forests, rivers, lakes, and seas with boats sailing in the distance.[2] There are eight famous lonely places called *hakkei*, or eight views, in both Japanese and Chinese tradition, and these scenes are often painted and much admired.[3]

---

[1] Illustrated examples of mural paintings illustrating the four seasons are found in Takeda, *Kanō Eitoku*. In some cases the four seasons are depicted in one and the same painting.

[2] For illustrations of wall paintings depicting 'water tumbling from rocky crags' and 'recluses dwelling in the wilderness', see Takeda, *Kanō Eitoku*, pp. 78–9, 147, 148, 149.

[3] The Chinese Eight Views were originally painted during the Song dynasty (960–1279), and are sometimes called the Xiao-Xiang Eight Views as they depict scenes connected with those two rivers. Although the *hakkei* may depict various places, the list normally follows the same pattern. Rodrigues probably had in mind the Eight Views of Lake Biwa (*Ōmi hakkei*). These views were arranged following the Chinese pattern at the end of the 15th century, but his list differs somewhat both in content and order from the accepted Eight Views. He gives practically the same list, with Japanese titles, in *Arte grande*, f. 226v. For further information on the *hakkei*, see Edmunds, *Pointers*, pp. 370–71, and Joly, *Legend*, p. 385. For illustrations of the views in 16th-century mural decoration, see Rodrigues, *This Island*, p. 207, and Takeda, *Kanō Eitoku*, pp. 58, 86–7.

Plate 23: 'Landscape' by Tōzen
Hosetsu. Hanging scroll, ink on
paper, 16th century. 'They also
depict hermitages of recluses
dwelling in the wilderness, as well as
valleys, forests, rivers, lakes, and
seas with boats sailing in the
distance.' p. 315.
Honolulu Academy of Arts.
Martha Cooke Steadman Acquisition Fund,
1962 (3099.1)

316

The first scene is a certain famous place with the clear autumn moon reflected in the water. They go out on autumn nights to gaze at the moon in a sad, nostalgic mood. The second view is of a valley or remote wilderness where a hermitage bell, rung at sunset or at night, is heard sounding softly from afar. Their bells are rung from the outside with a log like a battering-ram, and produce a soft and mellow note, quite unlike the harsh sound made by a metal clapper.[1] Third, rain falling quietly at night in a certain lonely spot. Fourth, a ship sailing back from the distant high sea towards land. Fifth, the sight of a lovely fair held in certain mountains.[2] Sixth, fishing-boats returning together from the sea at sunset. Seventh, flocks of wild birds landing with their leader in a certain place. Eighth, snow falling on a high place in the evening or at night. All this is in keeping with their temperament, and makes them feel very nostalgic and quietly lonely.

They also paint famous stories and ancient things, such as the Twenty-Four Obediences, observed in rare circumstances by sons towards their old parents and also by parents towards their sons.[3] They do not hang tapestries or silk drapings on the walls, but everything is painted on the wall on to waxed panels with their laths, as we described when talking about their houses.[4] These paintings may also be found on *byōbu*, a kind of frame made of six or eight linked panels, which can be doubled up or stretched out at will. They place them along the walls of a house for decoration, or they use them as partitions in a house when privacy is required. There are various types of this useful article and they are extremely well made, and some have been sent to Europe.[5]

Finally, although they copy nature in their paintings, they do not like a multitude and jumble of things, but prefer to portray, even in gilded and lovely palaces, just a few solitary things with due proportion between them. Indeed, they distinguish themselves in this respect. But they show very little knowledge and proportion when they come to paint the human body and its various parts, and they can hardly be compared with our painters as regards the proportions among the parts of the body and in respect to the body itself. For they lack a true knowledge of shading figures, for it is this that makes them stand out and gives them strength and beauty.[6]

---

[1] This passing observation illustrates Rodrigues's appreciative insight into Japanese mentality. The deep-sounding bells of Buddhist temples are most evocative to the Japanese, and the famous preface of the classic *Heike Monogatari* appropriately begins with the sound of the temple bell solemnly echoing 'the impermanence of all things'.

[2] The reference to a *feira*, or fair, is obviously out of place in this context. In his list of the *hakkei* in *Arte grande*, f. 226v, Rodrigues refers to *sanshi*, meaning either mountain fair or mountain town. While translating the Japanese terms for this account in his *History*, he erroneously adopted the first, instead of the more appropriate second, rendering.

[3] The Twenty-four Paragons of Filial Virtue is a collection of Chinese stories illustrating filial love and obedience. For example, Rōraishi (Lao Laizi, in Chinese) dressed in baby's clothing at the age of 70 to delude his aged parents into thinking that they were still young. See Plate 25. For other illustrations, see Doi, *Momoyama*, plates 15 and 40, and Takeda, *Kanō Eitoku*, pp. 84–5, 150, 151, 160. The 24 Paragons are listed in Edmunds, *Pointers*, pp. 198–9, and Joly, *Legend*, pp. 400–403; details are provided in Ferguson, *Chinese*, pp. 161–6. The reference to 'parents towards their sons' is unclear, and the text may be corrupt.

[4] See pp. 150–51.

[5] For references to these *byōbu*, see p. 231, n. 2. The best-documented case of a *byōbu* arriving in Europe concerns the screens depicting Azuchi castle and city which the Japanese envoys (see p. 98, n. 3, above) presented to Gregory XIII in Rome on 3 April 1585. Fróis, *Première Ambassade*, p. 184, and Abranches Pinto and Bernard, 'Instructions', pp. 398–9.

[6] It is debatable whether Chinese and Japanese painters were ignorant of proportion and perspective. The painters sought 'the angle of totality' and tried to show man's relations with the things of nature. Sullivan, 'Heritage', p. 167; Sansom (*Western World*, p. 233) quotes a 19th-century Japanese painter as declaring that correct and realistic representation is work for artisans, not artists.

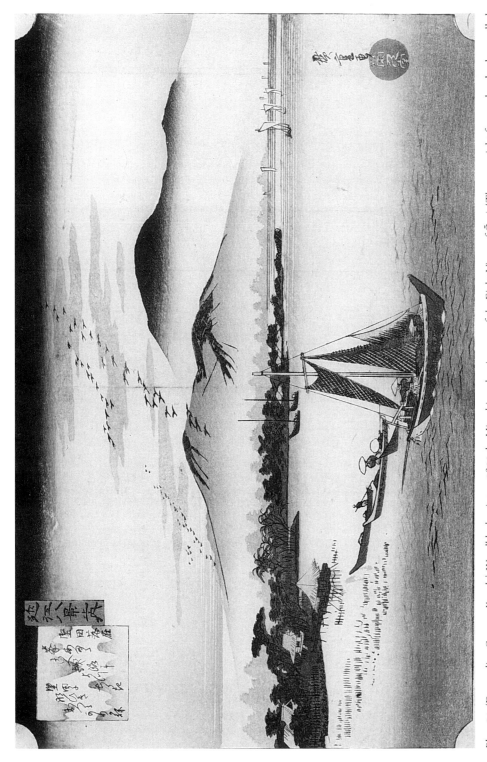

Plate 24: 'Descending Geese at Katada'. Woodblock print, c. 1833, by Hiroshige, showing one of the Eight Views of Ōmi. 'There are eight famous lonely places called *hakkei*, or eight views ..., and these scenes are often painted and much admired. ... Seventh, flocks of wild birds landing with their leader in a certain place.' pp. 315–17. *Honolulu Academy of Arts. Gift of James A. Michener, 1991 (23,215).*

Plate 25: An illustration of one of the *Twenty-Four Paragons of Filial Virtue*. Rōraishi plays like a child to make his aged parents think that they are still young. Rodrigues, *This Island of Japon*.

They are very skilful in the art of statuary and their statues, such as those of idols, both of wood or cast from metal, whether big or small, are well proportioned. They have such large statues in their temples that a man standing on the shoulder of one of them cannot touch its ear with his hand. The figure is seated on a proportionately large lotus flower with the legs crossed. The distance between the knees in 50 spans[1] and 32 spans from shoulder to shoulder, while the circumference of the seat that the body occupies is 150 spans. The palm of the hand is so big that it will hold a goodly number of people seated in it. But as the whole vast bronze structure and its parts have been cast with such proportion and measurement, it does not look so big as it really is. They say that they could make the whole body if they had only a small piece of one finger, because they have all the measurements worked out. There are three of these statues in various parts of Japan, and in their fashion they are like the Colossus of Greece.[2]

---

[1] The text gives 'five' spans here, but this must be a slip for 50.

[2] The three large Buddhist statues, or *daibutsu*, at Nara, Miyako, and Kamakura. The Nara statue in Tōdaiji dates from 749 and is 53 feet high. See Almeida, in *TCJ*, pp. 334–6. The Miyako statue was 63 feet high and was commissioned by Hideyoshi in 1588, but was melted down after being damaged in an earthquake in 1622. Berry, *Hideyoshi*, pp. 196–8; Almeida and Bermeo, in *TCJ*, pp. 334–7; Cocks, *Diary*, I, pp. 200–202. The Kamakura statue, cast in 1252 and 42 feet high, is decribed by Cocks (ibid., I, p. 194) as 'a mighty idoll of bras ... siting cros legged (telor lyke)...' Rodrigues went to see this statue while on his way to Edo in 1607. Guerreiro, *Relação*, III, p. 129. By his reference to people fitting into the palm of the statue, Rodrigues probably has the Nara statue in mind.

Plate 26: 'Birds and Flowers' by Kani Kōi (c. 1569–1636), six-fold screen, ink, colours, and gold on paper, early 17th century. 'They are also very skilful at painting realistically all kinds of trees, plants, flowers, birds, and animals.' p. 315. *Honolulu Academy of Arts. Gift of Mrs Charles M. Cooke, 1929 (4149).*

They have three kinds of painting, *iroe*, *sumie*, and *dei*.[1] They do not paint with oil, but grind the ink with glue. The first type is for cheerful things, and is in colour and gilded. The second is executed with black ink or water-colour, and they are very skilful and excellent in this. They like this style because it is keeping with their natural temperament, and among these paintings there are some by celebrated ancient artists who are highly esteemed, and they pay a high price for these. They use this kind in *suki* and *chanoyu*. The third kind of painting is done with powdered gold called *dei*, meaning lama or gold lama, and with this they produce very lovely and wholesome pictures, which are highly prized and dignified. These are combined with the water-colour painting or the painting in colours, instead of the gilded paintings.[2] They are very skilful and excellent in these, and it really is a certain kind of painting that we call illumination, albeit different from our kind.

The lords are wont to use these three kinds of painting in different rooms and apartments of their palaces in keeping with the purpose for which they are used. Thus, the rooms and apartments where guests are received are richly gilded with various paintings in colour. Inner rooms, where they gather to talk or conduct business among themselves, will be painted with ground gold and black ink, or with colours. Finally, other rooms will be excellently painted with black water-colour, and such is their skill that with the same black ink they seem to depict to the life even the same colour of the bird, tree, or any other thing.

[1] *Vocabulario*, ff. 134, 231, 71v: '*Iroe*. Something illuminated or painted in colours.' '*Sumie*. A water-colour painting in black ink.' '*Dei. Doro*. Mud or mire. Item, silver, gold, or brass ground and made like paste. *Dei wo kesu*. To make this ink or metal paste.' The last item is also called *deikin* (mud gold), used as a synonym for *kinpun*, gold dust or powdered gold.

[2] A literal rendering of a vague and perhaps corrupt sentence.

CHAPTER 3

THEIR OTHER MECHANICAL ARTS

They hold the art of architecture in wood in great honour and esteem, because as they build only with wood and the people are very grandiose and social, the craftsmen engaged in this art are most accomplished and skilful. Thus in general they can compete with anywhere as regards building with wood, and as they are so resourceful and skilful in mechanical arts they are greatly superior to the Chinese. Men who profess this art are considered nobler than the craftsmen engaged in other mechanical arts, and there is competition between them and the armourers. Hence it is not a base and lowly art as the others, and throughout the kingdom there are many people who profess this art and have pupils whom they teach. The Lord of Tenka has his Senior Carpenter or Architect, the head of all the others of the court and of all those engaged in royal works.[1] In addition to designing, he is very skilful in the art and is engaged in things of the greatest excellence, the dimensions of buildings, and the proportion between their parts. He usually does not toil himself, but has in his charge craftsmen skilled in every branch of this art, such as carving and gilding wood, and everything else. Each lord in his domain and house has a similar official, the Head Carpenter, who receives a salary and looks after all the buildings.

In the cities and towns all of these men are registered, and are organized in houses and subject to a head to whom they pay a certain fee. They have every kind of tool that we have, and very good and excellent ones at that, such as the adze, plane, and gradated square for measuring. They begin with the point, the smallest of all measurements and corresponding more or less to the mathematical degree. Ten of these make a unit like the distance between the two knuckles of the thumb, and ten of these equal one of their *covados* (cubit), which is a mathematical foot. Five of these make one ell, two ells one pole, and six-and-a-half feet make one *tatami*, or mat, so that with the help of the square they can determine all the measurements. They also have various chisels, saws, gimlets, and other tools, which we lack, for delicate work.[2]

All the houses are built according to certain measurements on account of the mats, or *tatami*, with which they are laid, for each of these mats has a certain measurement and size, eight spans long and four wide. In the rooms and compartments they always exercise great care that the mats, which are three fingers thick, are so close to each other that there are no gaps at all between them, just as if they were floorboards. The houses in which they dwell usually have only one storey, and the floor is raised four or five spans above the ground so that the house may be fresh and well aired underneath, and dampness avoided. There are,

---

[1] Probably a reference to the *daikugashira*, who supervised building projects, while below them the *daitōryō* were responsible for design and workmanship. Both offices were hereditary.

[2] For an illustrated account of traditional Japanese carpentry, see Coaldrake, *Way of the Carpenter*.

however, houses of more than one storey, as we have mentioned. The walls are made of wooden pillars, equally spaced out and resting on stone supports instead of being set into the ground, so that they will not rot. Each pillar is joined to the corresponding one in the opposite wall by a wooden transverse beam that rests in a hole that they make on top. In this way the house is stronger and firmer against the winds, storms, and earthquakes than it would be if it were made of stone, brick, or plaster. Although there are many great storms and earthquakes, the houses seldom collapse (unless they are already rotten) because the pillars are so strongly joined and fixed to each other. Thus they can easily move an entire house of this sort to another place nearby without dismantling it, apart from removing the roof from above because of its weight, and this we have seen them do many times.[1]

In the castle of the *kubō*, or Lord of Tenka, and in those of all the other lords of the kingdoms and states, there is generally a tower or a very strong, high, and big donjon of five, six, or seven storeys, which can be seen from afar. Such a keep will have eight roofs around the sides of each storey, and it is a truly wonderful and magnificent building, strong and impregnable.[2] They keep their treasure here, and it is here that they assemble with their womenfolk in time of siege. When they can hold out no longer, they kill the women and children to prevent their falling into the hands of the enemy, and then, after setting fire to the tower with gunpowder and other materials so that not even their bones or anything else may survive, they cut their bellies.[3]

The architecture of these buildings, the workmanship both inside and out, the decoration and proportion of the roofs, are truly wonderful to behold in every detail. Finally, they are so excellent in their art that every kind of carving, fitting, adjusting, and fortifying in their buildings leaves nothing to be desired. Thus in the construction of a fine chest or casket, they fit and join together the wood and boards in such a way that the joints are invisible and the wood appears to be fine-drawn, as if it were but one board or piece of wood.

After this comes the art of working iron, principally for the offensive weapons that the Japanese prize so highly. This art competes with the previous one as regards nobility and esteem, and there arise great disputes among them whether this art or architecture in wood occupies the first place among all the mechanical arts. In olden days there used to be great armourers who are very famous in this art, because their weapons are now of high value for their perfection in cutting and everything else — scimitars, daggers, the blades of lances and war-scythes,[4] arrowheads, and others that are valued. Some swords and daggers, as we have

---

[1] Practically all this material — linear measurements, the laying down of *tatami*, the transfer of houses, etc. — has already been mentioned in Book I, chapters 8 and 12.

[2] *Vocabulario*, f. 255v: '*Tenshu*. A multi-storeyed tower made of wood inside Japanese fortresses.' Each storey of the donjon generally had one roof on each of its four sides, plus two eave-like projecting roofs on opposite sides, thus making a total of eight roofs. As Rodrigues observes, such buildings looked truly magnificent, and Fróis (in *TCJ*, pp. 131–8) ecstatically describes the castles of Gifu, Azuchi, and Osaka. See plates 27 and 28.

[3] Rodrigues has already mentioned this point on p. 238, where he notes that besieged warriors performed the *sakazuki* ritual before dispatching themselves. His wording here is reminiscent of Fróis's dramatic report (in *TCJ*, p. 103) about Nobunaga's death in 1582. Caught by surprise, he fought for a while, and then retired to commit *seppuku* in the burning temple building. '… of this man, who made everyone tremble … , there did not remain even a small hair which was not reduced to dust and ashes.'

[4] *Vocabulario*, f. 174v: '*Naginata*. A kind of halberd, the blade of which is like a sickle.' Avila Girón (in *TCJ*, p. 142) describes this formidable weapon as 'blades fixed to hafts which they wield like broadswords. They are called *naginata* and the length of the blade is four spans or less, while the haft is some six spans long.' Illustrations in Sasama, *Nihon*, p. 238.

Plate 27: Himeji Castle, first built in the 14th century. Hideyoshi enlarged it, adding the magnificent *tenshu*, or donjon, in 1581. 'In the castle . . . there is generally a tower or a very strong, high and big donjon of five, six, or seven storeys, which can be seen from afar . . . it is a truly wonderful and magnificent building, strong and impregnable.' p. 323. *Beatrice Bodart-Bailey.*

Plate 28: The roofs of the donjon of Himeji Castle. 'Such a keep will have eight roofs around the sides of each storey.' p. 323. *Beatrice Bodart-Bailey.*

noted, are worth many thousands of crowns, and even nowadays throughout the whole kingdom there are craftsmen who are very skilful with these weapons. Experience has shown that Japanese weapons are in general the best and cut better than any others. One of their ordinary swords can cut a man through the middle in two parts with the greatest of ease, while a dagger (or sword of one-and-a-half, at most two, spans in length) will part a man's head from his neck, and a lance will do the same, for their blades are such that they not only wound with a thrust but also cut like swords. An arrow with a special head that has a wide moon-like mouth made for the purpose, will cut a man's throat when it is the product of a distinguished craftsman who is esteemed for this.[1]

Nor are the men whom we would call goldsmiths less skilled in the art of working gold, silver, and copper, and they are superior to the Chinese and other nations in this Orient as regards their excellence, the type of work, and the mixture of copper with silver and gold with which they make a third metal that they call black copper.[2] This is highly esteemed among the Japanese and they use it to make a certain instrument that they insert in sword

[1] There were half-a-dozen types of arrow heads with a moon-like form, although most were intended for use in hunting animals rather than in battle. See Sasama, *Nihon*, p. 223, for illustrations.

[2] Possibly a reference to *shakudo*, or *unkin*, used in the manufacture of sword mounts. Fine *shakudo* contains about 5% gold and is a perfect ground for inlaid gold, silver, and copper work. Boger, *Traditional Arts*, pp. 103–4; Rein, *Industries*, pp. 438–9.

scabbards and which is decorated with a flower or animal carved by very skilled craftsmen.[1] These men are highly regarded and enjoy much esteem in the art of working gold and silver. This sort of engraving various trees, plants, birds, water and land animals, and ancient legends on copper is extremely fine and lifelike in every detail. They greatly esteem such engraving done by hand, but this is not so of work that has been cast, however good it may be. They are incomparable in embellishing an engraving with gold and silver, or inlaying gold with silver, and silver and black copper with gold, and all of it engraved. This is something both excellent and attractive, and work of this kind is found only among the Japanese. A genuine, good, and choice item made by craftsmen outstanding in this art and esteemed by the Japanese has yet to find its way to Europe. Some crosses of black copper and silver inlaid with gold have gone over, but these were made by some of the many ordinary craftsmen throughout the kingdom.

In Miyako there is a certain family that is the head of this art. They make the things of the king, the *kubō* and Lord of Tenka, and other lords. However small it may be, their work is highly prized and valued both for the skill and excellence of the craftsmanship, and also for the perfection and combination of the materials. This family is called Gotō, and we saw some of their work that was of indescribable perfection and skill.[2] Even if such a small and minute thing were cast, it would not seem possible to produce so delicate a piece of work, all apart from the outstanding perfection of the parts. This is not exaggerated or excessive, and indeed it falls short of what could be said in all truth about the matter.

There is a universal art throughout the whole kingdom that has something in common with painting. This is the art of varnishing, which we call here *uruxar*, from the word *urushi*,[3] the varnish made from the gum of certain trees. They tap the trunk at a certain time of the year and draw off an excellent gum that is used as varnish. These trees are also found in China, Cauchi, Cambodia, and Siam. But of all these nations the Japanese stand supreme in this art, for they are so skilful that they can make a varnished object look as if it were made of smooth shiny ivory. The art is practised throughout the whole kingdom because all their tableware, such as bowls, tables, and other vessels and utensils, as well as the tables and trays from which they eat are painted with this varnish. The varnish is so hard and well applied that no kind of water, however hot it may be, damages these vessels and bowls at all if it falls on them, for they are just as if they were made of glazed clay. They also apply this varnish to the scabbards of katana and daggers, the handles of lances, and the sheaths of their blades, and a multitude of other things. For this reason it is the most universal art of the kingdom because it is used in practically everything.[4]

---

[1] *Vocabulario*, f. 340v: '*Kōgai-bitsu*. Certain place in the scabbard of a katana, in which is put the instrument called *kōgai*.' For these two small knives, called *kōgai* and *kozuka*, inserted within pockets let into the scabbard, see Robinson, *Arts*, pp. 69–70.

[2] Renowned for its skill in metalwork, this family was founded by Gotō Yūjō (1435–1512), who was employed in Miyako by the Ashikaga shogun. In Rodrigues's time the two outstanding members of the family were Eijō (d. 1617) and Kōjō (d. 1620). The family set the fashion in sword fittings until the mid-19th century. Boger, *Traditional Arts*, p. 104; illustrations in Robinson, *Arts*, p. 76.

[3] That is, the Japanese word was incorporated into the Portuguese spoken in Japan. Valignano uses another Japanese word in this way, *satorar*, adapted from the Japanese term *satori*, or Zen enlightenment. Valignano, *Sumario*, p. 62.

[4] Agreeing with Rodrigues, Vivero y Velasco (*Relación*, f. 72v) declares that Japanese lacquerware is without equal in any nation. The lacquer is produced from the sap of trees belonging to the Rhus family. Kaempfer (*Kaempfer's Japan*, p. 64) calls the lacquer tree 'the most noble tree of this country' and lists where it is to be found. An illustrated description of lacquerware is found in Casal, 'Japanese Art Lacquer', and Boger, *Traditional Arts*, pp. 353–64.

This has a certain affinity to the art of painting in that some of these craftsmen gild in a special way the finest examples of this work in the discovered world. Using pure gold powder, they paint various objects in which they set flowers made of gold and silver leaf and mother-of-pearl. They are so splendidly made that they have no superior, but they are very costly and only lords and the wealthy can afford them. There is, it is true, a cheaper kind of this work that looks more or less the same, but it is vastly different as regards workmanship, gloss, and price. The gentry and honourable people of the kingdom make much use of this type. Some escritoires and vessels of this kind were taken to Europe, but they were very inferior to the best of this second kind. There are also fakes that can deceive those who do not know much about this art.[1]

Although the Chinese have a large variety of gilded things and use a great deal of this varnish, they highly admire and value the gilt and varnish work of Japan, because for all their skill they cannot equal the Japanese in this art. The tree from which this varnish is taken bears a fruit that the Japanese boil to obtain a kind of wax from which they make their candles, and there is a great abundance of this in the kingdom.[2]

They also have the art of making fans from various materials for use all the year around. Men and women use them principally in the summer and the hot season, and nobody would go out into the street without one in his hand or tucked in his sash. This is especially true of bonzes and shaven people, who carry one out of politeness and as something to hold in their hands.

The ordinary fans are of cardboard made for this purpose by special craftsmen, while the framework of others may be of bamboo or precious wood. Those in ordinary and common use are painted with various suitable pictures or some legends or ancient palaces and other interesting things. Some are silvered, while others are beautifully speckled with gold, silver, and various other kinds of colours, for they are used throughout the kingdom and by every class of person, high and low. There are also fans gilded on both sides and bearing excellent pictures, and these are highly prized when the pictures are executed by accomplished and skilful artists. There is a custom of having a celebrated and fine calligrapher write on the fans a wholesome maxim, epigram, couplet, or sonnet of China, inscribed with the writer's name or mark or with his stamp or seal. As an aid to the memory, other fans bear a picture of the sixty-six kingdoms of Japan with all the islands in its seas and the boundaries separating the provinces and regions into which each kingdom is divided. Finally, people who have business matters and other things that they wish to remember write them down on their fans as a reminder against the time when they will be needed, for they are always carrying these fans about in their hands, opening them, shutting them, and looking at them.[3]

These fans are one of the usual gifts that they send each other as a sign of friendship, and to some extent they correspond to our gloves because they always carry them in their hands. They have other big and long ones used by the pages in hot weather to fan guests

---

[1] For the various techniques employed in *maki-e*, or gold lacquering, see Casal, 'Japanese Art Lacquer', part 1, pp. 16–22. The Japanese envoys gave the Archbishop of Evora a small lacquered box, and then presented a lacquered casket to Philip II on 14 November 1584. Fróis, *Première Ambassade*, pp. 45, 88. For other early examples of Japanese lacquerwork in Europe, see Boyer, *Japanese Export Lacquer*, along with a useful account (pp. 43–68) of lacquer techniques through the ages.

[2] See p. 107, n. 3.

[3] The folding fan is called *ogi*, while the rigid type is *uchiwa*. Fróis (*Tratado*, p. 110) stresses the universal use of fans in Japan. Rodrigues Giram (*Carta anua*, p. 104) mentions that Japanese desiring to become Christians would

while they eat and to fan the lords while they are speaking informally and resting. On public and social occasions it is a great discourtesy for an inferior to fan himself in the presence of a lord or noble, for this would be taking much liberty and would show but scant respect. No noble or courtier, unless he be a bonze or a *kuge*, uses a fan in the presence of the Lord of Tenka, or the *kubō*.

When bonzes preach, they carry in their right hand a closed fan with which they strike the table in front of them within the pulpit, instead of using the hand as we do. When in their fervour they begin to speak quickly in their sermons, they strike the table rapidly with their fans as if they were beating time with what they are saying. At the end they conclude by giving a great blow with the fan instead of the hand.[1] They do not use gestures or movements of the hand or body, as we do, in order to make a point, for this greatly astonishes them. Instead, they use special adverbs that greatly abound in their language, for their noise and sound explain the matter without any gestures or movement of the hands.[2] They use only the fan instead of a blow with the hand.

There are various other mechanical arts practised by craftsmen and are necessary for this nation, such as cobblers who produce sandals and makers of stockings of deer-skin and glove-leather, which are widely used throughout the kingdom. They produce some of this glove-leather handsomely painted with various colours and pictures, and these are used for stockings of young boys and children, and also for a certain kind of garment or jerkin worn in the countryside.[3]

The art of the dyers is also highly developed and widely practised among them, for they not only dye lengths of silk, cotton, and linen with various colours, but they are also wont to dye them and then add various roses and flowers of different colours on to the background of whatever colour. There are people who are very skilled in this art, especially with regard to silk robes. After the piece has been woven white, they dye it any desired colour with these flowers and many other patterns of various colours. They take great care with this work, for it is difficult to do and requires time. They have a certain kind of very strong paste with which they stop up the parts and blank spaces that they do not want to dye with that colour. After dyeing the desired parts, they remove the paste and cover up the part that has been dyed. Then they proceed to dye the remaining part as they wish, for the paste does not come off when it is dipped in the dye nor does it allow the dye to penetrate to the part that it is covering.[4]

They also practise the art of weaving lengths of silk with flowers, birds, and any other

---

write the *Pater Noster* and *Ave Maria* on their fans to remind them of these prayers. Valignano confirms this (*Sumario*, p. 164), adding the Creed and the Ten Commandments to the list. For descriptions and illustrations of fans, see Casal, 'Lore'; useful summary in Boger, *Traditional Arts*, pp. 307–10.

[1] Ricci (*Fonti*, I, p. 35, and *China*, p. 25) also compares the Chinese (and Japanese) custom of always carrying a fan to the European habit of holding gloves in the hands. For Fróis's accounts of Buddhist sermons in 1565, see *TCJ*, pp. 347, 352.

[2] Rodrigues describes such adverbs in some detail in *Arte grande*, ff. 73v–74. He tells readers that not only do these terms denote an action (as do European adverbs), but some are onomatopoeic or at least suggest the action in question. He provides some 60 examples of adverbs in duplicate form, such as *bata-bata*, 'helter-skelter', and *biku-biku*, 'timidly'. His remark that such adverbs take the place of European gestures is perceptive.

[3] Avila Girón (*Relación*, p. 23) mentions these *tabi*, or stockings made of soft leather, and describes how coloured patterns are printed on them.

[4] Avila Girón (*Relación*, p. 22) makes a passing reference to this resist method of dyeing, practised 'by putting paste in a very curious way on the parts which they do not wish to dye and then the cloth is extremely colourful.' Further details of this technique in Boger, *Traditional Arts*, pp. 284–5.

patterns as they do in China, and in the city of Miyako alone there are 5,000 silk looms on which these lengths are woven.[1] As their robes are of a certain size, the lengths of silk, silk floss, cotton, and hemp are all made to a certain size that will exactly make the robe of one person. For this reason, they do not sell it in ells as we do, but in complete lengths enough for one robe or garment, and these are given as gifts.[2] We refer here to the actual robe and not to all the clothes that they wear on the body, and these robes are like gowns with long sleeves.

[1] See p. 168, n. 3.
[2] Even today department stores in Japan sell gift packages containing just enough material to make up one shirt.

CHAPTER 4

THE LIBERAL ARTS OF JAPAN, AND FIRSTLY THE ART OF LETTERS

Among the liberal arts of the Chinese and Japanese, the first and principal place is taken by the art of their letters. Their invention and origin belong to China, whence they spread to the other nations that now use them, such as the Koreans, Japanese, Luchu, Cauchi, and a certain part of northern Tartary bordering on China. These letters are indeed one of the wonderful things to be found in the kingdom of China and in the other nations that use them, and you cannot form any adequate idea of them unless you see them or have experience of them at close hand. For you must know that the Chinese, Japanese, and the other nations that use these Chinese letters and characters, do not have an alphabet of separate letters like the European one. Instead, they are accustomed to writing with characters and figures that express things. Each word has one of these letters, and this is a token or sign of the thing. Some are like hieroglyphics of them, and of words and ideas, but not like Egyptian hieroglyphics that conveyed a meaning allegorically and enigmatically through certain pictures, human and animal figures, and others.[1] They use instead characters that spontaneously express their meaning.

There are as many of these characters as there are words in the Chinese language. They are like the ancient Hebrew letters that were lost in the captivity of the two tribes,[2] for each of these letters expressed a thing. What is even more surprising and apparently incredible is that as there are as many of them as there are words in the Chinese language (some seventy or eighty thousand of these figures can be found in their dictionaries), they discovered a way to invent this large number of different figures. It is also astonishing that they are learnt without great difficulty and are commonly used throughout the whole kingdom, both in scientific books and novels, as well as in letters and everything else.[3]

What is even more astonishing and seems almost impossible to human reason is that it is very seldom indeed to find somebody among the Chinese who does not know enough of

[1] Rodrigues is, of course, speculating – hieroglyphics, though they fascinated scholars from the Renaissance onwards, were not deciphered until the 19th century. Rodrigues's fellow Jesuit, the polymath Athanasius Kircher (1602–80) spent many years attempting a decipherment.

[2] There is no evidence that Hebrew letters or hieroglyphics existed before the captivity of the two tribes of Judea and Simeon by the Chaldeans.

[3] Ricci (*Fonti*, I, pp. 36–7, and *China*, pp. 26–7) compares Chinese characters with Egyptian hieroglyphics, and places the number of the former between 70,000 and 80,000. Nobody knew all these characters, but a knowledge of 10,000 was needed to write well. Mendoza (*History*, I, p. 121) and Cruz (in Boxer, *South China*, p. 162) mention the figures 6,000 and 'more than 5,000', but these presumably refer to the number in common use. Magalhães (*New History*, p. 68) offers an exact total of 54,409 letters, 'which express what they signifie with so much grace, vivacity

them for ordinary use. This is true of both the high and the lowly, peasants, artisans, country people and city dwellers, and even the fishermen who live with their families on the seas and rivers in their boats that serve them as ordinary houses. They learn these letters when they are children, and the length of time devoted to this study depends on their plans for profiting by them or following another pursuit. Their antiquity, according to the copious Chinese annals that they regard as authentic, goes back about 3,900 years up to the present year of 1620. This would be about a hundred years after the Confusion of Tongues in Babylon.[1] Thus they are as old as China itself, and they seem to have been the first letters in the world as soon as it began to be populated. Hence their invention must be attributed to those ancient Fathers even before the Flood, for according to what is said about the ancient Hebrew letters in use at the time of Solomon (they say that they were the invention of our first Father, Adam), there is a partial similarity between them in that each one separately expresses a thing, and in the various distinguishing figures, dots, and lines, or strokes of which they are composed. Not only is each of them a word or term expressing a thing, but there are also some that represent verbs and adjectives, and just one of these letters expresses a sentence or is a complete clause signifying true or false. Most of them have many different meanings, and the same letter is sometimes a verb, sometimes a noun, according to its position and context. The people who can best read, write, and understand the various hidden meanings locked up in the letters, and arrange their composition elegantly and place them correctly in their proper position, are regarded as sages and doctors. They are rather like the Hebrew scribes who were the doctors and experts of the Law, for they could skilfully read and write the characters, strokes, and dots used in ancient times, as well as understand the abundant meaning contained in a few letters.

The Chinese maintain that their first inventor, or the man who introduced and taught the use of these letters and characters, was one of their first sages, called Fuxi (in Japanese, Fukki), the ruler of one of the nine tribes that founded China. They number him as one of their first three kings who fashioned the nation and were contemporaries. He taught philosophy, natural magic, and astrology, conveying his teaching by figures, symbols, and odd and even numbers like the ancient Chaldeans. He is thus called the Heavenly King as he taught the things of Heaven.[2] The second was called Shennong (Shinnō in Japanese). He

and efficacy'. He later declares (p. 77) that Chinese is easier than any European language. Navarrete (*Travels*, II, p. 170) mentions a dictionary of 70,000 characters, remarking that a good scholar should know more than 10,000. Acosta (*Natural and Moral History*, II, p. 398) reports that a scholar should know no less than 120,000 characters, rightly adding, 'A strange and prodigious thing.' Six Chinese characters appeared for the first time in European publications in various books of Jesuit letters, e.g., *Cartas*, I, ff. 4–4v, reproducing those contained in a letter, dated 23 September 1555, by Balthasar Gago in Hirado. The characters are also given in Ruiz-de-Medina, *Documentos*, I, p. 564, and Lach, *Asia*, I, pp. 679–80. Three characters are contained in Escalante, *Discurso*, ff. 62–62v, but they are too distorted for recognition; the same is true of the characters in Mendoza, *History*, I, pp. 121–2.

[1] Rodrigues dates (see p. 11, n. 7) the Confusion of Tongues about 2400 BC. If the characters go back 3,900 years before 1620–21, when he wrote this part of the *History*, then they would have originated, as Rodrigues says, about a century after the Confusion.

[2] The traditional dates of the reign of Fuxi, the first of the five legendary emperors (see p. 24, n. 5), are 2953–2838 BC. He is said to have introduced hunting, fishing, music, cooking, the calendar, and written characters into China. Hirth, *Ancient Chinese History*, pp. 7–10; Giles, *Chinese Biographical Dictionary*, pp. 233–4.

Aparato breve, f. 12, has the following amplified account: 'Their records state that they call the first father of all men Pangu. He had three sons [*marginal note*: In general they call them *sanwang*, and in Japanese *sankō*, meaning the Three Supreme Kings]. They call the first by the honorific name of Tianwang (in Japanese, Tenkō), meaning Heavenly King; the second one, Diwang (in Japanese, Chikō), or Terrestrial King; the third one, Renwang (in Japanese, Jinkō), the Human King or King of Men. Each of them had a certain number of sons or families under him. Nine taught the way of rearing animals and working the land to grow food, for until then they lived on the fruit of the trees. For this reason they called him the Terrestrial King, for he taught the things concerning Earth.[1] The third was called Huangdi (Kōtei in Japanese), who taught the people to live in community, in houses and settlements, and to develop a civil and social life with laws, social customs, and dress. He brought order to the nation by establishing offices and administration. For up to that time the people dwelt in tree huts and in caves in the ground, and used the leaves of plants and trees for clothing. Thus they called him the Human King, because he taught them social matters concerning human relations.[2]

After this Fuxi there came other inventors of various sorts of letters, and each invented them with various shapes and figures. Some were made up of lines and strokes composing a figure, and this expressed various things according to the different ways and positions in which they were placed. Other letters imitated things, such as the arc of the moon with its two horns or points representing the moon, and a circle with a dot in the middle representing the sun.[3] There were other painted figures of animals that, when placed in a certain position, order, and number, expressed one thing, but placed differently they meant another thing. Others had the shape of trees and plants, which expressed things when they were arranged and placed in various ways. Finally there were other letters like ours that were connected or strung together, scattered and arranged among themselves in various ways and shapes. These served as letters expressing things. All this is recorded even now in Chinese books dealing with their antiquity, where they have many of them painted with their meanings. Among all of these letters, however, the most famous and suitable ones were those made up of various lines, strokes, and dots, and these are the letters that have lasted to this day. They seem to have been the first of all letters, and later in the course of time they have been perfected as regards their excellence and the depiction of their shape.[4]

As this composition of simple strokes, dots, and lines was too limited for them to be

---

families or leaders in this Orient originated from the descendants of the third king, and each of these nine had charge of a certain number of smaller families, which altogether totalled 140. These were the people who first populated this kingdom. At first they occupied only a small amount of territory, but as their numbers increased they extended over many of the neighbouring parts. They divided the territory they had populated into nine states according to the nine leaders or tribes. The Chinese call this Jiuzhou, and the Japanese, Kyūshū, meaning 'nine states'. This was the first name of this kingdom after being populated. We believe without any doubt that this first man was Noah.' Rodrigues then identifies the three sons as Shem, Ham, and Japheth.

[1] Shennong was conceived through the influence of a dragon. He reigned 2838–2698 BC, and is credited with the introduction of medicine and agriculture. Hirth, *Ancient Chinese History*, pp. 10–12; Giles, *Chinese Biographical Dictionary*, p. 646. The Portuguese text omits the Japanese version of his name and reads, '… whom the Japanese call, who taught the way…'. I have inserted the name Shinnō, which Rodrigues later gives on p. 349.

[2] Huangdi, the Yellow Emperor, reigned 2698–2598 BC, and is credited with introducing armour, wheeled vehicles, pottery, and a systematized written language. *Huangdi nei jing su wen* ('The Yellow Emperor's Classic of Internal Medicine') is attributed to him. Rada (in Boxer, *South China*, pp. 278–9) briefly mentions the Heavenly, Terrestrial, and Human Kings. Hirth, *Ancient Chinese History*, pp. 12–24; Giles, *Chinese Biographical Dictionary*, p. 338; Se-Ma Ts'ien, *Mémoires*, I, pp. 25–37. I have again supplied the Japanese version of the emperor's name, given later by Rodrigues on p. 350.

[3] Rodrigues displays his expert knowledge of the subject, as the character for 'sun' originally was indeed a circle with a dot inside, but later developed into its present form of a vertical oblong with a horizontal line through the centre. The circle and dot was also used as the symbol for the Sun in Greek, Arabic and Western astronomical texts, and is still so used.

[4] Magalhães (*New History*, p. 69) also mentions the origin of the characters depicting the sun and moon; he then goes on to talk about compound characters. For the origin and development of Chinese writing, see Wieger, *Chinese Characters*, especially pp. 5, 9, 165, 311.

able to form such a multitude of letters only by varying and combining their parts, they invented another composition in addition to this simple and primitive one in order to express other things not included in the first system. This is to form a letter from these simple letters (which were sometimes already composed of two) along with another letter, thus making only one letter out of two. This is done with great ingenuity and skill and not at all arbitrarily, but rather by going through various materials in the following way. For example, to express 'Heaven' (which they believe is fluid and the region of infinite air), they write the letter 'big' and over it add the letter meaning 'number one'. This letter, made up of 'one' and 'big', means 'the unique greatness' or 'Heaven', because Heaven is the biggest thing in existence. Then to write things connected with Heaven, its qualities and effects, they add another letter to 'Heaven' such as 'sun' or 'moon', and thus from the two letters form one expressing something to do with Heaven. When they want to express light, brightness, to dawn, to become clear, the morning, to be evident or obvious, they write the letter 'moon' at the side of the letter 'sun', and thus form one letter having the above-mentioned meanings, for the sun and the moon, the two celestial luminaries, are the source of light.[1]

In the same way, they go through the elements. Everything connected with fire, its qualities and effects (such as 'to burn', etc.) is expressed by the letter 'fire' along with another letter at its side. Things connected with the air or wind, which they believe is in the place of air because the air is the sky, are written with the letter 'wind' along with another. Things connected with 'earth' and 'water' are written in the same way. In this fashion they run through the substances and species of things such as metals, birds, plants, fishes, animals, rocks, etc. They take a generic letter and to this they add another, forming from the two letters one that expresses one of the species contained in such-and-such a genus. Thus every kind of tree and wooden thing connected with it is expressed by the letter 'wood' or 'tree', along with another.[2]

This combination of some letters with others has built up a skilful and scientific etymology of words, their meanings, properties, and emphasis, for not only can be seen in the letter the meaning of the thing but also the etymology of the word. These letters are quite admirable not only in all the respects that we have mentioned but also in their elegance and position one after another. Thus to learn these letters is also to learn at the same time natural and moral sciences and the art of rhetoric, for these are contained in the letters along with their many other properties.[3] This has so greatly quickened the wits of these nations using these letters here at the end of the world, where the people are out of contact with, and have no knowledge of, other world sages, that it seems we should attribute the sharp wits of the Chinese, Japanese, and Koreans to the exercise of these letters. The system also develops quite remarkably a retentive memory of things, as the letters are signs expressing the things in an almost natural way. If someone forgets, the mere sight of the letter reminds him of its meaning and significance when he sees the combination of one figure with another. They make up these combinations in four ways: by placing a suitable letter at the side of another, or on top of the other with one on top of the other, or below it, or inside the middle of the letter, for there is much empty space inside for this.

---

[1] Rodrigues uses the same example in *Arte grande*. See p. 334, n. 2, below, and also Plate 30.

[2] This explanation is correct. The generic part of a character is called in English the radical, of which there are generally reckoned to be some 200. The ideographs made up of one character are called *wen* in Chinese, while compound characters are known as *zi*. Further details in Wieger, *Chinese Characters*, p. 10.

[3] Writing in 1584, Mexia (in *TCJ*, p. 176) makes the same point: '… a person learns rhetoric and good breeding along with the language.'

According to their records, the Japanese received these Chinese letters from the kingdom of Korea in the Year of the Lord 285, or 290 according to other accounts, in the fifteenth or twentieth year of the reign of their sixteenth king, named Ōjin Tennō.[1] He is also known by the name of Hachiman Daibosatsu. The Japanese conquered the kingdom of Korea and made it a tributary in his time. Korea had long been a flourishing kingdom, and as it is very near, the Japanese had made earlier contact with this kingdom by trade and war than with China. Up to that time the Japanese had lacked the use of letters.

The Japanese also adopted the Chinese names of these letters or figures. These were according to the Chinese language, and this language is nothing more than the nouns and words of these letters. Both nouns and verbs are usually made up of one syllable, or sometimes two, but they are so corruptly pronounced according to the Japanese rendering that they bear little or no similarity to the present Chinese language, except for a few words. For the Chinese of today has changed somewhat from the ancient language spoken in that epoch. In addition to this Chinese name, they also put another Japanese one in their native language according to the meaning of the letter, and all the other nations that have taken over Chinese letters have done the same.[2] Each of these nations reads the same book, epistle, or anything at all written with these letters, according to its own native language, but all form the same idea. No nation can understand the words of other nations, but only its own. This is rather like the numerical ciphers among the European nations speaking different languages, or like the figures or characters of the celestial signs, the planets, and conjunctions, used by mathematicians. For each nation pronounces in its own language with a variety of words the symbols of numbers, signs, and planets, but they always mean and are worth the same idea in all these countries.[3]

This has resulted in a great benefit for these nations, because the books of each of them are written in these letters that are common to all, although they use different languages. It follows from this that they can also communicate among themselves, as indeed they do, by using only the same letters and books and not speaking by word. Thus embassies sent from one country to another communicate through the medium of these letters. Although they may not have an interpreter when they meet, they can make themselves understood through

[1] For the introduction of writing into Japan, see p. 47, n. 1; for Ōjin Tennō, see p. 97, n. 3. Rodrigues appears to have taken this sentence from his *Arte breve*, f. 1.

[2] The Chinese pronunciation of characters is called the *on* reading in Japanese, while the original indigenous pronunciation is the *kun* reading. In *Arte grande* (in *TCJ*, p. 172), Rodrigues calls them the *koe* and *yomi* readings. As a general rule, when a character appears in writing in combination with another, it is pronounced according to the *on* reading; when it stands alone, according to the *kun* reading. In his *Arte grande*, f. 185v, Rodrigues further explains that there are three types of *koe*, or *on*, readings according to the different pronunciations in the Han, Wu, and Tang dynasties. He gives as an example the Japanese word *akiraka*, 'bright', whose *koe* readings are *mei*, *myō*, and *min*, according to context. For a general account of Chinese characters and their readings, see *KEJ*, IV, pp. 141–3.

[3] The early Europeans in Japan and China often mention the fact that Asian nations using Chinese characters could read the same books but not speak the same language: Xavier, *Epistolae*, II, p. 292; Mendoza, *History*, I, p. 122; Cruz, in Boxer, *South China*, pp. 73, 162; Valignano, *Historia*, p. 254; Carletti, *My Voyage*, pp. 132, 165; Ricci, *Fonti*, I, p. 37, and *China*, p. 28. Acosta (*Natural and Moral History*, II, p. 398) also refers to the common numerical figures shared by all Europeans as an example of the universal nature of written Chinese: 'for this figure 8, wheresoever it be, signifies eight, although the French call this number of one sort and the Spaniards of another.' In this respect the characters were also useful within China itself. As Escalante, *Discurso*, f. 62v, explains, 'They all generally understand each other through writing as the same figure or character is used by all to signify something. They speak different languages in most of their provinces and so do not understand other people, just like Basques and Valencians.'

using only these letters, and through these letters they speak by writing down the idea or what they want to express.[1]

This in fact happens among the Chinese, Japanese, Koreans, and others who use these letters, although their own languages are so different. Hence books dealing with the things of our Holy Faith printed in China with their letters can be used by the Japanese and these nations, and it is not necessary to translate them into the native language of each nation. This is especially true of the *literati* who profess these letters. For this reason, all the books dealing with natural and moral sciences, ancient and modern history, and everything else written in either prose or verse, can be used by the Japanese, Koreans, and other peoples just as do the Chinese themselves. And the Chinese read the books of Korea and Japan that are written with their letters.

Although the number of these letters and figure is, as we have noted, as great as seventy or eighty thousand because each word has a letter, nevertheless for ordinary use and to understand the ordinary books of the schools, sciences, and things of the social and secular world, it is not necessary to learn and know them all, for it is usually enough to know ten thousand or a little more.[2] For if these are known well, many of the others are also known by their composition. If it is necessary to understand a certain one, they look it up in the copious and well-arranged dictionaries. These are classified according to their subject matter or in some other way, and with this exercise they are easily known.[3] The truth of this is borne out by their general use throughout the entire kingdom of China by every type of person, as we noted above.

In addition, to learn these letters and figures is not merely, as among us, to know how to read and use them as signs, but also to learn at the same time science and rhetoric with their composition and elegant style. For this reason, this nation has come to form with this kind of letters a beautiful, elegant, and compendious style, for they can say with a few words or even a few syllables just as much as we in our languages can express in many long speeches, for in their language each syllable is a word, noun, verb, adverb, interjection, conjunction, preposition, or any other part of speech. All their eloquence is found in this elegant, brief, and clear manner of composition, and in placing and arranging the letters with each other, and it is adorned with various figures and metaphors. Hence they have also many compendious maxims of two, three, or four syllables that in our language form only one word.[4]

Their way of writing and arranging the letter is contrary to ours, for they write and read from top to bottom, from right to left, so that their books begin where ours end, and end

---

[1] Cruz (in Boxer, *South China*, p. 162) gives a practical instance of communicating through the written, rather than spoken, language, a practice called *hitsudan* in Japanese. When his ship reached a port of Cauchi-China, the purser handed a list of required provisions to the local natives, explaining that they could understand his written, but not spoken, requests. Ricci (*Fonti*, I, p. 37, and *China*, p. 27) remarks that Chinese is essentially a written language. When a person's speech is not understood, he traces the characters on something with water, or with his finger in the air, or on the palm of the listener's hand.

[2] The text here has 'ten or a little more', an obvious slip for 10,000. For the number of Chinese characters, see p. 330, n. 3.

[3] The Jesuits themselves published at Nagasaki in 1598–9 *Rakuyōshū*, a dictionary of ideographs giving both their Chinese and Japanese readings. Laures, *Kirishitan Bunko*, pp. 58–60.

[4] Rodrigues seems to mean that the Japanese can express in a few syllables what Europeans say in one sentence, not one word. Concerning the brevity of Japanese, Caron (*True Description*, pp. 56–7) comments that 'truly it is admirable to see how full of substance, and with how few words these sort of writings are penned.'

Plate 29: The three styles of writing Japanese: *shin*; *gyō*; and *sō*. The characters read, *Nihon Kyōkai-shi*, 'The History of the Church of Japan', the title of Rodrigues's *History*. 'Each of the letters has three forms or ways of being written, although it always retains the same name, just as among us the same letter is written in various ways.' pp. 336–7. Rodrigues, *This Island of Japon*.

where ours begin.[1] It is not at all tiresome to learn and write them, for there is a certain kind of metre and attractive cadence in the Chinese language, and they learn and read them by half-singing them like verse. Their manner of writing is more like painting than writing inasmuch as painting and writing go practically togther. There is variety among the letters, both as regards their beauty, attractiveness, and also their style. The good writing of renowned calligraphers is more highly esteemed than a painting. They possess examples of the writing and lettering of people in ancient times who were renowned for their writing, and they esteem and value them as jewels. Even the most noble and important people take pride in writing well.[2]

We will now speak about the shape and delineation of these letters or characters of China, Japan, Korea, and the other nations that use them. Each of the letters has three

---

[1] The early Europeans often referred to the top-to-bottom way of writing Japanese; e.g., Xavier, *Epistolae*, II, p. 27; Fróis, *Tratado*, p. 212; Carletti, *My Voyage*, p. 132.

[2] The importance attached to good calligraphy often appears in Murasaki, *The Tale of Genji*, in which Prince Genji carefully studies the writing in letters from his various lovers. Waley (in *Pillow Book*, p. 10) remarks, 'it was as indispensable that a Japanese mistress should write beautifully as that Mrs Gladstone should be sound about episcopal succession'. See also Morris, *World*, pp. 183–7, on this subject.

Plate 30: Examples of written characters, showing in the left-hand column the generic 'radicals' meaning big, sun, fire, and tree, and then in the other columns words of related meaning formed by adding other characters to these radicals. 'For example, to express "Heaven" …, they write the letter "big" and over it add the letter meaning "number one". … When they want to express light …, they write the letter "moon" at the side of the letter "sun".' p. 333. Rodrigues, *This Island of Japon*.

forms or ways of being written, although it always retains the same name, just as among us the same letter is written in various ways. The first and proper way is the Roman, chancellary, or printed style in which everything is the same. Another is court hand or, as they say, notary script, which is a different style. Just as there are various ways and styles of writing the same letter in our alphabet, so also with the Chinese letters. But it is somewhat different, because in all three styles the same character is used, but they are more or less abbreviated with greater or less neatness or with fewer strokes or dots.

They call these three general writing styles *zhen*, *cao*, and *xing*, and in Japanese they are known as *shin*, *sō*, and *gyō*.[1] The first style, *zhen* or *shin*, meaning 'true', is the proper and original shape of the letter. It is well made and fashioned, and everything is done to perfection. All the strokes and dots are separate and in good order like a printed letter, and all of them are of the same size. Every kind of book is printed in this style. Even in this script there are various styles and fashions, but changes are made only as regard the style and elegance and not the actual shape of the letter. Thus one hand is admired more than another on account of a certain elegance that it possesses.

The second style (or the third in the order given above) is called *xing* or *gyō*, meaning 'to walk'.[2] The letters have the same form as before except for some alterations. The various

---

[1] The three styles of writing are known as the square, intermediate, and cursive respectively. Rodrigues (*Arte grande*, f. 55) goes into greater detail.

[2] More accurately, *gyō* means 'go, proceed', rather than merely 'walk'.

parts are not so clearly written and are joined to one another in what we would call a cursive script. This style is generally used for prologues of books, and when writing maxims and inscriptions on panels and fans, as well as for poems and things of that sort. There are various styles that they admire very much, and the valuable script of celebrated ancient scribes, and even modern ones, is written is this style.

The third style (the second in the order given above) is called *cao* or *sō*, meaning 'grass', and is even more flowing. It is the same as the first and second styles but with less strokes, and the letters are abbreviated and joined to each other. A person not well versed in this style may often fail to recognize a letter, because it bears but slight resemblance to its original form. This script is also used in writing prologues of books, inscriptions, and various other things, and it has many variations. The Japanese do not use the *shin* style in their social and ordinary dealings, for in Japan it is employed by the scholars of the sects, such as the bonzes and members of the Judō,[1] the sect of the Chinese *literati*, and by others in their books and commentaries and in the printing of books. Instead, they use the second or third writing styles, *gyō* and *sō*, in their letter-writing and other social matters. This is what the children learn to read and write at school, for this alone is in ordinary use throughout the kingdom. Those who know these two styles of writing will have no difficulty in recognizing and reading the original *shin* style.

This is why some people believe that the letters used by the Japanese are not Chinese, for they think that the *shin* style is Chinese and the two other styles are Japanese. In addition, the common people use certain syllables, also derived from Chinese letters, like an alphabet, as we shall presently explain.[2] But all these letters are Chinese and come from China.

---

[1] The Japanese term for Confucianism.
[2] A reference to the *kana* syllabaries, explained in the following chapter.

CHAPTER 5

ANOTHER SORT OF LETTERS, LIKE THE EUROPEAN ALPHABET
OF SEPARATE LETTERS, WHICH THE JAPANESE USE FOR
CERTAIN PURPOSES

Since its first foundation the kingdom of China has devoted itself to the study of letters and sciences that their first sages taught, for the administration of their nation depends on these as it is contained in them and has been founded on them. In all the Chinese reigns and monarchies people devoted themselves greatly to the study of letters and sciences, as may be seen in their annals. According to these, there have been many learned, renowned, and esteemed philosophers in China at various times. But it is in the present Daming, or Taimei, dynasty, which succeeded the Tartar dynasty 250 years ago,[1] that every type of person throughout the kingdom has given himself to the study of letters with much greater zeal. The reason for this is that the first king and founder of this dynasty did away with the noble ranks of the lords and grandees of the ancient families, in whose hands was the administration of the kingdom, and reduced them all to the status of ordinary common people, because they often instigated rebellion and treason.[2]

In order, therefore, that the kingdom might be governed by respected and prudent people of good customs, he decreed that all the common people (except for some notorious men) could advance to various literary degrees by means of letters and study. These degrees are arranged in various grades up to the highest one, and at the same time constitute the ranks of nobility and aristocracy in the royal household. This is done through various literary examinations and elections that he laid down for this purpose. He also decreed that only these people could be civil governors and magistrates of the kingdom, and hold all the offices and positions in the royal household. Each person by himself and by his own efforts was to rise to these positions by means of letters and not on account of the services and merits of his father and ancestors. These offices and ranks would die out with the same person, and their sons could not succeed to them.[3]

Hence all common people now devote themselves more than ever before to the study of letters with all possible diligence on account of the benefits and honours that can be obtained in this way. For these are the two motives that most animate a person to do something, however difficult it may be.

But in Japan letters do not carry this honour and advantage that would encourage their study, and so the secular gentry and people do not usually devote themselves to this with such zeal as do the Chinese. The *literati* of the sects are an exception, for they profess the

---

[1] That is, in 1368.
[2] A reference to Hongwu, the first Ming emperor. See p. 371, n. 1.
[3] Rodrigues has already mentioned this examination system on p. 35.

study of letters and thereby rise in rank and obtain ample means. The government in Japan depends more on weapons than letters, and, as we have said, they learn only those that will suffice in ordinary social use. But the common people experienced great difficulty in learning even the letters needed for ordinary use, such as informal letters, memos, and other such things.

So to make it easier and more convenient for the ordinary common people, in the Year of the Lord 810 a bonze named Kōbō Daishi,[1] the founder of the Shingon sect in Japan, took as a basis the five vowels of the Japanese language. In their due order these vowels are A, I, U, Ye, and Wo, as there is no E or O by itself.[2] These are joined with a consonant to form every type of syllable in the Japanese language, as every Japanese syllable is made up of a consonant and a concluding vowel. Then from among the Chinese letters of the third type, *sō*, mentioned above, he chose forty-seven letters, as there is that number of syllables and each Chinese letter is a syllable. He took away the original meaning of these letters and left them with only their name. He gave a name to each of them, and from them composed an alphabet of forty-seven elementary syllables.[3] When these are arranged together like the letters of our alphabet, the whole of the Japanese vocabulary can be conveniently written.

They arranged this alphabet in two ways. The first and principal way is to set down the forty-seven syllables, omitting numerical digits for each of these has its own character. They call this *i-ro-ha* because it begins with these syllables, and it runs as follows:

I	Ro	Ha	Ni	Ho	He	To
Chi	Ri	Nu	Ru	Wo	Wa	Ka
Yo	Ta	Re	So	Tsu	Ne	Na
Ra	Mu	U	Wi	No	O	Ku
Ya	Ma	Ke	Fu	Ko	Ye	Te
A	Sa	Ki	Yu	Me	Mi	Shi
Ye	Hi	Mo	Se	Su[4]		

In the second way, they arranged the same syllables by their five vowel sounds, placing below each vowel the syllables that end in that vowel. They are read back to front and from

[1] For Kōbō Daishi, see p. 95, n. 1. Rodrigues mentions him in connection with these letters in *Arte grande*, f. 55, and *Arte breve*, f. 6v.

[2] This is not true of modern pronunciation of Japanese. Early European accounts consistently refer to Vosaca and Yedo, instead of the modern spelling Osaka and Edo. Their references to Nobunanga (Nobunaga) and Firando (Hirado) indicate yet other changes in pronunciation.

[3] For the development of some of these *kana* letters from Chinese characters, see Sansom, *Japan*, p. 238. Thus the character for *chi*, 'wisdom', was simplified, deprived of its meaning, and now stands merely as a letter pronounced *chi*. Rodrigues fails to note here that there are in fact two types of *kana* letters: the cursive *hiragana* (attributed to Kōbō Daishi), and the angular *katakana* (attributed to Kibi Makibi, 693–775), but he makes this distinction in *Arte breve*, f. 6v. These *kana* letters transcribe foreign words and names better than do Chinese characters used for their phonetic value. Thus the enterprising Acosta (*Natural and Moral History*, II, pp. 400–401) asked a Chinese in Mexico to transcribe in characters a sentence in Spanish, 'whereupon the Chinois was long pensive.' Acosta observes that the Japanese can transcribe foreign words more easily by using their own kind of letters, that is, their *kana* script.

[4] Rodrigues fails to mention that the *i-ro-ha* table is an adaptation of a melancholy verse lamenting the transitoriness of human existence, so arranged that each syllable of the *kana* alphabet is used once and once only. An identical version, save for two slight differences, is given in *Arte grande*, f. 55v, and also by Carletti (*My Voyage*, p. 133), who omits the last line. The table, with the *kana* letters, is also given in *Arte breve*, f. 7.

top to bottom, as they are here. The order of the vowels is A, I, U, Ye, Wo, and the syllables below them are as follows:

A	I	U	Ye	Wo
Ka	Ki	Ku	Ke	Ko
Sa	Shi	Su	Se	So
Ta	Chi	Tsu	Te	To
Na	Ni	Nu	Ne	No
Ha	Hi	Fu	He	Ho
Ma	Mi	Mu	Me	Mo
Ya	Yi	Yu	Ye	Yo
Ra	Ri	Ru	Re	Ro
Wa	Wi	Wu	We	Wo[1]

But it is impossible to write all the syllables found in the pronunciation of their language with these forty-seven basic syllables just as they are. So they changed the pronunciation of some of them, although they kept the same shape of letter, and in this way they supplied all the missing syllables. For you must know that there are certain syllables in Japanese that change into a closer and more similar form to the syllable that follows.[2] They have fixed rules about this to determine when the syllables change and when they do not. The syllables that are altered and changed into other similar ones according to the following syllable, are listed below. This way of changing seems to exist in other languages as well, such as Greek and Hebrew, as regards certain words or syllables.

Ha		Ba & Pa	
He		Be & Pe	
Hi	are changed into	Bi & Pi	
Ho		Bo & Po	
Fu		Bu & Pu	
Cha		Ja	
Chi	into the syllables	Ji	they are pronounced as in the
Cho		Jo	Italian words *giorno*, *giudicio*
Chu		Ju	
Ka		Ga	
Ke		Ge	
Ki	are changed into	Gi	Ge, Gi are pronounced
Ko		Go	as in Italian and Latin.
Ku		Gu	

[1] *Vocabulario*, f. 121: 'Goin. ... The five vowels of Japan: A, I, U, Ye, Vo.' The full table is called the *gojūon*, 'the fifty sounds', although there are in fact only 47 sounds, owing to a repetition in the table. Rodrigues, *Arte grande*, f. 56, and *Arte breve*, 7v.

[2] Thus, the combination of the two characters *nichi* and *hon* is pronounced *Nihon*, Japan. The pronunciation of a syllable may also be modified by the preceding, as well as the following, syllable. Thus, the combination of *nichi* and *hon* may also be read as *Nippon*, and that of *setsu* and *fuku* as *seppuku*, the formal term for *harakiri*.

Sa		Za	
So	are changed into	Zo	
Su		Zu	

Ta		Da	
Te		De	
Chi	are changed into	Ji	
To		Do	
Tsu		Zu	

Sha		Ja	
She		Je	
Shi	are changed into	Ji	The J acts as a consonant in the
Sho		Jo	pronunciation.
Shu		Ju[1]	

Thus by changing and altering these original syllables, they provide other similar ones. The ordinary people use this sort of letter, and with it they write verses in the original native Japanese language. Women, especially ladies and nobles of gentle birth, also use it when writing letters. Cultured people and the gentry also use it, mixing and interspersing it with some characters. In this way they write their ordinary letters and simple books in the native Japanese language, as well as books of poetry and verse. Hence those people in Europe who wrote that the women of Japan used a certain sort of letter that the men did not understand were mistaken. They should have said that the women, especially the noble and high-born, use among themselves, in addition to the kingdom's ordinary language, many words, nouns, and verbs that the men do not ordinarily understand, and this in fact happens. When they converse with men, they use ordinary words, although they include some words proper to women that everyone understands because of their constant use.[2]

---

[1] In the Portuguese text, the fifth section has been erroneously copied, and I have corrected it in accordance with the identical table in *Arte grande*, f. 56v. The pronunciations in the right-hand column are called *nigori*. Rodrigues explains (*Arte grande*, f. 56v) that the verb *nigoru* means 'to muddy water', and that the syllables in the left-hand column are known as *sumi*, from *sumu*, 'to become clear.' Thus some *kana* letters could be pronounced in three different ways, for example, ha, ba, and pa. To indicate the correct pronunciation the Jesuit Press introduced the use of ° (for pa) and ″ (for ba), and these *handakuon* signs are still employed to this day. The Press also introduced *furigana*, that is, small *kana* letters printed by the side of a difficult character to indicate its pronunciation. Koda, 'Notes', pp. 380–81.

[2] The use of the prestigious Chinese characters (sometimes called *otokomoji*, 'men's letters') was considered proper only for men in past times, while the simple *kana* script was known as *onnade* ('women's hand'). The use of this unstilted script helps to explain the predominant role of women in Heian literature. Morris, *World*, p. 200. Rodrigues explains (*Arte grande*, ff. 202–202v, 205) that letters to and from women should be written in *kana* script, adding that they use various feminine words, such as *kukon* (instead of *sake*, 'wine'), *biyashi* (for *mizu*, 'water'), and *kachin* (for *mochi*, 'rice-cake'). *Vocabulario* also lists scores of women's words. But Valignano (*Principio*, f. 34v) points out that differences between the vocabularies of men and women are relatively few.

CHAPTER 6

THE PAPER, INK, AND OTHER INSTRUMENTS USED
IN WRITING

The things that necessarily accompany writing are chiefly the paper, inkwell, ink, brush, and the seals, or stamps, that they use. We shall say something about each of these things so as to give some idea of them and also of the skill that they put into them.

Firstly, as regards paper, its use goes back much further in these parts than in Europe. It was first used in China before anywhere else in this Orient, for the Chinese invented paper about 1,800 years ago in the Han (in Japanese, Kan) dynasty.[1] Up to that time they used cane tablets on which they wrote with iron punches,[2] or else other tablets on which they engraved the letters, as do even now the Brahmins and other nations of India who write on palm leaves with an iron stylus. They used this type of tablet for books, letters, and other writings and records. For some things they also used metal plates or vessels cast with these same letters, and there are still many preserved to this day. Some were made more than 3,000 years ago, and are very valuable and esteemed.[3]

But the use of these tablets is most difficult, both as regards learning the letters and making them available for many people, and producing lengthy writings and books, and so they invented paper, ink, and brush for writing. They made the paper from various materials, such as the wooden bark of canes, hempen cloth, and many other things, and it was introduced thence into Korea and from that kingdom to Japan.[4]

At the same time they invented the use of the black ink that they use in writing. The best kind is made from the smoke of sesame oil, but it is also made from other kinds of smoke. They collect the smoke that adheres to a vessel, and from this they make a paste. Using this paste, they produce sticks, some of them small, others long, and others round, in standard shapes, with a declaration printed on the actual stick indicating the quality and

---

[1] For the invention of paper, see p. 108, n. 4.

[2] For cane tablets, see *SCC*, V:1, fig. 1058.

[3] The oldest Chinese inscriptions are found on bronze vessels made during the Shang dynasty in the second millennium BC. Many of these characters resemble Egyptian hieroglyphics inasmuch as they pictorially represent their meaning. Some scholars maintain that these characters date as far back as 4,800 years ago. Watson, *Ancient Chinese Bronzes*, pp. 68–70.

[4] Mendoza (*History*, I, p. 123) states that Chinese paper is made from the pith of canes and can be used on only one side. Ricci (*Fonti*, I, p. 25, and *China*, p. 16) notes that it tears easily and is inferior to European paper. For modern accounts of Chinese paper manufacture, see Carter, *Invention*, pp. 3–8; for the different materials used in paper manufacture, see *SCC*, V:1, pp. 52–64. As regards Japanese paper, Kaempfer (*History*, III, pp. 249–62) provides a rambling account of its manufacture; for a more modern account, see Rein, *Industries*, pp. 390–98. As regards the introduction of paper into Japan, *Nihongi*, II, p. 140, records for the year 610: 'The king of Koryŏ [Korea] sent tribute of Buddhist priests named Tam-chhi and Pŏp-chŏng. Tam-chhi knew the five [Chinese] classics. He was moreover skilled in preparing painters' colours, paper, and ink.'

praising the ink. They are decorated with various flowers, serpents, and figures from ancient legends. Exteriorly this ink is very bright and even, and they add some musk while making the best sort so that it will smell sweetly when they write with it.[1] It is mixed with water inside a stone inkwell, and as they are so widely used in China and Japan there are craftsmen who earn their living by making and fashioning them. Their quills are small brushes, a span in length and as thick as the little finger. The tip with which they write is made of the fine hairs from the paunch of rabbits or other animals. They also make their painting brushes from this as well. There are craftsmen skilled in this art who earn their living from this because the use of brushes is so universal, and there are different brushes for various letters.[2]

The inkwells in which they grind the ink and in which they dip the brush in order to write, are of various kinds and are made of suitable smooth marmoreal stone. They are of different shapes, some being round and others proportionately oblong. It has a raised rim around the edge and a reservoir in the middle where the ink is ground. At one end of this there is a small, gracefully carved well wherein they pour the water with which the ink is mixed. After the ink has been ground and is sufficiently thick, it again collects in the well. They moisten the tip of the brush in the ink, and they sharpen and straighten the tip to a point within the reservoir. This is rather like the stone or palette in which artists prepare and mix the colours they use in painting. Some of these inkstands are highly esteemed and valued among the Japanese, and as they are used so much throughout the entire kingdom there are craftsmen who earn their living by making them.[3]

Finally, they use stamps or seals made of various materials, and there are many skilled craftsmen who cut them and thus make their living by practising this art. The letters that they cut on them have many meandering and intertwining strokes that are now no longer in use.[4] The use of these seals is far more widespread and general in China than in Japan, because they use them instead of their signature, although sometimes they do not use them. They use the seal by moistening it with black or vermilion ink and imprinting it on paper like a stamp, as in the prologues of their books, verses, poetry, pictures, drawings, and various other things.

The Chinese are wont to engrave on them their name and surname, and the rank, grade, or dignity they possess in the royal household. In addition to the inkstand, ink, and quills, the Chinese nobility keep on their table a tray bearing many seals, some of them big, others small, bearing various names and titles. They are made from various materials, such as precious stone, costly wood, ivory, metal, coral, crystal, jasper, or alabaster. The Chinese magistrates do not ordinarily write their signatures on official documents, but imprint them with their seal or stamp of office, given to them by the king, which bears the name of the office and the royal crest. The validity and force of all their official authority are contained in this royal seal. Hence magistrates of whatever rank observe great care and watchfulness so as not to lose them, for in such a case they immediately lose their office. They cannot

---

[1] Ricci (*Fonti*, I, p. 34, and *China*, p. 24) gives an account of Chinese ink, essentially the same as Japanese. The invention of this ink used in writing and printing is popularly ascribed to Weidan (179–253). Such ink is basically made of lamp-black and gum, and then poured into moulds. Carter, *Invention*, pp. 32–4, and *SCC*, 5:1, pp. 237–47.

[2] For the *fude*, or brush, see p. 232, n. 4.

[3] For these ink-stones, or *suzuri*, see p. 232, n. 4.

[4] This type of script is called *tensho* and is still used in formal Japanese seals. Copious examples are given in Gulik, *Chinese Pictorial Art*, pp. 442–9.

perform anything nor has anything any validity without the seal, because it is customary to place the seal, and not their signature, on all the documents and other things concerned with their office. When they formally leave their houses with their retinue and the insignia of their office, they are accustomed to having this seal carried in front of them in a chest slung from a pole carried by two men; they cover it with a sunshade of yellow silk out of reverence for the king, whom it represents.[1]

The Chinese call them *zhapiao* in the court language and *dzatpiu* in the rough language of Canton. Hence here in China the Portuguese call *chapas* every kind of warrant, patent, dispatch, safe conduct, and writ authorised by the king or his magistrates and judges, for they are stamped with these seals in red ink.[2] This is also true of Japan, where the royal patents and warrants and those of the *kubō* and Lord of Tenka are called *shuin*, meaning 'red seal', as they are stamped with red ink as in China. Other Japanese lords use only a black seal, and even the *kubō* or Lord of Tenka does this in private business, because red seals are used only in public and juridical matters.[3]

The Japanese place all their writing instruments in a beautiful varnished box made for the purpose, and nobles and the gentry have richly decorated boxes inlaid with gold and silver flowers on very delicate black lacquer. The interior of the box is divided into five compartments. In the centre and largest compartment is the inkstand, while in the others there are a small gilded copper vessel containing water to pour into the inkwell, the writing brushes, the ink, a small knife for cutting things instead of scissors, and a punch for closing letters, as well as everything also necessary, such as the seals.[4]

---

[1] Ricci (*Fonti*, I, pp. 33–4, 91, and *China*, pp. 24, 80) comments on the widespread use of seals in China, adding that mandarins have their seal carried before them when travelling and are said to sleep with them under their pillows. This information is confirmed by Cortes (*Viaje*, p. 143), who includes an illustration of two servants (p. 147) preceding a magistrate and carrying his seal as described by Rodrigues. See Carter, *Invention*, pp. 7–11. Gulik, *Chinese Pictorial Art*, pp. 417–42, deals in detail with Chinese seals.

[2] The usual Chinese term for a seal is *yinzhang* or *yinke*, but Rodrigues may have had in mind the term *qianji*. As this appears unlikely, I have left the two words as they are given in the Portuguese text. His suggestion as to the derivation of *chapa* is interesting, as most sources connect it with the Hindi term *chhāp*, printing, hence the Anglo-Indian term 'chop', meaning seal, licence, or passport stamped with a seal. Dalgado, *Glossário*, I, pp. 259–61; Yule, *Hobson-Jobson*, pp. 207–9.

[3] *Vocabulario*, f. 314: '*Shuin*. Seal stamped with red ink. Item, at the present time, a provision or licence of the Lord of Tenka, but this is not understood without *go-*. Thus, *goshuin*.' Further details in *Arte grande*, f. 196v, where Rodrigues notes that private black seals were called *kokuin*. Fróis (*História*, II, pp. 274–5) refers to the *goshuin* issued by Nobunaga in 1569 in favour of the Jesuits in Miyako. *Goshuin-chi* were temple lands confirmed with the shogun's red seal, while *goshuin-sen* or *goshuin-bune* were ships authorized with the red seal to sail abroad for trade.

[4] The writing box has already been mentioned on p. 232.

CHAPTER 7

THEIR WAY OF PRINTING

The method of printing books used by the Japanese is the same as in China, whence it passed to Korea and thence to Japan. It is more ancient in China than anywhere else, for the Chinese have been using it for more than 1,600 years.[1] Although the Japanese use printing, it is not so usual and general as in China, where innumerable books are printed. Nor is their printing so excellent and with such variety of letters as in China, where, as we said, they devote themselves to literature. But it is used in Japan, and they print all kinds of letters, both the Chinese ones as well as the sort used by the Japanese that are not hieroglyphic but are rather like our letters.[2]

The Japanese have three methods of printing that are also in use in China. The first method, and the most common one in China, is done with wooden blocks. They make the block the same size as the desired folio or page, and skilfully and swiftly carve on its surface the letters of the page, set out or written with its paragraphs, chapters, commas, full stops, and everything else in the following way. First of all, they take a sheet of paper the same size as the proposed book and write in fine lettering of the desired sort and style with the required number of lines, spaces, and everything else. They then glue this sheet face down on to the block and with great skill cut away all the blank paper, leaving only the black letters remaining on the block. They then carve these letters on the block with iron instruments, just as if they were composed in our way. They are so dexterous and skilful in this art that they can cut a block in about the same time as we can compose a page.

Once the letters have been cut out on the block, they dye it with black or other-coloured ink ground with water. They do not add oil as we do, but use ink prepared as if for ordinary writing.[3] Then they place the paper on top of the letters of the block and rub the top surface of the paper from side to side with an instrument so that the ink sticks to the paper and thus leaves an impression. There are as many blocks as there are folios or pages of the book. These blocks belong to the person who ordered them to be made and they last him a long time, so he can print as often and as many copies as he pleases. When a book is sold

---

[1] Block-printing is believed to have been invented about 712–56, and as early as 770 the Japanese Empress Shotoku had a million Buddhist charms printed. The oldest extant printed book dates to 868. Movable type, made of baked clay, was possibly used in China in the mid–11th century. The first movable-type book printed in Japan (excluding those of the imported Jesuit Press) was produced in 1595. But block-printing later became popular again because of the difficulty in making type for running script. Carter, *Invention*, pp. 41, 46–51, 212–3, 224, 230, 236. An overall account of printing in Japan is found in *SCC*, V:1, pp. 331–47.

[2] A reference to the *kana* syllables, mentioned earlier.

[3] Chinese ink was excellent for printing with wooden blocks and left a neat impression, but was not so satisfactory with metal blocks, on which it tended to form in globules. It is possible that the Chinese printers finally used a type of oily ink for metal blocks, as in Europe. Carter, *Invention*, pp. 32–3.

out, he can print it again because he always keeps the pages made up and ready. If there should be a mistake on the block, it can be easily corrected and changed according to his wishes. Both in Japan and in China there are printers who cut the blocks and print the books at their own expense and then sell them.[1]

The second method of printing uses movable type, each one made individually of wood or cast from metal.[2] They make up the page just as we do and then print it in the way already described. Afterwards they dismantle the page, wash the letters, and put them back in their places so that they can use them again whenever necessary. In this way they can dispense with the large number of blocks, which are made from a certain type of wood not easily obtainable.[3]

The third method of printing also uses blocks, or metal plates or smooth stone, on which they engrave the letters. This is the opposite of the technique employed in the first method, in which the surface of the block is cut away and the letters stand out in relief. In this third method, the surface of the block stands out and the letters are cut away and sunken.[4] In order to print, they moisten the paper lightly (as they also do in the other two methods) and then spread it over the block, plate, or stone. They then tap it with special soft-padded mallets so that the parts of the paper that lie over the engraved letters, strokes, and signs are pushed inside and moulded. They then ink the whole page over, except for the parts that were pushed into the letters. Thus the letters are left white and the background black. This method is not used for printing books, but for inscriptions and epitaphs, and pictures of men, flowers, plants, trees, animals, and other similar things, which are carved on blocks, plates, or stones. In this way they reproduce the celebrated letters that are on ancient stones and plates, and other pictures of ancient men, illustrious in this art, whom they greatly admire. This method is the opposite of printing with our plates, for they spread the ink on the empty spaces and clean the upper surface.[5]

The people who learn these letters in Japan are different from the Chinese (whom we have already mentioned), and in China itself the modern method is different from the ancient one employed before the present dynasty. For in ancient times in China (and even now in the kingdom of Korea) the people could not be promoted by means of letters and arms to the various degrees and ranks of nobles, posts in the royal household, and magistracies of the realm unless they were sons of lords and nobles possessing lands and revenues. But now in the present monarchy all the common people can be promoted in this way to the highest rank and dignity of the kingdom beneath the king. There are certain kinds of base people, however, who cannot be thus promoted. First of all, there are those

---

[1] A similar account is found in Ricci (*Fonti*, I, pp. 30–31, and *China*, pp. 20–21), who observes that a Chinese printer could engrave a block as fast as his European counterpart could set up a page of type, and could turn out 1,500 printed copies a day. For the techniques of Chinese block-printing, see Carter, *Invention*, pp. 34–5, and *SCC*, V:1, pp. 196–201.

[2] Metal movable type was never popular in China and Japan, although it was first cast in Korea in 1403 and later widely used there. Carter, *Invention*, pp. 223–30; McGovern, *Specimen Pages*, pp. 14, 19; *SCC*, V:1, pp. 211–22.

[3] The 'certain type of wood' used in block printing was usually cherry, pear, apple, or jujube wood. Ricci, *Fonti*, I, pp. 30–31, and *China*, pp. 20–21; Carter, *Invention*, pp. 211–19; *SCC*, V:1, p. 196.

[4] In this sentence the copyist makes a slip and then corrects himself. The text runs: '... the surface stands out and the letters are raised – I mean, cut away and sunken.'

[5] Ricci (*Fonti*, I, p. 31, and *China*, p. 21) describes the same way of reproducing epitaphs and pictures in China. For history and technique of this method, see Carter, *Invention*, pp. 19–23. The remainder of this chapter has nothing to do with printing, and presumably should have come in Book 2, Chapter 4, dealing with Chinese ideographs.

who look after the public women and earn their living thereby, and so are dishonourable.[1] Secondly, actors. Thirdly, catchpoles, butchers, executioners, etc.

In Japan, the sons of all the nobles, grandees, lords, and all the other gentry learn the letters. The sons of the lords are taught in their houses by instructors,[2] while all the other children go to learn at the monasteries of the bonzes. Some of them live there while they are studying, while others return home every day if the monastery is in the same place or nearby.[3] There are usually no public schools. After studying in these monastery schools, they become children of the devil on account of the many bad customs and vices that the bonzes teach the children there in their care. They not only do not feel these enormous vices to be wrong, but they teach them in such a way that it is considered a virtue to consent to them and a despicable vice to resist and oppose them as a weakness. What depths have the evil and blindness of men reached through sin![4] For this reason the Society, in keeping with its Institute, runs schools for sons of Christians in the areas where it has a house in order to counteract this evil, so they may learn Christian doctrine along with their letters. It was soon seen that the work of these schools produced excellent results in the young sons of Christians.[5]

These monasteries of bonzes also serve as universities for those who devote themselves to the study of sciences and philosophy, and wish to live in the ecclesiastical state. In the region of Bandō there is a university called Ashikaga in the kingdom of Shimōsa, and people from all over Japan gather there to study every kind of science, which they teach free. They have their rector called Gakkō. At present the university does not flourish so much as in the beginning, because it has been overrun and sometimes destroyed during the many continuous wars.[6]

---

[1] According to Saris (in Farrington, *English Factory*, II, p. 995), such people were despised, but only after death, also in Japan. 'When any of these Panders die, though in their life time they were received into company of the best, yet now, as unworthy to rest amongst the worst, they are bridled with a bridle made of straw, as you would bridle an horse, and in the cloathes they died in, are dragged through the streetes into the fields, and there cast upon a dunghill, for dogges and fowles to devoure.'

[2] A literal translation of the text would read: 'The sons of the lords have in their houses masters who teach their sons.'

[3] Most of the boys living in the monasteries were trained with a view to becoming monks. When Fróis visited Daitokuji temple in 1565 (in *TCJ*, p. 344), he noticed half-a-dozen boys who came out to see the foreigners. 'All of them are sons of nobles and they are brought up there to become bonzes and to occupy the high offices among them.' But Zen monks also ran *tera-koya*, where an elementary education was given to local boys. *Vocabulario*, f. 266: '*Tōzan. Yama ni noboru.* The attendance of boys at the *tera* [temples] of the bonzes in order to learn to read and write. When their fathers withdraw them from the *tera* (usually after three years), they say, "*Gezan suru*", that is, to leave the *tera* where they have learnt to read and write.' For the curriculum of the *tera-koya*, see Lombard, *Pre-Meiji Education*, pp. 100–107.

[4] A reference to pederasty. See p. 95, n. 1.

[5] Valignano (*Sumario*, pp. 170–75) points out the need for such schools and lays down the curricula for them. When he came to Japan in 1579, he planned three preparatory schools, or *seminarios*, although only two were in fact founded. Cieslik, 'Training', pp. 44–6; Schütte, *Valignano's Mission Principles*, I, pp. 326–7 and II, pp. 225–6. For Saris's description of the Azuchi school, 'a very stately colledge', where there 'are many Japonian children trayned up, and instructed in the rudiments of Christian Religion,' see Farrington, *English Factory*, II, pp. 1022–3.

[6] For the Ashikaga Academy, see p. 90, where the author correctly locates it in Shimotsuke, not Shimōsa.

CHAPTER 8

THE MATHEMATICAL ARTS OF JAPAN AND ALSO OF CHINA, WHENCE THE JAPANESE RECEIVED THEM

Just as the Japanese obtained from China their letters, sciences, and their many other social customs, so also they received thence many of their liberal and mechanical arts, and in particular mathematics, comprising of arithmetic, geometry, music, and astronomy. Although these nations have not developed these arts to the same perfection and degree as in Europe, nevertheless their practice is very widespread among them and, according to their records and first promulgators of these arts, much more ancient than among us. For it is by the antiquity attributed to these arts, principally astrology, that we must judge who were their first inventors. We can easily see that these were the first Fathers before the Flood, and this is also the opinion of the more learned Europeans. For when languages became confused at the Tower of Babel, Noah's descendants dispersed to various places in order to populate the world.

Now there were nine leaders of the same stock among them and each had 140 families in his charge. A certain number of them came to the Orient and peopled the kingdom of China. Among these 140 families, whose names still exist to the present day, there were three celebrated sages, and each of them was the leader of each of the families. We gather from their annals that they were contemporary, although in the course of time some succeeded others by succession instead of on account of learning.[1]

They gave form to the nation of China and set the country up with laws, government, letters, sciences, and liberal and mechanical arts. Their first form of government was tribal and quasi-aristocratic, and was conducted by the heads of families. But after they founded the kingdom, the monarchical system was introduced. Apart from the first man and woman, they have no record of anyone living before the first of these three sages. He was called Fuxi (the Japanese call him Fukki).[2] There were not even any houses in his time and the people dwelt in nests in the trees, and in huts, caves, and dens. They had no clothes, but used instead animal skins and the bark of trees and plants. At this time they began to use fire and water for cooking and other purposes, as they had thitherto subsisted on fruit from trees. He was the first among them to teach natural magic and astrology, and he expressed this with figures and odd and even numbers.

The second sage, who flourished after him, was called Shennong, or Shinnō in Japanese.[3] He taught the people the art of agriculture, of ploughing and sowing the land, and of

---

[1] Rodrigues has already mentioned these three sages on pp. 331–2. For a more detailed account of the legend of the 140 families in *Breve aparato*, see p. 331, n. 2.

[2] For Fuxi, see p. 331.

[3] For Shennong, see pp. 331–2.

rearing animals for its cultivation and the service of men, and also the art of medicine through a knowledge of the efficacy of herbs.

The third sage, who some say was the brother of this Shennong, was called Huangdi, in Japanese Kōtei, and was the first monarch. His descendants were all the other kings of the other monarchies and the lords of the kingdom.[1] He gave the kingdom the form of a nation with civil government and all the other liberal and mechanical arts. He divided the country into states and regions, and built cities in which the people dwelt in houses as communities. He arranged everything else necessary for a well-governed kingdom. Up to that time the people had lived very primitively, for everyone had been ruled by the head of his family and his heir, and there had been no laws or community. Now the things that he did will help us to understand better the antiquity of the mathematical arts, and we may thereby learn of their first inventors. We will therefore set down in order a detailed account of what he did and enacted as is found in the general histories of China, which, they say, were written more than 4,000 years ago. As we are now in the year 1620, they would date from 2,380 years before Christ our Lord.[2]

First of all, they had thitherto lived without houses, community, and laws. Each person was governed by his family, and the people by the doctrine of former sages. But as they were now ready for law and order, he distributed the land of China into states and regions to be possessed by lords with their vassals. He himself remained as monarch and supreme ruler of all. For the administration of the kingdom, he set up six bodies like general ruling councils, each of which was concerned with its own affairs. In imitation of this, there have been preserved in the kingdom to this day the councils of the treasury, state, rites and courtesies, civil and criminal justice, and general works. He laid down laws as well to govern the kingdom; he established houses and cities for the people to dwell therein in community, and he built royal palaces in which to live. He specified the robes suitable for each person's station, and the courtesies and etiquette to be observed among them. At the same time he distinguished the five colours, white, black, red, green, and yellow.[3] He introduced the use of fire and water for cooking and other uses.

Then, in the second place, he established letters, already in existence, and writing, and these seem to be the first known in the world. Thirdly, he chose from the wisest men six bodies or colleges with their presidents[4] for various liberal and mechanical arts. The first among these was the college or congregation of astrologers, who had a lofty tower to contemplate the stars and the celestial scene. They also had books that he compiled on this subject and, as their records affirm, these were the first of such books to exist. They may well be the first and most ancient writing in the world, because up to that time they used figures and odd and even numbers that to this day are found in their sciences.

---

[1] For Huangdi, see p. 332, n. 2.

[2] The text of the last sentence of this paragraph is somewhat incoherent, but its general meaning remains clear. It is difficult to determine to which annals Rodrigues is here referring. The first chapter of *Zhu shu ji nian juan*, or 'The Annals of the Bamboo Books' (Legge, *Chinese Classics*, III, pp. [108]–[110]) is devoted to a brief account of the reign of Huangdi, but this work, although ancient, does not date from the third millennium BC, and contains far less information about Huangdi than Rodrigues provides.

[3] The colour of an official's robe indicated his rank. These colours are mentioned in *Shujing*, II, 4, 4 (Legge, *Chinese Classics*, III, pp. 80–81). *Vocabulario*, f. 122: 'Goshiki. Itsutsu no iro. Five colours, i.e., *shō*, *ō*, *shaku*, *byaku*, *koku*. Blue, yellow, red, white, black.' As regards the difference of the first colour between this list and that given by Rodrigues, *shō* (or *aoi*) can mean either blue or green in Japanese.

[4] The Portuguese text has *perfeitos*, presumably a slip for *prefeitos*, mayors, governors.

They determined the seasons by which they were governed, and regulated them by the courses of the sun and of the moon. They divided the year into a solar year of 365¼ days with the four seasons.[1] They placed the beginning of the year at 15° of Aquarius, and this is when their spring begins and is 5th February.[2] They determined the four cardinal points of the two equinoxes and two solstices, and each of these points was the middle of one of the four seasons. They gave three signs of 30° each to every one of these.[3] They divided the sky into 12 equal parts, which they called houses or signs; they are also called hours because they give 12 hours to the natural day lasting the day and the night. The middle of their signs is the beginning of our signs in reverse direction.[4] They also arranged the lunar year of 12 months with an intercalary one every three years and two intercalary months every five years, so as to make it coincide with the solar year and to avoid a variation in the seasons. The ordinary lunar year has 354 days and an intercalary one has 384 days. Each lunar month lasts either 29 days, and this they call a small month, or 30 days, which they call a big month.[5]

They arranged the material sphere with its equinoctial circles, called the Red Path, and the ecliptical, called the Yellow Path;[6] they divided the whole sky into 365°25', each degree being worth 100' on the same sphere.[7] They plotted the course of the planets, placing the tropics at 24 of their degrees from the equinoctial, and the moon, which passes 6° away

---

[1] The length of the solar year is 365·24219 days, so the ancient Chinese were not far out in their calculations. *SCC*, III, p. 390. Here may I pay tribute to the late Joseph Needham and his monumental *Science and Civilisation in China* (modestly disguised in these pages under the rubric *SCC*), which has been of immense help in annotating the following material on Chinese astronomy.

[2] The Chinese, however, generally followed the lunar calendar, in which the year began when the sun entered the sign of Pisces, that is, between 20 January and 19 February. This was laid down by Emperor Wudi (d. 87 BC). Chalmers, *Astronomy*, p. [95], and Gaubil, 'Histoire', II, p. 6. For accounts of the Chinese way of determining the New Year throughout the ages, see Gaubil, 'Histoire', II, pp. 182–4, and Trigault, *Litterae*, pp. 129–30.

[3] The determining of the equinoxes and solstices is attributed to Emperor Yao, who commanded the brothers He and Xi to make these observations for the sake of agriculture. *Shujing*, I, 2, 4–8 (Legge, *Chinese Classics*, III, pp. 18–22). For a modern explanation of this ancient text, see *SCC*, III, pp. 245–6.

[4] The 12 signs are explained in detail by Chalmers, *Astronomy*, p. [95]; Saussure, *Origines*, pp. 309–51. This twelve-fold equatorial division is not identical with the 12 signs of the Graeco-Egyptian zodiac of the West. *SCC*, III, pp. 258–9, 404.

[5] *Shujing*, I, 2, 8 (Legge, *Chinese Classics*, III, pp. 21–2) records that Emperor Yao, who began his reign in 2357 BC, commanded astronomers to add intercalary months in order to synchronize the solar and lunar years. Avila Girón (*Relación*, p. 37) notes that the added month was called *urū-tsuki* in Japanese. This additional month was sometimes added after the third month, which was then counted twice, and sometimes after the eighth. The ordinary year of 354 days was called *heinen*, while that of 384 days was *urū-doshi*. When the solar year was so delayed that the 13th lunation did not reach the sign of Pisces, another month had to be added. At the end of the 19-year (Metonic) cycle, the solar and lunar years coincided exactly. Intercalary months were usually added in the 3rd, 6th, 9th, 11th, 14th, 17th, and 19th years. The 29-day month was called Small, and the 30-day one was Big; the intercalary month had 30 days. *Arte grande*, f. 230: 'Their months contain 30 days or 29. A month having 30 is called *dai*, or big, and 29 is called *shō*, or small.'

[6] For the meaning of *hesphera material*, see p. 11, n. 5. For the workings of the celestial sphere, see *SCC*, III, pp. 178–80. For the Red Path (*chidao*) and Yellow Path (*huangdao*), see ibid., III, p. 179; Maspero, 'L'Astronomie', pp. 274–5.

[7] In the books of the Han dynasty (206 BC–AD 220), the circuit of the heavens is divided into 365·25°, a degree of the heavens thus corresponding to a day of the calendar. The circle was also divided in the same way. When Ricci visited Nanjing observatory (*Fonti*, II, p. 57, and *China*, p. 330), he noticed an astrolabe divided into 365° 'and some minutes'. The change from decimal to sexagesimal gradation of the degree took place in China as late as the 17th century, principally as a result of the Jesuit astronomers, such as Ferdinand Verbiest (1623–88). *SCC*, III, p. 374, note b; Gaubil, 'Histoire', II, p. 6; Chalmers, 'Astronomy', p. [95].

from it.[1] They arranged the starry sky into constellations and figures into which they divided the stars, and they classed them in three colours and studied their influences.[2] For this purpose, they founded astrology after the fashion of the Chaldeans, and ever since then this has been greatly studied in the kingdom. They distributed along the zodiac 28 of the 240 or more pictures of the stars that they invented, and the sun passes through these during the course of the year.[3] They then established the colure of the winter solstice in the seventh degree of one of them,[4] for it seemed to them that it was perpetually at that point as they did not have any experience of the slow movement of the stars. In the same way, they fixed the other points of the solstices and equinoxes in the other figures, and took Ursa Major as a basis for all this according to the way it points and varies with the first star of the bow of the boat throughout the year.[5] They distributed all these stars in a planisphere, as we shall say later.

Fourthly, he arranged plain singing, distinguishing five notes like *do, re, mi, fa, so,* and *la,* along with twelve tones or pitches, and they always keep within this range. He also made musical instruments, such as the harpsichord of twelve or thirty-two strings, the flute, the shalm, and other instruments.[6] Fifthly, he established the art of arithmetic with its divisions after our fashion. Sixthly, he introduced the art of medicine and the method of taking the pulse. Seventhly, weights and measures. Eighthly, ships and oars, and the use of wagons and carts, beasts of burden, and the method of rearing silk worms and of working silk.[7] Ninthly and finally, the art of making vessels from clay and wood for ordinary use and service. So all these arts date from this time and are as old as China itself or even older. So that you may more easily see that their first inventors were the Fathers before the Flood, I will reproduce here what is recorded in the Chinese annals, for it presents a very clear argument for what we have said.

Accordingly, it may be noted how the Chinese historians refer to that first period in the

---

[1] The plane of the terrestrial equator is inclined to the earth's orbit at 23°27′, and this is generally called the obliquity of the ecliptic. Hipparchus (fl. 146–127 BC) calculated the angle of the moon's path with the ecliptic as 5°, while early in the 3rd century AD Liuhong arrived at the figure of 5°54′. The actual value is 5°08′. SCC, III, pp. 180–81, 421 note d. For early Chinese studies of the course of the moon and the planets, see ibid., III, pp. 392–3, 398–404.

[2] An interesting and correct observation. In the 4th century BC, the scholars Shishen, Gande, and Wuxian drew up separate catalogues of the stars. In the 5th century, the astronomer Qian Luozhi constructed an improvised planisphere, and marked in different colours the stars that the three scholars had noted – red for Shishen, black for Gande, and white for Wuxian. SCC, III, p. 263. For illustrations of these coloured charts, see Sun and Kistemaker, *Chinese Sky*, pp. 25–7; SCC, III, pp. 264–5.

[3] The angular value of the 28 mansions (*xiu*) is not equal and varies from 1° to 30°. The astronomer Chenzhuo made a star map at the beginning of the 4th century, incorporating all the stars noted by the three scholars mentioned in n. 2, above. They totalled 283 constellations and 1,565 (or perhaps 1,465) stars. Rodrigues later (p. 353) mentions a total of 284 constellations and 1,565 stars. SCC, III, p. 264; Chalmers, 'Astronomy', pp. [94]-[95].

[4] Rodrigues notes on the following page that the colure of the winter solstice is at 7° of the 11th mansion, called Xu. But owing to precession (see p. 353, n. 6), by the 1st century BC the colure fell between the 8th and 9th mansions, called Dou and Niu. SCC, III, p. 247; Forke, *World-Conception*, pp. 127–8.

[5] The role of the Great Bear constellation in Chinese astronomy and the Chinese names of its component stars are given in SCC, III, p. 232–3.

[6] *Vocabulario*, f. 354: 'Goin. The five musical notes or tones of Japan. That is, *kyū*, low tone or voice; *shō*, a little higher; *kaku*, higher; *chō*, much higher; *ū*, the very highest.' The gradation of these notes depends more on timbre than pitch. The complicated question of pitch or tone (*lu*) in Chinese music is explained in SCC, IV:1, pp. 160–71. The Chinese had instruments with varying numbers of strings. Rodrigues is possibly referring to the *guqin*, described in Gulik, *Lore*. See also SCC, IV:1, pp. 129–31, 140.

[7] For the invention of silk, see p. 11, n. 1.

time of this king and of the four who followed after him.[1] They distributed the stars among the 284 figures or constellations, and these stars numbered 1,565. Twenty-eight of these were distributed along the zodiac and were called houses, for during the course of the year the sun enters and moves among them. They assigned to each of them a smaller or greater number of degrees, and these total 365°25'.[2] These made up the ecliptic, starting from the star Spica Virginis, which is the beginning of the first constellation of the 28 figures of the zodiac.[3] In the same way, the rest of these constellations begin with other stars also known among us, such as Libra, Frons Scorpionis (which they also call Heart), Corpus Scorpionis, Cuspis Sagittae, Manus Sagittarii, Capricornus, the fourth star of Aquarius in the left shoulder, Aquarius, Aries, Hyades, Oculus Tauri, Orion, Geminorum Crura, and other known stars.[4] In keeping with this, they placed the two equinoxes and the two solstices at a certain degree in these figures, and the sun enters it at these points every year at that time. They believed that this was perpetual and invariable, for they did not have any experience of the slow movement of the stars from west to east which was subsequently discovered. Thus the colure of the winter solstice was placed in the seventh degree of one of their constellations called Xu, or in Japanese Kyo. This degree was 7° from the fourth star of the left shoulder of Aquarius, and it is from here that the constellations, occupying 9°25', begins.[5]

They continued in this way for many years until they began to notice that the colure of the solstice would change from that degree and that the stars had moved more than 25° towards the east up to that time. They have been observing this movement in all the cities since 103 before Christ our Lord right up to the present day. They discovered that it was sometimes slower and sometimes faster. Some people assigned 100 years to each degree, others 82, others 75, others 60, and finally others 50, which is the lowest that they found.[6]

---

[1] For these five emperors, see p. 24, n. 5. The first three were Fuxi, Shennong, and Huangdi, already mentioned, and they were followed by Yao (2357–2258 BC) and Shun (2258–2206). Rodrigues errs in making Huangdi the first of the five emperors, for in fact he was the third.

[2] For verification, see n. 3, below.

[3] The extent of each of the 28 mansions was measured from one determinative star to the next, the determinative star being usually (but not always) the most westerly star of the constellation that gave its name to the mansion. But because of precession (see n. 6, below), the relative position of some stars gradually changed, and certain determinative stars landed up in the sector of another mansion. At any rate, as Rodrigues correctly notes, Spica Virginis (or α Virginis) is the determinative star of Jiao, the first mansion. *SCC*, III, p. 235; Maspero, *L'Astronomie*, p. 284; Chatley, 'Ancient Chinese Astronomy', p. 68.

[4] Most of the Chinese mansions determined by these stars can be identified by reference to the table in *SCC*, III, pp. 235–7; for example, Libra is the determinative constellation of Di, and Frons Scorpionis (or σ Scorpii) determines Xin, which, as Rodrigues notes, means 'heart', etc. But the reference to Aries and Orion is too vague to determine the appropriate mansion with certainty. A table of the 28 mansions, together with their determinative stars in the year 1700, is given in Gaubil, 'Histoire', II, pp. 178–81. Several of these star names are not standard – it is possible that Rodrigues was mapping Chinese stars onto a Western star map or globe showing the pictorial representations of constellations. Corpus and Frons Scorpionis are not standard star names (but Allen, *Star Names*, p. 372, notes that the Arabs call Omega1 and Omega 2 Scorpionis 'Jabhat al 'Arab, the Forehead or Front of Scorpio; and the Chinese Kow Kin, a Hook and Latch'.), nor are Cuspis Sagittae, i.e. the Head of the Arrow, or Manus Scorpionis.

[5] The mansion called Xu, meaning 'emptiness', has as its determinative star β Aquarii, and extends 9·86°. *SCC*, III, p. 235.

[6] This phenomenon, called the precession of the equinoxes, is caused by the axis of the earth gyrating through a cycle of about 26,000 years. This motion causes a 50" shift in the relative position of the stars every year, or 1° in 71·6 years, or 31° in 22 centuries. To rectify this shift, the Taichu calendar reform took place in the 5th month of

So according to them, the colure of the solstice is now in the fourth degree from the constellation Ji (which is Cuspis Sagittae), from which it is separated by these four degrees.[1] This is also held by our mathematicians, who place the said colure in this year of 1620 slightly more than 4° from this star. Thus since that time to the present, they found that the stars had moved or changed 54°8' towards the east.

Now according to our modern mathematicians and the most expert members of their ranks today, the starry sky regularly moves one degree in 70 years and seven months.[2] Their observations also agree with this, because the mean of the difference occurring in a 100 years (which is the most) and 50 years is 25 years, which along with the 50 makes 75, and comes to more or less the same.[3] According to this, then, 3,892 years have passed from that time until the present, as any mathematician can easily confirm.[4] Now according to the Vulgate, 4,062 years elapsed from Adam until Christ our Lord; we follow this opinion here as it seems most probable to us and many grave authors.[5] When we add to them the 1,620 years from the time of Christ our Lord until now, we reach a total of 5,658 years up to the present time.[6] Subtracting from this 3,892, we get the 1,656 years that elapsed up to the Flood, plus the 131 more years from the Flood up to the Confusion of Tongues, and we come to three years after the said Confusion.[7] Now at that time the colure of the winter solstice was in the above-mentioned seventh degree from the fourth star of Aquarius, for the Chinese placed it there when they founded and established their kingdom.[8]

---

104 BC, under Emperor Wu. Precession was discovered in China by the astronomer Yuxi (4th century), who reckoned 1° shift every 50 years; later astronomers calculated 1° every 75, 83, or 100 years, until the figure of 66 years was finally acknowledged in Rodrigues's time. De Ursis (in D'Elia, *Galileo in China*, p. 78) mentions these different calculations and the agreement to accept 66 years. SCC, III, pp. 181, 200, 246–7, 250–51; Forke, *World-Conception*, pp. 126–9; Gaubil, 'Histoire', II, pp. 4–7.

[1] Ji is the seventh celestial mansion, and its determinative star is γ Sagittarii.

[2] *Breve aparato*, f. 12, states: 'Tycho Brahe [1546–1601] and other modern scholars now give 70 years and 7 months to each degree of this movement. Now any good mathematician can calculate that this dates back to about 3,950 years from the present, and this would be about the time of the Confusion of Tongues.' Brahe (*Opera omnia*, p. 176) gives 70 years and 7 months to the degree (as Rodrigues states), remarking that Ptolemy had given it 100 years. Brahe includes a short treatise on this subject in ibid., pp. 175–7.

[3] The text reads 25°, but this is an obvious slip for 25 years. Writing in 1925, Forke (*World-Conception*, p. 128–9) uses practically the same words as Rodrigues: 'Yü Hsi ... discovered that in fifty years the sun retrograded 1°. Ho Ch'eng-t'ien doubled this figure and made it one hundred years. T'ang Liu-ch'o took the average of these two numbers, fifty and one hundred, and made seventy-five years equal to 1°.'

[4] That is, if there is a shift of 1° in about 70 years, then it will take about 3,892 years to effect a change of 54°. According to my calculations, 54°08' multiplied by 70½ gives 3,820·9, not 3,892. My figures are later confirmed by Rodrigues, p. 391, who gives the figure of 3,822 years, not 3,892 as here.

[5] Rodrigues maintains (*Arte grande*, f. 239) that 4,074 years elapsed from the Creation until Christ. Presumably he understood that Adam was created 12 years after the Creation, and thus 4,062 years elapsed from Adam to Christ. According to the Introduction of Génébrard, *Chronographiae libri quatuor*, 1585, a work that Rodrigues later quotes, Christ was born in AM 4089. Rodrigues's Jesuit contemporary Jacques Salian (1558–1640) gives the date as 4052 in his *Enchiridium*, p. 326.

[6] An obvious slip for 5,682 years, mentioned later on p. 391.

[7] The reasoning here is as follows: From Adam to Christ, 4,062 years; from Christ to 1620, 1,620 years. So from Adam to 1620, 5,658 (*sic* – this should be 5,682) years. But it had taken 3,892 years for a precession of 54°. This precession therefore began 5,682 – 3,892 years after Adam, i.e., 1,790 years after him. This period of 1,790 years is made up as follows: Adam to Flood, 1,656 years (this agrees with *Arte grande*, f. 238v); Flood to Confusion, 131 years; plus an additional 3 years. Total, 1,790 years.

[8] That is, the colure of the winter solstice was originally in the Chinese mansion Xu of which β Aquarii is the determinative star (*SCC*, III, p. 235). This sort of calculation is not so far-fetched as it may seem, and scholars have

Hence it can be clearly shown that this is the most ancient observation to be found in the world, and it agrees with what Porphyrius says about Callisthenes, nephew and pupil of Aristotle:

When Callisthenes, disciple and nephew of Aristotle and companion of Alexander the Great in his wars, uncovered all the secrets and monuments of the Chaldeans, he succinctly wrote that these astronomical observations were the most ancient of all such records, although not older than 1,900 years. Hipparchus and Ptolemy also agree about the antiquity of these observations, which date from the time of Nebuchadnezzar, king of the Chaldeans, who began to reign about the 31st olympiad.[1]

Now Alexander the Great captured Babylon in the seventh year of his reign, which was AM 3681[2] From this we must subtract the 1,900 years that had elapsed, according to Callisthenes, since the Chaldeans began their observations of the Heavens. This leaves 1,781 years, which coincides exactly with the Confusion of Tongues, for this took place in AM 1787.[3] According to Pliny, the Chaldean genethliacal astrologers began with Jupiter Belus, father of Ninus, king of the Assyrians, and he states that he was the inventor of the science of the stars.[4] This Belus is the same as Nimrod, the grandson of Ham, from whom he learnt this science. He began to reign in AM 1791, which was just after the Confusion of Tongues.[5]

It can also be seen that the Chinese were the first settlers of this kingdom, coming from the Tower of Babel straight after the Confusion of Tongues, and that they were the first to develop, as we said above, astrology and other mathematical arts and other liberal and mechanical arts.

The third sage and king of China. ... They came before the Flood and were invented by

---

tried to date in this way a passage in *Shujing*. But it appears to be a hit-or-miss method. Biot places the date at about 2400 BC, while Maspero and others give the 8th century BC. According to Needham (*SCC*, III, p. 245–6), it is unlikely that the text refers to an event much before 1500 BC.

[1] This quotation, given in Latin, is presumably taken from a textbook of scholastic philosophy, but an extensive search has failed to trace its source. The Latin is corrupt and the translation therefore tentative. The work of Porphyrius from which this quotation was taken has been lost, but Simplicius, in his commentary on Aristotle's *De coelo* (2, 46), refers to this text, but mentions 3,900, not 1,900, years. Either Rodrigues or the Macao copyist erred when writing this passage. Some corrupt texts of Simplicius give 31,000 years. Heath, *Greek Astronomy*, p. xiv. Other references to the alleged antiquity of Chaldean astronomical observations were made by Cicero, *On Divination*, 1, 1; Diodorus of Sicily, 2, 31; Proclus, *Commentary on Plato's Timaeus*, 4. Nebuchadnezzar was king of Babylon 605–562 BC. The first year of the Olympiad is generally taken as 776 BC, so the 31st Olympiad would have been about 652 BC, which is 47 years before Nebuchadnezzar began to reign. Callisthenes (c. 360–327 BC) accompanied Alexander on his campaigns, but was executed because of his objection to prostrating himself before the throne. Douglas, *New Bible*, pp. 873–4; *Oxford Classical Dictionary*, pp. 59, 278.

[2] Alexander the Great succeeded to the throne in 336 BC, and captured Babylon in 331. Rodrigues clearly states (*Arte grande*, f. 239) that Christ was born in AM 4074. So 331 BC would correspond to AM 3743, and not 3681, as he gives here in the text.

[3] See p. 354, n. 7.

[4] Pliny, *Natural History*, VI, 30.

[5] Nimrod was the son of Cush, the son of Ham, and was renowned for his hunting skill (Genesis, 10, 8–10). Some scholars identify him with Sargon of Agade, a ruler of Assyria and a great hunter, who flourished about 2300 BC. Rodrigues has already noted that the Confusion of Tongues took place in AM 1787, which corresponds to about 2275 BC, and this date coincides with Sargon's time. The name Belus, or Belos, son of Nimrod according to some sources, is the hellenized form of Ba'al or Bel. Ninus is said to have been the son of Belus and to have begun his 52-year reign in 2189 BC: *Oxford Classical Dictionary*, p, 238; Douglas, *New Bible*, p. 888; Haskins, *Studies*, pp. 336–45.

the Fathers, and from them to Noah and his sons.[1] After the Flood his descendants and other families learnt these from them. They took them with them when they went out to populate the world and taught them to their descendants in the kingdoms that they peopled. They have been preserved until now here at the end of the world, where from that time to this, as their annals record, this nation has remained intact without any intermingling with any other, except for ninety years when they were overrun by the Tartars in these latter times.[2] But the Tartars took over their customs and not the Chinese theirs. Nor was it possible in such a brief, ignorant, and uncouth time for them to have invented them by themselves and to have had in these matters such sages, as we said, merely by experience. Nor could there have been such complete similarity between the things of Europe, Asia, Africa, or Egypt, whose origin is attributed among us to the first Fathers before the Flood.

For they divided the Heavens into twelve signs or parts through 365°25′, and the globe into equinoctial circles. They had the seven planets with the same qualities, names, and motion.[3] The same motion of the sun for 365 days and 25 minutes; the lunar year consisting of 12 months of 354 days, with the intercalary year of 384 days; the four seasons of the year, the solstices and equinoxes, the rules for calculating eclipses, and everything else of this kind. All this was so ancient and so similar to European science that it is evident that this was not invented here by chance, but both ours and theirs came from the same origin and source.

At the same time he also made them study judicial astrology here after the fashion of the Chaldeans with figures of odd and even numbers.[4] According to the authors, this science was spread throughout the world by Ham, son of Noah, and he taught it to his descendants so that they might learn it before the Flood from the sons of Ham who professed it. According to this and the other errors that they have held since then concerning God, the creation of the universe, spiritual substances, and the soul of man, as well as inevitable fate, the Chinese seem to be descendants of Ham, because he held similar errors and taught them to his descendants, who then took them with them when they set off to populate the world.[5]

---

[1] Although there is no gap in the text at this point, it is clear that the copyist has omitted some words, possibly a few lines. The text of the previous sentence also seems corrupt and can be translated only with difficulty.

[2] That is, the Yuan or Mongol dynasty, which began in 1279 and lasted 89 years until 1368 when it was succeeded by the Ming dynasty.

[3] As may be seen on p. 365, Rodrigues includes the sun and moon in the list of the seven planets as was normal in pre-Copernican astronomy, hence the Japanese term *shichiyō*, the seven luminaries. The five planets known to the Chinese were Mercury, Venus, Mars, Jupiter, and Saturn. For accounts of the Chinese understanding of these planets, see *SCC*, III, pp. 398–401; Maspero, 'L'Astronomie', pp. 295–318.

[4] As noted earlier, the odd numbers 1, 3, 5, 7, and 9 are *yang* in nature and are associated with Heaven, while the even numbers are *yin* and associated with Earth. Forke, *World-Conception*, pp. 77–8.

[5] Ham is associated with superstitious practices because his son Canaan was cursed by Noah (Genesis, 9, 25). According to Clement of Alexandria and other early Christian writers, Ham may be identified with Zoroaster. As Rodrigues later notes, the 5th-century monk and ascetical writer John Cassian asserts that Ham made a special study of astrology and that his descendants spread this knowledge throughout the world. See p. 378, below.

CHAPTER 9

CHINESE AND JAPANESE ASTROLOGY IN PARTICULAR

The Chinese, and also the Japanese who received them from them, divide their sciences into two categories. The first is natural magic, which deals with the production of the universe, the origins of natural things, generation and corruption of things, fate, and judicial and genethliacal astrology. We will describe this later in the treatise on the sects of these kingdoms.[1] The second is astronomy, which deals with the Heavens. Both are expressed by the two words *eki* and *reki,* or *yi* and *li* in Chinese. The first term means natural magic, and the second, astronomy.[2]

They divide astronomy into speculative and practical. Speculative astronomy deals with the structure of the upper and lower world; the Heavens and their movements; the rising and setting of the celestial signs and planets; the material sphere and its circles; the conjunctions of the planets and eclipses of the sun and moon; the planetary hours and time, and, after their fashion, everything else in this field that our astronomers also study. Practical astrology, which others call judicial, prognostic, or also divinatory, deals with good and bad days to work, and other contingent things that can be foretold by the celestial appearances and aspects, and the conjunctions of the planets among themselves and with the stars.[3]

As regards the unity of the world, we believe according to our faith that there is only one world. This is in keeping with natural reason that shows it to be so and at the same time shows that both the sky and Earth are round in shape.[4] Just as there were various theories held by ancient philosophers concerning the unity and form of the world, so also here among those of the sects. Some believe there to be only one world, others say that there are almost infinitely many. Some say that it is shaped this way, others say that way. Some say that Earth is square with six sides and the sky is round and fluid; others says it is pyramidal,

---

[1] This treatise, if written, has not survived.

[2] *Vocabulario*, ff. 321, 209: '*Eki*. A book or art that teaches the nature, qualities, and events of a man according to his birth. *Eki wo toru*. To guess or foretell by this book what is to happen to somebody, etc.' '*Reki. Koyomi*. Calendar of days, months, and year. *Item*, science of observing the stars, or planets, to know everyone's life and fortune.' While the term *eki* can be translated as 'divination', *reki* is generally rendered as 'calendar', thus showing how large was the calendar's role in oriental astronomical science.

[3] This division was also found in Western astronomy. According to Christopher Clavius (1537?–1612), the foremost Jesuit mathematician and a teacher of Ricci and much involved in the reform of the European calendar, theoretical astronomy deals with the movement, number, and size of the stars, while practical (or judicial) astronomy may be identified with what would now be called astrology. Clavius, *In Sphaeram*, p. 5.

[4] In 1593, Rodrigues debated with two Zen monks in Ieyasu's presence, and among the topics discussed was whether there is only one world or many. Rodrigues argued that there could be only one world under the heavens, citing reason and navigational experience. The monks told him that the books left by Shaka said there were other worlds, but they did not know whether this was true or not. Cooper, *Rodrigues the Interpreter*, p. 101.

high and low, with many Heavens like worlds. We put here briefly what these philosophers held over here, remarking in the first place that our philosophers who held the same opinion probably took it from the sages of these parts, just as they took other theories, principally from the Indian sect and that of the Chaldeans, which is the same as the sect of the Chinese astrological scholars. The reason for this is that the philosophers of these parts lived long before the others and even before the Greek philosophers.

Those among the ancient philosophers who believed that there were many worlds and even an infinite number of them were Democritus, Metrodorus, Anaximander, Anaximenes, Archelaus, Aristarchus, Xenophanes, Diogenes, Leucippus, Epicurus, and the Indian gymnosophist Anaxarchus.[1] Alexander the Great is said to have wept when he heard from this last man that there were many worlds, because he was not yet lord of even one of them.[2] There was also Shaka, or Shakia, also called Buddha, the founder of the sect of the gymnosophists of India. He advocates three worlds, and afterwards three thousand, and finally a quasi-infinite number of worlds.[3] He was followed by the Manicheans, who originated from this sect and took their principal dogmas from it, because Manes, the author of the Manichean sect, was, according to many authors, a Brahman by race. The three worlds laid down by Shaka are called *sangai*, that is, 'three worlds', and they place in each of these three worlds a certain number of Heavens to the total of thirty-three, with their inhabitants; some have a shorter life, others a longer, while others possess eternal life without end. They call the first of the three worlds *yokkai*, that is, world of concupiscence; the *shikikai* world is the corporeal world or with colour (which is the same among them); and the incorporeal world, or world without colour.[4]

In these three worlds Shaka places a mountain like a very high pyramid, called Shuminsan, or Xumisen in Chinese. It has four sides at the base, one facing the south, another towards the north, another towards the east, and finally another towards the west. In each one of these the inhabitants have differently shaped faces and bodies depending on the part to which they assign the particular figure. For example, the southern part is warm and they believe that it is the place for the element of fire and the pyramidal shape, and this is where the men of our world dwell. The northern part is the natural place for the element of water and a round shape; the western part is square or a cube of six sides, and this is where they place the water; the eastern part is a semicircle and they place the wind or locomotive power there.

Shaka holds that this mountain is separated from us by a great distance towards the north. He says that its foundations rest on three spheres supporting it. The first and lowest

---

[1] Rodrigues almost certainly took these names from *Commentarii*, p. 109, where there is an identical list of philosophers postulating an infinite number of worlds. This work was one of a series of commentaries on Aristotle, compiled and used at the Jesuit college in Coimbra, where Matteo Ricci had studied. There was at least one copy in China as Ricci's friend Li Zhizao translated it into Chinese, 'together with the questions, which are handled upon them by the Schoole of *Conimbra*,' (Semedo, *History*, p. 242). An account of ancient Western philosophers postulating a plurality of worlds is given in McColley, 'Seventeenth-Century Doctrine', pp. 385–92.

[2] This incident is mentioned in *Commentarii*, p. 109, although the classic reference to this episode is found in Plutarch, *De tranquilitate animi*, 466d.

[3] For the infinite number of world-spheres in Buddhist belief, see Bhadantācariya, *Path*, VII, 44 (p. 221).

[4] *Vocabulario*, f. 217v: '*Sangai. Buppō* [Buddhism]. *Mitsu no kai*. That is, *yokkai, shikikai, mushikikai*. Three kinds of world mentioned in Buddhism.' These are the three worlds of desire, form, and formlessness. The worlds are divided into 10, 18, and 4 heavens, giving a total of 32. In some lists an extra subdivision is added, thus reaching a total of 33. Vilela (Sakai, 15 September 1565, in *Cartas*, I, f. 194) mentions the Buddhist belief in 33 heavens. As regards Rodrigues's reference to the second world, *shikikai, shiki* can mean both carnality and colour.

one rests on the sphere of the wind, and on this the sphere of water, which surrounds all this mountain. The height of this mountain above the water is 46,080 leagues, and it has the same height below the water, making a total of 92,160 leagues. Above this mountain there are thirty-three Heavens divided into three orders, and the sun, moon, and stars move or revolve around this mountain. The mountain itself is thinnest in the middle and widest at the top and bottom, rather like an hourglass. From this arises the distinction between day and night, which are longer or shorter depending on whether the place where they move is thinner or thicker.[1]

In addition to these three worlds, they postulate three thousand others. The first is called the thousand small worlds, and this is made up of a thousand of these mountains and a thousand suns and a thousand moons. The second is called the thousand medium worlds, and this comprises a thousand smaller worlds. The third is called the thousand big worlds, and this consists of a thousand of medium size.[2] This is the form of the world according to Shaka and of the many worlds that he proposes, that is, the three thousand described above.

We are told in *Cursus Conimbricensis* that some of the ancient philosophers conceived the world as a pyramid:

> Some, such as Xenophanes, thought of it as a pyramid and believed that it remained at rest on account of its infinite depth. But Thales of Miletus believed that Earth was supported by water, rather like wood or something of the same sort floating in water. Anaximenes, Anaxagoras, and Democritus attributed the stillness of Earth to its breadth, and said that it was supported by air.[3]

As we have seen, this is the opinion of Shaka, who assigns a square or conical shape to the element of Earth and a pyramidal shape to the mountain, and says that the world is set deeply in the water that supports it.

But in truth both Shaka and the ancient philosophers who supposed many worlds postulated *in re* only one true world inhabited by men and animals, with only one sky, a sun, a moon, and stars. All the rest were mysterious and metaphorical fables concerning what happens within men. This can be clearly gathered from the doctrine of Shaka and from his texts and interpreters, where it is stated that these numerous worlds are enigmatic and symbolic. Hence it is most likely that all those who postulated many worlds took the theory

---

[1] *Vocabulario*, f. 396: '*Shishū. Yotsu no kuni*. As, *Shumi no shishū*. Four kingdoms that they think are on Mt Shumisan.' Quoting ancient Chinese texts about the mountain, called Sumeru in Japanese, Unno ('Japan', pp. 57–9) remarks that 'his [Rodrigues's] observations are generally correct.' Illustrations of Sumeru are given in ibid., pp. 58, 59, and also in Nakayama, *History*, pp. 206–7, 209. Fróis (*História*, I, p. 219) goes into some detail describing this mountain. 'In keeping with the teaching of Shaka, the Japanese believe that there is a mountain range to the north that reaches to the heavens and extends deeply into the earth. They call this Shumisen and it has the shape of an hourglass. They say that the sun always revolves around it, just like a child's spinning top, in such fashion that during its solar orbit every day the more the sun descends and draws near to the peak of the pyramid in the middle, the hotter the world gets and the warm winds become stronger and more intense. And when it later ascends and distances itself from us, more cold is felt because of its departure.' Without naming the mountain, both Ribadeneira (*Historia*, p. 364) and Ricci (*Opere*, II, p. 207) mention the myth that the sun revolves around a mountain, behind which it hides every night. The belief was inspired by reports of the enormous size of the mountain ranges north of India. For Japanese references, beginning in the 7th century, to belief in Mt Sumeru, see Unno, 'Japan', pp. 62–8.

[2] The description of these three worlds appears somewhat illogical and may well have been distorted by the copyist. It is possible to translate: 'The second is called the thousand medium worlds, and this consists of 2,000 smaller worlds.' But this version seems unlikely.

[3] Rodrigues gives these quotations in Latin, and they are rather free versions of statements found in *Commentarii ... de coelo*, pp. 379, 382.

from Shaka's doctrine and in the same enigmatic sense, for Shaka lived long before them and is the first to be found who postulates this multitude of worlds. Records show that many of these ancient philosophers were in communication with the Brahmans, disciples of Shaka's doctrine, and took from them many physical dogmas. As regards Anaxarchus, who told Alexander the Great that there were three thousand worlds, it is clear that he was speaking popularly and not materially, for he was a gymnosophist and a follower of Shaka's doctrine. This doctrine flourished at that time in India, and it clearly postulates the three worlds in a mysterious and metaphorical sense, but only one true world, which they call *isseikai*, that is, 'only one world'.[1]

The Chinese philosophers postulate only one world, consisting of Heaven and Earth. They believe that Heaven is round and Earth is square, surrounded on its four sides by four seas and situated in the middle of or within the sky. So on account of its shape, they say that it is motionless and only the upper part or surface is inhabited.[2] The Japanese follow this theory, and accordingly divide the structure of the world into celestial and terrestrial, or superior and inferior. The first[3] is expressed by the word 'Heaven', which they call *ten*, or *tian* in Chinese. They understand by this word all the ethereal and aerial world, the sky, stars, planets, the Heavenly influences, its five elements or five elementary qualities, that is, fire, wood, earth, water, and metal.[4]

According to their explanation, these correspond *in re* with hot, cold, dry, and wet. These are called elements, and they place them in the region of the air or ether, supported in the substance of the air in their appropriate places; fire in the south, water in the north, wood in the east, metal in the west, and Earth in the middle. They believe that these qualities correspond to the properties of the five planets: wood to Jupiter, fire to Mars, earth to Saturn, metal to Venus, water to Mercury, and so they call these planets by these names.[5] The sun and the moon are like a source and include these five qualities: the sun, hot and dry; the moon, wet and cold.[6]

---

[1] Rodrigues here shows his keen perception when stating that the numerous Buddhist worlds are merely 'enigmatic and symbolic', for few Europeans would have taken such a benign interpretation of Buddhist theology. Whether or not the plurality of worlds postulated by European philosophers was meant to be symbolic or not is discussed in McColley, 'Seventeenth-Century Doctrine', pp. 386–90.

[2] Of the several cosmological theories produced by the Chinese, the Gaitian theory seems best to fit Rodrigues's vague account. According to this system, the heavens were imagined as a hemispherical cover and Earth as a bowl turned upside down, thus forming two concentric domes. The heavens were circular, Earth was square and surrounded by water. *SCC*, III, pp. 210–15; Forke, *World-Conception*, pp. 12–18; Nakayama, *History*, pp. 24–35, provides much technical information. Ricci (*Opere*, II, pp. 175, 207) twice refers to the Chinese belief that Earth is flat and square, and the sky is a round canopy.

[3] The text appears corrupt here, and I have made some additions to the translation. A literal rendering would be: '… they divide the structure of the world into celestial and terrestrial, or in upper; they express the second…'.

[4] The five Chinese elements, or *wuxing*, are noted by Carletti, *My Voyage*, p. 174; Trigault, *Litterae*, p. 133; Ricci, *Fonti*, II, p. 51, and *China*, p. 327. These elements are listed in *Shujing*, V, 4, 5 (Legge, *Chinese Classics*, III, p. 325), where Legge rightly observes that the term 'element' is totally inadequate to express the Chinese concept. Accounts of the *gogyō*, as they are called in Japanese, are found in Forke, *World-Conception*, pp. 227–300, and *SCC*, II, pp. 232–44.

[5] Tables of the symbolic correlations are given in *SCC*, II, pp. 262–3. Not only were the five elements associated with the planets, the cardinal points of the compass, etc., as Rodrigues correctly observes, but each of them was associated with a taste, a part of the human body, a season of the year, a colour, a smell, a musical note, and an internal organ of the body.

[6] According to Chinese thought, the sun had a fiery *yang* nature while the moon had a watery *yin* one. The sun was called the Great Yang and the moon the Great Yin. The stars were accordingly called the Small Yang, and the planets the

The second region is expressed by the word *chi*, or *di* in Chinese, that is, Earth, by which they understand land, seas, rivers, lakes, stones, metals, trees, and all the rest contained therein. They believe that Earth is visible, and that water and fire are not elements but are compounds that are generated and corrupt like everything else corporeal.[1] They maintain this because the elements cannot be generated or corrupted, for they are the ingredients of which things are composed and into which they resolve by the corruption of the compound, and one is not generated from another.[2]

Small Yin. A distinction was thus made (knowingly?) between those bodies shining by their own light, and those only reflecting light. *SCC*, III, p. 227. For more on the principles of yin and yang, see *SCC*, II, pp. 273–8. See also p. 362, n. 4.

[1] The text is suspect at this point. By saying that the Chinese believe Earth to be visible, Rodrigues presumably means that they take a realist, not idealist, view of the world. But to add that water and fire are not considered elements in the second region is remarkable, and I find no confirmation of this view in Fung's standard work on Chinese philosophy.

[2] Here Rodrigues employs terms of scholastic philosophy, which he studied in preparation for the priesthood.

CHAPTER 10

HEAVEN IN PARTICULAR, AND THE DEGREES INTO WHICH THEY DIVIDE IT

As may be seen in their books, the Chinese and Japanese consider Heaven in various ways in keeping with the different theories that they form about it and the different aspects they attribute to it.[1] Thus, as there is numerically only one Heaven and only one substance, they give it various names by which these may be distinguished.

First of all, they consider it in general inasmuch as it embraces everything that is within it and is made in the region of air and aether, such as the substance of Heaven, its nature, operations, various qualities and arrangements, and the change that the sun in its orbit causes in the four seasons of the year, the aetherial influences, and everything else. From this point of view they call it *tendō*, or *tiandao* in Chinese, meaning the path, order, or science of Heaven.

Hence they divide all their science into three categories: *tendō*, celestial; *chidō*, terrestrial; and *jindō*, human or moral.[2] The subjects of these are the three principal things of the universe – Heaven, Earth, and Man – and they call this *sansai*, that is, the three accomplishments, or the three most excellent things.

Secondly, they consider Heaven from the point of view of its nature, disposition, properties, or power to act, or inasmuch as it contains the principle of constantly and perseveringly acting without any pause, and in this respect they call it *ken*, and *qian* in Chinese, and the Earth *kon* or *kun*. These mean Heaven and Earth insofar as its nature is strong and constant, and is perpetually in movement without stopping. As a result, it is the efficient principle and cause of everything generated and corrupted.[3] Hence they attribute to it active qualities, hot and dry and the same nature as fire. They also call it Father, male or masculine, and Lord, on account of its active and predominant power with which it produces things in spring, makes them bloom and reach their full strength in summer, ripens them in autumn, and finally perfects them and makes them reach their zenith. On the other hand, as far as its nature is concerned, Earth has the opposite qualities for it has passive and receptive power; its purpose is to receive and support, and for this reason it is called Mother and female.[4]

---

[1] Fung (*History*, I, p. 31) tabulates five (as opposed to Rodrigues's six) different aspects of Heaven: material Heaven, ruling Heaven, fatalistic Heaven, naturalistic Heaven, and ethical Heaven. These correspond to Rodrigues's categories fairly well. In the Portuguese text, *ceo* can mean either sky or Heaven, and I have generally used the latter version. In this context, 'Heaven' is of course devoid of the European concept of paradise.

[2] Already listed on p. 175.

[3] Rodrigues here introduces again terms from scholastic philosophy ('efficient principle', 'generated', 'corrupted') when explicating Asian astronomical theory.

[4] As early as 1556, the anonymous author of *Sumario de los errores* in Japan related that Earth was considered feminine, while the sky or Heaven was regarded as masculine. Ruiz-de-Medina, *Documentos*, I, p. 656. This distinction arose from the sun's *yang* nature and Earth's and moon's *yin* nature. *SCC*, III, p. 227; Forke, *World-Conception*, pp. 176–7.

Thirdly, they consider Heaven as regards its action and influence on the things below, and from this point of view they call it *mei* or *tenmei*, and *ming* or *tianming* in Chinese, the celestial influence from above. It is also called *tenri*, and *tianli* in Chinese, that is, *ratio coeli*, inasmuch as it is the universal efficient cause. It is called *tei* or *jōtei*, and *di* or *shangdi* in Chinese, that is, the dominion or predominant power over the things of below by continual movement without any intermission and the influence that it exerts. For the same reason, it is also called *tenshin* or *tentoku*, and *tianxin* or *tiande* in Chinese, meaning the spirit or soul of Heaven and the celestial virtue. It is not indeed a living soul, but it is thus called inasmuch as it invincibly operates on the things of below.[1] It is also called *kishin*, and *gueishen* in Chinese, that is, the good and evil spirit, which is the power with which it works and produces things like a soul, and with which it corrupts them. They believe that the good spirit or genius is the expansion and invisible strength of heat and its growth, which is brought about in the region of air by the approach of the sun towards us and by which things are produced. The evil spirit is the decrease and contraction of the same heat, and the cold that it causes with the departure of the sun, and things are thereby corrupted. The first belongs to heat and dryness; the second to cold and dampness.

Fourthly, they consider Heaven under different aspects and the different properties that it has in keeping with these, inasmuch as Heaven is fluid, diaphanous, transparent, and permeable air that yields without impeding, and an infinite space. They call this Heaven *taikū* or *taikyo*, and *taikong* or *taixu* in Chinese, meaning the great vacuum or incorporeal thing without solid shape or quantity. In comparison with Earth, it is superior and supreme, while Earth is inferior and lowly. Thus it is called *kō, ki, sō, sho*, and *gao, gui, cang, sheng* in Chinese, that is, high, supreme, sublime, noble, venerable.[2]

Fifthly, their ancient sages regarded the universe and the perpetual laws and order observed during the course of the four seasons as a moral imitation of Heaven and Earth.[3] The sun, approaching and receding, was considered as the universal mother and father of everything. They base all their moral and civil doctrine on this, imitating in their actions Heaven and Earth, the universal parents, whose progeny, they believe, was the first man and woman, the progenitors and ancestors of all other people. They believe that their legitimate successor is their king and so they call him Son of Heaven.[4]

Sixthly and lastly, they consider Heaven as regards its substance and material, and under this aspect they properly call it *ten*, and *tian* in Chinese, meaning 'Heaven'. They believe that this is numerically only one, without a multitude of different layers or spheres.[5] Its material, they maintain, is fluid air or ether without any bulk, and for this reason they call it

---

[1] For the Chinese belief in Heaven's ruling providence, see Forke, *World-Conception*, pp. 148–51.

[2] In the text, the third Japanese adjective is written *san* (or perhaps *son*), but in reference to the Chinese version, *sō* seems preferable. The literal meaning of the four terms is high, noble, luxuriant, and sacred. For the Chinese theory regarding Heaven as infinite, empty space, void of all substance, see *SCC*, III, pp. 219–21.

[3] A free translation of a sentence that literally reads: 'Fifthly, they considered it morally by their ancients the imitation of Heaven and Earth, and universal and perpetual laws and order…'.

[4] For Chinese theories regarding Heaven and Earth as father and mother, husband and wife, etc., see Forke, *World-Conception*, pp. 68–71. As regards *Tianzi*, or Son of Heaven, Semedo (*History*, p. 109) remarks: 'They call him also *Thien Zu*, which is to say, *Sonne of Heaven*; not because they believe him to be such, but because they hold, that *Empire* is a gift of heaven.'

[5] Needham (*SCC*, III, p. 223) remarks on the absence in Chinese thought of the Aristotelian cosmology adopted in medieval Europe in which the heavenly bodies were fixed to a series of concentric material spheres with the earth as their centre.

incorporeal, or without shape and different parts. The material or form of Heaven is comprised of the sun, moon, planets, and stars, for these have bulk and a manifestly spherical shape. They believe that the air or Heaven is in continual motion, but that this is not regular, just as the motion of the wind is not regular. But they attribute regular motion to the solar and lunar bodies, the planets and the stars, which they believe move along fixed paths in the same air with a certain limited motion, just as a fish swims in water.[1] They say that everything moves from east to west with both natural and rapt motion in a spiral, because, as they believe that the bodies of the stars move of their own accord and not with the motion of the Heavens, they could not understand how there could be two contrary movements simultaneously in the same body.[2]

Hence they believe that they move in a spiral, each day making their motion, rapt or diurnal, and at the same time descending or ascending towards one of the two tropics. Here they make the spring equinox in the east in Libra, and the autumn one in the west in Aries. In this way, contrary to our thinking, it moves from east to west. According to them, Heaven begins from the surface of Earth upwards, as everything that is not Earth and water is Heaven,[3] because, as has been said, the world is divided into Heaven and Earth. But usually and commonly they call Heaven the upper region of air where the planets and stars move along their paths. They maintain that Heaven in its outer surface and convex part, where the air ends, is mixed with the elementary qualities of a circular or round figure, and they believe that thence outwards there is infinite air and a most simple substance without any qualities or activity, just as we say that *materia prima* is pure substance. The concave surface of Heaven, which surrounds Earth, is square, according to them, just like Earth itself.

To understand this better, it should be noted that all these sects of philosophers in Japan and China firmly believe that *ex nihilo nihil fit*, nor did they know of any infinite power that could create out of nothing. Hence they postulated eternal matter *et a se ipsa*. They imagine this to be the infinite air in which, they say, there is perpetual movement. As a result of this motion in the midst of this infinite air, an infinite chaos was produced with elementary qualities, and it was like a sphere before it divided. They call this chaos by various names, such as *konton mibun*, that is, an indivisible conglobation or sphere. In the sect of the *kami* of Japan this is *keishi no gotoku*, that is, like a hen's egg that has a clear, thin, diaphanous shell[4] and an opaque and cloudy yolk, by which they signify the spherical shape and the confusion or parts therein.[5] It is also called *taikyoku*, and *taiji* in Chinese, meaning the great limit or

---

[1] This theory was a considerable advance on the medieval European view that the heavenly bodies were 'implanted, impressed, plastered, nailed, knotted, glued, sculptured or painted' (as Giordano Bruno scornfully described the system) on a series of concentric crystalline spheres. For centuries, Chinese astronomers spoke of a 'hard wind' (*gangqi* or *gangfeng*) that carried the heavenly bodies along their orbits. *SCC*, II, p. 483, and III, pp. 222–3, 440. For Western theories of concentric spheres, see Heath, *Aristarchus*, pp. 190–224.

[2] According to the Gaitian theory, the sun and moon travel eastwards by their own motion, but Heaven moves westwards and carries these bodies with it. To borrow an illustration found in both Chinese and Western literature, the heavenly bodies resemble ants creeping eastwards along a millstone or potter's wheel, which itself is turning more quickly westwards, and thus bears them along in that direction. *SCC*, III, pp. 210–16; Forke, *World-Conception*, pp. 12–14. An account of Chinese understanding of the course of the celestial bodies, with a wealth of technical detail, is given in *SCC*, III, pp. 392–401.

[3] The text at this point is repetitious, but the meaning remains clear.

[4] The text does not mention the word 'shell', but the context seems to require it.

[5] The anonymous author of *Sumario de los errores*, 1556, relates the theory that the world was once in the form of an egg; when this broke, the lighter white formed the sky, while the denser yolk formed the earth. Ruiz-de-Medina, *Documentos*, I, p. 656. This theory is also mentioned by Vilela (*Cartas*, I, f. 139), Ribadeneira (*TCJ*, 297);and Couto,

span, for it is infinite and the biggest thing in existence, and totally infinite air. And also *bukyoku*, and *wuji* in Chinese, meaning infinite or without limit. They also called it the unity or great unity, because it is uniquely big.[1]

With the continual movement, this chaos divided up. The pure, clear, and light parts ascended and became air or ether. This they call Heaven and it is most perfect as regards the four qualities – hot, cold, dry, and wet – and was changed into the planets and stars. The hot and dry were changed into the sun, and the cold and wet into the moon, and thus these two planets are the source of the four elementary qualities. The other five planets were each composed of the most perfect of one of these qualities, and the same happened for the stars. Some of them belonged to the sun on account of their quality and others to the moon. In the same way, the turbid, impure, and more gross and heavy descended to the middle of the chaos, where it condensed and became earth and water, and these also possessed the elementary qualities.[2]

With this mixture and the power of the celestial and terrestrial qualities, Heaven and Earth continued forming, and with their power later produced the first man and woman, and all the other things of the universe, acting like a universal father and mother.

From then onwards, with the movement of Heaven and the power of the sun, planets, and stars, it continued with the annual generation and corruption of the four seasons. They believe that this universe, from the time it began at its first production until it again finishes and returns to chaos, is to last twelve periods corresponding to the twelve signs of the zodiac. They give 10,800 years to each period or sign, and this makes a total of 129,600. They call this length of time the Great Year and they assign it months, days, and hours, which we describe separately elsewhere. Among us, this year is called the Platonic Year.[3] This year or space begins in the first sign of midnight, which is in the first degree of Capricorn. They believe that Heaven was produced in this sign, Earth was produced in the second towards the west, while man was produced in the third. In the fourth, which is in the east and the position of the spring equinox, all the other things were produced. From there until the first degree of Cancer, they believe that the world increases in perfection and size, and it begins to deteriorate thence onwards until reaching the place where it began. Here it completely ends, leaving nothing but the original chaos, as we shall say in the proper place.[4]

Década quinta, 8, 12 [f. 185]). The egg illustration is also found in the creation account in *Nihongi*, I, pp. 1–2. The same theory was advanced by the 1st-century philosopher Zhangheng and others. *SCC*, III, pp. 217–18; Forke, *World-Conception*, p. 20. For the ancient Taoist term *huntun* (*konton* in Japanese), see *SCC*, II, pp. 107–15.

[1] Similarities with various points of Rodrigues's account are found in Needham's exposition (*SCC*, III, pp. 219–24) of the teachings of the Xuanye school of thought, advocating the existence of infinite empty space. *Daiyi*, or Great Oneness, is mentioned in Wu Linchuan's 14th-century description of the origin of the universe. *SCC*, II, p. 486.

[2] The theory that the lighter mass rose and became Heaven, while the heavier mass sank and became Earth, is generally called centrifugal cosmogony, although, as Needham (*SCC*, II, pp. 371–4) points out, centripetal cosmogony would be an apter term.

[3] The period, called *yuan*, was to last 129,600 years, divided into 12 *hui* of 10,800 years each. The *yuan* was conceived as a quasi-infinite world period, similar to the Indian *kalpa*. One explanation of its length is that the *hui* lasts 360 x 30 years (or one generation). *SCC*, II, pp. 485–6; Forke, *World-Conception*, pp. 111–12. Heraclitus's Great Year was also to last for 10,800 years for the same reason. In his *Republic*, VIII:546, and *Timaeus*, 39, Plato mentions the same concept, but does not specify its duration. For a detailed explanation, see Taylor, *Commentary*, pp. 216–19. For the varying lengths given to the Great Year, see Heath, *Aristarchus*, pp. 61, 102, 129, 171–3, 314–16. Clavius (*In Sphaeram*, p. 56) reckons the Platonic Year as lasting 49,000 years, at the end of which all the stars return to their original places.

[4] According to Chinese thought, 5,400 years elapsed after the Great Beginning, or *taishi*, until the lightest part of the primaeval chaos rose in the middle of the first *hui* to form the sun, moon, stars, and planets. In the middle of the

The sects of the Indian gymnosophists teach this, and the same theory was held by many of the ancients, as may be seen in the authors:

> Anaximenes believed that air was the first principle of all things. He said that it was finite by nature, but possessed infinite qualities. He thought that everything came into being by the condensation and rarefaction of air, and that the great broad Earth was made in the first place from packed air, and therefore not without reason it is always encompassed by air.[1]

This theory that Heaven is one unit and fluid, or the very air, and the planets move therein like fish in water, is extremely ancient among the Chinese, and they have held this since their first foundation at the time of the Confusion of Tongues. It seems that all the earliest antiquity held the same opinion, and for this reason they attributed to Heaven the nature of fire, just as these did. Some modern astrologers in the northern regions follow this theory even now, for they are influenced by certain appearances that they have observed in the sky. They maintain that these cannot be explained unless Heaven is fluid, or at least the Heavens in which the planets move. But as it is too difficult to solve, they have not said anything yet about the eighth starry sphere where the stars are always at the same distance from each other and all move equally, both as regards their slow natural motion from west to east and also their rapt movement.[2]

The Moors and Arabs who profess Ptolemy's astrology in China have a royal college of mathematics in the court of Beijing.[3] They postulate nine Heavens, as did Ptolemy, but the Chinese have taken almost nothing from them, nor do they wish to mix their ancient astrology with that of the Moors. Although the ancient and modern Chinese books mention the nine Heavens, it is not because they postulate nine different spheres, but rather a fluid Heaven divided into nine parts or areas that they call nine Heavens.[4] They distribute the

---

second *hui*, the heavier mass condensed to form earth, rocks, water, and fire. After another 10,800 years, in the middle of the third *hui*, human beings were formed. At the end of a dozen *hui*, the universe will return to the original chaos. *SCC*, II, p. 486.

[1] This quotation, given in Latin, does not appear in *Commentarii*, and a search among other scholastic textbooks has not revealed its source. The Latin text is corrupt, and the word 'air' is added to the first line to make any sense of the translation. Anaximenes (fl. 546–25 BC) taught that air, when rarified, produces fire, and when condensed produces wind, clouds, water, earth, and stone in that order. *Oxford Classical Dictionary*, p. 86.

[2] In Ricci's *Mappamondo*, plate 4, there is a diagram illustrating the contemporaneous European (Aristotelian) concept of the movement of the celestial bodies. Earth is in the centre of nine concentric spheres, containing the stars, sun, moon, and planets. The ninth and last sphere contains the Primum Mobile circling from east to west in one day. All the other spheres move from west to east, but were presumed to be carried in the opposite direction by the ninth. This theory is mentioned (and rejected) in Clavius, *In Sphaeram*, pp. 46–8. See p. 364, n. 2, for the millstone simile.

[3] During the Mongol dynasty these so-called Moors and Arabs, presumably Persians and Central Asians, established themselves in the world of Chinese astronomy and technology. At Kublai's invitation, the Persian astronomer Jamāl al-Dīn arrived in Beijing in 1267, bringing astronomical instruments and a new calendar. In 1271, a Muslim astronomical institute (*Huihuisitianjian*) was established to work in parallel with the Chinese bureau. Ricci, *Fonti*, I, p. 41, n. 3; *SCC*, III, p. 49; Sugimoto and Swain, *Science and Culture*, pp. 122–3. For early references to the 'Saracen' astronomers, see Ricci, *Fonti*, I, pp. 41–2, and *China*, pp. 31–2; Trigault, *Litterae*, p. 127. According to Semedo (*History*, pp. 152–3), these 'Moors' had come to China from Turkestan some 700 years previously.

In a letter dated 12 May 1605, Ricci reports that the emperor maintains at great expense about 200 persons to prepare the calendar each year. There are two colleges: one follows Chinese canons, while the other, of lesser standing, adheres to the Muslim system. The two colleges are outside the imperial palace. There are two others, composed of eunuchs, within the palace. In Nanjing there are two more colleges. Quoted in Dunne, *Generation*, p. 210.

[4] In about 300 BC a theory was advanced in China suggesting the existence of nine layers or storeys (*jiuchong*) in the heavens, and this was somewhat similar to the Western concept of nine concentric spheres. *SCC*, III, pp. 198–9.

signs of the stars among them, dividing the torrid zone into eight parts and each part into 45°65′62″.[1] They call each of these parts a Heaven with its own proper name and quality, and distribute in them the 28 constellations or starry signs of the zodiac, most of these being stars of our twelve signs. The ninth part falls to the north, in which they place many other signs of stars. They also give special names to the sky in the four seasons of the year in accordance with the quality of that season, and so each season has a special name for the sky.[2] But in truth, it is but one Heaven and not many different spheres.

But this theory lost favour, and Rodrigues is referring to the nine regions of Heaven, according to the eight points of the compass plus the centre. These regions are listed in Forke, *World-Conception*, pp. 134–6.

[1] It must be recalled that the Chinese degree was divided into 100 minutes and the minute into 100 seconds. So 45°65′62″ multiplied by eight gives 365°24′96″, or 365·25°, which, as Rodrigues has said, makes up the Chinese circle.

[2] In spring the Blue Heaven, in summer the Luminous Heaven, in autumn the Gloomy Heaven, and in winter the High Heaven. Forke, *World-Conception*, pp. 133–4.

CHAPTER 11

THE DEGREES AND SIGNS INTO WHICH THEY DIVIDE THE SKY, AND THE EQUINOX AND THE ECLIPTIC

They do not think of the material of the sky as something solid but as fluid air, the depth of which cannot be recorded. Nor is there any definite beginning to it so that it may be measured and divided into degrees. They therefore divide and apportion the path of the sun, or the ecliptic (which they call the Yellow Path, or else the sun's path), the equinox, which cuts the sky through the middle and is called the Red Path, and also the moon's path, which they call the White Path.[1] The ordinary linear unit is also used to measure celestial things. The Japanese call it *shaku* and the Chinese *chi*, as we have already mentioned. This is, properly speaking, one of our mathematical feet, which equals four mathematical spans, each span comprising four fingers, each finger four degrees or points.

They divide the *shaku* according to the ancient fashion into 100 smaller parts or points, and they say that each point equals the thickness of 10 hairs of a horse's tail. Ten of these points make one *sun*, which is about the distance between the joints of the thumb; 10 *sun* make one *shaku*, 5 *shaku* one geometric pace or an ell of 5 feet; 10 *shaku* make one pole, etc., and thus it continues as has already been noted.[2]

To measure the degrees of the sky, however, they take as their unit the size of the sun, whose diameter, they say, is one degree long, and its circumference is 3°14′16″. They divide each degree into 100′, and each minute into 100″, and each second into 100 thirds, and thus they continue until ten.[3] They also believe that the moon is the same size as the sun, and they seemed to have adopted this view for the following reason.[4] Their ancient sages knew of only the movement from east to west, that is, the rapt movement of 13 hours,[5]

---

[1] For confirmation of these paths, see *SCC*, III, pp. 179, 278.

[2] Already noted on pp. 118–19. According to Chatley (*Ancient Chinese Astronomy*, p. 68), the Chinese reckoned celestial distances from star to star in 'feet', by comparison with a circle of 365·25 'feet' in circumference. This 'foot' therefore corresponded to a Chinese degree.

[3] The circumference of a circle is equal to its diameter multiplied by π, to which the Chinese gave the value of 3·142 as early as the 3rd century. *SCC*, III, p. 101. As regards Chinese calculations of the sun's size, in the 4th century Kehong held that its diameter was 1,000 *li* and its circumference 3,000 *li*, thus probably equating the 'size of the sun with one degree'. Forke, *World-Conception*, pp. 17, 60. Trigault (*Litterae*, p. 134) also mentions that the Chinese degree was divided into 100 minutes, their minute into 100 seconds, 'and so on'.

[4] Kehong, Bangu, and Xuzheng maintained that the moon was the same size as the sun, that is, they were both 1,000 *li* in diameter and 3,000 *li* in circumference. Forke, *World-Conception*, pp. 60–61. According to Ptolemy, the ratio of the diameters of the moon, Earth, and sun were 1 : 3.4 : 18.8. Heath, *Aristarchus*, p. 414. Whether Rodrigues's confused explanation of this point is correct is another matter.

[5] Presumably a slip for 12 hours.

which equal our 24, and the natural movement of each of the planets along its fixed path. Only the starry firmament moved through the air in a spiral until it returned to the place where it began its course. They also divide the ecliptic into 365° and 25' (or ¼°), and they give 365 days and three hours, or a quarter of a day, to the solar year. They therefore maintained that each day the sun, by its rapt movement, circled around[1] in twelve hours, and at the same time rose and set by its natural movement one degree equal to its size. Thus 365 solar diameters make one circle of 365°, and hence they say that the sun moves 366° in twelve hours throughout the day and night. Or perhaps they had another reason for this which we know nothing about.

They divide the equinoctial line (or Red Path, as they say) into a dozen equal parts that they call hours, giving a special name and character to each one.[2] Each of these parts is divided into 30°43'75", and the whole equinoctial circle into 365°25'; they assign to the diameter of this circle 121°75'. Each pole of the world is 91°31'25" distant from the equinox, and they are 182°62'50" away from each other.[3]

In the same way, they divide the ecliptic, or the Yellow Path, into another dozen equal parts, which they call houses in respect to the sun, planets, and starry signs, for the sun enters them in the course of the year. To each of these parts, or signs, they give the same name and character as the hours of the equinox. They divide each of these parts into 30°43'75", and the whole ecliptic into 365°25', and the sun traverses this in 365 days and three of their hours,[4] each day thus equaling a degree that the sun makes in its natural course. The ecliptic and the equinoctial cut each other at the two equinoxes of spring and autumn, and they separate from the equinoctial at 23°90'[5] towards the two poles of the world where they make two solstices, that is, the winter one, which they call the winter limit, and the summer one, the summer limit. They call these four the four fixed points.

In the same way, they divide the path of the moon, or White Path, into 365°25', and this cuts the ecliptic at two points, where they say the eclipses of the sun and moon are caused. This is what we call Caput and Cauda Draconis.[6] It separates from the ecliptic at 6°02' towards both poles of the world, and they thus make the length of the zodiac 12°04'.[7] They do not call it the zodiac, although that is what it is in actual fact.,

Each day the moon makes its rapt movement in 12 hours and travels 13°37' along its White Path.[8] They say that it completes its course in just over 27 days and that it makes its

---

[1] The text provides no main verb at this point, but the context demands some such word.

[2] Rodrigues provides a table of these signs at the end of the present chapter.

[3] As long as it is borne in mind that the Chinese used a decimal system of degrees (i.e., 30°43'75" equals 30·4375°) and that there were 365·25° to the circle, these figures quoted by Rodrigues are consistent. If the value of the diameter is given as 121°75', then in this instance the Chinese must have taken the value of π simply as 3·0, as indeed they often did (SCC, III, p. 99).

[4] As Rodrigues shows, the Chinese hour lasted twice as long as a modern European one.

[5] For the true value of the ecliptic angle, see p. 352, n. 1.

[6] These two points of the ecliptic are called the nodes of the moon. Concerning their association with Caput and Cauda Draconis, see p. 374, n. 1.

[7] Writing in 1086, Shen Gua pointed out that if the ecliptic and the moon's path coincided and there were no obliquity between them, there would be a solar eclipse every time the sun and moon were in conjunction, and a lunar eclipse every time they were in opposition. The actual angle between the ecliptic and the moon's path is 5°08'. SCC, III, pp. 415–16, 421 note d.

[8] According to the Xuanye school, the sun moved 1° every day and the moon 13°. SCC, III, p. 219; Forke, World-Conception, pp. 24, 59.

conjunction in just over 29 days 53 minutes.[1] The order of their signs and hours is the same, and they run from east to west, contrary to our signs. They are half a sign out of step with our signs, occupying 15° of one of ours and 15° of the next one. As a result, the four cardinal points of the solstices and equinoxes end up in the middle of their signs and hours, and the beginning of our signs occurs in the middle of theirs. Their first sign or hour begins at 15° of Capricorn. Its middle is the first degree of Capricorn, where they make the winter solstice and the middle of the night, and its end is at 15° of Sagittarius. The second begins at 15° of Sagittarius, its middle is at the beginning of the same sign, and its end at 15° of Scorpio. And so on in the others until the end.[2]

In ancient times they did not know about our signs and their names. But then the Moors came to China and translated the names of them into their language, and in order to show their superiority they joined them up with their own, running from east to west. But these seem to be the signs of the figures of the celestial stars that are in the zodiac, and for this reason they put them in their signs in the place where they are now found in the sky, for it is held to be separated towards the east by the slow movement of the stars.[3]

The degrees of the ecliptic begin the first degree of Capricorn in the winter solstice, whence it continues to ascend towards the east until the summer solstice. This arc is their ascendant and they call it *yō*, and *yang* in Chinese, that is, hot and dry, for these qualities begin to increase from the winter solstice onwards until the summer solstice, when they reach their due maximum. They call this *rōyō*, and *laoyang* in Chinese, meaning the old, or completed, hot and dry, because it thenceforth begins to decrease, while the contrary qualities, wet and cold, begin to increase until the sun reaches the winter solstice. This arc is their descendant and they call it *in*, meaning cold and wet, and when it reaches the solstice they call it *rōin*, or *laoyin* in Chinese, that is, old, or completed, cold and wet.[4] They attribute these qualities of *rōyō*, or *laoyang*, to the uneven number of nine, which multiplied by itself makes eighty-one.[5] Hence they declare that those who are born in it have the best possible destiny, and it is said among us that Plato was born in this to demonstrate his excellence over all other men. The Chinese hold that many of their illustrious men were born in this number or completed qualities, such as Rōshi, founder of the Dōkyō sect. The Chinese call him Laozi, that is, 'old son', giving the ignorant and common people to understand that he lived for eighty-one years in his mother's womb.[6]

---

[1] The sidereal month (i.e., the time taken for the moon to return to the same place among the stars) lasts 27·33 days, but the synodic month or lunation (i.e., the time between one full moon and the next) lasts 29·53 days (Rodrigues's '29 days 53 minutes'). The length of the lunation was accurately known in China in the 13th century BC *SCC*, III, pp. 239, 392.

[2] A table in Chalmers, 'Astronomy', p. [95], shows how the Chinese signs were out of step with the Western zodiac. This table gives the determinative stars and so must be read in conjunction with the table in Saussure, *Origines*, p. 279.

[3] A close translation of a typically vague sentence. Rodrigues seems to say that the foreign astronomers placed the determinative stars in the signs in which the stars were then found and not in their former positions, from which they had moved on account of precession (see p. 353, n. 6).

[4] For the interplay between *yang* and *yin* causing the various seasons, see Forke, *World-Conception*, pp. 177–83.

[5] According to traditional Chinese thought, Heaven is governed by the number 9, which number is also associated with the 'Old Yang'. Forke, *World-Conception*, pp. 77–8. Hence 81 (9 x 9) is considered an auspicious number, as may be seen in the examples quoted by Rodrigues. Gaubil, 'Histoire', II, p. 13.

[6] For Laozi, see p. 255. The characters of the name can in fact be literally translated as 'old son', but more correctly as 'Master Lao'.

They also believe that Hongwu was born in this. He was the founder of the present Chinese dynasty called Taimei, or Daming in Chinese. He was a poor man with a monstrously shaped face on which there were seventy-two pockmarks the size of a finger nail. The son of a peasant, he was a servant of the bonzes, or rather a cook, at the time of the Tartars, who had conquered China. He afterwards became a brigand and then a bandit chief, and he finally became so powerful that he drove the Tartars out of China, and was made the country's emperor in the year 1368. His descendants have reigned over this enormous empire ever since then until the present year of 1621, a total of 253 years.[1]

Their dozen signs or houses of the zodiac and of their dozen hours of the equinox, and the characters with which they write them both (for they are the same), are named after certain animals. These, along with our corresponding months, are given in Japanese, Chinese, and Portuguese, as follows:

The Characters of the Hours and Signs[2]

Japanese names	Chinese names	Our names	Our months	Japanese months or moons
ne	zi	Rat	December	11th
ushi	chou	Cow, bull	January	12th
tora	yin	Tiger	February	1st moon or month of the year
u	mao	Hare	March	2nd
tatsu	chen	Serpent	April	3rd
mi	si	Snake	May	4th
uma	wu	Horse	June	5th
hitsuji	wei	Ram	July	6th
saru	shen	Monkey	August	7th
tori	yu	Hen	September	8th
inu	xu	Dog	October	9th
i	hai	Wild Boar	November	10th

[1] Zhu Yuanzhang, better known by his reign title of Hongwu, was born of poor parents in 1328. He entered the Huangchueh monastery as a novice, but later left. He finally succeeded in overthrowing the declining Mongol dynasty. He had a 'rugged pockmarked face dominated by a jutting jaw, features so strange that they aroused awe …' Mote, 'Rise of Ming Dynasty', p. 44. As regards his being a brigand and bandit chief, 'In traditional Chinese historical materials, the words translated bandit … were applied to any person who defied legitimate authority … even to future founders of dynasties before they succeeded.' Ibid., p. 29. As Rodrigues correctly notes, Hongwu ascended the throne in 1368 and founded the Ming dynasty; he died in 1399. Giles, *Chinese Biographical Dictionary*, pp. 192–4.

[2] Both the Japanese and Chinese names are given fairly accurately in the text. Rodrigues may have copied the Japanese names out of his *Arte grande*, f. 231. The usual English translation of these names is: Rat, Ox, Tiger, Hare, Dragon, Snake, Horse, Goat, Monkey, Cock, Dog, Boar.

CHAPTER 12

THE ECLIPSES OF THE SUN AND MOON

The science of calculating the eclipses of the sun and moon is most ancient among the Chinese, and it is from them that the Japanese received the science. This is now very much in decline in these two nations as regards the theory of eclipses, for they are unaware of their principal cause.[1] But their ancient sages seemed to have had a complete understanding of this, but their writings were destroyed in the Burning of the Books, which a tyrannous Chinese king ordered 210 years before Christ our Lord in order to wipe out all memory of antiquity and to perpetuate his family, which had just tyrannized and usurped the kingdom.[2] But there have always remained traces of the science that they have worked on, and they have their ancient canons by which they calculate eclipses, albeit imperfectly, with such ease that even ignorant persons know how to do it by following these rules, as we often saw in Japan.[3]

Nor do the Chinese mathematicians now know how to rectify some problems that have arisen in the course of time concerning the hour, and still less do the Japanese know. For their ancient sages drew up their rules for the city now called Kaifengfu, the capital of Henan province and the ancient capital of Serica, or ancient China, at a position of $35\frac{1}{2}°$N and in that meridian.[4] In keeping with this, they still calculate the eclipses of the sun and moon throughout the whole kingdom, and from here the news is sent to the capitals of the provinces so that it may be communicated to the other cities therein. For this reason there are discrepancies as regards the hour and duration. In ancient times they carried the science from this city to Miyako, where the king dwells. The city is at the same latitude, but at about two hours further east.[5]

---

[1] One of the reasons for the demand for European Jesuits in China was their ability to forecast eclipses accurately. In early 1665 the Jesuits Ferdinand Verbiest and Adam Schall calculated more accurately the beginning of a solar eclipse than did the Chinese and Moorish astronomers. Rowbotham, *Missionary*, p. 85; Dunne, *Generation*, p. 362; G. Gabiani, *Incrementa Sinicae Ecclesiae*, Vienna, 1673, p. 228ff. Writing from Beijing in September 1612, Sabatino de Ursis refers to errors made in forecasting an eclipse in December 1610. More mistakes were made in June 1619. D'Elia, *Galileo in China*, pp. 67, 61. Further examples are given on p. 374, n. 3, below.

[2] For Shihuangdi and the Burning of the Books in 213 BC, see pp. 54–5.

[3] A correct understanding of solar eclipses can be traced back in China to about 20 BC, while an account of lunar eclipses may be dated AD 120. Eclipses could be approximately predicted by the 1st century BC, and by the 7th century further details, such as the extent or partiality, the times of the first and last contact, etc., could be predicted. But from the beginning of the Ming dynasty, there was a steady decline in the accuracy of prediction. *SCC*, III, pp. 410–14, 421–2, and Nakayama, *History*, pp. 50–52.

[4] A point also raised by Ricci (*Fonti*, II, p. 85, and *China*, p. 331; see also *Opere*, II, pp. 175, 224), who noticed that the astronomical instruments in Nanjing, at $32°04'$N, were set for a latitude of $36°$. This was because they had originally been made for a city in Shanxi province with a latitude of about $36°$. *SCC*, III, p. 368 note f.; Bernard, *Matteo Ricci's Scientific Contribution*, pp. 13–14.

[5] The position of Miyako (Kyoto) is $35°00'$N, $135°45'$E.

The Chinese make much account of the eclipses of the sun and moon, and, as is usual, there are many fables about them among the rustic common people, just as there are in Japan.[1] The royal mathematicians calculate them, and each year when they occur the royal board of rites sends the calculation beforehand to the capital of each province so that it may be communicated to all the other cities therein.[2] For it is a law of the kingdom that all the magistrates of the cities must gather with many common people in a certain place at the hour of the eclipse. From the time it begins and while it lasts they perform many ceremonies and have copper bells and cymbals struck with great noise, as if by so doing they help the planet that is suffering this defect. In the court of Beijing, all the lords and magistrates of the court assemble in the courtyard of the palace and all bow deeply to Heaven, praying that it may come to the help of the moon in its labour.[3] In ancient times they would list the eclipses in the kingdom's annual public records as a notable event, just as they note down all the other heavenly appearances of comets with two or three suns.[4] In Japan, when the king enjoyed authority and ruled the country, they also performed their ceremonies.[5] Even now they have their mathematicians who calculate eclipses and publish them in the annual calendar of the seasons, which is produced every year and distributed throughout the whole kingdom.[6]

In their mathematical books they agree with our mathematicians when they declare that the White Path, or the moon's path, is cut in two places by the Yellow Path, or ecliptic, and at the places where they cut eclipses occur. The eclipse will be lunar when the moon is full and in opposition, and solar when the moon is new and in conjunction.[7] Our mathematicians call these point of intersection Caput and Cauda Draconis. They lay down limits within which an eclipse can take place, and these are 13°5′ before and after the head and tail

[1] According to popular belief, solar eclipses were caused by a dragon devouring the sun. Another opinion held that the sun was eaten by a three-legged crow, and the moon by a hare or toad. *SCC*, III, pp. 409, 411, note a. Ricci (*Fonti*, I, p. 42, and *China*, p. 32) mentions the dragon myth.

[2] In a letter dated 25 January 1612 from Canton, Rodrigues goes into further details about this matter. 'Rodrigues in China', pp. 335–4.

[3] *Shujing*, IV, 2, 4 (Legge, *Chinese Classics*, III, p. 165) notes that during a solar eclipse, 'The blind musicians beat their drums; the inferior officers and common people bustled and ran about.' This practice is also mentioned by Ricci (*Fonti*, I, p. 42, and *China*, p. 32). For modern accounts, see Gray, *China*, I, pp. 367–8. According to Forke (*World-Conceptions*, p. 99), the ancient Romans clanged brass pots during an eclipse, and up to the 17th century people in Ireland and Wales beat kettles to assist the suffering luminary.

[4] The earliest record of an eclipse is found in *Shujing* (reference given in n. 3, above); this eclipse is traditionally dated in the 3rd millennium BC *SCC*, III, p. 409. Lists of some 924 solar and 574 lunar eclipses noted in Chinese records are given in Wylie, 'Eclipses'.

[5] Although not mentioning such ceremonies, *Nihongi* (II, pp. 166, 169, 333; 155, 167; 179, 349) records celestial phenomena in some detail. The sighting of comets in 634, 639 and 676 is duly noted, while solar eclipses are recorded in 628 and 636, and lunar eclipses in 643 and 680.

[6] For centuries the Kamo family drew up the official calendar, while the Abe was in charge of astrological prediction; in recent years the famous astrologer Abe no Seimei, 921–1005, has attracted much popular attention in Japan. In the middle of the 16th century, the Tsuchimikado family took over both functions, and was still active until the 1870s. Sugimoto and Swain, *Science and Culture*, pp. 123–5; Nakayama, *History*, pp. 21–2, 219. Further information about the history and work of the Divination Bureau, or Onmyōryō, is supplied in Butler, 'Way of Yin and Yang'. For the Chinese calendar and its adoption in Japan, see Nakayama, *History*, pp. 65–73.

[7] The points where the moon's path crosses the ecliptic are called the nodes. As already stated on p. 352, n. 1, the moon's path and the ecliptic are set at an angle of 5°08′. If there were no angular separation, there would be a solar eclipse at every new moon and a lunar eclipse at every full moon. *SCC*, III, pp. 410, 421.

of the Dragon. So the eclipse is total in the head or tail, and they say that it is greater or less inasmuch as it is nearer to or further from these limits.[1]

They are also careful in noting the signs where an eclipse occurs and the constellation and its degree in which it takes place, as well as its duration, that is, when it begins to enter the shadow, when it has completely entered, the middle of it, when it begins to emerge, and when it completely finishes. Now they divide the night into four watches and each hour into eight of our quarters, and at each quarter they ring a bell and beat a drum together a certain number of times and periods. They say that an eclipse will begin in the first or second quarter of a certain hour at a certain stroke of the drum and peal of the bell, as if we were to say …[2] But this great exactitude profits them but little, because there is usually a discrepancy of nearly half an hour either before or after the time announced.[3]

---

[1] Rodrigues has already stated (p. 369) that the moon's path and the ecliptic are inclined at an angle of 6°, but according to Chinese calculations 6°52½' must be postulated if the limits of an eclipse are 13°05'. Although the moon's nodes were represented by the head and tail of the Western constellation Draco, their position was entirely coincidental and had nothing to do with the Chinese dragon-theory of eclipses. *SCC*, III, p. 252 note c.

[2] There is a gap in the text at this point. The method of dividing the night watches is described later on p. 394.

[3] Rodrigues ('Rodrigues in China', p. 334) notes that the solar eclipse in China on 15 December 1610 began a full hour after the time forecast by the royal astronomers. Details about this eclipse, correctly calculated by Diego de Pantoia, are given in Bernard, *Matteo Ricci's Scientific Contribution*, pp. 73–4.

CHAPTER 13

THE STARS AND THEIR CONSTELLATIONS, THE NUMBER OF STARS, AND THE ORDER IN WHICH THEY DISTRIBUTE THEM ON THEIR CELESTIAL SPHERE

The constellations or figures in which they have distributed the stars of the sky, as mentioned above, are one of the oldest things among the Chinese, and their invention coincided with the foundation of China at the time of the Confusion of Tongues when the country began to be peopled. It seems more than likely that the figures of the stars used by the Chinese and the signs and constellations of our own mathematicians were not invented by astrologers after the Confusion of Tongues and the peopling of the world. All of them appear to owe their origin and beginning to the first Fathers before the Flood. This is in keeping with what scholars commonly understand of this matter, because there are various reasons for this assertion. For those Fathers lived to a great age and were strangers to cares produced by material possessions, and their long experience of the stars increased their knowledge and understanding of their qualities and influences.[1]

Such, for example, were the holy patriarch Seth, his son Enosh, and the rest of his descendants, such as Enoch and others. Genebrardus says in his *Chronology*:

> There is an old tradition that Seth and Enosh invented astrology, inscribed two pillars, and invented Hebrew letters. *See* Cedrenus, Josephus, and Rabbis.
>
> According to Suidas, Seth invented Hebrew letters and the names of the stars.
>
> The Books of Enoch are also cited by Origen in his 28th homily on the Book of Numbers, from which he says that knowledge was obtained not only of the regions of the sky but also of the stars and constellations. These books are in the Abyssinian language and are extant among the Ethiopians in the kingdom of the Queen of Saba.[2]

In his *Bibliotheca Sancta*, Sixtus of Siena says this about these books:

> The theme of this book is not known, but according to the testimony of the Fathers it appears to have contained some chapters, 'Concerning the Number and Names of the Stars, and Their Secret Power'. Thus, speaking about this subject in the 28th Homily on the Book of Numbers, Origen writes as follows:

---

[1] In his commentary on Sacrobosco, p. 3, Clavius makes exactly the same point. Rodrigues later quotes from Clavius's book.

[2] Rodrigues gives all these quotations in Latin. The first is found in Génébrard, *Chronographiae libri quatuor*, p. 5. Génébrard's reference to Cedrenus is in Cedrenus, *Annales*, p. 6, while the reference to Josephus is later given by Rodrigues on p. 376. The second quotation is taken from Génébrard, *Chronographiae libri quatuor*, p. 9. The reference to Suidas is from *Suidae historica*, column 849. The third quotation is an inaccurate paraphrase of Génébrard, *Chronographiae libri quatuor*, p. 14, who wrote that, according to Origen, the 3rd-century Christian writer, the secrets (*secreta*), not the knowledge (*scientia*), of the sky, etc., were obtained. The reference to Origen is correct.

He who made the multitude of the stars (as the Prophet declares) called them all by name. Now many hidden secrets concerning these names are contained in the books called Enoch. But because these books do not appear to have been recognized by the Hebrews, we will not quote their contents here as an example.[1]

Josephus speaks of the two pillars in his *Antiquities*, Book I:

The descendants of Seth invented the science of the stars and the knowledge of the celestial bodies. In order to prevent their discoveries from being forgotten by men and perishing before they became known (for they knew that Adam had foretold a general destruction of mankind, one by fire and another by flood), they erected two pillars and inscribed their discoveries on both of them. So if the brick pillar were lost in the flood, the stone one would remain to teach men and would show them what was graven thereon. They say that this stone pillar that they dedicated still exists to this day in the land of Syria.[2]

There is also a very ancient record of this matter, for some of these constellations and images of stars are mentioned in Holy Scripture in the Book of Job, where reference is made to the constellations Orion, Arcturus, Hyades, and Pleiades. These and many others are named in Homer and Hesiod, the ancient poets.[3] Above all, in this present year of 1620 the Chinese have had their constellations and number of stars with their properties and influences for almost 4,000 years. All this was at the same time as, or even before, the Confusion of Tongues. But they could not at that time have invented this, the movements of the planets, the material sphere, the division of time, and all the rest. It must have been invented by the Fathers before the Flood, as we have said.

The whole structure of the universe is like a composition of many parts, each of which is both useful and necessary for the perfection and conservation of the whole. In the same way, as all the parts of the Heavens are members of this universe, there is not a part or star, however small it may be, that does not possess its own proper power and influence needed for the perfection and permanence of the whole universe. For God our Lord, the Author of Nature, did not create things in vain. Indeed, as Holy Scripture says, He arranged them in number, weight, and measure.[4] So each one of these parts of the universe has a natural inclination to strive after the permanence of the whole, because they were created for its service. So as each of the stars, constellations, and planets is a member of this great body, they all act by disposing themselves towards its perfection inasmuch as it is the whole, because the

---

[1] The quotation is taken from Sixtus Senensis, *Bibliotheca sancta*, p. 69. Sixtus (1520–69) was born a Jew, became a Christian, was condemned to the stake for unorthodoxy, entered the Franciscan order, and died a Dominican. Rodrigues paraphrases his words, for Sixtus quotes a number of alleged titles from Enoch's work. Although Sixtus speaks about 'chapters' of Enoch, Rodrigues mentions the title of only one. In view of the earlier reference to Abyssinia, this reference is probably the apocryphal *Ethiopic Book of Enoch* (Enoch 1), Chapter 43, in which Enoch sees God naming all the stars. Charles, *Apocrypha*, II, p. 213. No text of Enoch in any version would have been available to Rodrigues. The quotation from the Prophet at the beginning of Origen's piece is from Psalm 147, 4.

[2] This quotation, given in Latin, corresponds to a passage in Josephus, *Antiquities*, 1, 2. Rodrigues's version is merely a paraphrase and was probably taken from a scholastic textbook. It errs in referring to Syria, instead of Josephus's Syrida. The quotation is given more accurately in Clavius, *In Sphaeram*, p. 3, a work from which Rodrigues later quotes on p. 389. Rodrigues's diffusionist theory, however, is greatly weakened because Josephus confused the biblical Seth with the legendary Seth, or Sesostris (perhaps Senwosri III?), the Egyptian king said to have erected some pillars in Ethiopia – see Strabo, *Geography*, XVI, 4, 4. For discussion of the Seth tradition see Klijn, *Seth in Jewish, Christian and Gnostic Literature*.

[3] Job 9: 9; Homer, *Iliad*, 22, 34–40; Hesiod, *Works and Days*, lines 609–17.

[4] Isaiah 45: 18; alternatively, Wisdom 11: 20.

existence of these parts depends on the permanence of the whole. Thus each of them communicates its power to these inferior things through the medium of movement, light, and influence. For the infinite divine knowledge has ordered the whole celestial body towards the production of all the natural events that we see, and towards the continual generation and corruption of elementary things. This is because Earth is a common receptacle receiving all of Heaven's influences in its lap. Hence the ancients and the Chinese call Earth mother and Heaven father.[1]

Through their wide experience acquired during their long lives, the Fathers before the Flood observed the effects of the Heavens. In this way they came to know about these things and their power, and the qualities that each of the constellations and planets infused into the elements and elementary things. For example, they found that every time the moon passed under the sign of Scorpion dampness increased or dryness decreased more or less in accordance with the position of Earth, the part of the world, the time of year, and other concurrences. They said that the sign of Scorpion infused dampness and cold.

In the same way, they noted that at the birth of Arcturus, Orion, and Hyades, there were usually wind storms. Whence they believed that these stars and constellations had the power of producing heat and dryness that caused hot and dry currents, and moved the air. They also found that rainy weather was caused when the planets Mars or Venus passed through Pleiades or Capella, and from this they supposed that these stars had the power of influencing dampness, and so on in the other constellations and planets. Using both reason and experience, they thus came to know the qualities that the celestial bodies infused in the things below. Whence they said that some signs and constellations produced some qualities, while others produced others, such as cold and heat, wet and dry.[2]

Thus they possessed the experience that had been gained by holy Seth, Enosh, Enoch, and Seth's other descendants. At the same time they were taught by Adam, whom God had created graced with all knowledge and understanding of the properties of things, including even the animals, on whom he placed fitting names in keeping with the nature of each species.[3] So they arranged the stars in figures, especially those of the Zodiac (through which the sun moves during the course of the year and causes various effects), as well as many others, and attributed to them various effects and influences. They carved them on two columns so that they might never be lost, and holy Enoch recorded them in his books, along with many other things concerning divine worship, as we said above.[4] The Apostle James quotes this book in his canonical epistle.[5]

Noah and his sons took all these things with them in the Flood and afterwards taught

---

[1] See p. 363.

[2] Some of these astrological indications of weather are mentioned in Shaw, *Manual*, I, pp. 48–9, 104–5, 107–8. For the ancient Western tradition, see Theophrastus of Eresus, *On Winds*, 36 and 55, and Aratus, *Phaenomena*, lines 778–908. For early Chinese tradition, see *Shujing*, II, 8, 3 (Legge, *Chinese Classics*, IV, p. 422): 'The moon also is in the Hyades, Which will bring still greater rain.'

[3] Genesis 2: 19–20.

[4] Chapters 72–8 of 1 Enoch, the Ethiopic version of the apocryphal *Book of Enoch*, contain much astronomical information concerning the sun, the moon and its phases, the lunar year, and intercalation. Charles, *Apocrypha*, II, pp. 237–44. 2 Enoch, the Slavonic version, contains similar information: Vaillant, *Le Livre des Secrets d'Hénoch*.

[5] *The Book of Enoch* is quoted, not by James, but by Jude, verses 14–15.

them to their descendants before the Confusion of Tongues. After the Confusion in Babylon these descendants dispersed to populate the world, and the wiser families took them with them and spread them throughout the world. In some places their memory and knowledge were lost on account of various events, but they were preserved in other places, such as China. This country has remained intact from its first foundation until the present day, for it never mixed with other nations, nor was it conquered and corrupted by them in its antiquity.

With this experience the same Fathers invented not only astronomy, dealing with the movements of the Heavens and planets, their various conjunctions, oppositions and confluences, but also judicial astrology, which is concerned with the effects caused by the movements, conjunctions, and aspects of the heavenly bodies on these inferior things. This science is natural and is founded on natural reasons acquired by experience. The Fathers considered that natural effects resulted from a mixture of the qualities of the elements (this is largely dealt with in the Chinese books of natural magic), and that these were mixed by virtue of the movement, light, and influence of the celestial bodies. For this reason, they diligently noted the natural effects that occurred in this elementary region, and the planets' aspects and conjunctions that simultaneously took place in the celestial region. They found that after these aspects and conjunctions had occurred together several times, the same effects followed more or less in keeping with them. Hence they believed that the influences of these aspects and conjunctions of the stars had the power to cause these results in things below. After many experiments they noted down this science, leaving it in writing so that others could profit from it.

In addition to this astrological truth acquired through experience by the good sons of Seth, the wicked sons of Cain invented many conceits, innumerable superstitions, and errors. Thus, contrary to all experience and reason, even human acts depending on free will, contingent things having nothing to do with such causes, and also each person's inevitable fate or destiny, were all subjected to the influence of the Heavens.[1] So with this excuse, they could commit many evil deeds and offences against God with the encouragement of the devil, to whom they had given themselves. For as it is written about him[2] and Cain, they were the first idolaters in the world and inventors of the magical arts. As he was evilly inclined, Ham, the son of Noah, was much given to this magical and judicial art, which he learnt from Cain's descendants before the Flood. Thus just as Cain had been leader of the apostates before the Flood, so after it Ham was the first to teach these arts and other superstitions to his descendants, and from him they spread throughout the whole world, as many grave authors have noted.

Hence Serenus the Abbot says in Cassian, Collation 8, Chapter 21:

It is recorded that the first authors and teachers of magical superstitions and deceptions were the wicked angels, and that Ham, the son of Noah, was most assiduous and skilled in these arts. He preserved them and saved them from perishing in the Flood by carving them on plates of various metals and on hard stone. After the Flood he taught them to his descendants and spread them throughout the world.[3]

So this science and the celestial figures and their natural powers were happily invented

---

[1] There is a gap in the text here. The literal translation runs: '... the inevitable fate or destiny that each one, were subjected...'

[2] This 'him' may refer to the devil, or possibly to Ham, who is mentioned in the next sentence.

[3] The reference to John Cassian is correct, although the quotation, given in Latin, is only a summary of Cassian's words. Rodrigues most probably took the passage from a scholastic textbook.

for a good purpose by Seth's descendants, but were then joined to vain and superstitious astrology.

According to what we have said, it seems certain that astronomy and wholesome judicial astrology have their origin in the first Fathers before the Flood. Before his sons and grandsons spread throughout the world, Noah taught them the art and science of letters or the art of inventing them anew. In addition, by means of figures or letters like hieroglyphics, odd and even numbers, and mathematical figures, he also taught them the sciences, the movements of the Heavens and the planets, their conjunctions and oppositions, the division of the parts of the Heavens by degrees, the material sphere to determine their movements, the division of time into the four seasons and months, the length of the year and hours, the lunar intercalary, the stars distributed in figures or constellations with their natural powers, and many other things, so that there might be uniformity among men in their way of life throughout all the world. Thus the heads of the families took at least this knowledge with them when they set out to populate the world. After Earth had been peopled, they continued improvising, increasing, and modifying this knowledge in keeping with what they newly observed. The people coming after them later regarded as their inventors the first men who taught such things, and put into practice what had already been invented.

Let us come down to detail. The ancient star map of the Chinese is a planisphere in which they distributed in figures the stars appearing in their hemisphere.[1] They took the elevation of the northern pole at 36° or 35½°, where Kaifengfu, the capital of Henan province and the most ancient capital and court of the whole of China or ancient Serica, is situated. They made all their observations at this latitude, and continue to do so even now, for they do not depart from ancient usage in any of this.[2] The southern stars that lie within the circle of 36° of the south pole are always hidden from them, for they always lie concealed below the horizon.[3]

---

[1] Charts of the heavens were constructed in China as early as the 3rd century; a planisphere prepared at the end of the 12th century shows 1,440 stars. *SCC*, III, pp. 276–82; Maspero, 'L'Astronomie', pp. 319–20. Illustrations of star maps made in the Han dynasty are given in Sun and Kistemaker, *Chinese Sky*, pp. 28–9; *SSC*, III, pp. 264–5.

[2] For Chinese astronomers' adherence to an outdated latitude, see p. 372.

[3] In the 1st century Zhangheng observed that there was a circle of 72° diameter around the South Pole that 'encloses stars which we never see'. As early as 724, a Chinese expedition went to the southern hemisphere to map the stars there and made observations within 20° of the south celestial pole. *SCC*, III, pp. 217, 274.

CHAPTER 14

EARTH AND WATER, THEIR SHAPE, AND THE DEGREES OF
ELEVATION IN WHICH THEY ARE SAID TO BE

As regards Earth and water, and the shape and size of these two elements, the Chinese, followed by the Japanese, propose some ridiculous things that are contrary to natural philosophy and experience. Everything that we set down here on this matter is taken from their
books written by the royal mathematicians, as we mentioned earlier when speaking about
the structure of the world.

The term 'Earth', as opposed to Heaven, is called by them *chi* or *ji*, and by the Chinese *di*,
and it includes the element of earth (which the Sacred Scriptures call *arida*,[1] the Japanese *do*,
and the Chinese *tu*), the rocks, mountains, trees, sea, rivers, lakes, and material or ordinary
fire. They call all of this 'Earth' and they imagine this to be square in shape and situated with
the water in the middle or centre of the sky, just as we say that the water and earth make a
round globe. They believe that the rocks and earth make up the body of Earth, and that this is
surrounded on its four sides by four seas, one on each side. They call this *shikai*, in Chinese
sihai, that is, 'the four seas', meaning the same as *tenka*, or lower world.[2] They say that the body
of Earth (and the rocks, which are properly Earth) is 24° in diameter from north to south and
that the complete square made up of Earth and water has a diameter of 131¼°, but I do not
know what this is based on.[3] They also hold that the waters of the four seas on the four sides
are supported by the air, and that part which is properly Earth (on whose surface men dwell)
is separated towards the north and west, and thus is not in the middle of Heaven, inasmuch as
they are in the northern tropic. The rest consists of sea containing some small islands.[4]

They say that the middle of the part that is properly the inhabited continent is
Kaifengfu or Yangcheng,[5] the metropolis and capital of Henan province, one of the fifteen
provinces into which China is at present divided. This is like the centre of the kingdom of

---

[1] Genesis 1, 9–10.

[2] *Vocabulario*, f. 299: '*Shikai*, or *Yotsu no umi*. The four seas lying in the four directions in respect to Miyako. *Itten
shikai*, The whole world.' In a wider context, the term refers to the four oceans around Mt Sumeru (see pp. 358–9),
and Rodrigues later points out on p. 384 that *shikai* came by extension to mean the whole world. Unno ('Japan', pp.
40–43) quotes this paragraph of Rodrigues's text and analyzes it in depth, pointing out that *shikai* originally meant
'four dark regions'.

[3] Here again Rodrigues seems to have the cosmological teaching of the Gaitian school in mind (see p. 360, n. 2),
for it taught that 'the earth is square like a chessboard'. *SCC*, III, p. 213; Forke, *World-Conception*, p. 13. The reference
to 24° is puzzling, but the author may have in mind the latitudinal limits of China, which he says are 23½° (p. 27, n.
2, and p. 383). If the value of π is taken as 3 (and the Chinese often took $\pi = 3$: *SCC*, III, p. 99), then a diameter
of 121·75° will give a circumference of 365·25°, and this is correct.

[4] Again, Unno ('Japan', pp. 43–5) quotes these lines and cites ancient Chinese sources in confirmation.

[5] Kaifengfu was certainly the capital of Henan province and later in this chapter (p. 382) Rodrigues repeats that it
was considered 'the centre of the inhabited world', probably when it was the Song capital in the 10th century. Yangcheng,

China, and in ancient times it was the court and capital of the whole kingdom. Ptolemy and the ancients called this Sera from the silk that it produced, and this is the same as Metropolis Sinarum found in Ptolemy, as we explained elsewhere.[1] They also believe that in the middle of the square structure of Earth (or more exactly, of the lower world in respect to Heaven) is a famous mountain in India extra Gangem,[2] a branch of Mt Caucasus in the province called Tebet by Marco Polo, next to the kingdom of Mien or of the Mongols.[3] The Chinese call this mountain Kunlunshan, and in Japanese Konronsan.[4] It is situated at 33°N and 123° of longitude, near the lake Xingsuhai, which is erroneously called Chiamay Lacus in the maps.[5] From this lake comes the River Huanghe of China, one of the two rivers mentioned by Ptolemy that water Serica. It passes next to this mountain, as you may see in the map placed at the beginning of this history.[6] The Venetian Marco Polo mentioned these mountain ranges in his Oriental History,[7] when recounting the journey he made from Kambalu, now Beijing, to India extra Gangem.

They believe that Earth is flat on its surface but one degree raised or higher towards the north and northeast, sloping towards the east and east-southeast and south. For them, this explains why the waters of the rivers in China ordinarily flow towards the east and south, and thence pour into the sea. But, as can be seen in their maps of the lands, the rivers of Tartary above China flow from the south into the Northern Sea, which we call the Sea of Ice

---

at 34°26′N and some 50 miles southeast of Luoyang, was for long regarded as the centre of the world or 'China's Greenwich', as it was considered to be located directly below the highest point of Heaven. Its giant tower for taking gnomon measurements still exists, and it was believed that the shadow of an eight-foot gnomon at Yangcheng would increase by 1 inch every 1,000 li north of the city. SCC, III, pp. 291 note b, 292, 296–7, 381 note b, and figures 115–17.

[1] See p. 24.

[2] The text is confused at this point. A literal translation reads: 'They also believe that the middle of the square structure of Earth, and more nearly, or of Earth (square structure, I mean) of the lower world in relation to Heaven, is a famous mountain. …' The 'square structure' of the lower world in relation to Heaven again indicates the Gaitian school of cosmology. See p. 360, n. 2.

[3] Polo describes Tibet in Book, II, chapters 45 and 46 (Yule, Book, II, pp. 42–52), and Mien (Burma) in Book, II, Chapter 54 (Yule, Book, II, pp. 109–14). See also p. 20, n. 5.

[4] The Kunlun mountain range forms the northern escarpment of the Tibetan plateau and runs through Tibet at about 36°N. Some have associated it with the mythical Mt Sumeru (see p. 359, n. 1). The Chinese name possibly expresses the spherical shape of the vault of the heavens, for as the mountains were situated at the limit of the Chinese known world, they were believed to touch the end of the world. SCC, III, p. 523; Saussure, 'L'Étymologie', pp. 370–71. A blank was left in the text and I have added the Japanese name.

[5] Lake Chiamay is shown on most of the early European maps of Asia, e.g., Ortelius, Theatrum, p. 63, at 23–25°N, and is often mentioned by writers of that period, e.g., Barros, Década primeira, 9, 1 (f. 177) and Década terceira, 2, 1 (ff. 37–37v). As this region contains the origin of five great rivers, it was presumed that an immense lake was there. Xingsuhai, or Starry Sea, was named in 1280 by officials sent by Kublai Khan to explore the sources of the Huanghe, or Yellow River. The lake is now shown on Western maps as Oring Nor. Bretschneider, Mediaeval Researches, II, pp. 204, 209; SCC, III, pp. 523–4. Ricci shows the position of Xingsuhai at 32–33°N, with the Kunlun mountains to the north of the lake, in Ricci, Mappamondo, plate 15. In a letter written in 1588, probably by Ricci, the lake is described and its name is correctly translated as 'stellarum et constellationum mare'. Ibid., p. 214, n. 201.

[6] As noted earlier, the map intended for the History has been lost. The course of the Huanghe, or Yellow River, and its changes in history are described and illustrated in Richard, Comprehensive Geography, pp. 24–7. For Ptolemy's reference to the river, see p. 29.

[7] Polo, Book, II, 42 (Yule, Book, II, p. 31) speaks of 'the great mountains and valleys which belong to the province of Cuncun [Kailun?]', although the region in question is usually taken as south Shanxi, which is considerably to the east of the mountains. When later describing Tibet in chapters 45 and 46, Polo makes no mention of mountains.

or the Scythian Sea.[1] They maintain that there is more land to the west of China, or of Mt Kunlunshan, the centre of the world, than to the east, for the land extends westwards from this mountain 30,000 of their *estados* called *li* (in Japan, *ri*); each one of these is 226 geometric paces of five feet, so this is more than 2,000 leagues. It extends 20,000 *li*, which is almost 1,500 leagues from the same place to the Eastern Sea. Thus the extent of the land surface from sea to sea, from east to west, would be 50,000 *li*,[2] which is more than 3,500 leagues. So the land extending from the centre towards the west is greater and the sea smaller, while the land towards the east is smaller and the sea bigger than the western sea.[3]

In keeping with this, their ancient authors did not concern themselves with the height or latitude of the land and the position of places with regard to the poles of the world and the equinox. They seem to have believed that the whole Earth was at the same northern latitude, because they held that it was flat and that the north pole arose 36° out of it.[4] They said that Kaifengfu, the court and capital of ancient China or Serica, was situated at this latitude. They believe that this was the centre of the inhabited world[5] or opposite the zenith, as they say, and it was on this latitude that they based all their observations concerning the length of the day and night, the hours, the duration of the eclipses, and everything else connected with the rising and setting of the planets and stars, and they do the same even now.

Hence they had nobody versed in the art and science of plotting the position of lands and places by latitude as they believed that it was all the same. But after the Moors, Arabs, and Persians came to China nearly 1,000 years ago,[6] they took the latitude of the principal cities of China and measured the longitude of the whole kingdom and the neighbouring countries. This happened principally in the time when the Grand Cham, King of the Tartars, reigned over China from the year 1205 until the 1368, a period of 163 years.[7] During this time he ordered a description of the whole of his empire tp be prepared, and he sent mathematicians as far as 65°N in the Northern Scythian Sea and as far south as 19°N in

---

[1] The alleged northern flow of Tartary rivers is shown in Ricci's *Mappamondo*, plate 15. For a mythological explanation of the eastward flow of Chinese rivers, see Fung, *History*, I, p. 397; *SCC*, III, p. 214. A more scientific explanation was advanced by Wu Zuohai, who wrote in the 1600 edition of Ricci's *Mappamundo*: 'Tradition tells us that the south-east spur of the K'un-lun Mountains penetrates the Middle Kingdom, and this explains why all the rivers flow towards the east.' D'Elia, 'Recent Discoveries', p. 92.

[2] The text gives the obviously mistaken total of 5,000 *li*. Rodrigues's figures of 20,000 and 30,000 *li* are confirmed by an entry in *Tu-shu-bian*, an illustrated encyclopaedia first published in 1613. Unno, 'Japan', pp. 49–50. For estimates of the length of Earth expressed in various Chinese sources, see ibid., pp. 52–3.

[3] A Chinese author in the 3rd century gave the east-west length of Earth as 28,000 *li*, while a later writer suggested 100,000 *li*. Other symbolic figures are recorded in Forke, *World-Conception*, pp. 59–60. In a map compiled in 801, Jiadan gives the east-west distance as 30,000 *li*. *SCC*, III, p. 543.

[4] In the 1st century, Zhangheng noted that the north pole was inclined at an angle of 36°. *SCC*, III, p. 217.

[5] Kaifengfu is situated at 34°43' N. Rodrigues has already mentioned earlier in this chapter (pp. 380–81) the belief that the city was the centre of the inhabited world.

[6] The influence of Persian and Arabic astronomers in China is discussed in *SCC*, III, pp. 49–50 and 372–82, with special reference to the Persian scientist Jamāl al-Din, who reached Beijing in 1267.

[7] Earlier, p. 356, Rodrigues has mentioned the 90 years of Mongol rule, that is, 1279–1368, when the Mongol rulers governed the entire country. His '163 years' here refers to Genghis Kahn's accession to Mongol leadership and occupation of part of China. In similar vein, Rodrigues writes in *Breve aparato*, f. 14, that the Tartars ruled China for 161 years from 1207 to 1378 (a slip for 1368), but again he does not have in mind the official Yuan dynasty, 1279–1368, but Genghis's partial occupation of the country. He clarifies the matter in *Arte grande*, f. 235v, by noting that it was not until 1278, in the time of Kublai, that the Song dynasty ended.

the province of Cauchi-China.[1] He commanded that a copious record with geographical maps should be made everywhere.[2]

The Chinese mathematicians, however, preferred to keep to their ancient ways rather than mix the mathematics of their forefathers with that of the Moors and Arabs. Thus it may be clearly seen that the calculations in their calendars are in error, for they were made at the above-mentioned latitude of 36°[3] for the whole kingdom. But some areas are more northerly, others less so; some are more easterly, others less so. For China begins at the south at 18½°N and ends in the north at 42°N; its longitude begins at the meridian of 123° and ends at 150°.[4] Japan begins its southern latitude at 30°N and ends in the north at 42½°N; its longitude begins at the meridian of 153° and ends at 168°.[5] But as their calendars are compiled in Miyako at 35¼°N and at the meridian of 162°,[6] they cannot be universal throughout the whole kingdom, and even less so in China where there are such distances in longitude and latitude.

Although they possess the same books of Chinese mathematics and geography, the Japanese do not know of latitude and gradations as do the modern Chinese, who learn these things from the Moors and from our Fathers of the Society. The latter have composed in the Chinese language and letters the books of our mathematicians and a gradated universal map of the whole world.[7] But the Japanese follow only what has been left them by their ancient predecessors, and all this is based on the position of Miyako according to their rules, but they do not know the reason for this.

Thus both the Japanese and Chinese in ancient times did not know of more than three kingdoms, which they believed made up all the land surface of the world. Everything else, they held, consisted of the sea surrounding the world on its four sides. The Japanese called these three kingdoms in general *sangoku*, that is, 'the three kingdoms', as if one were to say, 'all the inhabited world'. These were Japan, China, and India intra and extra Gangem, and the Japanese call them Nippon, Taitō, and Tenjiku in that order.[8] That is, Japan, China (including Korea and Tartary, both subject to China), and India intra and extra Gangem,

---

[1] I.e. Cochin-China.

[2] A reference to Genghis Khan (1162–1227), the Mongol ruler who by 1214 had occupied most of China north of the Yellow River. In 1218 he appointed surveyors to compile a map of the country, and explorers reached as far north as 67° and as far south as 19°N. Trigault, *Litterae*, pp. 126, 136; Douglas, *Life*, p. 84. Citing Chinese records, Rodrigues, *Nihon*, II, p. 184, n. 11, substantially confirms Rodrigues's statement, giving the figures 65° and 15°N. The Mongol rulers made great efforts to explore and map China and its environs, and in 1280–81 an expedition was sent to find the source of the Yellow River. Franke, 'Exploration', and *SCC*, III, pp. 524, 551–6.

[3] The text has 26° here, but as this is probably the copyist's slip, I have corrected the figure to 36°, which Rodrigues has already mentioned. See p. 372.

[4] Rodrigues has already given the limits of latitude and longitude of China on p. 26, where he places the western longitude at 125°E (as opposed to 123° here).

[5] Latitudes of 30½° and 42½°N, and longitudes of 153° and 168°E, are given earlier on p. 43.

[6] For the position of Miyako, see p. 372.

[7] In 1606–7, Ricci and Xu Guangqi (whom Rodrigues met about 1614) translated into Chinese the first volume of the 1589 edition of Clavius's *Euclidis elementorum libri XV*, and this was printed in 1607. Other works by Claver were also translated. Sommervogel, *Bibliothèque*, II, cols. 1215–18, and VI, cols. 1793–4; Ricci, *Fonti*, II, pp. 356–61, and *China*, pp. 476–7. Ricci's World Map was published in China in 1584, 1600, 1603 and 1608. An illustrated account of the 1602 edition is contained in Ricci, *Mappamondo*. See also D'Elia, 'Recent Discoveries'.

[8] Rodrigues has already mentioned the term *sangoku* on p. 66, where he lists the three countries as Tenjiku, Shindan, and Nippon. Taitō, defined in *Vocabulario*, f. 238, as 'The kingdom of China', literally means Great Tang (dynasty).

whence more than a thousand years ago arrived the sects of the idols that they worship. Before that time, the Japanese knew of only Korea and China.

The Chinese considered China alone as the whole world, and other countries were regarded as its outskirts, and so they called it by names that signify this. For example, Tianxia (Tenka in Japanese) means 'below Heaven', or 'the world'; also Sihai (in Japanese, Shikai) means 'the four seas', and this is the entire world. It is also called Zhonghua (in Japanese, Chūka), 'middle garden', and Zhongguo (Japanese, Chūgoku), 'middle kingdom'. Thus other countries were considered as mere tributaries and worthless. As Japan was at the end of the world and cut off from any communication with and knowledge of other kingdoms, as we have said, the Japanese have a high opinion of their kingdom and nation, and improperly call it Tenka or Shikai, which makes the Chinese laugh a great deal whenever they hear this.[1]

At the present time the arrival of the Law of God has given both the Chinese and Japanese complete knowledge of the universal world, its regions, and the various political nations that flourish as regards power, sciences, wealth, and magnificence, and they see all this in our general maps. They are astonished to see how small their kingdoms really are, for they had been believed to comprise the whole world in comparison with other nations.[2] Hence they have formed a different concept of other nations, and a lower one of their own kingdom, although they do not outwardly show this in front of foreigners. For they think that to do so would humble them, as these nations, principally China, have a very high opinion of themselves and a very low one of foreigners, whom they treat as basely and meanly as can be imagined.[3]

---

[1] Rodrigues gives all these and other Chinese and Japanese names for China in *Breve aparato*, ff. 12v–13. For the Chinese attitude, see Fitzgerald, *Chinese View*, especially pp. 22–32.

[2] But Ricci was sufficiently discreet to place China (and consequently Japan) in the centre of his World Map, with the prime meridian running through the country. Some Chinese were unwilling to accept the information on the map on the grounds that its compiler was a foreigner. But Ricci's friends declared that whoever had spent more than 20 years in China could no longer be considered a foreigner. D'Elia, 'Recent Discoveries', p. 97.

[3] Writing some 34 years after Rodrigues's death, Magalhães (*New History*, pp. 61–2) notes that the Chinese had a low opinion of foreigners, and it was often supposed that other countries were populated by dwarfs and monsters. 'They put the highest value imaginable upon their Empire and all that belongs to them; but as for strangers, they scorn 'em to the lowest pitch of contempt.' See p. 45, n. 1, and also Ricci, *Fonti*, I, pp. 102–3, and *China*, pp. 88–9.

CHAPTER 15

THE JAPANESE AND CHINESE DIVISION OF TIME

The division of time used by the Chinese, and also by the Japanese (who received it from them), is as ancient among them as the other celestial things that we have already mentioned, for they have used this division from their first foundation to the present day. Moreover, this division is the true and proper one, common to all developed nations, and is the most ancient one in existence. It was also used in the Sacred Scriptures and by the ancient Fathers before the Flood, as we shall say hereafter, and it is the most suitable one in existence. They divide time, then, into years, the four seasons, days, hours, quarters or minutes.

1. The year

The Chinese and Japanese have two kinds of year, the Small Year, which is the kingdom's common and usual year, and the Great Year, which we call the Platonic Year and will later describe separately.[1] There are two types of the Small Year. The first and principal kind is the solar year made by the sun in its revolution through the zodiac, beginning at one point and traversing the dozen signs or houses. According to them, this consists of 365 days and 25 minutes, or a quarter of a day, which equals three of their hours and six of ours.[2] The other kind is the common lunar year made up of twelve moons or lunar months. This year consists of 354 days or, in the case of an intercalary year, 384 days. This is the ordinary type used by the people, and it is in fact common to the rest of Asia. This has been in use since the earliest times; it was used by Sacred Scripture in the beginning, and later by the Jewish people when they founded a stable nation.

People over here use the intercalary month for the same reason as they [i.e. the Jews] did, that is, to harmonize the lunar year with the solar and the four seasons so as to avoid any discrepancy, and so they are very familiar with this matter of intercalation. As the solar year exceeds the lunar by eleven days, every three years they introduce an intercalary month and thus increase the year by a month so that it then has thirteen moons or months, and every five years they add two months. The circle of the zodiac has a cycle of 19 years, at the end of which time they coincide; during this period there are seven intercalations.[3]

The solar year is first of all divided into the four seasons, that is, spring, summer, autumn, and winter,[4] Each of these four seasons is divided into six quasi-months or inclinations of the weather, or qualities that reign supreme in every one of them. Each of these

---

[1] The Great, or Platonic, Year has already been mentioned on p. 365.

[2] As noted already (see p. 114), the '25 minutes' here refers to angular measurement, that is, 25′, which equals ¼°, or one-quarter.

[3] For confirmation of all this information, see p. 351, n. 5.

[4] The text mistakenly reads here, 'Summer or spring, summer, autumn, and winter.'

divisions lasts 15 days and 15 minutes.[1] There are 24 of these throughout the four seasons of the year, and they are called *nijūshi-ki* or *nijūshi-setsu*, meaning the 24 qualities or inclinations of the weather, or the 24 conjunctions into which they divide the whole zodiac. Each one begins when the sun enters it and each sign contains two of these 24 parts.[2]

2. The four seasons of the year and the 24 parts into which they are divided

As we have said above, they divide the zodiac into a dozen equal parts, or houses of the signs, out of step with our signs. So the beginning of our signs corresponds to the middle of theirs, and conversely the middle of theirs coincides with the beginning of ours. Hence the four cardinal times of the solstices and equinoxes fall in the middle of their four principal signs or the ascending arc of the zodiac. This begins in the winter solstice, its middle is in the spring equinox, and it ends and is consumed in the summer solstice. They call this arc *yō*, and *yang* in Chinese, and this embraces the two qualities of hot and dry. The descending arc, which they call *in*, meaning the two qualities of cold and wet, begins in the summer solstice, and its middle is in the autumn equinox. It finishes or is consumed in the winter solstice, when they say that these two qualities, cold and wet, begin to decrease and the two contrary ones start to increase.[3]

Now they divide the zodiac into four quarters, each of which embraces three of its signs and corresponds to one of the four seasons; thus the two equinoxes and two solstices are in the middle of each of these four seasons. The first quarter, corresponding to spring, starts in the beginning of their sign *yin*, that is, Tiger, in 15° of Aquarius on the fifth day of February, and finishes in their sign *chen*, that is, Serpent, at 15° of Taurus, on the sixth day of May.[4] They maintain that this period is characterized by three qualities, that is, partly cold because winter is so near, for in these parts at 32°N it sometimes snows in April; wet, because the rains begin to prevail in this period and dampness predominates; but it is also hot because summer is near, and at the equinox, the middle of their ascending arc, they believe that hot and dry are equal or in equal proportion to cold and wet.

The second quarter, corresponding to summer, begins at 15° of Taurus on the seventh day of May in their sign *si*. In the middle of this occurs the summer solstice, when hot and dry reach their maximum, and wet and cold are expended, but then begin to increase. The period ends in 15° of Leo on the sixth day of August. They hold that this period shares in the dampness of spring, for from the month of May onwards until past the middle of June they have the rainy season here and floods caused by the predominating southern monsoon wind and the sea wind, which bring many clouds. These rains are invariable in these parts,

---

[1] Literal translation: '15 days and as many minutes.' If each period lasts 15·15 days (for clarification of 'minutes' as a unit, see p. 385, n. 2), 24 of them would last for only 363·6 days. But if 15·15 is taken as a slip for 15·25, then a total of 366 days is reached. The periods in question last on average 15·218 days.

[2] Each of these 24 periods (called *qi* in Chinese) corresponds to 15° motion of the sun along the ecliptic. As examples of Rodrigues's 'qualities and inclinations of the weather', there are Summer Solstice, Lesser Heat, Greater Heat, Autumn Beginning, End of Heat, White Dews, Autumn Equinox, Cold Dews, Descent of Hoar Frost, etc. These periods are nos. 10–18 and last from 5 May to 23 October. A table of the 24 periods and further information are given in *SCC*, III, p. 405.

[3] This account of the increase and decrease of *yin* and *yang*, and the results produced on seasonal weather, is corroborated in Forke, *World-Conception*, pp. 177–85.

[4] Rodrigues here gives the names of these signs in Chinese; the equivalent Japanese names may be obtained from the table on p. 371. *Chen* (in Japanese, *tatsu*) is usually translated as 'dragon', but I follow here Rodrigues's version. Much of his information is confirmed in Kingsmill, 'Chinese Calendar', pp. 1–35.

and they note down beforehand in their calendars the times when they are to begin and when they are due to end. Rainy seasons in India and Cafraria[1] occur at this time, and this causes the River Nile to flood in Egypt because the river has its sources in that place. The period is also hot and dry, as has been said.

The third quarter, corresponding to autumn, begins in their sign *shen* in 15° of Leo, and ends in their sign *xu* in 15° of Scorpion. Its midpoint is the autumn equinox. They believe that this period shares in the heat of summer, and in the dry and the cold. The fourth quarter, corresponding to winter, begins in their sign *hai* in 15° of Scorpion and finishes in their sign *zhou* in 15° of Aquarius; its midpoint is the winter solstice. It is during this quarter that the cold and wet reach their maximum, and the spent hot and dry begin thenceforward to increase once more. The period shares in the dryness of autumn, and is very cold and wet.

They assign a quality to each of these periods. Thus, in spring there are buds and flowers; summer bears fruit or is laden with ripening fruit; in autumn the fruit is seasoned and is collected; in winter, the strength is hidden beneath the earth and collects in the roots of the trees.

They divide these four periods or the solar year into 24 conjunctions of time like months, each with its own name expressing the quality of such-and-such a conjunction or month. All of their signs are allotted two of these periods, each one lasting 15 days. Each of the four seasons contains six of these conjunctions. and their names are as follows. Beginning from the first of spring at 15° of Aquarius and the moon nearest to 15° of Aquarius, or the fifth day of February, when their third sign, the Tiger, begins. This ends in 15° of Pisces and is their first month of the year. They continue in this way through the rest of their signs so that each one of them corresponds to one of the dozen months by the conjunctions of the new moon that occurs in them. The names of the 24 months, or conjunctions and dispositions caused by the sun entering them on its course, are as follows.[2]

This was the first beginning that they gave to the solar and lunar year as soon as they had founded their kingdom after coming from Babylon to the Orient. But as they did not know about the slow movement of the stars from west to east but believed that they always kept the same place and order, they chose Ursa Major as a base in order to begin the year. They held that the day of the year when the tail of Ursa Major pointed after sunset to the third sign or hour after midnight (that is, four o'clock) would be the first day of the solar year or the beginning of spring.[3] The moon nearest to this was the first month of the year. As has been said, this was the fifth day of February, when the sun entered into 15° of Aquarius.

But nowadays, on account of the movement mentioned above, the tail of Ursa Major at the same time after sunset shows about three quarters after midnight, and this amounts to the 50° or so of difference described above.[4]

After this there followed the Chinese dynasty called Shang,[5] in which they started the year at 15° of Capricorn, which is about the fifth day of January. Then came the Zhou

---

[1] Rodrigues is referring to Africa by this term.

[2] A blank of practically half a page is left in the Portuguese text at this point, but no table is given. The relevant table is reproduced in Papinot, *Dictionary*, p. 383; SCC, III, p. 405.

[3] For the role of the Great Bear in determining the beginning of the seasons, see Chalmers, *Astronomy*, pp. [93]-[94].

[4] A reference to precession, noted on p. 353.

[5] A legendary dynasty beginning in 1766 BC, and lasting for 644 years. Varying dates and figures are given by different authors.

dynasty,[1] which began 1,123 years before Christ our Lord, in which they changed the beginning of the year and placed it in 15° of Sagittarius, which occurs about the seventh day of December. This continued in China and Japan until the Year of the Lord 1368 when the Chinese dynasty called Taimei,[2] which still reigns to the present day, began. This dynasty has restored the beginning of the year to the ancient date of the fifth day of February at 15° of Aquarius, and this has been observed in China and Japan from the above date until the present time.[3]

3. The manner of dividing the four seasons and of the beginning of the year appears the most suitable, and was used by the first Fathers before the flood

The manner of dividing the four seasons used by the Chinese and Japanese appears to be the same as that established and used by the Fathers before the Flood, and seems the most suitable one as regards the generation and corruption of things and the variety seen in the four seasons. It is the most natural of all methods, for although later astrologers for various reasons placed the beginning of the four seasons at the two equinoxes and solstices beginning from the 21st day of March onwards, nevertheless the system possessed by the Chinese from their first foundation at the time of the Confusion of Tongues seems more proper, natural, and suited for the purpose. It also appears to have been the first method employed by the Fathers before the Flood. It thus seems to have originated at that time, just as we said of the other celestial things mentioned above.

First of all, it is a certain and proved fact among the learned that the Fathers before the Flood used the lunar year and the solar year of twelve months, each month lasting 30 days, or some 30 and others 29½ days. This gives a solar year of 365¼ days, as in fact happens. They also used the division of the zodiac into 12 signs or parts that correspond to the twelve months of the year, during which the sun passes through them. Finally, they used the four seasons in the same form, manner, and time of the year as the Chinese and Japanese do.

According to the Fathers, all this may be understood from Sacred Scripture, for Moses says in Genesis, Chapter 1: 'Let there be lights in the firmament of the Heavens to separate the day from the night, and let them be for signs and for seasons and for days and years.'[4] Whence Cajetan says, 'That they might be the signs of the zodiac and of innumerable physical effects.'[5] St Basil says, 'That they might be for signs of the rains, the droughts, the wind, and storms.'[6] All this can be included in the phrase 'signs of the zodiac and rains', etc. As regards seasons, St Basil says, 'The four seasons of the year were made, and then the days by which the course of the year can be measured.'[7] The fact that the year then had

---

[1] The Zhou dynasty was founded in 1122 BC by Wuwang (mentioned on p. 53) and lasted until 255 BC, when it was succeeded by the Qin dynasty. It was during the Zhou dynasty that the three Chinese sages – Laozi, Confucius (Kongzi), and Mencius (Mengzi) – lived.

[2] The Ming dynasty. Rodrigues here uses its Japanese name.

[3] Most of what Rodrigues says in this section is confirmed by Trigault, *Litterae*, pp. 129–30; Kingsmill, 'Chinese Calendar', p. 6; Legge, *Chinese Classics*, V, pp. [90]-[92].

[4] Genesis 1, 14. It was formerly believed that Moses had written the Pentateuch. The quotations in this section are given in Latin.

[5] Vio, *Commentarii*, p. x. Tommaso de Vio (1469–1534), commonly known as Cajetan after his birthplace (Gaeta, Italy), was an illustrious Dominican Thomist scholar.

[6] The substance of this quotation is found in Basil, *Sixth Homily in Hexaemeron*.

[7] The substance of this quotation is found in ibid. Rodrigues probably took both these quotations from a scholastic textbook.

twelve months can be seen in the same Scripture of Genesis, which mentions them.[1] The fact that there were four seasons is clearly seen in Genesis, Chapter 35, where it says: 'Going forth Jacob came in the springtime to the land which leads to Ephrata.'[2] Mention of the seasons is made in Genesis, Chapter 8, 'All the days of Earth, seedtime and harvest, cold and heat, summer and winter, night and day shall not cease.'[3]

It can be proved that the beginning of their year and seasons occurred at the same time as that of the Chinese, as the same Chinese have used them from that time. Just as the other above-mentioned things of these regions cannot have been begun by them, neither can this be their invention, as the authors generally maintain that the sacred year or the year of the sacred things that God gave to the Jews when they departed from Egypt was standard among the Fathers before the Flood. This fell in the spring in March, and the one that the Jews used when they departed from Egypt, which fell in September, was proper to the Egyptians and not to the Jews. For until they entered Egypt the Jews did not have a nation of their own or a year proper to their nation, but instead they used the year of the land in which they dwelt, as Abraham the Chaldean used the year of the Chaldeans.[4] Hence in his *In Sphaeram Johannis de Sacrobosco*, Clavius says,

> It was God's wish that, after they had abandoned the errors of the Egyptians, the Jews should again begin their year in the spring. For it was in this season that the world was created and that it pleased Him to free them from harsh servitude.[5]

As some authors note, it happened that in very ancient times the Babylonians, Greeks, and Romans began spring on the seventh day of February, summer on the ninth day of May, autumn on the eighth day of August, and winter on the seventh day of November.[6] This corresponds exactly to the system used by the Chinese since their first beginnings, and it seems that in the beginning this was the common system in the principal nations, and that it had come down from before the Flood. But it was later changed in some nations because of various events that occurred. The astrologers who place the beginning of spring at the vernal equinox also agree with this to some extent.

The Chinese and Japanese prove by various reasons and from their experience of 4,000 years to the present day that this division of the year into four seasons according to their properties is the more probable and natural system than that used by astrologers of this time. We are speaking now of the places to the north and south of the tropics where this variation exists. First of all, they have observed (and we experience every day) that there is a notable and unfailing change and alteration of the weather at the beginning and end of many of the 24 periods into which they divide the year, and they note these down in their

---

[1] Various references are made in Genesis (e.g., 8, 13; 7, 11; 8, 4; 8, 5) to the 1st, 2nd, 7th, and 10th months, but I find no reference to the fact that the year has 12 months.

[2] Genesis, 35, 16.

[3] Genesis, 8, 22.

[4] Although the matter is far from clear, it appears that the Hebrew year formerly began in autumn. While the Jews were in Egypt, they may well have conformed to the solar year, but after the Exodus the religious year (although not necessarily the civil year) was appointed to begin in the spring. Douglas, *New Bible*, p. 178.

[5] Clavius, *In Sphaeram*, p. 265. This work is a commentary on a treatise on the sphere, *Sphaera mundi*, written by Joannes Sacrobosco (d. 1256). It was translated into Chinese by Li Zhizao under Ricci's supervision (see p. 358, n. 1).

[6] This is not accurate as far as the Greek and Roman seasons are concerned. Although there were many local variations, the Greek seasons began on 7 February, 10 May, 30 July, and 10 November; the Roman seasons on 7 February, 9 May, 8 August, and 9 November. Daremberg and Saglio, *Dictionnaire*, I, pp. 837–49.

annual calendars or almanacs. For instance, changes in the weather, climate, and wind, etc., are noted as something that begins then, for example, at *doyō-iri, doyō-zame, risshun, rikka, risshū, rittō*.[1] It is the same at the beginning of each of the four seasons. When one ends and another begins, a particular change is noticed in the weather and climate, and anyone experiencing and noticing it, invariably feels this.

In Japan and China the spring begins when the sun enters in 15° of Aquarius. The nightingale and other birds, which until then have been wrapt in silence with the winter cold, invariably appear and sing as if rejoicing. They indicate the arrival of spring, the season when the animals and all other things begin to revive, and the people regard this as a sign that spring has arrived. Also at the same time the plum, peach, pear, and other trees invariably bud and begin to flower, and as an infallible sign the mists (or *kasumi*) begin to appear. There are various poems about all this suited to the spring.[2] So in the Canticle the signs that spring has arrived and winter is now passed are given by saying:

> Winter is now past, the rain is over and gone.
> The flowers have appeared in our land.
> The voice of the turtledove is heard in our land.[3]

So for all these reasons it seems more likely that when the first Fathers arranged the seasons before the Flood and determined the equinoxes and solstices, the solar and lunar years with their intercalation, and the lunar months, they established the beginning of the solar year and of spring at 15° of Aquarius on the fifth day of February (the beginning of the third Chinese sign), starting from 15° of Pisces. The first Chinese placed it here, for it had thus come down by tradition until Noah and his sons, and they had received it from them and taken it with them when they came to people the Orient. For indeed the four seasons seem to be most suitable in this way as regards their effects and participate better in the qualities attributed to them. For spring is cold and wet because winter is still near, but it is also hot for the sun has now reached us, and the flowers and trees begin to bud and flower from February onwards. Summer is partly wet, hot, and dry, when the fruit is growing strong and ripening. Autumn is partly hot, dry, and cold, when the fruit is ripe and picked. Winter is partly dry, cold, and wet, when things are deadened and their vitality collects in the roots and under the ground.

In keeping with this, the star Aries was in the same 15° of Aquarius at the beginning of the world, if calculation is carefully made. For from the Confusion of Tongues until the

---

[1] *Arte grande*, f. 229v: 'Doyō. A certain conjunction thus called; they talk about *shi-doyō*, that is, the four of these conjunctions throughout the year. There is a *shiki-no-doyō* in each of the four seasons, and they last 18 or sometimes 19 days. They talk about *doyō-iri*, the beginning and when it starts, and *doyō-zame*, that is, when it finishes. The *doyō* of *rokugatsu* [the sixth month] coincides with our dog-days.' Avila Girón (*Relación*, p. 37) speaks about the four *doyō*, 'in which there is always a notable change [in the weather].' Nowadays the term *doyō* usually refers only to midsummer or the dog-days. *Risshun, rikka, risshū,* and *rittō* mean respectively the beginning of spring, summer, autumn, and winter. See the tables in Papinot, *Dictionary*, p. 838, and the Chinese equivalents in *SCC*, III, p. 405. The four terms are correctly defined in *Vocabulario*, ff. 211v, 374v, 375. In *Arte grande*, f. 229v, Rodrigues points out that as *risshun* depends on the solar year, it could occur either before or after the New Year, which was based on the lunar year.

[2] In his short treatises on Japanese poetry (*Arte grande*, ff. 181–4, and Rodrigues, 'Muse'), Rodrigues lists the various seasonal words used in poetry, and mentions that the words *uguisu* (nightingale), *ume* (plum blossom), *sakura* (cherry blossom), and *kasumi* (mist) are particularly appropriate to spring poems.

[3] Canticles, 2: 11–12.

present it has moved, as we have said, 54°08′ during a period of 3,822 years.[1] Now the Sacred Scriptures teach that 1,787 years passed from Adam to the Confusion of Tongues, during which period the stars are believed to have moved a little more than 25°.[2] If we add this to 54°08′, we get 79°08′ during the period of about 5,682 years from Adam to the present.[3] Now if we work backwards, the star Aries, which is now at 25°17′, and 97°08′ from the sign of Aries, was about 15° from Aquarius, and it was here at that time that the spring, as the Chinese placed it, began.[4]

Then there is also the common opinion of the authors who hold that the world was created in the spring equinox, which accordingly comes to be in the middle of the season, and this is the most suitable time of all.[5]

4. Their hours, weeks, days, and months

Like us, they consider the day in two ways, the natural day and the artificial day. Their natural day consists of one revolution of the sun and is made up of the interval of time elapsing between the sun moving from one base of the sky and returning to the same place. It begins at midnight and lasts until the following midnight. This is the same method employed by the Roman Church and seems to have been the first system to be used. It is the most proper and suitable method for the purpose. They divide this natural day into twelve equal hours called by the name of animals that we mentioned earlier. Each of their hours equals two of ours, and six of them make up the day and six the night, as if it were always the equinox. The day begins at the first morning hour, called Hare, when the night finishes, and this would be six o'clock in the morning. It finishes at sunset at the last hour of the afternoon, called Hen, and this is at six o'clock of the natural afternoon when night begins.[6] They divide the twelve hours of the natural day into 100 quarters, which the Japanese call *koku* and the Chinese *ke*. Each hour is divided into eight big quarters and two small quarters. Six of these small quarters make one big one and hence there are 100 big quarters in all. This is the ancient method, but the modern Chinese with their clocks give nine quarters to the hour at midnight and to the hour at midday, and also to those of six in the morning and six in the afternoon. All the other hours have eight quarters.[7]

The artificial day is called the common day by the Japanese and is the ordinary unit of

[1] For discrepancies in this calculation, see p. 354, n. 4.

[2] Rodrigues has already noted (p. 354) that the stars move 1° in 70 years and 7 months. So he correctly calculates that in 1,787 years, they would have shifted 25° (more accurately, 25·32°).

[3] See p. 354 for elucidation of these figures.

[4] This sentence is difficult to understand and the text may be corrupt. The argument seems to be that if there has been a recession of about 79° from the time of Adam to 1620, Aries, then 97°08′ distant from the sign Aquarius (not Aries, as in the text), would have been at the time of the Creation about 18° distant, 'or about 15° from Aquarius'.

[5] Cajetan, for example (Vio, *Commentarii*, p. 55) holds that the Creation probably took place in the spring. See also the quotation from Clavius to this effect on p. 389.

[6] Although Rodrigues speaks of the Hour of the Hen, it is more usual to call it the Hour of the Cock in English. As he later makes clear, the day begins in the *middle* of the Hour of the Hare and ends in the *middle* of the Hour of the Cock. For tables, see *Arte grande*, ff. 230v–1; Papinot, *Dictionary*, p. 840. It goes without saying that the Chinese hour was also twice as long as the European one.

[7] The division of the natural day into 100 quarters led to discrepancies, and systems of 120 quarters (1st century BC) and 96 quarters (6th century AD) were introduced in China, but later abandoned. De Ursis (in D'Elia, *Galileo in*

daily life. They begin moving about and conducting all their business and affairs in accordance with this day. It begins at sunrise and lasts until sunset, and the Chinese start it at four o'clock in the morning. The modern Chinese divide it in our way, counting the hours from midnight to midnight. The day lasts while the sun is up, and a greater or lesser number of hours is given to the night according to whether the day is short or long. They say that during the year the sun rises at such an hour or at so many quarters after it, and that it sets at such an hour. But the Japanese have retained the ancient Chinese method until now, and divide the artificial day and night from when the sun rises to when it sets. Whether the day be long or short, they give six hours to the day and six to the night. These are really the unequal planetary hours that the ancient Chinese, Babylonians, Chaldeans, and also the Hebrews used.[1]

Both the Chinese and Japanese count the hours by the names of animals. The artificial day begins at six o'clock in the morning when the sun rises in the middle of their hour of the Hare. Then follows the hour of the Serpent, which begins at seven o'clock and ends at nine; next comes the hour of the Snake, which begins at nine and ends at eleven. Then follows the hour of the Horse, which begins at eleven, reaches its midpoint at noon, and finishes at one. The hour of the Goat lasts from one to three, the hour of the Monkey from three to five. The last hour of the day, that of the Hen, begins at five, with the day finishing at six o'clock with the setting of the sun in the middle of this hour.[2]

Thus the artificial day is divided up into six of their hours or twelve of ours. After these six hours, night begins from six o'clock and continues in the same fashion until midnight and thence to six in the morning when the night comes to an end. Thus the night also lasts six of their hours, twelve of ours. They divide each of their hours into eight quarters which they call *koku*, or *ke* in Chinese, although in olden times they used to make ten divisions, that is, two short ones and eight long ones. The first four quarters, lasting until the middle of the hour, are called the first prime, the second prime, the third prime, and the fourth prime. Then comes the half-hour, followed by four quarters called the first, second, third, and four divisions after the middle. After that comes the name of the following hour.[3]

In addition to this method, the Japanese have another very common one, similar to that of the Hebrews, Chaldeans, and ancient Chinese, and the Church also uses it at present in the canonical hours. It runs as follows:

Prime, from sunrise to nine o'clock,
Then terce, from nine o'clock to midday.

China, p. 70) also reports on the Chinese months, days, and hours. For a useful account of Chinese time, see Needham, *Heavenly Clockwork*, pp. 199–205, as well as *SCC*, III, pp. 322, 398, note c.

[1] Needham (*SCC*, III, p. 313) confirms the existence of these two different systems in China and Japan. He further notes (ibid., III, p. 398, note c) that the Chinese may well have inherited the system of 12 equal double-hours from the Babylonians.

[2] All this information agrees with the table in *Arte grande*, f. 231v; Papinot, *Dictionary*, p. 840; Needham *Heavenly Clockwork*, p. 200. It is usual to refer in English to the hours of the Hare, Dragon, Snake, Horse, Goat, Monkey, and Cock. Discrepancies are due to translating Rodrigues's terms literally.

[3] This division of the double-hours into halves dates from early times. The first half was called *sho* (in Chinese, *chu*), while the second was *shō* (in Chinese, *zheng*). Needham, *Heavenly Clockwork*, p. 202. In the margin of the Portuguese text, the copyist has written: 'I.e., Hare, *shishi-ichi* 1st 1st, *sho-ni*, *sho-san*, *sho-shi*, *shō* or middle, *shō-ichi*, *shō-ni*, *shō-san*, *shō-shi*, *Tatsu*, *shosho-i*, etc.' These words may have been added as an afterthought or perhaps were accidentally omitted from the text. They indicate the divisions of time between the Hour of the Hare (starting at 5.00 a.m.) and the Hour of the Dragon (*Tatsu*, starting at 7.00 a.m.).

Then sext, from midday to three o'clock,

Then none, from three o'clock to six, which is vespers.[1]

At sunrise the Japanese say six, then follows the second hour which they call five;[2] this finishes at nine o'clock, which is the third; then follows the third hour, which they call four; then the fourth, which they call nine, and this is midday and our sixth. Then follows the fifth hour, which finishes at three o'clock; they call it eight and it is our ninth. Then follows the sixth hour, which they call seven and ends at five o'clock. Then comes the seventh hour, which they call six, in the midpoint of which is vespers.[3] Thus they again repeat 5, 4, 9, until midnight, and from then 8, 7, 5, 6, until sunrise, as may be seen in the diagram below.[4]

The Japanese do not have ordinary clocks with which to tell the time, but the bonzes have very ingenious fire-clocks in their temples in order to know the hour of prayer and when to ring or sound the hour. With these they measure the hours both of the long days as well as of the short ones, because for this purpose they have their fixed measurements in keeping with the length of the day, which they always divide into six hours, whether the day be long or short. They make the clock in this fashion. They take a square wooden box and fill it with a sort of fine sifted ash. This ash is very dry and they make its surface very smooth. On this surface they draw a continuous line of furrows of determined length, breadth, and depth in the form of a square, and they fill these furrows with a dry scented powder or flour, obtained from the bark of a certain tree. They set light to the end of one of the furrows, and the fire continues to burn very slowly so that one of them is consumed every hour. They can thus measure the time very accurately, for they know from experience how to regulate it so that the fire continues to burn in the same way and at the same rate. The furrow is made proportionately longer or shorter according to the length or shortness of the day and night.[5]

The Chinese have sun-clocks, titled towards the equinox according to the place's latitude, with a needle in the middle that points to both the poles. They divide the hours on this into quarters, as we said, but they make them all in respect to 35° of latitude, for they

---

[1] The text is unclear at this point, but this is the probable rendering.

[2] This is yet another Japanese method of calculating time, and a table setting it out is found in Papinot, *Dictionary*, p. 840. These hours also equal two European hours.

[3] A literal translation reads: '… the seventh hour, the middle of which they say six, which is the vespers.' I suspect the text is corrupt here and have translated freely. An alternative rendering would be: '… seventh hour, the middle of which is our sixth hour or vespers.'

[4] Three-quarters of a page is left blank in the manuscript at this point, but no diagram is supplied. Fróis (in *TCJ*, p. 229) refers to this system more succinctly: 'The Japanese count the hours in this way: 6, 5, 4, 9, 8, 7, 6, and so on.' In brief, 6th hour, 5.00–7.00 a.m. and p.m.; 5th, 7.00–9.00 a.m. and p.m.; 4th, 9.00–11.00 a.m. and p.m.; 9th, 11.00–1.00 a.m. and p.m.; 8th, 1.00–3.00 a.m. and p.m.; 7th, 3.00–5.00 a.m. and p.m. When the hours were struck on a bell, three preliminary strokes were rung as a warning; to avoid confusion, therefore, the 3rd, 2nd, and 1st hours were not counted. As an analogy, when a European clock strikes a single stroke, the hearer has no means of knowing whether this denotes 12.30, 1.00, or 1.30.

[5] Gabriel de Magalhães, who died in Peking in 1677, describes (*New History*, pp. 124–6) a similar device, in which sawdust paste is rolled into a rope and then coiled in the form of a cone. The rope, graduated to show the hours, is then set alight; some of the temple cones would burn for 30 days. See also *SCC*, III, p. 330, for Magalhães's text, and illustrations of metal fire-clocks. For devices of this kind, see Bedini, *The Scent of Time*. For the Jesuit clocks in China, see Needham, *Heavenly Clockwork*, pp. 142–50; Ricci, *Fonti*, II, pp. 123, 159. For the Jesuits' use of clocks as presents in Japan, see Fróis, in *TCJ*, p. 96; Cooper, *Rodrigues the Interpreter*, pp. 75, 83, 210–11, 216.

know of no other way, and they use them in the kingdom's cities that are situated at a greater or lesser latitude.[1]

They also possess water-clocks with which they measure the hours. These are made with great skill, and they take into consideration both the summer and the winter, so that the water always runs in the same way. These clocks have four or five measured and proportioned vessels with their spouts, and the water drops from one to the next. In the last one underneath there is a statue of a man with a small board in his hand. As the water gathers, he rises with the board on which are written with due proportion and measurement the hours and their quarters. Thus he comes out onto the surface or horizon of the containing vessel and shows the appropriate hour and quarter. But these clocks do not appear to be very accurate.[2] These clocks are found in a tower built over the main gates of the cities, and at each hour they hit a big drum with so many strokes so that the people may know the time. They also place over the same gate the hour and the quarters written in large letters on a board so that everyone can see the time. There are people seated there who are paid by the king and have the office of changing the boards according to the time.[3]

They also divide the night into four watches as we do. These are signalled by strokes on drums and bells according to the hour and quarter. They even divide the quarters into so many strokes on the drum and bell, which they strike from time to time. When one hour ends and another begins, they have another way of striking loudly, and after this come certain strokes so that people may thus know the hour and quarter of the watch.[4]

These same names of hours or animals are also applied to each year, and the year is called after it by adding another name to each. In this way, they make a cycle of sixty years, at the end of which they start again.[5] This is properly their method of reckoning years for they

[1] Ricci also mentions (*Fonti*, I, p. 33, and *China*, p. 23) these sundials, adding that no account was made of the varying latitudes of the places in which they were used. The 35° in the text here is doubtless a slip for 36° (see p. 382). Rodrigues's mention of the needle pointing to both poles is correct. In some sundials, the actual dial was graduated on both sides, and the needle, or style, extended right through the dial. The instrument was set at an angle to be in the plane of the equator, and thus could be read on both sides. *SCC*, III, pp. 307, 309.

[2] For the Chinese clepsydra, see *SCC*, III, pp. 313–29. Various intermediate vessels were required for accuracy because of the reduced pressure-head in the first vessel as the water emptied out. The viscosity of the water changed with the temperature, and efforts were made to keep the water temperature as constant as possible. See also Sun and Kistemaker, *Chinese Sky*, pp. 94–5, for illustrations of ancient clepsydra.

[3] Bartoli mentions (*Cina*, pp. 560–61) an ancient clepsydra in Hangzhou. Needham describes (*Heavenly Clockwork*, pp. 48–59) a remarkable clepsydra built in 1090 at Kaifeng. The clock was contained within a wooden tower more than 30 feet high and used about half a ton of water every nine hours. Manikins appeared ringing bells and holding tablets to indicate the time.

[4] The night was divided into five (not four) watches called *geng*, and each of these was divided into 5 *chou*. The watches ran from dusk to dawn and therefore varied in length according to season. Needham, *Heavenly Clockwork*, pp. 203–5; Wylie, 'Eclipses', p. 155. Both Pereira and Cruz affirm (in Boxer, *South China*, pp. 23, 101, 182) that in Chinese gaols the night was divided into five watches, although the latter states that there were six night watches in Canton. Magalhães (*New History*, p. 122) provides a detailed account of how the hours were struck on a drum and a bell in combination.

[5] The sexagesimal system of counting the years was composed of the duodecimal system named after animals, as Rodrigues notes, in combination with another system of 10 units, each two of which was named after one of the five elements. When these two systems were combined, a 60-year cycle was produced. The cycle is set out in a table in Papinot, *Dictionary*, p. 837. In a letter to Lord Salisbury, 10 December 1614, Cocks refers to the system named after animals: 'the Japons are accustomed to name (or calle) their yeares after the names of weild beastes & burdes.' He goes on to report that Ieyasu was born in a year of the Tiger, and as 1614 was also a year of the Tiger, soothsayers had predicted the ruler's death. Farrington, *English Factory*, I, p. 258. Ieyasu in fact died one year later.

lack eras; or rather, their eras are the name of the king reigning at that time, and there are as many eras as there have been kings. There are in fact even more eras than this, because on account of some misfortunes that occur, they often change the name of the era for another more propitious one, sometimes twice, three, or four times, and sometimes even twice in the same year.[1]

So this way of reckoning the year by these animals and this sixty-year cycle is like an era. They use it thus, beginning from the first animal year of the Rat, Cow,[2] Tiger, Hare, with its other accompanying word. Hence they say a man was born in the year of the Rat or of the Hare, with its qualifier. They thus know how old they are, and in this matter they are very skilful with their hands or fingers, just as we are as regards movable feasts.[3] They can easily know a year even though two sixty-year cycles have passed. In public and important documents they add it to the name of the king and of his family, and thus the reader knows in which reign the date occurred. In this reckoning they are most exact in their books and annals, and they say, 'He was crowned in the year of the Tiger, etc.'

They distinguish the big and long days with the entrance of the sun into the 24 conjunctions of the periods of the four seasons, each period lasting 15 days. Thus they say of the first of the 24 conjunctions that the sun rises in such-and-such a sign at so many quarters, and it sets in such-and-such a sign at so many quarters. The day has so many quarters and the night a proportionate number. But as they did not know about any latitude other than 35°N in which Miyako and the ancient capital of China are situated,[4] they calculated the length of the day and night according to this position. They divided the day into 100 quarters or into 96, giving the longest day of the year at the summer solstice 60 quarters and the night 40 quarters, or 58 to the day and 38 to the night. At the two equinoxes they assigned 50 or 48 quarters to the day and the same number to the night. In the winter solstice they allotted 40 or 38 quarters to the day, and 60 or 58 to the night. All this may be seen in the following diagram worked out by their ancient forefathers more than 3,822 years ago.[5]

---

[1] This system of eras was borrowed from China by the 36th emperor, Kōtoku (r. 645–54), who decreed that the first year of his reign should mark the beginning of the Taika era. Although his two successors abolished the system, it was restarted in 672 and continues to this day. As Rodrigues notes, *kaigen*, or name changes, could take place to commemorate a special occasion, and there were no less than eight *nengō*, or era names, in the reigns of Go-Daigo (1319–38) and Go-Hanazono (1429–65). Since the Meiji Restoration (1868), there has been only one *nengō* for each reign. Lists of era names in *Arte grande*, ff. 233–4v, and Papinot, *Dictionary*, pp. 823–4.

[2] Really the Ox, but Rodrigues writes 'cow'.

[3] Rodrigues is here probably referring to the mnemonic systems in both western and Orthodox Europe in which the joints of the hand were assigned numbers or letters in a variety of calendrical calculations or *aides-mémoire*.

[4] For the position of Miyako and Kaifeng, see p. 372, nn. 4, 5.

[5] Half a page is left blank at this point, but no table or diagram is supplied. The significance of 'more than 3,822 years ago', i.e., about 2200 BC, escapes me. Perhaps Rodrigues is thinking of Huangdi, in whose reign the division of the natural day into 12 hours was introduced (see p. 351). Rodrigues, *Nihon*, II, p. 210, n. 35, supplies a table providing the different lengths of day and night in the 24 divisions of the year, but does not explain the significance of 'more than 3,822 years ago'.

CHAPTER 16

THE PRACTICAL JUDICIAL ASTROLOGY OF THESE NATIONS, AND THE VARIOUS SUPERSTITIONS CONTAINED THEREIN

It is not easy to describe how much these nations of Japan, China, and Korea are given to the vain superstitions of judicial astrology, which depends on the aspects of the planets and stars, and of various other types of this sort, for they do not seem to take a single step that is not governed by it. It regulates their actions and even the state that they must accept for their whole life, as well as the place of residence and the work to which they must give themselves. Although the Japanese go to an excess in this regard, the Chinese, from whom they learnt this vain art, greatly surpass everyone else, and thus the ancient Chaldeans, from whom this art spread throughout the entire world, do not seem to have equalled them therein.

They have three principal sorts of judicial astrology, apart from various other superstitious devices that are all different from each other. The first is natural magic that the Chinese philosophers called *jasha*[1] practice, after the fashion of the ancient Chaldeans, Persians, and Babylonians. By means of a person's birth and natural temperament, which depends on the celestial influence received at his conception, they discern the nature of things, the fate or destiny that each person must have, and the good and evil fortune that he will accordingly enjoy in his free and contingent actions, for this will depend on whether such actions fit in with or oppose his inevitable fate.

The second is practical judicial astrology, by which they make their predictions and prognostications in accordance with the conjunctions and aspects of the planets and stars, and with other celestial appearances. They assign the good or so-called white days, and bad or black ones (the ancients also called such days *atri dies*),[2] the good or bad hour in which to do something or not to do it, such as to travel by horse, on foot, or by water, to marry, build, bury the dead, fight and overcome the enemy.[3] As they say that Earth is square and

---

[1] The text gives *jaxa*, which Rodrigues, *Nihon*, II, p. 211, interprets as an error for the Japanese word *juxa* (modern spelling, *jusha*). But this means Confucianist and does not seem to fit the context. In Japanese, the character read as *ja* has a pejorative meaning, e.g., *jadō*, an evil course; *jahō*, witchcraft, and thus *jasha* may mean a wizard, although admittedly the term is not found in dictionaries. Semedo (*History*, p. 143) gives the more familiar term *suanming* for a fortune-teller.

[2] Literally, 'coal-black days', because the Romans marked these unlucky days on their calendars with coal. A list of such days is given in *Works and Days*, lines 765 *et seq.*, by the Greek poet Hesiod, already mentioned on p. 376.

[3] Accounts of these lucky and unlucky days in China are given in Mendoza, *History*, I, pp. 46–9; Semedo, *History*, p. 93; Ricci, *Fonti*, I, pp. 94–5, and *China*, pp. 82–3; and Navarrete, *Travels*, II, p. 190. Ricci (*Fonti*, II, p. 500, and *China*, p. 548) notes a zealous Christian who deliberately set out on a journey on an unlucky day. De Ursis (in D'Elia, *Galileo in China*, p. 74) lists some of the restrictions in force on unlucky days. The subject is mentioned in Japan by Almeida (Shiki, 20 October 1566, in *Cartas*, I, f. 214v), and Kaempfer (*Kaempfer's Japan*, pp. 286–7), who supplies a table of unlucky days for traveling. In 1608, the high-ranking official Honda Masazumi discussed this matter with Rodrigues, who remarked that for a Christian an unlucky day was one on which he went on a journey and

has four corners (north-east, south-west, north-west, and south-east), they decide which of these directions or corners in any particular year is harmful to face when a person performs some natural or free action. In the same way, the appearances seen in the sky foretell whether and where there will be war, floods and droughts, epidemics, deaths, and calamities.[1] They divine lost things and innumerable other things.[2] A multitude of ignorant people, and even women, give themselves to this and earn their living thereby. For this reason there are many books dealing with this matter and the rules of the predictions that are to be made.

In Japan many of these soothsayers and sorcerers go about the cities and towns, practising this office and deceiving the wretched people who, in their desire to find out things for their own profit, patronize them and ask them such things so that they may be told their fate. If they do not know the year and month of their birth, the diviners will guess it for them, and then according to this they work out their fate. In the Chinese cities and towns there are many of these men, set up with their tables and chairs in the streets, shops, or crowded public places, and they keep many of these books on the tables to help them to guess and predict the things that people ask them.[3] The customers give each one some money every time. To show themselves wise, both in Japan and in China they examine the books and the diagrams therein, and face certain directions with various ceremonies, deceits, and pretences, and in this way they deceive the wretched people. These folk go off very happy with the prediction or forecast, but are out of pocket and no better off than at the beginning.[4]

The kings of China and Japan have colleges of judicial mathematicians, who are officials of the royal household and enjoy noble rank and revenue. Their principal task is to reckon the years, the eclipses of the sun and moon, arrange the intercalations and harmonize the lunar year with the solar, arrange the annual calendar or almanac, and everything else concerning astrology, both speculative and practical, or judicial. Such people still exist and work in Japan, and they have their quarters next to the Dairi's palace and also in other parts of the kingdom, such as in the kingdom of Izu, where they now compile and print the best calendars or almanacs every year.[5] But since the king and the grandees of the patrician order are excluded from the government, which was usurped by the *kubō* and the members of the

---

was caught in the pouring rain. Cooper, *Rodrigues the Interpreter*, pp. 250–51. For modern accounts, see Gray, *China*, II, pp. 13–15; Doré, *Recherches*, II, pp. 250–55.

[1] Needham notes (*SCC*, II, pp. 354–5) the celestial phenomena regarded by the Chinese as portents. Comets produced great fear, and caused one Japanese emperor to abdicate. Nakayama, *History*, pp. 52–3. Cocks (in *Diary*, II, p. 94) reports a 'comett (or blasing star)' seen in Edo, and some people believed that 'it did prognosticate som greate matter of warr.' When asked his opinion, Cocks said that comets were often seen in his own country, 'but the meanyng thereof God did know and not I.'

[2] Cocks records (*Diary*, II, p. 33) that a silver spoon was missing in his house and some of his staff went 'to a wis-szard to know whoe had taken it.' After a stone was heated to test by ordeal, a young servant confessed and was brought to 'disepline (or whiping cheare).'

[3] Even today in modern Japan fortune-tellers may still be seen in the evening sitting at small tables in city streets, waiting for customers wishing to learn their future.

[4] Ricci (*Fonti*, I, pp. 95–7, and *China*, pp. 83–5) describes Chinese soothsayers and fortune-tellers. *Vocabulario*, f. 321: '*Ekihakuji*. Sorcerer or diviner or astrologer, who knows what is to happen to a person from the conjunction of the stars in which he was born, etc.' '*Eki*. A book or art that teaches the nature and qualities and events of a person in keeping with his birth. *Eki wo toru*. To guess or foretell by this book what is to happen to somebody, etc.' For the art of calculating horoscopes in Japan, see Nakayama, *History*, pp. 58–63.

[5] Ferdinand Verbiest describes the Chinese calendar in his *Astronomia europaea*, pp. 69–78. He was well qualified to do so, for in 1669 he was put in charge of drawing up the official calendar for the whole of the Chinese Empire, and held this post until his death in 1688.

equestrian or military order, none of the offices of the royal household now functions publicly, and so these astrologers are much neglected and held in low esteem. In Japan they are called *tenbun hakase*, or *tenbun gakuji*, meaning 'astrologers', and the soothsayers practising natural magic are called *on'yōji*.[1]

They greatly flourish even now in China, and it is also an office there with rank and allowance from the royal household, and they succeed through inheritance from father to son. There is a law promulgated throughout the kingdom by Hongwu, the first king and founder of this present Daming dynasty, or Taimei as they say in Japan, which prohibits anyone from learning astrology without the king's permission, except those families who practise it as an office. For it is believed that this could be the means of seizing the kingdom through the knowledge and science obtained from their predictions and prognostications.[2].

In the court of Beijing there is a college of these royal mathematicians and another in Nanjing, in addition to a special one of eunuchs inside the palace and another of Moorish Arabs maintained by the state in Beijing.[3] The public astrologers have special palaces with high and exposed places therein where there are lofty towers and instruments, armillary spheres, and various other things to observe the Heavens. So they take it in turn day and night to keep continuous vigil, scanning the Heavens and the appearances thereof. When anything noteworthy occurs, they notify the king by a written memorial, adding at the same time what it presages.[4] The celestial appearances from which they make their predictions are primarily those concerned with the influences of the air, such as rain, thunder, lightning, snow, dew, which appear in the air or occur out of season or more excessively than usual. Secondly, the sun's appearances, of which they have twenty-eight different ones. Thirdly, the moon's appearances, of which they also have more than sixteen kinds.[5] Fourthly, those of the heavenly stars. Fifthly and finally, the appearances of comets of various shapes that appear in some of the twenty-eight starry signs or constellations of the zodiac.[6] All these phenomena and their interpretation are painted with figures in a book.

As regards this astrology and natural magic, it is common in these nations for each person to determine his fate or destiny from his birth with the help of these astrologers,

[1] Rodrigues (*Arte breve*, ff. 88–91) gives a long official list of the *hyakkan* ('hundred officials'), or civil servants. Towards the end of the list appear the offices of *Temmon*, or *Tembun, no hakase* ('a soothsayer') and *On'yō no hakase* ('an astrologer'). The second term means literally, 'Doctor of yin and yang'.

[2] Ricci (*Fonti*, II, p. 122, and *China*, pp. 370–71) once had his European astronomical books confiscated (but later returned) because, as he says, there was an ancient law forbidding under pain of death the study of astronomy, except in the case of the imperial mathematicians. Trigault (*Litterae*, pp. 125–6) confirms this, and mentions severe punishments for the publication of unofficial calendars. A decree of 840 ordered imperial mathematicians to keep their business secret. *SCC*, III, p. 193; Nakayama, *History*, p. 15.

[3] For these 'Moorish Arabs', see p. 366, n. 3.

[4] For the office and duties of the imperial astronomers, see *SCC*, III, pp. 189–92. The Astronomical Bureau went by various names, but from the 8th century it was usually known as the *Sitiantai*. *SCC*, III, p. 191, note a. For an illustrated account of the instruments, especially the armillary sphere, see ibid., III, pp. 339–90. Ricci (*Fonti*, II, pp. 56–8, and *China*, pp. 329–31) gives a detailed description of the instruments seen in the Nanjing observatory, and reports that there was a similar institution in Beijing. Identification of these instruments is given in *SCC*, III, pp. 369–70.

[5] While speaking about Chinese superstitions, Semedo, *History*, p. 93, mentions the 22 appearances of the sun and the 16 of the moon.

[6] So accurate and detailed were Chinese observations that the comets recorded in 240, 87, and 11 BC were undoubtedly Halley's comet. An extraordinarily precise account of the size and movement of a comet in 1472 is contained in the Ming annals. *SCC*, III, pp. 430–32.

and then arrange his life and work in accordance with the requirements of his fate so that everything may go well. For they believe that everything will go badly if they oppose and go against the decrees of fate. Thus many people, deceived by this foolishness of inevitable fate, choose a way of life suited to it, and some go on continual pilgrimage without ever remaining in their country, because this is what is decreed by their fate. The Japanese call this *honke*, and the Chinese, *benjun*.[1] Other people abandon the study of letters and weapons, and roam about even though they are nobles. Others become religious as their fate shows that they are not suited to secular things of this world, and there are a thousand and one other things of this sort.

The third kind concerns only the things of Earth, such as a good or bad site on which to build, the quality of the place in which to dwell, and the respect shown towards the good and bad directions of Earth, or the world. For they believe that some are very bad, harmful, and unlucky, while others are lucky and fortunate. So they choose sites for the tombs of their dead, because they hold that they communicate to them good or bad fortune and quality. In order to determine such things, they summon these soothsayers of Earth to inspect the site of the building, tomb, or house.[2]

These fortune-tellers possess various books and laws with which they deceive the people. In this regard, they also perform various ceremonies and superstitions, declaring to people that in such-and-such a place there will be sickness, death, and misfortune, and that they will be impoverished there and will not have any good luck, but quite the contrary.[3] Thus it comes about that these nations are extremely superstitious and attribute each and every misfortune or disaster to the site, so for this reason they move their dwellings to other places, and leave their houses empty. When somebody dies on them, these people (especially the Chinese) will never carry the corpse to the burial through the front door of the house, but use instead a side door or one at the back of the house; or else they make a new door for this purpose.[4]

There are other folk who throughout their entire lives will never pronounce the word 'death', which in Japanese is pronounced *shi*, nor will they use any other words similar in pronunciation but not in meaning. Instead of these modes of speech, they have special phrases by which they can express themselves. For example, instead of saying, 'He died,' they will say, 'He went on a long journey,' or 'He hid himself,' and other such phrases.[5]

They have various other means of predicting. For example, they can judge the state of a person and his good or bad fortune by the signs of his face and body. They can tell whether someone is rich or poor, and lucky by the lines on his hands.[6] This is so common among the

---

[1] *Vocabulario*, f.101v: '*Honke*. Astronomical line or point of those people whom astrologers examine as to which one they were born in, so as thus to judge someone's outcome, fortune, inclination, etc.' Rodrigues also argued with Honda Masazumi against the concept of *honke* (see p. 396, n. 3).

[2] References to the pseudo-science of geomancy, especially as regards the correct positioning of tombs, are given on p. 140, n. 1.

[3] A literal rendering of the conclusion of this sentence would read: ' ... sicknesses, deaths, without profit [?], and that they must impoverish themselves there without having good fortune, and the opposite of oestrus.' But the text may well be corrupt.

[4] A common custom observed in various parts of the world, but not noted by Groot, Gray, or Lay in their accounts of burials. But Semedo (*History*, p. 139) reports that the corpse of a prisoner was not removed from a Chinese gaol by the same gate through which he had entered alive.

[5] For references to this custom, see p. 192, n. 2.

[6] For *xiangshu*, or physiognomy, see *SCC*, II, pp. 363–4, and Doré, *Researches*, II, pp. 223, 232. Cheiromancy, or palmistry, is mentioned in *SCC*, II, p. 364, and Gray, *China*, II, p. 3. Other types of Chinese divination are described

Chinese that they immediately take a person's hand to examine it. It would take too long to recount their various methods of casting lots, how they are governed by them, the special persons who practise this divination, and the various other superstitions of this kind with which the devil lures this wretched and blind pagan people, dissatisfied with the temporal things of this life.

by Cruz, in Boxer, *South China*, pp. 214–15; Mendoza, *History*, I, pp. 46–9; Doré, *Researches*, II, pp. 239–49; Gray, *China*, II, pp. 8–13. Semedo (*History*, p. 94) relates with amusement that in 1630 a blind palmist warned the priest about the wayward conduct of his wife and two sons.

BIBLIOGRAPHY

1. Manuscripts
Lisbon: Library of the Ajuda Palace. *Jesuítas na Asia* series.
49–IV–51 Sebastião Gonçalves, SJ, *História dos religiosos da Companhia de Jesús.*
49–IV–53 João Rodrigues, SJ, *História da Igreja do Japão.* (Part 1, Books 1 and 2)
49–IV–57 Jesuit papers.
49–IV–66 Jesuit papers.

London: The British Library.
Add.MSS 9857 Alessandro Valignano, SJ, *Principio y progresso*, 1601.
Add.MSS 18287 Rodrigo de Vivero y Velasco, *Relación del Japón*, c. 1610.

Madrid: Library of the Real Academia de la Historia. *Jesuítas* series.
7236 João Rodrigues, SJ, *Bispos da Igreja do Japão.*
7237 João Rodrigues, SJ, *Breve aparato para a história de Japam*; also the Introduction and index of his *História.*
7238 João Rodrigues, SJ, *História*, Part 2, Book 1.

Rome: Jesuit Archives.
JapSin 25, 52, 54, 56, 57, 59. Jesuit letters and reports from Japan.

2. Books and Articles
Abranches Pinto, J. A. and Henri Bernard, '*Les Instructions du Père Valignano pour l'ambassade japonaise en Europe*', *MN* 6, 1943, pp. 391–403.
Acosta, José de, SJ, *The Natural and Moral History of the Indies*, ed. Clements R. Markham, 2 vols, Hakluyt Society, 1st series, 60, 61a, London, 1880.
Adams, William, *The Log-Book of William Adams, 1614–1619*, ed. C. J. Purnell, London, 1916.
Albuquerque, Afonso, *The Commentaries of the Great Afonso Dalbuquerque*, tr. Walter de Gray Birch, 4 vols, Hakluyt Society, 1st series, 53, 55, 62, 69, London, 1875–84.
Allen, R. H., *Star Names: Their Lore and Meaning*, New York, 1963 (1st edn 1899).
Alvarez-Taladriz, José Luis, 'Don Rodrigo de Vivero y Velasco et la destruction de nao "Madre de Deus"', *MN*, 2, pp. 479–511.
——, ed., *San Martín de la Ascensión y Fray Marcelo de Ribadeneira: Relaciones e informaciones*, Osaka, 1973.
——, tr., 'Perspectiva da la historia de Japón según el P. Juan Rodriguez, SJ', *Tenri Daigaku Gakuhō*, 4:2, 1952.
——, tr., 'Miyako visto por un europeo a principios del siglo XVII', *Ōsaka Gaikokugo Daigaku Gakuhō*, 2, 1953.

———, tr., 'La pintura japonesa vista por un europeo a principios del siglo XVII', *Más y Menos* (Ōsaka Gaikokugo Daigaku), 14, 1953.

———, tr., *Arte del cha*, Tokyo, 1954.

Anderson, Andrew Runni, *Alexander's Gate, Gog and Magog, and the Inclosed Nations*, Cambridge, Mass., 1932.

Andrade, Antonio de, *Nuevo descubrimiento del Gran Catayo*, 2 vols, Madrid, 1947.

Anesaki Masaharu, 'Kirishitan Missions in the Mines', *Proceedings of the Imperial Academy of Japan*, 3 (1927).

———, 'A Concordance of the History of the Kirishitan Missions', *Proceedings of the Imperial Academy of Japan*, 6 (Supplement), 1930.

———, 'Japanese Mythology', in *Mythology of All Races*, VIII, Boston, 1928.

Arnáiz, Greg. and Max van Berchem, 'Mémoire sur les antiquités musulmanes de s'iuan-Tcheou', *T'oung Pao*, 12, 1911, pp. 677–727.

Aurousseau, Léonard, 'Sur le nom de Cochinchine', *Bulletin de l'Ecole Française d'Extreme-Orient*, 24, Hanoi, 1925.

Avila Girón, Bernadino de, *Relación del reino de Nippon*, ed. Dorotheus Schilling, OFM, and Fidel de Lajarza, *Archivo Ibero-Americano*, 37, Madrid, 1934.

Ayres, Christovão, *Fernão Mendes Pinto e o Japão: Subsidios para a sua biographia e para o estudo da sua obra*, Lisbon, 1906.

Bagchi, Prabodh Chandra, *India and China: A Thousand Years of Cultural Relations*, Calcutta, 1981.

Bagrow, Leo, *History of Cartography*, revised by R. A. Skelton, 2nd edition, Chicago, 1985.

Ball, Samuel, *An Account of the Cultivation and Manufacture of Tea in China*, London, 1848.

Barbosa, Duarte, *The Book of Duarte Barbosa*, ed. M. L. Dames, 2 vols, Hakluyt Society, 2nd series, 44, 49, London, 1918–21.

Barros, João de, *Década primeira da Asia, Década segunda da Asia, Década terceira da Asia*, Lisbon, 1628.

———, *Década quarta da Asia,* Madrid, 1615.

Bartoli, Daniello, SJ, *Dell' historia della Compagnia di Giesu. Il Giappone, Secunda parte dell' Asia*, Rome, 1660.

———, *Dell' historia della Compagnia di Giesu. La Cina, Terza parte dell' Asia*, Rome, 1663.

Basil, *S.P.N. Basilii Opera omnia*, Patres graeci 29–32, 4 vols, Paris, 1857.

Beaglehole, J. C., *The Exploration of the Pacific*, 3rd edn, Stanford, 1966.

Beal, S., *Buddhist Records of the Western World*, 2 vols, London, 1884,

Bedini, Silvio, *The Scent of Time: A Study of the Use of Fire and Incense for Time Measurement in Oriental Countries*, Transactions of the American Philosophical Society, 53, 5, Philadelphia, 1963.

Bernard, Henri, SJ, *Matteo Ricci's Scientific Contribution to China*, tr. E. C. Warner, Beijing, 1935.

Berry, Mary Elizabeth, *Hideyoshi*, Cambridge, Mass., 1982.

Bhadantācariya Buddhaghosa, *The Path of Purification (Visuddhimagga)*, tr. Bhikkhu Nyanamoli, Colombo, 1964.

Blacker, Carmen, 'Forgotten Practices of the Past: Kaempfer's Strange Description of the Japanese Emperor', in Bodart-Bailey and Massarella, ed., *The Furthest Goal.*

Bodart-Bailey, B. M. and Derek Massarella, ed., *The Furthest Goal: Engelbert Kaempfer's Encounter with Tokugawa Japan*, Folkestone, 1995.

Bodde, Derk, *China's First Unifier*, Leiden, 1938.

Boethius, *De institutione arithmetica*, ed. G. Freidlein, Leipzig, 1867.

Boger, H. B., *The Traditional Arts of Japan*, London, 1964.

Boscaro, Adriana and Lutz Walter, 'Ezo and Its Surroundings through the Eyes of European Cartographers', in Walter, *Cartographic Vision*, pp. 84–90.

Boxer, C. R. *The Affair of the 'Madre de Deus'*, London, 1929.

———, 'Three Historians of Portuguese Asia', *Boletim de Instituto portugues de Hongkong*, 1 (1948), pp. 15–44.

———, *The Christian Century in Japan*, California, 1951.

———, ed., *South China in the Sixteenth Century …*, Hakluyt Society, 2nd series, 106, London, 1953.

———, *The Great Ship from Amacon*, Lisbon, 1959.

Boyer, M., *Japanese Export Lacquer from the 17th Century in the National Museum of Denmark*, Copenhagen, 1959.

Braga, J. M. 'Jesuitas na Asia', *Boletim eclesiástico da diocese de Macau*, 53, January 1955.

Brahe, Tycho, *Opera omnia, sive astronomiae instauratae progymnasmata*, Frankfurt, 1648.

Bretschneider, E., *Mediaeval Researches from East Asiatic Sources*, 2 vols, London, 1910.

Brown, Delmer M., *Money Economy in Medieval Japan*, Connecticut, 1951.

Brown, Lloyd A., *The Story of Maps*, Boston, 1950.

Bunbury, E. H., *A History of Ancient Geography*, 2 vols, London, 1883.

Butler, Lee A., 'The Way of Yin and Yang: A Tradition Revived, Sold, Adopted', *MN*, 51:2, 1996, pp. 189–217.

Cabezón, Jose Ignacio, ed., *Buddhism, Sexuality, and Gender*, New York, 1992.

Cambridge History of China, ed. Frederick W. Mote and Denis Twitchett, Cambridge and New York, vol. 7, 1988.

Cambridge History of Japan, ed. John W. Hall et al., 6 vols, Cambridge and New York, 1990–99.

Cardim, Antonio, SJ, *Elogios e ramalhete de flores borrifado com o sangue dos religiosos da Companhia de Jesu …* , Lisbon, 1650.

Carletti, Francesco, *My Voyage Around the World*, tr. H. Weinstock, London, 1965.

Caron, François and Joost Schouton, *A True Description of the Mighty Kingdoms of Japan and Siam*, ed. C. R. Boxer, London, 1935.

Cartas que os padres e irmãos da Companhia de Jesus escreverão dos reynos, de Japão e China …, 2 vols, Evora, 1598. Facsimile edition, Tenri, 1972.

Carter, T. F., *The Invention of Printing in China*, revised by L. Carrington Goodrich, New York, 2nd edition, 1955.

Casal, U. A., 'Some Notes on the *Sakazuki* and the Role of *Sake* Drinking in Japan', *Transactions of the Asiatic Society of Japan*, 2nd series, 19, 1940, pp. 1–186.

———, 'Japanese Art Lacquers', *MN*, 15, 1959–60, pp. 1–34 and 225–56.

———, 'The Lore of the Japanese Fan', *MN*, 16, 1960, pp. 53–117.

———, 'Japanese Cosmetics and Teeth-Blackening', *Transactions of the Asiatic Society of Japan*, 3rd series, 9, 1966, pp. 14–17.

———, *The Five Sacred Festivals of Ancient Japan: Their Symbolism and Historical Development*, Tokyo, 1967.

Cassian, *Opera omnia, PL* 49 and 50, 2 vols, Paris, 1846.

Castanheda, Fernão Lopes de, *Historia de descobrimento e conquista da India pelos Portugueses*, 4 vols, Lisbon, 1833.

Cedrenus, Georgius, *Annales, sive historiae ab exordio mundi ad Isacium Comnenum usque compendium*, Basle, 1566.

Chalmers, John, 'Astronomy of the Ancient Chinese', in Legge, *Chinese Classics*, 3, 1, pp. [90]–[102].

Chamberlain, Basil Hall, 'Wasabisuwe, the Japanese Gulliver', *Transactions of the Asiatic Society of Japan*, 7, 1879, pp. 285–312.

——, 'The Luchu Islands and Their Inhabitants', *The Geographical Journal*, 5,1895.

——, and W. B. Mason, *A Handbook for Travellers in Japan*, London and Yokohama, 1907.

Charles, R. H., ed., *The Apocrypha and Pseudoepigrapha of the Old Testament in English*, Oxford, 1964.

Chassigneux, Edmond, 'Rica de Oro et Rica de Plata', *T'oung Pao*, 30, 1933, pp. 37–84.

Chatley, H., 'Ancient Chinese Astronomy', *Occasional Notes of the Royal Astronomical Society*, 1:5, 1939.

Cieslik, Hubert, SJ, 'The Great Martyrdom of Edo, 1632', *MN*, 10, 1954, pp. 1–44.

——, *Hokuhō Tankenki* [Records of the Exploration of the Northern Regions], Tokyo, 1961.

——, 'The Training of a Japanese Clergy in the Seventeenth Century', in Roggendorf, *Studies in Japanese Culture*, pp. 41–78.

Clavius, Christopher, *Christopheri Clavii Bamburgenensis ex Societate Iesu in Sphaeram Ioannis de Sacro Bosco commentarius*, Lyons, 1594.

Clavijo, Ruy Gonzales de, *Narrative of the Embassy of Ruy Gonzalez de Clavijo to the Court of Timour, at Samarcand, A.D. 1403–1406*, tr. C. R. Markham, Hakluyt Society, 1st series 26, London, 1859.

Coaldrake, William H., 'Edo Architecture and Tokugawa Law', *MN*, 36, 1981, pp. 235–84.

——, *The Way of the Carpenter: Tools and Japanese Architecture*, New York, 1990.

——, *Architecture and Authority in Japan*, London, 1996.

Cocks, Richard, *The Diary of Richard Cocks*, ed. N. Murakami, 2 vols, Tokyo, 1889.

Colin, Francisco, SJ, *Labor evangélica de los obreros de la Compañía de Jesús en las Islas Filipinas*, ed. Pablo Castells, SJ, 3 vols, Barcelona, 1903–4.

Collingridge, George, 'The Early Cartography of Japan', *The Geographical Journal*, 3, 1894, pp. 403–9.

Columbus, Christopher, *Raccolta di documenti e studi publicati dalla R. Commissione Columbiana*, 6 vols in 11, Rome, 1892–4.

Commentarii Collegii Conimbricensis Societatis Jesu, in II libros de generatione et corruptione Aristotelis Stagiritae, Coimbra, 1597 (edition cited, Cologne, 1600).

Commentarii Collegii Conimbricensis Societatis Jesu, in Quatuor libros de coelo Aristotelis Stagiritae, Cologne, 1600.

Cooper, Michael, 'The Early Jesuits and Zen', *The Month*, May 1962, pp. 261–74.

——, ed., *They Came to Japan: An Anthology of European Reports on Japan, 1543–1640*, California, 1965; Michigan, 1995.

——, 'João Rodrigues, SJ, and His Description of Japan', doctoral thesis, University of Oxford, 1969.

——, *Rodrigues the Interpreter: An Early Jesuit in Japan and China*, Tokyo, 1974, 1994.

——, ed., *The Southern Barbarians: The First Europeans in Japan*, Tokyo, 1971.

——, 'The Early Europeans and Tea', in Varley and Kumakura, *Tea in Japan*, pp. 101–33.

Cortazzi, Hugh, *Isles of Gold: Antique Maps of Japan*, Tokyo, 1983.

Cortes, Adriano de las, SJ, *Viaje de la China*, ed. Beatriz Moncó Rebollo, Madrid, 1991.

Cortesão, Armando, and A. Teixeira da Mota, *Portugaliae monumenta cartographica*, 6 vols, Lisbon, 1960.

Couto, Diogo da, *Década quarta da Asia. Década quinta da Asia. Década sexta da Asia*, Lisbon, 1602–15.

Cros, Léonard, SJ, *Saint François de Xavier, sa vie et ses lettres*, 2 vols, Paris, 1900.

Cunningham, Alexander, *The Ancient Geography of India*, London, 1871.

Curzon, G. N., *Persia and the Persian Question*, 2 vols, London, 1892.

Dahlgren, E. W., *Les Débuts de la cartographie du Japon*, Upsala, 1911.

——, 'Contribution to the History of the Discovery of Japan', *Transactions and Proceedings of the Japan Society*, 11, 1912–13.

Dalgado, S. R., *Glossário Luso-asiático*, 2 vols, Coimbra, 1919–21.

Danvers, F. C., *The Portuguese in India*, 2 vols, London, 1894.

Daremberg, G. and E. Saglio, ed., *Dictionnaire des antiquités grecques et romaines*, 9 vols, Paris, 1897–1917.

Davenport, F. G., *European Treaties Bearing on the History of the United States*, 4 vols, Washington, 1917–37.

Davies, C. Collin, *An Historical Atlas of the Indian Peninsula*, Oxford, 1949.

Davis, T. L., 'The Tomb of Jofuko or Joshi', *Ambix*, 1, 2, December 1937.

Dawson, Raymond, ed., *The Legacy of China*, Oxford, 1964.

D'Elia, Pasquale M., SJ, *Galileo in China: Relations through the Roman College between Galileo and the Jesuit Scientists-Missionaries (1610–1640)*, tr. Rufus Suter and Matthew Sciascia, Cambridge, Mass., 1960.

——, 'Recent Discoveries and New Studies (1938–1960) on the World Map in Chinese of Father Matteo Ricci, SJ', *Monumenta Serica*, 20 (1961), pp. 82–164.

Dening, Walter, *The Life of Toyotomi Hideyoshi*, London, 1930.

Doi Tadao, 'Das Sprachstudium der Gesellschaft Jesu in Japan im 16. und 17. Jahrhundert', *MN*, 2, 1939, pp. 437–65.

——, *Kirishitan Gogaku no Kenkyū* [A Study of Kirishitan Linguistics], Osaka, 1943.

Doi Tsugiyoshi, *Momyama Decorative Painting*, tr. Edna B. Crawford, Tokyo and New York, 1977.

Doré, Henri, SJ, *Recherches sur les superstitions en Chine*, 3 vols, Shanghai, 1911–12.

Douglas, J. D., ed., *The New Bible Dictionary*, London, 1962.

Douglas, R. K., *The Life of Jenghiz Kahn*, London, 1877.

Dumoulin, Heinrich, SJ, *A History of Zen Buddhism*, tr. P. Peachey, London, 1963.

Dunne, G. H., SJ, *Generation of Giants*, London, 1962.

Edmunds, W. H., *Pointers and Clues to the Subjects of Chinese and Japanese Art*, London, 1934.

Eitel, E. J., *Feng-shui, or the Rudiments of Natural Science in China*, London, 1873.

Elison, George, *Deus Destroyed: The Image of Christianity in Early Modern Japan*, Cambridge, Mass., 1973.

——, and Bardwell L. Smith, ed., *Warlords, Artists, and Commoners: Japan in the Sixteenth Century*, Honolulu, 1981.

——, 'Hideyoshi, the Bountiful Minister', in Elison and Smith, *Warlords*, pp. 213–44.

Elman, Benjamin A., *A Cultural History of Civil Examinations in Late Imperial China*, Berkeley, 2000.

Enciclopedia italiana di scienze, lettere et arti, 40 vols, Milan and Rome, 1929–61.

Escalante, Barnardino de, *Discurso de la navegacion que los Portugueses hazen a los reinos, y provincias del Oriente, y de la noticia q se tiene de las grandezas del reino de la China*, Seville, 1577. In Sanz, *Primera historia*.

Fairbank, J. K. and S. Y. Tang, 'On the Transmission of Ch'ing Documents', *Harvard Journal of Asiatic Studies*, 4, 1939, pp. 12–46.

Faria, Manoel Severim de, *Vida de João de Barros*, Lisbon, 1778.

Farrington, Anthony, ed., *The English Factory in Japan, 1613–1623*, 2 vols, London, 1991.

Ferguson, J. C., 'The Chinese Foot Measure', *Monumenta Serica*, 6, 1941, pp. 357–82.

——, 'Chinese Mythology', in *The Mythology of All Races*, VIII, Boston, 1928.

Fitzgerald, C. P., *China: A Short Cultural History*, London, 1935.

——, *The Chinese View of their Place in the World*, London, 1964.

——, *Barbarians Beds: The Origin of the Chair in China*, London, 1965.

Forke, Alfred, *The World-Conception of the Chinese*, London, 1925.

Foust, Clifford M., *Rhubarb: The Wondrous Drug*, Princeton, 1992.

Franke, Herbert, 'The Exploration of the Yellow River Sources under Emperor Qubilai in 1281', Chapter 9 in Franke, *China under Mongol Rule*, Aldershot, UK, 1994.

Fróis, Luís, SJ, *De rebus japonicis historica relatio anni 1591 and 1592*, Cologne, 1596.

——, *Die Geschichte Japans 1549–1578*, tr. Georg Schurhammer, SJ, and E. A. Voretzsch, Leipzig, 1936.

——, *Segunda parte da Historia de Japan, 1578–1582*, ed. J. A. Abranches Pinto and Y. Okamoto, Tokyo, 1938.

——, *La Première Ambassade du Japon en Europe, 1582–1592*, ed. J. Abranches Pinto, Y. Okamoto and Henri Bernard, SJ, Tokyo, 1942.

——, *Tratado en que se contem muito susinta e abreviadamente algumas contradições*, ed. J. F. Schütte, SJ, Tokyo, 1955.

——, *História de Japam*, ed. José Wicki, SJ, 5 vols, Lisbon, 1976–84.

——, *Luís Fróis: Proceedings of the International Conference, United Nations University*, Tokyo, September 24–26, 1997, Tokyo, 1999.

Fuchs, Walter, *The 'Mongol Atlas' of China*, Peking, 1946.

Fung, Y., *History of Chinese Philosophy*, tr. D. Bodde, 2 vols, London, 1952–3.

Galvano, Antonio, *The Discoveries of the World*, Hakluyt Society, 1st series, 30, London, 1862.

Gaubil, Antoine, SJ, 'Histoire abrégée de l'astronomie chinoise', *Observations mathématiques, astronomiques, tirées des anciens livres chinois*, ed. H. Souciet, SJ, 3 vols, Paris, 1729–82.

Geerts, J. A., 'Preliminary Catalogue of the Japanese Kinds of Woods', *Transactions of the Asiatic Society of Japan*, 4,1875, pp. 1–26.

——, 'Useful Minerals and Metallurgy of the Japanese', *Transactions of the Asiatic Society of Japan*, 3:1, 1875, pp. 1–16, 27–51 and 85–97.

Geil, William Edgar, *The Great Wall of China*, London, 1909.

Génébrard, Gilbert, *Chronographiae libri quatuor*, Paris, 1585.

Giles, N. A., *A Chinese Biographical Dictionary*, London, 1898.

Gómez, Pedro, SJ, *Compendium catholicae veritatis*, 3 vols, Tokyo, 1997.

Gonçalves, Sebastião, SJ – *see under* Manuscripts.

Grande enciclopédia Portuguesa e Brasileira, 40 vols, Lisbon and Rio de Janeiro, n.d.

Gray, John Henry, *China: A History of the Laws, Manners, and Customs of the People*, 2 vols, London, 1878.

Gribble, Henry, 'The Preparation of Vegetable Wax', *Transactions of the Asiatic Society of Japan*, 3:1, 1874, pp. 98–101.

——, 'The Preparation of Japanese Tea', *Transactions of the Asiatic Society of Japan*, 12:1, 1885, pp. 1–84.

Groot, J. J. M. de, *The Religious System of China: Its Ancient Forms, Evolution, History, and Present Aspect Manners, Customs and Social Institutions Connected Therewith*, 6 vols, Leiden, 1892–1910.

Guerreiro, Fernão, SJ, *Relação Anual das Coisas que Fizeram os Padres da Companhia de Jesus nas suas Missões ...*, ed. Artur Viegas [António Antunes Vieira, SJ], 3 vols, Coimbra, 1930–32, Lisbon, 1942.

Gulik, Robert van, *Mi Fu on Ink-Stones*, Peking, 1938.

——, *The Lore of the Chinese Lute*, Tokyo, 1940.

——, *Chinese Pictorial Art*, Rome, 1958.

Guzman, Luis de, SJ, *Historia de las misiones que han hecho los religioos de la Compañía de Jesús ...*, 2 vols, Alcalá, 1601.

Hakluyt, Richard, ed., *The Principal Navigations Voyages Traffiques and Discoveries of the English Nation*, 12 vols, Glasgow, 1904–5.

Hall, D. G., *A History of South-East Asia*, London, 1955.

Hall, J. C., 'Japanese Feudal Laws. III, The Tokugawa Legislation. Part IV, The Edict of 100 Sections', *Transactions of the Asiatic Society of Japan*, 41 (1913), pp. 683–804.

Hall, John W. and Toyoda Takeshi, ed., *Japan in the Muromachi Age*, Berkeley, 1977.

Hansen, Thorkild, *Arabia Felix*, London, 1965.

Haskins, Charles H., *Studies in the History of Mediaeval Science*, Cambridge, Mass., 1927.

Hattori Shiro, 'The Relationship of Japanese to the Ryukyu, Korean and Altaic Languages', *Transactions of the Asiatic Society of Japan*, 3rd series, 1, 1948, pp. 101–33.

Hayashi Razan, *Baison Saihitsu*, in *Nihon Zuihitsu Taisei*, ed. Hayakawa Junzaburō, vol. 1, Tokyo, 1928.

Hayes, L. N., *The Great Wall of China*, Shanghai, 1929.

Hazard, B. H., 'The Formative Years of the *Wakō*, 1223–1263', *MN*, 22:3–4, 1967, pp. 260–77.

Heath, Thomas L., *Aristarchus of Samos, the Ancient Copernicus: A History of Greek Astronomy to Aristarchus*, Oxford, 1913.

——, *Greek Astronomy*, New York, 2nd edition, 1969.

Heike, The Tale of, tr. Helen Craig McCullough, Stanford, 1988.

Hinago, Motoo, *Japanese Castles*, tr. and adapted by William H. Coaldrake, Tokyo, 1986.

Hirai Kiyoshi, *Feudal Architecture of Japan*, tr. Hirosaki Sato and Jeannine Ciliotta, Tokyo and New York, 1973.

Hirth, Friedrich, *The Ancient History of China to the End of the Chou Dynasty*, New York, 1923.

Hitomi Hitsudai, *Honchō Shokkan* [A Mirror of Our Country's Food], ed. Shimada Isao, 5 vols, Tokyo, 1976–81.

Hookham, H., *Tamburlaine the Conqueror*, London, 1962.

Hucker, Charles O., 'Governmental Organization of the Ming Dynasty', *Harvard Journal of Asiatic Studies*, 21, 1958, pp. 1–66.

——, *The Censorial System of Ming China*, Stanford, 1966.

——, *A Dictionary of Official Titles in Imperial China*, Stanford, 1985.

Hulbert, H. B., 'National Examination in Korea', *Transactions of the Korean Branch of the Royal Asiatic Society*, 14 (1923), Seoul.

Humbertclaude, Pierre, *Recherches sur deux catalogues de Macao (1616 et 1632)*, Tokyo, 1942.

——, 'Supplement aux "Recherches sur deux Catalogues de Macao"', *MN*, 6, 1943, pp. 435–44.

Hunter, Dard, *Papermaking through Eighteen Centuries*, New York, 1930.

Imperial Gazeteer of India, Oxford, 1907.

Inoue Mitsusada, 'The Century of Reform', *Cambridge History of Japan*, I, pp. 163–220.

Isidore, *Etymologiarum … libri XX*, in *PL* 82.

Jackson, Peter, 'Marco Polo and his "Travels"', *Bulletin of the School of Oriental and African Studies*, 61:1, 1998, pp. 82–101.

Jacobson, Robert D., ed., *The Art of Japanese Screen Paintings: Selections from The Minneapolis Institute of Arts*, Minneapolis, 1984.

Joly, Henri L., *Legend in Japanese Art: A Description of Historical Episodes, Legendary Characters, Folk-Lore Myths, Religious Symbolism Illustrated in the Arts of Old Japan*, Tokyo, 1967.

Josephus, *The Works of Flavius Josephus*, tr. William Whiston, London, 1906.

Kaemmerer, Eric A., *Trades and Crafts of Old Japan*, Tokyo, 1961.

Kaempfer, Engelbert, *The History of Japan … 1690–1692*, tr. J. G. Scheuchzer, 3 vols, Glasgow, 1906.

——, *Kaempfer's Japan: Tokugawa Culture Observed*, ed. and tr. Beatrice M. Bodart-Bailey, Honolulu, 1999.

Kammerer, Albert, *La Découverte de la Chine par les Portugais au xvième siècle et la cartographie des portulans*, Leiden, 1944.

Kamo no Chōmei, *The Ten Foot Square Hut*, tr. A. L. Sadler, Westport, Connecticut, 1970.

Karrow, Robert W., Jr, *Mapmakers of the Sixteenth Century and Their Maps*, Chicago, 1993.

Kawazoe Shōji, 'Japan and East Asia', in *Cambridge History of Japan*, III, pp. 396–446.

KEJ. See *Kodansha Encyclopedia of Japan*.

Kingsmill, T. W., 'The Chinese Calendar: Its Origin, History and Connections', *Journal of the North China Branch of the Royal Asiatic Society*, 32, 1897, pp. 1–35.

Kircher, Athanasius, SJ, *China illustrata*, tr. Charles D. Van Tuyl, Muskogee, Oklahoma, 1987.

Kish, George, 'Some Aspects of the Missionary Cartography of Japan during the XVIth Century', *Imago Mundi*, 6, 1949, pp. 39–47.

Kitagawa, Kay, 'The Map of Hokkaidō of G. de Angelis ca.1621', *Imago Mundi*, 7, 1950, pp. 110–14.

Klijn, A. F. J., *Seth in Jewish, Christian and Gnostic Literature*, Supplement to *Novum Testamentum*, XLVI, Leiden, 1977.

Koda Shigetomo, '*Notes sur la presse jésuite au Japon et plus spécialment sur les livres imprimés en caractères japonais*, *MN*, 2, 1939, pp. 374–85.

Kodansha Encyclopedia of Japan, 9 vols, Tokyo, 1983.

Kojiki, or Record of Ancient Matters, tr. B. H. Chamberlain and W. G. Aston, Kobe, 1932.

Kokushi Daijiten (Yoshikawa), Tokyo, 14 vols, 1979–93.

Kracke, E. A., 'Family vs. Merit in the Civil Service Examinations under the Empire', *Harvard Journal of Asiatic Studies*, 10, 1947, pp. 103–23.

Kreiner, Josef, 'European Maps of the Ryūkyūs from the Sixteenth to the Mid-Nineteenth Century', in Walter, *Cartographic Vision*, pp. 77–83.

Kumakura Isao, 'Sen no Rikyū: Inquiries into His Life and Tea', in Varley and Kumakura, *Tea in Japan*, pp. 33–70.

Kuno, Y. S., *Japanese Expansion on the Asiatic Continent*, 2 vols, Berkeley, 1937.

Lach, Donald F., *Asia in the Making of Europe,* 3 vols, Chicago, 1965–93.

Lapide, Cornelius à, *Commentarii in Scripturam Sanctam,* Paris, 1875.

Laufer, Berthold, 'The Name "China"', *T'oung Pao,* 13, 1912, pp. 719–26.

Laures, Johannes, SJ, *Kirishitan Bunko,* 3rd ed., Tokyo, 1957.

Lay, A. H., 'Japanese Funeral Rites', *Transactions of the Asiatic Society of Japan,* 19, 1891, pp. 507–44.

Le Bar, F. M., ed., *Laos: its People, its Society, its Culture,* New Haven, 1960.

Legge, James, tr., *The Chinese Classics,* 5 vols, Hong Kong, 1960.

Lewis, C. T. and C. Short, *A Latin Dictionary,* Oxford, 1958.

Linschoten, J. H. van, *Discours of Voyages into ye Easte and West Indies, Devided into Foure Books,* London, 1598.

Liu Xinru, *Ancient India and Ancient China: Trade and Religious Exchanges, AD 1–600,* Delhi, 1988.

Lombard, F. A., *Pre-Meiji Education in Japan,* Tokyo, 1913.

López-Gay, Jesús, SJ, 'La primera biblioteca de los Jesuítas en el Japón (1556): Su contenido y su influencia', *MN,* 15, 1959–60, pp. 350–79.

Lucena, João de, SJ, *Historia da vida do Padre Francisco de Xavier,* Lisbon, 1600.

Ludwig, Theodore, 'Before Rikyu: Religious and Aesthetic Influences in the Early History of the Tea Ceremony', in *MN,* 36:3, 1981, pp. 367–90.

Mackenzie, Donald A., *Myths of China and Japan,* London, n.d.

Maffei, Giovanni P., SJ, *Historiarum Indicarum libri XVI,* Florence, 1588.

Magalhães, Gabriel de, SJ, *A New History of China,* London, 1688.

Magini, Giovanni A., *Geographia universae veteris et novae absolutissimum opus,* Cologne, 1597.

Magino, Leo, *Pontificia Nipponica,* 2 vols, Rome, 1947–8.

——, 'A contribução dos Portugueses para o conhecimento da Ilha de Iesso, no Japão, no séc. XVI', *Actas de Congresso internacional da história dos Descubrimentos …,* III, Lisbon, 1961.

March, A. L., 'An Appreciation of Chinese Geomancy', *Journal of Asian Studies,* 27, 1968, pp. 253–67.

Markham, Clements R., tr. and ed., *Early Spanish Voyages to the Strait of Magellan,* Hakluyt Society, 2nd series, 28, London, 1911.

Marsh, Robert M., *The Mandarins,* Glencoe, Ill., 1961.

Martini, Martinus, SJ, *Novus atlas sinensis,* Amsterdam, 1655.

——, *Bellum Tartaricum, or the Conquest of the Great and Most Renowned Empire of China, by the Invasion of the TARTARS …,* London, 1655. [Second part of Semedo, *History,* with continuing pagination.]

——, *Description géographique de l'Empire de la Chine,* in *Relations de divers voyages curieux,* III, Paris, 1666.

Maspero, Georges, 'Le Royaume de Champa', *T'oung Pao,* 11 and 12, 1910–11, pp. 153–202.

Maspero, Henri, 'L'Astronomie Chinoise avant les Han', *T'oung Pao,* 26, 1929, pp. 267–356.

McColley, G. 'The Seventeenth-Century Doctrine of a Plurality of Worlds', *Annals of Science,* I (1936), pp. 385–92.

McCrindle, J. W., *Ancient India as Described by Ptolemy,* Bombay, 1895.

McCullough, Helen C., 'Aristocratic Culture', in *Cambridge History of Japan,* II, pp. 390–448.

McCullough, William H., 'The Capital and Its Society', in *Cambridge History of Japan,* II, pp. 97–182.

McGovern, Melvin P., *Specimen Pages in Korean Movable Types*, Los Angeles, 1966.

McNeil, William H., 'The Historical Significance of the Way of Tea', in Varley and Kumakura, *Tea in Japan*, pp. 255–63.

Meijer, M. J., 'A Map of the Great Wall of China', *Imago Mundi*, 13, 1956, pp. 110–15.

Mendoza, J. Gonzalez de, *The History of the Great and Mighty Kingdom of China and the Situation Thereof*, tr. Robert Parke, ed. George T. Staunton, 2 vols, Hakluyt Society, 1st series, 14, 15, 1853–4.

Mercator, Gerard, *Atlas, or a Geographicke Description of the Regions, Countries and Kingdomes of the World*, tr. Henry Hexham, Amsterdam, 1636.

Mercer Dictionary of the Bible, ed. Watson E. Mills, Edgar V. McKnight, Roger A. Bullard, Macon, Ga,1991.

Michael, Franz, *The Origin of the Manchu Rule in China*, Baltimore, 1942.

Mills, J. V., 'Notes on Early Chinese Voyages', *Journal of the Royal Asiatic Society*, 1951, pp. 3–25.

Miyazaki, Ichisada, *China's Examination Hell: The Civil Service Examinations of Imperial China*, tr. Conrad Schirokauer, New Haven and London, 1981.

MN = Monumenta Nipponica

Montanus, Arnoldus, *Atlas Japannensis. Being Remarkable Addresses by Way of Embassy from the East-India Company of the United Provinces to the Emperor of Japan*, tr, John Ogilvie, London, 1670.

Monumenta Ignatiana. Scripta de Sancto Ignatio de Loyola, I, Madrid, 1904.

Morejon, Pedro de, S.J., *Historia y relación de lo sucedido en los reinos de Iapon y China*, Lisbon, 1621.

Morita, Kiyoko, *The Book of Incense*, Tokyo and New York, 1992.

Morris, Ivan, *The World of the Shining Prince: Court Life in Ancient Japan*, New York, 1969.

Morris, V. Dixon, 'The City of Sakai and Urban Autonomy', in Elison and Smith, *Warlords, Artists, and Commoners*, pp. 23–54.

Morse, Edward S., *Japanese Homes and Their Surroundings*, London, 1886.

Mote, Frederick W., 'The Rise of the Ming dynasty, 1330–1376', in *Cambridge History of China*, VII, pp. 11–57.

Moule, A. C., *Quinsai, with Other Notes on Marco Polo*, Cambridge, 1957.

Moura, Carlos Francisco, *Roteiros de Japão: I, O primeiro roteiro de Nagasáqui*, Evora, 1970.

Mundy, Peter, *The Travels of Peter Mundy in Europe and Asia*, ed. Richard Carnac Temple, 6 vols, Hakluyt Society, 2nd series, 17, 35, 45, 46, 55, 78, London, 1907–36.

Murai Yasuhiko, 'The Development of *Chanoyu*: Before Rikyū', in Varley and Kumakura, *Tea in Japan*, pp. 3–32.

Murase, Miyoko, *Byōbu: Japanese Screens from New York Collection*, New York, 1971.

Murdoch, James, *A History of Japan to 1542*, London, 1949.

——, *A History of Japan during the Century of Early Foreign Intercourse (1542–1651)*, Kobe, 1903.

Nakamura Hiroshi, *East Asia in Old Maps*, Tokyo, 1964.

Nakayama, Shigeru, *A History of Japanese Astronomy: Chinese Background and Western Impact*, Cambridge, Mass., 1969.

Navarrete, Domingo, O.P., *The Travels and Controversies of Friar Domingo Navarrete (1618–1686)*, ed. J. S. Cummins, 2 vols, Hakluyt Society, 2nd series, 118–119, Cambridge, 1962.

Needham, Joseph, *Science and Civilisation in China*, 6 vols, Cambridge and New York, 1954–1996.

——, 'Science and China's Influence on the World', in Dawson, *Legacy*, pp. 234–308.

——, et al., *Heavenly Clockwork: The Great Astronomical Clocks of Mediaeval China*, Cambridge and New York, 1960.

Nihongi, Chronicles of Japan from the Earliest Times to 697 A.D., tr. W. G. Aston, 11th printing, Tokyo, 1998.

Nishigōri Takeka, *Kokon Fukusō no Kenkyū* [A Study of Ancient and Modern Costumes], Osaka, 1927.

Nishiyama Matsunosuke, *Edo Culture: Daily Life and Diversions in Urban Japan, 1600–1868*, tr. and ed. Gerald Groemer, Honolulu, 1997.

Nordenskiöld, Nils Adolf Erik, *Facsimile-atlas to the Early History of Cartography with Reproductions of the Most Important Maps Printed in the XV and XVI Century*, tr. Johan Adolf Ekelof and Clements R. Markham, reprint, New York, 1961.

——, *Periplus: An Essay on the Early History of Charts and Sailing-Direction*, tr. Francis A. Bather, Stockholm, 1897 (reprint, New York, n.d.)

Norton, Luis, *Os Portugueses no Japão*, Lisbon, 1952.

Nuttall, Zelia N., 'The Earliest Historical Relations between Mexico and Japan', *University of California Publications in American Archaeology and Ethnology*, 4, 1, 1906.

Ogasawara Shorei Daizen [The Complete Ogasawara Book of Etiquette], ed. Kitahashi Oyokuzan, Tokyo, 1881.

Origen, *Opera omnia*, PG 12, 2 vols, Paris, 1857–60.

Orta, Garcia de, *Colloquies on the Simples and Drugs of India*, tr. Clements Markham, London, 1913.

Ortelius, Abraham, *Theatrum orbis terrarum*, Antwerp, 1570.

Oxford Classical Dictionary, ed. Simon Hornblower and Antony Spawforth, 3rd edition, Oxford and New York, 1996.

Oxford English Dictionary. The New Shorter Oxford English Dictionary, ed. Lesley Brown, 2 vols, Oxford, 1993.

Pacheco, Diego, SJ, 'The Founding of the Port of Nagasaki', *MN*, 25, 1970, pp. 303–23.

Pacheco, Joaquin F., *Colección de documentos inéditos relativos al descubrimiento, conquista y colonisación de las posesiones españolas en America y Oceanía* …, 42 vols, Madrid, 1864–84.

Paine, R. T. and A. Soper, *The Art and Architecture of Japan*, Harmondsworth, 1960.

Palme of Christian Fortitude or the Glorious Combats of Christians in Iaponia, Douai, 1630.

Pan Ku, *The History of the Former Han Dynasty*, tr. H. H. Dubbs, 3 vols, Baltimore, 1938–44.

Pandey, Rajyashree, '*Suki* and Religious Awakening: Kamo no Chōmei's *Hosshinshū*', *MN*, 47:3, 1992, pp. 299–321.

Papinot, Edmond, *Historical and Geographical Dictionary of Japan*, Tokyo, 1976 reprint.

Partington, J. R., *History of Greek Fire and Gunpowder*, Baltimore and London, 1960, 1999.

Paske-Smith, M., *Western Barbarians in Japan and Formosa in Tokugawa Days, 1603–1868*, Kobe, 1930.

Pelliot, Paul, 'L'Origine du nom de "Chine"', *T'oung Pao*, 13, 1912, pp. 727–42.

Pérez, Lorenzo de, O.F.M., *Cartas y relaciones de Japon*, 3 vols, Madrid, 1916–23.

Perrin, Noel, *Giving Up the Gun: Japan's Reversion to the Sword, 1543–1879*, Boston, 1979.

PG = J. P. Migne, *Patrologiæ cursus completus … series græca*, Paris, 1857–1912.

Philip G. (ed.), *Philip's Historical Atlas*, London, 1927.

Phillips, George, 'The Identity of Marco Polo's Zaitun with Changchau', *T'oung Pao*, 1, 1890, pp. 218–38.

——, 'Two Mediaeval Fuh-kien Trading Ports, Chüan-chow and Changchow', *T'oung Pao*, 6, 1895, pp. 449–63, and 7, 1896, pp. 223–40.

Pigafetta, Antonio, *Magellan's Voyage Around the World*, ed. J. A. Robertson, 3 vols, Cleveland, 1906.

Pinto, Fernão Mendes, *The Travels of Mendes Pinto*, ed. and tr. Rebecca D. Catz, Chicago and London, 1989.

Pires, Thomé, *Suma Oriental of Tomé Pires*, ed. Armando Cortesão, 2 vols, Hakluyt Society, 2nd series, 90–91, London, 1944.

PL = J. P. Migne, *Patrologiæ cursus completus ... series latina*. Paris, 1844–64.

Polo, Marco, *The Book of Ser Marco Polo*, ed. Henry Yule, 2 vols, London, 1903.

Ponsonby-Fane, R. A. B., *Kyoto, Its History and Vicissitudes since its Foundation in 792 to 1868*, Hong Kong, 1931.

——, *The Imperial Family of Japan*, Kobe, 1915.

——, *Studies in Shinto and Shrines*, Kyoto, 1953.

Pratt, Peter, *History of Japan, Compiled from the Records of the English East India Company*, 2 vols, Kobe, 1931.

Prévost, Antoine François, *Historische Beschryving der Reizen ...*, XVII, Amsterdam, 1758.

Purchas, Samuel, *Purchas His Pilgrimage, or Relations of the World ...*, London, 1613.

——, *Purchas his Pilgrimages in Japan*, ed. Cyril Wild, Kobe, 1939.

Pyrard, François, *The Voyage of François Pyrard of Laval to the East Indies, the Maldives, the Moluccas, and Brazil*, tr. Albert Gray, 3 vols, Hakluyt Society, 1st series, 76, 77, 80, London, 1887–90.

Rachewiltz, Igor de, 'Marco Polo Went to China', *Zentralasiatische Studien*, 27, 1997, pp. 34–92.

Redesdale, Lord, *Tales of Old Japan*, 1910, London.

——, *Memoires*, 2 vols, n.d., New York.

Rein, J. J., *The Industries of Japan*, London, 1899.

Renondeau, G., *Le Shugendō, histoire, doctrine et rites des anchoretes dits Yamabushi*, Paris, 1965.

Ribadeneira, Marcelo de, OFM, *Historia de las islas del Archipélago Filipino y reinos de la Gran China ... Japón*, Madrid, 1947.

Ricci, Matteo, SJ, *Opere storiche del P. Matteo Ricci, S.J.*, II: *Le lettere della China (1580–1610)*, ed. F. Tachi Venuri, SJ, Macerata, 1913.

——, *Il mappamondo cinese del P. Matteo Ricci, S.I.*, ed. P. N. D'Elia, SJ, Vatican, 1938.

——, *Fonti Ricciane*, ed. P. N. D'Elia, SJ, 3 vols, Rome, 1942–9.

——, *China in the Sixteenth Century ...*, tr. L. J. Gallagher, SJ, New York, 1953.

Richard, L., *Comprehensive Geography of the Chinese Empire and Dependencies*, tr. M. Kennelly, SJ, Shanghai, 1908.

Robinson, B. W., *The Arts of the Japanese Sword*, London, 1961, 1970.

Rockhill, W. W., 'Notes on the Relations and Trade of China with the Eastern Archipelago and the Coast of the Indian Ocean during the Fourteenth Century', *T'oung Pao*, 15, 1914, pp. 419–47.

Rodrigues, João, SJ, *Arte da lingoa de Iapam* [= *Arte grande*], Nagasaki, 1604–8.

——, *Arte breve da lingoa japoa...* [= *Arte breve*], Macao, 1620.

——, *Arte del cha*, ed. J. L. Alvarez-Taladriz, Tokyo, 1954.

——, *História da Igreja do Japão pelo Padre João Rodrigues Tçuzzu, SJ*, ed. João do Amaral Abranches Pinto, 2 vols, Macao, 1954–5.

——, *Nihon Kyōkai Shi* [Japanese translation of *História*, Part 1, Books 1 and 2, and Part 2, Book 1], tr. Doi Tadao et al., 2 vols, Tokyo, 1967–70.

——, 'The Muse Described: João Rodrigues's Account of Japanese Poetry', tr. Michael Cooper, *MN*, 26, 1971, pp. 55–75.

——, *This Island of Japon: João Rodrigues' Account of 16th-Century Japan*, tr. Michael Cooper, Tokyo, 1973.

——, 'Rodrigues in China: The Letters of João Rodrigues, 1611–1633', tr. Michael Cooper, in Doi Tadao, *Kokugo-shi e no Michi* [The Road to the History of the Japanese Language], II, Tokyo, 1981, pp. 353–224.

——, *see also under* Manuscripts.

Rodrigues Giram, João, SJ, 'Carta anua da Vice-Província do Japão do ano de 1604', ed. António Baião, Coimbra, 1933.

Roggendorf, Joseph, SJ, ed., *Studies in Japanese Culture*, Tokyo, 1963.

Rotours, Robert des, *La Traité des fonctionnaires et Traitée de l'armée*, 2 vols, Leiden, 1947–8.

Rowbotham, A. H., *Missionary and Mandarin*, California, 1942.

Rubruck, William of, *The Journey of William of Rubruck to the Eastern Parts of the World, 1253–55*, tr. William Woodville Rockhill, Hakluyt Society, 2nd series, 4, London, 1900.

Ruiz-de-Medina, Juan, SJ, ed., *Documentos del Japón, 1547–1557 and 1558–1562*, 2 vols, Rome, 1990–95.

Sadler, A. L., *Cha-no-yu: The Japanese Tea Ceremony*, Kobe, 1934.

——, *The Maker of Modern Japan: The Life of Tokugawa Ieyasu*, London, 1937.

Salian, Jacques, SJ, *Enchiridium chronologicum sacrae et profanae historiae, a mundo condito ad Christii Domini Ascensionem*, Cologne, 1638.

Sande, Edwardus, SJ, *De missione legatorum japonensium ad Romanam Curiam ...*, Macao, 1590. Facsimile edition, Tokyo, 1935.

Sansom, G. B. *The Western World and Japan*, New York, 1951.

——, *Japan, A Short Cultural History*, Stanford, 1952.

——, *A History of Japan to 1334*, Stanford, 1958.

——, *A History of Japan, 1334–1615*, Stanford, 1961.

——, *A History of Japan, 1615–1867*, Stanford, 1963.

Sanz, Carlos, ed., *Primera historia de China*, Madrid, 1958.

Sasama Yoshihiko, *Nihon Gassen Tsuten* [Illustrated Dictionary of Japanese Battles], Tokyo, 1997.

Saussure, Leopold de, 'L'Étymologie du nom des monts K'ouen louen', *T'oung Pao*, 20, 1921, pp. 370–71.

——, *Les Origines de l'astronomie chinoise*, Paris, 1930.

SCC. See Needham, *Science and Civilisation in China*.

Schalow, Paul Gordon, 'Kūkai and the Tradition of Male Love in Japanese Buddhism', in Cabezón, *Buddhism*, pp. 215–30.

Schlegel, G, 'Etymology of the Word Taifun', *T'oung Pao*, 7, 1896, pp. 581–5.

Schurhammer, Georg, SJ, *Shintō, the Way of the Gods in Japan*, Leipzig, 1923.

——, *Die Disputationen des P. Cosme de Torres, SJ, mit den Buddhisten in Yamaguchi im jahre 1551*, Tokyo, 1929.

——, *Orientalia*, Rome and Lisbon, 1963.

——, 'Doppelganger in Portugiesisch-Asien', in *Orientalia*, pp. 121–47.

——, 'O descobrimento do Japão', in *Orientalia*, pp. 525–79.

——, 'P. Luis Frois SI, ein Missionshistoriker des 16. Jahrhunderts in Indien und Japan', in *Orientalia*, pp. 581–604.

——, 'P. Johann Rodriguez Tçuzzu als Geschichtschreiber Japans', in *Orientalia*, pp. 605–18.

——, 'Das Stadtbild Kyōtos zur Zeit des Heiligen Franz Xaver (1551)', in *Orientalia*, pp. 619–82.

——, 'Kōbō-Daishi', in *Orientalia*, pp. 683–703.

——, 'Die Yamabushis', in *Orientalia*, pp. 705–30.

——, *Francis Xavier: His Life and Times*, tr. M. Joseph Costelloe, 4 vols, Rome, 1973–82.

Schütte, Josef F., SJ, 'Map of Japan', *Imago Mundi*, 9, 1952, pp. 73–8.

——, 'A história inédita dos "Bispos da Igreja do Japão" do P. João Rodrigues Tçuzu, SJ', *Actas de Congresso internacional de história dos Descobrimentos ...*, V, Lisbon, 1961.

——, *Documentos sobre el Japón conservados en la colección 'Cortes' de la Real Academia de la Historia*, Madrid, 1961.

——, *El 'Archivo del Japón'*, Madrid, 1964.

——, *Introductio ad historiam Societatis Iesu in Japonia 1549–1650*, Rome, 1968.

——, *Textus catalogorum Japoniae ...*, Rome, 1975.

——, *Valignano's Mission Principles for Japan*, tr. John J. Coyne, SJ, 2 vols, St. Louis, 1980–85.

Se-Ma Ts'ien, *Les Mémoires historiques*, tr. Edouard Chavannes, 5 vols, Paris, 1895–1905.

Semedo, Alvaro, SJ, *The History of the Great and Renowned Monarchy of China ...*, London, 1655.

Shasekishū [A Collection of Sand and Stones], Nihon Koten Bungaku Taikei 85, Tokyo, 1966.

Shaw, W. N., *Manual of Meteorology*, 4 vols, Cambridge, 1942.

Shimizu, Yoshiaki and John Rosenfield, *Masters of Japanese Calligraphy*, New York, 1984.

Sicardo, José, OSA, *Christianidad del Japon, y dilatada persecución que padeció*, Madrid, 1698.

Silverberg, Robert, *The Great Wall of China*, Philadelphia and New York, 1965.

Sixtus Senensis, *Bibliotheca sancta. A.F.Sixto Senensi, Ordinis Praedicatorum, ex praecipuis Catholicae Ecclesiae auctoribus collecta, et in octo libros digesta*, Lyons, 1591.

Skene Smith, Neil, ed., *Tokugawa Japan*, London, 1937.

Smith, Bradley, *Japanese History Through Art*, London, 1954.

Smith, D. Howard, 'Zaitun's Five Centuries of Sino-Foreign Trade', *Journal of the Royal Asiatic Society*, 1958, parts 3 and 4, pp. 165–77.

Sommervogel, Carlos, SJ, ed., *Bibliothèque de la Compagnie de Jesus*, 12 vols, Brussels and Paris, 1890–1960.

Stein, Aurel, *Innermost Asia*, 4 vols, Oxford, 1928.

Stone, L. H., *The Chair in China*, Toronto, 1952.

Sugimoto, Masayoshi and David L. Swain, *Science and Culture in Traditional Japan*, Rutland, Vermont and Tokyo, 1989.

Suidas, *Suidae historica, caeteraque omnia quae ulla ex parte ad cognitionem rerum spectant*, Basle, 1581.

Sullivan, Michael, 'The Heritage of Chinese Art', in Dawson, *Legacy*, pp. 165–233.

Sun Xiaochun and Jacob Kistemaker, *The Chinese Sky during the Han: Constellating Stars and Society*, Leiden and New York, 1997.

Szcześniak, Boleslaw, 'The Seventeenth Century Maps of China: An Inquiry into the Compilations of European Cartographers', *Imago Mundi*, 13, 1956, pp. 116–36.

Taiheiki, The: A Chronicle of Medieval Japan, tr. Helen Craig McCullough, New York, 1959.

Takahashi Kenji, *Rekisei Fukushoku Zusetsu*, 2 vols, Tokyo, 1929.

Takayanagi Shun'ichi, 'The Glory that Was Azuchi', *MN*, 32:4, 1977, pp. 515–24.

Takeda Tsuneo, *Kanō Eitoku*, tr. and ed. H. Mack Horton and Catherine Kaputa, Tokyo and New York, 1977.

Takekoshi T., *The Economic Aspects of the History of the Civilization of Japan*, 3 vols, London, 1930.

Tarn, W. W., *The Greeks in Bactria and India*, Cambridge, 1938.

Taylor, A. E., *A Commentary on Plato's Timaeus*, Oxford, 1928.

TCJ. See Cooper, *They Came to Japan*.

Teleki, Paul, *Atlas zur Geschichte der Kartographie der Japanischen Inseln*, Budapest, 1909.

Teng Ssu-Yu, 'Chinese Influence on the Western Examination System', *Harvard Journal of Asiatic Studies*, 7:4, 1943, pp. 267–312.

Toby, Ronald P., 'Why Leave Nara? Kammu and the Transfer of the Capital', *MN*, 40:3, 1985, pp. 331–47.

Tokugawa Jikki, Kuroita Katsumi, ed., 14 volumes, Tokyo, 1976 reprint.

Tooley, R. V., *Maps and Map-Makers*, London, 1961.

Torsellini, Orazio, SJ, *De vita Francisci Xaverii*, Rome, 1594.

Trigault, Nicholas, SJ, *Litterae Societatis Jesu e Regno Sinarum …*, Antwerp, 1615.

——, *Rei Christianae apud Iaponios commentarius ex litteris annuis Societatis Iesu annorum 1609. 1610. 1611. 1612*, Augsburg, 1615.

Trinidade, Paulo da, *Conquista espiritual do Oriente*, 2 vols, Lisbon, 1961.

Totman, Conrad, *Tokugawa Ieyasu: Shogun*, Union City, Ca., 1983.

Tsukahira, T. G., *Feudal Control in Tokugawa Japan*, Cambridge, Mass., 1966.

Tsunoda R., tr. and ed., *Japan in the Chinese Dynastic Histories*, California, 1951.

Üçerler, M. Antoni, S.J, 'Jesuit Humanistic Education in Sixteenth-Century Japan', in Gómez, *Compendium*, III, pp. 11–60.

– 'Sacred Historiography and its Rhetoric in Sixteenth-Century Japan: An Intertextual Study and Critical Edition of *Principio y progreso de la religión christiana en Jappón …* (1601–1603) by Alessandro Valignano', doctoral thesis, University of Oxford, 1998.

Unno, Kazutaka, 'Japan before the Introduction of the Global Theory of the Earth: In Search of a Japanese Image of the Earth', *The Memoirs of the Toyo Bunko*, 38, 1980, pp. 39–69.

Vaillant, A., *Le Livre des Secrets d'Hénoch*, Paris, 1952.

Valignano, Alessandro, SJ, *Historia del principio y progreso de la Compañía de Jesús en las Indias Orientales (1542–1564)*, ed. J. Wicki, SJ, Rome, 1944.

——, *Il ceremoniale per i missionari del Giappone*, ed. J. F. Schütte, SJ, Rome, 1946.

——, *Sumario de las cosas de Japon (1583); Adiciones del Sumario de Japon (1592)*, ed. J. L. Alvarez-Taladriz, Tokyo, 1954. See also under Manuscripts.

Vaporis, Constantine Nomikos, *Breaking Barriers: Travel and the State in Early Modern Japan*, Cambridge, Mass., and London, 1994.

Varley, Paul, 'Ashikaga Yoshimitsu and the World of Kitayama', in Hall and Toyoda, *Japan in the Muromachi Age*, pp. 183–204.

——, *Warriors of Japan as Portrayed in the War Tales*, Honolulu, 1994.

——, 'Cultural Life in Medieval Japan', in *Cambridge History of Japan*, III, pp. 447–99.

——, and George Elison, 'The Culture of Tea: From Its Origin to Sen no Rikyū', in Elison and Smith, *Warlords*, pp. 187–222.

——, and Kumakura Isao, ed., *Tea in Japan: Essays on the History of Chanoyu*, Honolulu, 1989.

Verbiest, Ferdinand, SJ, *The Astronomia Europaea of Ferdinand Verbiest, SJ*, tr. and ed. Noel Golvers, Monumenta Serica Monograph 28, Nettetal, 1993.

Vio, Tommaso de, OP, *Commentarii illustres planéq. insignes in quinque Mosaicos libros, Thomae de Vio, Caitani quondn Cardinalis Sancti Xysti*, Paris, 1539.

Visser, M. W. de, *Ancient Buddhism in Japan*, 2 vols, Paris, 1928–35.

Vivero y Velasco, Rodrigo de – *see under* Manuscripts.

Vizcaino, Sebastian, *Relación del Viaje ...*, in Pacheco, *Colección*, VIII, 1867.

Vocabulario da lingoa de Iapan con adeclaração em Portugues ..., Nagasaki, 1603–4.

Wagner, H. R., 'Marco Polo's Narrative Becomes Propaganda to Inspire Colón', *Imago Mundi*, 6, 1949, pp. 3–13.

Waley, Arthur, *The Opium War through Chinese Eyes*, London, 1958.

Walter, Lutz, ed., *A Cartographic Vision: European Printed Maps from the Early 16th to the 19th Century*, Munich and New York, 1994.

Wang, Yi-T'ung, *Official Relations between China and Japan*, Cambridge, Mass, 1953.

Warner, L., *The Enduring Art of Japan*, New York, 1952.

Watsky, Andrew M., 'Commerce, Politics, and Tea: The Career of Imai Sōkyū', *MN*, 50, 1995, pp. 47–65.

Watson, William, *Ancient Chinese Bronzes*, London, 1962.

Werner, E. T. C., *A Dictionary of Chinese Mythology*, New York, 1961.

Wheatley, Paul, *The Golden Chersonese*, Kuala Lumpur, 1961.

Wieger, Léon, SJ, *Chinese Characters, Their Origin, Etymology, History, Classification and Signification*, New York, 1965 reprint.

Wong, K. and Lien-teh Wu, *History of Chinese Medicine*, Shanghai, 1936.

Wood, Frances, *Did Marco Polo Go to China?*, London, 1995.

Wylie, A., 'Eclipses Recorded in Chinese Works', *Journal of the Royal Asiatic Society (North China Branch)*, 4, Shanghai, 1868.

Wyngaert, A. van den, OFM, *Sinica Franciscana*, vol. 2, Florence, 1933.

Xavier, Francis, *Epistolae S. Francisco Xaverii aliaque ejus scripta*, ed. G. Schurhammer, SJ and J. Wicki, SJ, 2 vols, Rome, 1944–45.

———, *Francis Xavier, His Life, His Times*, by Georg Schurhammer, SJ, tr. M. Joseph Costelloe, SJ, 4 vols, Rome, 1973–82.

Yetts, W. P., 'Taoist Tales, III', *The New China Review*, 2, Shanghai, 1920.

Yule, Henry, *A Narrative of the Mission ... to the Court of Ava*, London, 1858.

———, ed., *The Book of Marco Polo*, 2 vols, London, 1903.

———, and A. C. Burnell, ed., *Hobson-Jobson: Being a Glossary of Colloquial Anglo-Indian Words and Phrases*, London, 1903.

———, *Cathay and the Way Thither*, 4 vols, Hakluyt Society, 2nd series, 33, 37, 38, 41, London, 1913–16.

Zi, Etienne, SJ, *Pratique des examens littéraires en Chine*, Shanghai, 1894 (reprint Taipei 1971).

———, *Pratique des examens militaires en Chine*, Shanghai, 1896 (reprint Taipei 1971).

INDEX